CONTENTS

List of Maps vii

LIST OF MAPS

HOW TO CONTACT US

In researching this book, we discovered many wonderful places—hotels, restaurants, shops, and more. We're sure you'll find others. Please tell us about them, so we can share the information with your fellow travelers in upcoming editions. If you were disappointed with a recommendation, we'd love to know that, too. Please write to:

Frommer's Vietnam with Angkor Wat, 4th Edition
John Wiley & Sons, Inc. • 111 River St. • Hoboken, NJ 07030-5774
frommersfeedback@wiley.com

AN ADDITIONAL NOTE

Please be advised that travel information is subject to change at any time—and this is especially true of prices. We therefore suggest that you write or call ahead for confirmation when making your travel plans. The authors, editors, and publisher cannot be held responsible for the experiences of readers while traveling. Your safety is important to us, however, so we encourage you to stay alert and be aware of your surroundings. Keep a close eye on cameras, purses, and wallets, all favorite targets of thieves and pickpockets.

FROMMER'S STAR RATINGS, ICONS & ABBREVIATIONS

Every hotel, restaurant, and attraction listing in this guide has been ranked for quality, value, service, amenities, and special features using a **star-rating system.** In country, state, and regional guides, we also rate towns and regions to help you narrow down your choices and budget your time accordingly. Hotels and restaurants are rated on a scale of zero (recommended) to three stars (exceptional). Attractions, shopping, nightlife, towns, and regions are rated according to the following scale: zero stars (recommended), one star (highly recommended), two stars (very highly recommended), and three stars (must-see).

In addition to the star-rating system, we also use **seven feature icons** that point you to the great deals, in-the-know advice, and unique experiences that separate travelers from tourists. Throughout the book, look for:

special finds—those places only insiders know about

fun facts—details that make travelers more informed and their trips more fun

kids—best bets for kids and advice for the whole family

special moments—those experiences that memories are made of

overrated—places or experiences not worth your time or money

insider tips—great ways to save time and money

great values—where to get the best deals

The following abbreviations are used for credit cards:

AE	American Express	DISC Discover	V Visa
DC	Diners Club	MC MasterCard	

TRAVEL RESOURCES AT FROMMERS.COM

Frommer's travel resources don't end with this guide. Frommer's website, **www.frommers. com**, has travel information on more than 4,000 destinations. We update features regularly, giving you access to the most current trip-planning information and the best airfare, lodging, and car-rental bargains. You can also listen to podcasts, connect with other Frommers. com members through our active-reader forums, share your travel photos, read blogs from guidebook editors and fellow travelers, and much more.

THE BEST OF VIETNAM

Clinging to the coast of Southeast Asia like a rearing dragon, Vietnam is a fiercely independent country, as anyone familiar with its history will know. Its unique culture is evident in the dress, cuisine, and manners of its hospitable people, and the country's varied topography creates the ideal backdrop for an unforgettable adventure.

Cities Vietnam's two major cities provide convenient bases for exploration of this long, thin country. In the south, **Ho Chi Minh City** is an unlikely mix of ancient, Chinese-style temples, fancy French colonial architecture, and modernist glass and steel. Thousand-year-old **Hanoi** in the north is the country's administrative capital, with a bustling Old Quarter and tranquil lakes that reflect gleaming office towers.

Countryside **Vietnam's** countryside runs the gamut from mangrove swamps in the south to rugged peaks in the north, with a huge variety of landscapes in between. Trekking to villages around **Sapa** is a popular activity for visitors; **Dalat** is the country's adventure-sport capital; and the **Mekong Delta** provides an endless panorama of rice paddies and fruit orchards.

Coast **Nha Trang,** located about halfway along the coastline, is Vietnam's leading beach resort, though nearby **Mui Ne** is giving it some fierce competition these days. The offshore islands of **Phu Quoc** and **Con Dao** are making a name for themselves as idyllic getaways, but the World Heritage Site of **Halong Bay** is still the top attraction along Vietnam's coast.

Eating and Drinking Whether slurping spicy noodles from Saigon street stalls or savoring French croissants in a Hue patisserie, you'll find Vietnamese cuisine to be full flavored, fascinating, and affordable. The national dish is *pho bo,* sliced beef in an aromatic noodle broth, garnished with a fistful of herbs.

THE best VIETNAM EXPERIENCES

o **Eat on the Street:** "Real" Vietnamese food is best at street side or in small market areas, and though it might be a little grungy or off-putting to some, dining alfresco in old Indochina offers the most authentic and delicious meals. Prepare yourself for some adventurous dining. In either Hanoi or Ho Chi Minh City, try Quan An Ngon Restaurant (p. 83 and p. 306) for a safe overview of Vietnamese fare.

o **Get Lost in the Markets:** In Vietnam, the market—spelled *cho* and pronounced like the beginning of the word *could*—is the epicenter of culture and commerce. The most convenient market for tourists is Ben Thanh Market (p. 309) in Saigon, which caters to foreign visitors with low-cost T-shirts, souvenirs, and local treats, though everything there now is sadly fixed price. Every town has a market: check out Dalat's market, with its delicious strawberry preserves; Hoi An's busy riverside fish market and wholesale silk market; Hanoi's sprawling Dong Xuan Market (p. 110); and the hilltribe markets of Sapa and Bac Ha in the far north.

o **Visit Hilltribe Groups:** Vietnam's remote mountain regions, the Central Highlands and the far north, are home to a patchwork of ethnic minorities. Ethnic hilltribe people still practice animism and wear colorful traditional clothing. Travelers among them, in places such as Sapa and Bac Ha in the far north or near Buon Ma Thuot or Kontum in the Central Highlands, can even experience a homestay in some villages through eco-tours and trekking companies. See chapters 6 and 10.

o **Witness a Water Puppet Show:** This is a bit touristy, but the Thang Long Water Puppet Theater (p. 112) in Hanoi and the Golden Dragon Theater (p. 310) in Ho Chi Minh City present a magical performance. Intricate puppets controlled by an ingenious system of rods and pulleys dance across the surface of a watery stage, telling tales of old Vietnam. Don't miss it.

o **Take a Wild Ride:** Whether through Hanoi's narrow alleyways and mazelike neighborhoods or on the broad boulevards of busy Ho Chi Minh City, the traffic in Vietnam is a trip. Darwinian road rules mean that any ride by motorcycle, car, or bus is a test of faith, as drivers swerve and angle through some of the world's craziest traffic. In Vietnam, "getting there" is an adventure in itself. See "Getting There" sections in the following chapters for more information.

o **Celebrate the Tet Holiday:** This Lunar New Year celebration (p. 24) in late January or early February is the most important event on the calendar. Should you be in Vietnam at this time of year, you'll experience a wave of excitement throughout the country. However, it's not the best time to travel around, as seats on planes, trains, and buses are booked up long in advance.

THE best SITES (ACCORDING TO UNESCO)

o **Halong Bay:** Just a few short hours from Hanoi, the bay at Halong, with its craggy limestone towers dotting the wide-open bay all the way to the horizon, has long inspired Vietnamese poets and philosophers. A ride on the bay these days is a rather busy, crowded affair, but some luxury tours and a few eco-tour operators can take you to the back of beyond, exploring hidden lagoons by kayak or climbing up sheer cliff faces. See chapter 7.

o **Phong Nha—Ke Bang National Park:** These massive caves (some of the biggest in the world) are about halfway between Hue and Vinh, and rarely visited. You have to arrange your own transport or go with a tour. See p. 173.

o **Hoi An:** Tourism has exploded on the ancient streets of Hoi An. A hub of international craft and commerce since the 14th century, this is where Vietnamese, Chinese, and even Japanese tradesmen made and sold their designer wares. Many shops are still-operational wood, stone, and ceramic workshops, but now among them are fine-dining outlets, funky hotels (as well as new resorts on the outlying beach area of Cua Dai), and lots of bespoke tailors. Shoppers swoon. See chapter 9.

o **My Son Sanctuary:** The Cham people, an Indonesian group that arrived by ship from the Malay Peninsula, held sway over most of central Vietnam for several centuries and built arching hilltop towers. My Son is the finest example of Cham architecture. See "An Excursion to My Son," in chapter 7.

o **Hue Monuments:** The Nguyen Kings—the last and perhaps the most glorious (or grandiose) of Vietnam's dynastic rulers—built grand monuments to themselves in the countryside around the massive Hue Citadel. The elaborate kings' tombs make for a very interesting visit. See chapter 9.

THE best TEMPLES & ARCHAEOLOGICAL SITES

o **The Cao Dai Holy See:** The spiritual home base of the Cao Dai religion, a unique contemporary faith, the Holy See is a fantasyland of colored mosaics and elaborate painting. Followers are dressed in white turbans during the daily service. See p. 316.

o **Tomb of Khai Dinh:** The egotistical, eccentric emperor Khai Dinh left behind a tomb that is a gaudy mix of Gothic, baroque, and classical Chinese architecture. See p. 188.

o **The Tunnels of Vinh Moc and Cu Chi:** During the war with the United States, both of these sites supported large groups of Communist soldiers and civilians who used the tunnels as supply lines, escape routes, and bases for waging a devastating guerilla campaign against U.S. forces. Day trips to either site are memorable. See p. 194 and p. 316.

o **Hoa Lo Prison (aka Hanoi Hilton):** Home to U.S. pilots—including John McCain—who were shot down during the Vietnamese war with the U.S., Hoa Lo Prison is now a small museum (most of it was demolished for a high-rise). It offers a good glimpse into Vietnam's grisly past. See p. 99.

o **Temple of Literature:** The site of Hanoi's first university is as old as the city itself and the most important religious site in the entire country. See p. 98.

THE best MUSEUMS

o **War Remnants Museum** (Ho Chi Minh City): Formerly called the Museum of American War Crimes, this collection is the face of Vietnam's war-torn past. Exhibits are insightful and certainly rife with rhetoric, but offer a unique glimpse at propaganda from "the other side," and a yin to the heavy yang of Western reporting and documentation of the war years. A must-see. See p. 314.

o **The Cham Museum** (Danang): This open-air colonial structure houses the largest collection of Cham sculpture in the world. Many of the 300-plus Hindu-inspired carvings are captivating. See p. 202.

o **Vietnam National Museum of Fine Arts** (Hanoi): This large colonial structure houses a fine collection of new works, historical lacquer and silk paintings, woodblocks, and folk and expressive works in oil. See p. 97.

o **Ho Chi Minh Museum** (Hanoi): Like the War Remnants Museum, the Ho Chi Minh Museum is a battleground of ideology. Located adjacent to his very tomb, the museum tells the tale of the revolutionary from cradle to grave. See p. 96.

THE best BEACHES

o **Nha Trang:** Vietnam's Ocean City is very crowded in the summertime with domestic tourists, but it's a great escape. The city boasts some of the best-value lodgings in the country, and a fantastic range of cuisine, with seafood the top choice. See p. 257.

o **Mui Ne Beach, Phan Thiet:** Just a few hours from Saigon, Mui Ne is the perfect getaway for Saigon residents. Get your kicks windsurfing or kite-surfing, playing golf, or taking day trips to remote sand dunes and small fishing villages. See p. 274.

o **Phu Quoc Island:** Phu Quoc features vast tracts of interior forestland and far-flung beaches great for exploring by motorbike. There's a growing number of resorts nestling along its soft-sand beaches, and the imminent opening of an international airport can only make it more popular. Get here fast. See p. 348.

THE best OF THE OUTDOORS

o **Kayaking in Halong Bay:** Often in conjunction with luxury cruises, kayaking in Halong Bay means going through low caves at low tide to get to hidden lagoons at the center of limestone rings, where walls of jungle vegetation tower hundreds of feet overhead and crawl with monkeys, snakes, and rare animals. Kayaks are the only way to get up close. See chapter 7.

o **Adventure Sports in the Central Highlands:** Opportunities abound for trekking, rock climbing, canyoning, and mountain biking. Just contact one of the many small outfitters in Dalat (all are a copy of Phat Tire, a Vietnam pioneer). See chapter 10.

o **Cycling the Mekong Delta:** The best part about cycling in the Mekong Delta is that the routes are quite flat. Adventure-tour outfitters in Ho Chi Minh City (see "Visitor Information & Tours," in chapter 12) can make any arrangements for a customized tour of any length, even providing a support van, and going by bike gives you a close-up view of it all. See chapter 13.

o **The Central Highlands or the Far North by Motorbike:** The rural back roads of Vietnam beg to be explored, and going by motorbike, though dangerous, is a great way to do it. From Dalat in the Central Highlands, arrange a ride with an Easy Rider (p. 228), motorcycle guides who can take you up the Ho Chi Minh Highway to Danang and Hoi An. In the far north, the Russian Minsk motorbike is the workhorse of the hills, and you can rent your own bike or go with a guide out of Hanoi and visit some incredible terrain. See chapter 10.

o **Taking On Fansipan or Trekking the Far North:** The very top of Vietnam, **Mount Fansipan** (p. 118) is a multiday adventure and only for the hearty, but the views afforded and the experience itself are amazing. There are lots of outfitters in the popular tourist town of Sapa, and you can arrange any number of treks to ethnic hilltribe villages, even overnights and homestays. See chapter 6.

o **Rock Climbing in Halong Bay:** Cat Ba is the base for such companies as Slo Pony Adventures to explore the endless potential for rock-climbing routes on thousands of islands in the bay. Experienced climbers and beginners are both welcome. See chapter 7.

o **Cuc Phuong National Park:** A great little overnight from Hanoi for nature lovers, Cuc Phuong hosts a primate-research center, has good accommodations, and offers lots of hiking trails. Guides are on hand to assist or hire for the day. See p. 116.

o **Cat Tien National Park:** Bird-watcher heaven, little Cat Tien is halfway between Saigon and Dalat, and an overnight stay includes night spotting, rustic accommodations, and a morning hike. The place is crawling with jungle animals, birds, and lots of naturalists and ornithologists chasing after them with binoculars. See p. 334.

THE best LUXURY ACCOMMODATIONS

o **Hilton Hanoi Opera** (www.hilton.com; ✆ 04/3933-0500): With a fine blend of traditional design and modern facilities, spot-on service, and a location next to the Opera House, the Hilton is an obvious choice in Vietnam's ancient capital. See p. 68.

o **Sofitel Metropole Legend Hanoi** (www.sofitel.com; ✆ 04/3826-6919): The best hotel in Vietnam for luxury, service, style, and a connection to the history of Hanoi. See p. 68.

o **The Nam Hai** (Hoi An; www.thenamhai.com; ✆ 0510/394-0000): This resort is the most luxurious, over-the-top destination in Vietnam. A premier spa, three outdoor infinity pools, and private pool villas highlight a list that goes on and on. See p. 205.

o **Ana Mandara Villas Dalat** (http://anamandara-resort.com; ✆ 063/355-5888): This is the most charming hotel in Vietnam, with 17 lovingly restored French colonial villas nestled upon a hill in the Central Highlands. See p. 230.

o **Dalat Palace** (www.dalatpalace.vn; ✆ 063/382-5444): There's nothing like this converted palace of the last emperor of Vietnam, Bao Dai. Retro-style rooms come with fireplaces, divan beds, claw-foot tubs, and great artwork. Fine dining and a high standard of service round out the package. One of those special finds. See p. 230.

o **Six Senses Con Dao** (Con Son Island; www.sixsenses.com; ✆ 064/383-1456): Dat Doc Bay provides the perfect setting for the latest Six Senses resort in Vietnam. Live the dream in a private pool villa, with a personal butler at your beck and call. See p. 331.

o **Princess d'Annam** (Phan Thiet; www.princessannam.com; ✆ 062/368-2222): This sparkling resort is a breathtaking beauty in the middle of nowhere. Luxurious suites and villas are nestled around a tropical garden, with picturesque oceanside dining, an outdoor infinity pool, and a three-story spa rounding out the indulgence. See p. 276.

o **La Veranda** (Duong Dong Beach; www.mgallery.com; ✆ 077/398-2988): This stately colonial resort with pristine views of the ocean and gourmet dining on a relaxing terrace is one of Vietnam's premier island getaways. See p. 351.

o **Park Hyatt Saigon** (www.saigon.park.hyatt.com; ✆ 08/3824-1234): This luxury hotel has a prime downtown location overlooking the Saigon Opera House. The interior is sophisticated and modern, and the decor is luxurious without being chintzy. The hotel also has some of the best dining options in Saigon. See p. 293.

- **Caravelle Hotel Saigon** (www.caravellehotel.com; ☎ 08/3827-2828): Former hangout of journalists covering the American War, the Caravelle is currently the city's flagship five-star property. Check out the breezy Saigon Saigon rooftop bar, and write your own report for the folks back home. See p. 289.

THE **best** MIDRANGE ACCOMMODATIONS

- **Hanoi Moment** (www.hanoimomenthotel.com; ☎ 04/3923-3988): This stylish hotel in the Old Quarter features crisp lines and soft lighting, and offers a taste of luxury at midrange prices. See p. 72.
- **Topas Ecolodge** (Sapa; www.topasecolodge.com; ☎ 020/387-2404): Topas Ecolodge has the best mountain and rice paddy views in Sapa. Nestled in a misty valley away from the din of Sapa town, the lodge is also an ideal jumping-off point for treks and hikes. See p. 125.
- **Life Resort Hoi An and Quy Nhon** (www.life-resorts.com): Whether at the more isolated beachside resort in Quy Nhon (☎ 056/384-0132) or at the fine resort in Hoi An (☎ 0510/391-4555)—the very closest resort to town—Life Resort sets a new standard. See p. 206 and p. 254.
- **Sheraton Nha Trang** (www.starwoodhotels.com; ☎ 058/388-0000): Off for a beach vacation with the kids? You won't find a more welcoming or convenient spot than this new place, located smack in the center of Nha Trang's sweeping beach. See p. 262.
- **Asian Ruby** (Ho Chi Minh City; www.asianrubyhotel.com; ☎ 08/3827-2839): One of a chain of minihotels offering a degree of luxury at midrange prices. Rooms are very cozy, and the location is ideal to get to the shops and sights. See p. 296.
- **Victoria Chau Doc and Can Tho** (www.victoriahotels-asia.com): These two riverside classics are worth the trip. Chau Doc (☎ 076/386-5010) is a renovated old administration building, and Can Tho (☎ 0710/381-0111) is a retrofitted grande dame. Take great day trips and enjoy slow, riverside living. See p. 347 and p. 343.

THE **best** DINING

- **Green Tangerine** (Hanoi; ☎ 04/3825-1286): This lovely restored colonial building on the fringe of the Old Quarter is a great setting for some sensational tastes, whether you go for the set menus or a la carte. See p. 77.
- **La Badiane** (Hanoi; ☎ 04/3942-4509): The hottest table in town, La Badiane offers affordable French cuisine in an atmospheric colonial mansion. See p. 77.
- **Mango Rooms** (Hoi An; ☎ 0510/391-0839): The atmosphere is fast and furious as hip young owner Duc slings a unique brand of Asian-fusion fare, heavy on grilled items and delicious light ingredients. See p. 212.
- **Le Rabelais** (Dalat; ☎ 063/382-5444): Fine French cuisine served with real panache at one of Vietnam's most luxurious rural hotels. See p. 233.
- **Xu** (Ho Chi Minh City; ☎ 08/3824-8468): This stylish downtown restaurant is the place to taste innovative versions of traditional Vietnamese cuisine. Serious dining upstairs and a hip lounge downstairs. See p. 305.

VIETNAM IN DEPTH

Despite its "in-depth" subtitle, this chapter only briefly skims the surface of a rather deep reservoir; literary and nonfiction works about the Vietnam War era alone are legion, and Vietnam's cultural heritage goes back thousands of years. With its distinct, very sophisticated traditions of painting (particularly lacquer painting), crafts such as weaving and woodcarving, theater, opera, dance, and water puppetry, Vietnam's cultural landscape is as varied and colorful as its topography. And despite centuries of occupation by foreigners, Vietnamese cultural traditions have survived. Opportunities abound to explore trade villages, learn about Vietnamese cooking, witness the country's performing arts, catch a traditional opera, or look over the shoulder of artists at work in studios or at street side.

WHO ARE THE VIETNAMESE?

More than 90% of Vietnamese people are Viet, or *Kinh,* people, descendants of the indigenous race, but with the many violent and migratory incursions over the centuries, as well as the southward expansion of Vietnamese territory into Cambodia, modern Vietnamese are a combination of many races and cultural influences. Chinese, Khmer (or Cambodian), Cham, and indigenous groups in the north, central mountains, coast, and far south were all one-time enemies turned allies and comprise the melting pot of modern Vietnamese.

So who are the Vietnamese? A people trying to find that out themselves, really. With the opening of their doors in the late 1980s, capitalism came trickling in and now flows like a tidal wave, and the "comrades" of old now strive to become "consumers" who participate in the global market. The contradictions are sometimes absurd.

The dominant group, the ethnic Viet or Kinh people, inhabit the prime lowland rice-growing territories and are a very lopsided majority. Kinh people are descendants of inhabitants of the provinces of southern China.

Vietnam's tapestry of ethnic minorities spreads across the vast tracts of the Central Highlands and the far north (for more information about the specific hilltribe groups in each region, see the related boxes in chapters 6 and 10). Known under French governance and during the U.S. war years as Montagnards, ethnic hilltribe people and their myriad subgroups in Vietnam divide the mountainous areas of the country into a colorful patchwork of disparate languages, cultures, and traditions. A visit to the regions in the far north or Central Highlands, best when accompanied by a guide who can make introductions, is a unique glimpse of the diversity and fortitude of these resilient groups, who have been immigrating from

China and nearby Laos for hundreds of years. Ethnic Khmer, or Cambodian people, live in large communities in the south, mostly along the Cambodian border and on the Mekong Delta. Ethnic Cham people, the Muslim descendants of the 15th-century Champa Kingdom that once ruled the far south, live mostly in isolated fishing communities in the coastal south.

A few million ethnic Chinese make up a strong merchant class centered in the major cities. Ho Chi Minh City has a teeming and prosperous Chinatown, and Chinese merchants have lived for generations and plied the same trades for hundreds of years in Hanoi's Old Quarter. As one-time conquerors and colonists, and contemporary enemies, ethnic Chinese have been persecuted since the expulsion of American forces and reunification of Vietnam in 1975. Many Chinese in Vietnam fled, joining the deluge of Vietnamese "boat people" escaping persecution.

Today ethnic tensions in Vietnam are limited to the majority government, with its fear of and disputes with ethnic minority people in the Central Highlands and the far north. Only recently, a contingent of refugees fleeing persecution in Laos—Vietnam's cousin in paranoia about hilltribe insurgency—found refuge in the Central Highlands, only to suffer suspicion, searches, and bullying from the Vietnamese. Still smarting from hilltribe group complicity with French and U.S. forces during the Vietnam War, the government is wary of these stubborn, autonomous people, placing them into controlled village units of "enforced primitivism" and forbidding tourists from entering their villages unless chaperoned by a government guide.

Vietnamese family units are tight. Generations live together and practice the same trade, usually rural farming, but merchants and shopkeepers also work together generation after generation. Population density is high because wherever there are no mountains, the land is either developed or cultivated; flat, arable ground is at a premium. Collectivization and cooperation in villages have always been the norm—some argue that some form of socialism was inherent in the Vietnamese makeup. Vietnam nearly collapsed in abject poverty under Communism, but with its return to the market economy, village units have formed again and rural life has improved. Although material wealth eludes most, the standard of living is on the rise. Though the country is in a mad dash of modernization, the economy has remained largely agrarian, with farmers, fishermen, and forestry workers accounting for more than half of the workforce in a mostly rural demographic.

The French categorized the country into three distinct regions—Cochin China in the south, Annam in the center, and Tonkin in the north—and it's important to note that Vietnam was unified under one name only after the departure of Japanese and French troops at the end of World War II. It took years of fighting—first with the French, then with the Americans—before the nation was united, and even today Vietnamese from the north and the south are quite distinct.

Traditional village life once centered on the *dinh,* or small shrine honored as the god of the village or the mountains, now a Confucian altar to the generations that came before. Young Vietnamese are increasingly seeking higher-paying jobs in cities, but most return home or support their extended families from afar.

Hospitality is very important to Vietnamese, and travelers often find themselves as guests in local homes and offered the choicest pieces of a humble repast, or sharing rice whiskey and laughter. Vietnamese are very kind and playful. Children are doted upon. Families are close and supportive, and adopt new members all the time (you'll be taken in, too). Accept invites whenever possible.

It's easy to know a lot about Vietnam and Vietnamese culture, but much harder to really *understand,* say many longtime expats. Learning about the concept of "saving face," for example, often takes some painful lessons in "losing face," but a trip to Vietnam is a great way to get perspective on our own cultural programming.

VIETNAMESE RELIGION

Religion in Vietnam was stifled for many years by the Communist authorities, but these days the traditional rituals, including visits to the local temple, are once again practiced. More than 75% of Vietnamese follow a mix of **Confucianism** and its tenets of ancestor worship, as well as **Buddhism** and **Taoism.** Buddhism came to the region via China in the 2nd century A.D., a form of Mahayana Buddhism, or "The Big Vehicle," in which the belief is that all sentient beings will attain enlightenment en masse. There are some pockets of Theravada Buddhists, mostly among ethnic Khmer communities in the south, who are proponents of the "Small Vehicle" belief—inherited from India via Thailand and Cambodia—in enlightenment on a person-by-person basis. Daoism, a Chinese traditional belief in the harmony of nature, also influences belief, and a small sect of Hoa Hao Buddhists believes strongly in ancestor worship.

Only a small percentage of Vietnamese are **Protestant,** but **Catholicism** came ashore with missionaries as early as the 17th century and found a firmament in Vietnam that lasts to this day, particularly in the south (in fact, after the withdrawal of the French and partitioning of the country at the 17th Parallel, the majority of northern Catholics fled south). There are a number of Catholic vestiges in the Central Highlands and far north where missionaries did some of their hardest work, and devotion to this day, now led by a Vietnamese bishop, is still strong. Every city has a Catholic cathedral, and church services are well attended and quite fervent.

Unique is the **Cao Dai** faith, a homegrown religion that embraces all faiths and philosophies, and even ranks scientists, such as Pasteur, as saints. There are more than two million Cao Dai worshippers in Vietnam, predominantly in the south, and their colorful Holy See near Tay Ninh is a popular day trip from Ho Chi Minh City.

A small percentage of Vietnamese, mostly the Cham people living along the coast in central Vietnam, follow the tenets of **Islam.**

A LOOK AT THE PAST: VIETNAM THE COUNTRY, NOT THE WAR

The war in Vietnam is written large on the collective consciousness of the last few generations in the West, but Vietnam's scope of history spans thousands of years and has seen the rise and fall of many empires and conquerors. Not to minimize the devastating effects on both sides during what the Vietnamese call "The American War," but the conflict that ended now more than 30 years ago is far in the past for most Vietnamese, many of whom consider the time as just another in a very long series of incursions by a foreign foe. Search for volumes of Vietnamese history in your local library in the West, and you'll find literally hundreds of tomes about the war with the United States but little about the scope of Vietnam's 1,000 years of struggle with foreign powers. Vietnam's recent struggles are so close, so well documented, that our image of the country is intimately connected to footage of napalm-strafed hillocks, suicide attacks in Saigon, prolonged bombing campaigns, prisoners of war in the most desperate straits, the Vietnamese "boat people" of the 1970s and 1980s, or returning U.S. veterans with PTSD (post-traumatic stress disorder), the likes of Robert De Niro

Dong Son Culture: Vietnam's Non-Chinese Origins

First discovered in 1924 near the Ma River in the far north near Dong Son (thus the name), Dong Son Drums are large, ornate brass kettles supposedly dating as far back as the 7th century B.C. But early research of these sites was shoddy, and the French Ecole d'Extrème Orient used some rather loose evidence to posit the existence of a unified society throughout the region and named the culture Dong Son after its first discovery. So the truth about these ancient and obviously well-organized civilizations is still in question, and although Vietnamese cling to the Dong Son Drum as evidence of an early, very advanced, and, most important, autonomous (read "not Chinese") civilization, questions remain. Many archaeologists believe that the Dong Son cultures originated from outside incursions of Austronesian groups.

What we do know for sure is that the drums were produced by a very advanced early civilization (from the 7th c. B.C. to the 1st and 2nd c. A.D.) and made from sandstone and terra-cotta molds. Each drum is unique, with some commonalities, like the small sculptures of frogs around the faces of some drums, as well as images of the sun and of the Lac Bird.

in the *Deer Hunter* or Sylvester Stallone in *Rambo*. But talk to Vietnamese about the "American War," and you'll hear little recrimination. In fact, Vietnam's war record and persistence in the face of an economically superior foe is its greatest source of strength in a long history of prevailing against the odds—or an "ongoing revolution," according to Marxism.

Vietnamese history can be broken into six distinct eras: 1) prehistory until the first of the vaunted Hung Kings (like the British legends of Arthur); 2) the Chinese millennium from 189 B.C. to A.D. 939; 3) 1,000 years of Vietnamese autonomy and wars with the Khmer and the Cham to the south, as well as ongoing border scraps with China until the late 19th century; 4) colonization of Vietnam, again, under the French for 80 years; 5) war with the United States; and 6) years of hard-fought independence that began with Ho Chi Minh's Declaration of Independence but wasn't cemented until the fall (or liberation, depending on your perspective) of Saigon in 1975 and a reunified Vietnam.

EARLY HISTORY

Early history is steeped in legend, and even the most reliable documents are but secondhand musings in the footnotes of ancient Chinese texts. The earliest kingdom, the Van Lang, was formed by the legendary **King Hung Vuong,** the Vietnamese equivalent of Arthur and his Knights of the Round Table. For some 2,000 years until the 3rd century B.C., the mythical Hung dynasty prospered in the Red River Delta concurrently with early Bronze Age cultures, and later the Dong Son Bronze Age culture, which dated from 850 to 300 B.C. (see the box on Dong Son culture, below).

Legend has it that Hung kings had magical powers, and their story is shrouded in myth; but, particularly under the later Hung kings, there was relative stability and progress. Communal life centered on wet rice cultivation, a model that has stood through the ages, and early Vietnamese under the Hung also raised cattle; fostered the growth of weaving, pottery, and building skills; and developed intricate bronze-smith technology. The Hung dynasty crumbled under repeated incursions from China in the 3rd century B.C. (culminating in collapse in 258 B.C.).

Under the leadership of **An Duong Vuong,** a small kingdom of ethnic Viet tribes called **Au Lac** formed in the 3rd century B.C. The tiny kingdom centered on the ancient capital near Co Loa, north of present-day Hanoi. The Au Lac were eventually absorbed into the Chinese Qin dynasty in 221 B.C., but as that dynasty crumpled, a Chinese general by the name of Chao Tuo, or Trieu Da in Vietnamese, conquered the northern regions in 207 B.C. and established Nan Yueh, a Chinese term meaning "Far South" (called *Nam Viet* in Vietnamese), an autonomous principality that would be handled as a "rogue territory" by the Chinese for hundreds of years to come.

THE CHINESE MILLENIUM

From 111 B.C., Vietnam was under Chinese rule, this time as part of the Han Empire. Vietnam would remain part of greater China for the next thousand years. The Chinese form of writing was adopted (to be replaced by a Roman alphabet in the 17th c.), Confucianism was instated as the leading ideology, and Chinese governors were installed as local rulers. The Chinese were heavy-handed colonists, seeking to profit on the backs of the conquered Vietnamese, imposing forced labor, and extracting high taxes at sword point.

For centuries, few effectively challenged Chinese rule until the **Ba Trung** sisters, Trung Trac and Trung Nhi, took the place of their executed dissident husbands and, in a wave of popular support and revolutionary spirit that is revered to this day, staged the **Hai Ba Trung Rebellion** (literally, the "Two Sister's Rebellion") in A.D. 39. The sisters, leading an angry horde, expelled the Chinese and ruled the northern kingdom for just 3 years before the Chinese resumed control; the sisters, in their shame, drowned themselves. The Hai Ba Trung Rebellion stands out only because of its brief success and was really just an early incarnation of the many rebellions against Chinese rule that would follow—rebellions that, despite their tenacity, all ended under the brutal thumb of tyrannical Chinese rule.

THE VIETNAMESE MILLENIUM

One of the greatest triumphs of the loosely unified Viet people came in A.D. 939 when **Ngo Quyen** defeated the Chinese at **Bach Dang,** a naval battle of legend in which the Vietnamese surprised their enemy by placing massive pikes in the waters of Halong Bay, where the Chinese boats were run aground and ransacked. Although Ngo Quyen died and Vietnam fell into a prolonged civil war under the Ngo dynasty, Vietnam was finally free of China.

In A.D. 968, **Dinh Bo Linh** pacified, unified, and made extensive treaties to keep Vietnam a fully autonomous Chinese vassal state. So began the ascendancy of Vietnam's mandarins, a high caste of intelligentsia who created special schools for promising Vietnamese to be groomed into the country's elite. All education was conducted in Chinese by Chinese (see "Temple of Literature and National University [Van Mieu–Quoc Tu Giam]," in chapter 5), and Mandarins exerted great influence. These concessions meant that Vietnam was free to run its affairs independent of the Chinese, other than the regular tolls it paid to mother China. Vietnam benefited from this adoption of China's educational system, as well as inherited technologies of math and science, the lunar calendar, and both legal and educational systems. The Chinese imprint is still visible today in Vietnam's Confucian traditions, architecture, and even today's pell-mell thrust toward a market economy.

Vietnam's long period of autonomy was not without peril, however, as incursions from the Cham in what is now central Vietnam and the Khmer in the far south put pressure on the burgeoning united state. The kingdom flourished and strengthened, enough for the Vietnamese to repel the intrusion of Mongol invaders under Kublai Khan from the north, and armies from the kingdom of Champa from Danang and the east, in the mid–13th century. Vietnam gradually absorbed the Cham Empire and made progressive claims on Khmer land as far as the Mekong Delta.

In 1400, China once again occupied Hanoi, reclaiming its foundering vassal as its own, until, in that same year, a peasant uprising changed everything, something like the popular movement of the two Trung sisters. Socialist historians pointed to this as evidence of the true revolutionary spirit among Vietnamese.

Even after the shortest trip in Vietnam, you'll recognize the name **Le Loi** from street signs everywhere. Le Loi was a rich landowner who organized resistance to the occupying Chinese forces from a base high in the mountains. In 1426, he achieved a great military victory at Sontay and at Lam Son in the far north, vanquishing the Chinese and paving the way to his becoming emperor, renaming himself **Le Thai To.** He reigned from 1428 to 1433 and heralded what many call a "golden age" in Vietnam under the Le Kings, a time where the country came into its own, developing a new education system and penal code, especially under the rule of **Emperor Le Thanh Tong.**

Instability at court was rife, however, and the country was eventually split along north-south lines in 1545; the north followed the Le dynasty, and the south followed the Nguyen, with ongoing conflict between the two.

Europeans, particularly the French, seized upon Vietnamese instability, and Catholic missionaries and European traders began to come ashore. French Jesuit Alexandre de Rhodes arrived in Vietnam in the 17th century and created a Romanized Vietnamese script, an important milestone in Vietnamese literacy and accessibility to the West.

Continued clan tension between the north and south led to numerous failed peasant revolts, until the **Tay Son Rebellion** in central Vietnam near the town of Quy Nhon saw the ascendancy of **Nguyen Hue,** who proclaimed himself the **Emperor Quang Trung** and fought to obliterate the Nguyen in the south and the Trinh in the north, effectively uniting Vietnam under one banner.

When Quang Trung died without an heir in 1792, **Nguyen Anh,** a southerner, declared himself king in 1802 and adopted the name **Gia Long.** For the first time, he called the country **Vietnam.** The **Nguyen Capital** was in **Hue,** and the Citadel and grand tombs of the fallen Nguyen kings still stand.

By the 1850s, the French had already settled in the region, the arms of the Catholic Church reaching far and wide and exacting more and more influence. The French pressed for further control and, in 1847, attacked Danang, which became the French city of Tourane. Three decades later—after first capturing Saigon, then Cambodia, then central Vietnam (or Anam), and later the north—France signed a treaty as the official protectorate of Vietnam in 1883. And so began some 80 years of colonial rule once again in Vietnam.

FRENCH COLONIAL RULE & THE FIRST INDOCHINA WAR

Some books and movies, the likes of Graham Green's *The Quiet American* (made into a film with Michael Caine in 2001) or Erik Orsenna's *Indochine,* portray colonial Vietnam as an ephemeral time of gentle European eccentrics and explorers in starched white collars (usually sweaty) traipsing around an exotic landscape of cacophonous streets or padding about dark opium dens among erotic temptresses in the traditional *ao dai* dress, a romanticized image of Vietnam as a land of exotic pleasures. Missing are scenes of Vietnamese under the lash of the colonists, desperate peasant revolts, poverty, and forced labor. By the 1900s, a fragile truce existed between the Vietnamese and their occupiers, who painted themselves as benevolent benefactors of culture and education, who were embarked on a *"mission civilisatrice."* But it was that education, and the writings of French patriots, such as Rousseau and Voltaire, that fueled Vietnamese ire over French subjugation. The fighting was soon to follow.

Early-20th-century resistance, such as the **Quan Phuc Hoi** movement that sought restoration of an autonomous Vietnam or the **Tonkin Free School Movement** that preached ascendancy of Vietnamese traditions and culture, imminently failed or was brutally crushed by the French, and the numbers in the notorious prisons, such as the **Maison Centrale** (later dubbed "the Hanoi Hilton" by Americans held there), swelled to breaking points. The proud people of Vietnam bristled under colonial rule, and in 1930 revolution found fertile ground to establish a nationalist movement, especially with the return of **Nguyen Tat Thanh,** otherwise known as **Ho Chi Minh.** Uncle Ho rose from relative obscurity and a long life as an expatriate and exile (read the story of Ho Chi Minh in chapter 8). He overcame the limitations of his rather frail carriage and bearing to become the leader of decades of struggle. World War II and occupation by the Japanese in 1940 helped fuel the movement by creating chaos and nationalist fervor, and in celebration of the retreat of the Japanese, Ho Chi Minh declared Vietnam an independent nation in August 1945.

However, the French returned and took the north as their own once again, infuriating Communists who had, but briefly, seen a window of opportunity for self-governance. The French didn't agree with Ho Chi Minh's cleverly versed plea for autonomy and democracy. On September 2, 1945, he began with the famed quote from the U.S. declaration that "All men are created equal." Despite international pressure for full French withdrawal from their interests in Indochina, the French—under leadership of plucky Gen. Charles de Gaulle, in an effort to restore French colonial glory—sent a large expeditionary force. Guerilla fighting in all of the provinces escalated, and in November 1946, in reaction to Vietnamese attacks, the French shelled Haiphong, the major port city in the far north, killing an estimated 6,000 and kicking off what is now often referred to as the First Indochina War. After 7 years of French/Viet Minh conflict—and despite heavy backing by Eisenhower (the U.S. supplied planes and 80% of the war costs)—the French, dug in at Dien Bien Phu, made the fatal blunder of being cavalier about their enemy's capacities: They chose a wide, shallow valley where they assumed that their superior artillery could handle any attack.

General Giap, Vietnam's top strategist, had acquired heavy artillery from China and, with a huge heroic effort of human will, hauled his new hardware over mountain passes to surround the wide valley at Dien Bien Phu. The French were completely surprised. In short order, the airstrip was destroyed and the French were cut off. Supplies and new troops arrived via airlift, but the Viet Minh were relentless, engaging a vicious trench ground war—Vietnamese proudly declare that the siege of Dien Bien Phu was won not by bullets and bombs, but with Vietnamese resolve and the shovel. Brave French and South Vietnamese paratroopers dropped into the battle site in the 11th hour when hope was surely lost, but on May 7, 1954, the Viet Minh made their final assault. The battle lasted almost two months, with Viet Minh troops winning by inches, but with heavy casualties on both sides. When the smoke cleared, North Vietnamese rejoiced to what looked like the end of a foreign empire.

Meeting in Geneva, all sides agreed that Vietnam would be partitioned at the 17th Parallel (a line that would come to mark the front in the next war), and the country would hold free elections 2 years hence. The north would be ruled in the interim by Ho Chi Minh, the leader of the Viet Minh, and the south by Ngo Dinh Diem, a U.S.-backed expatriate politician.

When election time arrived, Diem, facing likely defeat from the populist candidate Ho Chi Minh, withdrew from the election, breaking his promise at the Geneva Convention, and so began the struggle that pitted a reluctant superpower against a headstrong nationalist movement. The Viet Minh became the Viet Cong, and the war of attrition was on.

THE SECOND INDOCHINA WAR: VIETNAM & THE UNITED STATES

In 1961, in the hopes of supporting democracy in South Vietnam, President John F. Kennedy tentatively escalated U.S. involvement in Vietnam based on fears of the domino effect, a phrase set forth by former President Eisenhower and popularized by Robert McNamara, then U.S. secretary of defense. The idea was that with the support of "Red China," the countries of Southeast Asia, mostly poor, developing nations with large rural populations, were susceptible to Communist ideology, then the greatest perceived evil for U.S. politicians. Vietnam—being closest to China and heavily reliant on Chinese aid—would, the theory went, be the first to fall. The domino effect meant that Vietnam's fall would trigger grass-roots Communist movements in neighboring Laos, Cambodia, Thailand, and Burma, and on to the rest of South Asia. Vietnam, and specifically the 17th Parallel, is where U.S. ideologues chose to draw the line in the mud.

In its earliest stages, U.S. involvement was meant to "win the hearts and minds of the people." Hoping to showcase the benefits of capitalism and lead the fight with humanitarian efforts, there were many doctors and educators among early advisors, but most met with skepticism and armed resistance from a peasantry well versed in taking bonbons from imperial forces by day and practicing subterfuge by night.

Southern president Diem was an unpopular, heavy-handed ruler. In the early 1960s, southern Buddhists began to protest against Diem's unfairness and persecution of Buddhists and rural people (Diem was a staunch Catholic). In a famous image from the war, an elder monk set himself aflame in Saigon on June 11, 1963. Unrest in the south was growing, but the U.S. still backed Diem right up until the coup d'état in November 1963 and Diem's demise. Three weeks later, President Kennedy was assassinated.

The **Gulf of Tonkin Incident** was a watershed moment in the Second Indochina War (better known as the Vietnam War in the West, and, for obvious reasons, the American War in Vietnam itself). In August 1964, two U.S. ships, the *Maddox* and the *Turner Joy,* were reportedly attacked while patrolling the Gulf of Tonkin near Hanoi. In response, President Lyndon Johnson bombed Hanoi, the first of many large-scale bombing campaigns; the U.S. Congress also passed the Gulf of Tonkin Resolution, giving the U.S. president broad powers to wage war in Vietnam. Though hardly the sinking of the *Lusitania* or the attack on Pearl Harbor, the incident at Tonkin set off an irreversible chain of events. U.S. bombing campaigns increased in 1965 with the hopes that the North Vietnamese would just surrender or come to the bargaining table—in fact, they never would, and the many civilian deaths caused by **Operation Rolling Thunder** merely steeled northern resolve. War protests in the U.S. began as early as 1965 with the Students for a Democratic Society march on Washington, D.C.

Official war was never declared in Vietnam, but on March 8, 1965, President Johnson dispatched the first full contingent of more than 3,000 American combat troops to Danang to prop up the south. The Soviet Union and China weighed in with assistance to the north. The rest is history. You couldn't turn the TV on without seeing what would be called the "Living Room War," the first combat to be reported on television nightly, and the first to be so hotly debated in public consciousness. Americans had always believed that they fought, and won, wars that were justified, but Vietnam was a confounding exception. Early images of U.S. troops burning villages raised more questions than support at home, and just as the number of U.S. casualties increased, so did youthful protest and dissent. Vietnam divided the United States for generations, and many see the years of discord between political "hawks and doves" as molding political consciousness and public activism in America.

The statistics tell this story best: 2.5 million U.S. military personnel served during the 15-year conflict—58,000 gave their lives in action, some 300,000 were wounded, and countless numbers suffered post-traumatic stress disorder (PTSD). The war cost the United States over $900 billion. U.S. planes dropped 8 billion pounds of bombs (more than four times the tonnage of all of World War II), and along with Operation Ranch Hand, the systematic spraying of carcinogenic defoliants, Vietnam was left a virtual wasteland.

Around three million lives were lost on the Vietnamese side, of whom more than half were civilians. After the war, hundreds of thousands of South Vietnamese were put in reeducation camps, and an untold number of "boat people" fleeing oppression died at sea due to storms or at the hands of the South China Sea's rabid pirates (most of the lucky few who made it languished in a refugee camp for years before being able to find placement abroad). Tens of thousands of deaths were due to land mines and UXO (unexploded ordinances) in Vietnam since 1975, and tens of thousands more still suffer deformities because of exposure to U.S. chemical defoliants.

U.S. troops numbered just 200,000 in 1965, but by the end of 1968, the totals were more than 540,000. In November 1965, the United States claimed success in the first open battle of the war in the Ia Drang Valley in the Central Highlands. With its superior firepower and air support, the United States inflicted heavy losses on the Viet Cong. Though the United States also suffered heavy casualties, the superior "body count" at Ia Drang bolstered U.S. resolve that the war could be won.

But Vietnam was a guerrilla war, an episodic war against an enemy happy to win by inches, to suffer major casualties in order to break American resolve, to attack, retreat, and wait. The Viet Cong troops, with basic support from China, could subsist, they said, on a cup of rice and a cup of bullets each day, and the Ho Chi Minh supply line, a trail "complex" more than a road, could never be stopped by U.S. might. The North Vietnamese were also able to attack and retreat into neighboring Laos and Cambodia. Clever "tiger traps" and antipersonnel mines and snares set by the North Vietnamese troops were also demoralizing to a mostly drafted (that is, nonvoluntary) U.S. force. The Vietnamese built elaborate tunnel complexes and had many spies in the ranks of the south.

The mountainous jungles of Vietnam meant that the United States could not use tanks or armored personnel carriers in combat. U.S. techniques were to use defoliants, establish defoliated perimeters around fixed positions, and patrol to hunt down an enemy—tactics that played right into the Vietnamese strategy of attack and retreat.

U.S. soldiers fought valiantly, but the strategy of a "limited war" meant that the army had to fight one-handed and was unable to mount a full attack, mostly for fear of reprisals from nearby China or the Soviet Union. The U.S. was losing the "war of attrition" to a highly motivated North Vietnamese force, while the Army of the Republic of Vietnam (ARVN), the troops who fought alongside the U.S. GIs, was notoriously indifferent.

The tide of the war turned with the **Tet Offensive** in late 1968. U.S. Gen. William Westmoreland put all of his eggs in one basket, amassing the bulk of U.S. forces along the demilitarized zone (DMZ) at the 17th Parallel in expectation of a full frontal attack from the north. However, after major diversionary attacks at Hue, just south of the DMZ, North Vietnamese forces instead made an end run through neighboring Laos and Cambodia, connected with troops loyal to the revolution embedded in the south, and penetrated into the heart of Saigon, even taking the U.S. Embassy briefly. Northern General Giap's tactics were a great risk, and losses on the North Vietnamese side were heavy, but the Tet Offensive was the beginning of the end of the war—at home in the United States and on the ground in Vietnam.

After Tet came the devastating My Lai Massacre on March 16, 1968, where a platoon led by Lieut. William Calley went on a rampage that left 500 villagers dead and a world wondering what was happening in Vietnam. "The whole world is watching!" the demonstrators shouted at the 1968 Democratic convention—and it was. U.S. troops returning to the United States were met with jeers. There were "two wars," actually: the military war of bombs and guns in Vietnam, and the political war in the United States, a country undergoing drastic social changes.

The Paris Peace Talks began in the same year that the U.S. election brought Richard Nixon to the stage, and troop reductions began just a year later. Ho Chi Minh died in 1969 of natural causes, but his memory was a rallying cry, while back in the United States, protests became violent at Kent State University, where in 1970 national guardsmen shot and killed four unarmed protestors. The **Paris Peace Accords** finally became a success, and the United States ceased bombing North Vietnam. A massive exchange of prisoners took place at the DMZ, and "Vietnamization" of the war began—in other words, U.S. combat ended and turned the war over to the South Vietnamese.

After more than a decade of fighting, the Communists took Saigon on April 30, 1975, and in 1976 the north and south were officially reunited.

MODERN VIETNAM

Rather than enjoying the newfound peace after driving out the United States, Vietnam invaded Cambodia after border skirmishes in 1978. China, friend of Cambodia, then invaded Vietnam in 1979 (sometimes called the Third Indochina War).

At home, Communist ideology didn't fill the people's stomachs, and international trade embargoes and faltering support from the Soviet Union made life extremely difficult for the Vietnamese. In fact, life got worse for most people after the victory; millions were starving and inflation neared 1,000%. Desperate boat people, many of the unfortunate Vietnamese who had complied with the Americans, took to the seas on leaky boats, and many met horrible fates at the hands of the South China Sea's deadly pirates.

Faced with disaster, the Vietnamese government began implementing the new ideas of *Doi Moi,* a free-market policy that decentralized business, allowing private citizens and farmers to own land and the Vietnamese currency to trade on international markets. To ingratiate itself with the international community in the hope of aid and trade, Vietnam withdrew its army from Cambodia in 1989, and as the 1990s began, the country began opening to the world. After peace with Cambodia and

Vietnam's move to market economy, the United States lifted its long-standing trade embargo against Vietnam in 1994, and the two countries established diplomatic relations in 1995. Vietnam also joined ASEAN (Association of Southeast Asian Nations), and recent years have seen one milestone after another toward cooperation: a visit by President Bill Clinton in 2000, huge economic aid packages and commitments to cooperation, answers to long-standing questions about U.S. POWs, and U.S. assistance to victims of Agent Orange. Vietnam hosted the Asian Games in 2003, putting its best foot forward in what was a coup for international opinion. American Secretary of Defense Donald Rumsfeld met with Vietnam's defense minister in Washington, D.C., in 2003, and the USS *Vandergrift* pulled into port in Ho Chi Minh City at about the same time, the first U.S. Navy ship to dock in a Vietnamese port since hasty withdrawal in 1975. Telling signs, indeed.

The per-capita income of Vietnam (currently around $1,300) may seem low by Western standards, but the number is steadily rising each year. Unfortunately, the gap between urban and rural incomes remains noticeably large: inhabitants of Ho Chi Minh City earn about three times as much as their compatriots elsewhere. Vietnam's gross domestic product (GDP) in 2010 ranked it as the 42nd richest country in the world—unthinkable just a decade ago. Meanwhile, the country's status as an Asian "Tiger Economy" was solidified with its ascension to the World Trade Organization in early 2007. Shortly afterward, President Nguyen Minh Triet became the first Vietnamese head of state to visit Washington since the war ended. These are exciting times for Vietnam. And while Communist rhetoric still exists as an all-encompassing nationalism, the Vietnamese look toward a bright and very different future in the free market.

VIETNAMESE CUISINE

Gourmets have discovered Vietnam's light, subtle cuisine everywhere from Los Angeles to London, and are making their own long-haul flights to experience the real deal. Dining is often a highlight for visitors to Vietnam, and to ensure you're getting the most from your meals, dine with locals whenever possible; even if you foot the bill for the whole table, the cost is still a pittance.

TYPICAL INGREDIENTS

Vietnamese cuisine relies heavily on fresh ingredients and the right mix of herbs and spices. Look for the following in any dish you experience in the country: *Mang* (bamboo shoots) are the tender young stalks of a thick bamboo that's usually sliced thin and served fresh, dried, boiled, or as pickles; *bap chuoi* (banana blossom) is a red flower bud used in salads or as garnish; *la chuoi* (banana leaves) are used to wrap small portable meals of cakes or meats; and *kho qua* (bitter gourd) is used as a garnish. *Ot* (red chilies) are a common ingredient and add a real zing to any Vietnamese dish.

Fresh fish is available anywhere in Vietnam—you're never very far from the sea or a river—and meat and poultry are locally farmed.

Herbs and fresh vegetables are used both in cooking and as condiments at the table. With most Vietnamese meals, you'll be offered a plate of *rau que* (raw basil), which comes in several varieties, as well as *ngo* (coriander) and lettuce. The use of lemongrass, mint, coriander, ginger, basil, and garlic creates light, fresh, and flavorful fare.

Sadly, MSG (monosodium glutamate) is used widely in Vietnamese fare. In fact, the *Agi No Moto* ("More Taste") brand from Japan is offered on some local tables as a condiment. If you have a hard time processing MSG (that is, you get headaches, short-ness of breath, or MSG "seasickness"), ask for food without it *(khong co bot ngot).*

Nuoc mam is the famous—or notorious—Vietnamese fish sauce; its pungent flavor (and more pungent aroma) sets Vietnamese food apart. Simply put, it is fish that has been fermented in saltwater, but the subtleties to *nuoc mam* production are as calculated as the making of fine wine or olive oil. **Nuoc cham** is the most popular tabletop alternative, and mixes the pungent standard *nuoc mam* with sugar, vinegar, and seasonings for a more pleasant introduction to this unique Vietnamese flavor—you gotta try it once.

DINING & ETIQUETTE

Vietnamese are very hospitable, and there's a good chance you'll be invited to eat with a local family or join a Vietnamese group at a restaurant—you don't want to pass up the opportunity if it presents itself.

Etiquette is a rather casual affair, but there are a few things to remember. First and foremost, eating in Vietnam is a communal, not an individual, experience. The order of who is served, of who is given the choicest delicacies, and of who eats first is very important. When in doubt, wait. It's best to see that the eldest member of the group is served first and given the choicest fare—a whole egg from the top of a hot pot, a shrimp, or piece of steak.

Meals are slow, friendly affairs surrounding a banquet, usually on the floor, with everyone sitting in a circle. Courses come out of the kitchen in succession, and don't expect to get away with just eating like a bird. Food in shared dishes is picked up with either chopsticks or spoons, and eaten in a small hand-size bowl. It's okay to sip or slurp from the bowl, and shovel the last bits of a meal using your chopsticks. In fact you'll find it much easier to hold your bowl up near your chin rather than leaving it on the table. *Also note:* It's okay—customary even—to wipe utensils before eating.

POPULAR DISHES

Authentic Vietnamese cuisine is best enjoyed alfresco at street side, where food is cooked fresh and served on squat stools at a low table, often under an umbrella—a great way to meet locals. Below are a few of the kinds of dishes you can sample. Get adventurous. Go where locals go. Look for stalls that are packed, or storefront restau-rants that have a line out the door. Walk in, smile, and point or just say, "One, please," holding up a finger. Dishes are usually $2 or less.

PHO Classic Vietnamese noodle soup. **Pho bo** (noodle soup) is a dish of wide or narrow rice noodles done in a beef broth; flavored with ginger, black pepper, lemon, and shallots; and topped with thin slices of roast beef and fresh greens such as basil or coriander. **Pho ga** (noodle soup with chicken) is the same as *pho bo,* but with shredded chicken on top.

COM The very definition of "eating" is to *an com,* or "eat rice," And Vietnam's staple plays a part in nearly every meal. *Com* (the *o* in *com* is pronounced like the elongated *ou* in the word *should*) restaurants serve all manner of stir-fries or curries, often quite spicy in the south.

BUN Vietnamese *bun* (the *u* in *bun* is pronounced like a shortened *oo* in *wood*) is rice vermicelli, a fresh, light rice noodle with a slightly pungent aroma to it. Bun-style dishes are many, usually a mix of herbs and spices served with broth as a one-dish meal. **Bun bo** is rice vermicelli with shredded beef, usually in a fiery sauce. **Bun rieu** is a hearty stew of paddy crabs cooked in curry and shrimp paste and served with

For Vegetarians

Any dish can be altered for vegetarians, and good vegetable dishes such as *rau mouang xao chau* (fried morning glory with oyster sauce) or the standard *rau* *xau* (mixed fried vegetables) are available anywhere; just say *"An chay"* ("I eat vegetarian").

fresh rice vermicelli and greens. Avoid the various pig intestine varieties of bun dishes, the likes of *bun moc* or *bun gio heo.*

NEM RAN (CALLED CHA GIO IN THE SOUTH) The classic fried Vietnamese spring roll with ground meat or fish in a thin rice wrapper.

BANH XEO A thin pancake of rice flour folded with chicken or pork.

BANH CUON A variant of the standard spring roll made with a thick rice wrap and stuffed with chicken, beef, or shrimp (lots of varieties) and steamed.

CHA CA A delicious meal of delicate whitefish, fried at high heat in gobs of peanut oil with dill, turmeric, lemon shrimp paste, and a dash of rice whiskey.

NEM NUA Fresh spring rolls you make yourself that are popular all over Vietnam and a great light, low-budget snack.

DAOFU CHIEN A basic dish of fried tofu with lemongrass, delicious with rice and a side of *rau mouang xao chau,* fried morning glory (a kind of stringy spinach) with oyster sauce.

CHA TOM Ground, seasoned shrimp grilled on a stick of cut sugar cane.

BO BAY MON This is "beef served seven ways." A Saigon specialty, this succession of beef dishes includes fondue, fried, barbecued, and soup.

GOI NGO SEN A lotus root salad served with pomelo.

CA HAP Steamed fish served as you like.

Always look for regional specialties. **Hue cuisine,** for example, is famous for its light specialties, such as *bun bo hue* and good spring rolls. In **Hoi An,** try the Vietnamese raviolis, and in **Hanoi** the great *pho,* dog-meat dishes (if you dare), and *cha ca* (see above). Keep your eyes open for the fish sauce of Phan Thiet and Phu Quoc; duck dishes and spicy curries in **Saigon;** and many other regional favorites.

DRINKS

Tea follows hundreds of years of Chinese tradition—under Chinese tutelage—in the provinces of Thai Nguyen and Lao Cai, for example, where estates date back centuries. Vietnam's plantations produce all varieties, standard black and green as well as fine jasmine tea, and fine teas are imported from China.

Small cups of hot, **bitter Chinese tea** (called *tra*) are de rigueur for a first meeting, for a business situation, and for just killing time, and this casual offering of is an important component of hospitality. *Note:* When pouring more, fill your host's cup first and your cup last.

Tra da is iced tea, a standard pot of bitter Chinese tea poured over ice, usually unsweetened. Local restaurants serve *tra da* gratis from large pitchers.

EEW, WHAT'S that?

Vietnam is home to some of the world's most exotic fare. **Thit co (dog meat)**—a delicacy of the north—is usually eaten family style, almost exclusively by men to celebrate business deals (the meat is said to increase one's virility). Similarly, **thit ran (snake meat)** is a popular dish in Hanoi and is served in the Le Mat section north of Hanoi (see the box, "Have You Tried the Snake?" on p. 87).

One of Vietnam's rarest culinary oddities is **cafe cut chon.** The beans of this coffee are served after being digested and passed—I choke on that euphemism—by a weasel or civet. The taste? Earthy and strong.

Local **bia hoi,** a cheap draft beer of watery lager made in every region, is served cold on tap in every town, usually in small storefronts crowded with squat stool tables and lots of revelers.

Vietnamese whiskey, called **ruou,** comes in many varieties, and most of it could thin paint and is sure to cross your eyes in due time—go easy with the stuff. *Nep moi* is the standard variety, and it's sold in stores throughout the country, as well as in most *bia hoi* bars and roadside restaurants. In the Central Highlands, don't miss an opportunity to slurp from a long reed straw from a massive pot of **ruou can,** a particularly potent local brew made by ethnic-minority groups.

Vietnam is the second-largest **coffee grower** in the world, and though roasting techniques are primitive, choice Vietnamese Robusta coffee is delicious. Look for the **Trung Nguyen** brand, Vietnam's Starbucks. Also look for the fine **Highland Coffee** outlets in Hanoi and Ho Chi Minh City.

Vietnamese coffee is usually served with **sua,** or very sweet condensed milk. Say *"Ca phe sua chut-chut"* if you want only a little of the saccharine sweet stuff, or order a *"café den"* for black coffee. To order ice coffee at a local alfresco stand, just say *"Ca phe sua da"* and wait for the drip and pour it on ice.

Nuoc khoang is Vietnamese for "drinking water," which is available in bottles everywhere. Just say **"Cho toâi nuoc khoang"** (pronounced *Jya toy nook kwang*). Even locals drink bottled water (tap water is never potable), and all ice or drinking water provided is usually boiled or filtered and is just fine. Kids love the popular **nuoc mia,** or sugar-cane juice. Also popular are cool drinks with lemon: **Nuoc chanh** is lemonade, and **soda chanh** is a lemon soda. Ask for it with or without sugar (*duong*). This is the hip expat drink of choice.

DESSERT

Che is a popular dessert dish of rice gelatin sweetened with Chinese litchi fruit and sugar. **Kem** (ice cream) is available everywhere, both Western-style ice cream (as taught by French colonists) and the local variety made with soy and coconut.

Sinh to is a delicious soy-based sweet shake made with the fruit of your choosing. Tropical Vietnam offers a wide variety of fruit, sometimes served with *da ua* (fresh yogurt), and is affordable and available everywhere.

WHEN TO GO

Think Vietnam, and you might imagine a steamy jungle and hot sun—and you'd be mostly right. But even though Vietnam is tropical, you'll find a real range, from chilly mountaintops and cool highland areas to sun-drenched coastline and, yes, that steamy jungle, too, laced with the swampy rivers you've seen in movies.

Opposing monsoon seasons in the north and south mean that seasonal changes are different in north, central, and south Vietnam. The good news for travelers is that this means it's always high season *somewhere* in Vietnam, and the tropical south is always warm. Vietnam can be broken into three **distinct geographical and climatic zones** as follows: north, central, and south.

The **north** is cooler than the rest of the country. Winter months, from November until January, can be quite chilly, especially in mountainous areas. Northern temperatures range from 60°F to 90°F (16°C–32°C). If you are going far north to **Sapa** or **Dien Bien Phu** along the China/Laos border, be sure to take a pullover and jacket with you; near Sapa is Fansipan, Vietnam's highest point, and there are even the occasional freeze and snow at this altitude. **Hanoi,** the capital, and nearby coastal regions around **Haiphong** and **Halong Bay** experience relatively high humidity year-round and a rainy season from May to October. Winter months are cool (as low as 57°F/14°C) and somewhat damp, but the heat starts to pick up in April and makes for a hot, wet summer (many Hanoians get out of town, to the mountain towns or nearby beaches off Haiphong or Vinh). The best time to visit the north, though cold in midwinter, is from November to the end of April.

The **Central Coast** follows an opposing monsoon pattern to the north, with warmer weather during the July-to-October high season, and wet, colder weather from November to May. **Coastal Vietnam**—Quy Nhon and Nha Trang—experiences steamy temperatures like the far south (70°F–90°F/21°C–32°C), but coastal wind can have a cooling effect. Raging storms and frequently large typhoons strike the coast from September to December; often during this season, the surf is too rough for swimming.

The **Central Highlands,** just inland and on the southern end of the **Annamese Cordillera** range, receives nearly double the rainfall of the national average, and this plateau, in towns such as **Dalat** and **Pleiku,** is cool throughout the year.

The **south,** the region around **Ho Chi Minh City** and the **Mekong Delta,** is steamy hot year-round with only periods of rainy and dry weather. Temperatures range from 70°F to 90°F (21°C–32°C), with a hot, dry period from March to May seeing temperatures in the 90s (30s Celsius). Summers are hot, humid, and rainy.

Because of the regional variations in weather, a part of the country is seasonable at any time of year. Most travelers in Vietnam trace a north-south or south-north route with flights connecting on either end (or adding continued travel to Cambodia or China). Depending on the duration of your stay, you can plan to "follow" the good weather, hitting Saigon in February or March and tracing warmer weather up the coast.

Note: **Avoid travel during the Tet holiday** in January or February (see calendar of events, below). Tet is a Christmas and New Year's celebration rolled into one, and anyone and everyone is going "over the river and through the woods" to their respective grandmother's house. Transport is always fully booked. Unless you're lucky enough to enjoy Tet with a Vietnamese family, be forewarned: During this time, many travelers find themselves stranded, hotels completely full, and roadways crowded with traffic and revelers.

Below are the monthly weather charts for the major cities of the northern, central, and southern regions of Vietnam (Hanoi, Danang, and Ho Chi Minh City, respectively). Rainfall daily averages are accurate to within 1 millimeter.

LESS IS MORE: packing & CLOTHING IN THE TROPICS

Keep it light and loose. You are sure to hit hot, sticky weather on any route in Vietnam. The old traveler rule "less is more" applies here; bulky luggage is an albatross in Vietnam. Fast and light is best. Loose, long-sleeve shirts and long pants, preferably cotton, are recommended. Shorts are good for swimming but not great for the backcountry, where mosquitoes are ferocious. Also note that shorts are generally worn by children, not adults (although long shorts are more accepted, especially for young men), and for women only rarely (with

sporting events being the exception). Foreign visitors are somewhat exempt from these conventions, but why not go local where we can? A wide-brimmed hat is essential protection from the sun, and some even carry an umbrella to be used either as a parasol or as cover from sporadic rains. Sandals are acceptable in most arenas. Affordable laundry service is available everywhere, and thin cotton dries quite quickly—great for a bit of sink-washing instead of carrying around heaps of laundry.

Average Daily Temperatures (°F/°C) & Monthly Rainfall (mm/in.)

		JAN	FEB	MAR	APR	MAY	JUNE	JULY	AUG	SEPT	OCT	NOV	DEC
Hanoi	**Highs**	66/19	67/19	72/22	80/27	87/31	90/32	90/32	89/32	88/32	82/28	76/24	71/22
	Lows	58/14	60/16	65/18	71/22	77/25	80/27	80/27	80/27	78/26	73/23	66/19	60/16
	Rainfall	18/	28/	38/	81/	196/	239/	323/	343/	254/	99/	43/	20/
		0.7	1.1	1.5	3.2	7.7	9.4	12.7	13.5	10.0	3.9	1.7	0.8
Danang	**Highs**	77/31	79/32	83/34	87/34	91/33	93/31	93/30	92/30	89/30	85/31	81/30	77/30
	Lows	67/16	69/21	71/24	75/24	78/24	79/24	79/24	78/24	76/23	75/23	72/23	68/19
	Rainfall	102/	31/	12/	18/	47/	42/	99/	117/	447/	530/	221/	209/
		4.0	1.2	0.5	0.7	1.9	1.7	3.9	4.6	17.6	20.1	8.7	8.2
Ho Chi Minh City													
	Highs	88/31	90/32	92/33	93/34	92/33	89/32	89/32	88/31	88/31	87/31	87/31	87/31
	Lows	72/22	73/23	76/24	79/26	79/26	77/25	77/25	77/25	76/24	76/24	74/23	72/22
	Rainfall	15.2/	2.5/	10.2/	50.8/	213.4/	309.9/	294.6/	271.8/	342.9/	261.6/	119.4/	45.7/
		0.6	0.1	0.4	2.0	8.4	12.2	11.6	10.7	13.5	10.3	4.7	1.8

Vietnam Calendar of Events

In their daily lives, Vietnamese people follow the standard 12-month calendar, otherwise known as the Gregorian or solar calendar used in the West. However, most of Vietnam's small village fetes and holidays follow the traditional Chinese calendar, which has 355 days and adds a "leap month" every 3 years or so to keep up with the solar calendar. Following the Chinese lunar calendar means that most holidays correspond with the full moon (on the 15th of each lunar month) or no moon (on the 1st); it also means that holidays fall on different calendar dates each year. For example: **Tet,** the Lunar New Year and Vietnam's biggest holiday, will be on January 23, 2012, and February 10, 2013.

There is a variety of regional celebrations and local festivals among the ethnic majority Vietnamese. Add to that the many disparate holidays and practices of Vietnam's 54 ethnic groups, and you have holidays left and right; any rural trip means a good chance of stumbling onto something interesting. Vietnamese are inclusive about their celebrations; **Tet,** for example, is a family holiday, but a few shouts of *Chuc Mung Nam Moi* (Happy New Year!) usually mean getting swept up in the fervor. Surrender to it.

Be sure to ask around about market days in the Northern Highland areas—when a big, traveling goods market comes into town (usually Sun). Also look for the likes of modern city festivals, such as the hugely popular **Hue Festival** (see the box in the Hue section of chapter 9). Below are the major national holidays and festivals.

JANUARY/FEBRUARY

New Year's Day. Everything but Dick Clark. January 1.

Anniversary of the Founding of the Communist Party. Nationwide. Celebrated everywhere; expect parade grounds in any city to be busy with cultural shows and speechmaking. Waving massive red flags in open-air shows in the evening is always the finale. February 3.

Vietnam Traditional Lunar New Year Festival (Tet Nguyen Dan). Countrywide. This 4-day national holiday, Tet, usually falls in late January or early February. The festivities begin on New Year's Eve and the first 3 days of a Lunar New Year, but most people celebrate for a week or more. It's a time to be with family members. For detailed information, see the box on Tet, below. The first day of the first lunar month (Jan 23, 2012; Feb 10, 2013).

MARCH/APRIL

Festival at the Perfume Pagoda. Near Hanoi. Buddhists from all over Vietnam make a pilgrimage to the deep cave at the apex of this holy mountain at the half-moon of the second lunar month (Mar 7, 2012; Mar 26, 2013).

Hmong Spring Festival. In the far north. Hmong populations across the north converge for colorful parades and market days. Fifth day of the third lunar month (Mar 26, 2012; Apr 14, 2013).

Gio To Hung Vuong. Nationwide. This new holiday (added in 2007) commemorates the death of Emperor Hung. According to legend, Emperor Hung ruled over what is now modern Vietnam some 50 centuries ago. Tenth day of the third lunar month (Mar 31, 2012; Apr 19, 2013).

Saigon Liberation Day. Nationwide. Celebrated with lots of parades and commemorative TV programming. Apr 30.

MAY

International Labor Day. Nationwide. The Communist marching day around the world. Celebrations and parades in central squares nationwide. May Day, May 1.

Birthday of President Ho Chi Minh. Nationwide. Cultural performances and candlelight vigils are held across the country. The major sights in Vinh, Ho Chi Minh's birthplace, are overrun, and Ba Dinh Square, Hanoi, where Ho's body is held in state, is mobbed. May 19.

AUGUST/SEPTEMBER/OCTOBER

Tet Trung Nguyen. Nationwide. A time to give thanks to the ancestors. Families gather, remember those who have died, eat, and visit grave sites. Half-moon of the seventh lunar month (Aug 31, 2012; Aug 21, 2013).

National Day. Nationwide. Celebrates the rise of the Socialist Republic of Vietnam. Local parades, pomp, and circumstance. Sept 2.

Do Son Buffalo Fighting Festival. Near Haiphong. A riot for everyone (except the buffalos). The ninth day of the eighth lunar month (Sept 24, 2012; Sept 13, 2013).

Mid-Autumn Festival. Nationwide. This colorful celebration is a popular one for kids, with dance and special sweet cakes. Half-moon of the eighth lunar month (Sept 30, 2012; Sept 19, 2013).

DECEMBER

Christmas. Nationwide. Most widely celebrated in the south, where Christian populations are largest. Although Vietnam's recent plunge into capitalism means more and more American-style Santa-focused decorations and shopping in the major cities; you can still expect some ho-ho-ho Ho Ho Ho Chi Minh style. Dec 25.

For an exhaustive list of events beyond those listed here, check http://events.frommers.com, where you'll find a searchable, up-to-the-minute roster of what's happening in cities all over the world.

Imagine an American Thanksgiving, Christmas, New Year's Eve, and Easter all rolled into one—that's Tet. This megaholiday on the Vietnamese calendar is a time for pilgrimage to the family stamping grounds. Everyone, including the many young Vietnamese who have left the rice fields for work in the big cities, goes home (travel is a nightmare and best avoided). Food is the focus, and everyone hustles home to try Grandma's *chung* cakes—small square cakes made of glutinous rice—after a real feast of down-home cooking (regional variations are many). This is a time to honor ancestors; offerings of fruit and flowers, whole feasts even, are placed on family altars. The 23rd day of the 12th lunar month hosts a ceremony of farewell for last year's "Kitchen God." The 29th and 30th days are a time to say farewell to the old year and hello to the new, with all the fanfare and hoopla you can muster; streets are crowded with motorbikes, and the rice wine and *bia hoi* (local draft beer) flows freely. Folks go a-visiting on the first day of the lunar New Year, sharing food and fellowship among neighbors. Tet is also a celebration of Vietnamese strength and autonomy. On the fifth day of the Tet holiday, people raise a glass (or two) to freedom fighter **Quang Trung,** who defeated the Chinese at Dong Da near Hanoi, and spurred them on with cries of, "And then we'll go home for some of Grandma's *chung cakes*!"

THE LAY OF THE LAND

Vietnam is an S-shaped strip of land that borders China in the north, Laos in the west, and Cambodia in the southwest. Covering about 331,520 sq. km (129,293 sq. miles), it is roughly the size of Italy. It has a varied and lush topography, with two deltas, tropical forests, craggy mountains, rock formations, and a coastline that stretches for 3,260km (2,021 miles), much of it white-sand beaches. Vietnam also claims thousands of islands off its coast.

THE REGIONS IN BRIEF

THE NORTH The scenic northern highlands have craggy mountains hovering over sweeping green valleys. The inhabitants of the region are predominantly ethnic minorities, scratching out a living from subsistence farming and still somewhat isolated from civilization. Popular tourism destinations are **Sapa** and **Dien Bien Phu,** the former French military garrison. Vietnam's tallest mountain, Fansipan (3,143m/10,309 ft.), hovers over Sapa near the border with China in the northwest, part of the mountain range the French dubbed the "Tonkinese Alps." The **Red River Delta** lies to the east of the highlands. It is a triangular shape off the **Gulf of Tonkin,** an extension of the South China Sea. In the gulf is spectacular **Halong Bay,** 3,000 limestone formations jutting from still blue waters. South of the highlands but still in the northern region is **Hanoi,** Vietnam's capital city.

THE CENTRAL COAST South of Hanoi is the central coastline, location of major cities **Hue, Hoi An,** and **Danang.** Hue is Vietnam's former capital and Imperial City (1802–1945). Hoi An, a major trading port in the mid–16th century, still shows the architectural influences of the Chinese and Japanese traders who passed through and settled here, leaving buildings that are perfectly preserved. Danang, Vietnam's fourth-largest city, is a port town whose major attractions include the museum of Cham antiquities and nearby China Beach.

THE SOUTH-CENTRAL COAST & HIGHLANDS   The central highlands area is a temperate, hilly region occupied by many of Vietnam's ethnic minorities. Travelers are most likely to visit historic **Dalat,** a resort town nestled in the Lang Bien Plateau, established by the French at the turn of the 20th century as a recreation and convalescence center. On the coast is **Nha Trang,** Vietnam's preeminent sea resort.

THE MEKONG DELTA   Farthest south, the Mekong Delta is a flat land formed by soil deposits from the Mekong River. Its climate is tropical, characterized by heat, high rainfall, and humidity. The delta's sinuous waterways drift past fertile land used for cultivating rice, fruit trees, and sugar cane. The lower delta is untamed swampland. The region shows the influences of ancient Funan and Khmer cultures, as well as the scars from war misery, particularly in battles with neighboring Cambodia. **Ho Chi Minh City (Saigon),** Vietnam's largest cosmopolitan area, lies just past its northern peripheries.

SUSTAINABLE TOURISM

As a relatively new vacation destination—and a developing country, to boot—Vietnam puts little pressure on the tourism industry to develop sustainable practices. There is virtually no backlash for hotels' and resorts' profligate energy usage. Meanwhile, the enthusiasm of international hotel chains and local developers has led to massive development of once-public, pristine beaches in places such as Phu Quoc, Mui Ne, and Danang. The end result may well be ghettos of five-star resorts and golf courses guzzling large quantities of energy.

For individual travelers, cranking up the air-conditioning is a knee-jerk reaction when vacationing in Vietnam. Sure, there are some cool respites in the north and central parts of the country, but for the most part, your vacation is going to be a hot one. But bear in mind that it takes massive amounts of energy to keep hotel rooms and indoor areas cool. To make your Vietnam vacation a little bit greener, take the initiative and turn down the air-conditioning when staying at high-end hotels—these places often keep rooms at a chilly 66°F (19°C).

A few notable outfits are also making conscious efforts to reduce their impact on the surrounding environs. The guys at **Vietnam Vespa Adventure** (see chapter 12) use biodiesel made from refined vegetable oil waste to run their multiday tours on vintage Vespa scooters. Over in Phnom Penh, the **Quay** (see chapter 14) bills itself as a "carbon-friendly" boutique hotel, buying carbon credits to offset the hotel's emissions.

Finally, when traveling to far-flung places, be mindful of local customs. Be very cautious about taking photographs among Vietnam's ethnic hilltribe minorities in the far north and Central Highlands. Ask first, respect an answer of "no" (true anywhere), and avoid photographing sacred shrines of hilltribe people.

SPECIAL-INTEREST & ESCORTED GENERAL-INTEREST TOURS

Special-Interest Trips

ACADEMIC TRIPS & LANGUAGE CLASSES

A visit just to **Hanoi** puts vast resources at your fingertips—from museums to vestiges of architecture as far back as the 11th century. Walking tours of the Old Quarter, an area of the city that a curious traveler could literally pick apart block by block, are

responsible TOURISM

Tourists in Vietnam are a relatively new species, and it's important to respect local culture and try to minimize our impact on the country. In Vietnam, try to keep personal ideologies and political debate quiet. Vietnamese are proud of their triumph over outside threats, autonomy that came at a great cost in lives and suffering, and the doors are just opening after a long period of isolation (because of both external sanctions and internal policies). The common sentiment among Vietnamese, more than half of whom were born after the end of conflict with the United States, is to forget the past and push on into an ever brighter future, economically and socially. There are, however, many monuments to Vietnam's years of struggle. When visiting monuments to war—or one of the many sights that depict or revisit the years of struggle against the Chinese, French, or Americans—it's important to practice restraint. Refrain from jokes, try to go in smaller groups, and engage in debates or personal feelings in discreet tones or at a later time. In places such as **Ho Chi Minh's Mausoleum** in Hanoi, the monument to the **My Lai Massacre** in central Vietnam, the tunnels of **Cu Chi** and **Vinh Moch,** the

Hanoi Hilton, or the **War Remnants Museum,** discretion is not only requested, it's often enforced (visitors have been known to receive actual hand slaps and barked orders at Ho Chi Minh's Mausoleum, for example).

Our strongest impact as visitors is through our money and how we spend it. Giving gifts in Vietnam, particularly to young people or the many who approach foreign visitors with calls of help, is a double-edged sword. Where it might gratify in the short term to help someone and fill a few outstretched hands with sweets or school supplies, it sets up a harmful precedent and props up the image of foreign visitors as walking ATMs—to be bilked, begged, and bamboozled at every turn. You will be followed and harried in Vietnam quite a bit, and in some areas, particularly Hanoi, the young book-and-postcard salesmen and touts are part of organized gangs and very persistent (although the hard sell has lessened with the increased number of tourists). Saying a polite but firm "No" or "Maybe later" to persistent hawkers goes a long way to alleviating the problem.

Among **Vietnam's ethnic minorities** in the Central Highlands and the far

like a giant textbook. Here you'll learn about early Vietnamese commerce, the colonial administration of the French, early Vietnamese unrest, and eventual insurgency, not to mention the more heavy-handed legacy of a triumphant Vietnam under the leadership of Ho Chi Minh in the vestiges of his mausoleum and museum.

Asia Transpacific Journeys (see the listing under "Escorted General-Interest Tours," below) is quite typical of the many international tour agencies running trips to Vietnam. They offer specialized itineraries focused on Vietnamese culture—such as the ancients, the Cham people, vestiges of the Chinese millennia, and the years under French colonialism.

Hanoi Language and Culture Tours (℘ 09/1352-2605; www.hanoilanguage tours.com) offers multiday courses that range from quick 2-day affairs to arm you with Vietnamese basics, to language and travel courses that offer the opportunity to practice your newly learned linguistic skills in a Vietnamese homestay.

north, be most careful about your impact. These communities are on the fringe of Vietnamese culture, distinct enclaves where ancient practices of animistic faiths still hold sway. Photographers should be sure to ask before snapping portraits or images of ceremonial sights; increasingly, asking for permission to photograph is met with pleas for money, but say no and move on. It's important not to assault locals with a camera, however uniquely attired and exotic they may be. Gifts of clothes or medicines might seem helpful but only diminish already-eroding ancient cultures and customs of clothing manufacture—where, in fact, one's clothing is an integral part of status in the community—and traditional medicines, erasing ancient traditions passed on from the time of migration from China. Learn about these people and their traditions as much as you can before traveling among them—in fact, your knowledge about any place that you travel makes you less likely to make uncomfortable blunders. Keep an open mind, and be ready to learn, not teach. Below are a few good guidelines for environmental and cultural stewardship.

Don't litter: Sounds simple, but in a country where you will rarely find a public trash receptacle (most things are discarded on the street and swept up en masse), it is difficult. As unimportant as it might feel to drop a gum wrapper, more important is your example of *not* dropping a gum wrapper. On rural hiking trails or in national parks, tie a garbage bag to the outside of your pack and pick up wrappers along the way. Don't preach, but if locals ask what you are doing—and they certainly will—explain that you are keeping the park clean and that it is something that anyone can do.

Wherever possible, try to **support the local economy**—eat at local joints, buy essentials such as bottled water and soap at small mom-and-pop shops instead of big air-conditioned department stores, even try public transport (if you are a hearty soul). Don't buy any animal products, even the likes of snake wines or lizard-skin bags, and try to find out if souvenirs are produced locally.

Your behavior as a tourist also reflects on the many tourists who will come after you. Set a good precedent, even when if doesn't feel important.

ADVENTURE & WELLNESS TRIPS

If you like to get out into the countryside, you can find much to do in Vietnam. Consider first the kind of terrain you'd like to explore—ranging from dense jungle to high mountains, coastal estuaries to inland rivers on flooded rice plains. Next, choose your preferred method of transport: kayak, mountain bike, motorcycle, jeep, hiking boots, or flip-flops.

The best areas for good trekking are in the **far north** and **Central Highlands** of Vietnam; both regions have large populations of minority ethnic hilltribes, and the scenery—rice terraces and spiked peaks—is stunning. Highlights include visiting **Halong Bay** and the country's many national parks.

In the north of Vietnam, the folks at **Handspan** (© 04/3926-2828; www. handspan.com), as well as **Buffalo Tours** (© 04/3828-0702; www.buffalotours. com), put together exciting kayaking adventures in Halong Bay. In the far north, they offer good hiking trips to Sapa and by jeep up to Dien Bien Phu. For a rock climbing

GENERAL RESOURCES FOR green travel

The following websites provide valuable wide-ranging information on sustainable travel. For a list of even more sustainable resources, as well as tips and explanations on how to travel greener, visit www.frommers.com/planning.

o **Responsible Travel** (www.responsibletravel.com) is a great source of sustainable travel ideas; the site is run by a spokesperson for ethical tourism in the travel industry. **Sustainable Travel International** (www.sustainabletravelinternational.org) promotes ethical tourism practices. Both of these sites have extensive directories of sustainable properties and tour operators around the world.

o In the U.K., **Tourism Concern** (www.tourismconcern.org.uk) works to reduce social and environmental problems connected to tourism. The **Association of Independent Tour Operators** (**AITO;** www.aito.co.uk) is a group of specialist operators leading the field in sustainable tourism.

o In Canada, **www.greenliving online.com** offers extensive content on how to travel sustainably, including a travel and transport section.

o In Australia, the national body that sets guidelines and standards for eco-tourism is

Ecotourism Australia (www.ecotourism.org.au). **The Green Directory** (www.thegreen directory.com.au), **Green Pages** (www.thegreenpages.com.au), and **Eco Directory** (www.eco directory.com.au) offer sustainable travel tips and directories of green businesses.

o **Carbonfund** (www.carbonfund.org), **TerraPass** (www.terrapass.org), and **Cool Climate Network** (http://coolclimate.berkeley.edu) provide info on "carbon offsetting," or offsetting the greenhouse gas emitted during flights.

o **Greenhotels** (http://greenhotels.com) recommends green-rated member hotels around the world that fulfill the company's stringent environmental requirements. **Environmentally Friendly Hotels** (www.environmentallyfriendly hotels.com) offers more green accommodations ratings.

o For information on animal-friendly issues throughout the world, visit **Tread Lightly** (www.treadlightly.org).

o **Volunteer International** (www.volunteerinternational.org) has a list of questions to help you determine the intentions and nature of a volunteer program. For general info on volunteer travel, visit **www.goabroad.com** and **www.idealist.org**.

adventure in Halong Bay, your best bet is **Slo Pony Adventures** (℃ **091/376-0025;** www.slopony.com). In central Vietnam, the old French colonial hill station of Dalat plays host to a great outfitter, **Phat Tire Ventures** (℃ **063/3829-422;** www.phattireventures.com), where you can rock-climb, mountain-bike, or trek with the most professional guides and experienced technicians.

Off-road adventures on **motorbike** and **by jeep** abound along the length of Vietnam. See chapter 6 for more extensive information on motorbike and jeep touring north of Hanoi along the **Dien Bien Phu Loop** or up to **Cao Bang.** Small outfitters in Hanoi can help with rentals or guide hires.

In the **Central Highlands,** hiring an **Easy Rider** motorcycle guide out of Dalat is all the rage. (See chapter 10 for contact information.) Riding a big (for Vietnam) 125cc Honda Bonus—you sit on the back—the Easy Riders, some of whom retired from the South Vietnamese Army and speak English well, will take you across the ridge of the highlands all the way through **Buon Ma Thuot** and on to **Kontum,** where the Ho Chi Minh Highway leads to Danang or Hue and eventually Hanoi. Easy Rider can make arrangements for groups and even rent motorbikes if some members of the group want to ride their own bikes alongside a guide. The same routes can also be done by jeep.

In **Ho Chi Minh City,** seek out **Vietnam Vespa Adventure** for a memorable trip on a lovingly restored vintage Vespa scooter (see chapter 12 for contact information). These guys will take you off the beaten track around the beach resorts of Mui Ne or Nha Trang.

FOOD & WINE TRIPS

Sampling Vietnamese cuisine is a highlight of any trip, so why not learn to make it yourself? The **Hanoi Cooking Centre** (✆ **04/3715-0088;** www.hanoicooking centre.com) is a popular choice in the nation's capital. The city's first purpose-built cooking center runs hands-on classes out of a restored colonial building near Truc Bach Lake. In Hoi An, in central Vietnam, Ms. Vy at **Morning Glory Restaurant and Cooking School** (✆ **0510/224-1556;** www.restaurant-hoian.com) runs great programs of varying length.

ESCORTED GENERAL-INTEREST TOURS

Escorted tours are structured group tours with a group leader. The price usually includes everything from airfare to hotels, meals, tours, admission costs, and local transportation.

Whether you want to ride an elephant through the jungle, trek among indigenous people, shake hands with a gibbon, swim beneath a waterfall, snorkel in a clear blue lagoon, lounge on a white-sand beach, or wander through exotic markets, there's a Vietnam tour packager for you, offering a wide range of travel options using the finest and most reliable travel services available in the region.

Among the most experienced and knowledgeable tour operators specializing in Vietnam and Southeast Asia are **Absolute Asia** and **Asia Transpacific Journeys.** In-country tour providers **Diethelm** and **Exotissimo** can do anything from arranging deluxe tours to just helping out with any small details or bookings. Most companies allow clients to design their own trips or deviate from exact schedules (often at a small cost). Companies such as **Intrepid,** among others, offer unique itineraries for solo travelers. Many in-country tour operators are listed in the book's following chapters, but here are the top outfitters:

Abercrombie & Kent   Well-known luxury-tour operator Abercrombie & Kent offers Southeast Asia programs with numerous comprehensive itineraries, including expansive tours to Vietnam and Cambodia. A journey with A&K includes the best dining and luxury transport, as well as high-end stays at the finest hotels in Southeast Asia and Vietnam, such as the Metropole in Hanoi or the finer beach resorts near Nha Trang. In the United States: 1411 Opus Place, Executive Towers West II, Ste. 300, Downers Grove IL 60515-1098; ✆ **800/554-7016;** fax 630/725-3401; www. abercrombiekent.com.

Absolute Asia   Founded in 1989, Absolute Asia offers an array of innovative itineraries, specializing in individual or small-group tours customized to your interests,

VIETNAM WITH kids

If you have enough trouble getting your kids out of the house in the morning, dragging them thousands of miles away might seem like an insurmountable challenge. But family travel can be immensely rewarding, giving you new ways of seeing the world through smaller pairs of eyes.

The rough roads of Vietnam can be a bit much for little ones, and concerns about communicable diseases in rural areas should certainly be weighed (be sure to check with your healthcare provider and be vigilant about updating all vaccinations). However, more accessible destinations and larger cities offer a glimpse into ancient civilization and varied culture that delights the kid in all of us.

Traveling families report no unique hassles to bringing the kids along to Vietnam. Most families choose to fly from place to place within the country, though, and avoid overcrowded local transport (though the trains, especially to Sapa in the far north, are pretty doable and a good adventure). Most hotels can arrange extra beds at little additional cost (in some places kids stay free), and connecting-room capability is common. To locate accommodations, restaurants, and attractions that are particularly kid friendly, refer to the "Kids" icon throughout this guide.

The larger resort destinations—the better hotels in **Nha Trang, Hoi An,** and the **Furama Resort in Danang**—are quite kid friendly. Many families choose a comfortable hotel and make **culturally rich Hanoi** a hub for trips to **Halong Bay** and **Sapa,** but the whole length of Vietnam's coast is open to exploration by the adventurous traveling brood. Kids love eating ice cream in the many open-air joints surrounding Hoan Kiem Lake in Hanoi, and war tourism seems to spark something in boys (of all ages). The **War Museum** in Ho Chi Minh City—with tanks, planes, and artillery in the large courtyard—seems to delight kids and is a highlight, but be forewarned: There are also many grisly images in this museum. Kids love crawling through the tunnels in **Cu Chi** or **Vinh Moc** and clambering up the steep hills in the Central Highlands town of **Dalat,** which, with its

with experienced local guides and excellent accommodations. Talk to them about tours that feature art, cuisine, religion, antiques, photography, wildlife study, archaeology, and soft adventure—they can plan a specialized trip to see just about anything you can dream up for any length of time. They can also book you on excellent coach programs in Vietnam or throughout Indochina. In the United States: 15 Watts St., 5th floor, New York, NY 10013; © **800/736-8187;** fax 212/627-4090; www.absoluteasia.com.

Asia Transpacific Journeys   Coordinating tours to every corner of South and Southeast Asia and the Pacific, Asia Transpacific Journeys deals with small groups and custom programs that include luxury hotel accommodations. The flagship package, the 23-day Passage to Indochina tour, costing around $8,000, takes you through Laos, Vietnam, and Cambodia's major attractions with a well-planned itinerary that also promotes cultural understanding. A highly recommended choice. In the United States: 2995 Center Green Court, Boulder, CO 80301; © **800/642-2742** or 303/443-6789; fax 303/443-7078; www.asiatranspacific.com.

Backroads   For those who want to explore Vietnam by bike, cycling and hiking specialist Backroads has a 12-day Vietnam tour, among others. Check out their tattered Disney-like sights and fun day hikes, is a favorite for kids. Kids always enjoy rapping with the **hilltribe people in Sapa**—a fun clash of culture because the young ethnic hilltribe folks speak English well and are eager to chat with foreigners their age—this also means that your kids might come home with a few words of Hmong, Dao, or Vietnamese, and maybe even a pen pal.

The big hotels all have pools, oceanside resorts are great places to play, and every major city has a big water park that, though sometimes a bit grungy, is an appealing option to both parents and kids wanting to escape from the heat and connect with locals. You'll find willing—and affordable—babysitters in even the smallest hotel or guesthouse, and Vietnamese dote on children, meaning your clan will get lots of attention everywhere you go. Some parents are surprised at how easily kids adapt—much better than parents sometimes—adventurously hopping on boats and fearlessly meeting with locals.

A note of warning: People generally love kids in Vietnam, and foreign children are sure to attract lots of attention—sometimes far too much, actually, and it can be a bit overwhelming. With the most friendly of intentions, Vietnamese often like to touch foreign kids, tousle their hair, or brush a cheek and dote like your favorite auntie does back home, which can be disconcerting or confusing for kids (even from auntie). It's a good idea to warn your kids that this might happen, and it's also okay to step in front of people and kindly but firmly say no or *khong tich* (he/she doesn't like that) while brushing away a hand. You might also find yourself in "walking zoo" moments, where groups of Vietnamese tourists want photos of themselves—and this is most common at the big sights—with foreign people. Again, this can be irritating, and saying no is fine, but you could also make their day by giving them a few moments for a cheesy snapshot. As much as possible, talk with people; this takes away the freaky "sideshow" vibe and puts you on a level of "relating," as all parents do, rather than comparing your differences.

website; they're always coming up with new innovative itineraries in the region. In the United States: 801 Cedar St., Berkeley, CA 94710-1800; ✆ **800/462-2848** or 510/527-1555; fax 510/527-1444; www.backroads.com.

Exotissimo A French outfit and outbound (in-country) agency with offices in every major city in the region, Exotissimo has excellent on-site guides. Agents can arrange all-inclusive tours and help with all travel details, from ticketing to visas. See the office locations in each relevant chapter: 80–82 Phan Kich Long St., Phu Nhuan District, Ho Chi Minh City; ✆ **08/3995-9898;** fax 08/3995-9184; www.exotissimo.com.

Imaginative Traveller This U.K.-based firm gets rave reviews every time for organizing all sorts of cycling, trekking, and motorcycling adventures throughout the region, particularly in Vietnam and Cambodia. In the U.K.: 1 Betts Ave., Martlesham Heath, Suffolk IP5 3RH; ✆ **1473/857-535;** www.imaginative-traveller.com.

Intrepid This popular Australian operator is a good choice for getting off the beaten track on a tour of Vietnam. Intrepid caters tours for the culturally discerning, those with humanitarian goals, adventurers, and people on a budget. Their motto is their name, and with some of the best guides in Asia, these folks will take you to the back of beyond safely, in style, and with lots of laughs. A fun, fraternal vibe pervades

TOURS FOR vietnam veterans

A good percentage of visitors to Vietnam are American Vietnam War veterans. It's not unusual to run across groups or individuals as you make your way through the country, some simply seeing how the story ended or others on more somber missions, such as staging memorial services.

But why would a veteran want to return to Vietnam, the scene of such tragic events? Most say they seek closure and that only by finally crossing the 17th Parallel can they find that; many also say that a trip to Vietnam gives them a chance to truly experience Vietnamese culture this second time around and visit peaceful villages devoid of barbed wire, mines, and terror.

Tours of Peace (TOP), a nonprofit organization started by Jess DeVaney, a retired U.S. Marine, arranges tours of Vietnam for veterans not only to come to terms with their past but to participate in the future. DeVaney's tours bring friends and family to points of historical or personal significance, but what is unique here is their humanitarian focus: The folks at TOP believe that through helping others, we heal ourselves, so humanitarian-aid projects are part of every tour. TOP visits orphanages, homes for the elderly and the homeless, leprosy communities, poor rural villages, and schools, providing food, medicine, and supplies that save lives and give hope. Participants have a chance to return again to the scene of bygone battles, only this time they are able to help and spread kindness. Trip participants say that the tour is a great step in their recovery and toward acceptance of the past.

According to a spokesperson, "TOP participants come home from Vietnam this time feeling whole and understood. Vietnam is no longer a secret and a source of nightmares for them. A Tour of Peace helps participants exorcise the demons of war and find peace of mind." TOP offers financial assistance for those who need it and organizes tours year-round.

Applications for a Tour of Peace can be printed from TOP's website, **http://topvietnamveterans.org**, or by writing to TOP Vietnam Veterans, 8000 S. Kolb Rd., Ste. 43, Tucson, AZ 85756-9275.

Also consider **Vets with a Mission,** a large nonprofit that has been in business more than 20 years and runs annual trips for veterans only to Vietnam. Like Tours of Peace, Vets with a Mission—as their name suggests—is a group out to make a difference on their trips, and they bring large medical donations and services. The group helps veterans cut through the outmoded notion of heavy remorse and gives them a chance to weigh in with their actions. Go to **www.vwam.com**, or contact the group by snail mail at Vets with a Mission, P.O. Box 202, Newberry, SC 29108.

A few tour operators cater to veterans and can tailor individual tours to follow a division's history or customize travel for a returning veteran's wishes. Most groups visit general operating areas. An itinerary may start out in Saigon with an excursion to the Cu Chi Tunnels, going down to the Mekong Delta, then heading up to Quy Nhon and to the Central Highlands and Pleiku, and then moving on to Danang, China Beach, Hue, and, of course, the demilitarized zone (DMZ).

Contact **Global Spectrum,** 3907 Laro Court, Fairfax, VA 22031 (© **800/419-4446;** www.asianpassages.com).

these tours; it's especially great for the hearty adventurer looking to join a group. In Australia: PO Box 2781, Fitzroy DC, VIC 3065; © **613/9473-2626;** fax 613/9419-4426; www.intrepidtravel.com.

PROS & CONS OF ESCORTED TOURS

Many people like the ease and security of escorted trips. Escorted tours—whether by bus, motorcoach, train, or boat—let travelers sit back and enjoy their trip without having to spend lots of time behind the wheel or worrying about details. You know your costs upfront, and there are few surprises. Escorted tours can take you to the maximum number of sights in the minimum amount of time with the least amount of hassle—you don't have to sweat over the plotting and planning of a vacation schedule. Escorted tours are particularly convenient for people with limited mobility. They can also be a great way to make new friends.

On the downside, an escorted tour often requires a big deposit upfront, and lodging and dining choices are predetermined. You'll get little opportunity for serendipitous interactions with locals. The tours can be jampacked with activities, leaving little room for individual sightseeing, whim, or adventure—plus they also often focus only on the heavily visited sites, so you miss out on the lesser-known gems.

Before you invest in an escorted tour, ask about the **cancellation policy:** Is a deposit required? Can they cancel the trip if they don't get enough people? Do you get a refund if they cancel? If *you* cancel? How late can you cancel if you are unable to go? When do you pay in full?

Note: If you choose an escorted tour, think strongly about purchasing trip-cancellation insurance, especially if the tour operator asks you to pay upfront. (For information on traveler's insurance, trip cancellation insurance, and medical insurance while traveling, please visit www.frommers.com/planning.)

You'll also want to get a complete **schedule** of the trip to find out how much sightseeing is planned each day and whether enough time has been allotted for relaxing or wandering solo.

The **size** of the group is also important to know upfront. Generally, the smaller the group, the more flexible the itinerary, and the less time you'll spend waiting for people to get on and off the bus. Find out the **demographics** of the group as well. What is the age range? What is the gender breakdown? Is this mostly a trip for couples or singles?

Discuss what's included in the **price.** You may have to pay for transportation to and from the airport. A box lunch may be included in an excursion, but drinks might cost extra. Find out if you will be charged if you decide to opt out of certain activities or meals.

Before you invest in a package tour, get some answers. Ask about the **accommodations choices** and prices for each. Then look up the hotels' reviews in a Frommer's guide and check their rates online for your specific dates of travel. You'll also want to find out what **type of room** you get. If you need a certain type of room, ask for it; don't take whatever is thrown your way. Request a nonsmoking room, a quiet room, a room with a view, or whatever you fancy.

Finally, if you plan to travel alone, you'll need to know if a **single supplement** will be charged and if the company can match you up with a roommate.

For more information on escorted general-interest tours, including questions to ask before booking your trip, see www.frommers.com/planning.

SUGGESTED ITINERARIES IN VIETNAM

The narrow S-curve of coastal Vietnam makes itinerary planning quite simple: You're going either south to north or north to south. Though some travelers enter Vietnam overland at one of the many international borders with Laos, Cambodia, and China, the great majority of visitors arrive in Vietnam by air into Hanoi or Ho Chi Minh City, so these are the logical places to begin a tour, and where you'll find all the tour operators. These pulsating cities provide a baptism of fire for new arrivals, who are sometimes overwhelmed by the chaotic traffic, busy markets, pesky touts, and hot weather—hang in there, it just takes a bit of getting used to.

If you have just a few days, immerse yourself in either Hanoi or Ho Chi Minh City and choose from the day trips and overnights listed in chapters 5 and 14. With any itinerary of a week or more, try to give yourself a good amount of flextime for days of rest at a beach, tummy trouble, or chance meetings, side trips, and inspirations along the way. With a couple of weeks, you can fit a lot more in; and with prudent use of domestic flights, it's possible to have a glimpse at rarely visited provinces, too. While in the country, you're bound to bump into backpackers taking at least a month (if not more) to see the entire country, going by "open tour bus" and/or other local transport.

The most important thing to consider when planning a visit is weather. The country's opposing monsoonal systems in the north and south may sound a bit complicated, but here's what you need to know in a nutshell:

The south, including **Ho Chi Minh City (Saigon)** and the **Mekong Delta,** is always hot, with a rainy season (ranging from afternoon thunderstorms to all-day downpours) from May to October. The **Central Highlands** is best during their "somewhat" dry season from January to May. Along the coast in **central Vietnam,** the monsoon season is inverted, and though the temperature is steady and warm, you can experience rain from October to February (and some tropical storms in between). The **north** is much cooler, with a wet and cold winter from December through February (quite cold in the mountains, and there's even snow) and a very hot summer with rains (best time to visit is in the fall, Sept–Oct). Consult individual destination chapters for more details. You can catch high season in multiple regions if you visit on the cusp of seasons: For example, travel in the north in November before you head south.

Important note: If you're landing directly in Vietnam after a long-haul flight from Europe or the U.S., know that **jet lag** is a formidable foe. You might hit the ground running on your first day and then feel exhausted on day 2 or 3—especially due to the heat and chaos of urban Vietnam. Try to get onto Vietnamese time immediately (go to bed at a reasonable hour even if you're not tired, and wake up in the morning); some people also say that taking melatonin, an herbal supplement, helps with jet lag. All of the itineraries below assume that you're rested and ready to go, so you might want to factor in some downtime at the start of your trip to get rested.

THE REGIONS IN BRIEF

The Lay of the Land

Vietnam is an S-shape peninsula that borders China to the north, Laos to the west, and Cambodia to the southwest. Covering about 331,520 sq. km (129,293 sq. miles), it's roughly the size of Italy, but only a small percentage of the land is arable and habitable because of the Annamese Cordillera and other steep mountain ranges and mountain terrain. Vietnam has a varied and lush topography, with two massive deltas (one in the north and one in the south), tropical forests, craggy mountains and rock formations, and stunning coastline. Vietnam is only about 1,613km (1,000 miles) north to south as the crow flies, but by road and along the stretch of coastal highway, it's about 3,260km (2,021 miles). Vietnam also claims thousands of islands off its coast.

Rice is the staple of Vietnam, and the economy and society relies heavily on its production. The shape of Vietnam is often compared to a common sight in any Vietnamese market: the tenuous balancing of a bamboo pole slung over one woman's shoulder as she hangs pendulous bundles on either side of her body. The thin central coast of the country is the bamboo shaft of the fragile contraption, and the productive rice-growing regions of the Red River Delta in the north and the fertile Mekong Delta in the far south are the overflowing "bread baskets" that hang from the pole. But drawn to scale, it might be a bit lopsided—the Mekong is exponentially more productive.

THE NORTH *Bac Bo* is the Vietnamese term for the north, the cradle of Vietnamese civilization along the country's own version of the Tigris and Euphrates, the **Red River Delta.** Called the *Song Hong* in Vietnamese, the river is the epicenter of prehistoric culture and early empires, where organized wet rice cultivation, done on flooded paddies and requiring extensive community cooperation, began. The Red River Delta gave birth to the first Au Lac dynasty and earliest capital at Co Loa—just north of Vietnam's current capital, **Hanoi,** which lies at the heart of the region. Just east of Hanoi, the busy port of Haiphong leads the way to the 3,000 islands of the stunning **Halong Bay;** the islands are a stunning set piece of towering karst, or limestone, formations shrouded in jungle. Where Hanoi's creation myth speaks of the ascending dragon *Thang Long,* the mountains of the bay are said to be the footprints of the descending dragon, or *Ha Long,* as it went to its home in the ocean deep.

The northern highlands, occupying the northwest tip of Vietnam, are known for their beauty, with jagged mountains rising over sweeping green valleys. The inhabitants are mostly ethnic minority hilltribes still somewhat isolated from civilization. Popular tourism destinations are **Sapa, Mai Chau,** and **Dien Bien Phu.** Vietnam's tallest mountain, Fansipan (3,143 m/10,309 ft.), overlooks Sapa, part of the mountain range the French dubbed "The Tonkinese Alps."

CENTRAL Central Vietnam, or *Trung Bo,* flanks the long line of the Trung Son Mountain range, also called the Annamese Cordillera. In this volume, I divide the center into the north central region, where you'll find the city of Vinh; the central region, which includes Hue, Danang, and historic Hoi An; and the south central region, where you'll find the beach community of Nha Trang. Set inland from the coast is the temperate, hilly Central Highlands region, with small towns such as Kontum and the city of Dalat.

Traveling south from Hanoi, most visitors trace the central coastline, location of major cities Hue, Danang, and Hoi An. The small town of **Vinh,** birthplace of Ho Chi Minh, is just halfway between Hanoi and Hue. And **Hue** (pronounced *Hway*), a name familiar from the war years for its strategic location near the 17th Parallel, is Vietnam's former capital and imperial city (1802–1945). Going south from Hue, after crossing over (or through a tunnel under) the Hai Van Pass, you come to **Danang,** Vietnam's fourth-largest city and a port town whose major attractions include the museum of Cham antiquities and nearby China Beach. Nearby **Hoi An,** a major trading center from the mid–16th century, shows the architectural influences of Chinese and Japanese traders who passed through and settled here, leaving perfectly preserved buildings. It is now once again a center of cultural exchange and commerce, but is tourist-focused with souvenir centers and tailor shops (also lots of new resorts on nearby Cua Dai Beach).

Tracing the coast farther south from Hoi An, pass through the small port city of **Quy Nhon,** off the tourist trail but with a few nice new resort offerings, and then on to **Nha Trang,** Vietnam's preeminent sea resort, where new upmarket offerings are popping up like mushrooms on a log. Just inland from the south-central coast area, you'll find the Central Highlands area, a temperate, hilly region occupied by many of Vietnam's ethnic minorities. Most popular and developed for tourists is historic **Dalat,** a resort town nestled in the Lang Bien Plateau, established by the French at the turn of the 20th century as a recreation and convalescence center. The scenery looks something like Switzerland in summer, with high hills studded with tall pines and peppered with quaint, French villas, some renovated and others in a sad state of decay. North of Dalat, the Annamese Cordillera mountain range hosts the coffee capital of Buon Ma Thuot, as well as Pleiku and Kontum, names familiar from the war era and home to some of the hottest fighting at that time.

THE SOUTH Southern Vietnam, called *Nam Bo,* is home to Vietnam's largest city, bustling **Ho Chi Minh City,** also known as **Saigon.** Vietnam's largest cosmopolitan area is like a region unto itself, with a population of more than eight million spreading out over a wide area of urban and suburban sprawl. **Tay Ninh** is a town just to the north and west of Saigon that's home to the unique Cao Dai sect and the end of the Ho Chi Minh Trail at the Black Mountain. Some of the heaviest fighting during the war took place here, much of it planned from the tunnels of **Cu Chi.** The south is hotter, in climate as well as cuisine.

South of Ho Chi Minh City is the **Mekong Delta,** where, after a 4,500km (2,790-mile) journey from the mountains of Tibet, the mighty Mekong splits into nine smaller branches and a wide alluvial plain as it deposits its silt on the way to the South China Sea. The well-irrigated delta is the most agriculturally productive region of Vietnam, where most of the country's rice is grown, and where the population has swelled in recent years with increased productivity and industries such as fish farming and shrimp cultivation. The climate of the delta is tropical; the lower delta is untamed swampland. The region shows the influences of ancient Funan and Khmer cultures, as well as the scars from recent wars (the Viet Cong used the delta as a secret base) and battles with neighboring Cambodia.

DOING IT ALL: VIETNAM & CAMBODIA IN 28 DAYS

The following tour is the most comprehensive one in this chapter, and it still hits only the highlights. You can combine any itineraries listed with the side trips and specialty itineraries at the end of this chapter, and lots of Vietnamese destinations are conducive to further in-depth study or relaxed lingering.

Day 1: Arrive in Hanoi

"Honey, were there five people on that motorcycle?" Yes, dear, there were. Welcome to Hanoi. Even your ride from the airport can be tiring; plan to rest a bit when you first arrive. If you can swing it, stay at the **Sofitel Metropole Legend** (p. 68) in the heart of the city, and kick off your stay with an evening meal at the sophisticated **Press Club** (p. 77), located just around the corner.

Day 2: Hanoi

Take a Hanoi City Tour starting at Ba Dinh Square, including the **Ho Chi Minh Mausoleum, House,** and **Museum** (p. 96) as well as the **One-Pillar Pagoda** (p. 97). Then hit **Van Mieu,** the Temple of Literature (p. 98), in the afternoon. Take a tour of the **Old Quarter** (p. 87) on foot (with or without a guide) or by cyclo. In the evening, take in the **Thang Long Water Puppet show** (p. 112).

Day 3: Hanoi to Halong Bay

Leave early in the morning for a 3-hour drive to the pier at Halong City (p. 151) and then board an overnight boat in the bay—best is the luxury *Emeraude,* and one notch down is Buffalo Tour's *Jewel of the Bay* or Handspan Tour's *Indochina Sails* (p. 156). You will cruise for a few hours with stops at various cave sites, and then dine and sleep onboard the boat moored in a quiet bay. Itineraries vary, but most include time for kayaking to caves and island lagoons and swimming.

Day 4: Halong Bay to Hanoi

Awaken to sunlight reflecting off the high limestone formations of stunning Halong Bay. Most trips include a morning kayak adventure or tai chi practice and a few stops before returning to the pier and making the 3-hour road connection to Hanoi. Overnight in Hanoi. **Note:** Some adventure itineraries include extra days for more far-ranging kayak exploration, or include an extra night on **Cat Ba Island** (p. 157).

Day 5: Hanoi

Enjoy another near full day in Hanoi. Wake up early (dawn) and exercise with locals around **Hoan Kiem Lake** (p. 99), check out the lakeside temples, and take a stroll around the French Quarter, to the south of the lake. Here you can check out **Hoa Lo Prison Museum** (once dubbed the **Hanoi Hilton;** p. 99), as well as the **History Museum** (p. 100) and the **Opera House** (p. 99). After lunch at **Pane e Vino** (p. 82), take a cab or walk to **St Joseph's Cathedral,** then browse the colorful boutiques and inviting cafes on Nha Tho Street. In the evening, catch the overnight train from Hanoi to Lao Cai (p. 117).

Day 6: Lao Cai to Sapa

Arrive in Lao Cai at 6am and hop on a bus for transfer to Sapa. Check in to your hotel—I recommend the **Victoria Sapa** (p. 125)—and take an afternoon walk down into the valley lined with rice terraces to the **Cat Cat Village** (p. 128).

Day 7: Sapa

Spend a full day trekking—best arranged through an outfitter in Hanoi or with **Topas** or **Handspan** (p. 124) in Sapa. The **Lao Cai–to–Ta Van Walk** is popular, but there are many options to visit Hmong and Dao villages. Snuggle in to the **Nature Bar & Grill** (p. 127) in the evening to recharge those flagging batteries.

Day 8: Sapa to Hanoi

Should you time it right on a Sunday, you can make a round-trip to the **Bac Ha Market** (p. 128) in the early morning before returning by overnight train to Hanoi. Otherwise, arrange a short day trek or rent a Minsk motorcycle to explore farther afield on your own before you get on the overnight train from Lao Cai back to Hanoi.

Day 9: Hanoi

When you arrive in Hanoi, you'll likely be tired after trekking and the overnight train. Rest in the capital for the morning, and then take a day trip to the **handicraft villages** outside of Hanoi.

Day 10: Ninh Binh (or the Perfume Pagoda)

Take a day trip out of the big city. Connect with a good tour provider for a full-day trip south of the city to the **Ninh Binh** area, with the grottoes of **Tam Coc** (p. 165; similar to Halong Bay's, but along a river), and nearby **Hoa Lu,** a former capital of the country. You can also include a visit to **Cuc Phuong National Park** (p. 167), though it's best as an overnight so that you can go jungle trekking in the morning, when it's cool and the wildlife is active. Another option is to take a full-day tour to the **Perfume Pagoda** (p. 115), about 60km (37 miles) south of Hanoi. Return to Hanoi and make reservations for dinner at **La Badiane** (p. 77) before some final souvenir shopping.

Day 11: Hanoi to Hue

Fly to Hue in the morning. After checking in at your hotel, take a tour by bicycle or cyclo to the central **Hue Citadel** (p. 186) and the ruins of the old **Imperial City** (p. 186). This should occupy you for most of the day. In the evening, enjoy

Suggested Itineraries

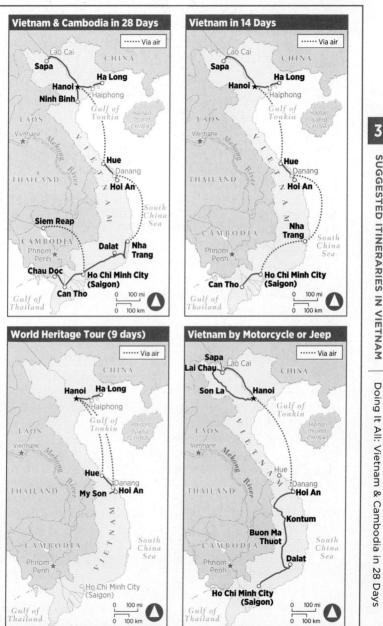

Vietnam & Cambodia in 28 Days

······ Via air

Lao Cai
CHINA
Sapa
Ha Long
Hanoi ★
Haiphong
Ninh Binh
Gulf of Tonkin
Hainan Island CHINA
LAOS
Vientiane ★
Mekong River
THAILAND
Hue
Danang
Hoi An
South China Sea
Siem Reap
CAMBODIA
Phnom Penh ★
Dalat
Nha Trang
Chau Doc
Ho Chi Minh City (Saigon)
Can Tho
Gulf of Thailand
0   100 mi
0   100 km

Vietnam in 14 Days

······ Via air

Lao Cai
CHINA
Sapa
Ha Long
Hanoi ★
Haiphong
Gulf of Tonkin
Hainan Island CHINA
LAOS
Vientiane ★
Mekong River
THAILAND
Hue
Danang
Hoi An
Nha Trang
South China Sea
CAMBODIA
Phnom Penh ★
Ho Chi Minh City (Saigon)
Can Tho
Gulf of Thailand
0   100 mi
0   100 km

World Heritage Tour (9 days)

······ Via air

CHINA
Hanoi ★
Ha Long
Haiphong
Gulf of Tonkin
Hainan Island CHINA
LAOS
Vientiane ★
Mekong River
THAILAND
Hue
Danang
My Son
Hoi An
CAMBODIA
South China Sea
Phnom Penh ★
Ho Chi Minh City (Saigon)
Gulf of Thailand
0   100 mi
0   100 km

Vietnam by Motorcycle or Jeep

······ Via air

Sapa
Lao Cai
CHINA
Lai Chau
Son La
Hanoi ★
Gulf of Tonkin
Hainan Island CHINA
LAOS
Vientiane ★
Mekong River
THAILAND
Hue
Danang
Hoi An
Kontum
Buon Ma Thuot
South China Sea
CAMBODIA
Phnom Penh ★
Dalat
Ho Chi Minh City (Saigon)
Gulf of Thailand
0   100 mi
0   100 km

dinner at **Tropical Garden** (p. 184). After your meal, stroll along the **Perfume River** near the **Trang Tien Bridge** (p. 176).

Day 12: Hue to Hoi An

In the morning, take a boat trip to the **Thien Mu Pagoda** (p. 190) and visit a few of Hue's many **imperial tombs**—best are the tombs of **Khai Dinh** and **Minh Mang.** In the afternoon, leave by car or minivan for **Danang** (p. 197). Along the way, stop at **Lang Co Beach** (p. 196) and the overlook at **Hai Van Pass** (p. 194). Visit the **Cham Museum** (p. 202) in Danang and, time permitting, the **Marble Mountains** (p. 202). Overnight in Hoi An. If you arrive before the shops close, place an order for your tailored clothes.

Day 13: Hoi An

Buy a ticket for a tour of the central area of Hoi An (p. 202), stopping at **ancient attractions** including the Chinese pagodas and congregation halls, the Japanese Bridge, and the many museums and old shop houses. In the afternoon and evening, take an improvised stroll around the old town or scoot out to **Cua Dai Beach** (p. 218), a short car ride from town, to dip your toes in the South China Sea. Shop 'til you drop in the evening until around 9pm, when shops close.

Day 14: Hoi An

Take a day of leisure and shopping—get that suit fitted properly—or beachcombing at **Cua Dai Beach,** or opt for the all-day jaunt to **My Son** (p. 218), the most famous relics of Cham civilization.

Day 15: Hoi An to Nha Trang

Fly from Danang (after a trip to the **Marble Mountains,** p. 202, in the morning if you've yet to go) and get settled in Nha Trang for a few days of beach time. Rest and relax at the **Ana Mandara** (p. 261) if you can afford it; if not, good budget options abound, too.

Day 16: Nha Trang

You have plenty of options here: take a scuba course, hop on an all-day boat trip to outlying islands, or hit the city's few nearby sights (the **Po Nagar Cham Towers,** p. 269, or the **National Oceanographic Institute,** p. 269). Or alternatively, find a patch on Nha Trang's lovely beach on which to while away the day reading, snacking, and being massaged. Nha Trang is a great place to kick back, eat good seafood (check out **Ngoc Suong,** p. 267, for some delicious dishes), and rest.

Day 17: Nha Trang to Dalat (or Stay in Nha Trang)

Note: This trip to Dalat is optional; you might prefer to spend an extra night in Nha Trang before flying to Ho Chi Minh City. A 3-hour drive on a spanking new highway takes you to mountainous **Dalat** (p. 226). If your budget allows for it, stay at the luxurious **Dalat Palace** (p. 230) or the **Ana Mandara Villas,** tucked away on a hilltop overlooking the city center (p. 230).

Day 18: Dalat

Take a fun day tour of the breathtaking (some, rather hokey) sights around Dalat. Hire an **Easy Rider** (p. 228) and watch out for the bugs hitting your teeth as you smile, bouncing around hilly Dalat on the back of a motorbike (tour options by van and car are also available; see p. 228). Alternatively, try an all-day adventure of rock climbing, canyoneering, or mountain biking with **Phat Tire Ventures** (p. 229).

Day 19: Dalat to Ho Chi Minh City (Saigon)

Starting in the morning, drive overland from Dalat. (***Note:*** Naturalists, birders, and nature photographers will want to add a day at the **Cat Tien National Park,** about halfway btw. Dalat and Saigon; see p. 334.) Arrive in **Ho Chi Minh City** (p. 281) in the late afternoon, check in somewhere near central **Dong Khoi Street,** and then explore the downtown area near **Lam Son Square,** the central **Opera House,** and busy **Le Loi Street.** Lots of good shopping, dining, and nightlife.

Day 20: Ho Chi Minh City Tour

In the morning, get an early start at **Giac Lam Pagoda** (p. 315), Ho Chi Minh City's oldest pagoda, and then tour **Chinatown** (p. 314) and some temples, as well as the large Chinese market, **Binh Tay Market** (all in far-off District 5), before returning to the city center and **Ben Thanh Market** (p. 309)—a good place to wander and pick up a few trinkets and stop for lunch at **Pho 2000** (p. 307), just adjacent to the market. In the afternoon, hit the **War Remnants Museum** (p. 314) and, time permitting, the **Reunification Palace** (p. 311). In the evening, enjoy a meal at **Quan An Ngon Restaurant** (p. 306), Vietnam's finest purveyor of authentic Vietnamese cuisine in a local setting (there are lots of gussied-up high-end Vietnamese restaurants in town, but funky Ngon takes the cake).

Day 21: Cu Chi Tunnels and the Cao Dai Holy See

Try to catch the midday service of the unique world religion of **Cao Daism** (p. 316) in their Technicolor temple. Then make your way to the **Cu Chi Tunnels** (p. 316), where North Vietnamese guerrillas waged war on American and South Vietnamese forces from a vast, hidden complex of tunnels near the terminus of the Ho Chi Minh Trail.

Day 22: Ho Chi Minh City to Chau Doc

Note: Take a guided tour to the Mekong Delta. Most tour providers offer different versions of the same trips, with 1-, 2-, or 3-night stays. Go for at least 2 nights. For an unforgettable journey, sign up for the **Bassac** cruise (see p. 344).

Your first stop will probably be the **Cai Be Floating Market** (p. 340) for a boat ride among the busy river throngs. From here move on to **Chau Doc,** just a short hop from the Cambodian border, where you should stay at the **Victoria Chau Doc** (see p. 347).

Day 23: Chau Doc to Can Tho

In the morning, take a boat trip across the Mekong River to the floating villages of ethnic **Cham** (p. 347)—you'll see fish farms and riverside temples and mosques near Chau Doc. Then, time permitting, trek up little **Sam Mountain** (p. 347), a Buddhist pilgrimage peak with views all the way to Cambodia. Afterward, make your way to Can Tho. Overnight at the **Victoria Can Tho** (p. 343).

Day 24: Can Tho to Saigon

Take a morning boat tour to **Cai Rang Floating Market** and along the many canals around Can Tho (p. 344), visiting craft communities, rice-cake and toffee factories, and raw-rice granaries (photographers will be click-click-clicking) before making your way back to Saigon.

Days 25 to 28: Saigon to Siem Reap (Angkor Wat)

Take a morning flight from Saigon to Siem Reap, Cambodia, the support town for the stunning temples of Angkor Wat. Give yourself a few days to take in all of the sights at Angkor (see "A Side Trip to Cambodia," later in this chapter, and "Siem Reap & Angkor Wat," in chapter 14). You might even consider going to Angkor Wat from Saigon via the Cambodian capital of Phnom Penh (you can go by boat from Chau Doc on the Mekong Delta).

Important note: When you leave Vietnam, you will need a multiple-entry visa or to apply for a new tourist visa to reenter. You can enter and exit Cambodia at designated points (overland or by air) and receive a visa upon arrival. You can fly from Siem Reap to Bangkok for onward international connection.

VIETNAM IN 14 DAYS: NORTH TO SOUTH

This is a truncated version of the 28-day itinerary. You can see quite a lot in 2 weeks and catch the major sights along the coast. See information at the bottom of this section for advice on doing this same itinerary in reverse, from south to north.

Day 1: Arrive in Hanoi

Get settled somewhere cozy (I recommend the **Sofitel Metropole Legend,** p. 68), and then take a walk (or cyclo ride) around the **Old Quarter** and **Hoan Kiem Lake** (p. 87 and p. 99).

Day 2: Hanoi to Lao Cai (Sapa)

Enjoy a morning of touring the main sights in Ba Dinh Square, including **Ho Chi Minh's Mausoleum** (before 11am), **House,** and **Museum** (p. 96), and the **One-Pillar Pagoda** (p. 97). In the early evening, catch the overnight train for Lao Cai (best on a **Victoria** sleeper car; see p. 122).

Day 3: Lao Cai to Sapa

Arrive in Lao Cai at 6am and hop on a bus for transfer to Sapa. Check in to your hotel—I recommend the **Topas Ecolodge** (p. 125)—and take an afternoon walk down into the valley lined with rice terraces, or sign up for a guided trek to a **Red Dao village.** Alternatively, just pay a visit to the central market in Sapa, crowded with **Black Hmong** people.

Day 4: Sapa to Bac Ha and back to Hanoi

If it's a Sunday, take a day trip to the market town outside of Lao Cai called **Bac Ha** (p. 128), where the **Flower Hmong** are the region's most colorful dressers.

Otherwise, plan to spend part of the day trekking (contact **Topas** or **Handspan,** p. 124) or exploring by motorbike, and then catch an early evening overnight train from Lao Cai back to Hanoi (factor in the few hours from Bac Ha or Sapa to Lao Cai station).

Day 5: Hanoi

Arrive at 6am in the capital and take some time to rest in comfy city digs. Explore the **French Quarter** with its colonial architecture, then do a bit of shopping along **Nha Tho Street** in the shadow of **St Joseph's Cathedral.** Catch a show at the **Thang Long Water Puppet Theater** (p. 112) in the evening, or hit some of the town's fine-dining establishments or nightlife (see chapter 6).

Day 6: Hanoi to Halong Bay

Leave early in the morning for a 3-hour drive to the pier at Halong City, and then board an overnight boat in the bay—best aboard the luxury *Emeraude* or *Halong Ginger;* one notch down is Buffalo Tour's *Jewel of the Bay* or Handspan Tour's *Indochina Sails* (p. 156). You'll lunch aboard the ship, cruise for a few hours with stops at various cave sites, and then sleep aboard the boat moored in a quiet bay. Itineraries vary, and most include time for kayaking to caves and island lagoons and swimming.

Day 7: Halong Bay to Hanoi and on to Hue

Awake to sunlight reflecting off the high limestone formations of stunning Halong Bay. Most trips include a morning kayak adventure and a few stops before returning to the pier and making the 3-hour road connection to Hanoi. Catch the evening (8:10pm) flight from Hanoi to Hue (or overnight in Hanoi and fly in the morning).

Day 8: Hue

Set out on a tour by bicycle or cyclo to the central **Hue Citadel** and the ruins of the old **Imperial City** (p. 186). In the afternoon, you can arrange a boat to see the likes of the **Thien Mu Pagoda** (p. 190) and a few of Hue's many **imperial tombs**—best are the tombs of **Khai Dinh** and **Minh Mang** or **Tu Duc.** In the evening, enjoy dinner at **Tropical Garden** or **Hoa Mai Restaurant** (p. 184 and 183), and then stroll along the **Perfume River** near the **Trang Tien Bridge** (p. 176).

Day 9: Hue to Hoi An

In the afternoon, leave by car or minivan for **Hoi An** (p. 202). Along the way, stop at **Lang Co Beach** (p. 196), the overlook at **Hai Van Pass** (p. 194), the **Cham Museum** in Danang (p. 202), and, time permitting, the **Marble Mountains** (p. 202). Overnight in Hoi An (p. 205). If you arrive before the shops close, place an order for your tailored clothes.

Day 10: Hoi An

Follow **Day 13** in the 28-day itinerary, above, exploring the old town or hitting the beach.

Day 11: Hoi An to Nha Trang (via Danang)

Fly from Danang (via a trip to the **Marble Mountains,** p. 202, in the morning if you've yet to go) and settle in Nha Trang for a few days of beach time. Rest and relax at the **Evason Ana Mandara Resort** (p. 261) or one of the many good budget options around (see chapter 11).

Day 12: Nha Trang

Take a scuba course, hop on an all-day boat trip to outlying islands, or hit the city's few sights (the **Po Nagar Cham Towers,** p. 269, or the **National Oceanographic Museum,** p. 269). However, you could be forgiven for doing none of the above, and instead staking a claim to a small patch of the beach, then whiling away the day sunbathing, snacking, and snoozing. In the evening, head for a sumptuous seafood dinner at **Ngoc Suong** (p. 267) before dancing the night away at one of the venues on the beach or Biet Thu Street (p. 272).

Day 13: Nha Trang to Ho Chi Minh City

You might consider adding a few days at this point and scoot up to the temperate hill town of **Dalat** or tour part of the **Central Highlands.** Otherwise, fly to Ho Chi Minh City.

Day 14: Ho Chi Minh City

In the morning, get an early start at **Giac Lam Pagoda** (p. 315), Ho Chi Minh City's oldest, and then tour **Chinatown** (p. 314) and some temples, as well as the large Chinese market, **Binh Tay Market** (all in far-off District 5), before returning to the city center and **Ben Thanh Market** (p. 309)—a good place to wander and pick up a few souvenirs. Stop for lunch at **Pho 2000** (p. 307), just adjacent to the market. In the afternoon, take in the **War Remnants Museum** (p. 314) and go on to the **Reunification Palace** (p. 311) if there's time. Enjoy a meal at **Quan An Ngon Restaurant** (p. 306), where you can enjoy authentic Vietnamese cuisine in a local setting (there are lots of gussied-up high-end Vietnamese restaurants in town, but funky Ngon takes the cake). Depart.

Going South to North

Note: If arriving in the south (most likely in Ho Chi Minh City), you can reverse this 2-week itinerary. Many travelers include a trip to the **Mekong Delta,** staying 1 night in **Can Tho** and exploring the river markets in the area (see **Days 22 and 23** in the 28-day itinerary, above) instead of going to Sapa in the far north.

WORLD HERITAGE TOUR (9 DAYS)

This trip takes you to the main **UNESCO World Heritage Sites** of Vietnam, including **Halong Bay, Hue, Hoi An,** and **My Son.**

Day 1: Hanoi

After you arrive and settle in to your hotel, take a cyclo tour or walk around Hanoi's busy **Old Quarter** (p. 87). See the **Thang Long Water Puppet show** (p. 112) in the evening.

Day 2: Hanoi to Halong

In the early morning, take a walk around central **Hoan Kiem Lake** (p. 99) and the **Old Quarter** (p. 87), and then visit historic Ba Dinh Square—with **Ho Chi Minh's Mausoleum, House,** and **Museum** (p. 96), as well as the **One-Pillar Pagoda** (p. 97). In the late afternoon, head to **Halong City** (p. 151) or **Cat Ba** (p. 157) for an overnight. (**Note:** My preference is to overnight on one of Halong's better boat trips, but this journey requires a full 2 days.)

Day 3: Halong to Hanoi

Take an early morning boat cruise on **Halong Bay,** stopping at some of the main cave sights (p. 153). Check out **Thien Cung Grotto (Heavenly Cave)** or **Surprise Cave,** and enjoy lunch aboard the ship before returning to Hanoi in the late afternoon.

Day 4: Hanoi to Hue

Take an early morning flight (6:10am) to **Hue** (p. 175), the old Imperial City in central Vietnam, and check in at **La Residence Hotel** (p. 181). Visit the **Hue Citadel** (p. 186), taking in some of its renovated buildings such as the **Thai Hoa Palace** and the **The Mieu Temple;** this will probably occupy you for most of the day, but if you have time, lounge by the pool for an hour in the afternoon. In the evening, enjoy Hue cuisine at one of the popular downtown tour restaurants (p. 183).

Day 5: Hue to Hoi An

Take a morning boat ride to visit the **Thien Mu Pagoda** (p. 190), and the Imperial tombs of **Khai Dinh** and **Minh Mang** (p. 188), set in attractive countryside around the city. In the afternoon, leave by car or minivan for **Hoi An.** Along the way, stop at **Lang Co Beach** and **Hai Van Pass.** Overnight in Hoi An. (If you get here in time, place an order for your tailored clothes.)

Day 6: Hoi An

Take an all-day tour of the **Ancient Town,** stopping at Chinese pagodas and congregation halls, the Japanese Bridge, and the many museums and old shop houses. If you have time in the afternoon, scoot out to **Cua Dai Beach** on a bicycle or motorbike to wriggle your toes in the sand and cool off in the ocean. Shop 'til you drop in the evening.

Day 7: Hoi An to My Son

Set out in the morning for an all-day trip to the impressive Cham temple remains at **My Son** before returning to Hoi An.

Day 8: Hoi An to Hanoi (via Danang)

Head to Danang in the morning, making stops at the **Marble Mountains, China Beach,** and the **Cham Museum,** where you'll see all the relics that were removed from My Son, before flying from Danang to Hanoi (last flight 9:35pm).

Day 9: Hanoi

Spend your last morning before departure in Hanoi doing some souvenir shopping on **Hang Gai** in the Old Quarter.

GET YOUR MOTOR RUNNIN'— VIETNAM BY MOTORCYCLE OR JEEP

To rent your own motorbike and drive the length of the country, contact tour agencies in Ho Chi Minh City and Hanoi. If you go this route, Vietnam is your oyster—you can go where the road and your fancy takes you. Below is a trip that combines destinations in the **Central Highlands** and the **Northern Highlands**—also doable by rented jeep as well. Start your engines, and prepare for some memorable adventures.

Day 1: Arrive in Ho Chi Minh City (Saigon)

Get acclimated and explore the downtown area of Ho Chi Minh City, along Dong Khoi. If time permits, go to the **Reunification Palace** (p. 311) or **War Remnants Museum** (p. 314).

Day 2: Saigon to Dalat

Fly or ride from Saigon to the mountain town of Dalat, and if you didn't rent a bike before leaving Ho Chi Minh City, head for **Peace Cafe** (p. 235) to arrange your trip with an **Easy Rider** (expect to pay about $60 per day to ride on the back with a guide, budget accommodations included). In the evening, check out the **Dalat Market** (p. 236).

Day 3: Dalat to Buon Ma Thuot

Start early, catching the sights around Dalat that interest you, such as **Xuan Huong Lake, Bao Dai's Palace,** and the Art Deco **railway station** (p. 236). Then follow rolling hills of coffee plants and stunning pine-dotted vistas as you ride to **Buon Ma Thuot** (p. 239). Pause at **Lak Lake** (p. 244) and take an **elephant ride** to visit **M'nong Communities** (p. 244). It's possible to overnight in the comfy **Bao Dai Villa** or in a rustic M'Nong **longhouse** (p. 244). Otherwise, press on to Buon Ma Thuot and the **Damsan Hotel** (p. 241).

Day 4: Buon Ma Thuot to Kontum

Ride north across the **Dak Lak Plateau,** passing regimented rows of **rubber trees** and coffee bushes on the way to Pleiku, capital of Gia Lai Province. There are no sights to see here, but it's a good meal stop before riding on to **Kontum,** where the towering **communal houses of the Bahnar people** are one of the Central Highlands' most distinctive features. Overnight at **Family Hotel** (p. 247) in Kontum.

Day 5: Kontum to Hoi An

Visit **Dak To** (p. 249) and **Charlie Hill** (p. 249), two important battle sites, before hopping on Highway 14 (the Ho Chi Minh Hwy.) for a ride all the way to Hoi An. For an overnight stay, try one of the resorts along **Cua Dai Beach** (p. 209), and settle in for a day of well-earned relaxation.

Day 6: Hoi An

Take a tour of the **ancient town** (p. 204) or rest up on **Cua Dai Beach** (p. 218).

Day 7: Hoi An to Hanoi

Fly to the capital via Danang. Get oriented with a cyclo or walking tour of the **Old Quarter** (p. 87).

Day 8: Hanoi

Take a tour of Hanoi starting in Ba Dinh Square; visit the **Ho Chi Minh Mausoleum, House,** and **Museum** (p. 96), and the **One-Pillar Pagoda** (p. 97). See **Van Mieu,** the Temple of Literature (p. 98), in the afternoon. In the evening, take in the **Thang Long Water Puppet show** (p. 112).

Day 9: Hanoi to Son La

Hit the highway on your rented **Minsk** motorcycle, with or without a guide (check with rental agencies in Hanoi; p. 132). Breeze through little **Mai Chau** (p. 131), take a walk to the ethnic villages outside of town, and then spend the night in Son La at the **Trade Union Hotel** (p. 135). If you have time, visit the **Son La Prison** (p. 136).

Day 10: Son La to Muong Lay

Follow **Route 6** in its most dynamic climb up from Tuan Giao and along a high mountain area to the town of **Muong Lay** (p. 140). Stay at the little **Lan Anh Hotel** (p. 140) and take a late-afternoon (or tomorrow-morning) trek to the nearby **White Thai villages** (p. 131).

Day 11: Muong Lay to Sapa

The all-day ride from Muong Lay to **Sapa** (p. 118) follows the **Da River** (p. 140) along a very picturesque stretch. Just before Sapa, you'll climb up stunning **Tram Ton Pass** (p. 141), which offers some of the most picturesque landscape in Vietnam. Put your feet up in Sapa (I recommend **Topas Ecolodge,** p. 125) and swap tales of your adventure.

Day 12: Sapa

Enjoy a full day of trekking—best arranged through an outfitter in Hanoi or with **Handspan** or **Topas** (p. 124) in Sapa. The **Lao Cai–to–Ta Van Walk** is popular, but there are many options to visit Hmong and Dao villages. Wrap up warm in the evening, and enjoy a hearty meal at the **Nature Bar & Grill** (p. 127).

Day 13: Sapa to Hanoi

If it's a Sunday, check out the **market** (p. 128) in the town of **Bac Ha.** Otherwise, explore **Sapa market** and buy a few souvenirs before the short few hours to **Lao Cai** (p. 117). From here, you can put your motorcycle on the train for Hanoi and ride in comfort on the overnight, best in a luxury sleeper car.

Intrepid riders who didn't get enough of the open road can forgo the train back to Hanoi from Lao Cai and head east, reaching **Ha Giang**—gateway to Vietnam's northernmost province—or even continuing farther to **Cao Bang** (p. 143) in a day.

Ban Gioc Waterfall outside of **Cao Bang** is spectacular, and the road to **Lang Son** (p. 145) is a great ride (lots of hilltribe markets). From **Lang Son** to Hanoi is a wide highway (for trade with China). Budget 3 extra days of hard riding if you want to include Cao Bang and Lang Son on your way back to Hanoi.

Day 14: Hanoi

Arrive in Hanoi station at 6am. After a day's stay at a hotel to get cleaned up and do some last-minute shopping, depart for your next destination.

A SIDE TRIP TO CAMBODIA

The majestic temples of Angkor Wat are just a short flight from Ho Chi Minh City or Hanoi, and many travelers extend their trip to visit this archaeological wonder.

Day 1: Ho Chi Minh City/Hanoi to Siem Reap

Fly from Hanoi or Ho Chi Minh City to **Siem Reap.** Get comfortable at your hotel: The **Raffles Grand Hotel d'Angkor** (p. 398) is a palace, and **Hôtel de la Paix** in town (p. 397) is a contemporary luxury.

Day 2: Angkor Wat

Set out for the temples before dawn, taking in the morning glow from atop **Bakeng Hill** (p. 410). Visit the main temples, including the many sights of **Angkor Thom** (p. 410)—including the **Bayon,** the **Baphuon,** the **Terrace of the Leper King,** and the **Elephant Terrace**—and then hit **Preah Khan** (if you have time) before lunch. In the afternoon, take in the site's eponymous temple, **Angkor Wat** (p. 408), where you can spend hours gazing at relief carvings such as the **Churning of the Ocean of Milk.** Take a guided tour to get the most out of this experience. Climb the three tiers of the temple (careful, the steps are steep) and enjoy the sunset from the top.

Head back to **Siem Reap** (p. 392) to enjoy a fine meal. For cheap, local fare, try **Khmer Kitchen** (p. 406), where you can down a few beers and join in the backpacker babbling. For something more cultural, book a seat for the evening **Apsara dance show** and buffet at the **Raffles Grand Hotel d'Angkor** (p. 398).

Day 3: Angkor Wat

Watch the sunrise illuminating the outline of **Angkor Wat,** and then hit your favorite temple again or any you missed in the main Angkor compound. Many use Day 3 for trips out to the likes of the **Roluos Group** (p. 417) or as far as the crumbling jungle temple of **Beng Melea** (p. 416). Watch the sunset from Bakeng Hill, but be prepared for lots of company. Catch a morning or afternoon flight back to Ho Chi Minh City or Hanoi.

Option: Add an extra day and hop on a flight to Cambodia's capital **Phnom Penh** (p. 369), and visit the **Royal Palace and Silver Pagoda** as well as the **National Museum** (p. 382). If you've got a strong stomach, you might also like to take in the rather grim sights focused on the Khmer Rouge genocide in Cambodia: **Tuol Sleng Museum** (p. 382) and the **Killing Fields** (p. 381).

ACTIVE VACATION PLANNER

Just 40 years ago, the only action a foreigner was likely to see in Vietnam was on a battlefield. Visitors today, however, can choose from a wide range of outdoor activities, including kayaking and kite surfing, mountain biking and trekking, diving and rock climbing.

The diverse topography of this amazing country lends itself to all kinds of adventurous experiences, and this chapter points out some of the most popular options for an active vacation here, along with contact details for reliable companies that organize specialized trips.

ORGANIZED ADVENTURE TRIPS

While many people who enjoy outdoor activities are independent-minded travelers, there are several reasons why it makes sense to arrange a trip through an adventure tour operator.

First and foremost is time. Organized tours help you make the most of your precious vacation time by arranging quick and smooth transfers to the locations where the fun begins, and taking care of everything else including accommodation and eating. Second is the practical consideration of equipment; it's hardly worth taking a kayak or heavy diving gear halfway around the world when you can rent it locally at very reasonable rates. Third, organized adventure trips bring together like-minded people for a shared experience that often results in long-lasting friendships.

Two points to keep in mind when choosing an adventure tour are the difficulty level and the number of people in a group. Some tours are only for the dedicated and superfit, while others brand themselves as "soft adventure tours," which promise adventure and discovery without the need to be in tiptop physical condition. Knowing your limitations is an important part of choosing the tour that is right for you.

Whether to book your tour through an in-country or an international tour operator is a matter of taste and budget. Some travelers take comfort in signing up with international operators that have a track record of providing safe transport, knowledgeable guides, and comfortable accommodation, though there's no doubt such tours come with a hefty price tag attached. With the Internet, however, it's easy to find details of tours offered by in-country operators and get any queries answered before committing yourself to a particular tour, and their prices are significantly lower. Below I've listed the best operators based both in and outside Vietnam.

Vietnamese Adventure Tour Operators

Sinhbalo Adventure Travel ★★★ (☏ 08/3837-6766 in Ho Chi Minh City, or **888/661-0808** in the U.S.; www.sinhbalo.com) is run by the enthusiastic and knowledgeable Sinh (founder of Sinh Café), and specializes in biking tours and cus-tomized tours to anywhere in the country.

Handspan ★★ (☏ 04/3926-2828 in Hanoi; www.handspan.com) offers small group tours and tailor-made trips that include trekking, kayaking, and mountain bik-ing; they have a commitment to sustainability and the principles of responsible travel.

Buffalo Tours ★★ (☏ 04/3828-0702 in Hanoi; www.buffalotours.com) oper-ates tours throughout Indochina. In Vietnam, their adventure tours feature trekking, mountain biking, and rock climbing.

Active Travel Vietnam ★ (☏ 04/3573-8569 in Hanoi; www.activetravelvietnam.com) is one of the newer in-country adventure tour operators, and offers a wide range of adventure sports on its package and customized tours.

International Adventure Tour Operators

Intrepid Travel ★★ (☏ 800/970-7299 in the U.S.; www.intrepidtravel.com) features a range of tours for travelers with a yearning to get off the beaten track, last-ing from 4 days to a month.

Geographic Expeditions ★★ (☏ 800/777-8183 in the U.S.; www.geoex.com) is an award-winning travel adventure operator offering several tours in Vietnam, including a week of trekking in the north.

Journey International ★ (☏ 800/255-8735 in the U.S.; www.journeys.travel) is a family run tour company that offers biking in the Mekong Delta, kayaking in Halong Bay, or trekking around Sapa among their many tours.

ACTIVITIES A TO Z

This section lists the most popular activities that visitors to Vietnam can participate in, along with the best locations to partake in that activity and details of specialist tour operators that can take you there.

As you'll notice, these activities run the gamut, from what might be called passive, such as bird-watching, to extremely demanding sports such as rock climbing. If you are considering any of the more challenging activities, be realistic with yourself about your abilities. Every year there are fatalities because participants push themselves too hard—don't become part of these statistics.

Biking

Biking, in particular mountain biking, is one of the most popular outdoor activities in Vietnam, and understandably so. The entire road network of the country is waiting to be explored, but I'd advise against biking in the big cities or along major highways, such as the coast road between Hanoi and Ho Chi Minh City, as the traffic is danger-ously unpredictable. However, this still leaves lots of places where biking is a pure joy.

One of the most popular destinations, especially for inexperienced cyclists, is the Mekong Delta, which has the advantage of being flat, so you won't strain your muscles grinding up and down hills. Tours between 1 day and a week are easy to organize, and mostly involve biking along country lanes and dirt tracks, where motorized traffic is minimal or nonexistent. Bicycle tours of the Delta are often combined with a night in a homestay, where you can learn something about the local culture.

Other popular destinations for biking tours are the area around Hoi An and Hue, which combines healthy exercise for the body with stimulation for the mind as you learn about the former trading port and imperial capital. Tours here usually include a visit to My Son with its relics of the Cham civilization that once inhabited the area.

There's no doubt that the most challenging itinerary for cyclists in Vietnam is a tour of the Tonkinese Alps in the northwest; be prepared for long slow climbs up daunting mountain slopes, but you'll also be rewarded with vistas stretching out forever.

TOUR OPERATORS

Cycling Vietnam ★★★ (© 08/3837-6766 in Ho Chi Minh City; www.cycling vietnam.net) is one of the country's leading biking tour operators, using the latest bikes and led by experts; customized tours to the Delta or anywhere upcountry.

Vietnam Backroads (© 08/3601-7671 in Ho Chi Minh City; www.vietnam backroads.com) offers tours ranging from 1 day to 2 weeks in all regions of the country.

Spice Roads ★★ (© 02/712-5305 in Thailand; www.spiceroads.com) focuses exclusively on bicycle tours in Asia, with a range of appealing itineraries.

Roadmonkey ★ (© 323/924-8351 in the U.S.; www.roadmonkey.net) describes its tours as "philanthropic adventure expeditions," and combines biking with do-good activities such as building playgrounds or organic farms to help local communities.

Bird-Watching

Vietnam is an exciting destination for bird-watching because of its huge variety of species (more than 850 recorded), which includes some that are very rare and a dozen that are endemic to the country, such as the Annam partridge and the Vietnamese greenfinch.

As you might imagine, the country's national parks are the best place to go for the best sightings, though the wetlands of the Mekong Delta also attract many colorful species. These include the endangered sarus cranes, with their distinctive red heads and black-tipped wings, which visit the Tram Chim National Park annually. The Tra Su Cajuput Forest is another magical place in the Delta that echoes with the calls of numerous birds; you can combine a visit with a biking trip organized by Cycling Vietnam (see above).

TOUR OPERATORS

Grandeur Journeys ★★ (© 08/3820-0257 in Ho Chi Minh City; www.grandeur journeys.com) organizes bird-watching trips to Tra Su Cajuput Forest and to Cat Tien National Park.

Vietnam Birding ★★ (© 08/3827-3766 in Ho Chi Minh City; www.vietnam birding.com) is dedicated exclusively to birding tours, which run from 10 to 24 days and cover most of the country, focusing on national parks.

Cooking

Vietnamese cuisine is enjoying a wave of popularity in the West, so it's hardly surprising that many visitors want to learn the secrets of its fresh ingredients, subtle flavors, and varied textures. This is the type of activity that you don't have to dedicate your entire vacation to, as courses generally last for just a day or half-day.

Several five-star hotels offer courses, such as the Sofitel Metropole Legend, which are generally more expensive than the schools that focus entirely on cooking. A typical class involves a trip to the market to buy fresh ingredients, followed by observing the teacher, making the recipe for yourself, and then tasting your own creation.

COOKERY SCHOOLS

Vietnam Food Tour (© 04/3929-0270 in Hanoi; www.vietnamfoodtour.com) is an umbrella organization that can arrange cookery classes at schools in Hanoi, Ho Chi Minh City, Hoi An, and Hue.

Hanoi Cooking Center ★ (© 04/3715-0088 in Hanoi; www.hanoicooking centre.com) offers classes in street food, Northern specialties, and the famed spring roll. Classes take place in the morning and early evening, and cost around $50 per person.

Morning Glory Cookery School ★★ (© 0510/224-1556 in Hoi An; www. restaurant-hoian.com) is run by the tireless Ms. Vy, who operates several of Hoi An's most successful restaurants (p. 213).

Red Bridge Cooking School ★ (© 0510/3933-222 in Hoi An; www.visit hoian.com) offers half-day courses at their delightful out-of-town location (p. 213).

Diving & Snorkeling

With its tropical climate and more than 3,000km (1,864 miles) of coastline, Vietnam is a magnet for divers from around the world. There's a wide variety of colorful fish flitting around the coral reefs, and you may even spot whales, sharks, and manta rays. Dive operators offer courses for beginners that lead to PADI certification, as well as a variety of fun dives for experienced divers. Even if you don't want to go below the surface, you can sign up for one of these tours at a cheaper rate and just go snorkeling in some memorable locations. Nha Trang is the main dive center for the country, where the season runs from March to October, but because of the different climate, Phu Quoc Island, another popular dive destination, is best from November to March. Other good dive sites are the Con Dao archipelago and the Cham Islands, near Hoi An.

DIVE OPERATORS

Rainbow Divers ★★★ (© 090/878-1756 in Nha Trang; www.divevietnam.com) is the longest-established and most trustworthy dive company in the country. They can arrange trips to any of the country's top dive sites.

Sailing Club Divers ★★ (© 058/352-4628 in Nha Trang; www.sailingclub divers.com) is another reliable setup that offers dives around Nha Trang at similar prices to Rainbow.

Cham Island Diving Center ★ (© 0510/3910-782 in Hoi An; www.cham islanddiving.com) is the best operator for trips to the Cham Islands due to their local expertise.

Kayaking

Vietnam's most popular location is without doubt Halong Bay, with its towering karst outcrops. At low tide it is possible to enter hidden lagoons in these outcrops, where it feels like you've slipped through a gateway to another world. Kayaking is often offered on tours in combination with a cruise on a junk, or with trekking in Cat Ba National Park or rock climbing on the islands in the bay.

Other popular places for kayaking are in the narrow channels of the Mekong Delta and on Tuyen Lam Lake near Dalat in the Central Highlands.

TOUR OPERATORS

Kayak Halong Bay (© 04/3573-8569 in Hanoi; www.kayakhalongbay.com) can arrange 3-day cruises around Halong Bay that include a day of kayaking for around $260 per person.

Phat Tire Ventures ★★ (© 063/382-9422 in Dalat; www.phattireventures. com) offers 1-day kayaking trips as well as other adventure sports such as rock climbing, canyoning, and white-water rafting.

Kite Surfing & Windsurfing

Mui Ne is the Mecca for windsurfing and kite surfing in Vietnam, and in fact conditions are so good (more than 200 days a year with winds greater than 12 knots) that this growing resort hosts annual events on the Professional Windsurfers Association (PWA) Tour each February. Instruction and rental of state-of-the-art equipment is available, and you can get a week's stay in a fancy resort with windsurfing or kite-surfing rental for $400 to $700.

TOUR OPERATORS

Jibe's Beach Club ★★★ (© 062/384-7405 in Mui Ne; www.windsurf-vietnam. com) is the longest-running and most professional outfit in Mui Ne, run by a fanatical French windsurfer.

Storm Kiteboarding ★ (© 062/384-7440 in Mui Ne; www.stormkiteboarding. com) is based at the plush Mia Resort (formerly Sailing Club) and offers similar courses and rates to Jibes.

Motorcycling

The motorbike is the most popular form of transport in Vietnam, and you'll be amazed at the greeting you get if you head off on the country's back roads and stop in remote villages. Not only will you feel you're traveling as the locals do, but if you run into a mechanical problem you'll soon find someone who can fix it for you.

Motorbike tours go all over the country, but the most popular region by far is the northwest, where the Tonkinese Alps provide challenges and great rewards with stunning views around each bend. The best way to go is on a rented Minsk (see box on p. 132), but tour operators offer a variety of machines if you'd prefer something else.

If the idea of a motorbike tour appeals but you don't want to ride yourself, your best option is to hook up with the **Easy Riders** in Dalat (see box on p. 228), who will prepare a customized itinerary for you (usually heading up through the Central Highlands to Hoi An or Hanoi) and act as your personal rider and guide for the trip.

TOUR OPERATORS

Offroad Vietnam ★ (© 04/3926-3433 in Hanoi; www.offroadvietnam.com) specializes in tours on reliable Hondas around the north, including the stunning Dong Van Karst Plateau Geopark in Ha Giang province.

Explore Indochina ★★ (© 091/309-3159 in Hanoi; www.exploreindochina. com) has been mapping routes around North Vietnam since 1994 and runs small-group motorbike tours (maximum six riders), providing all equipment such as storm-proof wet-weather gear.

Rock Climbing

Rock climbing is one of the newest adventure sports to arrive in Vietnam, launching in Dalat in the Central Highlands about a decade ago. A few years later, perceptive climbers realized that the vertical and overhanging cliffs of Halong Bay make for ideal rock climbing, and now several companies offer beginner through advanced rock-climbing courses, often run in combination with kayaking and trekking in Cat Ba National Park.

TOUR OPERATORS

Slo Pony ★ (✆ 091/376-0025 on Cat Ba Island; www.slopony.com) is the best of several operators offering rock climbing programs in Halong Bay, along with kayaking and trekking tours

Phat Tire Ventures ★★ (✆ 063/382-9422 in Dalat; www.phattireventures.com) was the first company in Vietnam to offer rock climbing in the hills around Dalat. They still run canyoning and rappelling activities up in the highlands, though their main climbing walls are now near Hoi An, where they also have a branch.

Trekking

Since travelers first started coming to Vietnam in the early 1990s, one of the most popular activities has been trekking, particularly in the northwest around Sapa; these days, though, treks around Kon Tum in the Central Highlands are attracting more and more people.

The joys of trekking are clear for all to see. Anyone can do it, as long as they are left to their own pace. You need no special equipment apart from a sturdy pair of hiking boots and perhaps a stick to steady you. And best of all, you get to see scenes that are impossible from the road, including colorful hilltribe markets in remote villages. Trekking tours can last from a day to a week, with accommodation usually provided in simple huts along the way and a guide to help you communicate with the locals.

The toughest trek in this area is to the summit of Mount Fansipan at 3,143m (10,309 ft.), which takes at least 4 days and is not advised in inclement weather, which unfortunately occurs often. Nevertheless, there are plenty of options to choose from, and for many a trek in the northern hills is the highlight of their stay in Vietnam.

TOUR OPERATORS

Topas Adventure Travel ★★ (✆ 020/387-2404 in Sapa; www.topasecolodge.com) offers packages that include a stay in their remote ecolodge with trekking to minority villages to visit the Black Hmong and Red Dao.

Handspan Travel ★★ (✆ 020/387-2110 in Sapa; www.handspan.com) is one of Vietnam's biggest tour operators with a local office from which they arrange treks and mountain biking tours of the region.

Lotussia ★ (✆ 04/2249-4668 in Hanoi; www.hikingvietnam.com) offers trekking tours countrywide, including the Central Highlands.

HANOI

Residents of Hanoi, which recently celebrated its 1,000th birthday, know a thing or two about hospitality, and you'll find them eager to help in any way, from directing you somewhere to negotiating a fare with a cyclo rider for you. You could spend days in the **Old Quarter,** but save some time to explore the **French Quarter,** the city's **lakes,** and **Ba Dinh Square,** where you'll learn about the country's greatest hero, Ho Chi Minh.

Things to Do   The **Old Quarter,** a maze of commercial streets dating from the 13th century, is Hanoi's one unmissable sight. Nearby **Hoan Kiem Lake** is a great place for a stroll; keep your eyes open for the lake's giant turtles. Another sightseeing highlight is the **Temple of Literature,** a sanctuary of Confucianism and Vietnam's seat of learning for almost 1,000 years.

Restaurants & Dining   Hanoi's finest local food is served at small, one-dish restaurants; don't miss the ubiquitous *pho,* **noodle soup** served with slices of beef *(bo)* or chicken *(ga),* which can be found anywhere. The city also boasts some elegant spots for a special night out, such as **Bobby Chinn's** and **Wild Lotus.**

Nightlife & Entertainment   Hanoi is the best place to experience **traditional Vietnamese arts** such as opera, theater, and water puppetry; everyone loves performances at the **Thang Long Water Puppet Theater.** The city also has a variety of pleasant little watering holes; take a stroll along **Ma May Street** in the Old Quarter or **Nha Tho Street** by St. Joseph's Cathedral and duck in any welcoming door.

Active Pursuits   In the morning, the walkway encircling **Hoan Kiem Lake** becomes a training camp, with locals working up a sweat performing **tai chi** or calisthenics. Otherwise, **walking** is the best way to tour the winding passages of the Old Quarter. More intrepid souls **bike** around town to beat the chaotic traffic, and most hotels have cycles to rent.

ORIENTATION
Getting There & Away
BY PLANE

Hanoi, along with Ho Chi Minh City, is a major international gateway. Hanoi's **Noi Bai International Airport** (✆ **04/3886-5060**) is about a 45-minute drive outside the city. If you haven't booked a hotel transfer through your hotel, an airport taxi costs 300,000 VND for a sedan taxi, or a bit more for a van. To save a few dollars, you can take the Vietnam

flying dragons & THIEVING TURTLES: HANOI'S FOUNDING

Originally, at its prehistoric founding as Thang Long, Hanoi was called **"The Ascending Dragon."** The dragon that ascended, so the story goes, created civilization as we know it along the Red River Valley and then plunged to his sleep in Halong Bay, thereby creating the grand karst slopes—today a UNESCO World Heritage Site. The dragon is the symbol of the city, and you'll find references to it wherever you go.

Hanoi's other important creation myth is one oddly echoed by the legend of King Arthur and his rise to the throne after receiving the sword Excalibur from the Lady of the Lake. "Strange women lying in ponds distributing swords is no basis for a system of government," says Michael Palin's character in *Monty Python and the Holy Grail*, the spoof of the Arthur legend, and Hanoi's mandate granted by a giant turtle in Hoan Kiem is equally ridiculous, but a great one for putting the kids to bed at night.

Le Loi, the first king of a united Viet people, asked the powers in heaven to help him vanquish the Chinese in the 2nd century A.D. His answer came from a giant turtle that rose from the depths of Hoan Kiem Lake and offered him the sword that he would use to drive out the Chinese. (Vietnamese history is full of valiant tales about driving out the Chinese.) When Le Loi returned to the lake to give thanks, the turtle rose again out of the water and took a firm jaw hold of the sword and dragged it to the watery depths, a sign that the citizens could lay down their arms and the city would prosper in peace. The turtle fooled old Le Loi, because the Vietnamese would suffer under Chinese oppression for centuries to come. The myth is best depicted at the Thang Long Water Puppet Theater (p. 112). And watch for a unique breed of giant lake turtles—if you're lucky you might see them basking on the central island (one was captured and treated for injuries in early 2011). See the "Hoan Kiem District" section under "Attractions," later in this chapter, for details of the lake's temples and sights, and note that most addresses in this chapter are given in relation to the lake, so you should get to know it during your stay in the Vietnamese capital.

Airlines minivan into town. It costs $2 for a drop-off at the Vietnam Airlines office, but sometimes, for an extra buck, you can get the driver to drop you at your hotel if it's along the way. From town to the airport, shuttles depart from the Vietnam Airlines office and cost 35,000 VND. Call ☎ **04/3832-0320** to get departure times.

To contact international carriers in Hanoi, try the following: **Aeroflot,** 360 Kim Ma (☎ 04/3771-8542); **Air Asia,** 30 Le Thai To (☎ 04/3928-8282); **Air France,** which has a helpful customer service desk on the southwestern edge of Hoan Kiem Lake, 1 Ba Trieu (☎ 04/3825-3484); **All Nippon Airways (ANA),** 9 Dao Duy Anh (☎ 04/3934-7237); **British Airways,** 9 Dau Duy Anh (☎ 04/3934-7239); **Cathay Pacific,** 49 Hai Ba Trung (☎ 04/3826-7298); **China Airlines,** 6B Trang Tien (☎ 04/3936-6364); **Emirates Airlines,** 9 Dao Duy Anh (☎ 04/3934-7240); **Japan Airlines (JAL),** 63 Ly Thai To (☎ 04/3826-6693); **Jetstar Pacific Airlines,** 152 Le Duan (☎ 04/3851-5350); **Lao Airlines,** 40 Quang Trung (☎ 04/3942-5362); **Malaysia Airlines,** 1/F Hanoi Towers, 49 Hai Ba Trung (☎ 04/3826-8820); **Singapore Airlines,** 17 Ngo Quyen (☎ 04/3826-8888); or **Thai Airways,** 44B Ly Thuong Kiet (☎ 04/3826-7921). Note that if you work with a local ground operator for day tours and trips in Vietnam, most will help with any reconfirmation or flight changes free of charge or for just the cost of necessary local calls.

For domestic connections, your best option (and, as luck would have it, a good and affordable one) is **Vietnam Airlines,** though Jetstar Pacific and Air Mekong are other possibilities. The main, and most convenient, Vietnam Airlines office in Hanoi is at 25 Trang Thi, a street that runs directly west from the southern end of Hoan Kiem Lake (℃ **04/3832-0320**). Ticket purchases are made on the second floor (at a good discount from prices quoted at storefront travel agents), and it's an orderly business where you pick a number and wait for the next teller. They accept major credit cards as well as either U.S. dollars or Vietnam dong. The office is open from 7am to 6:30pm Monday to Friday, and in front of the building is a convenient stand of minivans that make regular connections with the airport for just 35,000 VND. A tourist information kiosk is also at the airport, as well as a **lost and found** (℃ **04/3884-0008**).

BY TRAIN

Hanoi Railway Station, on the western edge of Hoan Kiem District (120 Le Duan; ticket office ℃ **04/3942-3949**), is a terminal stop on the Reunification Railroad. A comfortable, air-conditioned soft berth to Hue costs 600,000 VND, and it's 1,300,000 VND to Ho Chi Minh City. Buying tickets at the station is easy (but time-consuming), and any travel agent can handle it for a small fee. Both standard and luxury trains from Hanoi to Lao Cai, the jumping-off point for the popular hill town of Sapa, can be booked at traveler cafes in the Old Quarter and from any travel agent; often you can get a special rate on a deluxe overnight train to Lao Cai and your overnight accommodations in Sapa. Slow trains also connect with Haiphong and even to Cao Bang and Lang Son, but these are the kinds of rides that are for train buffs only.

BY BUS

Budget traveler cafes in the Old Quarter, mostly along Hang Bac or Hang Be streets, offer low-luxe seat-in-coach tours. Services and prices are similar: About $30 to $40 gets you an open-tour ticket from Hanoi to Saigon with all stops in between. See the section "Budget Tourist Cafes & Open Tours," below.

Local buses arrive at and depart from the following stations: **Gia Lam Station** (Nguyen Van Cu St., Long Bien District—across the Long Bien Bridge and a few miles to the east of town) runs minibuses and coaches to Haiphong, Halong Bay, Lang Son, and some destinations in the far northwest; **Luong Yen Station;** 3km (2 miles) southeast of the Old Quarter runs regularly to destinations in the north and northeast, including Cao Bang and Ha Giang, as well as southern destinations such as Nha Trang and Ho Chi Minh City; **Ben Xe Phia Nam (Southern Bus Station)**, 5km (3 miles) south of the Old Quarter on Duong Giai, serves destinations to the north, east and south; while the **My Dinh Station,** 7km (4 miles) to the west of the city center, serves places such as Mai Chau, Dien Bien Phu, and Buon Ma Thuot.

Visitor Information & Tours

There are a number of good, high-end tour operators in Hanoi, all offering similar tours throughout the north—to Halong Bay, Ninh Binh, and the Dien Bien Phu loop. Operators can usually assist with city day tours and arrange internal flights, hotels, and countrywide tours, as well as handle any onward connections in the region or back home. Most visitors contact these providers before arriving in Vietnam, but if you land at their counter on any given day, the folks at the tour companies below can help. With prices only a hitch above the midrange operators, the following six providers are a cut above others in their efficient service, creative and adventurous itineraries, and quality guides.

- **Ann Tours,** 77 Pham Hong Thai St., Truc Bach Ward, Ba Dinh District (② 04/3715-0950; www.anntours.com). Based in Ho Chi Minh City, Ann Tours also has an office in Hanoi and offers private deluxe tours to Halong Bay and elsewhere. Frommer's readers have written to share their good experiences with this operation.
- **Buffalo Tours,** 94 Ma May (② 04/3828-0702; fax 04/3826-9370; www.buffalo tours.com.vn). This reputable outfit offers a range of standard tours and some good ecoadventures, including cycling, trekking, and kayaking trips from the Mekong Delta in the south to the hilltribe hills along the China border in the far north. Their boat, the *Jewel of the Bay,* is a great choice for trips in Halong. The friendly and professional staff can handle any eventuality, including onward travel and connections in the region.
- **Exotissimo,** 26 Tran Nhat Duat (② 04/3828-2150; fax 04/3828-2146; www. exotissimo.com). You'll get comprehensive service throughout the region from this company.
- **Handspan,** 78 Ma May St. (② 04/3926-2828; fax 04/3926-2383; www.handspan. com). This is an excellent option for organized trips around Hanoi, in the northern hills, and to Halong Bay, plus some great adventure options. Their Halong Bay boat is one of the most popular, and their eco-friendly adventures throughout Vietnam usually mean you'll break a sweat and get out to see the "real" Vietnam. They have an office next to the popular Tamarind Café (p. 84).
- **Queen Travel,** 65 Hang Bac St. (② 04/3826-0860; fax 04/3826-0300; http:// azqueentravel.com). With upmarket private tours at midmarket prices, Queen Travel is a reliable operator based in the Old Quarter. The company can arrange almost anything and put together specialized itineraries on demand.
- **Topas Outdoor Adventures,** 52 To Ngoc Van St. (② 04/3715-1005; fax 04/ 3715-1007; www.topastravel.vn). This Danish company is very professional and extremely friendly. They are best known for their outdoor/trekking tours (to Sapa and other parts of Vietnam), and their guides are well trained and knowledgeable.

MIDRANGE LOCAL TOUR OPERATIONS

- **I Love Vietnam,** 4th floor, 277 Doi Can St., Ba Dinh District (② 04/3722-5648; www.ilovevietnamtravel.com). I Love Vietnam is a popular Vietnamese/ Australian joint venture with good local and regional tours for small groups.
- **TNK Travel,** 56 Hang Be (② 04/3926-4386; fax 04/3926-4396; www.tnktravel. com). Offering all basic services, including budget transportation options such as those offered at Hanoi's tourist cafes (see below), TNK leads good private tours.
- **Ethnic Travel,** 35 Hang Giay St., Hoan Kiem (② 04/3926-1951; fax 04/3926-1950). A relatively new but extremely efficient tour operator that specializes in educational and active holidays, with a strong ecofriendly stance. They also have an office in Sapa.
- **ET Pumpkin,** 89 Ma May St. (② 04/3929-5571; fax 04/3926-2085; www. et-pumpkin.com). Offering adventure travel and all of the usual northern itineraries, ET Pumpkin is a dependable organization catering to groups and individuals.
- **Kangaroo Cafe,** 18 Bao Khanh, west of Hoan Kiem Lake (② 04/3828-9931; www.kangaroocafe.com). A long-popular tour operator and cafe run by Australian expats, the Kangaroo Cafe is a good, safe choice for midmarket tours anywhere in the north and in southern Vietnam as well. The staff speaks a cool Aussie slang, some mixed with a nasal Vietnamese accent, and they make you feel at home (their breakfasts aren't too bad, either).

MAKE FRIENDS WITH VIETNAM heritage

Friends of Vietnam Heritage (www.fvheritage.org) is a group of Hanoi residents and expatriates who get together to celebrate Vietnamese culture and history in informal gatherings in the hopes of preserving its rich tapestry and introducing it to the uninitiated. They hold events, show films, and host special lectures, in addition to offering many group meetings: a pottery group, a museum group, a cultural history and civilizations group, a traditional-medicine group, and a Buddhist group, among other informal gatherings. The organization has published a few useful guides to local temples and pagodas, and sponsors a small resource center on the fourth floor of the Hanoi City Library, 47 Ba Trieu, which is open from 8am to noon and 1:30 to 5:30pm Monday through Friday. It's a great way to connect with some friendly and very engaged Hanoi residents and expatriates.

o **Hidden Hanoi,** 137 Nghi Tam (© **091/225-4045;** www.hiddenhanoi.com.vn). Hidden indeed, this small tour provider runs unique walking tours around the Old Quarter and around the city's most important pagodas and temples. With a focus on connecting with Vietnamese culture, the company teaches language and cooking at their center north of the city near West Lake. Arrange to meet up with their good walking tours in town at preordained meeting places.

o **Vietnam Indochina Travel,** 5-239/71 Bo De, Long Bien (© **04/3872-7754;** fax 04/3872-2319; www.vietnamholidays.biz). This private operator offers the standard set of day trips and excursions, with personalized and attentive service.

BUDGET TOURIST CAFES & OPEN TOURS

Tourist cafes are small eateries and travel agents rolled into one. Tours are often barebones and services are basic—and often crowded—but the cafes are a good option for tours and transport or for 1- or 2-day excursions to sights such as Halong Bay, the Ninh Binh area, or the far north. For higher-quality information and service, I recommend the companies in the sections above. But tourist cafes get you where you want to go, have consistent daily departures, and cost peanuts.

Hanoi is the home base of many of Vietnam's large **tourist cafes** that sell budget **"Open-Tour Tickets,"** which are no-frills seat-in-coach tours to just about anywhere along the country's length (for more information, see "Getting There & Getting Around," in chapter 3). Below are the best of the many:

o **Sinh Café,** 52 Luong Ngoc Quyen St. (© **04/3926-1568;** fax 04/3926-1621; www.thesinhtourist.com). This is the biggest and most popular cafe tour company in all of Vietnam. Their services are good throughout the country, and their offices are quite helpful elsewhere; sadly, in the north, things get a little confusing with this outfit. Just about anybody with red paint and a paintbrush is putting up the distinctive Sinh Café logo above shops in the Old Quarter. Most do, in fact, act as consolidators for the company, but often what you get is not the genuine item or, worse, a really bad local company taking advantage of you. What complicates the matter is that Sinh Café is in cahoots with Hanoi Toserco, a big government travel agency, and the two cooperate in a number of offices, the largest at 48 Hang Bac St. I've heard some bad reports about the Toserco trips, so try to book through the main Sinh office on Luong Ngoc Quyen.

○ **Kim Tours,** 137 Hang Bac (© **04/3993-5766;** fax 04/3926-4651; www.kimtours. net). Like the other tourist cafes, the folks at Kim Tours have reliable transport services. Their office in Hanoi is just one of many throughout the country, and they offer open bus tours as well as package tours countrywide.

City Layout

Hanoi is divided into four main sectors: Hoan Kiem, Ba Dinh, Hai Ba Trung, and Dong Da (see the section, "The Neighborhoods in Brief," below). Metropolitan Hanoi includes a number of outlying areas that were once provinces, but as the population expands in number and large-scale development seeks new land, the city's perimeter widens.

The Neighborhoods in Brief

HOAN KIEM DISTRICT Most foreign visitors to Vietnam spend their time in the heart of Vietnam's ancient capital, Hoan Kiem District. Between the shops and restaurants around busy central **Hoan Kiem Lake,** the very lungs of the city and the most popular strolling spot in town, and the **Old Quarter,** there is wandering aplenty. Most of the prewar colonial buildings in this area are still intact, even if exteriors are faded and crumbling or being encroached on or crowded out by newer concrete construction. Hanoians are getting hip to the historical cachet they have in this district, and you'll find more and more buildings being preserved for the public, whether as restaurants or as tour sights (for details, see "Walking Tour: The Old Quarter," in the "Exploring Hanoi" section, later in this chapter). In and among the Old Quarter's busy streets, you'll find the guildhalls of each individual trade once practiced there, as well as community halls and Chinese temples tucked behind ancient willow trees and down quiet alleys. Hoan Kiem hosts a number of markets, including Dong Xuan, the city's largest. The southern edge of Hoan Kiem District is the French Quarter, where streets were reordered under French rule. Here you'll find the old **Opera House** and a number of museums. On the western edge of Hoan Kiem, you'll see a number of important pagodas, including the city's most prominent, **Quan Su,** as well as the famous prison the **Hanoi Hilton,** now mostly replaced by an office complex. Traffic in this district is about as busy as it gets.

BA DINH DISTRICT The farthest northwest sector of Hanoi, Ba Dinh begins at the line demarcated by the train station and train line running north-south through the city. This is where you'll find the **Hanoi Citadel,** now rebuilt and housing the **Ho Chi Minh Mausoleum,** as well as his house and the **Ho Chi Minh Museum.** The nearby **One-Pillar Pagoda** is one of the city's oldest, dating from the 11th century. The **Army Museum** and **Fine Art Museum** are also in Ba Dinh.

HAI BA TRUNG DISTRICT Once where foreign visitors were more or less sequestered (or limited to), this area to the south of Hanoi is where you'll find some impressive colonial mansions and **Thong Nhat Park** (formerly Lenin Park).

DONG DA DISTRICT Where Quang Trung, one of the leaders of the Tay Son Rebellion, defeated the Chinese—the event is celebrated every year during the Tet holiday—Dong Da is also home to the city's **Van Mieu Temple of Literature,** the home base of the Mandarins who once governed Vietnam.

GETTING AROUND

Hanoi is divided into districts. Most sights and accommodations are in Hoan Kiem District (downtown), centered on picturesque Hoan Kiem Lake and Ba Dinh (west

⚠ RIGGED taxi METERS

Be sure to go with an accredited taxi company, either one mentioned above or a company connected with your hotel. Smaller companies and individual operators sometimes rig the meter and charge up to double the price. If you protest, these shifty characters just point to the meter as evidence. If you think you're being overcharged, don't pay, but ask the driver to wait while you get someone from the front desk of your hotel to verify the rate.

of town) or Hai Ba Trung (south) districts. Most addresses include a district name. You'll want to plan your travels accordingly because getting from district to district can be time-consuming and expensive.

By Bus

Hanoi has a number of local **buses** that ply regular routes through the city, but Hanoi's smoke-belching trucks are extremely crowded, and using them is difficult if you don't speak Vietnamese. With the ready availability of fast, affordable local motorbike taxis and good metered taxis (see below), few tourists bother with local buses.

By Taxi

Taxis can be hailed on the street, at hotels, and at major attractions. The meter should read between 10,000 VND and 15,000 VND (depending on the company and size of the cab) to start, and 12,000 VND to 14,000 VND for every kilometer (about ½ mile) thereafter. The three most reputable companies are **Hanoi Taxi** (✆ 04/3853-5353), **Airport Taxi** (✆ 04/3873-3333), and **Mai Linh** (✆ 04/3822-2666). You (or the concierge) can call ahead for pickup. Make sure the cabbie turns on the meter. Be sure to get your change; drivers often seek a surreptitious tip by claiming that they don't have the right amount to give back. Smile. Tell the driver that you'll wait until it's obtained, and it will materialize. Tips are greatly appreciated, but don't feel pressed to give any certain percent; just round up the meter or offer 5,000 VND, and you are being quite generous by local standards.

By Car

Renting a car is convenient, but driving yourself is not recommended. Book a car with a driver from $60 a day (or $10 per hour). If an upscale hotel quotes you more, call one of the **tourist cafes** or any of the travel agents listed above. A rented car or shared taxi is a great way to make your own itinerary around the city or to destinations throughout the north. Note that in the city center, however, a big car can get stymied by the heavy traffic, so if your constitution is hearty and you like to throw caution to the wind, go for a cheap and maneuverable motorbike taxi to get you through the city traffic and small alleyways of the city (see below).

By Motorbike

Motorbike taxis are a cheap and easy way to get around the city, but drivers go like madmen. *Be forewarned:* This is transportation for the brave. Haggle hard with these guys. No matter the distance, drivers will start off asking for a few dollars, but with relentless haggling (you'll have to walk away a few times) they'll come down as far as 15,000 VND for short trips. Motorbike taxi drivers in Hanoi can also be hired by the hour for 40,000 VND to 50,000 VND, and showing the driver the written address of where you want to go is a better alternative than trying to have your bad Vietnamese understood. I've even given a driver a day's worth of addresses and had him create my itinerary because these drivers know the streets and the traffic best. Give a tip and you've got a friend for life, or at least someone who'll show up at your hotel the next day to see if you need any further assistance.

If you're feeling especially brave, you can **rent your own motorbike.** Navigating Hanoi's busy streets is harrowing, though, and most motorbike riders use their rented two wheels to get out of town instead of around in town (see chapter 7 for more detailed information on motorbike touring in the north). Most tourist cafes and mid- to low-range hotels can arrange rentals, and there are a few good storefront rental agencies. Try **Mr. Cuong's Motorbike Adventure,** at 1 Luong Ngoc Quyen St., on the east side of the Old Quarter near the city's major ring road (© **04/3926-1534**)—the best place to rent a big honkin' Russian Minsk motorbike for $7 per day—or **Mr. Hung's Vietnam Adventure Tour,** at his in-town office just north of Hoan Kiem Lake, 5A Dinh Liet St. (© **04/3926-0938**), or at his repair shop on the city ring road at 162 Tran Quang Khai St. (Mr. Hung's provides bike rentals as well as comprehensive in-town and rural tour options and guides.) One-day rentals of 100cc motorbikes start at $6. A 1-month rental of a little hair dryer–style model (a Honda Dream or Wave) can cost as little as $100. Wear a helmet (it's now a well-enforced law, and all the locals are doing it), go slow, honk to alert other vehicles when passing, and stay alert. Inexperienced riders might want to think twice about cutting their teeth on a motorbike in crazy Hanoi traffic.

Warning: Riding on a motorbike, whether your own or on the back, presents a Catch-22: It's the fastest and most affordable way to navigate city roads, but it's also your best bet for a trip to the emergency room or worse. Take caution and, wherever possible, try to put as much steel between you and the chaos of the road as possible. In other words, take buses and cars when possible.

By Cyclo

Cyclos are two-seated carts powered by a man on a foot-pedal bike riding behind you. You can flag them down anywhere, particularly near hotels and tourist attractions, where they're certain to find (or follow) you. Being trundled along among whizzing motorbikes isn't always very comfortable, but it can be a nice choice for touring the Old Quarter's narrow streets. Bargain with the driver before setting out. You can pay as little as 20,000 VND for a short ride, and 30,000 VND for a longer haul. You can also hire by the hour for about $3 to $5. If you're inclined, most drivers will even let you take the handlebars for a souvenir photo or a short ride—around the block or so—just for fun.

By Bicycle

Rental costs for a bike are about $1 per day from a hotel or tourist cafe. The traffic is daunting, but the brave quickly learn how to just stay to the right and join the flow. Helmets are generally not available.

[FastFACTS] HANOI

ATMs Most major banks in Hanoi and even country-wide now have ATMs. Look for **Vietcombank** and **Incombank** branch locations throughout the city. New ATMs are popping up all over. Ask any hotel concierge where to find one.

Consult with your bank at home to inquire about international ATM usage fees. Most range from just $1 to $3. For more information, see the "Money & Costs" section in chapter 3.

Banks & Currency Exchange The best service (24-hr. ATMs with guards) is at the **Australia New Zealand Bank (ANZ),** 14 Le Thai To St. (✆ **04/3825-8190**); **Citibank,** 17 Ngo Quyen St. (✆ **04/3825-1950**); and **Vietcombank,** 198 Tran Quan Khai (✆ **04/3934-3137**). Most banks will exchange foreign currency, either U.S. dollars or euros, during normal banking hours. You'll also find a few money-changing storefronts along Hang Bac Street in the Old Quarter and around the edge of Hoan Kiem Lake.

Avoid exchanging on the black market. Black-market money-changers will approach you outside of the major banks; in the past, you could get a much improved rate from them, but today the advantage is nominal and travelers often find themselves left with a few counterfeit or out-of-circulation notes in the mix—it's not worth the trouble.

Business Hours Most Hanoi shops and offices are closed for lunch, usually from 11 or 11:30am to 12:30 or 1pm. Hanoians wake up very early to take advantage of cooler weather, and an early lunch is followed by some rest time in the heat of the day.

Most offices close at 5pm and are shut on Sunday.

Car Rentals Contact any tour operator or hotel concierge about booking a car with driver for day trips or to sights farther afield. Expect to pay about $50 to $60 per day, and $20 for a guide to accompany you.

Climate Hanoi experiences relatively high humidity all year and a rainy season from May to October. Winter months are cool and damp (rarely below 57°F/14°C), but the heat starts to pick up in April and makes for a hot, wet summer (a popular time to hit cooler climates, such as Sapa in the far north, or enjoy the offshore breezes in Halong).

Doctors & Hospitals International SOS, at 1 Dang Thai Mai St., just beside West Lake, is your best bet for emergency services and travel illness. Contact their 24-hour service center at ✆ **04/3934-0666,** or visit the website at www.internationalsos.com. International SOS is part of a worldwide international service that you can join for a fee and be covered anywhere they offer services. The organization has a capable staff of expatriate and Vietnamese doctors, with specialists ranging from pre- and post-natal care to tropical infectious disease experts, good eye doctors, and dentists. They work in collusion with most major insurance companies and can contact your provider

to let you know if you are covered.

Hanoi Family Medical Practice, at Van Phuc Diplomatic Compound, 298 Kim Ma (✆ **04/3843-0748**), is another walk-in clinic, like International SOS, that caters to Hanoi's growing expatriate community. They have a good dental center.

Another good choice for comprehensive service is the **Hanoi French Hospital,** south of the town center at 1 Phuong Mai (✆ **04/3577-1100**). As the name suggests, the hospital caters to Francophones, and a knowledge of French is a plus, but doctors and staff can speak English as well. Service is very professional, efficient, and much more accessible and affordable than at the town's two international clinics.

Embassies & Consulates Your country's embassy is your home base in the event of any instability, political situation, or emergency (either medical or legal). It's not a bad idea to register with your embassy when you arrive in Hanoi or Ho Chi Minh City, or through the embassy website before you leave home. Embassies are also a good place to pick up the most current information on regional crises, health issues, political hot spots, and advice on travel. If you are in Vietnam during one of your country's national holidays, check for any special events held at an embassy compound (there's nothing like Thanksgiving among Americans or Victoria Day with fellow Canadians, for example). The following is a list of the major international embassies in Hanoi: **Australia,** 8 Dao Tan (☎ 04/3831-7755); **Canada,** 31 Hung Vuong (☎ 04/3734-5000); **European Union,** 83B Ly Thuong Kiet (☎ 04/3946-1702); **New Zealand,** 63 Ly Thai To (☎ 04/3824-1481); **United Kingdom,** 31 Hai Ba Trung (☎ 04/3936-0500); **United States,** 170 Ngoc Khanh St. (☎ 04/3850-5000).

Note that most storefront travel agencies can handle visa services for a nominal fee, but when arranging visas and gathering information about travel in nearby countries, you can also contact the following embassies: **China,** 46 Hoang Dieu (☎ 04/3845-3736); **India,** 58–60 Tran Hung Dao (☎ 04/3824-4989); **Japan,** 27 Lieu Giai (☎ 04/3846-3000); **Laos,** 22 Tran Binh Trong (☎ 04/3942-4576); **Malaysia,** 45 Dien Bien Phu (☎ 04/3734-3836); **Myanmar,** 298A Kim Ma (☎ 04/3845-3369); **The Philippines,** 27B Tran Hung Dao (☎ 04/3943-7948); **South Korea,** 360 Kim Ma (☎ 04/3831-5111); **Thailand,** 63–65 Hoang Dieu (☎ 04/3823-5092).

Internet   Internet service in Hanoi is provided free of charge in most budget and midrange hotels, in the form of either ADSL cables or Wi-Fi. Strangely,

top-end hotels are still charging for this service, at the exorbitant rate of around $15 a day. Due to its universal availability, most Internet cafes in Hanoi have now closed, though there are still a few on streets such as Hang Bac and Ma May that cater to young Vietnamese playing games all day. Rates at these shops are around 5,000 VND per hour.

Maps   The **Tourist Information Center** (7 Dinh Tien Hoang St.; ☎ **04/3926-3366**) has excellent free tourist maps, and several tour agents sell a good map of the city and surrounding area published by the Ban Do Publishing House for just $1.

Newspapers & Magazines   The **Vietnam News** is available free at most upmarket hotels and can be purchased at most bookstores and at magazine shops near Hoan Kiem Lake; written by Vietnamese, its local news is more or less propaganda ("We are successful and our economy is growing"), but the paper does cover the major international wire-service news items of the day and lists current events in the country.

A number of cheap and/ or free local magazines are geared toward tourists and business visitors. You can pick up either of the following at travel agents, popular restaurants, bars, hotel lobbies, and bookstores: the **Guide,** which is a travel and tourism glossy supplement published

monthly by the **Vietnam Economic Times** that provides useful listings of hotels, restaurants, and happenings (pick it up for free or for $5 with the VET); or **The Word: Hanoi** (www.wordhanoi.com), which also includes extensive listings as well as articles on aspects of the city and Vietnamese culture. Another publication, less frequently seen these days, is **Vietnam Pathfinder,** which is a small tourism magazine with an expatriate section featuring good insider tips on tours, travel, dining, and shopping.

Pharmacies   Vietnamese pharmacies are the "diagnose yourself" variety. Got a bad cough and think it's an infection? Pound the table and ask for antibiotics. So much for discouraging antibiotic-resistant illnesses. Pharmacies are on every street corner and, even if the folks there don't speak English, they can help if you mime your disease (I once did an interpretive dance I call "nonstop diarrhea"), or for the less theatrical, they usually have an English-to-Vietnamese dictionary with medical terms listed. Ask for foreign-made drugs, best from France, as Vietnamese versions of medicines, though cheap, are often inferior. I recommend heading to the SOS International Clinic, which has a pharmacy on-site (see "Doctors & Hospitals," above).

Police   Yes, you may call them if you have

something stolen, and they can fill out a report for insurance purposes, but the Hanoi police are best avoided; in fact, the only reason to see them is if you're bribing your way out of something (a traffic violation, for example). In Vietnam's rapidly changing economic and social climate, laws are mutable and, in fact, the rule of law is still uncertain. Traffic police crack down on motorbike drivers without helmets, but in general, foreign visitors have no contact with the grim lads in khaki.

Post Office The **General Post Office** is located at 6 Dinh Le St., Hoan Kiem District (✆ **04/3825-2030**). It's open daily from 7am to 8pm. You can also send faxes and make international phone calls there. **FedEx** (✆ **04/3557-8899;** daily 8am–6pm) is located at 5A Le Van Thiem St., in the Thanh Xuan District. You can find a **UPS** office at 26 Pham Van Dong St., Tu Liem District (✆ **04/3514-2888;** daily 7:30am–6pm) and a branch of **EMS** at 1 Tan Xuan (✆ **04/3757-5577;** daily 7am–9pm). Expect to pay anywhere from $35 to $80 per kilo (2.2 lb.), depending on expediency of service.

Safety Hanoi, like the rest of Vietnam, is safe. The only concerns for visitors are pickpockets and minor local scams (see "Rigged Taxi Meters," under "Getting Around," earlier in this chapter). Keep an eye on your valuables; store traveler's checks and money in your hotel safe or, if you must bring them with you, keep cash and important documents safe in a travel wallet under clothing and out of sight of the clever hands of thieves. Take care if out clubbing late in Hanoi, and avoid dark streets and walking alone, as you might in any place in the world. But in general, you're free from violence in the Vietnamese capital.

The city is not without hassles, though. You will be harassed by book, magazine, and souvenir sellers. The entreaties of these relentless entrepreneurs can get pretty tiresome. Remember that they're just kids, most of whom work under the pressure of local mafia, and it is their job to sell you; take time to talk with them if you have it, but remember that any conversation is geared toward getting the greenbacks out of your pocket. If you're not interested in their goods, let them know,

but these guys rarely leave it at that. A firm "No!" doesn't hurt anyone's feelings. If you stop at intersections and look at maps, know that the motorbike taxi guys will swarm you. I always try to have a look at the map before I get to any intersection so that I know what street I'm looking for and can proceed through intersections as if I know where I'm going.

Telephone The city code for Hanoi is 04. Most hotels provide **international direct dialing (IDD),** although none allow you to access an international operator or AT&T (whose Vietnam access code is ✆ **01/201-0288**). To do that, you will have to go to the post office. You'll find public phone booths throughout the city for local calls that accept phone cards purchased from the post office. **Internet "telephony"** is the cheapest option and is available in convenience stores throughout the city. Connecting through a designated ADSL line, phone service through the Internet from Hanoi is quite good, with the annoying delay effect at a bare minimum. Phone calls via **Skype** are usually much clearer, and free as well.

WHERE TO STAY

From historic charm to slick efficiency to budget hole-in-the-wall accommodations, you'll find what you want in Hanoi. Amenities and cleanliness levels are high across-the-board, and your dollar, yen, or euro goes quite far, so indulge in an upgrade. Most hotels costing more than $20 a night will have a phone, air-conditioning, in-room safes, and hair dryers. Children 11 and under usually stay free. Ask for discounts.

Hanoi

PHUC XA

To Tay Bac,
Hai Phong
& Lang Son

Nguyen Truong To

Yen Phu

Quan Thanh

Long Bien Bridge

See "Hanoi: Old Quarter" and
"Old Quarter Walking Tour" maps

Hang Dau

Gam Cau

PHUC TAN

Tran

Nhat Duat

THE OLD QUARTER

O QUANG
CHUONG

Chuong Duong Bridge

Ly Nam De

Phung Hung

Hang Luoc

Cha Ca

Hang Ma

Hang Chieu

Duong Bach Dang

Hanoi

Cua Dong

H. Phen

Hang Can

L. Van Can

HOAN
KIEM
DISTRICT

Ng Huu Huan

Tran Quang Khai

Ly Nam De

Phung Hung

Hang Dieu

Hang
Bo

H. Quat

H. Gai

Hang Bong

Ly Quoc Su

Le Thai To

Hoang

Chuong
Duong

Lake
Hoan
Kiem

Tran Nguyen Han

13

St Joseph's
Cathedral

Nha Chung

Huong River

Trang Thi

Dinh Tien

14

15

Quan Su

Hang Khay

Main
Post
Office

Ly Thai To

20

16

18
18

19

Trang Tien

21

22

17

Tho Nhuom

Hai Ba Trung

24

25

26

27

29

30

Pham Ngu Lao

Tran Khanh Du

Duong Bach Dang

23

Tran Hung Dao

Ly Thuong Kiet

28

Hang Bai

31

Ngo Quyen

Phan Chu Trinh

33

Le Thanh Tong

Tran Khanh Du

Nguyen Du

Quang Trung

32

Ba Trieu

Lake
Thien Quang

35

34

Le Van Hu'u

36

Tran Nhan Tong

HAI BA TRUNG
DISTRICT

THONG
NHAT PARK

Nguyen Dinh Chieu

Hue

Ngo Thi Nham

37

Lake
Bay Mau

To Hien Thanh

Nguyen Cong Tru

Prices shown here are high-season rack rates; discounts of up to 50% are available. Hotels charge a VAT of up to 20% except where noted.

Very Expensive

Hilton Hanoi Opera ★★ The Hilton is a reproduction colonial that makes an elegant arc around the perimeter of the splendid Hanoi Opera building. The inside matches the fine facade, with a lobby done on a grand scale. Rooms are outfitted with richly colored carpet, unique cushioned wallpaper, subdued lighting, and faux Chinese lacquer cabinets. Those on the fifth floor have balconies. Suites are much larger and nicely appointed. Daily newspaper delivery, voicemail, and in-room broadband Internet access keep business travelers up to speed. Leisure travelers can enjoy the inviting courtyard pool, get tips from the helpful concierge, and take advantage of in-house tour services with Exotissimo (daily 8am–8pm).

1 Le Thanh Tong St., Hoan Kiem District, Hanoi. www.hilton.com. ℂ **800/774-1500** in the U.S., or 04/3933-0500. Fax 04/3933-0530. 269 units. $200 double; $275 executive room; from $320 suite. AE, MC, V. **Amenities:** 2 restaurants; bar; cafe; babysitting; concierge; executive-level rooms; fitness center; outdoor pool; room service; rooms for those w/limited mobility. *In room:* A/C, satellite TV, hair dryer, Wi-Fi.

Hotel Nikko Hanoi ★★ The folks at the Hotel Nikko take care of the most discerning of all international visitors: the high-powered Japanese businessman. As a result, the place has every detail right—an immaculate, modern, streamlined design throughout, rooms so tidy you could eat sushi right off the floor, and comfort at a premium. Dining outlets are superb. It is a business hotel, but I include it here for the discerning travelers who like their accommodations peppered with a little bit of wabi wabi: the Japanese way of precision, quiet, and emptiness (with a little bling-bling thrown in). Nikko is located on the north end of sprawling Thong Nhat Park (formerly Lenin Park) overlooking Bay Mau Lake, a good distance south of the busy tourist area of Hanoi, but that might be one of the hotel's greatest assets.

84 Tran Nhan Tong St., Hai Ba Trung District, Hanoi. www.hotelnikkohanoi.com.vn. ℂ **04/3822-3535.** Fax 04/3822-3555. 255 units. $180–$350 double; $250–$1,500 suite. AE, MC, V. **Amenities:** 3 restaurants (Japanese, Chinese, and Continental); 2 bars; babysitting; concierge; health club; outdoor pool (4th floor); room service; spa. *In room:* A/C, satellite TV, fridge, hair dryer, minibar, Wi-Fi.

Sofitel Metropole Legend Hanoi ★★★ Hanoi's top choice. Built in 1901, the Metropole is a historic treasure. It's where invading, liberating, or civil armies have found billet and raised their flags, where the first film was shown in Indochina, where Charlie Chaplin spent his honeymoon, where Jane Fonda and Joan Baez took cover in a bomb shelter, and where heads of state and embassy officials resided for many years. In fact, the history of the Metropole is the history of the last 100 years in Hanoi.

The hotel has been through numerous renovations, and a new building was added in 1994. Rooms in the newer wing are more spacious, but go for the old wing and walk into a bit of history: Your medium-size room will have wood floors, cane furniture, classic fixtures, and high ceilings. The staff couldn't be nicer or more efficient. The pool is small, but the adjoining Bamboo Lounge is an oasis of calm in the city center. Le Beaulieu is popular for classic French fare, while the Spices Garden is a great place to sample local delights (the lunch buffet is a safe and tasty place to try Hanoi street fare including *pho* and *bun cha*). The downtown location can't be beat, and there's a nice mix of tourists and businesspeople here.

15 Ngo Quyen St., Hoan Kem District, Hanoi. www.sofitel.com. ℂ **800/221-4542** in the U.S., or 04/3826-6919. Fax 04/3826-6920. 364 units. $230–$410 double; from $580 suite. AE, DC, MC, V. **Amenities:** 3 restaurants; 3 bars; babysitting; concierge; top-notch health club & spa; nice courtyard pool;

room service; smoke-free rooms; Wi-Fi. *In room:* A/C, satellite TV, fridge, hair dryer, high-speed Internet, minibar.

Sofitel Plaza Hanoi ★　If you've come to Hanoi for real Sofitel charm, your best bet is the downtown Sofitel Metropole (see above). The big drawback of this hotel is location, which resembles a Florida suburb, but for familiar comfort and a bit of breathing room from downtown chaos, the Sofitel Plaza is a good bet. The hotel towers over the southern end of West Lake, which is about a 10-minute ride on Hanoi's ring road to the north of downtown, but this hulking plaza hosts such a high standard of rooms and services that you won't mind the slight inconvenience. Views from upper floors to the nearby lake and surrounding city (no buildings obstruct the views from here) are great. Rooms are large and decked out in sumptuous fabrics, rich rugs, and fine furnishings. The commute to the Old Quarter is about 40,000 VND in a taxi, and after wandering around there, you might be pleased to be whisked out of the chaos to air-conditioned comfort.

1 Thanh Nien Rd., Ba Dinh District, Hanoi. www.sofitel.com. © **04/3823-8888.** Fax 04/3829-3888. 317 units. $180–$200 double; $250–$1,000 suite. AE, MC, V. **Amenities:** 2 restaurants; 3 bars; concierge; health club; Jacuzzi; outdoor pool; room service; spa. *In room:* A/C, satellite TV, fridge, hair dryer, high-speed Internet, minibar.

Expensive

De Syloia ★　The De Syloia is a cozy little treasure just south of the city center. Rooms aren't especially luxurious for the price, but they're large, clean, and comfortable, with tidy carpet and dark-wood furniture. The large bathrooms have tubs (deluxe rooms and suites have Jacuzzis). The lobby is compact and clean but not particularly atmospheric, and the whole setup is a Hanoi minihotel gone upscale. Amenities are limited, but the staff is friendly on a good day, and this is a popular choice away from the downtown traffic. Check the website for discounted rates.

17A Tran Hung Dao St., Hoan Kiem District, Hanoi. www.desyloia.com. © **04/3824-5346.** Fax 04/3824-1083. 33 units. $100–$120 double; $130 suite. AE, MC, V. **Amenities:** Restaurant; bar; minigym; Internet. *In room:* A/C, satellite TV, fridge, hair dryer, minibar, Wi-Fi.

Hanoi Horison Hotel ★　This massive midrange number is far south of the tourist area of Hanoi, but the Hanoi Horison attracts international businesspeople as well as a burgeoning leisure market, and covers all the bases. This is a good choice for comfort and, for some, a welcome distance from "tourist Hanoi" (but just a short cab ride to the sights). Horison is built around a 14-story tower of glass, with an elevator open to the views of the busy street scene below and two massive wings extending from the glass centerpiece. The service is effusive from the moment someone opens the door for you. Deluxe rooms are very large, and a much better deal than standard rooms, certainly worth the upgrade. The rooms are decorated in a cozy, contemporary style with funky white floor lamps that shine mellow, indirect light and big, comfy beds. Swimming in the pool gives you a commanding view of the busy intersection below.

40 Cat Linh St., Dong Da District, Hanoi. www.accorhotels.com. © **04/3733-0808.** Fax 04/3733-0888. 247 units. $100 standard double; $120 deluxe double; from $200 suite. AE, MC, V. **Amenities:** 2 restaurants; 2 bars; concierge; concierge-/club-level rooms; health club; Jacuzzi; outdoor infinity pool and city view; room service; sauna; smoke-free rooms; spa; tennis court. *In room:* A/C, satellite TV, fridge, hair dryer, Internet, minibar, Wi-Fi.

InterContinental Hanoi Westlake ★★　The InterContinental offers a sweet resortlike atmosphere in busy little Hanoi. The hotel is Hanoi's newest and best five-star. For a romantic treat, splurge on a suite on one of the island pavilions connected to the main building via Venetian-style bridges. All rooms come with private balconies, and most have fabulous views of West Lake. Rooms on the top floor ("Atelier rooms") have high, sloping ceilings, giving the space a cozy cabin feel. Located about a 20-minute cab ride away from Hanoi's Old Quarter, this hotel is a perfect getaway from the hustle and bustle of city life. The outdoor Sunset Bar is a popular destination for hip locals and expats alike.

1A Nghi Tam, Tay Ho District, Hanoi. www.ichotelsgroup.com. ℂ **04/6270-8888.** Fax 04/6270-9999. 359 units. $120–$170 double; from $220 suite. AE, MC, V. **Amenities:** 3 restaurants; outdoor bar; cafe; lounge; babysitting; concierge; executive-level rooms; health club; Jacuzzi; outdoor pool; room service; sauna; smoke-free rooms; spa. *In room:* A/C, satellite TV, fridge, hair dryer, minibar, Wi-Fi.

Maison d'Hanoi ★★   This is a very comfortable option right in the heart of the city. Opened in December 2008, the Maison d'Hanoi has all the fun stuff you expect from a boutique property in Hanoi—contemporary decor with a flair of Vietnamese style, comfy wood floors, and great service. Bathrooms are small but comfortable. Double rooms are spacious, and the beds come with mattress pads that leave them incredibly soft and comfortable. Oversize, thick silk headboards are both sleek and functional, doing a good job of muffling sounds of nearby rooms. The breakfast is nothing special, but there's enough available to satisfy morning hunger pangs. Tea and coffee are served throughout the day.

35-37 Hang Trong St., Hoan Kiem District, Hanoi. www.hanovahotel.com. ℂ **04/3938-0999.** Fax 04/3938-0989. 55 units. $140–$180 double; $200–$220 suite. AE, MC, V. **Amenities:** Restaurant; bar. *In room:* A/C, satellite TV, fridge, high-speed Internet, minibar, Wi-Fi.

Mövenpick Hotel Hanoi ★★   The newly renovated Mövenpick is a sleek affair of modern comforts and swish decor. This is a better deal than other hotels in this category, such as the Hilton and the Daewoo, which look and feel quite dated in comparison. Rooms are spacious, with warm, dark wood–finish floors and splashy accent furniture such as French-style dressers painted in silver and gray, and black Art Deco rugs with a bit of lime thrown in. It's a careful balance of classic and contemporary, and the overall feel is excellent. Bathrooms are a bit on the small side, with no separate tubs, but there is a good-size shower cubicle outfitted with a rain shower. Watch out for the water temperature—it gets hot very quickly. The service is very friendly, if sometimes a bit eager.

83A Ly Thuong Kiet St., Hanoi. ℂ **04/3822-2800.** Fax 04/3822-2822. 154 units (some with shower only, some with shower and tub). $150–$170 double; from $230 suite. AE, MC, V. **Amenities:** Restaurant; bar; concierge; health club; dry sauna; smoke-free floors. *In room:* A/C, satellite TV, fridge, hair dryer, minibar, Wi-Fi.

Sheraton Hanoi ★   Just a 10-minute ride north of town, this smart, upscale hotel sits on a peninsula jutting into Hanoi's picturesque West Lake in a neighborhood popular with the local expat community (which means good restaurants and services in the area). The hotel makes up for any inconvenience of being far from town by being completely self-contained, with fine dining options, a top fitness center, and services that cover all bases, from local touring to business support. Rooms are done in an ultratidy, contemporary style typical of Sheraton hotels—certainly nothing spectacular, but cozy and familiar nonetheless. All units have fine views of the lake. Bathrooms are large, with big tubs, separate showers, and wood and granite detail. In-house dining is tops; a shuttle bus to town runs three times daily and taxis are available 24 hours.

K5 Nghi Tam, 11 Xuan Dieu Rd., Tay Ho District, Hanoi. www.sheraton.com. ℂ **04/3719-9000.** Fax 04/3719-9001. 299 units. $119–$190 double; from $325 suite. AE, DC, MC, V. **Amenities:** 2 restaurants;

bar; babysitting; concierge; executive-level rooms; health club; Jacuzzi; outdoor pool; room service; sauna; smoke-free rooms; tennis court. *In room:* A/C, satellite TV, fridge, hair dryer, minibar, Wi-Fi.

Zephyr Hotel ★★ 🎁 This downtown boutique property is a real find. Nine floors overlook the southern end of central Hoan Kiem Lake. It's perfect for luxury travelers who want to be in the middle of things but can't bear the thought of an Old Quarter minihotel (though many of these hotels are being upgraded, they can still be pretty beat-up and rooms very noisy from the busy streets below). Thin office-style carpets in rooms are a drawback, but beds have big fluffy duvets, and the built-in wooden cabinetry is sleek and contemporary. Deluxe rooms are quite luxurious, and two of them have balconies. Upper floors are best—some have great views. The first-floor restaurant serves international fare and a very good buffet breakfast. The place is like a large international hotel stuffed into the space of a Hanoi minihotel. The staff is very efficient, and you couldn't ask for a better downtown location.

4 Ba Trieu St., Hoan Kiem District, Hanoi. www.zephyrhotel.com.vn. © **04/3934-1256.** Fax 04/3934-1262. 43 units. $123 superior double; $143 deluxe double; $178 Zephyr suite. AE, MC, V. **Amenities:** Restaurant; bar (top-floor lounge); exercise room. *In room:* A/C, satellite TV, fridge, high-speed Internet, minibar.

Moderate

Army Hotel ★ 🍴 In a sprawling complex owned by the Vietnamese military—thus the name—there's no need to salute here and the friendly staff won't ask you to drop for 20 push-ups. For comfort and value close to downtown (and a nice pool), the Army Hotel is good value. Located on a quiet street just a short walk east of downtown (behind the Opera House), Army is popular with long-term visitors. Rooms vary, so ask to see one before you check in; most are large and clean, with tile floors and nice-size bathrooms with a tub/shower. Each room has a balcony, some with direct pool access. The staff is friendly, the lobby business center is convenient, and the pool is inviting and unique in this price range. Ask about their eclectic suites, some with Japanese-style rooms, and a larger private balcony.

33C Pham Ngu Lao St., Hanoi (just behind the Opera House). armyhotel@fpt.vn. © **04/3825-2896.** Fax 04/3826-5541. 70 units. $60 double; $100 suite. AE, MC, V. **Amenities:** Restaurant; babysitting; exercise room; outdoor pool; room service; sauna. *In room:* A/C, TV, fridge, hair dryer, Wi-Fi.

Church Hotel This was the first of the downtown, boutique hotel trend in the nation's capital, and the Gothic windows reflect the hotel's name. Rooms are smallish but bright and have all amenities, including Internet access. Staff members are helpful, but somewhat begrudgingly so. However, the hotel still sits right in the middle of the action on busy Nha Tho Street, a popular cafe-and-shopping area near Hanoi's large Catholic cathedral. The lobby is spotlessly clean, with modern Vietnamese oil paintings adorning the walls. It remains a good choice for comfort and downtown convenience.

9 Nha Tho St., Hoan Kiem District, Hanoi. www.churchhotel.com.vn. © **04/3928-8118.** Fax 04/3828-5793. 16 units. $50–$55 double; $82 suite. Rates include breakfast. MC, V. **Amenities:** Restaurant. *In room:* A/C, satellite TV, fridge, hair dryer, high-speed Internet.

Galaxy Hotel ★★ Popular with tour groups, the Galaxy is on a busy corner just north of the Old Quarter—a good spot to begin exploring this colorful part of the city. Converted from a 1929 factory, the building is colorless but comfortable. The carpeted rooms are a decent size, with armchairs and desk, and bathrooms all have tubs. Corner suites are a great option, with windows facing two directions over the Old Quarter. A good Asian restaurant is on the premises, as well as an inviting lobby bar. Friendly staff members will remember your name and can suggest good places to dine and city tours.

1 Phan Dinh Phung St., Hanoi. www.tctgroup.com. © **04/3828-2888.** Fax 04/3828-2466. 60 units. $70 double; $100 suite. Rates include breakfast. AE, DC, MC, V. **Amenities:** Restaurant; bar; room service. *In room:* A/C; satellite TV, fridge, hair dryer, minibar, Wi-Fi.

Green Mango ★★ 🎁   Tucked away in the labyrinthine streets of the Old Quarter, this little gem is a one-stop sleep, eat, and party location. With just a handful of stylish rooms upstairs and one of the city's most celebrated restaurants and bars downstairs, this place is ideal for short-stay visitors who prefer to avoid getting caught up in the city's traffic. Most rooms are compact but well-equipped, with wooden floors, flatscreen TVs, and Wi-Fi. If you prefer a bit more space, go for the Deluxe Sweet room. Rates include a delicious breakfast, and airport pickups can be arranged for $20.

18 Hang Quat St., Haon Kiem District, Hanoi. www.greenmango.vn. © **04/3928-9916.** Fax 04/3928-9915. 7 units. $50–$100 double. MC, V. **Amenities:** Restaurant, bar, room service. *In room:* A/C, cable TV, minibar, Wi-Fi.

Halong Hotel   This long-standing hotel has just received a makeover and is now worth considering as a reasonably priced place to base yourself in Hanoi. Its location on the northern fringe of the Old Quarter is both convenient yet away from the rowdy corners, and staff can help you with almost any request. Rooms are traditionally furnished, with all fixtures and fittings in good condition, and satellite TV and Wi-Fi are available, too. A buffet breakfast is served on the top floor, from where there are sweeping views of the Old Quarter.

77 Hang Luoc St., Old Quarter, Hanoi. www.halonghotel.com. © **04/3828-3525.** Fax 04/3828-3526. 18 units. $35–$55 double. MC, V. *In room:* A/C, satellite TV, Wi-Fi.

Hanoi Moment ★   One of the newest hotels in the Old Quarter, this boutique-style place offers a taste of luxury at midrange prices. Polished wood floors, dark wood furniture, and black, gray, and white decor, along with mood lighting, give rooms a modern feel, and comfy beds with crisp linen promise a sound sleep. Some rooms have glassed-in balconies that add lots of extra space. Double glazing on all windows helps to keep out the noise of honking horns in the street below, and things such as free daily newspapers, buffet breakfast, and computers for guests' use in the lobby make it a home away from home.

15 Hang Can St., Old Quarter, Hanoi. www.hanoimomenthotel.com. © **04/3923-3988.** Fax 04/3923-3989. 16 units. $60–$75 double; $100–$110 suite. MC, V. **Amenities:** Restaurant; room service. *In room:* A/C, satellite TV (DVD player in some), Wi-Fi.

Hoa Binh Hotel   Built in 1926, the Hoa Binh is a good, atmospheric choice. Comfort and history meet here, and whether you're walking up the big, creaky grand staircase or opening French doors onto a balcony overlooking the busy street, you know that you're in Hanoi. Sizable rooms have original light fixtures, molded ceilings, and gloss-wood furniture, though they are beginning to look a bit battered from the constant stream of guests. Everything is done a bit "low luxe," but the shiny polyester bedspreads, velveteen drapes, and spongy mattresses detract from the overall effect. Bathrooms are plain and small but spotless. The hotel, popular with tour groups, is in a prime downtown location, and the bar has a view of the city. Ask to see a room before checking in, because they vary in size, shape, and degree of cigarette smell.

27 Ly Thuong Kiet St., Hoan Kiem District, Hanoi. www.hoabinhhotel.com. © **04/3825-3315** or 3825-3692. Fax 04/3826-9818. 100 units. $85 double; $130–$150 suite. Rates include breakfast. AE, MC, V. **Amenities:** 2 restaurants; 2 bars; concierge; room service; sauna; smoke-free rooms. *In room:* A/C, TV, fridge, hair dryer, Internet, minibar.

Hanoi: Old Quarter

RESTAURANTS ◆
Café des Arts **21**
Garden Restaurant **27**
Green Tangerine **19**
Highway 4 **16**
Mediterraneo **25**
New Day **13**
Pineapple **7**
Restaurant 69 **12**
Tamarind Café **14**
Tandoor **17**

PHUC TAN

Long Bien Bridge

Quan Thanh
Phan Dinh Phung
Hang Than
Nguyen Thiep
Tran Nhat Duat
Hang Dau
Gam
Hang Cau
Hang Giay
Dong Xuan
Hang Khoai
Cao Thang
Dong Xuan Market
Thanh Ha
Hang Ma
Chieu
Ly Nam De
Phung Hung
Hang Cot
Hang Luoc
H. Ruoi
Cha Ca
Hang Dong
Hang Ga
Ngo Gach
Nguyen Sieu
Dao Duy Tu
Cho Gao
O QUANG CHUONG
Tan
Chuong Duong Bridge
Huong River
Lo Su Dong
Hang Ren
Bat Su
Thuoc Bac
Lan Ong
Hang Buom
Ma Chinh
Hang Ca
Lo Su
Hang Ma
Hang Vai
Cua Dong
H. Phen
Bat Dan
Hang Bo
Luong Ngoc Quyen
PHO CO
Nguyen Huu Huan
Hang Bac
Hang Be
H. Mam
Hang Giay
Hang Ngang
Hang Dao
Hang Can
Luong Van Can
Dinh Liet
Gia Ngu
Tran Quang Khai
Hang Tre
Hang Quat
H. Thiec
H. Non
Hang Dieu
Duong Thanh
Yen Thai
H. Manh
H. Hom
Hang Gai
Hanh
Cau Go
Water Puppet Theater
Hang
Lo Su
Hang Da Market
Ngo Tram
Ha Trung
Hang Bong
Phu Doan
Ly Quoc Su
Hang Trong
Hang Hanh
Le Thai To
Ben Ngo Son Pagoda
Lake Hoan Kiem
Dau Tien Hoang
Ly Thai To
Hang Voi
St. Joseph's Cathedral †
Nha Tho
Tran Nguyen Han
Quan Su

0 200 yds
0 200 m

5

HANOI | Where to Stay

HOTELS ■
Camellia 3 Hotel **23**
Church Hotel **26**
Classic Street Hotel **18**
Galaxy Hotel **1**
Green Mango **28**
Halong Hotel **3**
Hanoi Backpackers Hostel **6, 24**
Hanoi Moment **11**

Hong Ngoc Hotel **15**
Maison d'Hanoi **22**
Majestic Salute Hotel **4**
New Century **5**
Prince Hotel 1 **2**
Prince Hotel 2 **8**
Queen Hotel **20**
Quoc Hoa **10**
Sunshine Palace **9**

Majestic Salute Hotel ★   The Majestic's lobby has a funky 1960s retro feel, the kind of place where Austin Powers might feel at ease after a night at the clubs. Rooms are large and cozy, a basic high-end minihotel standard. The thin office-style carpeting in both public and private spaces is unfortunate, but some rooms have neat anterooms and are quite spacious. The hotel is just north of the main action in the Old Quarter, with entrances onto both Hang Duong, a street that becomes a walking district on weekend nights, and Cha Ca Street (near the popular restaurant Cha Ca La Vong, a Hanoi institution). Double-glazed windows throughout the hotel mean that though the hotel is sandwiched between some of the Old Quarter's busiest (honk-honk) streets, rooms are quite quiet.

54-56 Hang Duong/19 Cha Ca St., Hoan Kiem District, Hanoi. www.mssalutehanoihotel.com. © **04/3923-0036.** Fax 04/3923-0037. 37 units. $85–$102 double; $120 suite. MC, V. **Amenities:** 2 restaurants; lobby lounge bar; health club; room service. *In room:* A/C, satellite TV, fridge, minibar, Wi-Fi.

Queen Hotel ★   Typical of many lodgings in the Old Quarter, this former backpacker's haunt has been made over and reborn as a classy boutique hotel with a distinctive lobby where vintage bicycles and scooters are on display. The central location is ideal and the breezy roof garden and cozy communal lounge make it feel like home. Rooms are equipped with wooden floors and traditional furnishings, and each has a small balcony. Rooms out back are a bit quieter, away from the traffic noise. The owner is both an architect and one of the city's most knowledgeable tour operators, so it's well worth signing up here for a customized tour of the north.

65 Hang Bac St., Hoan Kiem District, Hanoi. www.azqueentravel.com. © **04/3826-0860.** Fax 04/0826-0300. 15 units. $65–$100 double. Rates include breakfast. AE, MC, V. **Amenities:** Rooftop garden; communal lounge. *In room:* A/C, satellite TV, DVD player, hair dryer, minibar, Wi-Fi.

Quoc Hoa ★   The Quoc Hoa is a cozier, more upmarket choice than your average Old Quarter minihotel. Standard rooms are clean and have many amenities, but they're crammed into a smaller space. Superior rooms are worth the extra $20: They're larger and have nicer furnishing and amenities. Deluxe rooms are just slightly larger than standard rooms. The contemporary design isn't flashy, but crisp and inviting. Service is good—in fact, the Quoc Hoa caters to a large contingent of Swiss and Japanese business visitors on a regular basis—some long-staying customers—and the front-desk staff really snaps to and even anticipates guests' needs. A tiny fitness center is on the top floor, and the smart restaurant (La Dolce Vita) on the same floor enjoys great views. There's also a relaxing cafe/bar on the ground floor. Your minihotel neighbors will be envious.

10 Bat Dan St., Hoan Kiem District, Hanoi. www.quochoahotel.com. © **04/3828-4528.** Fax 04/3826-7424. 46 units. $65–$100 double; $150 suite. MC, V. **Amenities:** Restaurant; bar; fitness center; Jacuzzi; room service. *In room:* A/C, satellite TV, fridge, hair dryer, minibar, Wi-Fi.

Inexpensive

Camellia 3 Hotel ★ 🛎   For simplicity and comfort, this minihotel, just a short walk north of Nha Tho Street and the old Catholic cathedral—now a popular gallery-and-cafe area—is a no-frills choice that fires on all cylinders. The best of the Camellia Group's three hotels (the others are numbers 4 and 5) in town, this one is down a quiet side street and offers guests a clean, quiet room with air-conditioning, hot water, and cable television. Deluxe rooms with a balcony and windows facing the street are just $45, an excellent value, and the family room is a good deal, too. Breakfast is included. Staffers are very helpful, will take care of any extra bags you leave while on overnight trips, and are very prompt about laundry service. A great choice for a simple, affordable home base while traveling the north. Should you speak French or Chinese, you might even make a few new friends, as the little lobby is always abuzz with expat comings and goings.

12c Chan Cam St. (just north of St. Joseph's Cathedral), Hanoi. www.camelliahanoihotel.com. © **04/3828-5936.** Fax 04/828-9409. 17 units. $25–$45 double; $50 family room. Rates include breakfast. No credit cards. **Amenities:** Restaurant (breakfast only). *In room:* A/C, satellite TV, fridge, Wi-Fi.

Classic Street Hotel 🛎   Furnished like a traditional Vietnamese house, this place makes guests feel at home right away and offers some quiet sitting areas apart from the cozy, carpeted rooms. Lodgings are not luxurious but are very adequate for the price and include all major comforts such as bathtubs, hot-water bathrooms, and cable

TV. There's a small restaurant where guests can enjoy a free breakfast before heading out to explore—and one of this hotel's best points is that it is right in the heart of the action, on the edge of the Old Quarter and a few steps from Hoan Kiem Lake.

41 Hang Be St., Hoan Kiem District, Hanoi. www.classicstreet-phocohotel.com. © **04/3825-2421.** Fax 04/3934-5920. 22 units. $33-$38 double. MC, V. **Amenities:** Restaurant, room service. *In room:* A/C, cable TV, fridge, hair dryer, Wi-Fi.

Hanoi Backpackers' Hostel ★ The explosion of the Hanoi Backpackers' Empire reflects the popularity of Hanoi for young backpackers; they now have more than 30 dorms, each sleeping six to eight people (some females only, some mixed), as well as about 30 private rooms, spread between three buildings, and they're always full. There's now a second branch almost opposite the original site on Ngo Huyen, and in late 2010 a huge third branch opened on a prime spot in the middle of Ma May in the Old Quarter. Hostel staff have got all travelers' needs covered; cheap beds with lockers and showers, free computer use, bar with generous happy hours, restaurant, "rock long, rock hard" tours of Halong Bay, and even souvenir T-shirts. More than anything, people come here to meet others, to share travel experiences, and make new friends. In order to help them do that, staff arrange games and parties almost every evening.

31 and 48 Ngo Huyen St. (down a small road just north of St. Joseph's, the big Catholic cathedral), Hoan Kiem District, and 9 Ma May. www.hanoibackpackershostel.com. © **04/3828-5372.** $6-$9 dorm bed; $25-$40 double. No credit cards. **Amenities:** Restaurant, bar, chill-out lounge with pool tables; computers and Internet use; tour services. *In room:* A/C, cable TV, Wi-Fi, no phone.

Hong Ngoc Hotel ★★ With four locations right in the heart of the Old Quarter, this is a good no-frills option close to Hoan Kiem Lake. The staff has an amazingly friendly, can-do attitude and can help you with any detail, such as renting a car, motorbike, or bicycle. Rooms are compact but all have the quality amenities of a proper hotel. For those traveling with their own computers, the budget locations (Hang Bac St. and Ma May St.) offer in-room wireless connections; the other locations have faster ADSL connections. Larger suites are a good choice, and all rooms are done in dark wooden trim. Bathrooms are small and clean. This is an affordable minihotel with attitude—like a terrier that thinks it's a Great Dane.

14 Luong Van Can St., Hoan Kiem District, Hanoi. hongngochotel@hn.vnn.vn. © **04/3826-7566.** Fax 04/3824-5362. 34 Hang Manh St., Hoan Kiem. © **04/3828-5053.** Fax 04/3828-5054. 99 Ma May St. Hoan Kiem. © **04/3828-3631.** 39 Hang Bac St., Hoan Kiem. © **04/3926-0322.** 97 Nguyen Truong To. © **04/3829-2025.** Total of 110 units. $30-$45 double at the budget locations; $50-$125 double at other locations. MC, V. **Amenities:** Restaurant; Internet; room service. *In room:* A/C, satellite TV, fridge, Internet, minibar.

New Century ★ 🍴 Formerly the Thien Tan Hotel, this well-maintained minihotel is one of the best deals in town. Though there's no elevator—you'll have to drag your bags upstairs—the rooms are particularly well equipped for this price, with computers and flatscreen TVs, and most are quite bright. The service staff is super friendly and genuinely concerned about meeting your needs (they'll look after your bags for a few days if you go away on a trip), and the tour desk can help with any sightseeing arrangements.

12 Cha Ca St., Hoan Kiem District, Hanoi. www.hanoinewcenturyhotel.com. © **04/3824-4005.** Fax 04/3824-4004. 8 units. $25-$40 double. MC, V. **Amenities:** Restaurant. *In room:* A/C, satellite TV, computer, fridge, high-speed Internet, minibar.

Prince Hotel I & II This is a classic minihotel in the Old Quarter. Nothing frilly, rooms at the Prince Hotels are basic decorless spaces with dark-wood furnishings, tile floors, air-conditioning, and hot water. The front-desk staff might at first appear helpful until you realize they're trying to sell you the kitchen sink in terms of tours and rentals, but that's their job. The place is a good budget base for exploring the area. Rooms at the back, away from the busy street, are your best bet. They have two addresses, both nearby in the heart of the Old Quarter.

Prince I: 51 Luong Ngoc Quyen St., Old Quarter, Hanoi. www.hanoiprincehotel.com. © **04/3828-0155.** Fax 04/3828-0156. Prince II: 42B Hang Giay St., Old Quarter, Hanoi. © **04/3926-1203.** Fax 04/3926-1205. $20–$30 double. Total of 26 units. MC, V. In room: A/C, satellite TV, fridge, minibar.

Sunshine Palace ★ 🍷   The newest of five hotels run by the Sunshine group, this small minihotel offers great value and an ideal location in the heart of the Old Quarter. It bills itself as a three-star hotel, and indeed the rooms are well equipped with stylish furnishings, computers, satellite TV, massage showers, and Jacuzzis, which you wouldn't find elsewhere at this price. A buffet breakfast is included in the price. Staff are extremely attentive and ready to assist guests with any request, from advising them where to buy an umbrella to organizing a trip to Halong Bay.

52 Ma May St, Old Quarter, Hanoi. www.hanoisunshinehotel.com. © **04/3926-4920.** Fax 04/3926-4921. 31 units. $25–$40 double; $60–$70 suite. Rates include buffet breakfast. MC, V. **Amenities:** Restaurant; concierge; babysitting; room service. In room: A/C, satellite TV, computer, hair dryer, minibar, Wi-Fi.

WHERE TO EAT

It's hard to have a bad meal in Hanoi. Almost every ethnic food variation is well represented in the city—from Italian and India, to vegetarian options and familiar Western fare. Years of brutal colonial rule by the French left many resentments, but no amount of antiforeign revolutionary zeal could overcome Vietnamese culinary traditions borrowed from their one-time oppressors. The baguette lives on, and the legacy of fine French cuisine can be found in every quarter (and the French chefs are coming back to train this next generation as well). In Hanoi, look out for both classical French and Vietnamese fusion fare, all priced for varying budgets. The city now hosts a number of fine high-end Vietnamese restaurants where you can try local specialties without worrying about getting dysentery. But for authentic Vietnamese fare, try the squat stool places at street side. Check the special sidebar below for good no-frills local dining options. Hanoi is a great place to eat adventurously and belly up to good local cuisine.

Expensive

Café des Arts ★ FRENCH   Located near the northwest corner of Hoan Kiem Lake, this classy and expensive eatery, run by French expats, makes for a memorable evening meal. Spacious, with tiled floors and shuttered windows looking into the narrow Old Quarter street below, the cafe has solid furniture and a long, inviting bar, and it doubles as an art gallery, which explains the interesting paintings hanging throughout. Go for the set menu, or sample one of the tempting alternatives from the a la carte menu. There is also a good range of wines available. If prices seem a bit steep, check out the ground floor **Stop Café** (8am–11pm), under the same management, where the menu is more varied and prices are more down to earth.

11B Ngo Bao Khanh, Hoan Kiem District (in the Old Quarter). © **04/3828-7207.** Set menus $30–$48. Main courses $13–$38. MC, V. Daily 11am–11pm. Bar open until midnight.

Club de L'Oriental ★★★ VIETNAMESE   This is upscale Vietnamese food at its best—beautiful colonial decor, properly trained staff, and amazing food. The fresh spring rolls are the best in town, though I can never choose between those and the deep-fried Imperial-style spring rolls, so I often order both and end up stuffing myself before the entrees arrive. For mains, I highly recommend the grilled chicken in lemon leaves served with a dipping plate of salt and pepper in a sprinkle of lime juice, a light but savory dish. On the richer side, try the sautéed prawns in tamarind sauce. The main floor has a handful of tables set up around an open kitchen, seats around which are perfect for couples or single diners. For an intimate but chilly experience, reserve a table in the wine cellar.

22 Tong Dan, Hoan Kiem District. ✆ **04/3826-8801.** Reservations recommended. Main courses $9–$65; set menu $35 lunch, from $45 dinner. AE, MC, V. Mon–Sat 11am–2:15pm and 5:45–11:15pm; Sun 5:45–11:15pm.

Green Tangerine ★★ FRENCH The Green Tangerine is set in a lovingly restored 1928 colonial in the southeast corner of the Old Quarter. Its small courtyard, just a few steps off busy Hang Be, is great for an afternoon drink, while the air-conditioned dining room is a real sanctuary for a luxurious meal. It's very popular with expats, and that makes for a constantly evolving menu to keep up with repeat customers. Dishes might include a lovely bass enhanced with ginger served with slices of zucchini and potatoes piled like a layer cake. The creamy Cointreau-flavored frozen yogurt served in a green tangerine shell is delicious and refreshing. The set menus are popular and good value. Everything here is rich and delicious.

48 Hang Be, Hoan Kiem District. ✆ **04/3825-1286.** www.greentangerinehanoi.com. Main courses $13–$26. AE, MC, V. Daily 11am–10:30pm.

La Badiane ★★ FRENCH Local chef Benjamin Rascalou's new restaurant is a tasty addition to Hanoi's fine-dining scene. La Badiane is housed in an old colonial villa divided into a small garden courtyard on the ground floor and a pair of intimate dining rooms upstairs. The three set-price dinner menus include flavorful options such as roasted lamb shank. Service is also top-notch here, which is quite an accomplishment for such an intimate place. This is Rascalou's first restaurant, but he is well respected in the local foodie community for his stunning work at the Green Tangerine, where he served as head chef for 6 years prior to opening La Badiane.

10 Nam Ngu St. ✆ **04/3942-4509.** Reservations recommended. Main courses $20–$35; set menus $13 lunch, $33 dinner. AE, MC, V. Mon–Sat 11:30am–2pm and 6–10pm.

La Verticale ★★ FUSION Chef and owner Didier Corlou has lived in Vietnam for many years and has a clear love affair with spices. Not only do magical spice combinations make appearances in La Verticale's tasty food, but they are also infused into the restaurant's decor—tables are sprinkled with star anise, chopsticks rest on curls of cinnamon, and colorful peppercorns lie in shallow bowls. The menu changes by season, but expect to find inventive dishes marked with a strong Vietnamese base. If it's available, I highly recommend the pork served five ways. The succulent fatty cubes braised in red sauce are divine, as is the thin loin strip marinated in soy sauce.

19 Ngo Van So St. ✆ **04/3944-6317.** Reservations recommended. Main courses $17–$36. AE, MC, V. Daily 11am–2pm and 6–10pm.

Press Club ★ CONTINENTAL Don't be fooled by the elite address and elegant atmosphere: The Press Club is the kind of place that impresses, but it's far more affordable and accessible than its reputation and stylish dining room might indicate. The old-boys' network still digs it, but the Press Club is also attracting a younger, hipper crowd. The indoor restaurant is sizable yet private, done in dark tones of

THE BEST authentic LOCAL FARE

Hanoi's local cuisine is some of the best in Vietnam, and the finest local dishes are served at small one-dish restaurants, usually just open-air joints at street side, where you might wonder why there's a line out the door. To Vietnamese, it's about the food, not the atmosphere. Some of the best meals in the capital—or anywhere in Vietnam, for that matter—are eaten on squat stools with disposable chopsticks. Standards of hygiene might appear poor, but do as locals do and wipe down bowls and chopsticks with a napkin before digging in. Yes, eating on the street does mean you might have some tummy trouble, but if you stick to the few places recommended below, you should be okay.

The ubiquitous *pho*—noodle soup served with slices of beef *(bo)* or chicken *(ga)*, fresh bean sprouts, and condiments—can be found anywhere. And don't miss *cha ca,* Hanoi's famed spicy fish fry-up (see below).

Banh Cuon ★, 14 Hang Ga St., consists of minced pork and mushrooms rolled into soft rice crepes topped with crispy fried garlic and coriander. Cut-up pieces are dipped in a tasty fish sauce. The stuffing-to-crepe ratio at this streetside eatery is a bit on the low side, but it is still great value for money, at 30,000 VND a plate.

Bun Bo Nam Bo ★★, 67 Hang Dieu St., serves only one main course: *bun bo,* a dish of fresh rice noodles topped with crisp fried garlic, bean sprouts, peanuts, basil, and beef, that costs only 40,000 VND. Sound simple? It is. It is the subtlety of the flavors of this dish and the

stock that brings 'em here in droves. Just order by holding up as many fingers as you want bowls of *bun bo,* take a seat at the low tables in the brightly lit interior, and wait. A spartan atmosphere, but a rich and delicious dish worth hunting down. No credit cards. Daily 7am to 10:30pm.

Cha Ca La Vong ★★, 14 Cha Ca St., is on a street called Cha Ca, and it serves one dish—you guessed it—*cha ca* (150,000 VND per person). So what's the story with *cha ca?* Very simple: It's a delicate whitefish, fried at high heat in peanut oil with dill, turmeric, rice noodles, and peanuts—and it's delicious. The place is pretty grungy, and to call the service "indifferent" would be to sing its praises, but that's the beauty here: It's all about the food. You order by saying how many you are and how many bottles of beer or soda you'd like. Then it's do-it-yourself, with some gruff guidance, as you stir in the ingredients on a frying pan over a charcoal hibachi right at the table. It's a rich dish and great with some hot sauce (go easy on it at first), and it makes for a fun and interesting evening. Just say "Cha Ca" and any cabdriver can take you there. Avoid copycats: There are a few copycat "Cha Ca La Vong" restaurants on the same street serving this dish on electric grills, so make sure you've got the right address before you sit down and order. No credit cards. Daily 11am to 2pm and 5 to 9pm.

Gia Truyen Pho (Noodle Soup) ★★, 49 Bat Dan St. (on the west side of the Old Quarter near the old citadel wall), is a

maroon and forest green with solid wood furniture and detailing. Outdoor seating is available on the terrace facing a large stage that features occasional live music acts. The service is impeccable. The menu is full of sumptuous Continental standards: antipasto starters, goat-cheese salad, tuna steak, and various wood-grilled imported steaks and meat dishes. Savory entrees include the Australian beef tenderloin and very popular storefront *pho* noodle soup stand in Hanoi's Old Quarter. If you've seen the Japanese film *Tampopo,* about the making of the perfect noodle soup, or saw the *Seinfeld* episode about New York City's "Soup Nazi" who, because of his quality broth, chose his customers instead of vice versa, you'll have an idea what it's like. The line is around the block day and night, as Hanoians of all stripes humbly line up for a taste of the best. The formula is simple: delicious cured beef, fresh noodles, and spices—done the same way, over and over, for years. Just order "One please" (it is *pho* with beef or nothing) and pay the surly lady, who might even let a few customers go ahead of you if she doesn't like the cut of your jib. Unlike in most *pho* joints, no one serves you, so you have to carry your own bowl to an open slot at a crowded table (if you come with a friend, you might have to separate), and the place is as grotty as any little noodle stand, but when you pull those first noodles off the chopsticks and follow with a spoonful of broth, you'll know why you came. No phone. One bowl of beef *pho* is 30,000 VND. Daily 6 to 11am and 6 to 11pm.

Lan Chin, 15 Hang Tre, in the southeast corner of the Old Quarter, is a fun adventure. It's not exactly a hole in the wall; in fact, its two expansive floors can seat hundreds of diners, and it's one of the best places in town to enjoy the real *lau,* or Vietnamese hot pot. Go with a Vietnamese friend or be open to some creative charades with your waitress; there's no English menu, and foreign visitors are rare. The official directions

for cooking hot pot? As my friend says, "You just put." Add whatever you like—fresh seafood, beef, poultry, and vegetables—to a shared pot of boiling broth on a hot plate in the center of the table. They also can bring out a barbecue setup for small kabobs. You order like you would order dim sum, choosing plates of raw ingredients off a tray. The place is packed in the evenings, especially in the winter (this is Vietnam's version of stew) and on weekends. The local draft beer flows freely, and though it costs a little more than the stuff on the street, is a cut above. Expect to pay about $5 per person in a group. No credit cards. Daily 11am to 11pm.

Nguyen Sinh Restaurant Francais, 17–19 Ly Quoc St., directly north on the street that runs in front of the Nha Tho Cathedral. What is so Vietnamese about this French restaurant? Everything. Founded in 1950, these folks were the ones (among many) who kept alive the art of baking bread and cooking French foods. Vietnamese French has its own bend, say French expats, and in Hanoi it's a cuisine of its own. This little storefront offers good imported cheese and wine; it's sort of like Hanoi's de facto New York deli (it'll do in a pinch, anyway, for that late-night snack). Here you can get a delicious baguette with cheese and pâté for just 40,000 VND, or a savory, French-style steak fry-up. You'll find locals in berets trying out their newest licks on the saxophone, and French expats getting a little taste of home, chatting with the Francophone clientele. *Très* chic. Daily 7am to 10pm.

sautéed duckling breast. For dessert, try the tiramisu with raspberry essence and passion fruit ice cream. On the same (third) floor, there's a casual and cozy coffee corner called the **Deli** (see "Snacks & Cafes," later in this chapter).

59A Ly Thai To St., Hoan Kiem District. © **04/3934-0888.** www.hanoi-pressclub.com. Reservations recommended. Main courses $30–$40. AE, MC, V. Daily 6.30am–10:30pm.

Wild Lotus ★★ CONTEMPORARY VIETNAMESE   City sounds—and smells— melt away as you climb up a marble staircase, past two small lotus ponds and a water- fall, to get to the main floor of this restaurant, housed inside an old French building. The ambience is upscale Asian chic, with a bouquet of lotuses on every table, wooden furniture, and original art pieces on the wall by established Vietnamese artists such as Vo Van Long. From the kitchen comes gorgeous Vietnamese food with added hints of spices from Thailand. I highly recommend the peanut-crusted shrimp with green mango salad, and grilled fish tikka in pandanus leaves with tartar and sweet chili. Both are light dishes that carry just the right amount of spunk, thanks to the tart green mango and sweet chili sauce. *Tip:* The restaurant serves portions that are meant to be shared, so if dining alone, ask about half-portions so you can try more than one dish.

55A Nguyen Du St. ℂ **04/3943-9342.** Fax 04/3943-9341. Main courses 180,000 VND–320,000 VND. MC, V. Daily 10am–11pm.

Wild Rice (Lá Luá) ★ ASIAN FUSION   Nothing about Lá Luá portends to be authentic Vietnamese; everything from the decor to the dining is, in fact, an amalgam of traditions and customs. The place looks like an upmarket L.A. bistro borrowing Japanese themes, with tall stands of bamboo encased in glass, slate floors, and bright white walls that shine with the mellow glow of indirect lighting. The food is good Vietnamese-influenced fare. My grilled chicken in chili with lemongrass was deli- ciously spicy and savory. Try the barbecued squid or beef with coconut. Presentation is Zen simple: white linen with black chopsticks, a plate, a bowl, and a candle on the table, and it's as if the staff is playing a game of chess on your table, rearranging things as if they'd rather not disturb the utensil still life. It's all a bit studied, really, but the food is very good.

6 Ngo Thi Nham St., Ba Trung. ℂ **04/3943-8896.** Fax 04/3826-6299. Main courses $8–$25. AE, MC, V. Daily 11am–2pm and 6–10pm.

Moderate

Al Fresco's ☺ TEX-MEX   Run by Australian expats, Al Fresco's is the flagship of a growing chain that includes Jasper's and Pepperoni restaurants. Al Fresco's had six outlets at the last count, so check out their website for other locations. This one occupies two floors and offers friendly, casual dining. With checkered tablecloths, good oldies music, and a great view from the second floor to the street below, this is the place to bring the kids (or yourself) when they're in need of a slice of home. The only reason to visit this place is for the ribs, which are a house specialty. Desserts, such as brownies a la mode, are good standbys. The wine list is heavy on Australian and inexpensive South American reds. If you've had enough of fried rice or noodle soup, come here for something to stick to your ribs.

23L Hai Ba Trung St., Hoan Kiem District. ℂ **04/3826-7782.** www.alfrescogroup.com. Main courses 150,000 VND–180,000 VND. MC, V. Daily 8:30am–11pm.

Club Opera ★ VIETNAMESE   Just next to the Press Club and across from the Sofitel Metropole, this exclusive little bistro, like its sister, the Emperor, serves deli- cious Vietnamese food that's a bit dolled up for the foreign palate—and priced to the foreign wallet. They have all kinds of Vietnamese fare, from Hue specials such as crispy fried spring rolls to delicate, smaller versions of *banh khoi* (fried doughy pan- cakes filled with vegetables, herbs, and shrimp). You'll also find stir-fries and hot-pot specials, as well as grilled chicken in lemon grass and rich fried squid. The atmo- sphere is a retro French villa, with lots of cozy romantic nooks and candlelight.

59 Ly Thai To St., Hoan Kiem District. © **04/3824-6950.** Main courses 210,000 VND-320,000 VND. AE, MC, V. Daily 11am-2pm and 6-10:30pm.

Garden Restaurant ★ VIETNAMESE   The Garden Restaurant is a low-luxe, authentic Vietnamese restaurant that attracts a few tourists (and small tour groups) in the know. With cool courtyard seating and cozy inside dining, this is a good place to try real Hanoi cuisine—stir-fries and roast dishes, as well as curries and specialties such as whole fried river fish or sautéed shrimp with tamarind sauce. Bring friends and settle in for a long repast. The young waitstaff are eager to practice their English and aim to please.

36 Hang Manh (west of the lake and just north of Hang Gai). © **04/3824-3402.** Main courses 110,000 VND-270,000 VND. MC, V. Daily 10am-2pm and 5-10pm.

Highway 4 ★ VIETNAMESE   Named after the highway that snakes through north Vietnam, this place is more than a restaurant—it's a complete dining experience. Explore a range of traditional Vietnamese dishes such as steamboat and oven-baked clay pot, while relaxing in a typically Vietnamese interior. If you are suitably impressed by the quality of the food, you can also sign up for cookery classes here. To complete the cultural immersion program, choose one of the Son Tinh rice wines in herbal and fruit flavors—a range of liquors produced exclusively by Highway 4. They claim that the high quality of distillation and absence of artificial additives guarantees a clear head the next day, though if you want to be sure, stick to the herbal teas or fruit juices. There are now five branches (see website for details of others); this one is conveniently located on the eastern side of the Old Quarter.

3 Hang Tre St. © **04/3926-4200.** www.highway4.com. Main courses 50,000 VND-365,000 VND. AE, MC, V. 10am-midnight.

Hoa Sua Training Restaurant ★ FRENCH/VIETNAMESE   Do a good deed, enjoy a great feed. You'll find lots of good French and Vietnamese dishes at this popular cafe that recently moved out near West Lake. Started in 1995, Hoa Sua is an NGO and training school for disadvantaged youth, and every year it recruits around 500 students who go on to all kinds of careers. Because working at the restaurant is like a final exam for these students, the young staff is as friendly as they come and every detail is well attended to. The food is great, the atmosphere is very laid back, and the price is right. Everything—from good steak and sandwiches to Vietnamese curry specials and fried seafood—is delicious. Best of all, the profits go to good use, providing scholarships for students and upgrading the school's service standard.

34 Chau Long St. © **04/3942-4448.** www.hoasuaschool.com. Main courses 50,000 VND-210,000 VND. MC, V. Daily 11am-10:30pm.

Jaspas ★ INTERNATIONAL   One of two Jaspas in town, this is part of the Al Fresco's Group that has been so successful in Vietnam. Set on the fourth floor of Hanoi Towers, a popular executive service building and apartment block, Jaspas is a sleek and stylish spot—elbow to elbow during postwork happy hours—and the menu features great imported steaks, fry-ups, pizzas, and some good local offerings. The glass-and-steel open area of the restaurant overlooks the nearby pool. In the evening, it's popular for dinner, drinks, and negotiations between international partners, and in the morning, it's the spot for a good fry-up breakfast.

4th floor, Hanoi Tower, 49 Hai Ba Trung. © **04/3934-8325.** Main courses 185,000 VND-485,000 VND. MC, V. Daily 6am-midnight.

Khai's Brothers ★ VIETNAMESE   Buffet only, Brothers is an inexpensive starting point to explore gourmet Vietnamese cuisine. Lunch includes dishes such as salted chicken, sweet-and-sour bean sprouts, shrimp, noodles, and spring rolls; a full dessert table of sweet tofu, sweet baby rice, dragon fruit, and other exotic offerings; and fresh lemon or melon juice. Dinner features grilled items—shrimp, fish, lamb, and pork— and a glass of wine. There are faux street stalls encircling the garden, with Vietnamese favorites such as *pho* (noodle soup) and *bun cha* (cold rice noodles, spring rolls, and lettuce eaten by dipping into a slightly sweet sauce with meat). ***But be forewarned:*** The place is virtually overrun by tourist buses during peak lunch- and dinnertimes.

26 Nguyen Thai Hoc. 📞 **04/3733-3866.** www.brothercafe.com. Lunch $13; dinner $18. AE, DC, MC, V. Daily 11:30am–2pm and 6:15–10pm.

Khazänna ★★ NORTHERN INDIAN   This restaurant changes names and owners every 2 years, but the current incarnation serves a fine menu of good north Indian dishes. You'll find tidy Indian-themed Western decor here with excellent service and presentation: The curries are served in small metal crocks with brass ladles. The affordable lunch menu brings in crowds of businesspeople. In the evening, choose from an extensive menu of curries, grilled dishes, and good *naan* breads.

1C Tong Dan St., Hoan Kiem District. 📞 **04/3934-5657.** Main courses $6–$12. MC, V. Daily 11am–2:30pm and 6–10:30pm.

Pane e Vino ★ ITALIAN   Set in a cozy backstreet location near the Opera House, this small Italian restaurant turns out consistently good pastas and pizzas, and features a good range of wines, too. The three-course set lunch menu is an excellent value, at 150,000 VND, and more than enough to fuel a traveler who's been walking all over Hanoi for the better part of 4 hours.

3 Nguyen Khac Can. 📞 **04/3826-9080.** Main courses $4–$18. MC, V. Daily 7:30am–11pm.

Restaurant Bobby Chinn ★★ CALIFORNIA/FRENCH/VIETNAM-ESE   Bobby Chinn's new place out in Xuan Dieu is a minireplica of the style and panache that made him famous in the Old Quarter, and the new streamlined menu is significantly cheaper. The main floor, with its cozy gray couches and intimate bar, is perfect for predinner cocktails. Upstairs in the main dining area, maroon cloths hang in twisted knots from the ceiling and are draped over walls, providing stark backgrounds to the restaurant's stylish selection of local art. As for food, vegetarian quesadillas served with mango salsa are an excellent starter, and from the short menu of fusion dishes, my favorite entree is the decidedly Western rack of lamb and mashed potatoes. Polish the meal off with the trio of crème brûlée and one last cocktail downstairs, and you won't regret schlepping out to the new location.

> **Restaurant Tip**
>
> Note that many upscale restaurants in Hanoi levy a 5% service charge on top of the 10% government tax.

77 Xuan Dieu, Ba Dinh District. 📞 **04/3934-8577.** www.bobbychinn.com. Reservations recommended. Set lunch 300,000 VND. Main courses 150,000 VND–450,000 VND. AE, MC, V. Daily 11am–midnight. Bar until 11:30pm.

Inexpensive

Chim Sao (L'Oiseau Siffleur) ★ 📷 VIETNAMESE   This charming restaurant serves authentic Vietnamese dishes in a home-style ambience. Rotating art hangs on unfinished walls, and guests have to remove footwear before heading upstairs to sit on floor pillows and dine over squat tables. The English translations of dishes rarely do them justice—the "tofu with egg salted" is actually a delightful dish of cubed, battered tofu that is flash-fried for a crisp exterior. Other must-try dishes are the caramelized pork served in a piping hot clay pot, and the "mountainous flower rice," which is sticky rice served with a sprinkle of crispy fried garlic.

65 Ngo Hue, Hoan Kiem District. ℭ **04/3976-0633.** Main courses 60,000 VND–100,000 VND. No credit cards. Daily 11am–2pm and 6–11pm.

Mediterraneo ★ ITALIAN   A tasty but typical range of northern Italian fare is served at this mellow streetside cafe on Nha Tho, Hanoi's stylish cafe area (called Church St.). Prosciutto with melon, and tomato and mozzarella are good starters. Follow with homemade pasta, a grilled dish, or pizza. You'll also find daily specials and a good wine list. This is an affordable, cozy, and casual spot.

23 Nha Tho St., Hoan Kiem (near the Old Church). ℭ **04/3826-6288.** Main courses $5–$14. MC, V. Daily 9am–11pm.

New Day ★★ 🍴 VIETNAMESE   Right across from Restaurant 69 on Ma May, this no-frills place lives up to its slogan ("The best foods, the cheapest price") and packs in locals and tourists alike throughout the day. In fact, it's so popular that if you turn up alone, you'll probably need to share a table with others, but this is half the fun. The extensive menu features every kind of Vietnamese specialty, but the staff are understanding of foreigners' unfamiliarity with local dishes, and welcome diners to take a look in the kitchen at prepared dishes, too. Try the spare ribs with New Day sauce and the ever-reliable deep-fried Hanoi spring rolls; you won't be disappointed.

72 Ma May, Old Quarter, Hanoi. ℭ **04/3828-0315.** Main courses 35,000 VND–115,000 VND. No credit cards. Daily 8am–10:30pm.

Pineapple ★ VIETNAMESE   This tiny place only has a frontage of a few feet and just a couple of tables by the busy street, but upstairs are two relaxing dining rooms. The tasteful lemon and apricot decor and smart appearance of waitstaff makes it seem that it should be much pricier than it is. Come here for the great-value set lunch (100,000 VND), which provides a taste of several traditional dishes, or choose from the wide-ranging a la carte menu. Don't miss out on the delicious fruit juices and shakes.

35 Hang Buom, Old Quarter, Hanoi. ℭ **04/3935-2316.** Main courses 50,000 VND–130,000 VND. No credit cards. Daily 10am–11pm.

Quan An Ngon ★★★ VIETNAMESE   *Ngon* means "delicious" in Vietnamese, and this lively restaurant and its extensive menu live up to its name, though it's so popular it can get quite a crush at peak eating times. Sit at the elbow-to-elbow tables in the open air or else inside, where it's cooler and quieter. The bustling courtyard, filled with Vietnamese professionals and students, is surrounded by well-stocked, clean food stalls, reminiscent of what you might find at random, on the street, but without some of the, uh, hygiene concerns. My personal favorites are the pounded shrimp fried on sugar cane, served with greens that you then wrap in the accompanying rice paper, and the sautéed beef with salad greens. Prices are incredibly reasonable, and this is a great place to explore a wide-ranging sample of Vietnamese fare.

18 Phan Boi Chau St., Hoan Kiem District. ℭ **04/3942-8162.** Main courses 32,000 VND–135,000 VND. MC, V. Daily 7am–10pm.

Restaurant 69 ★ VIETNAMESE   The number is the address on busy little Ma May Street, right in the heart of the Old Quarter tourist area. Set in an old converted traditional shop house, Restaurant 69 is worth it if only for the atmosphere. Go for a table on the second-floor balcony, if you can. There's a novella of a menu with lots of local specials, anything from *pho* (Vietnamese noodle soup) and *bun bo Hue* (a dish of rice vermicelli and beef popular in the town of Hue in central Vietnam) to good stir-fries and seafood hot pots. The clay-pot dishes are popular, too. Soups, salads, and sandwiches pretty much cover all the bases, and the friendly staff makes this a welcome place to beat the heat (or get warm) and have a snack while touring the Old Quarter.

69 Ma May St., Hoan Kiem. ℂ **04/3926-1720.** Main courses 75,000 VND–130,000 VND. No credit cards. Daily 10:30am–11pm.

Tamarind Café ★★ VEGETARIAN Tamarind is a laid-back, friendly spot, and even if you're not a vegetarian, this welcoming cafe's inventive menu will tickle your fancy. Soups such as vegetarian wonton and two-color (spinach and sweet potato) take the chill off Hanoi winter nights and go great with the selection of sandwiches. Other inventive options here include "Ratatofu," ratatouille over tofu, and the tamarind salad—diced onions, cucumber, tomatoes, mango, and avocado over a bed of crisp lettuce served with honey vinaigrette—makes a fabulous summer lunch. Fruit shakes and excellent teas round out the meal. It's not only a great place to take a break from the hectic traffic of the Old Quarter and relax but a good place to meet other travelers and pick up advice. The cafe is full early in the morning, when large groups of travelers setting out with **Handspan Travel** meet here for breakfast before their trips.

80 Ma May St., Hoan Kiem District. ℂ **04/3926-0580.** Set lunch $7. Main courses $4–$8. MC, V. Daily 5:30am–11pm.

Tandoor ★ INDIAN Tandoor is a long-popular Indian-food enclave, popular with both young travelers looking for a bit of a curry fix after weeks on the road with nothing but rice and noodle dishes, as well as expats feeding a family (they have free delivery service and takeout). Try the delicious kabobs served from an authentic *tandoor* oven—hence the name—and any of the delicious curries. *Thali* set menus for 95,000 VND (vegetarian) and 125,000 VND (with meat) are affordable and offer a good range of dishes, hitting all the right points on your palate, from spicy, to salty, to sweet. Go for the prime balcony table on the second floor overlooking the busy street out front.

24 Hang Be St., Hoan Kiem District. ℂ **04/3824-5359.** Main courses 55,000 VND–250,000 VND. MC, V. Daily 11am–10:30pm.

> **A Scoop**
>
> **Check out the local ice-cream shops along Trang Tien Street between the lake and the Dan Chu Hotel. For 4,000 VND, enjoy a cone and be part of the local scene.**

Snacks & Cafes

Life moves fast in the busy city, but Hanoians are fond of their coffee and taking time to sit back and watch it go by. Below are just a few of the many cafes in town. Hanoi's cafes open early for breakfast (about 7am) and close around 9pm. Bring cash; only larger places accept credit cards.

Ciao Café An outlet of this popular Saigon chain, Ciao Café is a cool two-story place just south of the lake, with cozy booths and a funky, Art Deco style all its own. It attracts mostly locals, making it a fun hangout and people-watching perch.

2 Hang Bai St. ℂ **04/3934-1494.** Daily 7am–11pm.

The Deli   Located on the third floor of the Press Club (p. 114), the Deli is a good place to grab a local or international paper and enjoy a relaxed lunch of sandwiches and gourmet pizzas, not to mention the Aussie pie with chips or "Mom's Meatloaf." It's a bit pricey, but there's free Wi-Fi, so bring your laptop and get connected.

59A Ly Thai To St., Hoan Kiem District. ✆ **04/3934-0888.** www.hanoi-pressclub.com. Daily 7am–10pm.

Fanny's Ice Cream ★★   One of the main attractions around Hoan Kiem Lake (for me) is Fanny's Ice Cream on the west side of the lake. They serve exquisite gelato-style ice cream.

48 Le Thai To (on the western edge of Hoan Kiem Lake). ✆ **04/3828-5656.** Daily 8am–11pm.

Highland's Coffee ★   Highland's is the local version of Starbucks—a popular place to beat the heat and have a good, strong cup of coffee. The best location is lakeside on the third floor of the massive wedge-shaped building that overlooks a busy traffic circle and the north end of the lake. Red couches are set up in intimate arrangements on platforms overlooking the busy anthill below: a good meeting point. Alternatively, head to their hip outdoor courtyard between the Hilton and the Hanoi Opera House (✆ **04/3933-4947**). This is a great place to enjoy any kind of espresso or cappuccino, Italian sodas, snacks, sandwiches, pizzas, and good breakfasts, all while looking out over the lake or watching the hustle and flow of traffic below.

3/F 1-3-5 Dinh Tien Hoang St. (across the street from northeast corner of Hoan Kiem Lake). ✆ **04/3936-3228.** Daily 7am–9pm.

KOTO (Know One Teach One) ★   Why not put your ice-cream money to work for a good cause? KOTO is an acronym for "Know One Teach One," and like Hoa Sua (p. 81), the cafe is just one arm of a grass-roots humanitarian program to train Hanoi kids in the service industry. The program teaches English, comportment, food preparation, and service skills at the cozy little storefront. Just around the corner from the Temple of Literature in Dong Da District (p. 98), KOTO is the best choice for refreshment after touring the sight. Pop in for good soups and sandwiches, as well as a host of sweet treats and good coffee.

59 Van Mieu St., Dong Da District. ✆ **04/3747-0337.** Fax 04/3747-0339. www.koto.com.au. Tues–Sun 7am–10pm; Mon 7am–3:30pm.

La Place   Tucked in a quiet alleyway just off the square out in front of St. Joseph's Cathedral (Nha Tho), La Place is a lounge cafe with free Wi-Fi, good coffees, mellow music, great breakfasts, and desserts.

6 Au Trieu. ✆ **04/3928-5859.** Daily 7:30am–10:30pm.

Little Hanoi   Just north of the lake, this local-style fast-food joint has basic but tidy bamboo-and-wood decor. Overlooking the busy street, it's a good place for breakfast and to watch the world roar by on motorbikes. A limited menu offers local favorites such as banana flower salad and noodle soup. Little Hanoi makes a good central meeting point.

23 Hang Gai St. ✆ **04/3828-8333.** Daily 7:30am–11pm.

Moca Café ★   For some good coffee and desserts, or to just sit, rest, and watch the world go by along busy Nha Tho Street, stop in at Moca Café, one of the city's popular traveler hangouts. This area is infamous for its bohemian community of artists and expatriate English teachers (many of whom use the cafe to give private lessons).

14-16 Nha Tho. ✆ **04/3825-6334.** Daily 7:30am–11pm.

Paris Deli ★ Just across from the Moca (see above) on Hanoi's tranquil and chic little "Church Street," you'll find this well-liked air-conditioned storefront that serves good pastries, proper croissants, breads, and deli sandwiches, plus all the coffee and cool fruit drinks you'll need to wash it down. This is a good place to beat the heat and take a rest from shopping or walking the city center.

13 Nha Tho St.📞 **04/3928-6697.** Daily 7:30am–11pm.

Pepperoni's Pepperoni's serves tasty comfort food in several outlets around town, including the popular Bao Khanh Street area (across from Le Café des Arts in and among many popular nightlife spots). There are special deals every day that allow diners to eat their fill of pizza, pasta, and salad for a few bucks.

31 Bao Khanh.📞 **04/3928-7030.** Daily 8am–11pm.

Pho 24 This popular national chain serves good Vietnamese *pho* (noodle soup) as you like it—make your own creation by ticking boxes off a punch list of ingredient choices. The beauty of Pho 24 is its high standard of cleanliness.

31 Hang Khay St. (at the southern end of Hoan Kiem Lake).📞 **04/3824-7044.** Daily 7am–11pm.

Puku ★ 🍴 NEW ZEALAND Advertising "couch-surfing food and Wi-Fi-enabled coffee," this switched-on cafe recently relocated to trendy Tong Duy Tan, and now offers its range of sandwiches, burgers, and Asian specials 24 hours a day. The Kia, a grilled open-faced sandwich topped with pesto, chicken, and cheese, and served with saffron mayo and a small green salad, is a hearty lunch. There's a real laid-back vibe here, and the place is popular with local expats.

16–18 Tong Duy Tan St., Hoan Kiem District.📞 **04/3838-1745.** Daily 24 hr.

Thuy Ta Cafe On the water at the northwest end of the lake, this cafe has great views and an extensive menu. The best choice is a good ice cream or coffee while taking in the lake's scenery. Because of its excellent location, it's often busy with locals and tourists alike.

1 Le Thai To St., Hoan Kiem District.📞 **04/3828-8148.** Daily 6am–11pm.

EXPLORING HANOI

Hanoi is a good place to get out and tour on your own. Start in the Old Quarter with a morning walking tour—especially in the summer months, when you'll want to take advantage of cooler weather. If you're game, get up really early and join in with morning exercise at lakeside. If sleeping a bit later sounds better, start at Hoan Kiem, hit the major sights in the Old Quarter, including **Bach Ma Temple,** and then take in the Hanoi Citadel area. *Remember:* If you want to catch a glimpse of the embalmed Ho Chi Minh in his mausoleum in the very center of the Citadel, you have to get there before 11am. Catch Ho's mausoleum, museum, and his very spartan home, as well as the One-Pillar Pagoda. Then hit the Temple of Literature, a short cab/motorbike ride away. From there, it's a matter of preference: shopping options galore around the central lake, French colonial buildings south of the lake and the Opera Building, a trip to the Catholic cathedral of Nha Tho and the surrounding cafe area, or further exploration of the Old Quarter or the Dong Xuan Market. You can get well acquainted with Hanoi in a day or two, but it takes a lifetime to know.

While sightseeing, remember that state-owned attractions will usually close for lunch from 11:30am to 1:30pm. Be sure not to accept any extraneous pamphlets or unwanted guides at sights; all come with a nominal, but frustrating, fee.

HAVE YOU TRIED THE snake?

Six kilometers (3¾ miles) to the east of Hanoi, across the Red River, is the town of Le Mat, also known as the "Snake Village." Among shanty houses and winding alleyways, you'll find Chinese-style roofs sheltering elegant dining areas, all strangely tucked away. What's the big secret? This town is the hub of the very taboo snake industry, and it's the place to try fresh *Tit Ran,* or snake meat. The Vietnamese taboo is not much different from that in the West—something like "Eat snake? Ooooh, yuck!" Snake is also considered a male aphrodisiac, a kind of fried Viagra, so at night it's not uncommon to see groups of businessmen drunk as skunks piling into these places for a bit of medicine.

Here's the drill: Finding it is half the battle (or adventure). Any taxi driver will be happy to take you to his friend's place in anticipation of a commission. Feel free to ask to see another restaurant (some of them are pretty grotty), but expect to pay about $6 to get there. There are lots of restaurants in Le Mat, but one to try is **O Sin** (© **04/3827-2984**).

You'll be greeted by a friendly owner who'll usher you back to the cages and put on quite a show of stirring up the snakes before selecting one he thinks will feed your party. He'll then quote you

a ridiculous price, but expect to pay somewhere between $7 and $15 per person after bargaining.

Then the show begins. You'll be seated and, before your eyes, the owner will adeptly kill the snake, drain the blood into a jar of rice whiskey, and systematically disembowel the animal, extracting the liver and showing you the still-beating heart before adding it to the whiskey/blood concoction. The guest of honor eats the heart and takes the first sip of whiskey before circulating the bottle. Thus begins a lengthy seven-course meal, starting with fried snake skin, grilled snake filet, snake spring rolls, snake soup with rice cake, minced snake dumpling, copious amounts of rice whiskey, and orange wedges for dessert. It's a decent meal, really, and certainly something to remember.

Be warned that many of these places are part of the underground market in endangered species, selling bear paws and rare jungle animals thought to have medicinal benefits. But the snakes are common cobras found everywhere in Vietnam, and a trip here makes for an interesting night. Be clear with the driver about where you want to go (for example, not to a brothel afterward), and don't pay until you arrive at the destination.

The Old Quarter

Hanoi would not be Hanoi without its **Old Quarter,** a maze of streets dating back to the 13th century, its present-day chaos just a different version of the old chaos, when specialized trade guilds were responsible for each street. The quarter is exhausting ("What's with all the honking?" my friend asks) and crowded; you'll be jostled by passing motorbikes, cyclos, and hawkers with shoulder poles hanging pendulous burdens of local produce. The quarter is one of those places that grows on you the more you experience it.

Said to resemble a tree sprouting from the cool waters of Hoan Kiem Lake, the streets are like chaotic branches and tendrils as they fan out in jagged patterns across the area north of Hanoi's famed lake. Limited on one side by the Red River and on the other by the once-great Hanoi Citadel, whose walls are still standing in some areas, the Old Quarter is, as the name denotes, the oldest area of the town and has long been an important economic center. In its earliest inceptions, the Old Quarter was accessed by a series of canals on its northeast edge that led to regional waterways. The western end of the quarter was developed in the early 19th century when the completion of the Hanoi Citadel left open areas that were settled by outlying villages and tradespeople. The quarter hosts the city's largest market, Dong Xuan, and welcomes the bulk of foreign visitors to the city with its maze of streets, multitude of services, and great hotel and restaurant "finds." Getting lost in the maze is one of the biggest joys of Hanoi.

Most interesting are the **Communal Houses** set up by the guilds in each area. Like small temples to honor a local god, many to the Bach Ma, or "White Horse," who represents the city of Hanoi, these little courtyard areas are usually protected from the street and often have hidden entrances or just humble low roofs out front that give way to elaborate interior courtyards and temple buildings. Aside from communal houses, you find standard **Buddhist and Taoist temples** among the city's crooked streets. Most notable is the **Bach Ma Temple** right in center of the quarter.

Keep an eye out for the classic Old Quarter **tube house,** the best and most accessible example of which is at 87 Ma May St. or at 38 Hang Dao (directly north of the lake). Tube houses are so named because they are just that: a long, narrow tube of space that is subdivided into sections that served the family's every need. Why so narrow? And, in fact, why do Vietnamese still build so narrow and high today? Properties were taxed on the basis of their street frontage, and real estate has always been expensive in this bustling quarter (real estate prices in Hanoi rival any city in the West these days). Tube houses are divided into sections. The front is the business office, where any goods are displayed and where business is conducted. In a succession of courtyards and interior spaces, some two stories, a tube house has areas set aside for gardening and for servants, and, at the back, private family quarters with the kitchen and the toilet, which was traditionally nothing more than a large latrine pot that fit into a nook and had to be emptied regularly. You can spot the few remaining traditional homes by their low tile roofs parallel to the street.

European buildings of the French are more elaborate, usually two-story structures, with architectural flourishes, such as overhanging bay windows and a high sloping roof, some of the mansard variety. The more time you spend in the Old Quarter, the more adept you get at finding the old among the new. In fact, many shops with the most modern, neon-lit storefronts on the first floor, in fact, are old colonials, so be sure to keep an eye on the roofline to spot some antique gems among the clutter.

The Old Quarter evolved from workshop villages organized by trades, or guilds, and even today, streets are dedicated to a product or trade. Some streets still offer the services of old—for example **Hang Thiec Street,** or Tinsmith Street, is still the place to buy tin receptacles and for sheet-metal work—but others have changed: **Hang Vai,** or Cloth Street, is now home to the bamboo trade, and many old streets support new trades. You won't find anything named "Motorcycle Seat Repair Street" or "Cheap Plastic Toys Imported from China Street," but they do exist. It's a fascinating slice of centuries-old life in Hanoi, including markets that are so crowded that the streets themselves narrow to a few feet.

Hanoi's Old Quarter is also where the seeds of Communist revolution were sown—starting in 1907 with the Tonkin Free School Movement, a program of study at a school in the Old Quarter, just north of Hoan Kiem Lake, which focused on Vietnamese traditions instead of the *de rigueur* French curriculum. The Old Quarter school was closed down by French officials, but the patriotic zeal that founded it would never die and instead produced small workers' strikes throughout the 1920s, many of which brought bloodshed. Old Quarter trade guilds were fertile ground for the worker's revolution, spawning independent presses; over time, Communist cells emerged that would unite during the August Revolution of 1945. The Old Quarter was, in fact, Vietnamese turf during violent skirmishes with the colonial French in their bid to control the upstart colony from 1945 until complete Vietnamese victory at Dien Bien Phu and French withdrawal.

The following is a translation of just some of the streets and the trades that were practiced in the Old Quarter. Some of the streets below still sell or produce the same items; others have evolved to more modern goods, but the clumps-of-industry principle remains. Look for the following:

Street Name Translations of Old Quarter Trades

STREET NAME	TRADE
Hang Bac	silver
Hang Be	rattan rafts
Hang Bo	baskets
Hang Bong	cotton
Hang Buom	sails
Hang Ca	fish
Hang Can	scales
Hang Cot	bamboo mats
Hang Da	leather
Hang Dao	silk
Hang Dau	beans
Hang Dieu	bongs and pipes
Hang Dong	brass
Hang Duong	sugar
Hang Ga	chicken
Hang Gai	hemp and rope
Hang Giay	paper
Hang Hom	coffins
Hang Khoai	sweet potatoes
Hang Luoc	combs
Hang Ma	paper replicas/toys
Hang Mam	fish
Hang Manh	bamboo shades
Hang Muoi	salt
Hang Non	conical hats
Hang Quat	fans
Hang Than	charcoal
Hang Thiec	tin
Hang Thung	barrels
Hang Tre	bamboo
Hang Trong	drums
Hang Vai	cloth

I had the good fortune of meeting an American *Viet Kieu,* or returning Vietnamese, on a trip in Halong Bay and hearing about his life in old Hanoi and his impressions now. Born on Hang Bong (Cotton St.) in the Old Quarter, he grew up in a house near West Lake but had spent a lot of his youth careening about the commercial streets at the town center while his mother worked as a seamstress. Asked what was different between the old Hanoi and the new (this was his first time back since taking flight after the Geneva Accords divided the country), the kind gentleman talked only of the similarities, saying that his home out near West Lake is just as it was (and the owner abruptly slammed the door on him when he told her why he'd knocked, for fear he'd come back to reclaim his house). He said that the Old Quarter, barring the proliferation of motorbikes, neon, and improved pavement, was exactly as it was when he left Vietnam in the mid-1950s. For those who decry the cacophony and chaos of motorbikes, cars, and trucks in the district, it's important to remember that the Old Quarter is a market area, a place for business, and business in Vietnam is conducted at high decibels. The streets of the Old Quarter have always been busy and noisy, only now it is modern traffic that makes the racket, not shouting hawkers pulling bullock carts.

Note: There is an initiative to make the Old Quarter a pedestrian-only zone, and on weekend nights, the length of pavement along central Hang Ngang and Hang Dương is closed to car and motorbike traffic. A night market has opened up with lots of flea market–style sellers of tourist trinkets.

WALKING TOUR: **THE OLD QUARTER**

START:	**North end of Hoan Kiem Lake (at the Ngoc Son Pagoda).**
FINISH:	**Return to the north end of Hoan Kiem Lake (to the Dong Kinh Nghia Thuc Sq.).**
TIME:	**1½ hours without stops; up to 3 hours with exploring, coffee, and chatting.**
BEST TIMES:	**From early morning.**
WORST TIMES:	**Middle of the day (too hot).**

The best way to really experience Hanoi's Old Quarter is on foot. As you explore the route below, stop for coffee at a local cafe or a storefront geared to tourists in the backpacker area of the quarter. Stop for a chat; folks are busy but friendly if you take the time to connect. Photographers will want to set out early and catch the dynamic colors of the morning sun, which set off the rich yellowed plaster of older buildings and make the colors of produce in the markets more vibrant.

This route is a large clockwise circle through the Old Quarter. Walking times vary depending on your clip and your interest in the details, but generally, allow a few hours. **Note:** Try to study the map discreetly and know your next turn before arriving at an intersection. If you ask for directions, motorbike taxi drivers will just implore you to hire them for a ride and even try to confuse you. Learn to look for distinct rooflines. Just a short time in the Old Quarter will have you distinguishing a Chinese temple or community house from a tube house or more French-influenced construction.

1 Hoan Kiem Lake

Start with a visit to the **Ngoc Son** pagoda on the north end of the lake. Cross the red **Bridge of the Rising Sun** to reach the temple. From this most

Walking Tour: The Old Quarter

1 Hoan Kiem Lake
2 Hang Gai Street (Hemp St.)
3 Tam Thuong Alley
4 Hang Da Market and
   Hang Dieu Street
5 Bun Bo Nam Bo ☕
6 Bat Dan Street
7 Hang Phen Street
8 Phung Hung Street
9 Hang Vai
10 Lan Ong Street
11 Cha Ca Street
12 Hang Duong Street
13 Hang Chieu
14 Infinity Cafe ☕
15 Nguyen Sieu Street
16 Bach Ma Temple
   (The White Horse Temple)
17 Hang Buom Street
18 Ma May Street
19 Tamarind Café ☕
20 Hang Bac Street
21 Hang Dao
22 City View Café ☕

prominent point in the city, follow the northern edge of the lake heading west and cross over the busy traffic circle. This busy square is known as the **Dong Kinh Nghia Thuc Square** (the **Tonkin Free School Movement Sq.**), named for the early-20th-century nationalist movement that would eventually spawn grass-roots Communism in Vietnam.

West from the square is:

2 Hang Gai Street (Hemp St.)

This busy avenue marks the southern boundary of the Old Quarter. Hang Gai no longer supports hemp outlets as in days of old (the street would also host print shops and bookstores in the 19th c.), but is lined with boutique shopping, galleries, and silk tailors. Just a few hundred meters west of the traffic circle (on the left), you'll find a large **banyan tree** out in front of what was once a prominent communal house at no. 85 Hang Gai. The tree is one of the finest specimens of an old banyan in the city, a perfect example of nature's adaptability as heavy roots cleave large stones, and masons have built around the old tree for centuries. The sight is like a small temple, with sticks of incense and flowers wedged between knobs of the tree and offerings of rice whiskey sometimes lining the base of the tree.

Turn right off of Hang Gai and look for a small street sign pointing to:

3 Tam Thuong Alley

Follow a few crooks in this quiet little alley, and you come to the **Yen Thai Communal House,** a classic low tile roof over a wooden entry that gives way to a quiet courtyard. Just across the street are a few cheap and quiet guesthouses. Tam Thuong terminates at **Yen Thai Street,** where you'll make a left and, in the morning, walk through a small open-air market with great morning light for photography.

Turn right at the end of Yen Thai Street onto Hang Da Street:

4 Hang Da Market and Hang Dieu Street

At the intersection of Yen Thai and Hang Da is the former site of **Hang Da Market,** a large, local dry-goods and clothing market. Sadly, the old four-story yellow stone building was recently torn down, and the new Hang Da Market is a sterile shopping mall. After a quick look, head north on Hang Da—don't miss the large **bird shop** with a wall of bamboo cages on the northern corner of Hang Da and Hang Dieu.

Continuing north, Hang Da becomes Hang Dieu Street. Hang Dieu was traditionally the area for tobacco and pipe sellers.

5 Bun Bo Nam Bo 🍵

Bun Bo Nam Bo, 67 Hang Dieu St. (✆ 04/3923-0701), serves one of Hanoi's most popular one-dish noodle specialties.

Turn right off of Hang Dieu onto:

6 Bat Dan Street

This street once housed sellers of clay bowls that were brought to the city from riverside workshops along the Red River. No. 33 Bat Dan is a very ornate and colorful communal house.

Turn left (go north) on Thuoc Bac Street, once an area for traditional medicines. Then turn left (west) on:

7 Hang Phen Street

At the corner of Hang Phen and Bat Su, look for a preserved traditional house, characterized by its low tile roofline, at **no. 52 Bat Su** (also note the cozy little coffee shops a few steps south, good for a rest and to watch the busy street life).

Carry on along Hang Phen until it becomes **Cua Dong Street,** which brings you to the eastern edge and wall of the Hanoi Citadel built by the Nguyen dynasty in the 1800s. Cua Dong Street terminates at the wall of the Hanoi Citadel.

Turn right off of Cua Dong onto:

8 Phung Hung Street

Running along the wall of the city's old citadel, what marks the western edge of the Old Quarter, Phung Hung Street is a notable sight among Vietnamese tourists for the publication offices of an important Communist paper at **no. 105 Phung Hung.** There's a plaque that notes this spot as a historical vestige, but if you spend too much time studying the shuttered colonial edifice, local folks might get edgy, thinking you're a spy of sorts.

Turn right off of Phung Hung onto:

9 Hang Vai

Translated as "Cloth Street," Hang Vai is the **bamboo district.** The busy exteriors of small warehouses are lined with stands of cut bamboo poles, some more than two stories in height. This is the raw material for those wonderful Dr. Seuss scaffoldings you see on construction sites. The shops also sell bamboo tobacco pipes of the "bong" variety, some quite elaborate. At the corner of Hang Vai and north-south Hang Ga, keep an eye out for the **communal house** at no. 16D Hang Ga St.: A corner door cut into the white plaster and flanked by Chinese script ushers you into a small courtyard area with a bo tree and a small temple to Bach Ma, the "White Horse," a god associated with Hanoi (see Bach Ma Temple, below). Carrying on east on Hang Vai, look for the entrance to the **communal house** at **no. 7 Hang Vai.**

Heading east, Hang Vai becomes:

10 Lan Ong Street

One of the most interesting parts of the Old Quarter, Lan Ong Street is still home to a large enclave of ethnic Chinese who sell the herbs and medicines of old from small storefronts that date back to the origins of the quarter. The best shops are on the right side as you head east. Here you'll find picturesque little interiors with walls lined in massive dark-wood cabinets with tiny drawers and buckets and bins all around, with the most curious assortment of dried goods you'll ever see. This is the kind of place where, sadly, you might be able to buy a bear's gall bladder or a monkey's paw. The buildings all along this short stretch are originals dating back as far as the 17th century. Look for the busy elementary school at **no. 40 Lan Ong,** which was once the **communal house** of the area's Chinese population. Just across from the converted communal house and all along the length of the street, look for low roofs and narrow entries, as these are original Chinese homes.

A quick left (north) turn brings you to:

11 Cha Ca Street

Following Lan Ong Street, heading east, cross the famous **Cha Ca Street (Fish St.).** Make a left (north) and look for the **Cha Ca La Vong** restaurant (p. 78), which serves one of Hanoi's most famed dishes.

Returning to eastbound Lan Ong, turn left (north) onto Hang Duong.

12 Hang Duong Street

Hang Duong Street (Sugar St.) is lined with traditional constructions, foremost of which is the **communal house** on the left as you go north at **no. 38 Hang Duong St.** It has a dark, alluring charm to its smoky interior. *Note:* Hang Duong is a **pedestrian area** on weekend nights and becomes a busy night market for tourist trinkets and local goods.

A short detour off of Hang Duong is the 13th-century **Thanh Ha Communal House,** just a short walk east on **Ngo Gach Street (Brick St.).**

Continue north on Hang Duong, and then turn right on:

13 Hang Chieu

Follow **Hang Chieu** east across the northern end of the Old Quarter to **Quan Chuong Gate,** the only remaining gate of the city's once-formidable fortifications. From here, go right (south) onto **Dao Duy Tu Street** and look for the small entrance to the **Huong Nghia Communal House** at 13B on the left side near the corner of Cho Gao Street. The communal house has an entrance open to visitors who bring offerings and light incense.

14 Infinity Café 🍹

To the right of the temple entrance is the Infinity Cafe, where you can get a shot of strong Vietnamese coffee or a soft drink.

Turn right onto Nguyen Sieu.

15 Nguyen Sieu Street

Nguyen Sieu is a street named for a noted 18th-century scholar and lined with colonial buildings (your architecture-spotting muscles must be strong by now). On the right, keep an eye out for the small alley entrance to the **Co Luong Communal House,** a colorful temple surrounded by modern relief sculptures.

Turn left (south) on Hang Giay Street. Go straight 1 block. Then turn left on Hang Buom Street. After 1 block on your left is the important:

16 Bach Ma Temple (The White Horse Temple)

Located at no. 76 Hang Buom St., the Bach Ma Temple is open from 8 to 11am and 2 to 5pm Tuesday to Sunday (until 9pm on holidays). Built in A.D. 1010, the temple is dedicated to the White Horse of legend, which, it is said, helped the early king of the Viet people, Ly, decide where and how to defend his city. The temple interior is a grand courtyard of massive red pillars and large Buddhist statuary and altars.

Continue east along:

17 Hang Buom Street

From the Bach Ma Temple, continue east on Hang Buom (Sail St.). Once adjacent to a small tributary of the To Lich River, which brought goods to the city, Hang Buom was where local merchant vessels came to refit their ships. Look for the many colonial buildings and traditional Vietnamese houses, as well as a communal house at **no. 28 Hang Buom,** which now hosts performances of **Ca Tru music** on Saturday nights.

As Hang Buom curves to the right (south), it becomes:

18 Ma May Street

Ma May is the beginning of the busiest budget tourist areas of the Old Quarter, and you'll notice a sudden increase in the number of Western faces around here. In and among fashion shops and tourist restaurants, you'll find good examples of traditional and colonial buildings. The **Huong Tuong Communal House** is at **no. 64 Ma May,** and one of the most interesting sights in the city can be found at **no. 87 Ma May,** a refurbished and restored traditional house. Here, for a fee of just 5,000 VND, a young docent dressed in a traditional flowing *ao dai* gown will take you on an informative tour of the building and can explain important details about life in the Old Quarter in centuries past. With the careful renovations done by a UNESCO-funded, French- and Canadian-backed organization, this classic home offers a unique opportunity to have a close look at the interior detail of a traditional Old Quarter home. Also see the similarly renovated property at 38 Hang Dao St. (see below).

19 Tamarind Café 🍽

Ma May is home to the popular Tamarind Café (p. 84), a perfect place to kick off your shoes, order a fresh fruit smoothie, and recharge for the last leg of this walking tour.

Heading south on Ma May, turn right at its terminus with:

20 Hang Bac Street

Heading west on Hang Bac, you're in the heart of the backpacker area. Here you're sure to be assailed on all sides by touts and hucksters and have your pick of budget tours from the many storefronts that line this busy street. Hang Bac means "Silver Street," and the silver these days is mostly the stuff coming from your pocket and falling into tour operators' hands, though you still can find some silver (and gold) jewelry makers and sellers.

As you approach the intersection of Dinh Liet Street, look right and you'll see the large **Chuong Vang Theater** at **no. 72 Hang Bac,** which was the stronghold of troops who laid siege to the French after the August Revolution in 1945.

You'll find good shopping and lots of goods and services in this area. You can finish the tour here or check out one more sight worth seeing.

Head west on Hang Bac. Turn left (south) on:

21 Hang Dao

Immediately on your right, don't miss another fine example of a **restored traditional Old Quarter house,** much like the one on Ma May. **No. 38 Hang**

Dao is a two-story home that was once owned by silk merchants. It's quite spacious and elaborate (silk merchants were wealthy); you'll see how an Old Quarter house was set up, including where the worship area was set (now an office), as well as where the family lived, cooked, and worked. Entry is free between 9 and 11am and 2 and 5pm, and boards explain restoration techniques used, though unfortunately only in French (the restoration was carried out with French assistance).

Hang Dao continues south and ends at Hang Gai and the **Dong Kinh Nghia Thuc Square** (the **Tonkin Free School Movement Sq.**). Look for the large ocean-liner-shaped building that overlooks the square and Hoan Kiem Lake to the south.

22 City View Cafe 🍺
On the fifth floor of the most prominent building on Dong Kinh Nghia Thuc Square, find the popular City View Cafe, a good place to meet up after your walk or to rest your bones after completing the circle.

Attractions
BA DINH DISTRICT
Army Museum ★★   This museum presents the Vietnamese side of the country's struggle against colonial powers. There are three buildings of odds and ends from both the French and American wars here, including evocative photos. Most interesting, though, is the actual war equipment on display, including aircraft, tanks, bombs, and big guns, some with signs indicating just how many of which enemy the piece took out. Outside sits a spectacular, room-size bouquet of downed French and U.S. aircraft wreckage. Also on the grounds is Hanoi's ancient flag tower (Cot Co), constructed from 1805 to 1812. The exhibits have English translations, which makes this an easy and worthwhile visit.

28A Dien Bien Phu St. ☎ **04/3823-4264.** Admission 20,000 VND; camera 20,000 VND. Tues–Thurs and Sat–Sun 8–11:30am and 1–4:30pm.

Ho Chi Minh Museum ★★   English-language explanations help to piece together the fragments of Ho's life and cause at this museum tribute, and there are personal items, photos, and documents detailing the rise of the nation's Communist revolution. The rhetoric is laid on a bit thick, but all in all it's an interesting and informative display. Completely unique to Vietnam are the conceptual displays symbolizing freedom, reunification, and social progress through flowers, fruit, and mirrors.

19 Ngoc Ha (left of One-Pillar Pagoda, near Ba Dinh Sq.), Ba Dinh District. ☎ **04/3846-3752.** Admission 15,000 VND. Daily 8–11:30am; Tues–Thurs and Sat–Sun 2–4pm.

Ho Chi Minh's Mausoleum ★★   In an imposing, somber, granite-and-concrete structure modeled on Lenin's tomb, Ho lies in state, embalmed and dressed in his favored khaki suit. He asked to be cremated, but his wish was not heeded. A respectful demeanor is required, and the dress code mandates no shorts or sleeveless shirts. Note that the mausoleum is usually closed in October and November, when Ho goes to Russia for body maintenance of an undisclosed nature. The museum might be closed during this period as well. Note that the mausoleum is open only in the mornings.

On Ba Dinh Sq., Ba Dinh District. Free admission. Tues–Thurs and Sat 8–11am. Last visitors admitted at 10:15am.

Ho Chi Minh's Residence ★★   Ho's residence, the well-known house on stilts, is behind the Presidential Palace, a gorgeous French colonial building built in 1901 for the resident French governor. In stark contrast to the ostentatious palace, Ho's house is pure simplicity, and he lived here from 1958 to 1969. Facing an exquisite landscaped lake, the structure does have its charm, and the spartan room is an interesting glimpse into the life of this enigmatic national hero. The basement was a meeting place for the politburo; upstairs are the bedroom and a study, and little details such as his phone and walking cane are kept behind glass. Behind the house is a garden of fruit trees, many of them exotics imported from other lands, including miniature rosebushes and areca trees from the Caribbean.

Behind the Presidential Palace at Ba Dinh Sq. Guided tour 15,000 VND. Daily 8–11:30am; Tues–Thurs and Sat–Sun 2–4pm.

Hun Tiep Lake and the Downed B-52   This is not a sight that will knock you off your feet for its size or beauty: In fact, what brings many here is that it's an ordinary neighborhood, a maze of quiet lanes broken only by a small pond and, in the brackish water, the wreckage of an American B-52 shot down during the Christmas air raids of 1972. Many folks, veterans among them, find that a visit here puts a perspective on the war and that the rusting wreckage brings our abstract historical impressions back to the concrete present; others see landing gear, struts, and metal sheathing in a grungy pond. Most taxi drivers know it, or some creative charades will get the point across. Drivers will drop you off at the head of the alley (Lane 55) leading to the sight (a handwritten sign reads B-52 with an arrow).

Located just south of West Lake along Hoang Hoa Tham Rd., and a short walk down Lane 55 heading south. Free admission.

One-Pillar Pagoda ★   To the right of the Ho Chi Minh Museum is the unique One-Pillar Pagoda, a wooden structure originally built in 1049 that sits on a single concrete pillar in a tiny pond. A king of the Ly Dynasty, Ly Thai Thong King had it built after having a dream in which the bodhisattva Avalokitesvara, the goddess of mercy, presented him with a lotus flower. The existing pagoda is a miniature reproduction of the original, which was said to represent a lotus emerging from the water. It is certainly interesting, and a prayer here is said to bring fertility and good health. It's best to wear something full length (skirt or trousers), not shorts.

Right of Ho Chi Minh Museum, near Ba Dinh Sq., Ba Dinh District. Free admission. Daily 6–11:30am and 2–6pm.

Vietnam National Museum of Fine Arts ★★   This very worthwhile arts museum features Vietnamese art in all its forms, such as painting, sculpture, weaving, and lacquerware. Entire rooms are devoted to the Vietnamese style of lacquer and silk painting, woodblock, and folk art. Techniques are explained—a nice touch. Interesting also are the modern works of wood statuary interspersed among the exhibits. Some are patriotic in nature, depicting daily life or events during the war or done in Soviet-influenced caricature with heavy-limbed peasants striking triumphant poses or depictions of the brotherhood of the army and the working class. The top floors are devoted to prehistoric artifacts and Buddhist sculptures, some of which are huge and impressive. Don't miss the famous 11th-century goddess of mercy Guanyin (Quan Âm in Vietnamese), with her thousand arms and eyes, in the far-left room on the second floor. Best of all, the museum itself is in an old colonial, and, unless there's a tour group milling around, you can stroll around in relative serenity and rest on one of the many benches provided (no napping). The gift shop has some modern works of well-known artists for sale and will also sell works displayed in thematic exhibitions. The museum will then register and grant a certificate for the piece.

66 Nguyen Thai Hoc. © **04/3733-2131.** Admission 20,000 VND. Daily 8:30am–5pm.

West Lake ★★   Covering a broad area north and west of central Hanoi, West Lake is home to lots of recent housing developments. In fact, the east shore of West Lake is more or less the "Beverly Hills" of Hanoi, where the best and brightest young Hanoians and expats call home. The lake is also steeped in legend and is bordered by several significant pagodas. Vietnam's oldest pagoda, **Tran Quoc,** was built in the 6th century and is located on Cayang Island at the southeast end of the lake, a beautiful setting. An actual fragment of the bodhi tree under which Buddha achieved enlightenment was given as a gift from the prime minister of India in 1959 and now grows proudly in the main courtyard. Constructed by an early Zen sect and a famous center for dharma study, and later as an imperial feasting ground, the temple has a visitor's hall, two corridors, and a bell tower; it still houses a group of diligent monks who carry out elaborate rituals for the dead on auspicious days (if a ceremony is underway, be conscientious and keep a distance, but visitors are welcome to observe). Here, as at other temples, it is impolite to wear shorts. All around the little peninsula that the island temple and its manmade walkway has created, you'll see fishermen busy with long bamboo poles and oversize hand reels; they essentially twirl a large spool by hand, something that's fun to watch, especially if they pull in something big.

Farther south, **Quan Thanh Temple** was built during the reign of King Le Thai To (1010–28). It's dedicated to Huyen Thien Tran Vo, the god who reigned over Vietnam's northern regions. Renovated in the 19th century, the impressive temple has a triple gate and courtyard, and features a 3.6m (12-ft.) bronze statue of the god. West Lake is also a hub of local activity, particularly on weekends, when families go paddleboating on it.

Bordered by Thuy Khue and Thanh Nien sts. Quan Thanh Temple 2000 VND.

DONG DA DISTRICT

Temple of Literature and National University (Van Mieu-Quoc Tu Giam) ★★   If Vietnam has a seat of learning, this is it. There are two entities here: Van Mieu, a temple built in 1070 to worship Chinese philosopher Confucius; and Quoc Tu Giam, literally "Temple of the King Who Distinguished Literature," an elite institute established in 1076 to teach the doctrines of Confucius and his disciples. It existed for more than 700 years as a center for Confucian learning. Moreover, it is a powerful symbol for the Vietnamese, having been established after the country emerged from a period of Chinese colonialism that lasted from 179 B.C. to A.D. 938. It is a testament to the strong cultural heritage of the Mandarins. As such, it stands for independence and a solidifying of national culture and values.

What exists today is a series of four courtyards that served as an entrance to the university. Architecturally, it is a fine example of classic Chinese with Vietnamese influences. Still present are 82 stone stelae—stone diplomas, really—erected between 1484 and 1780, bearing the names and birthplaces of 1,306 doctor laureates who managed to pass the university's rigorous examinations. Beyond the final building, known as the sanctuary, the real university began.

The main focus of attention for visitors is the Temple of Confucius in the heart of the complex, where a resplendent red and gold statue of the great philosopher takes pride of place. Most visitors will also enjoy a brief presentation of traditional Vietnamese music played in the adjoining music room. They may not be so happy to be forced to leave the complex via a gaggle of souvenir vendors trying desperately to make a sale.

Quoc Tu Giam St. ℭ **04/3845-2917.** Admission 10,000 VND. Apr 15–Oct 15 daily 7:30am–5:30pm; Oct 16–Apr 14 8am–5pm.

HOAN KIEM DISTRICT

Hanoi Opera House   This gorgeous, historic Art Nouveau building was built near the turn of the 20th century. Unfortunately, to get inside, you'll have to attend a performance, which are usually enjoyable (p. 111) but few and far between. The steps out front are a popular local hangout to sit and watch the world go by, and the fountain of the nearby Hilton Hanoi Opera, a building that fits like a jigsaw puzzle piece around the old opera, is, more than the opera building itself, a popular place for domestic tourists to get their photos snapped.

1 Trang Tien St. (intersection of Le Thanh Tong and Trang Tien sts., District 1). ℭ **04/3933-0113.**

Hoa Lo Prison (Hanoi Hilton) ★★   For sheer gruesome atmosphere alone, this ranks near the top of the must-see list. It was constructed by the French in 1896 mainly to house political prisoners, and the Vietnamese took it over in 1954. It was subsequently used to house prisoners of war. From 1964 to 1973, it was a major POW detention facility. U.S. Sen. John McCain was a particularly famous inmate, as was Pete Peterson, the ambassador to Vietnam, and Lt. Everett Alvarez, officially the first American pilot to be shot down over Vietnam. Their stories are told from the Vietnamese perspective in photographs and writings grouped in one small room. To the west is the guillotine room, still with its original equipment, and the female and Vietnamese political prisoners' quarters. The courtyard linking the two has parts of original tunnels once used by a hundred intrepid Vietnamese revolutionaries to escape in 1945. Only part of the original complex is left; the rest of the original site was razed and is ironically occupied by a tall, gleaming office complex (Hanoi Towers) popular with foreign investors. There are basic English explanations, but this is a good spot to have a guide, who is certain to be armed with a tale or two.

1 Hoa Lo St., off Quan Su St. ℭ **04/3824-6358.** Admission 10,000 VND. Daily 8am–5pm.

Hoan Kiem Lake ★★★   Hoan Kiem Lake is the center of the city, both literally and figuratively. The lake is the city's most popular strolling ground and a lovers' lane at night, with couples locked in embrace on benches or parked motorbikes looking out over the placid waters, the shadows of overhanging willows cast by moonlight. In the morning, the lake area is crowded with folks out for their morning exercise—running or walking in a circle around the lake or joining in with the many tai chi, martial arts, calisthenics, aerobics, and even ballroom dancing groups that meet in the open areas at water's edge. Hoan Kiem Lake is also the site of the city's own creation myth: the Legend of the Lake of the Recovered Sword. In the mid–15th century, the gods gave Emperor Le Thai To a magical sword to defeat Chinese invaders. While the emperor was boating on the lake one day, a giant tortoise reared up and snatched the sword, returning it to its rightful owners and ushering peace into the kingdom. Stroll around the lake in the early morning or evening to savor local life among the willow trees and see elders playing chess or practicing tai chi. In the center of the lake is Thap Rua, the Tortoise Tower; on the northern part is **Ngoc Son** pagoda, reachable only by the stunning **Bridge of the Rising Sun,** a long, red arch typical of Chinese temple compounds. Ngoc Son is a working temple, meaning that you might walk into a local ceremony of chanting monks and kneeling supplicants. The temple grounds offer great views of the surrounding lake, and the little lakeside park on the island is a popular place for elderly men to enjoy a game of Chinese chess. There's also the preserved carcass of one of the lake's giant turtles in the last room of the complex.

Hoan Kiem is a useful locator for navigating the city; for addresses downtown, people generally give directions in relation to it. It's good to know how to get from the lake to your hotel. The lake is also the jumping-off point for exploring the Old Quarter, Hanoi's labyrinth of traditional craft streets in a sprawling maze on the north end of the lake (see the walking tour in the Old Quarter, p. 90). Lakeside is also a good place to find a bench and rest your toes after trundling around town, and you can find some good little cafes, particularly on the north end. Grab an ice cream and take time to stroll, or stop and watch the moon reflect off the surface of this magical lake. You might even spot one of the giant turtles that took back the sword of Le Thai To to herald peace in Vietnam; sightings of this rare breed of turtles are quite common. Willows hang over the lake and reflect in the rippling light of dusk.

Thap Rua, or Tortoise Tower, was built in 1886 by an obscure Mandarin official. The temple was at first despised and involved in a scandal in which the official tried to have his father's bones laid to rest at the pagoda base. But over time, tiny Thap Rua, which sits on a small island at the very center of the lake, has become something of the city's Leaning Tower of Pisa, Statue of Liberty, and Eiffel Tower all rolled into one though it is off-limits to visitors. Consisting of three tiers of window galleries, the temple commands great respect, and it's a popular focal point for swooning lovers at lakeside in Hanoi's "Central Park"—the lungs of the city. The turtles that can be seen on rare occasions basking at the temple's base are said to be up to 500 years old and the very species that stole the sword and founded the fair city. Hanoians love their stupa of peace; in fact, recent initiatives to have the aging pagoda painted and restored—the small stupa is covered in moss and is overgrown with weeds—were met with staunch disapproval from Hanoi citizens. And so it is as it always was.

At city center, bordered by Le Thai To and Dinh Tien Hoang sts. Entrance fee to Ngoc Son Temple 10,000 VND; daily 7:30am–5:30pm.

National Museum of Vietnamese History This is an exhaustive repository of Vietnamese ancient and historical relics nicely displayed with some bare-bones explanations in English. Housed in a building that was the French consulate until 1910 and a museum in various incarnations since, this collection walks you from prehistoric artifacts and carvings to funerary jars and some very fine examples of Dong Son drums from the north, excavations of Han tombs, Buddhist statuary, and everyday items of early history. It's the kind of place where schoolchildren are forced to go (and be careful if you see buses out front), and for anyone but history buffs, you might feel just as bored as the kids. For those on any kind of historical mission in Vietnam, I recommend contacting a tour agency and booking a knowledgeable guide for an excellent overview and a good beginning to any trip.

1 Trang Tien St. (just east of the opera). ℭ **04/3825-3518.** Admission 20,000 VND; camera 15,000 VND. Daily 8am–4:30pm.

Quan Su Pagoda ★ Quan Su is one of the most important temples in the country. Constructed in the 15th century along with a small house for visiting Buddhist ambassadors, in 1934 it became the headquarters of the Tonkin Buddhist Association, and today it is headquarters for the Vietnam Central Buddhist Congregation. It's an active pagoda and usually thronged with worshipers; the interior is dim and smoky with incense. To the rear is a school of Buddhist doctrine. For good luck (or for fun), visitors of any faith are welcome to buy sticks of incense and make offerings at the various altars and sand urns. It's easy to follow suit, and folks will be glad to show you what to do.

73 Quan Su St., as it intersects Tran Hung Da, Hoan Kiem District. Free admission. Daily 8–11am and 1–4pm.

Revolutionary Museum The revolution will not be televised; however, afterward we'll have lots of old beat-up museums that celebrate the ongoing class struggle and inevitable triumph of a unified proletariat over the running dog bourgeoisie capitalists and their elitist, oppressive schemes to keep the common man in chains. Or so runs the old party line. What is best about the Revolutionary Museum is that it's a little run down, a telling sign of where the nation's revolutionary zeal has gone in the wake of a booming capitalist economy. Uncle Ho's ideas were quickly lost in the shuffle when affordable motorbikes and TVs came on the scene. But to the elder generation of Vietnamese, those who were born before 1975 and experienced Vietnam's great struggle, places such as the Revolutionary Museum are important reminders of the legacy. The revolution that started with Ho Chi Minh is celebrated now less with socialism in mind than with celebrating the nation's hard-fought autonomy. The museum houses an interesting collection of photos and memorabilia not only chronicling the life and ascendancy of Nguyen Tat Tanh, otherwise known as Ho Chi Minh, but of the many early revolutions at the turn of the 20th century. Oil paintings retell the struggles and, literally, paint a grisly picture of life in colonial·jails on Con Dao Island or Phu Quoc Island in the south. The museum route starts on the first floor with the 1945 August Revolution, photos and relics of victory at Dien Bien Phu, good background on the conflict with the United States, and the obligatory color photos of a prosperous Communist Vietnam as the revolutionaries envisioned. Party rhetoric is heavy here, and a big part of the allure of trundling around these big halls (once a French administrative building) is looking for words such as "running dog" and finding artifacts such as an old Budweiser can that was bent into a lantern for Viet Cong troops. Fun if you're a war buff.

26 Tran Quang Khai St., Hoan Kiem (east of the lake near the ring road and just adjacent to the old Opera Building). ℭ **04/3825-4151.** Admission 10,000 VND. Daily 8–11:30am and 1:30–4:15pm.

Women's Museum After a total renovation, this is now one of the city's most interesting museums, with lots of video presentations about various aspects of women's roles in Vietnam. Communism of the Ho Chi Minh variety was an egalitarian movement where all men and women were created equal, and revolutionary women were on the front lines throughout Vietnam's long conflicts with foreign powers. Whether pushing overladen bicycles along the Ho Chi Minh Trail Network or packing a pistol through the cave complexes outside of Saigon, Vietnamese women were a little more proactive than America's "Rosy the Riveter" of World War II fame, and Hanoi's Women's Museum celebrates their pivotal contribution to the war effort and to the growth of a modern, stable Vietnam. The entrance is a large rotunda with a great golden statue of the oversize and overmuscled Soviet school of propaganda depicting a triumphant woman facing a great wind with a small child balanced on her shoulder. The first floor, "Women in Family," focuses on the role of women in the home, as well as the problems faced by single mothers. The second floor, "Women in History," recounts their heroic deeds during the struggle for independence and reunification, while the third floor focuses on women's fashion, particularly the splendid garments worn by the various ethnic minority groups. Western visitors often used to criticize this museum for its patronizing attitude, but that aspect has disappeared completely during the renovation and visitors are now likely to leave with renewed respect for Vietnamese women. A popular coffee shop is just opposite the entrance to the museum, a good place to chat and connect with locals.

36 Ly Thuong Kiet St., Hoan Kiem District. ✆ **04/325-9936.** Admission 30,000 VND. Tues–Sun 8am–4:30pm.

Sights Outside the City Center

Ho Chi Minh Trail Museum   A museum dedicated to the war of inches and supplies along the borders of Vietnam, Laos, and Cambodia. The museum is far out of town but worth the trip, especially if you are on the way to Mai Chau, as you'll pass right by. Three floors are crowded with exhibits of photography, as well as lots of war machinery. The trucks that traveled parts of the Ho Chi Minh Trail are parked in a shaded area in the courtyard out front. Visitors are first taken up to the second floor to watch a 20-minute video that gives an overview of the construction of this trail, which was in fact many trails that took years to get connected, and proved to be perhaps the single most significant factor in the outcome of the war. The revolutionary rhetoric is heavy at this museum, and the focus is on the sacrifice of the many who shoveled, dug, fought, and scraped by to get supplies of rice and ammunition to North Vietnam's frontline forces, including a stress on the efforts of women to keep the supply lines open. Among the exhibits, look out for the 60-kilo (132 lb.) anti-shrapnel coat worn by commanders, and the oil drums covered in bamboo slats that common soldiers jumped in when the bombs rained down. The weapons on display are a testament to human cruelty, and include vicious-looking nail bombs and cigarette bombs. Out back, there's a reconstruction of an underground command center, but it's not very convincing.

14km (8¾ miles) southwest of Hanoi along Rte. 6 (heading toward Hoa Binh). Admission 20,000 VND; camera 10,000 VND. Mon–Sat 7:30–11:30am and 1:30–4:30pm.

Vietnam Ethnology Museum ★★   If you're interested in learning more about the 54 ethnic minorities populating Vietnam's hinterlands, make the jaunt out to this sprawling compound (go by cab). Vietnam's different ethnic groups, their history, and customs are explained in photos, videos, and displays of clothing and daily implements. Out back are a number of re-creations of the village homes, from a low Cham house to the towering peak of a thatched Banhar communal home. You come away with a good historical perspective on the many groups you meet in the far north and in parts of neighboring Laos and Cambodia.

Nguyen Van Huyen, 6km (3¾ miles) west of town. ✆ **04/3756-2193.** www.vme.org.vn. Admission 25,000 VND. Tues–Sun 8:30am–5:30pm.

OUTDOOR ACTIVITIES & OTHER FITNESS PURSUITS

Hoan Kiem Lake

Along with being the cultural center of Hanoi, from predawn until about 6 to 7am, the lake becomes something like an Olympic training camp. Hordes of locals work up a sweat going along the walking paths and wide road that circles the lake, taking advantage of the morning cool and greeting the day with, as a Vietnamese friend put it, "a breath of fire." Groups doing calisthenics and light aerobics to loud taped music stand next to ranks of white-clad, slow-moving tai chi practitioners, martial arts groups, and even ballroom-dancing clubs. Joggers and speed-walkers circle the lake, and you'll spot solo exercisers doing all kinds of strange contortions or practicing meditation.

Join in. It's a great way to start the day and get into the rhythm of Hanoi life (you'll be wanting a siesta after lunch, like most locals), and it's a unique time when you can travel anonymously, unharried by souvenir sellers. You always find someone going your speed, and if solo at the beginning, you're sure to meet up with friendly locals along the way. Hoan Kiem at dawn is a real scene and a great place for people-watching and a little morning wake-up. It's a similar scene near the Botanical Gardens and in Thong Nhat Park (formerly Lenin Park) overlooking Bay Mau Lake in the south end of town. Get your run in before 6:30am, though, when traffic starts to snarl.

Bicycles are easily rented from almost any hotel for about $1 a day, and though Hanoi motorbike traffic is chaos defined, you can pick your way through traffic and see more of town with your own wheels. Take extreme caution.

Spas & Fitness

The fitness center at **Metropole Legend Hotel** (✆ **04/3826-6919**) has top-end equipment, a sauna, and a Jacuzzi, with day rates for nonguests.

Vietnam hasn't quite kept up with Asia's current spa revolution, but most hotels offer basic massage services, and the larger upmarket properties have deluxe spas. Try the Metropole Legend, the Hanoi Horison, and the Nikko Hotel.

Small massage storefronts (the nonseedy variety) are all over town. Affordable and convenient to the town center for a rest while shopping or exploring the city is **Salon** (15 Ma May St.; ✆ **04/3926-2036**), where a 60-minute Swedish massage costs just $10. It's open daily from 9am to 9pm.

A couple of good day spas are **Orchids Spa** (34 Luong Ngoc Quyen; ✆ **04/3926-48620;** www.orchids-spa.com), which offers several spa treatments as well as facials and waxing, and **Zen Spa** (Alley 310, Nghi Tam, Tay Ho; ✆ **04/3719-9889;** www.zenspa.com.vn), in a beautiful location near the banks of the Red River, where you can choose from a range of five-element spa packages.

Golf

King's Island Golf Resort and Country Club is just 35km (22 miles) north of Hanoi and offers your best chance to hit the links near Vietnam's capital. A fine international course is set among the Ba Vi Mountains, and the club (open to visitors) has a whole range of services, from bungalow rentals to good pro services, equipment rentals, and dining. The course is in the town of Son Tay in Ha Tay Province. Call for reservations at © **033/3686-555** or 04/3944-8690 (in Hanoi), or visit their website (www.kingsislandgolf.com).

Chi Linh Star Golf and Country Club is just east of King's Island, some 68km (42 miles) from Hanoi, on the road to Haiphong. The club recently hosted the Carlsberg Masters Open. With two fine courses, Chi Linh also offers a host of services and welcomes day guests. It costs $80 for 18 holes on a weekday and $100 on the weekend. Contact the office in Hanoi at © **04/3939-3100,** or book through the useful website www.chilinhstargolf.com.vn.

SHOPPING

Hanoi is like Bangkok for the sport shopper: a good choice for the last destination before flying home, if you want to easily buy and fill an extra suitcase in just a few days. Note that affordable, knockoff bags are for sale on the northeast end of Hoan Kiem Lake (where Lo Su St. terminates at lakeside). Most airlines on long-haul flights have high weight limits for each of your two check-in bags (some airlines allow as much as 36kg/79 lb. per bag), but note that regional flights, particularly on Vietnam Airlines, impose more strict limits; you might be able to bring just two 20-kilogram (44-lb.) bags with you to Bangkok, while it's double that if you go on directly to Frankfurt. Just be sure to check.

What to Buy

Hanoi is a fine place to shop for silk, silver, lacquerware, embroidered goods, and ethnic-minority crafts. Silk is good quality and an easy buy. (If you're unsure of the quality, pluck a few strands and burn the fibers; if it smells like burned hair, it's silk.) Shops will tailor a suit in as little 24 hours, but allow extra time for alterations. Many of the shops are clustered along Hang Gai Street, whose name translates as Hemp Rope Street. It once housed ship-rigging shops but is now unofficially called Silk Street. A silk suit here will run from about $50 to $100, depending on the silk, and a blouse or shirt will cost $20 to $30. Virtually every shop takes credit cards (MasterCard and Visa). Bargain hard for all but the silk; offer 50% of the asking price and end up paying 70% or so. Most shops are open from 8am to 8pm, though those in tourist areas may stay open later.

Antique Regulations

Note that the sale of antiques is a simple matter, but carrying them out of the country is another question, and many tourists have gone smiling through Customs to declare their Buddha—only to discover that they can't bring the statue home with them. Dealers are not always forthcoming because they're more concerned with making the sale, but for larger, more expensive purchases, a dealer will get involved and help with the process.

SILK & EMBROIDERY

In addition to the shops mentioned below, also consider **Thanh Ha Silk,** 114 Hang Gai St. (☎ **04/3928-5348**), and **Oriental House,** 28 Nha Chung (☎ **04/3828-5542**).

Craft Link   Put your money to a good cause. This not-for-profit store has a nice collection of silk notebooks, accessories, minority art and clothing, and lacquer plates and bowls. The store is spread out over two floors of a charming, restored colonial building. The Clintons visited Craft Link during their tour through Vietnam, and there's an enlarged photo on the second floor to prove it. 43 Van Mieu St. ☎ **04/3733-6101.**

Hanoi Silk   Hanoi Silk has a collection comparable to Khai Silk (see below) and carries good ready-to-wear as well as tailors' silk garments. Sheraton Hotel at 11 Xuan Dieu Rd. ☎ **04/3719-2434.** www.hanoisilkvn.com.

Khai Silk   With branches and small outlet corners in various hotel lobbies around town—also in Saigon—Khai Silk is the largest retail silk outlet in Vietnam and offers a good, high standard of silk ready-to-wear and bespoke tailored clothing. You might find better deals, but Khai Silk is justly famous for its selection, silk quality, and chic store layout. Main store is at 96 Hang Gai St. ☎ **04/3825-4237.** 26 Nguyen Thai Hoc St.: ☎ 04/3733-3866. 113 Hang Gai: ☎ 04/3928-9883. www.khaisilkcorp.com

New Collection: Hoa Sua Embroidery and Sewing Showroom   Like their affiliated restaurants and cafes in Hanoi (and in Sapa), the folks at the Hoa Sua Showroom are an outlet for disadvantaged children, many of whom are hearing-impaired, to receive on-the-job training and placement in a career. The shop here carries a nice collection of daily-use items, tablecloths, and slipcovers, as well as made-to-order goods. An expat favorite, and your money goes to a good cause. 21D Ha Hoi, Hoan Kiem District. ☎ **04/3822-6912.**

Tan My ★★   This shop states they are the oldest store in Hanoi. History claims aside, it stocks some of the finest threads in this overcrowded shopping district. Come here to buy beautiful cotton or linen pieces with subtle or quirky embroidery. I love their simple white pieces marked with a single flower in a corner, and their adorable children's wear makes perfect pint-size gifts. You can also bring in photos or a design you fancy, and the shop can reproduce them into a woven picture or a motif for tablecloths and accompanying dinner napkins ($40). There are several locations of Tan My shops around town, but the best selection is at their flagship on Han Gai Street. 66 Han Gai St. ☎ **04/3825-1579.** Fax 04/3824-7522. www.tanmyembroidery.com.vn.

TRADITIONAL ITEMS, ANTIQUES & SOUVENIRS

For silver, antique oddities, and traditional crafts, try **Hong Hoa,** on 18 Ngo Quyen St. (☎ **04/3826-8341**). **Giai Dieu,** 82 Hang Gai St. (☎ **04/3826-0222;** also at 93 Ba Trieu St.), has interesting lacquer paintings and decorative items.

For fine ceramics, look to **Quang's Ceramics,** at 95 Ba Trieu St. (☎ **04/3945-4235**), in the Old Quarter.

For decorative items and souvenirs, look to the streets surrounding Hoan Kiem Lake. A good place to start is **Nha Tho Street,** also called "Church Street," as it terminates in the town's huge cathedral. Here you'll find silk and housewares designers in and among quiet cafes. **Delta Deco** (12 Nha Tho St.; ☎ **04/3828-9616**), a large dealer of lacquerware and fine furnishings, is a popular choice. Its Chinese-influenced modern designs are especially attractive. The area all around the lake is lined with budget souvenir shops offering the likes of lacquer painting of the French cartoon character Tin Tin and carvings and trinkets. Other outlets are listed below.

Hanoi Moment ★ A small selection of porcelain and lacquer flatware is sold in this smartly laid-out store. Rather than leaving you to dig through assorted stacks of plates and bowls, Hanoi Moment displays a small selection of pieces arranged in eye-pleasing display areas. 101 Hang Gai St. ℂ **04/3928-7170.** www.hanoimoment.vn.

La Casa This store uses traditional Vietnamese crafts and combines local materials with a modern edge. It's an excellent place to scope out little gifts to bring back home that people will actually like. 15 Nha Chung St. ℂ **04/3828-9616.** http://lacasavietnam.com.

Maroon Conveniently located in the heart of the Old Quarter, this place is a treasure trove of easy-to-carry items of home decor such as lacquer picture frames and silk bedding. 156 Hang Bong. ℂ **04/3928-7264.**

Van Loi You'll enter past one of Hanoi's classic banyan trees along Hang Gai (see the walking tour of Hanoi, p. 90) into the interior of Van Loi, which centers on a large circular staircase and open gallery space filled with fine furnishings and handicrafts, mostly in wood. 87 Hang Gai. ℂ **04/3828-6758. www.vanloi.com.**

Vietnamese House A good little collection of gems, handicrafts, small ceramics, jewelry, and antiques. 92 Hang Bac St. ℂ **04/3826-2455.** www.vietnamesehouse.com.

STYLE: CLOTHING, ACCESSORIES & DECOR

For luxury foreign goods, and/or for a glimpse of Vietnam's burgeoning mall culture, check out the renovated **Trang Tien Plaza,** a large, three-story complex on the southeast corner of Hoan Kiem Lake, which features budget clothing, and real name-brand fashion and electronic goods, the likes of Levi's and Sony.

Hang Dau Street, on the northeast corner of Hoan Kiem Lake (near the intersection Lo Su), is positively **"shoe heaven"** and carries a wide selection of men's and women's shoes. The lads will be sad to note that you won't find many sizes over 43 centimeters (about an American size 9), and the sneakers and tennis shoes are often "pleather" and not the best quality, but women, particularly those ascribing to the Imelda Marcos school of shoe acquisition, are in heaven with these underpriced (bargain hard) creative outlets. Most are good knockoffs or rejects of goods made in factories east of Hanoi. Also throughout the area, especially where Lo Su Street meets the lake, you'll find **bag sellers** with loads of medium- to good-quality reproductions of your favorite brands, such as North Face or Adidas. Five dollars gets you a reasonable copy of a bag that might cost $100 or more at home, but the zippers give out pretty quickly.

Hanoi, once a bastion of hard-line Communism and rigid control over a corrupt free market, is now giving way to fashion. Led by its pop-culture benefactors—nearby South Korea and Hong Kong—Vietnam is growing its own base for pop culture alongside a burgeoning (Uncle Ho wouldn't like it) middle class of consumers, and areas such as Hanoi's **Nha Tho Street** are leading the way. Close on its heels, in the expat district near West Lake, is **Xuan Dieu Street,** which has quirky, Western-friendly stores. Meanwhile, high-end flagship stores such as **Burberry** (oddly enough, across the street from midrange San Francisco chain **Esprit**) are congregating at the corner of Ly Thai To, between the Metropole and the Hilton. Here's a rundown of the city's best:

Galerie Royal ★   This small boutique is sandwiched between the Hilton and the Metropole and caters to high-end shoppers. They carry three lines only: Kenzo, Korloff, and La Perla. The La Perla lingerie and swimsuit selection is top-notch. 60 Ly Thai To St. ℰ **04/3936-6672.**

Ipa Nima and Tina Sparkle   You've come to the right place for gaudy little Zakka fashion bags and accouterments for the ladies. Run by jet-setting Hong Kong lawyer–turned-designer Christina Yu, the place is popular with Japanese and Singaporean ladies and has managed to cause a small stir in other international markets. Celebrities Jamie Lee Curtis and Kelly Osbourne (admittedly, not your typical fashion icons) have been known to sport an Ipa Nima creation or two. Yu herself admits that you either love it or hate it. Her bags are creative, glitzy affairs adorned with rhinestones, metal grommets, and contrasting materials. They have two stores: a flagship Ipa Nima store in the south end of town, and Tina Sparkle, in the heart of the popular Church Street cafe area. Ipa Nima: 34 Han Thuyen St., Hai Ba Trung District. ℰ **04/3933-4000.** www.ipa-nima.com. Tina Sparkle: 17 Nha Tho St., Hoan Kiem District. ℰ 04/3928-7616.

Ha Truong Studio ★   Young designer Ha Truong's creations are, according to her slogan, "understated, artful, contradictory." As the founder of her own studio, she has made some small waves on the international scene. Truong freely mixes and matches (for example, a wraparound dress made in multicolored lace paired with solid-colored, netted silk sleeves) and creates interesting cuts that work well on many body types. Check her website for updates. No fixed store hours. 278 Nghi Tam St., Tay Ho. ℰ **04/3710-0675.** www.mirror-design.com.

Mosaique   Here is a popular little boutique and a great place to pick up some designer silver jewelry, silk hangings, or ready-to-wear items, as well as home goods from furnishings to lamps. Major credit cards are accepted. 22 Nha Tho St., the heart of chic "Church St." ℰ **04/3928-6181.** www.mosaiquedecoration.com.

Nagu   Think cute gifts, such as passport holders and notebooks in linens and silk. Nagu also carries a small selection of clothing (modern with a Vietnamese touch) at the back. The changing room appears by unfolding strips of cloth from a high wire—not a lot of privacy for trying on the goods. 20 Nha Tho St. ℰ **04/3928-8020.** www.zantoc.com.

Song ★   This boutique (whose name means "life" in Vietnamese) carries original designs offering a modern twist on classic Vietnamese styles. They are a bit on the pricey side, but the clothing is thoughtful and well cut. Everything is a creation of established designer Valerie Gregori McKenzie, who first began designing in France and continued her trade in California. Her clothing and home collections are a mix of Vietnamese classical styles and a tropical bohemian chic look. 27 Nha Tho St. ℰ **04/3928-8733.**

Tan My Design   This new store showcases work from talented local designers, both expat and Vietnamese. Expect modern twists on styles of the past—mandarin collars mixed with contemporary silks or fine embroidery in quirky designs. 61-65 Hang Gai St. ℰ **04/3938-1154.** www.tanmyembroidery.com.vn.

Things of Substance ★   An excellent place to find original designs, and all reasonably priced. The store has a lovely sense of humor, as evidenced by their motto: "Western sizes . . . Vietnamese prices" and their small selection of souvenir T-shirts ("Vietnam, One Party since 1975"). Things of Substance sells mostly women's cotton and linen separates with a touch of Eastern influence—the type of clothing that is perfect for the hot weather and could transfer easily to an office setting. They also have a small handful of funky accessories, such as canvas yoga bags embroidered with a big dragon or bohemian-style leather shoulder bags made of pigskin. 5 Nha Tho. ✆ **04/3828-6965.**

Three Trees ★   This specialty store showcases original jewelry designs by a Belgian expat. Showpieces in the front display cases are oversize but still delicate. Designs often feature floral motifs (which balance out the chunkier shapes and sizes) in gold, interlaced with well-placed, small-cut diamonds. 15 Nha Tho St. ✆ **04/3928-8725.** Also has boutiques at the Hilton and the Sheraton.

ART

Vietnam has a flourishing art scene, and Hanoi has many galleries of oil, silk, water, and lacquer paintings. Don't forget to bargain, and know that, in most cases, the paintings you buy are not originals, but copies of well-known Vietnamese artists. Even places that like to offer a "certificate of originality" are selling you a line of bull along with the certificate and a copy of a work by a famous Vietnamese artist. The good news is that the better galleries do carry the originals, and Vietnam is now home to some international names. Try to meet the artist, if you can, and stick with the larger dealers, who are less likely to pull a fast one. All galleries will ship from door to door at a cost of about $150 for a medium-size canvas. Listed below are a few reliable stops. Galleries are mainly in the Old Quarter and along the shores of central Hoan Kiem.

Apricot Gallery   This large, well-lit, air-conditioned space holds some works by Vietnam's most well-known contemporary lacquer painter, Dinh Quan, as well as other artists of the current vanguard (all priced accordingly, of course). Apricot Gallery carries 80% famous artists and 20% upcoming artists. See if you can spot which paintings fall into which categories. The gallery has hosted several international customers, including former President Bill Clinton, who purchased a landscape piece by Hoang Hai Anh. Hoang, naturally, falls into the 80% group. 40B Hang Bong St. ✆ **04/3828-8965.** www.apricotgallery.com.vn.

Art Vietnam   One of the city's premier galleries, Art Vietnam is set in a large contemporary space on Nguyen Khac Nhu and run by a longtime expat, collector, and steward of Vietnamese art, Suzanne Lecht. Find Suzanne at the gallery most days, and take any opportunity to chat with her and pick her brain about art in Vietnam—she also has some good tales to tell. 7 Nguyen Khac Nhu ✆ **04/3927-2349.** www.artvietnam gallery.com.

54 Traditions Gallery ★★   This gallery is more like an ethnographic museum, library, and gallery all rolled into one. The space is divided into five theme rooms (such as "Functional Objects" and "Shamanism"), and co-owner Mark Rapoport is more than happy to play guide for a day. Rapoport is a self-described collector: baseball cards when he was a kid, African art while living in New York, and then Vietnamese minority art when he moved to Hanoi. Rapoport has a natural gift for bringing the artifacts to life, and given the range of affordable pieces (small mounted prints made from antique stamps or seals go for less than $10) and exquisite antique artifacts, few people walk away empty-handed. 30 Hang Bun St. ✆ **04/3715-0194.** www.54traditions.com.vn.

Hanoi Gallery   Different from all the rest, by virtue of the fact that this little open-air storefront sells only old Communist propaganda posters, mostly artful copies that are "worried" to look old (the difference is obvious), but the stark images are quite appealing. 42 Cau Go St. (directly north of the lake). ✆ **04/3824-1854.**

Mai Gallery ★   Like the Apricot Gallery and Art Vietnam, this gallery carries a good deal of work by well-known and established Vietnamese artists. It also has a handful of exclusive artists, whose works are available only at their gallery. These include the latest darling of Vietnamese landscapes, Phan Thu Trang, a young painter (born in 1981) who has been with Mai Gallery since 2004 (you'll see reproductions of his work in hotels throughout the country). Staff here is helpful and the gallery has an excellent layout, with good lighting for easy viewing. 113 Hong Bong St. ✆ **04/3938-0568.** www.maigallery-vietnam.com.

Viet Fine Arts Gallery   Just north and east of the church area is this high-end collection of works bearing the authentic stamp of local painters. The gallery has an imposing storefront and an extensive collection. 96 Hang Trong St. ✆ **04/3928-6667.** www.vietfinearts.com.

Also look for **Thanh Mai,** 64 Hang Gai St. (✆ **04/3825-1618**); **Bui Gallery,** 23 Ngo Van So St. (✆ **04/3944-8595**); and **Van Linh Gallery,** 13 Hang Gai St. (✆ **04/3928-7013**), in the Old Quarter.

Trang Tien Street, the heart of the French Quarter just east of the southern end of Hoan Kiem, is full of galleries and showrooms. The road was once home to the French colonial administration buildings, and these grand facades have long been places for commerce in foreign goods (thus the many English-language bookstores and galleries). **Van Gallery,** the sister shop of Van Linh Gallery in the Old Quarter, is at 25–27 Trang Tien, near the Dan Chu Hotel. Below are just a few others.

Hanoi Art Contemporary Gallery   This large corner space carries a large collection. The friendly staff greets you with smiles. Here you'll find standard copies and some very unique pieces. 36-38 Trang Tien St. ✆ **04/3934-7192.** www.hanoi-artgallery.com.

Life Photo Gallery   This gallery carries the works of two prominent Hanoian photographers whose color prints of the Vietnamese hinterlands, including some of the finest portraits and scenes from the hilltribes of the far north and Central Highlands region, have been published widely. You'll find some of their best prints here, framed and at prices unheard of in the West. Pick up a great souvenir or get some inspiration for your own snapshots. The eccentric photographers themselves, Mr. Le Quang Chau and Mr. Do Anh Tuan, are often on hand and happy to chat. 39 Trang Tien St. ✆ **04/3936-3886.**

BOOKS

For foreign books in Hanoi, check out one of the few shops lining **Trang Tien Street,** the only place where you could find a book, even a simple English or French grammar book, during the years of austere Communist control. Nowadays there are a few large state-sponsored bookstores, each with a simple collection of English-language books, a few shelves of the classics, and a useful section with books about travel and the culture of Vietnam, as well as a selection of coffee-table books and language-learning texts that are geared to the local market.

The **Bookworm** ★ (44 Chau Long St., to the southeast of the lake; ✆ **04/3715-3711;** http://bookwormhanoi.com) is a longtime expat favorite that has recently relocated and carries a good collection of international bestsellers, classics, and books on culture and travel. It's your best bet for unique finds (short of swapping with fellow travelers). They do trades of the two-for-one variety, and the expat staff is friendly and helpful (there's also a useful bulletin board of local events and things for sale).

In the Old Quarter on **Hang Bac Street,** you'll find backpacker book repositories; it's a good place if you're looking to trade books (especially if you find another traveler there doing the same and can make a private deal; otherwise, it's usually two-for-one at the store counters). Try **Love Planet Tours and Books,** 25 Hang Bac (✆ **04/3828-4864**), a longtime traveler favorite (they'll try to sell you all kinds of tours along with your tome, too). Also try one of the similar budget shops on **Bao Khan Street,** a popular nightlife area on the northeast corner of the lake.

Note that most high-end hotels (see the Sofitel Metropole, the Hilton Hanoi Opera, and the Daewoo, earlier in this chapter) have lobby book nooks with some palatable volumes and international news sources.

Also note that **Hanoi's wandering booksellers,** once the plague of the city, especially near Hoan Kiem Lake, where the hassle of tourists was legendary, are less in evidence these days. These lads sell the likes of *The Sorrow of War,* by Bao Khanh, as well as popular phrase books, guidebooks, and the obligatory *Quiet American,* or now the popular *In Retrospect,* by the Vietnam War's architect, Robert McNamara. Just $2 gets you a photocopied edition (some are rife with mistakes), and the biggest fun of all is bantering with these kids, all of whom have a good, funny line or two to get your money out of your pockets. If you haven't read these classics on Vietnam, this is a good place to pick one up (or a map or a postcard). It's almost obligatory, or at least your savvy salesman will make you feel like it is.

Traditional Markets

Dong Xuan Market is the city's largest traditional market and a highlight of a visit to the Old Quarter. A massive indoor pavilion is surrounded by streets teeming with sellers day and night (early morning is best to visit). Find lots of Chinese knockoff goods, produce, and stuff for everyday use in homes—but there are plenty of neat trinket shops tucked down the narrow lanes of this maze of commerce, and just the experience of walking around (or photographing the chaos) is a reason to visit.

Cho 19–12 (the **19–12 Market**) is one of Hanoi's most interesting markets. Just west and in the shadow of the Melia hotel, you'll find this labyrinth of local goods, produce, and oddities. On the south end of the market, near the main entrance, is the "whole roasted dog" aisle, with crispy Fidos stacked one atop the other. A bit of a shock, really. In the heart of the market are all kinds of *che* (Vietnamese custard) shops and local food stalls, as well as meat and produce stands. You won't be able to get over all the dogs here.

Photo Stores

Got a memory card full of images that you want to print or back up on CD? Looking for good film cheap, or good processing equally cheap? Hanoi's many photo stores can do it all. Try any of the following, all within a baseball throw from the lake: **A Dong Photo Company** (128 Hang Trong St.; ✆ **04/3826-0732**), **Konica Digital**

Photo Center (3B Le Thai To St.; ☎ **04/3825-8517**), or **Nguyen Cau Digital Camera Lab** (1 Ba Trieu St.; ☎ **04/3936-1516**).

Convenience

To pick up good snacks for a long train or bus ride, check out **The Croissant** or **The Deli** (see "Cafes," p. 84), or even stock up at any street stall selling baguettes with pâté and salad fillings. Another good place for deli treats is **Au Delice** (19 Han Thuyen St.; ☎**04/3971-5753;** www.au-delice-online.com), who claim to have the city's widest range of cheeses.

For wines and imported meats, cheeses, and breads, try **Hanoi Gourmet** (1B Ham Long St; ☎ **04/3943-1009**). For fine wines from the choicest regions of the world, as well as any kind of liquor or aperitif, stop in at **La Cave** (57 Trang Thi St.; ☎ **04/3934-4083**). In the heart of the Old Quarter, the **Warehouse** ★ (59 Hang Trong St.; ☎ **04/3928-7666;** www.warehouse-asia.com) also has an extensive wine selection. The **Gourmand Shop** (56 Ly Thai To; ☎ **04/3826-6919,** ext. 8702) is located on the first-floor area on the east side of the grand Sofitel Metropole hotel (p. 68) and carries a fine collection of wines, cheeses, treats, and gifts. It's open from 7am to 9pm, and whatever they don't have, they can point you in the right direction to find.

HANOI AFTER DARK

Hanoi hosts a variety of pleasant little watering holes and even a few rowdy dance spots that stay open far past when the Communist cadres deem decent (thank goodness for kickbacks and corruption). A growing number of expat residents means that options abound, particularly in the Old Quarter. You have your pick of some cool lounge bars or local draft beer for pennies a pitcher at the popular streetside *bia hoi* stalls, where patrons hunker down on squat stools for a long night of boozing and chat (this is the top choice for connecting with local folks).

Hanoi is the best place in Vietnam to experience **traditional Vietnamese arts** such as opera, theater, and water puppet shows. Invented during the **Ly Dynasty** (1009–1225), the art of water puppetry is unique to Vietnam and a highlight of any visit to the city. The puppets are made of wood and really do dance on water. The shows feature traditional Vietnamese music and depict folklore and myth. Book tickets for the popular puppets at least 5 hours ahead. Check the listing below for more information.

Theater & Performance

The **Hanoi Opera House** (Hanoi Municipal Theatre), 1 Trang Tien St., Hoan Kiem District (☎ **04/3933-0113;** www.hanoioperahouse.org.vn), hosts performances by local and international artists. Check their website or ask any hotel concierge to see if any performances coincide with your stay, and be sure to book in advance. The **Hanoi Traditional Opera,** 15 Nguyen Dinh Chieu, Ba Dinh District (☎ **04/3943-7361**), has shows on Monday, Wednesday, and Friday at 8pm. The ancient song tradition known as **Ca Tru,** which flourished in the 15th century, has seen something of a revival in Hanoi due to funding from UNESCO (in 2009, *ca tru* was inscribed on the UNESCO list of Intangible Cultural Heritage in Urgent Need of Safeguarding). You can witness a performance of this hauntingly beautiful music each Saturday evening at 8pm at the **Ca Tru Singing House ★★**, a traditional house at 28 Hang

Buom (in the Old Quarter). Admission is $10 and the performance lasts an hour, including a short intermission, when the instruments are introduced.

Central Circus, on the north end of Thong Nhat Park (formerly Lenin Park), across from the Nikko Hotel, Hai Ba Trung District (℃ **04/3822-0277**), has shows at 8pm Wednesday through Sunday, and an extra show at 9am on Sundays that is geared toward children. It's a real circus done on a small scale, so see it only if you're desperate to entertain the kids. As in so many isolated Communist blocks in the world, the circus was once the only game in town. But now, with the proliferation of televisions in homes, online gaming, and movies, young Hanoians have myriad options in the entertainment realm, so visiting Russian troupes don't draw a crowd. It's sad that the art is dying (be sure to check with your concierge to see if shows are running), but many foreign visitors to this circus report being saddened by the brutal treatment of trained animals.

Thang Long Water Puppet Theater ★★★ 🎁 Shows are three times daily, at 5:15, 6:30, and 8pm. This might sound like one for the kids, but there is something enchanting for everyone in the lighthearted comedy and intricately skilled puppetry of this troupe. They perform numerous vignettes of daily life in the countryside and ancient tales, including the legend of Hoan Kiem Lake and the peaceful founding of the city of Hanoi. Puppeteers use bamboo poles to extend their puppets from behind the proscenium and up through the surface of a small pond that forms the stage. You will be amazed at their ingenuity, and it doesn't take much to suspend disbelief and get caught up in a magical hour of escape. The kids will love it, too. Buy tickets early in the high season. The theater is poorly raked, and that means that, though seats in the front cost a bit more, you'll have a better view—and not look at the back of someone's head—from the middle or the back (pick from a seating chart at the ticket office). You also get a more realistic effect from the back.

57B Dinh Tien Hoang St., Hoan Kiem District. ℃ **04/3824-9494.** Fax 04/3824-5117. www.thanglong waterpuppet.org. Admission 40,000 VND–60,000 VND; extra for camera or video. Shows at 3:30, 5, 6:30, 8, and 9:15pm.

Cinema

Who knew you'd be watching a Spanish film and chatting with an elite group of *cinéastes* in a courtyard cafe in the middle of Hanoi? Life is a mystery. This little theater is more or less kept a secret—not for long, though. Popular with expats, the tiny screen of the **Hanoi Cinematique** imports some interesting work from all over the world and holds showings nightly. To see a film here, you have to follow some funny rules. The government forbids charging money to see foreign titles (information that is beyond the censor's grasp), so the theater is, in fact, classified as a club and part of the adjacent cafe; membership is just 20,000 VND. Tickets aren't bought; they're invitations that come with a suggested donation of 50,000 VND. The best part about the Hanoi Cinematique is meeting up with Hanoi's growing bevy of wild-eyed artists and the likes of hotel general managers mingling in one space—all for the love of the cinema. And very good cinema, indeed. Showtimes vary. Call ℃ **04/3936-2648,** or just stop by the cafe, which is at the end of a long, narrow alley off of 22A Hai Ba Trung (in the area south of Hoan Kiem Lake).

Bia Hoi, Bars & Pubs

Nightlife in Hanoi is more raucous than you might imagine of a town known as an austere Communist outpost. Midnight is the generally held strict closing time, but a few choice places rock until dawn. Traveler cafes in the Old Quarter are known to burst out in wild parties (I once enjoyed a rollicking Christmas Eve dinner and dance party in a travel agent's office), and there are lots of little restaurants and bars open late.

One good way to connect with local expats and be guaranteed a swilling good time is to contact the **Hash House Harriers** (www.hanoih3.com), a drinking fraternity for folks who like to work up a bit of a sweat before hitting the suds. The Hanoi group is quite family friendly, however, and they have fun runs every Saturday.

The best place to have a wild night—local style—is to pull up a little plastic squat stool on a street corner or in one of the many open-air bars serving the local brew, *bia hoi,* translated as "fresh beer" and otherwise known as draft beer. The kegs flow as long as folks are drinking, and sitting among locals in these cozy little joints is an infusion of local culture, where you can make friends and get close to Hanoi street life. You'll find *bia hoi* just about anywhere in Vietnam, in even the tiniest hamlet, but in Hanoi your best bet is on **the corner of Ta Hien Street and Luong Ngoc Quyen,** in the heart of the Old Quarter. Try the stalls where you see foreigners frequenting, and you're most likely to meet willing English speakers, both staff and patrons. One glass costs just a few thousand dong, so why not have another? How about one more? Stay away from the local rice whiskey unless you have an iron gut.

Bao Khanh Street ★   For nightlife geared to the expat or tourist, busy little Bao Khanh Street is a good place to start. Tucked behind a block of buildings down a short lane in the northwest corner of Hoan Kiem Lake (look for Café des Arts on the map of Hanoi, p. 73), the street is home to lots of popular bars and late-night spots. Some are a bit seedy, but there are a few comfortable laid-back places, and the street is lined with lots of open-air eateries, cafes, and bars geared to locals.

One of several popular bars on Bao Khanh Street is the **Factory,** 11A Ngo Bao Khanh (℃ **04/3938-1756**); they have live music and a welcoming atmosphere. Also check out **Polite Pub,** 5 Bao Khanh (℃ **04/3825-0959**; daily 5pm–2 or 3am), a popular gay men's hangout, but pretty "straight friendly," too. All of these spots are open late, and the street's always hoppin'. There are lots of nearby dining options as well (see Pepperoni's, p. 86, and Café des Arts, p. 76).

Binh Minh Jazz Club ★   Jazz aficionados are in for a rare treat at this new venue for Hanoi's preeminent saxophonist, Quyen Van Minh. Just walk through the Hot Life Café and go up to the third floor, and settle in for some fine versions of jazz classics between 9 and 11pm. Minh is always backed by a proficient band, and sometimes his son takes the stage as well. Open daily 8:30 to 11:30pm. 65 Quan Su. ℃ **04/3851-4969.** www.minhjazzvietnam.com.

Eté   This place lures a diverse expat crowd for its labor-intensive fresh fruit cocktails, tasty pub food, and impromptu dance parties. The spacious alfresco areas make this one of the best bars outside of the Old Quarter. Open daily 8am to midnight. 95 Giang Van Minh St. ℃ **04/7675-1331.**

Funky Monkey   Recently removed from its snug spot on Bao Khanh Street, this dim-lit music lounge will be hoping its fortunes continue in its new location in the southeast of the Old Quarter. Open 6pm to late. 31 Hang Thung St. ☏ **04/3928-6113.**

Hair of the Dog   If you believe that the perfect cure for a hangover is another shot of whatever gave you that headache, then try it out at this well-named watering hole. Just don't expect any service before 6pm. Open daily 6pm to late. 27 Hang Giay St. ☏ **09/3838-5382.**

Half Man Half Noodle   A welcoming watering hole that draws its fair share of locals, expats, and curious travelers, this place tends to get busier as the evening wears on. It's tucked away between Ta Hien and Ma May streets, but not exactly hidden. Open daily 6pm to late. 62 Dao Duy Tu. ☏ **04/3926-1943.**

Le Pub   Just a friendly little storefront bar in the heart of the backpacker area, Le Pub is a good vantage point on street life in the Old Quarter and a good meeting point when exploring town; there's a second branch near West Lake. The beer here is well chilled, and the staff is quite helpful. Open daily 7am to late. 25 Hang Be St. ☏ **04/3926-2104.** 9 Xuan Dieu St. ☏ 04/6674-6140. www.lepub.org. Daily 7am–11pm.

Ma May Street   The Old Quarter's epicenter for budget hotels is fast becoming the epicenter for nightlife, especially since the opening of **Hanoi Backpackers' Hostel** at number 9 (p. 75), where happy hour sees guests spilling (literally) out onto the street. Almost directly in front of the hostel, at 32 Ma May, is the **Bucket Bar,** which opens at 6pm and closes "when the last person's no longer standing"—you get the message. Just down the road at number 55, **EZ Rider** also comes to life after dark, offering cocktails, dance music, and shisha pipes (flavored tobacco smoked with water pipes) out front.

Nha Tho (Church Street)   Nightlife along Hanoi's Church Street, Nha Tho, which extends from the town's largest Catholic cathedral, is quite inviting and laid-back. The area is lined with boutique shops and galleries, and there are a few popular restaurants, such as Mediterraneo (p. 83), as well as Paris Deli (p. 86) and Moca Café (p. 85), which attract tourists and expats. A good place to meet up before going out is **La Salsa,** which serves fine cocktails in a chic streetside overlook. 25 Nha Tho. ☏ **04/3828-9052.** Nha Tho (Church St.) extends from Vietnam's largest Catholic cathedral, St. Joseph's, on the west side of Hoan Kiem Lake.

Press Club   Don't be put off by the seeming exclusivity of this old-boys' club; nothing could be further from the truth. Press Club is a cozy bar and upscale eatery, but with all kinds of affordable snacks and dishes. Both the snazzy bar area and laid-back patio seating area are anything but stuffy. You'll find regular events and live music here, and it's a good place to connect with "connected" expats to find out what's going on in town. The first Friday of every month, the terrace buzzes with some big event, be it a huge outdoor barbecue or an all-out dance party. Don't miss it if you're in town. Open daily 11am to 3pm and 5pm till late. 59A Ly Thai To. ☏ **04/3934-0888.**

Ta Hien Street   It's just a narrow alley in the Old Quarter, but it's lined with a clutch of bars that spring to life after dark. Just take a walk down and stick your nose in anywhere to see what's happening. A few that are often worth checking out are **Cheeky Quarter** (at number 1; ☏ **09/0403-2829**), **Funky Buddha** (at number 2; ☏ **04/3292-7614**), and **Mao's Red Lounge** (at number 7; ☏ **04/3926-3104**).

Sunset Bar ★ Overlooking tranquil West Lake, Sunset Bar is an absolute gem. Rattan couches and cozy daybeds run the circumference of the bar's fabulous wooden deck. It's a popular hangout with hip locals and expats; just don't forget your insect repellant. Open daily 4:30pm to midnight. 1A Nghi Tam St. ℂ **04/6270-8888.**

DAY TRIPS FROM HANOI

Hanoi is a good base for longer explorations of the north and northeast. **Halong Bay** is by far the most popular day trip, or overnight trip, for visitors to Vietnam's capital, and detailed information about boat trips there and to nearby **Cat Ba Island** can be found in chapter 8. For other destinations farther afield, see chapters 7 and 9. Below are the most convenient trips from Hanoi.

Cruise the Red River

Ask the friendly folks at **Buffalo Tours** (94 Ma May; ℂ **04/3828-0702;** www. buffalotours.com) about their popular *Jewel of the Delta,* a small but cozy river cruiser that takes you from Hanoi along the busy flood plain of this life-giving river. The Red River Delta is a very productive rice-growing region, and the riverside fields are lush with green. The day tour starts early, stopping to explore **But Thap Pagoda** by bicycle (double-check to make sure they have a bicycle for your height before leaving Hanoi), then on to various handicraft villages, and cycling to small off-the-beaten-path villages connected by narrow paddy dikes. On board the boat, enjoy a nice lunch and some time to rest before hitting the village of **Bat Trang,** an important commercial hub as early as the 15th century, and now a center for the production of fine pottery. You'll have plenty of time to rest and enjoy the sun on the boat's spacious sun deck before returning to Hanoi in the late afternoon.

Perfume Pagoda

Just 60km (37 miles) south of Hanoi is this stunning area of limestone peaks surrounding a lowland waterway through the rice fields. Visitors in groups of seven foreigners and seemingly limitless Vietnamese board low rowboats for a short river ride to the temple area. The river trip is a highlight, a relaxing ride where you can take it all in and snap photos to your heart's content, or even get a chance to try the funky forward stroke of the typical Vietnamese small boat. The area looks a lot like the dynamic Tam Coc grottoes near Ninh Binh; if you've been there, don't bother with the Perfume Pagoda—Tam Coc is more beautiful.

The best part about visiting the Perfume Pagoda is the hearty climb, some 30 to 60 minutes of scrambling up to the stadium-size mouth of the mountain's holy cave (there's a cable car alternative if you feel lazy). The site is home to a number of important temples and shrines, and the area is worth a wander. Tours leave early in the morning for the 2-hour drive to My Duc.

Ninh Binh Area

Just a few hours south and east of Hanoi, you'll find the town of Ninh Binh—a good home base for some interesting day trips (you might make it an overnight). But the town isn't much, and touring the sights is really best done on good organized tours based out of Hanoi. For detailed information, check out chapter 9.

The area is home to **Cuc Phuong National Park,** the nation's first park (from 1964) and a vast expanse of wilderness. The park also supports an important primate rescue and reintroduction program. Ninh Binh's popular **Tam Coc (The Three Grottoes),** with its towering limestone karst towers, is considered the "Halong Bay of the Rice Fields." Visitors can see the sight from small local rowboats. **Hoa Lu,** the ancient capital area, connects with Tam Coc via a scenic little back road; the temples themselves are 17th-century re-creations of the originals but are quite lavishly decorated. **Ken Ga** is another scenic area, but for its busy riverside market that's very much unlike Tam Coc's peaceful charm. Just south of Ninh Binh Town is **Phat Diem,** once home to a large population of French missionaries. The town's famous cathedral is a highlight.

THE NORTHERN HIGHLANDS

The far north is where the rubber meets the road for hard-core adventure junkies. If you were born to be wild, take your own Minsk motorbike; if you weren't, go with a jeep and driver.

This chapter is broken into four sections: **Lao Cai, Sapa,** the **Northwest Highlands,** which includes the Dien Bien Phu Loop; and the **North-Central Highlands,** a shorter route including Ba Be Park and the small towns of Cao Bang and Lang Son.

In addition to breathtaking landscapes of the **Tonkinese Alps** and off-the-map destinations such as **Dien Bien Phu,** one of the main attractions in the region is the **villages of the ethnic minority hilltribes.** The weather is much cooler here than in Vietnam's often sultry lowlands and coastal plains, so bring some layers, and be ready for some good adventures.

The region's most accessible and popular choice for luxury travelers, backpackers, and tour groups, **Sapa** can be reached by overnight train from Hanoi. With a range of good accommodations and dining, Sapa is a good base for trekking to hilltribe villages or as the first or last destination on a rugged highland adventure.

Below I've outlined the long loop round the northwest starting in Hanoi and including the towns of **Hoa Binh, Mai Chau, Son La, Dien Bien Phu** (where the French forces in Indochina fell), and **Muong Lay** before crossing the high pass to **Sapa.** The trip is a real hoot and takes from 4 days to 1 week of adventurous road travel along some treacherous tracks through beautiful mountain scenery in the heart of the Tonkinese Alps. A trip around this loop is a great chance to experience Vietnam "off the track" and have contact with ethnic hilltribe culture.

Another route included in this chapter leaves Hanoi and heads directly north via the town of **Thai Nguyen** to the **Ba Be Lake National Park,** then to the riverside town of **Cao Bang,** where rural day trips take you to a stunning waterfall and to hilltribe markets, and finally to **Lang Son,** a provincial outpost, before returning to Hanoi. Different hilltribe groups call this region home, and weekend markets abound.

LAO CAI

300km (186 miles) NW of Hanoi

The access town for visitors to Sapa and Bac Ha, Lao Cai is really just a stopover, a place to catch the bus to the hills or to catch the train back to

Hanoi. You won't find much to see or do, but you should know a few things in case you get stuck here for a while. The **train station** is in the heart of the town, and you can buy onward tickets here easily, though it's best to book sleeper berths a day in advance.

A few hotels are also near the station, if you miss your train or want to get a jump on travel to Bac Ha from Sapa for the weekend market there. Your best bet is the **Thien Hai** (306 Khanh Yen St.; ✆ 020/383-3666), immediately on your left as you exit the station. It's not exactly luxurious, but the carpeted rooms are neat and tidy. For dining and information, the best place to visit is the family run **Hai Nhi Restaurant** (337 Nguyen Hue St.; ✆ **020/383-5901**), which is right next door to the Thien Hai Hotel. This is the town's traveler central, where shuttle buses drop off groups of tourists waiting to board the night trains back to Hanoi. If you're passing through, stop in for a good meal; the friendly proprietor and his family can help out with any detail (they helped me empty the gas out of my motorbike, and even took me to their house for dinner).

Lao Cai is also a gateway to China, and many travelers make this their last stop before going on to the Middle Kingdom. *Important note:* You must have a **prearranged visa** for China before crossing at the checkpoint. (For more about obtaining visas, see "Visas," under "Entry Requirements," in chapter 15.) From Lao Cai, it's a short walk or ride on a motorbike taxi to the border area and on to China. Once across the border in China, you can catch an onward train or bus into the heart of the country (but that's another story for another guidebook).

SAPA

337km (209 miles) NW of Hanoi; 37km (23 miles) E of Lao Cai

Sapa is a small market town that has been a gathering spot for many local hilltribes for nearly 200 years. Hmong and Dao people, among others, still come here to conduct trade and socialize. They also used to attend an ephemeral **"love market,"** where young men and women would choose one another for marriage, but they are understandably shy about courting under the gaze of camera-toting tourists, so you'll have to hunt elsewhere to find such rituals nowadays. But seeing this behavior as early as 1860, French missionaries said *"Mon Dieu!"* and set up camp to save souls; their stone church still stands sentinel at the center of town. Sapa, with its mercifully cool climate, became a vacation escape for French colonists, complete with rail connection, upscale hotels, and a tourist bureau as early as 1917. The outpost was retaken by the Vietnamese in 1950, attacked and destroyed later by the French, and left in ruin, only briefly occupied by Chinese troops in 1979. The town reopened for tourism in the 1990s and has been developing at a headlong pace since then.

Now connected via Lao Cai by luxury train with Hanoi, Sapa boasts good accommodations and is a great starting point for trekking and eco-tours. Even a 1- or 2-day trip, bracketed by overnight train journeys from Hanoi, will give you a unique glimpse of local hilltribe culture. Trek out to nearby villages with a guide (it's actually illegal to trek without a licensed guide, and you may find yourself a very unwelcome guest in a village that does not accept tourists), or meet with the many hilltribe people who come to town to sell their wares.

The Tonkinese Alps are a feast for the eyes; hills striated by terraced rice farms in vast, green valleys are like a stairway up to **Mount Fansipan,** which is Vietnam's tallest mountain, at 3,143m (10,309 ft.). Climbing Fansipan is a multiday trip, requiring

hilltribes IN NORTHERN VIETNAM

Population estimates of the diverse groups of ethnic minorities in the far north of Vietnam range widely, mainly because these independent and often elusive minority groups defy central authority, living autonomously in rural areas beyond reach of the census takers' clipboards. Including disparate groups in the Central Highlands (see chapter 10), the current estimate is around nine million, or about 10% of Vietnam's population.

Vietnam's hilltribe ethnic minority groups originally came from Tibet and near Burma, and arrived in Vietnam via China, though a few groups in the Central Highlands are of ancient Indonesian descent. Some hilltribe groups have been in Vietnam for thousands of years, but others migrated as recently as 100 years ago or as a result of Chinese political pressure in the last 50 years.

Under the rule of the 19th-century Nguyen dynasty, the majority ethnic Vietnamese were given districts, and in exchange for paying some obeisance to the king, hilltribe groups were given near autonomy. Since the fight for independence in 1955, the Hanoi government has sought fruitlessly to portray its ethnic groups as a vanguard of the ongoing agrarian revolution, but in truth hilltribe groups have always been separate. Vietnam's ethnic minorities played a major role as converts and allies of the French missionaries and colonialists, and later as foot soldiers for the American military and CIA. Knowing no boundaries (even to this day), these groups could fight in Vietnam and then flee to safety behind the mountainous Laos border. Both the United States and the Viet Cong fought for the loyalty of these groups. Sadly, many of the hilltribesmen who cooperated with the Americans, particularly the Hmong, were left high and dry after the hasty American pullout, and some Hmong refugees still fight for survival in the border areas in nearby Laos.

Assimilation with ethnic Vietnamese has brought improvements such as the availability of electricity, Western-style medicine, and education—but it has come at the expense of traditional identity. Tourism, too, is exacting a strong cultural toll; the young Hmong souvenir sellers in Sapa who talk with tourists on a daily basis are getting a new worldview, and one day the valley might not look big enough to them. Among some groups, only the women wear traditional clothing—men dress in the same fashions as the majority of lowlanders.

The groups of the far northwest have more in common than anything, and many do business together and intermarry (particularly the Hmong and the Dao [Zao]). Most hilltribe groups farm small hillside slash-and-burn plots and wet rice terraces in the valleys and tend domestic animals. Groups use **central marketplaces** (such as the famed markets of Sapa and Bac Ha) not just as opportunities for commerce, but for forming friendships and alliances, courting, and building a shared culture. Be sure to catch a market day in the north. Each group has a distinct **language.** Some groups fight to keep alive ancient traditions of transcribing their native phonemes into Chinese characters, but the practice is dying out in favor of learning Vietnamese and, increasingly, English.

Northwestern hilltribe people are mostly **animist,** except for the groups that fell under the sway of French missionaries. Hilltribe religion honors the natural world by building small shrines and carving totems. *Important note:* When out in the country, **do not photograph** or touch any carved bamboo totems and sculptures, especially near village gates, and always ask before taking someone's portrait.

A first visit to this region excites a certain awe in travelers, and photo-clicking tourists usually flip at the seeming exoticism of ethnic minority folks, especially in and around Sapa. It's important to remember that these are people, not circus sideshow acts. Do not pay anyone to take his or her photo. Do not give gifts. Should you find something interesting, buy souvenirs at a fair price. Go with a good guide who can make introductions and explain the subtle differences in these distinct cultures. Below is a short breakdown:

Dao (Zao) Mostly in the regions around Sapa and Lao Cai, Dao people are notable for their elaborate dress, including the massive red headdresses and silver jewelry worn by women.

Hmong The Hmong came from China some 500 years ago, and many settled in the area around Sapa. On a short visit to the region, if visiting just the hill town of Sapa, for example, you're most likely to run into Black Hmong folks, distinguished by their indigo-dyed clothing hung with elaborate embroidery, copious silver jewelry, and high headdresses for women (Hmong men commonly wear Western clothes). Many Hmong fought alongside American and South Vietnamese troops during the war, and there are large Hmong communities—those who escaped—in parts of the United States. Hmong practice wet rice cultivation where possible, usually just one crop per year, and slash-and-burn elsewhere. The most savvy of hilltribe businessmen, Black Hmong people lead the pack in selling trinkets and souvenirs to tourists—the friendly English speakers who sidle up to your table in Sapa are most likely Black Hmong.

Nung Populous along the Ba Be-to–Cao Bang route, Nung people have much in common with their Tay neighbors, practicing wet rice cultivation and growing vegetables and other crops with the aid of water-wheel irrigation (some of these wheels are quite dynamic). Nung live in mud huts instead of stilt houses and are Buddhists.

Tay Similar to Kinh people, Vietnam's ethnic majority, with an estimate of more than one million people, Tay live in the most prime turf: the fertile lowland areas of the far north (Tay were some of the earliest settlers in the region). Successful wet rice cultivators and growers of cinnamon and tobacco, Tay people are much like ethnic Vietnamese, practicing the standard mix of Buddhism and Confucianism, and enjoying the benefits of progress such as improved irrigation and even some luxury items such as motorbikes. Few Tay men still wear their characteristic indigo-dyed pajamalike clothes, although Tay women commonly wear the traditional headscarf and silver jewelry. Tay villages are getting wealthier, with concrete and brick structures displacing the traditional wood stilt houses. The Tay have their own written language and strong literary traditions. **Muong** people are much like the Tay people.

Thai Totaling more than 60 million people in Southeast Asia, mostly in Thailand and nearby Laos, the Thai ethnic group in Vietnam is second only to the Tay in population (also at an estimate of more than one million people) and can be divided into two distinct subgroups: the Black Thai and the White Thai. The distinction is nominal apart from minor variations in dress. The Black Thai are characteristically all in black with colorful headdresses, while the White Thai have small white swatches hanging from their belts. Thai houses are still mostly made of wood, and Thai groups practice both wet rice cultivation in the lowlands and slash-and-burn in the highlands. Black Thai are commonly seen around Son La and Dien Bien Phu, while White Thai populations are largest in and around Mai Chau.

If you can, time your trip to Sapa right before or during rice harvesting (Sept–Nov). Rice terraces are planted at intervals, allowing farmers to reap the fields over a period of several months. During the fall season, the valley will be painted various shades of green. The colors signal to farmers when a field is ready to be harvested. Along with the vibrant green colors, the valley will be dotted with bright colors of red or indigo, as many female farmers still wear their traditional ethnic minority clothing while working the land.

a guide and gear—best arranged through one of the tour operators listed, and only for the hearty. *Note:* Bring a few layers; it can get quite chilly here, especially in the winter months.

Sapa has gotten busier year by year, and concerns are coming from Hanoi that the growth in tourism is unsustainable and does not benefit local people, but instead lines the pockets of slick financiers. In response, every hotel in town seems to have jumped on the bandwagon of working to preserve local culture rather than to make money. You can do your part by educating yourself about some hilltribe traditions—be very cautious around any animistic totems, ask before taking photos, be careful where your money goes, and try not to encourage a culture of begging.

Getting There

BY TRAIN   Don't miss a chance to ride **Victoria's Express** train from Hanoi to Lao Cai (from there, it is a 1½-hr. ride to Sapa), though you'll need to book a room at the hotel as well. With wood-paneled luxury sleeping cars and a restaurant billed as the finest dining between Hanoi and Sapa, this is an exciting option. Trains now run daily, except for Saturday, when cars are closed for maintenance and service. A four-course meal is offered aboard their dining cars (available on a rotational basis) for an additional $25. Menus are designed by Victoria Sapa Hotel's resident executive chef, and a la carte options are also available. The train's soft duvets, fluffy pillows, and hand-knit bags containing towel, toothbrush, and bottled water make the deflated pillows and thin comforters of the standard tourist trains look second-rate indeed. Round-trip prices range from $115 to $290. *Note:* If you want one of the train's few two-berth sleepers, book at least 6 months in advance. Contact Victoria Sapa (② 020/387-1522; www.victoriahotels-asia.com) for details and reservations.

A number of standard and tourist trains also make the overnight run from Hanoi. You can make arrangements with any travel agent for a small fee, or do it yourself at the Hanoi Railway Station (where the western edge of Hoan Kiem district meets Dong Da district at 120 Le Duan; ② 04/3942-3949). Prices range from 290,000 VND for a hard sleeper in a six-bed berth with air-conditioning to 380,000 VND for a soft sleeper in a two-bed berth with air-conditioning. **Tulico Trains** (② 098/815-8565) is another good bet, just one notch above the regular sleeper cars. All cars have four-sleeper berths in a pretty cramped space. If you like your privacy, buy yourself your own private car (and some breathing room) by purchasing all four beds and using only two of them.

Onward transport to Sapa leaves regularly from just outside the station. When the train arrives from Hanoi in the morning, you have your pick of transport, and friendly touts will tug and pull you to their rickety shuttle buses. The 1½-hour trip costs just

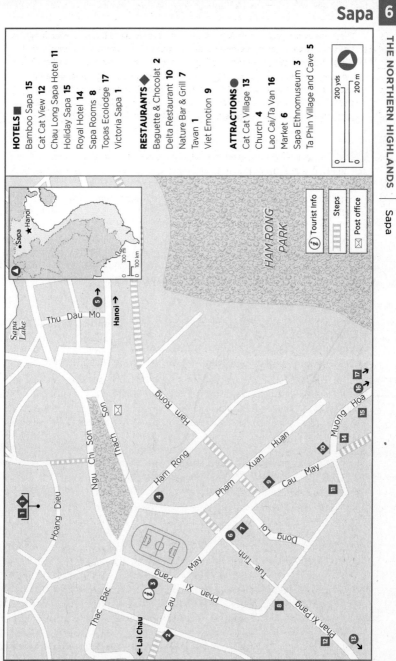

HOTELS ■
Bamboo Sapa **15**
Cat Cat View **12**
Chau Long Sapa Hotel **11**
Holiday Sapa **15**
Royal Hotel **14**
Sapa Rooms **8**
Topas Ecolodge **17**
Victoria Sapa **1**

RESTAURANTS ◆
Baguette & Chocolat **2**
Delta Restaurant **10**
Nature Bar & Grill **7**
Tavan **1**
Viet Emotion **9**

ATTRACTIONS ●
Cat Cat Village **13**
Church **4**
Lao Cai/Ta Van **16**
Market **6**
Sapa Ethnomuseum **3**
Ta Phin Village and Cave **5**

0 ──── 200 yds
0 ──── 200 m

ⓘ Tourist Info
▥ Steps
✉ Post office

HAM RONG PARK

Sapa Lake

Thu Dau Mo

Hanoi →

← Lai Chau

← Hanoi

50,000 VND. The road is cut into the hillside and is bumpy and windy, but the views of the terraced rice farms of the valley are beautiful as you ascend (ride on the left side).

Note: All trains to Lao Cai leave from the **Hanoi Railway Station** at 120 Le Duan St., which is often confused with Hanoi's other station. Be sure to show any taxi driver the address.

BY BUS Hanoi's tourist cafes all run frequent buses to Sapa for around 300,000 VND one-way. Some include Sapa as a stop on a seat-in-coach tour around the Dien Bien Phu loop (usually a 4- or 5-day adventure stopping in Mai Chau, Son La, Dien Bien Phu, Muong Lay, and Sapa before returning to Hanoi). The train is, however, the best option if just connecting from Hanoi.

BY CAR Any tourist cafe or travel agent in Hanoi can arrange trips by private jeep or a combo jeep-and-train tour. Apart from Sapa, the vast tracts of the north are best visited through a tour company. **Ann Tourist, Buffalo Tours,** and **Handspan** all offer comprehensive itineraries. Especially for areas off the beaten track, avoid the temptation to book budget tours with the tourist cafes. In addition to the following section, see "Visitor Information & Tours" in chapter 6 for more information and options.

Visitor Information & Tours

For tours and trekking in the region, the Danish outfit **Topas Adventure Travel** (24 Muong Hoa, Sapa; ✆ 020/387-2404; fax 020/387-1405; www.topasecolodge.com), with offices worldwide and experienced guides, is one of your best options (with Handspan being your other best choice). Office managers are usually tour leaders with regional experience who have been dispatched from Denmark and have worked with Topas for several years. Whether it's a day trek to nearby villages, an extended tour with homestays in villages, or the 5-day push to the top of Fansipan, these guys cover it.

Handspan—a large eco-tour outfit based in Hanoi with a good branch office overlooking the valley—is the most consistent choice for arranging day treks and transport. Find them in the Chau Long Hotel at 24 Dong Loi (✆ 020/387-2110; www.handspan.com).

Small budget-trekking offices line busy Cau May Street in Sapa, and you have your pick of guides and guided tours at budget prices. Just about anyone can hook you up with a Minsk motorbike for a 1-day rental or connect you with a guide. One of long standing and with a good reputation is **Dan Trung Auberge** (7 Muong Hoa St.; ✆ 020/387-1243). Francophones mostly, there is also a good contingent of English speakers, and they can arrange the standard itineraries at midrange prices from their busy little guesthouse, restaurant, and tour center (long a Sapa fixture).

New is the **Tourist Information Center** (2 Phan Xi Pang, in the center of town; ✆ 020/387-1975; fax 020/387-1976), which can arrange a guide ($25) for 1-day treks. And you'll support local villagers by booking through this center: Guides are local ethnic-minority members, few of whom speak English, but all of whom can take you on the classic day treks around the valley. The agency supports sustainable tourism in the valley and works with large international relief agencies to minimize the impact of tourists on the surrounding hilltribe cultures and customs.

BANKS & COMMUNICATION There's a post office on Cau May Street (✆ 020/382-1206), but most hotels can send postcards and letters and have stamps for sale. Just about every hotel provides free high-speed Internet and Wi-Fi. The more expensive hotels provide exchange service for traveler's checks and even credit card cash advances. There is a local **bank** on Cau May where you can cash traveler's checks for the same 2% fee as at your hotel. There are two reliable ATMs in town, one in front of the Royal Hotel and another one 500m (1,640 ft.) north of the hotel on Cau May Street.

Where to Stay
EXPENSIVE

Topas Ecolodge ★ For people who really want to get away from it all, Topas Ecolodge offers a clean break from TVs, telephones, and all the hustle and bustle of modern life. The lodge is made up of 25 individual bungalows encircling a hilltop about a 45-minute drive from Sapa. The silence and breathtaking mountain and valley views are unrivaled. The lodge bills itself as an eco-tourism experience; heating and light are provided by solar panels placed behind each bungalow, and it uses a wastewater facility that ensures no or minimal pollution of the local area. Stone paths snake out from the main building (paved with stones from local stonemasons), and picturesque greenery with bright blue hydrangeas marks the way to each bungalow. Large windows in each room let in plenty of sunlight, and the design is a simple affair of wicker furniture, red-tile flooring, and whitewashed stone-cut walls. Rates include breakfast, and unless you're out for the day, you'll be eating a set lunch ($12) and dinner ($17) at the resort as well.

Located 18km (11 miles) from Sapa town. Shuttles to the lodge depart from Topas Adventure Travel's office, at 24 Muong Hoa, Sapa, Lao Cai Province. www.topasecolodge.com. ✆ **020/387-2404.** Fax 020/387-1405. 25 units. $99–$125 double (including train to Sapa and SUV transport to and from resort). AE, MC, V. **Amenities:** Restaurant; Wi-Fi in main building. *In room:* Fridge, no phone.

Victoria Sapa ★ ☺ This is Sapa town's crème de la crème. Situated around a cozy courtyard, all rooms have balconies with wood-spindled railings and, inside, deep-toned wood floors offset by saturated wall colors, cane and fine wooden finish work, and local weavings and art. If you're here with the kids, family rooms are huge, with up to six beds (they can be rearranged), and are a great option. For a luxe local encounter, the hotel can arrange an overnight Victoria-style homestay package (complete with the hotel's housekeeping services, mattresses, slippers, and a morning croissant) in nearby Muong Hum village. If you want rooms with a view, head to Topas Ecolodge (see above) or the Hmong Mountain Retreat (see below); new budget hotels and ongoing town construction have blocked the once-clear view to Mount Fansipan.

At the top of the hill overlooking town, Sapa district, Lao Cai Province. www.victoriahotels-asia.com. ✆ **020/3871-522.** Fax 020/3871-539. 77 units. $195–$205 double; $295 suite (promotional rates available). AE, DC, MC, V. **Amenities:** Restaurant; bar; children's playroom; fitness center; indoor heated pool; sauna; smoke-free rooms; spa; tennis court. *In room:* Satellite TV, DVD (in suites), fridge, hair dryer, minibar, movie library, Wi-Fi.

MODERATE

Bamboo Sapa This large concrete block suspended over the valley near the town center is a decent midrange choice, though a bit overpriced. Rooms are clean and large, and the royal-blue trim is a nice change from the dingy pink at nearby Holiday Sapa. Most have balconies (sadly, too small to fit chairs), and all are oriented to the valley view. Bathrooms contain showers and are large and clean; mattresses are sturdy, hard foam; the staff is quite friendly; and the hotel has a good in-house tour operator (**Sapa Trekking Tour**) that can plan any trip. There is an open-air restaurant under the lobby, and they hold frequent, fun cultural dance shows.

18 Muong Hoa St. www.sapatravel.com. ℂ **020/387-1076.** Fax 020/387-1945. 45 units. From $75 double; $215 suite. MC, V. **Amenities:** Restaurant; bar; motorbikes. *In room:* TV, fridge, Wi-Fi.

Chau Long Sapa Hotel ★   A tour-group favorite, the old wing of the Chau Long has the look of an old hilltop castle in Europe, but that's just the facade. Down a quaint alley near the main road, the hotel consists of two buildings, with the new one being the best choice for facilities and views. Rooms are cleanly crafted in dark wood with small, tidy bathrooms. Most in the new building have balconies with good views, but many of those in the old building do not, so be sure to ask to see the room before checking in. The friendly staff will bend over backward to make your stay fun. Be sure to say hello to their dog, whose fur has been carefully shaved, leaving a mane that is dyed bright orange: the techno-colored lion-dog of Sapa.

24 Dong Loi. www.chaulonghotel.com. ℂ **020/387-1245.** Fax 020/387-1844. 89 units. $45–$120 double; $150 suite. MC, V. **Amenities:** Restaurant; bar; bike and motorbike rental; Internet; pool; relaxing room for early arrivals; room service. *In room:* Satellite TV, fridge, hair dryer.

Holiday Sapa   Most rooms here are clean and spacious, though you should avoid the standard rooms, which are tiny and have no view. The best deal is the corner room on the sixth floor (602), which is spacious, has a fantastic view, and features a gigantic corner balcony fitted with a cozy wooden bench. The only drawback is the bathroom, which is the all-in-one kind with no separate tub or shower cubicle. Deluxe rooms and up have separate tubs. Staff here is very friendly and speaks good English.

16 Muong Hoa St. www.holidaysapa.com. ℂ **020/387-3874.** Fax 020/387-2788. 45 units. $35–$70 double; $100 suite. AE, MC, V. **Amenities:** Restaurant; babysitting; gym; pool; room service; Wi-Fi. *In room:* TV, fridge, hair dryer, minibar.

Sapa Rooms ★★   This place's self-description as a boutique hotel is a bit generous, but it definitely wins for being the most contemporary and stylish option in town. Rooms are a good size, with plush, brightly colored rugs thrown over marble floors, as well as colonial-era wood furniture. Bathrooms are luxurious for this price, with a stylish shower lined with wooden floors. Rooms also come with dehumidifiers, a major plus in a place as damp as Sapa. The ground-floor restaurant is a Thai-inspired area with dark-colored walls and cozy seats. They also operate the **Hmong Mountain Retreat,** located in an idyllic spot 6km (3¾ miles) out of town, which has a handful of simple bamboo and thatch cottages and hosts cookery classes. See their website for more details.

18 Phan Xi Pang. www.saparooms.com. ℂ **020/650-5228.** Fax 020/626-4020. 6 units. From $57 double; $75 suite. MC, V. **Amenities:** Restaurant; bar; bike and motorbike rentals; Internet; room service. *In room:* TV, hair dryer, Wi-Fi.

INEXPENSIVE

Cat Cat View ★   The view—that's what it's all about here. At this popular guesthouse, buildings are stacked like an unlikely pile of children's blocks against a steeply sloping hill, and rooms range from those that are tiny and spartan to a two-room apartment that is quite luxurious. It's a bit of a hike up a long flight of steps, past the more eccentric rooms to the large guesthouse block and popular restaurant at the top of the hill (best views and comfort). Cheaper rooms are concrete and plain, a backpacker standard, but most have big windows and balconies. You're sure to meet other travelers who'll be saying, "Did you check out the view from the top?" Stop by for a coffee even if you don't stay.

46 Phan Xi Pang. (at the base of the town on the way down to Cat Cat Village). www.catcathotel.com. ℭ **020/387-1601.** Fax 020/387-1133. 40 units. $30–$60 double; $160 apt. MC, V. **Amenities:** Restaurant; bar; Internet. *In room:* TV, fireplace (some), Wi-Fi (some).

Royal Hotel It's backpacker central at this picturesque five-story tower in the heart of town, the very terminus of central Cau May Street. With just the right blend of comfort and affordability, this hotel is a real budget-traveler favorite. If you aren't a real budget traveler, you might be a bit turned off by the sparse tile-and-concrete decor, busy hallways, and hit-or-miss service. The hotel's Friendly Café is aptly named: Waitstaff here seem to be chosen for their desire (read: not ability) to speak English, and the food is basic, affordable traveler fare (fried rice, fried noodles, and beer). Every room has a balcony, and electric blankets are provided, too.

54B Cau May St. www.royalsapahotel.com. ℭ **020/387-1313.** Fax 020/387-1788. 29 units. $15–$30 double. No credit cards. **Amenities:** Restaurant; bar; Internet. *In room:* TV, fridge, Wi-Fi.

Where to Eat

Baguette and Chocolat ★ FRENCH   The folks from **Hoa Sua** (p. 81), a popular restaurant designed as a training center for disadvantaged youth, have done an excellent job with this cozy cafe. Open sandwiches, pizzas, salads, and omelets top a fine menu heavy on good French cuisine. Seating is in a cool "no shoe" area with rattan couches and white pillows (be sure to tidy up if coming from a day in the hills), or you can sit outside. The sandwiches here are okay, but accompanying french fries are excellent. What really attracts folks to this little cafe are the pastries and good, strong coffee; you won't find espresso and cappuccino like this elsewhere in town. They serve good, inexpensive breakfasts: a pastry and coffee costs only 48,000 VND, and a European breakfast costs 80,000 VND. The friendly folks at Baguette and Chocolat can also arrange picnic lunches that you can take while trekking, even for large groups if you contact them in advance.

Thac Bac St., near the hilltop terminus of central Cau May St. ℭ **020/387-1766.** www.hoasuaschool. com. Main courses 60,000 VND–120,000 VND. No credit cards. Daily 7am–9pm.

Delta Restaurant ★ ITALIAN   Come here for the post-trek or post-long-haul-to-Sapa pizza. Right in the center of town on the corner across from the Royal Hotel, this place has wide glass doors that they can close on windy or foggy nights. Upstairs is a chic little wine bar with booths: cozy and romantic. The menu features the likes of gazpacho, bruschetta, good fresh salads, pasta, lasagna, ravioli, Australian steaks, and chicken dishes, but the pizza reigns supreme. Thin crust topped with light and fresh ingredients and real cheese. The Cappriciosa pizza I ordered was topped with tomato, eggplant, mushroom, olive oil, and gobs of good mozzarella. Prices are high for this little backpacker town, but that just keeps the backpackers out.

33 Cau May St. (just cater-cornered to the Royal Hotel). ℭ **020/387-1799.** Main courses $6–$14. MC, V. Daily 7:30am–10pm.

Nature Bar & Grill ★★ VIETNAMESE   This is the best restaurant on Cau May Street. The specialty here is fresh, tasty Vietnamese dishes served piping hot on stone plates. The grilled beef is a good bet, as is the deer, if you like gamier meat. Vietnamese staples, such as fried rice, *pho,* and spring rolls, round out the menu. The ambience is a cross between a country lodge and a backpacker haunt, with a giant brick fireplace in one corner and Bob Marley tunes piped in over the speakers.

24 Cau May St. ℭ **020/387-2094.** www.naturebarandgrill.com. Main courses 60,000 VND–115,000 VND. AE, MC, V. Daily 7am–10pm.

Tavan ♨ FRENCH/VIETNAMESE   The most elegant dining in the Tonkinese Alps comes with high prices and average food. You are essentially paying New York prices for small portions of underwhelming fare. The menu is rich with imports: everything from lamb, to filet, to salmon steaks. There are Vietnamese specials on an evolving menu, but I actually prefer the local specialties at Nature Bar & Grill. The pastas are a good bet—homemade and filling. The dining room is dimly lit and romantic, done up with burgundy walls, rich wood floors, and local hangings surrounding a central fireplace. They do make a mean cocktail here, so indulge in predinner drinks.

At the Victoria Sapa Hotel. ✆ **020/387-1522.** Main courses $15–$45. AE, MC, V. Daily 6:30am–10pm.

Viet Emotion ★ 🎁 INTERNATIONAL/VIETNAMESE   This cozy, welcoming, bistro-style place on Cau May is the ideal spot to snuggle up on a cold morning or evening in Sapa. The menu covers every need, from hearty omelets to homemade soups, tasty tapas such as garlic prawns, and tempting mains including salmon with sticky rice. They have Wi-Fi, books, and games in case you want to settle in for a while.

27 Cau May St. ✆ **020/387-2559.** www.vietemotion.com. Main courses 130,000 VND–270,000 VND. MC, V. Daily 7am–10pm.

Attractions

Though most visitors spend their days out of town trekking, the town itself has a few points of interest. **Cau May Street,** the main drag, and the **central market area** (at the top of Cau May) are, on any given day, teeming with hilltribe folks in their spangled finest, putting on and practicing the hard sell with some great weaving, fine silver work, and interesting trinkets such as mouth harps and flutes. Especially on the weekend, it can be quite a scene. The small alleys and streets of the town are extremely wanderable, and a short walk in any direction offers great views. For a general introduction to the region, drop by the **Sapa Ethnomuseum,** located behind the Tourist Information Office at 2 Phan Xi Pang, where you can learn more about the ethnic minorities and the town's history. Admission is free, and it's open daily from 7:30 to 11:30am and 1:30 to 5pm.

Bac Ha Market ★★   Some 100km (62 miles) from Sapa, this is the most famous market in the region and more along the lines of what Sapa was once like. Here, various hilltribes, but most notably the Flower Hmong, converge every Sunday morning to conduct commerce. As a visitor, you're part of the trade here because folks are keen to sell you their wares, but this market isn't as much about the tourist buck (yet) as it is about small-time business and fellowship. Bring a camera. Sunday morning from dawn to late morning is prime time, but the market continues until about noon. Most visitors make the 3-hour drive from Sapa in the early morning.

Join a minibus tour from Sapa for around $20. Can also be arranged from nearby Lao Cai (contact Hanoi travel agents).

Cat Cat Village ★   At the base of the hill below the town of Sapa, this Hmong village is accessible by rough-paved road most of the way, and cement path for the rest. The small waterfall here is a good spot to kick back and rest—quite dynamic in rainy season. From there, follow the narrow cement walkway up a long set of steps until the path terminates in another part of Cat Cat Village. From there you can hop on a waiting motorbike taxi for the ride back up to Sapa (30,000 VND). The trip can be made in just a few hours and offers a unique glimpse of rural life. Some travelers walk the whole valley top to bottom and back—a good way to get your lungs up to speed for later treks in the valley.

Entrance fee (paid at the top of the hill) 20,000 VND. You can walk all the way down or hire a motorbike/car taxi to pick up and drop off.

Coc Ly Flower Market Also some 100km (62 miles) from Sapa, this is a lesser-known market than Bac Ha (see above), which means it attracts fewer tourists. It runs Tuesday mornings, when members of various minority groups sell flowers at the roadside. However, because it is about a third the size, it also attracts few locals and is a bit less varied and lively than Bac Ha. Tour operators in Bac Ha combine a visit to this market with a boat ride and an overnight in a homestay in a minority village for around $30 per person.

Ta Phin Village and Cave Okay, so this one is a bit canned. You'll be mobbed at the entrance to the village by young Dao women in their elaborate regalia, high red headdresses and all, selling weavings and other wares. The ladies will keep an eye on your motorbike or car for you and offer to take you on a guided tour "for free," with only the hope that you'll perhaps look at some of their items for sale at the end of the tour. The women of Ta Phin are nice enough—some speak English well and can provide some useful insight into Dao and Hmong culture—but the whole experience is a bit pushy. At the end of it, you're expected to drop a big wad of dough on some pretty pathetic-looking weavings. Not worth it. Best to just say "No, thank you" to offers of a village tour.

The cave at the apex of the town requires a guide with a lantern to lead you through, but one is rarely available. Bring your own flashlight to explore deep in the cave.

TREKKING & HIKING Hiking in Sapa's picturesque landscape and among Vietnam's traditional ethnic minorities is one of the main reasons visitors flock to this northern region. Convenient to the town center, the **Lao Cai–to–Ta Van** day trip from Sapa is a chance to traipse around the rice terraces and experience a bit of rural village life. Unfortunately, the convenience also means there are many tourists around. Visitors are often assaulted by (mostly Hmong) villagers trying to sell their handicrafts and wares, and many do not accept no for an answer. This is a tour to do only if you are pressed for time. Hire a car or motorbike for the 9km (5½-mile) road down the valley from Sapa to the Hmong village of Lao Cai (some folks even walk it); it's a nice ride in itself, with great views of the lush terraces. From there, just follow the valley for a few miles to the next town of Ta Van. Along the way, you'll walk through terraced rice fields and among some picturesque villages, and experience a bit of rural life. (Entrance fee is 20,000 VND. Drop-off at Lao Cai and later pickup at Ta Van is about $5 with a motorbike taxi and $30 for a jeep.)

As you **walk through different hilltribe villages (Hmong and Dao people),** it's helpful to have a guide to explain customs or practices to you and perhaps translate. Farther afield, I found hikes 2 to 3 hours **north of Sapa,** among the **Tay villages,** to be less traveled; the Tay people were more shy and respectful of passersby (that is, no trinket sellers following you doggedly for hours on end). You'll still be greeted with a hearty *"Hello! Allo!"* wherever you go, though.

Ask at your hotel front desk, or contact Topas Adventure Travel (p. 124) for longer, less touristy treks. It is in fact illegal to hike without a guide, and you may find yourself a very unwelcome visitor in a village that does not accept tourists. Besides, local guides are knowledgeable about levels of difficulty and which hikes are more secluded and less touristy.

Shopping

The streets of Sapa are lined with small, local boutiques, and more are setting up each day. But the real shopping and good bargains come from roving groups of ethnic hilltribe women, many just young girls, who are sure to find you—some are true polyglots and masters of the hard sell. The best boutique in town is **Indigo ★** (12 Duong Muong Hoa; ℭ **020/387-2568;** daily 7am–9pm), a store run by Tanh, a local Hmong minority, and her Japanese expat husband (they met and fell in love while he was visiting to look into the textile industry). Indigo offers simple, modern takes on traditional ethnic clothing. Most pieces are solid-colored cotton or linen, and dyed using natural vegetable dyes. Unlike many pieces sold at markets or by street sellers, Indigo's pieces are properly dyed to ensure colors won't run when thrown in the washing machine. The boutique is a fair trade company that orders fabric and various motifs from local villages, and employs local disadvantaged workers (deaf-mute graduates of the Hoa Sua school in Hanoi) to sew and embroider their clothing and wares. The Indigo line is also sold at the Victoria Sapa Hotel gift shop.

THE DIEN BIEN PHU LOOP

Tired of tourist trails? Here's a great opportunity to get off the track and into rugged terrain that is little affected by tourism or the world economy. In an area along the border of China and Laos, rugged roads traverse high mountain passes, cling to the side of steep mountains prone to landslide, and peer down over deep river gorges. The major thoroughfares are paved and in good condition in the dry season, but do keep an ear to the ground before setting out during or just after the summer rains (check in at **Highway 4,** a popular bar and meeting spot in Hanoi, for the most updated information; for the bar's location, see p. 81).

Travel in this region offers the best opportunity to meet and greet people of ethnic-minority hilltribe groups, from the timid White Thai to the gregarious Hmong. But remember that responsible tourism is crucial; our collective interaction with isolated ethnic minorities lays the groundwork for their future survival (or demise). Hire guides if you are going off into the boonies or out among ethnic groups. Your impact, especially if your travels take you to real rural parts, is important. (See the "Responsible Tourism" sidebar, p. 20.)

When Traveling in the Northern Highlands . . .

Bring cash. You can find local banks in each of these little towns to exchange U.S. greenbacks, but usually at a much less favorable rate. Apart from in Sapa and Lao Cai, there are few **ATMs** in the region. Just bring enough Vietnam dong to cover expenses (on your own, plan to bring about 500,000 VND, preferably in small bills). Even the smallest hamlet in Vietnam has good postal service, you can make calls via an international phone, and the Internet is accessible in the smallest town, but service tends to be slow, even in Sapa. **Medical services** are not up to par, even for Vietnam. You can fly yourself out of Dien Bien Phu if you're in real trouble, but you're more or less on your own out on the roads. Bring a good first-aid kit for incidental cuts and scrapes, and be sure to carry stomach medicine, bug spray, and sunscreen.

Give yourself **5 or 6 days** for the loop from **Hanoi to Sapa;** anything shorter means you'll spend all of your time on the road, with little respite or time to explore.

The best way to do this loop is by motorbike, as two wheels will take you to small villages and off the main road—places that are off-limits to a jeep. But jeeps are also a good—and certainly safer—option. A few good outfitters can arrange tours by motorbike, with or without guides, or jeep (see information on renting a Minsk below). All of the traveler cafes in Hanoi run trips up this way, but it's worth it to go with a midrange or high-quality tour provider (see Queen Travel, p. 58, or Buffalo Tours, p. 58); you'll get more individual attention, follow more-out-of-the-way routes, and enjoy unique itineraries with professional guides.

Between Hanoi & Mai Chau

The hardest part of the trip is getting out of Hanoi. From the city center, one-way streets actually abut one another and the traffic must disperse in either direction—it's very strange. The roads out of town going southwest, either Ton That Tung or Tay Son, are a sea of motorbikes; crossing traffic is heavy and unpredictable. If you're going more than 30kmph (19 mph), you're going too fast. At the farthest edge of the city, traffic thins out, and once you pass the Ho Chi Minh Trail Museum (p. 102) some 14km (8¾ miles) south and west on Route 6, you're in the clear. (The museum is a good rest stop after the long road of city traffic.) From here, you're in the boonies and the fun begins. You can drive up to 70kmph (43 mph), but about 50kmph (31 mph) is best.

Before you reach the town of **Hoa Binh,** you'll pass through an area of towering limestone peaks—a first taste of the dramatic landscapes in store on this ride. The town of Hoa Binh is not worth a stop—it's just a typical Vietnamese city of cement row houses and honking motorbikes—but it's the dropping-off point for trips on the large **Da River** (or *Song Da*) **Reservoir,** which powers the town's large hydroelectric plant. Past Hoa Binh, you'll enter the landscape typical to this region, with large hills cut by streams and lined with terrace rice farms.

Most stunning is the high pass you cross on the way to Mai Chau. The road is chiseled into the mountain's rock face, and the debris that resulted from the blasting forms a wide skirt at the foot of the mountain.

Mai Chau

150km (93 miles) W of Hanoi; 170km (105 miles) E of Son La

Mai Chau makes a good overnight after the shakedown cruise from Hanoi (about a 5-hr. ride). The town center is a rather dull strip of small shops and a few *pho* and *com* stands (noodle soup or rice), but there are two White Thai villages just outside of town where both solo travelers and group tours commonly stay. You can take short boat trips on the **Da River Reservoir** from the pier just near the turnoff road to Mai Chau (best arranged through a tour).

WHERE TO STAY

In addition to the recommendation below, the other option in town is to stay at one of the nearby **White Thai villages** of **Ban Lac** of **Pom Coong.** If you travel through this way on tour, you will most likely be spending the night at one of these local homestays, sleeping under a thatch roof on bamboo woven floors. Tourists have been staying here a while, and there are now more than 30 homestays in Ban Lac alone. All homestays have electric lights and Western-style toilets, and guests are

THE MINSK: A GUIDE TO RENTING & ENJOYING YOUR BIG HONKIN' SOVIET motorbike

So you want to really get out and see the far north on your own? Well, one way to do it is to get yourself a Minsk. Built in Minsk, Belarus, by the Motovelo corporation, these sturdy 100cc machines come in two different models: 1) the older **classic Minsk,** which is a model of Soviet-style "function, not form" design principles; and 2) the **sport Minsk,** which came around due to late Soviet innovations and the fall of the iron curtain, and is a higher-profile bike with better suspension, something like a standard motocross bike, but with the same engine as the classic Minsk.

Sure, you'll see lots of 100cc scooters out on these roads, but a Minsk is still your best bet for reliability, durability, and easy fixability, as they are well known, so most mechanics can help you with even major repairs. Hairpins and bailing wire often suffice as replacement parts, and even the smallest little country repair shop is staffed with someone who can tap apart the crank case and fix major problems. Stop on the most deserted stretch of mountain trek, and you'll be amazed when, after only a brief pause, you'll be greeted by Montagnards (who've been watching you the whole time), who come down out of the hills to diagnose and fix a sick Minsk with little more than their farming machetes. Locals appreciate your adventurous spirit (or call you crazy) for striking out on these old hunks of metal to explore their country. Once a security guard at a hotel gave my bike a full tune-up just for the love of the bike and to ensure I'd have a safe trip. And these bikes will make a mechanic out of you: The principles of the internal-combustion engine couldn't be clearer than if Fred Flintstone himself designed it.

Be sure to learn the phrase *xang fa dao* (sounds like "sang fa zow"), which means "gas with oil," and *nam fa jam,* which means "5%." Minsks are two-stroke, or two-cycle, motors (something like your lawn mower, weed whacker, or go-kart back home), and you need to mix 5% oil with the gas. In the countryside, folks at gas stations are very adept at this because they're used to dealing with Minsks and other two-stroke machines, but be careful in cities, where gas station attendants know only scooters. Be vigilant to ensure your bike gets the right mix of gas and oil, as not doing so is the easiest way to give yourself problems down the road. When filling up with gas, be sure to turn off the fuel line connecting to the engine, and help the attendant, who will either measure a cup of oil and then thin it out by adding gas directly to the cup, suspended over a funnel into your tank (and a few extra hands are appreciated for this little operation), or mix the oil and gas in a separate can. In either case, watch closely and see that the bike gets oil. When you start off, keep the fuel line closed and make some slow, swerving turns to mix the gas; then open the fuel line to the normal setting.

There are lots of kind strangers on the roads of the northeast, and relying on your Minsk and a bit of "trail magic" is certain to get you there.

There are two good **rental** agencies in Hanoi:

○ **Mr. Cuong's Motorbike Adventure** (1 Luong Ngoc Quyen St., on the east side of the Old Quarter near the city's major ring road; ✆ **04/3926-1534**) is the best place for straight-up rental. Cuong is a mechanic and keeps a large stable of Minsks in good condition. Each bike is nearly rebuilt after every rental. You'll pay the standard $7 per day, which includes a good helmet, but that's where service stops. Mr. Cuong's place is open daily from 8am to 6pm, and he's a very understanding man, cutting you little breaks, such as charging for a half-day if you bring it back early, and lending extras at no cost to you.

- **Mr. Hung's Vietnam Adventure Tour,** on the other hand, provides motorbike rentals as well as comprehensive guide services. For just $30 per day, you can hire a bike and an accompanying guide with his own bike. Choose from a number of well-planned routes around the north, enjoying ease of navigation and easier connection to locals. If you're considering going it alone, some folks have reported that Hung's bikes aren't quite as well maintained as those at Cuong's (see above), but if you're looking for more of a tour, Mr. Hung's is the place to start. Find him at his small storefront travel agency just north of Hoan Kiem Lake at 5A Dinh Liet St. (© **04/3926-0938**), and someone there can take you to his repair shop on the city ring road at 162 Tran Quang Khai St. (just around the corner from Mr. Cuong's).

Most shops ask that you pay in advance and sign a contract that gives you complete responsibility (to the tune of $350–$500, depending on the bike) for the bike's well-being. Demand a lock and use it when leaving the bike for long intervals (most Minsks do not have key ignitions and therefore are easily started by anyone).

Safety   Demand a helmet and wear it; go slow; and honk to alert other vehicles when passing. Stay alert! Vietnamese roads are chaotic, and something or somebody is always leaping out onto the roadway or veering into your lane. The hardest part about any trip in the north is navigating Hanoi's crazy traffic and finding your way out of the city; in fact, both Mr. Hung and Mr. Cuong are given to leading their more inexperienced clients out of the city center to more sane open roads.

What to Bring   In the little metal storage cases on the side of the bike (for older models) or under the seat, pack an extra tube, a patch kit, a few spark plugs, a spark-plug wrench, and a crescent wrench; most rental shops will provide it all, but be sure to ask. Minsks leak oil—in fact, just getting close to the bike usually means you get a few smudges on you—so bring two sets of clothes: one grungy pair of long pants, T-shirt, and light jacket that you won't mind getting covered in oil and road splatter during the day, as well as a clean set of dry clothes, including something warm, such as a sweatshirt or fleece, for those chilly highland nights. Minsks can be outfitted with handy saddlebags, or else you can bungee your gear onto the rack at the back of the bike. I take everything I want to keep dry, wrap it in plastic, and tuck it into the bottom of the saddlebag or bungee it tight to the back of the bike. I then keep a light day pack of daily-use items (camera, journal, wallet, and so on) on my back or at the top of the saddlebags. A "dry bag" is good to have at the ready should you hit some rain and want to just tuck away readily used items and valuables (I also drop my money belt into the dry bag if the rain starts). Be sure to bring bug repellent, a flashlight, and a hat for day hikes and cave exploring. Wear long pants, preferably jeans, when riding, and wear boots, if possible, and at least shoes or sneakers, if not (no sandals), but bring something light, such as flip-flops, for the evening.

provided with a mattress and mosquito net in a dorm-style setup. You'll dine either with a family or with your group if you're on a tour, and probably witness a traditional dance performance after dinner. The people of these villages are White Thai, and most of the women still wear traditional dress. A stay or a brief visit is a good glimpse into White Thai culture, and a rustic overnight in the village is a memorable experience. However, if you don't want to sleep with a crowd of others, opt for Mai Chau's only decent hotel, the Mai Chau Lodge.

Mai Chau Lodge ★   This is Mai Chau's most luxurious accommodation option, offering stylish rooms with wooden floors and trim; some have fabulous views over the rice paddies. Room rates here are a bit steep, but all rooms are well equipped with flatscreen TVs and smart, modern furnishings. Facilities include an attractive swimming pool, a sauna and steam room, a reading room, and bicycle rental. The Lodge's restaurant serves set lunches and dinners in a traditional open sided area or on a breezy terrace with superb views of the valley around.

At the farthest end of town, Mai Chau, Hoa Binh. ✆ **0218/8386-8959.** 16 units. From $130 double; $150 suite. MC, V. **Amenities:** Restaurant; bar; bicycle rental; pool; reading room; sauna. *In room:* Satellite TV, hair dryer, Internet, minibar.

WHERE TO EAT

Dinner in Mai Chau (or "Your Chow," as my punny travel companion pointed out) is offered at just a few small local storefront restaurants, though visitors arriving on organized tours generally eat in the stilthouses (food is included in the price of the tour). For something a cut above the tourist fodder dished up for tour groups, head round to the Mai Chau Lodge, where set dinners are priced at $20 a head. If you explore the local restaurants, be armed with a few phrases on food such as *com trung* (fried egg with rice), *rau xau* (mixed vegetables), or *pho bo* (noodle soup with beef). For more language help, see chapter 16. A few Internet outposts are in the town, but service is rather slow.

ATTRACTIONS

The villages of **Ban Lac** and **Pom Coong,** where most people stay, are great for a morning wander, whether you spent the night in a village homestay or at the Lodge. The villages are touristed-out, meaning that the little dusty streets are now paved, and though the hospitality is genuine, the folks here lead with handfuls of souvenir items for sale and not a handshake. Some items are just tacky tourist souvenirs, but if you rummage around you may find some well-made garments in striking colors at reasonable prices (don't forget to bargain!). The surrounding valley is green with rice fields and laced with fun little tracks that are great to explore; in fact, tours out of Hanoi usually include a few-hour trek around the area in the itinerary. Bring a camera and your sense of adventure, and get lost out on the paddies for a few hours before heading on to Son La. Try to avoid visiting at the weekend if you can, as the place gets overrun with students from Hanoi, and their noisy city ways stand in contrast to the locals' laid-back manner.

From Mai Chau to Son La

Take a detour near Mai Chau and hop a ride on the **Da River Reservoir.** In fact, many tours include a long boat ride between Mai Chau and Hoa Binh; but if you just want to catch a glimpse of the water, turn right at the Tong Dau junction just before Mai Chau and drive 5km (3 miles) to Bai Sang. The road from Mai Chau to Son La is lined with Montagnard villages and some fine areas of karst limestone outcroppings.

Son La

320km (199 miles) NW of Hanoi; 170km (106 miles) W of Mai Chau

Son La is a small city set in a narrow valley at the foot of low hills. A short walk up to the town's famous hilltop prison or to one of the viewpoints in the hills above gives you a good perspective on the two busy streets that make up downtown. Both accommodations and dining are rather limited, but this is a popular (pretty much essential) stop on any tour of the northeast.

A testament to the wily French colonists and their love of brutal prisons (also see Con Dao and Phu Quoc Island in the far south; between the American and the French prisons, you can, in fact, tour a prison in just about every province), Son La was home to one of the country's worst facilities, the end of the line for Vietnam's early-20th-century dissidents. A letter from French brass talking of Son La Prison's brutal effectiveness says, "The malaria and toil here would break the revolutionary zeal of any man."

FAST FACTS   The **Agribank** (8 Chu Van Thinh St.) has an ATM and can cash traveler's checks. Most hotels provide Wi-Fi or ADSL connections, but if you need an Internet shop, look along To Hieu Street, near the corner where Route 6 enters the town of Son La. The post office is also on To Hieu in the center of town.

WHERE TO STAY

Most accommodations in Son La are basically of the same low-end minihotel standard, though the Hanoi Hotel (see below) is a welcome addition.

Hanoi Hotel 🛍   Son La's newest hotel is located just south of the town center and offers good-size, comfortable rooms with firm beds and smart, modern furnishings. Doubles are a good value here, but if you plan to spend any time in your room, spring for a VIP room, as these have fabulous views over the rice paddies around town, as well as carpets and comfy sofas. All bathrooms have tubs and granite counters. There are extensive sauna and massage facilities as well as a good restaurant and bar, and staff can help arrange trips to local villages.

228 Truong Chinh St., Son La. www.hanoihotel299.com. © 022/375-3288. Fax 022/375-3277. 50 units. From $30 double; from $50 VIP room. MC, V, AE. **Amenities:** Restaurant; bar; room service; sauna. *In room:* A/C, satellite TV, minibar, Wi-Fi.

The Trade Union Hotel (Cong Doan)   Son La's aging standby, the Trade Union has simple white-tile rooms with cool canopy beds and ornate ceilings of white plaster, rimmed with heavy ornamental trim. The place is always busy with Vietnamese tour groups. The staff speaks English well, but they use it to press you into using their services—"You rent car? You eat here?"—though all done a bit tongue-in-cheek. The folks at Trade Union Hotel take good care of your car or motorbike—they even give it a free power-wash. The restaurant is bland, but the best choice for the familiar.

04 Son Thuy, Son La. www.sonlatradeunion.com.vn. © 022/385-2804. Fax 022/385-5312. 70 units. $25–$40 double. No credit cards. **Amenities:** Restaurant; bar. *In room:* A/C, satellite TV, fridge, minibar.

WHERE TO EAT

At Truong Chinh Road, near the intersection of To Hieu Street and on the corner where Route 6 enters the town of Son La, you'll find a number of **small storefront eateries,** most of which are cafeteria style, where you can put together a meal by pointing to what appeals to you, usually a choice of boiled eggs, vegetables, pork in broth, fried fish, or tofu fried in lemon grass, all accompanied with rice. These same shops can cook to order the likes of fried noodles or omelets upon request, but suffice it to say that dining in little Son La is far from gourmet; think of it more as a place to just fill your tummy before heading off on the road the next day. Your best bet for being understood and getting a reasonable meal is at the hotel of your choice.

ATTRACTIONS

Son La Prison Hilltop **Son La Prison** is an important historical vestige. Some parts were destroyed by the French, and later by the Americans, but many of the ramparts have been rebuilt, and some interiors have been done over so that visitors get the full effect. The museum at the back tells—in cases of artifacts, translated documents, pictures, and creative renderings—the story of how prisoners marched in chains for more than 220km (137 miles) and then were entombed here. (Having just gone over it by car or motorbike, think of walking the same route in chains over a 2-week period.) Expressive plaster statuary and oil paintings of scenes inside the prison express the prisoners' plight. Like many war sites or prisons in Vietnam, Vietnamese visit here as a way of remembrance, to honor and give thanks to those who have sacrificed. Find displays of prisoner shackles, photos of prison life, and weapons used by prisoners during the many uprisings, including the 1945 revolt that shut down the prison for good. The museum has a model of the prison rooms as they were, with slat beds and floor toilets. Out back, don't miss the tree of **To Hieu,** a survivor and the namesake of the town's main thoroughfare who returned in the 1950s and planted a small peach tree to celebrate peace. The tiny, gnarled tree is behind a wall just to the right of the entry to the main prison compound. The basement of the main prison building houses eerie solitary-confinement chambers and rebuilt "Tiger Cage" cells. Don't go alone unless you can handle the chill.

Adjacent to the prison area, there is a two-story museum in a more modern compound. You'll find rather tatty but organized displays on local hilltribe culture, a room dedicated to the life and legacy of Ho Chi Minh, and ubiquitous sun-bleached photos of industrial projects indicating Vietnam's victorious rise of the working man and progress into the future (seen one, seen 'em all). There's also a room of stone and ancient artifacts, including some fine examples of Dong Son drums, evidence of Vietnam's earliest Bronze Age culture. *Note:* The promenade near the museum is more or less the city's "inspiration point" in the evening.

Admission 10,000 VND. Daily 7:30–11am and 1:30–5:30pm.

Between Son La & Dien Bien Phu

The road gets more mountainous and curvy as it traces vast river valleys and brings you among more Montagnard groups. In fact, a stop just about anywhere brings you into some *National Geographic*–like moments. Be sensitive when taking pictures of hilltribe people; some groups have superstitions about photo taking. Be sure to ask first, and honor the wishes of anyone who declines to have his or her photo taken, however front-page-worthy. Do not offer money to take someone's photo. The road traces some high ridges, which also means some hard climbing, with jeeps and motorbikes digging down into second gear, but you're rewarded along the way with stunning viewpoints over broad valleys of terraced rice farms.

Route 6 terminates at the town of Tuan Giao, itself just a place for a little coffee or a local lunch of rice or noodles; from here, a right turn takes you some 98km (61

Route 6 cuts across a stunning mountainous patch, a narrow ribbon of paved and broken-paved road that is more often just a shelf cut into the rock. Overlooking broad valley scenery, you'll pass through quaint hilltribe villages all along the path. The road terminates in **Muong Lay (p. 140)**, where you can find lodging for the night before pushing on to Sapa. *Note:* Even if you decide to go to Dien Bien Phu, see if you can find the time to travel the head of this stunning road for at least a few kilometers, to get a taste of the stunning scenery (drive up from either Tuan Giao or, on the other side, Muong Lay).

miles) to Muong Lay along a stunning stretch of Route 6, and a left is just 80km (50 miles) to Dien Bien Phu. Most tours take you to Dien Bien Phu, but should you be so lucky/brave/foolish to be on a motorbike, I recommend you skip a visit to Dien Bien Phu, which, short of its historical significance, is just a dusty border outpost, and head over Route 6 to Muong Lay on one of Vietnam's most beautiful roads.

Dien Bien Phu

475km (295 miles) W of Hanoi; 150km (93 miles) W of Son La; 105km (60 miles) S of Lai Chau

Toward the end of World War II—after the withdrawal of all Japanese forces from Vietnam, and the August 1945 reading of the Vietnamese Declaration of Independence and the resultant August Revolution—the French colonial mission in Vietnam was nearly over. French forces were down to a skeleton crew after years of attrition under Japanese rule in Indochina, but despite international pressure, Charles De Gaulle sent a force of 70,000 to old Indochina under the command of General LeClerc in the 1950s. Efforts at building a French-Vietnamese coalition including Ho Chi Minh were ill-fated and failed as soon as they were implemented. Guerilla fighting and terrorist attacks by the Viet Minh forces throughout the north soon led to the full-scale Indochina War.

First, a massive French bombing campaign of northern supply lines in Haiphong, attacks that killed thousands of innocents, gave way to a long succession of bloody battles and many casualties on both sides. Nearing some truce in the conflict in 1953, the French put all of their eggs (or most of them) in one basket and chose Dien Bien Phu as the best place to intercept supply lines to rebel groups. Hoping to provoke a classic pitched battle instead of hunting terrorists, the garrison at Dien Bien Phu was surrounded by fire stations, or fortified outposts, in the hills above, supported by heavy air transport and, by 1954, manned by some 16,000 seasoned French Foreign Legion fighters. The impoverished Vietnamese guerrilla forces looked cut off, and the French expected to go to the bargaining tables with some real leverage. How wrong they were.

The battle lasted from March 13 until May 8, 1954, with Vietnamese forces surrounding the valley and pummeling French forces with artillery dragged, by hook or crook, over hill and dale from China. The French were completely surprised. Though French expeditionary troops fought valiantly, with some truly fearless French units parachuting into the crippled encampment long after the runway was destroyed, supply lines were cut and all looked lost. Strategists likened the battle to a fight between a jungle tiger and an elephant, where the Vietnamese tiger strikes at intervals and leaves its larger, stronger prey to bleed to death. Without any official surrender, the French laid down their arms and were completely overrun. The first Indochina War was over, and Dien Bien Phu would forever be a rallying cry for Vietnamese sovereignty.

The town of Dien Bien Phu itself is just a wide avenue lined with Soviet-era construction. There are a few decent hotels, but mainstream tourism is far from overrunning Dien Bien, a town whose greatest moment in history was, in fact, when it was overrun. War memorials, including a good museum, are what attract mostly war buffs and French tour groups to this outpost on the Lao border. The highlights can be seen in a casual afternoon before pressing on to Lai Chau or Sapa the following day.

GETTING THERE BY AIR

There are regular flights on Vietnam Airlines that connect Dien Bien Phu with Hanoi. The small airport is just north of town on the road to Lai Chau. **Vietnam Airlines** has a booking office at the airport (℃ **0230/382-4948**) or nearby on Rte. 12 (℃ **0230/382-4948**).

ORIENTATION

The city center lies on the eastern shore of the Nam Rom River. The road from Son La and Tuan Giao, Route 12, enters to the north of the city (some of the better accommodations are along it), and the central avenues of Le Trong Tan and Nguyen Chi Thanh make up the busy downtown. The history museum and A-1 hill are on the south end of town, and a few important military sites—bunkers and abandoned artillery and tanks—are on the west shore. The airport is just north of town on the west bank of the river, along the road to Muong Lay.

FAST FACTS You can exchange money at the **Agribank** (3 Duong 7–5; ℃ **0230/382-5786**). There are lots of local Internet storefronts along the main drag. Slow connection is the rule. Better to wait until Sapa unless you're in a pinch. The main post office is just south of the Agribank.

WHERE TO STAY & DINE

There are no **dining** venues geared to tourists in Dien Bien Phu; you're left to your own devices among the town's rice and noodle shops. But assuming you've come this far over land, you'll be an expert with the basics in local cuisine (for a few pointers, look in chapter 16). The best shops are near the main intersection in town; try the **Cong Hoan** on the south side of Muong Thanh Road, about 500m (1,640 ft.) west of the Muong Thanh Hotel, where there's an English menu of sorts featuring hot pots, stir fries, and *bia hoi* (draft beer). The Dien Bien Phu Hanoi Hotel (see below) serves good one-dish meals at their cozy little coffee shop on the first floor, and the Muong Thanh Hotel (see below) also has an in-house restaurant.

Dien Bien Phu Hanoi Hotel　Plain, clean, and large, the Dien Bien Phu Hanoi Hotel is a government-run place that's quite similar to all the others in the center of town, but the location is central and staff is helpful. There's a downstairs coffee shop, in-house restaurant, and massage parlor (wink-wink), all popular for regional businessmen. It has a good standard of basic, carpeted rooms with air-conditioning, and simple wannabe-luxe decor, but I recommend the Muong Thanh (see below) over this one.

849 7-5 Rd., Street 6, Dien Bien Phu. ℃ **0230/382-5103.** Fax 0230/382-6290. 39 units. 350,000 VND–450,000 VND double. No credit cards. **Amenities:** Restaurant; cafe; sauna. *In room:* A/C, TV, fridge, minibar.

Muong Thanh Hotel　About 1km (½ mile) outside of town on the road from Son La, this hotel has always been popular, but now it has been completely reborn as Bien

Phu's only luxury option. Though the new building itself is a characterless monolith, the entrance is memorable for its quirky statues of dragons and folk heroes around the pool and intriguing wall patterns formed of various stones. The spacious rooms are thoughtfully designed and well furnished, and facilities include a business center. Because of its popularity, it sometimes hosts noisy wedding parties, but rooms out back are well away from it all. From the smartly dressed bellboy to the smiling receptionists, the staff is eager to please and generally very efficient.

514 7-5 Street, Dien Bien Phu (on the main road outside of town). www.muangthanhdienbienhotel.com. ✆ **0230/381-2556.** Fax 0230/381-0713. 150 units. From $60 double. AE, DC, V. **Amenities:** Restaurant; bar; pool. *In room:* A/C, satellite TV, fridge, minibar, Wi-Fi.

ATTRACTIONS

The sites in Dien Bien Phu require a lot of imagination, really. Visualize, if you will, the French dug in all around town, completely cut off from the rest of the world. Bolstered by their surprise battery of Chinese artillery, and seemingly eager to endure casualties, Vietnamese troops came in waves. Losses were devastating on both sides. The story of this important moment in history is told in the many monuments and museums and the town cemetery—but the modern concretized trade town of Dien Bien Phu is not so interesting. Take a ride across the small bridge at the southern end of town and look for the rusting gun emplacements and a re-creation of the **Bunker of Colonel Christian De Castries,** who killed himself when he finally realized that all was indeed lost.

A-1 Hill and the Dien Bien Phu Cemetery   This highest point at the center of town was a holdout of French troops and a hard-fought-for hill. Today you'll find a memorial and a quiet park that makes a good perch to get the lay of the land. Just south, at the foot of the hill, is the **Dien Bien Phu Cemetery,** with mostly unmarked graves of the fallen. A grand compound at the entrance is the Vietnamese version of the Wall in Washington, but here are the names of soldiers who died at Dien Bien.

Daily 7–11am and 1:30–5pm.

Dien Bien Phu Museum   This long, low building is a bit beat-up (and could use a weed whacker out front), but the Dien Bien Phu Museum houses important relics, photos, and displays that chronicle the long struggle of revolution and the big Vietnamese victory over the French in 1954. There are photos of tanks that were airlifted in pieces, as well as grinning American advisors and confident French troops. The artifacts tell a story of massive artillery sledges designed to carry the big guns in pieces over the mountains from China. You'll see shoulder slings, the very shovels that dug the trenches or cleared the paths, and even the smudged clothes and field maps of troops. The Vietnamese win was the genius of North Vietnam's eminent strategist, Gen. Vo Nguyen Giap, and his life and works are celebrated at the museum.

At the town center. Admission 5,000 VND. Daily 7–11am and 1:30–6pm.

Between Dien Bien Phu & Muong Lay

Except for some construction spots, the road is in fairly good shape up to Muong Lay. About 300km (186 miles) from Dien Bien Phu to Sapa, many travelers make the trip in 1 day, but it's actually a bit much, considering the big climbs and descents along the way. Also, if you go from Dien Bien Phu to Sapa in 1 day, you pass through the **Tram Ton** pass to Sapa in the evening (assuming you make lunch and photo stops along the way); this pass is one of the highlights of any trip in the north, and it's a

When plans were laid to transform the Da River into a massive reservoir to provide much-needed power for the country, the authorities, for some reason, decided to re-name many of the towns in the affected region. Such changes are not unusual in Vietnam, but in this case many names were switched from one town to another, causing considerable confusion. Thus the town formerly known as Lai Chau is now Muong Lay, what was once Phong Tho has become Pa So, and the town formerly known as Tam Duong is now Lai Chau. Sadly, the authorities have been slow to change signposts, leading locals to get on the wrong bus home and tourists to scratch their heads at road junctions.

shame to get there too late in the day, when the towering peaks are in clouds. Stay the night in Muong Lay or Pa So, if you can spare the time, so you'll get to the pass and to Sapa at midday. Both towns are surrounded by towering hills and make good places for an improvised stroll.

Muong Lay

105km (61 miles) N of Dien Bien Phu; 180km (110 miles) SW of Sapa

Muong Lay, formerly Lai Chau, was set in the valley of the Dong Da River that has now been flooded to form part of the Da Reservoir, so all homes had to be demolished or taken apart and rebuilt higher up the hills. At the time of this update, a huge bridge over the reservoir was almost complete and reconstruction of the town was beginning. The town is the terminus of Route 6 from Tuan Giao, a shortcut over the mountains from Son La and one of the loveliest stretches of mountain road in Vietnam. It's a logical stop if you're coming from Dien Bien Phu and don't want to bust all the way to Sapa in 1 day. (**Note:** If you cross the Tram Ton pass to Sapa too late in the evening, you will likely miss the most spectacular scenery. Many therefore opt to stay in Lai Chau and cross to Sapa the next day.) The little Lan Anh Hotel, recently moved up the hill, is your only choice for a home away from home here.

Once reconstruction is complete, there should be no problem finding **banks** or **Internet connections.** For information about good places to trek in the region, ask at the **Lan Anh Hotel.**

WHERE TO STAY

Lan Anh Hotel   Muong Lay's longest standing hotel was being rebuilt farther up the hillside at the time of this update and should be fully functional by early 2012, but check their website for the latest news. **Mr. Trang** is the owner and manager of the hotel; he organizes local treks and offers helpful advice and information for onward travel. The in-house restaurant/bar has a good English menu.

Central Lai Chau near the riverside (about 1km/½ mile west of the main road; large signs point the way). www.lananhhotel.com. ✆ **0230/385-2370.** Fax 0230/385-2290. 58 units. $15–$20 double; $35 suite. No credit cards. **Amenities:** Restaurant/bar; Internet (spotty); motorbike rental. *In room:* A/C (in some, mostly fan only), minibar, no phone.

From Muong Lay to Sapa

The road out of Muong Lay follows the **Da River Valley** as the water widens in broad valleys and narrows to small rapids through precipitous gorges. Several other dam projects are in progress along the way. The road is well paved and not as steep as other spots on the route, but it's not straight.

One possible detour on the route north to Sapa is the village of **Sin Ho.** Some 30km (19 miles) up a dirt track just east of the main road, Sin Ho is a quiet, isolated Thai village well worth the visit for an amateur ethnologist or an adventurer looking to see what their motorbike can "really do." *Warning:* This is well off the beaten track, so be sure you have all the requisite gear to fix any flats or major problems; there won't be any helpful strangers wandering down this rugged road. From Sin Ho, there's a road that connects to the north and with the town of **Pa So** on the way to Sapa, but note that during the rains it's more or less a rutted track.

Most travelers pass Sin Ho and opt to follow the Da River in a picturesque climb toward Sapa. In this case, you'll pass through **Pa So,** which has one little riverside hotel run by the same folks as Lan Anh Hotel in Lai Chau (see above), and then hit **Lai Chau** (formerly **Tam Duong**), a town where you might catch a glimpse of colorful Hmong and Dao people at roadside. There are a few hotels and guesthouses in Lai Chau, but it is so close to Sapa that you might as well press on. From Lai Chau, you climb among stunning peaks on one of the most beautiful stretches of road before hitting the massive switchback of the **Tram Ton Pass,** which brings you up and over to the town of Sapa.

Note: Many travelers who do this route by motorbike opt to ride the short stretch from Sapa to Lao Cai, and then put their **motorbike on the train** for the overnight back to Hanoi. The road from Lao Cai to Hanoi via **Yen Bai** is rural and quite pretty, but nothing compared with the mountain roads of the highland area. It's worth saving the gas, exhaustion, and hassle to just toss it onto the train for around $10. In Lao Cai, stop in to see the friendly folks at **Hai Nhi Restaurant** (337 Nguyen Hue St.; ✆ 020/383-5901), who can help you out with the details. *Important note for Minskers:* You have to remove all of the gasoline from your motorbike, so find a local with a Minsk motorbike and make his day by donating your gas to him.

THE NORTHEASTERN HIGHLANDS LOOP

Less popular than the rural regions of the far northwest, the mountainous area north of Hanoi is attractive because of its paucity of other travelers—though this also means a matching paucity of decent hotels, restaurants, and services. Roads are rough and prone to landslide, and many are under construction. It's best to hit this loop on a Minsk motorbike (for the adventurous only) or a jeep. If you're really adventurous, head straight up to **Ha Giang** on Highway 2, get a permit to travel through the province, and then set off through the wonderland that is now called the **Dong Van Karst Plateau Geopark.** From here you can drop down via Bao Lac to **Ba Be National Park,** a cache of protected land around a large lake and inland waterway. The shores of Ba Be Lake and the nearby town of Cho Ra are both good places to stay overnight. From there, explore the park, and then return to the main road north and head to **Cao Bang,** a riverside provincial center that is a good base for exploration to surrounding hilltribe villages. Outside of Cao Bang, you can visit the **caves** where **Ho Chi Minh** holed up after returning from China, as well as one of the region's most stunning waterfalls, **Ban Gioc.** From Cao Bang, return directly to Hanoi, or set out east to the unremarkable city of **Lang Son,** a journey that is "about the journey, not the destination." The ride itself, dotted with ethnic hilltribe villages, is what's worth seeing, not provincial Lang Son. The road between Lang Son and Hanoi is a superhighway and a good choice back to the capital (there is also a slow train service).

Ha Giang &the Dong Van Karst Plateau Geopark

310km (192 miles) north of Hanoi

Ha Giang is Vietnam's northernmost province and so far remains largely untouched by tourism, partly because this border region is considered a sensitive area and foreigners need to obtain a permit ($10) from the immigration office in Ha Giang to travel through the province. However, recent road improvements and the newly named **Dong Van Karst Plateau Geopark** make this region very appealing, as the scenery is probably the most dramatic in the entire country. **Dong Van** is the country's northernmost town, and hosts a bustling hilltribe market on Sundays. The ride there from Ha Giang is a breathtaking experience as the road switchbacks up and over mountain ridges and reveals superb views of rice terraces and jagged peaks. A side trip from Dong Van to **Luong Cu** takes you to the a flag tower that marks the northernmost point of the country, and the road south to **Meo Vac** passes through the country's deepest canyon, where the **Nho Que River** snakes its way south. From Meo Vac, head south to **Bao Lac** and then on to **Ba Be Lake.**

GETTING THERE

Follow Highway 2 directly north from Hanoi or join a tour group. The journey takes about 6 hours.

WHERE TO STAY & DINE

This region has not yet developed for tourism, so visitors need to put up with fairly basic facilities in hotels and eat local food. When traveling between Ha Giang and Dong Van, most people make a lunch stop in **Yen Minh,** though you'll need to use your phrase book or point. Dong Van has just one restaurant, the **Au Viet,** in the middle of the main street, that has an English menu and can cater for foreign visitors, though the restaurant at the **Rocky Plateau Hotel** serves a limited number of dishes too.

Rocky Plateau Hotel   The best choice of Dong Van's few hotels, this place is not at all luxurious, but it does have all the basic facilities, such as air-conditioning and hot water, as well as solid wood furnishings. The helpful staff can suggest what you should see around town.

At the top of the main street, next to the market. © **0219/385-6868.** 14 units. $13–$19 double. No credit cards. **Amenities:** Restaurant. *In room:* A/C, TV, Wi-Fi.

Ba Be Lake & Cho Ra Town

270km (168 miles) north of Hanoi

Cho Ra is the small town servicing **Ba Be National Park,** just 14km (8¾ miles) to the west. Cho Ra is one of the best places to overnight before a day tour in the park and an afternoon ride on to Cao Bang (or back to Hanoi), though most people on tours out of Hanoi stay in **homestays** in villages beside the lake such as **Pac Ngoi. Cho Ra** is just a quiet little outpost, one busy main street surrounded by rice fields and mountains. Surrounded by diverse ethnic hilltribes, mostly Thai, the town's central market is very busy on weekends, when rural villagers trek to town to sell produce, as well as weaving and needlework. **Ba Be Park** is a great place to enjoy an all-day boat ride and trekking to remote villages in the surrounding hills.

Come prepared for self-sufficiency: There are few facilities in tiny Cho Ra. You can usually pay with U.S. dollars at the hotels, but be sure to also carry Vietnamese dong.

GETTING THERE

Go by car or motorbike north from Hanoi some 200km (124 miles), and then follow signs to Cho Ra.

WHERE TO STAY & DINE

Dining is pretty minimal in this area. Even travelers staying in homestays tend to be served rather safe (read bland) versions of Vietnamese cuisine. If you stay in the park, there's a canteen with basic, overpriced grub, but it's rarely busy, so it's kind of an ad hoc operation. You're on your own in Cho Ra Town, really, and any Vietnamese-language basics (*"com trung"* for rice and eggs, for example) or knack for charades will help out at the few little *com* (rice) and *pho* (noodle soup) stands along the main drag near the central market (at the corner where the road splits north to Cao Bang, west to Ba Be Lake, and south to Bac Can).

The most convenient place to stay is at the **National Park Guest House** (✆ **0281/389-4099;** www.babenationalpark.org), which was under renovation at the time of this update. Expect to pay around $40 for a well-equipped and comfortable double. At park headquarters you can also arrange to stay in a **homestay,** probably at **Pac Ngoi,** which nestles beneath a dramatic cliff at the southern end of the lake. For around $10 a night, you'll get a mattress, mosquito net, and space on the floor with fellow travelers, as well as dinner and breakfast.

Thuy Dung Guesthouse   This is currently the most popular guesthouse in Cho Ra town, and the friendly staff can help organize boat trips on the lake. Rooms are cozy and clean, and those out back have great views. Breakfast is included in the price, and it's a good place to meet up with other travelers and arrange day tours on the river and lake. The welcoming restaurant has an English menu.

In Central Cho Ra. ✆ **0281/387-6354.** 7 units. $18 double. Rates include breakfast. No credit cards. **Amenities:** Restaurant. *In room:* A/C, Wi-Fi, no phone.

ATTRACTIONS

Ba Be National Park   Just 20,000 VND to enter—plus an additional 2,000 VND for a motorbike—Ba Be National Park surrounds central Ba Be Lake, the starting point for adventurous trips to the park's more far-flung destinations. Best if organized through a tour company, you'll find many options for rugged travel here. Some start near the town of Cho Ra in a little area called **Pak Kaw,** and then spend all day on **long-tail boats** exploring the small river as it snakes among hilltribe villages before emptying into the lake. The remote caves and far-flung villages are all best visited with a guide. Standard group tours commonly hop a boat just past the park entrance (half-day trips are $20; full-day trips $35).

Cao Bang

285km (177 miles) N of Hanoi

This provincial outpost lies in a picturesque crook in the Bang Giang River. Few foreigners get up this far, and the state of hotels and services might indicate why, but rugged travelers are in their element. The city alone is worth a wander, especially its large, unruly riverside market, and sunset in Cao Bang is an event, best viewed from the bridge or walking along the riverside promenade. From here, you can watch water buffalos grazing and locals paddling low skiffs to bring their produce to market. What brings people to Cao Bang, apart from the call of the fun rural roads in the region, is the famed **Ban Gioc Waterfall** northwest of town, one of the most photographed waterfalls in the world. Also northwest of Cao Bang are the **Pac Bo Caves** where Ho Chi Minh hid out upon returning from China. On designated days, usually on weekend mornings, you are sure to come across **hilltribe markets** in the towns outside of Cao Bang (on your way to Pac Bo or Ban Gioc)—a photographer's dream.

There's an **Agribank ATM** machine outside the Bang Giang Hotel, and most hotels will exchange currency, but it's best to bring U.S. greenbacks or dong with you from Hanoi. There are a few Internet spots, including one very good storefront right next to the Hotel Hoang Anh. The post office is on central Hoang Dinh Gong Street.

GETTING THERE

Cao Bang connects directly north of Hanoi on Route 3. Local buses leave from the Long Bien Station and are pretty uncomfortable. Best to go by motorbike or hired car. The road from Ba Be is quite spectacular.

WHERE TO STAY

Cao Bang's **Thanh Loan Hotel** used to be the top dog, commanding the most prime real estate overlooking the river at the very center of town (near the bridge), but this big government-run calamity has fallen into disrepair. Some tours will try to stick you here. Don't buy it. Instead, go for the **Hoang Anh Hotel** (131 Kim Dong; ✆ **026/385-8969**), where the smart rooms, some with wonderful river views, have cable TV and Wi-Fi, all for $15.

Dining is limited in Cao Bang. Go for "point-and-shoot"–style dining at the little local buffet at riverside, **Huong Sen Restaurant.** "Point" at what you want and say "Shoot!" when they charge you double for it. But even at double the price, it's still a bargain. They've got fried egg, tofu dishes, vegetables, fried river fish, and rice.

On the main drag, there are lots of good local coffee joints, the best of which is the **Trung Nguyen Coffee Shop** at town center. For a good, familiar snack, look for **89 Kim Dong St.,** where there is a good little stand selling *banh mi* (bread) and pâté. They'll make you a great little savory sandwich from just 10,000 VND.

ATTRACTIONS

Both the journey *and* the destination in Cao Bang offer attractions. The caves at **Pac Bo** are of little interest to foreign visitors, but the waterfall at **Ban Gioc** is quite a stunning sight during and after the rains (July–Nov) and worth the effort to see. The best part is that the roads to both sights pass through beautiful mountain landscapes among **ethnic hilltribe villages.** Especially on weekends, you are likely to pass through seemingly impromptu **hilltribe markets,** the roads lined for miles with Tai and Nung people in traditional wear marching their product to market. Ask at your hotel about any scheduled markets (they are often held on auspicious days in the lunar calendar).

Ban Gioc Some 85km (53 miles) of mountain road—more than a 4-hour drive one-way—east of Cao Bang brings you to one of the most well-known waterfalls in Asia. People don't know it by name, but once you tick this sight off your list, you'll be able to spot glossy photos of it in Chinese restaurants and hotel lobbies everywhere. The multitiered falls are fueled by the Quay Son River spilling into Vietnam from China. The French originally built small villas on the banks at the base of the falls.

Vietnamese tourists now come to this beautiful place in big groups, especially on weekends, and the place is crowded with happy picnics, drinking, and chatter. Sit for a while, and you might be invited to join in. **Nguom Ngao Cave** (admission 20,000 VND) is just a few miles past the falls, and the cavernous space is well worth the visit.

Important: You have to arrange a **special permit** (just a bit of a bureaucratic hang-up) to get to the falls. Don't try to do it yourself—a waste of time, really—just arrive in Cao Bang the night before you plan to see the falls and have your hotel make arrangements (for a small fee). The cost for the permit is $10 per group, whether the group is of 1 or 20.

Daily 7:30am–5:30pm; admission 15,000 VND.

Pac Bo (Ho Chi Minh's Hide-Out)   Most sights dedicated to Ho Chi Minh are geared to Vietnamese tourists and are of little interest to Westerners. Pac Bo follows the party line. Pac Bo is the site where, returning to Vietnam after more than 30 years of exile, a fired-up Ho Chi Minh began planning the revolution in 1941, living in caves and protected by local people. The approach to the site is lined with big concrete pavilions and walkways. An open parking area gives way to paved paths along the picturesque **Lenin River** at the foot of the **Karl Marx Mountain** (Ho Chi Minh named them himself). Paths take you to some small cave sites, and signs lead the way to places where Ho wrote, slept, and ate; but the real business at Pac Bo is family swimming and picnicking. It's a great place to meet Vietnamese tourists.

Lang Son

150km (93 miles) N of Hanoi

The city of Lang Son is connected to Hanoi by a broad, flat highway, and is more or less a food stop after the stunning ride from Cao Bang, before you make your way back to the capital just a couple of hours away. Dining and accommodations options are many, but only the few that are acceptable are listed below. The city is known for being overrun, repeatedly, by the Chinese over the centuries—most recently in 1979 as retribution for Vietnam's invasion of Cambodia. Things are quiet now—so quiet, in fact, that you'll probably just pass on through, whether going back to Hanoi or to the border town of **Dong Dan** and on to China. (*Important:* You must have a prearranged Chinese visa to travel to China; see "Visas," under "Entry Requirements," in chapter 15, for more information.)

The **Vietin Bank,** 51 Le Loi, has an **ATM,** and next door is the **post office** at 49 Le Loi St. You can get **online** at the Van Xuan Hotel (see below), which has a few terminals in the lobby.

GETTING THERE

The road from Cao Bang, Route 4A (though never marked as such) is a stunning drive. Route 1 is a wide highway that runs straight north from Hanoi (better to trade with China, my pretty).

There are two very slow **trains** connecting Lang Son with Hanoi daily. The train station is on Le Loi Street. Most go by the highway, however.

Onward connection to or from China is via the town of **Dong Da,** some 18km (11 miles) north of Lang Son. A motorbike taxi will run you there for about 50,000 VND.

WHERE TO STAY & EAT

Next best to Van Xuan Hotel (see below), and a similar standard, is **Hoang Son Hai Hotel,** near the town's central square (57 Duong Tam Thanh; ✆ **025/371-0479**).

Rooms are priced the same, but they don't see many foreign visitors here and have no services.

New Century VIETNAMESE   At the very center of town, just across the market area, is this hulking restaurant that's full of comings and goings. On a small island in Phai Loan Lake—connected by a walkway—the place hops in the evenings, with karaoke rooms, a beer hall area, and large banquet-style dining. Quieter tables at the lakeside sit under the twinkling lights hanging from trees. An English-language menu presents the standard Vietnamese fare of stir-fries, noodle dishes, and rice, as well as more exotic offerings such as bees, rabbit, and turtle. Cute beer hostesses in miniskirt outfits emblazoned with local beer logos sling the suds, and the waitstaff is friendly, but nobody savvies much English—just point to menu items and smile. The place is adjacent to the Van Xuan (see below).

Phai Loan Lake at the center of town. ℂ **025/389-8000.** Main courses 45,000 VND–220,000 VND. No credit cards. Daily 7:30am–10pm.

Van Xuan Hotel   Of the slim pickins in Lang Son, Van Xuan is top of the heap. This five-story riverside complex has a friendly(ish) front-desk staff and an elevator (unique in this category) that connects you with their large, clean, basic tiled rooms. It uniquely offers movie channels on TV, and the rooms are cozy (though the foam beds are kind of a drag). Compared with others in town, this is far and away the best.

147 Tran Dang Ninh St. ℂ **025/371-0440.** Fax 025/371-0436. 29 units. 320,000 VND–500,000 VND. No credit cards. **Amenities:** Restaurant; bar. *In room:* A/C, satellite TV, fridge, minibar, Wi-Fi.

NORTHEASTERN COAST

Named by French colonists, the stunning Tonkin coast—which extends from Haiphong and Halong Bay all the way to central Vietnam—will forever be associated with the disputed 1964 artillery exchange between U.S. and Vietnamese ships off the Gulf of Tonkin. The altercation ultimately led to the Tonkin Gulf Resolution and opened the door on the whole Vietnam shootin' match. What puts this region on the map now, though, is the likelihood that the sneakers or sandals you're wearing, or the shirt on your back, were put together in one of the large factories that line the road between Hanoi and the sea.

Boat tours of the UNESCO World Heritage Site **Halong Bay,** with its legendary limestone peaks and miles of calm waters, are the highlight. The small city of **Haiphong** has its own colonial-throwback kind of charm, and little **Cat Ba Island,** with its national park, is commonly included in itineraries with Halong Bay. You can also now reach Cat Ba by high-speed ferry from Hanoi.

There are also some good "off the map" destinations in this region, including **Bai Tu Long Bay,** just north of Halong (best visited on an organized tour), and **Do Son Beach,** just south of Haiphong. The Tonkin Coast area is just a few short hours by good road from Hanoi, and an overnight should suffice to experience any of these stops. Just about anybody in Hanoi sells tours to Halong and Cat Ba, with service ranging from Hanoi's ultrabudget-traveler cafe trips on old, beat-up junk boats to luxurious packages on the *Jewel of the Bay* (p. 156) and the *Emeraude,* a replica of an old colonial steamer.

HAIPHONG

100km (62 miles) E of Hanoi

With its wide avenues and grand parks, lined with colonnaded buildings of yellowed, aging stucco, Haiphong is like a smaller, more manageable version of Hanoi. You won't find jaw-dropping sights, but the town is worth a wander and not a bad stop on the way to or from the likes of Cat Ba or Halong Bay. Architectural sights include the classic old city theater, the town's large cathedral (Nha Tho Lon), an eclectic museum of history, and a museum of the navy. Central An Bien Park is also worth a wander, and the town boasts a few good hotels. Do Son Beach is just 21km (13 miles) southeast of Haiphong and a popular getaway for locals or Hanoi weekenders; the beach town hosts the annual Do Son Buffalo Fighting Festival, which is more or less a gory game of bull-baiting, but with lots of pomp and circumstance.

On your way to Haiphong from Hanoi, you'll pass through Binh Duyen, the industrial district east of Hanoi, where big, belching factories churn out Nike and Adidas shoes or name-brand shirts. There's an enormous Ford factory and other automotive and technical production facilities as well. Nearby, some farmers still use manual scoops to "cup" water from one rice terrace to the next, true manual irrigation, while just a stone's throw away, intricate pumps for automotive engines are manufactured by the thousands. It's a mad world.

Getting There

BY BUS   Buses make the 2-hour connection from Hanoi's Luong Yen Station to Haiphong frequently throughout the day. Haiphong also connects by bus with Halong City. The Haiphong bus station, Tam Bac, is just a 10,000 VND ride from the city center. One way to avoid the hassle is to book with **Hoang Long Bus Company** (in Hanoi, 28 Tran Nhat Duat, ✆ **04/3928-2828;** in Haiphong, 4 Le Thanh Tong, ✆ **031/355-2866;** in Cat Ba, 223 1 April Rd. ✆ **031/268-8008**), which runs a very fast bus service and high-speed boat four times daily from Cat Ba back to the mainland at Haiphong and on to Hanoi. Call directly, or ask your hotel's front desk to arrange pickup.

BY TRAIN   The **Haiphong Railway Station,** 75 Luong Khanh Thien St. (✆ **0313/920-025**), is the terminus of the eastern spur from Hanoi. Daily connections leave from the Hanoi station in the morning and in the evening. Because good roads now connect with Haiphong, this trip is more or less for the train buff.

BY BOAT   Boats regularly connect with Cat Ba Island from Haiphong's ferry pier on the northernmost tip of the town peninsula. You can book at any hotel front desk for the boat and bus trip with **Hoang Long Bus Company** (3 Tran Nguyen Han; ✆ **031/370-0778**) or with local high-speed boats. Just hop on whichever boat is heading out next.

FAST FACTS   You'll find an **ATM** and a place to cash traveler's checks at **Vietcombank** in Haiphong (11 Hoang Dieu St.; ✆ **031/384-2658**). Open Monday to Saturday from 8am to 4pm, but closed for lunch 11:30am to 1:30pm. You'll find a few budget **Internet** outfits on Dien Bien Phu Street. The main **post office** is at 3 Nguyen Tri Phuong St. (✆ **031/382-3789**).

Where to Stay
MODERATE
Harbour View Hotel ★★   Done in a cool retro French-colonial style, Harbour View is the town's most impressive address. The hotel is set up to meet and greet foreign business dignitaries—the folks who come over to check on the works of their nearby textile, shoe, and auto-part factories—and as such, the staff are practiced at rolling out the red carpet. This place has panache without being pretentious. Elegant wooden entries give way to large rooms, conservatively decorated in a plain chain-hotel fashion with fine wood furnishings. Bathrooms are large and clean, with granite. Don't miss the classic car out front, which is not just the hotel's mascot, but can be rented for transfers and city tours at just $25 per day.

4 Tran Phu St., Haiphong. www.harbourviewvietnam.com. ✆ **031/382-7827.** Fax 031/382-7828. 122 units. $115–$155 double; $185–$230 suite. AE, MC, V. **Amenities:** 2 restaurants; bar; fitness center; small outdoor pool; room service. In room: A/C, TV, fridge, hair dryer, Internet, minibar.

INEXPENSIVE

If you're in a pinch and the two hotels below are full, try **Hotel (Kach San) Kim Thanh** (67 Dien Bien Phu; ☏ 031/374-5264), which is a rabbit warren of less-than-average rooms starting at $17.

Bach Dang Hotel   One of the best of the town's hotels in this category, Bach Dang is set on a busy corner of Dien Bien Phu Street, just adjacent to the town's popular Maxim's Restaurant (see below). Old but clean rooms come in all shapes and sizes; be sure to have a look first. The hotel was a proud supporter of athletes during the Asia Games, and the staff speaks English and can help sort out any travel arrangements. A large restaurant and massage parlor (kind of sleazy) are just around the corner.

40 Dien Bien Phu St., Haiphong. bachdanghotelhp@hn.vnn.vn. ☏ **031/384-2444.** Fax 031/384-1625. 34 units. 350,000 VND–500,000 VND double. MC, V. **Amenities:** Restaurant; bar. *In room:* A/C, TV, fridge, minibar, Wi-Fi.

Maxim Hotel   Maxim is the best minihotel in town. It's a far better choice than the beat-up old business hotels at the town center that charge more than double the price for musty rooms. Maxim also hosts one of the town's best restaurants on its second floor, as well as the popular Maxim's Restaurant (run by the same owner) just down the street. Rooms are small but have good modern conveniences such as satellite TVs and clean bathrooms done in designer tile. There's a second branch, **New Maxim,** around the corner at 31 Dien Bien Phu St., with comparable rates.

3K Ly Tu Trong St., Haiphong City. maxim@vnn.vn. ☏ **031/374-6540.** 30 units. 250,000 VND–850,000 VND double. No credit cards. **Amenities:** Restaurant (see review of Truc Lam, below); bar. *In room:* A/C, TV, fridge, minibar, Wi-Fi.

Where to Eat

For a taste of local fare in "real" local atmosphere, head to tiny **Hoa Dai Do**—just north of the park at 40 Le Dai Hanh St. (☏ **031/381-0452**)—which slings Vietnamese-style hash, good stir-fries, noodle soups, roasted dinners, fried rice, and noodles. They march out an English menu when you arrive, but you can also have a peek in the kitchen to see what looks familiar or appetizing.

In the park adjacent to the high-end **Harbour View Hotel** (see above), find **Van Tue Restaurant** (1A Hoang Dieu; ☏ 031/374-6338). This oversize garden restaurant caters mainly to big wedding parties and other special events, but they do have some private rooms and serve delicious fresh seafood (by weight) from a limited English menu. It's a bit pricey but good, especially with a group.

Maxim's Restaurant and Bar ★   Try this place for a familiar Western meal in a casual coffee-shop setting. Little extras (linen tablecloths, flowers on the table, surly waiters) add to an old-school diner feel. The menu features Vietnamese versions of Western favorites—good sandwiches, pizza, and steaks—as well as a host of affordable Vietnamese fare. Breakfasts are hearty, the coffee is strong, and they change the TV to CNN when foreign visitors arrive.

49 Dien Bien Phu St. ☏ **031/382-2934.** Set menu 65,000 VND–120,000 VND. MC, V. Daily 6:30am–11:30pm.

Truc Lam   *Truc Lam* means "Bamboo Forest" and refers to an old Chinese legend about travelers lost in the woods (the owner will patch the story together for you). On the second floor of the Maxim minihotel (see above), Truc Lam serves classic Vietnamese cuisine and offers special imports on occasion such as salmon from Norway

HOTELS ■
Bach Dang Hotel **4**
Harbour View Hotel **1**
Maxim Hotel **2**

RESTAURANTS ◆
Maxim's Restaurant and Bar **3**
Truc Lam Restaurant **2**

ATTRACTIONS ●
Haiphong museum **5**
Municipal theater **6**

or beef from New Zealand. Meals are tastefully presented on oversize crockery, and tables are draped in linen. The narrow interior's dark red walls are bisected by heavy shelves displaying oversize pottery, and some fine examples of local painters works hang here. This restaurant is always full and seems to attract a unique mix of expats and locals. The only drawback to the dining experience is the secondhand smoke, so go for a seat near the veranda (and certainly not back near the small bar). They regularly feature live music, too.

36 Le Dai Hanh St. ✆ **031/384-2487.** Main courses 60,000 VND–200,000 VND. MC, V. Daily 6am–midnight.

HALONG CITY

160km (99 miles) NE of Hanoi

Halong City, a jumping-off point for trips to the bay, has grown in direct proportion to increased tourism, and you'll find a number of fine hotels to choose from, though it tends to accommodate more Asian tourists than Westerners, whose tastes are better catered for at Cat Ba (p. 157). Many visitors choose to overnight on one of the cruisers in the bay (p. 158) or take a full-day boat trip that ends at Cat Ba Island. But if you're not keen on sleeping on the ocean blue or overnighting in an island outpost, Halong City might be just the ticket. Most visitors here are part of Vietnamese and Chinese tour groups, especially in the summertime, when Hanoians want to get out of the humid capital.

The town is divided into **Bai Chay,** the main tourist strip of hotels and boat piers for trips to the bay, and **Hong Gai,** a more local area that's connected by a new suspension bridge. Hong Gai has just a few minihotels and local restaurants geared mainly to Chinese tour groups. The local Halong City culinary specialty is *gio,* a minced pork dish popular with Chinese tourists.

FAST FACTS A **Vietcombank** branch in Bai Chay, along Halong Road near the main pier (☎ **033/381-1099**), has an **ATM** and can cash traveler's checks. Open Monday to Saturday 8am to 4pm, but closed for lunch 11:30am to 1:30pm. The outlet adjacent to the post office offers the best **Internet** service. The main Halong **post office** is at the intersection of Vuon Dao and Halong Road at seaside.

Where to Stay

Below, I've listed the three best hotels of the many in Halong City. Because few tour groups stay in town (most opt for overnights on boats in the bay), the city attracts more regional tourists and larger Chinese tour groups. There isn't much to see in town, but the hotels are good.

If you're looking for something a little lighter on the wallet, check out **Sunlight Hotel,** 88 Hung Thang, Group 8 Section 9A Bai Chay (☎ **033/384-4479**), just around the corner from the Mithrin Hotel (see below). It has clean, basic rooms—not to mention a helpful tour desk—from as low as $25 a night.

Halong Dream Hotel ★   Near the boat pier for Saigon tourists, the Halong Dream is the last decent hotel option before you get to the town's northern terminus and bridge. The large rooms have fluffy duvets and marble bathrooms; suites are much larger versions of the same chain-hotel-style decor. There's a small spa and fitness center, and the midsize pool is not bad for kicking back for an afternoon. Good views from the upper floors showcase the busy bay and distant Halong.

10 Halong Rd., Bai Chay Ward, Halong City. www.halongdreamhotel.com.vn. ☎ **033/384-9009.** Fax 033/384-4855. 184 units. $115–$185 double; $210–$290 suite. MC, V. **Amenities:** International restaurant; bar; lobby lounge; health club; Jacuzzi; outdoor pool; room service; sauna; small spa. *In room:* A/C, TV, fridge, minibar, Wi-Fi.

Mithrin Hotel   Sticking out like a sore thumb, obtrusively over the undeveloped southern end of the Halong City strip, Mithrin was built with unflagging optimism that this town will boom and the hotel will be the center of a little skyscraper village (for now, it's still a barren salt flat). Managed by Swiss-Belhotel International, a company of good reputation in the region (see the Hanoi Horison, p. 69, and the Golden Sand in Hoi An, p. 209), the Mithrin covers all the bases: It has a small pool, salon, gym, small spa with sauna and Jacuzzi, and a very helpful and accommodating staff. Rooms are large and rather dull, a typical businessman's hotel with lots of disinfectant sprayed about, but they're clean and pleasant enough, with cable and standard in-room amenities. Bathrooms are small.

Hoang Quoc Viet Rd., Halong City. www.mithrinhotelhalong.com.vn. ☎ **033/384-8090.** Fax 033/384-1770. 88 units. $85–$95 double; $165 suite. MC, V. **Amenities:** Restaurant; bar; Jacuzzi; outdoor pool; room service; sauna; tennis. *In room:* A/C, TV, fridge, minibar, Wi-Fi.

Novotel Halong Bay ★★   It only takes a glance at the lobby to realize this is the best place to rest your head in Halong City, and comes with the usual Accor guarantee of reliable service and comfortable in-room facilities. The rooms are thoughtfully lit and feature thick mattresses and crisp sheets. Modern furnishings have minimalist lines, and there's a feeling of harmony about the space. Most rooms have wood floors and balconies with views out across the bay. There's a huge swimming pool and spa facility, too. In addition to tours of Halong Bay, they can organize trips to Bay Tu Long Bay, kayaking and rowing, and cookery classes.

Halong Rd., Bai Chay Ward, Halong City. www.novotelhalongbay.com. ✆ **033/384-8108.** Fax 033/384-8018. 214 units. $140–$155 double; $180 executive room; $250 suite. MC, V, AE. **Amenities:** Restaurant; bar. *In room:* A/C, satellite TV, fridge, minibar, hair dryer, Wi-Fi.

Saigon Ha Long Hotel ★   This massive hotel on a hill above the bay (and across from a private jetty for Saigon tourist boats) is government owned, which is usually a bad thing, but not here: all the bases are covered, and it's quite cozy. The hotel attracts huge groups, and the front-desk staff handles the rush with aplomb. Deluxe rooms have large balconies and good views (go for the 14th floor, which is the highest one here). The pool in a small courtyard is near an outdoor restaurant that overlooks the street below.

168 Halong Rd., Bai Chay Ward, Halong City. www.saigonhalonghotel.com. ✆ **033/384-5845.** Fax 033/384-5849. 222 units. $95–$125 double; $225 suite. MC, V. **Amenities:** 2 restaurants; 3 bars; babysitting; small health club; Jacuzzi; outdoor pool; room service; sauna; tennis courts. *In room:* A/C, TV, fridge, minibar, Wi-Fi.

HALONG BAY

175km (109 miles) E of Hanoi; 55km (34 miles) NE of Haiphong

The light playing on the arching rock formations of Halong Bay is never the same, painting rich colors on a stunning landscape, which attracts many artists and photographers. A Vietnamese fable says that the towering limestone-karst rock formations at Halong were formed with the crash landing of a dragon sent by the prehistoric gods of early Vietnamese animism to protect the country from an invading navy. The picturesque area did, in fact, play host to some important Vietnamese naval victories against Chinese forces (a fact that is proudly broadcast to all visitors), but the bay is most famous for its emerald green water and more than 3,000 islands of towering limestone in the Gulf of Tonkin.

The total area of the bay is 1,553 sq. km (606 sq. miles), but only 434 sq. km (169 sq. miles) are part of the UNESCO World Heritage Site (designated as such in 1994). Of the more than 700 islands and islets in this area, only a few are habitable. Some islands were originally named by local fisherman, usually based on their shape. You'll find the likes of Tea Pot Island, Mother and Child Island, and Stone Dog Island.

The bay's topography developed over 250,000 years, from when Earth's crust was unstable. Originally deep under a prehistoric ocean, the area formed layers of limestone sediments that slowly weathered and receded. Limestone being porous, it created mountains that look a bit like Swiss cheese, laced with hundreds of caves. More than 20 caves in the bay are open to visitors.

Tran Hung Dao had his great standoff with the Chinese in this area. Anticipating the Chinese attack, the story goes that wily Tran Hung Dao had his men place long

How Halong Got Its Karst

Karst—a name derived from a limestone plateau in Slovenia—refers to outcroppings of readily soluble rock, commonly limestone, that are eaten away by chemical reactions catalyzed by dripping water. The karst outcroppings in Halong—and in places such as Guilin, China or Phang Nga Bay, Thailand—are made of this porous sedimentary rock and tend to develop dynamic caves that drip minerals and form stalactites and stalagmites. Other features of limestone karst deposits and erosion are wide fissures and underground streams—in short, a constantly changing, dynamic landscape caused by chemical erosion. Some of Halong's many caves are actually "dead," meaning that the leaching process is over, but others are constantly changing.

bamboo stakes in the bay, and when the Chinese ships arrived at low tide, they were pierced and thus easily attacked by the fearless Vietnamese hero and his men. You'll see Tran Hung Dao's statue in nearly every town in Vietnam, and the story of his clever foiling of the Chinese (not, of course, their subsequent return and rule of Vietnam for nearly 1,000 years) is the stuff of real glory. **Do Go,** or the Cave of Stakes (see "Attractions," below), is the reputed resting place of the stakes that foiled the Chinese.

Hundreds of thousands of visitors have climbed aboard the tour boats making the rounds of the sights. The crowds at the overstuffed ferry pier in Halong City are a bit much (you're never alone out on the bay), but the water is flat, great for kayaking and swimming, and a visit here is a real highlight of any tour of Vietnam. Of course, the experience depends on the weather, which is more unpredictable in Halong Bay than elsewhere in Vietnam. Spending a day watching drizzle running down the porthole is not much fun.

A visit to Halong Bay—about a 4-hour drive from Hanoi—usually includes an overnight stay (though it can be done in one very long day, it's not advisable). Given the logistics, the trip is best done through an agent or with a group. When you book a tour with an overnight stay, you'll probably cruise on a junk for 4 to 6 hours along the bay, stopping to explore two or more grottoes and other sights along the way. You might pause for swimming or kayaking, depending on the operator (some offer just cruising; others have extensive adventure agendas). Overnight trips can cost anywhere from $20 to upward of $150. It depends on whether you hire a bus or a private driver, where you stay, and what you eat. Sinh Café does a reasonable job on the low end, but don't expect much more than the ride and a surly guide. In fact, there are definite dangers in going with a cheap tour; in February 2011, 11 foreigners and a tour guide drowned when their boat sprang a fatal leak at night and sank before they could get out of their cabins. Good luxury options abound (see below).

The best time to visit is from May to October, though it's impossible to guarantee good weather. The weather's at its hottest at this time, but it's your best chance for good visibility. *Note:* With hundreds of boats heading out into the bay every day, the amount of garbage being discarded into the bay's waters by thoughtless tourists is beginning to spoil the otherwise magical views. This is one reason to join a tour that explores lesser-frequented parts of the bay, such as **Bai Tu Long Bay,** just north and east of Halong. The area is a busy fishing zone, and the scenery is not quite as dynamic as in Halong, but many visitors appreciate the absence of huge tour groups. Contact a tour agency in Hanoi for information.

More active trips include **rock climbing** the beautiful, steep karst outcrops of the bay, or a 2- or 3-day **sea-kayaking** tour. Contact BlueSwimmer Adventures or Slo Pony, both based on Cat Ba (see below), for exciting half-day to multiday trip packages.

The Boats of Halong Bay

Halong Ginger ★★ 👔 Unlike the *Emeraude* (see below), *Halong Ginger* is a small, intimate affair, equipped with only 10 cabins all pushed to either side of a central deck to ensure each room has a private, unobstructed view of the ocean. Deluxe rooms come with three large windows, letting in plenty of light and ocean sounds. Rooms have huge bathrooms, especially for a boat, and marble countertops.

Halong Ginger's cruising route moves away from the traffic of Halong Bay, and unlike other junks in the bay, it doesn't retrace its path. Passengers board the boat between 11:30am and noon, with staff on hand to carry suitcases to your cabin so that you can enjoy a welcome drink on deck. The boat sets off at 12:30pm and a set menu of local seafood is served for lunch half an hour later. The boat docks at Soi Sim, an island in the heart of Halong Bay, where you either take a dip or go for a trek to a viewpoint. Then it's off to Lan Ha Bay, south of Halong Bay, where you are taken into a traditional fishing village. If you opt for kayaking, you can kayak yourself through the village. From here, it's time to board bamboo boats to maneuver through narrow waterways into a secluded cave.

Dinner aboard the boat is a sumptuous set seafood menu. Finish your evening with drinks on the upper deck. Then it's a dreamy sleep in your luxe cabin before the early morning tai chi class. After a visit to a grotto, the second day is a simple, relaxing cruise back to the hectic pace of land life. The price of *Halong Ginger*'s overnight cruise is hefty, ranging from $419 to $493. Book through their website at www.cruisehalong. com, or call their offices at ✆ **04/3933-5561** (fax 04/3984-4538). They also have two newer junks, the **Halong Jasmine** and the **Halong Violet,** both of which are smaller, more exclusive, and (incredibly enough) more expensive than the **Halong Ginger.**

Emeraude ★★ For a unique high-end experience, book passage aboard the *Emeraude,* a copy of a French steamer that once plied these waters in the early 20th century. Certainly the largest of the luxury boats, at 55m (180 ft.), the elegant *Emeraude* has 38 cabins, a fine-dining outlet, and plenty of room to stretch your legs. The luxury trip comes with a price tag, of course, but the 2-day, 1-night cruise is well worth it.

Leaving Hanoi at 8am, you'll check in at a private pier and be walked to the boat. Compact rooms are decked out in hardwood, with nice fixtures such as air-conditioning, a private reading lamp, slippers for shuffling about the decks, and a tidy bathroom area with toilet, shower, and a separate room for a small sink stand. Everything on board is retro, which means pleasing hardwood, brass, and fine linens. The oversize wicker chairs on the top deck are cozy, and you'll find shaded areas as well as sunworshiping space. A casual, friendly atmosphere pervades, especially when the corks start popping.

Dining on board is a delicious buffet, and most guests find themselves sharing a meal with new friends. Lunch on Day 1 is followed by a stop at the Surprise Cave (see "Attractions," below), then an afternoon of cruising and great views of the islands. The boat docks in a quiet harbor, and guests have an opportunity to, on their own or with a guide, explore nearby Trinh Nu and Hang Trong, the Virgin Cave and the Cave of the Winds, or take a dip in the bay. Dinner is a sumptuous affair of fine local cuisine (heavy on seafood) and good Western options. Enjoy drinks on the upper deck as you watch the moonlight glisten off the bay.

Day 2 starts with tai chi classes on the sun deck as a brilliant sunrise (hopefully) paints its colors on the arching canvas of high limestone peaks jutting from the glassy waters. After your exercise, tuck in to a hearty Western-style breakfast. The boat returns to the dock by 9:30am, and a direct transfer finds you back in Hanoi by lunchtime. The trip is quite memorable, and a ride on this retro ship, outfitted to the nines, is unique to Halong Bay. The price for the overnight cruise is $370 for a superior cabin for two and $550 for the one-suite room, but discounts for larger groups are available. Shuttle bus transfer from Hanoi costs $40. Check the website at www. emeraude-cruises.com, or call their office in Hanoi (© **04/3935-1888**).

Jewel of the Bay ★   Another highly recommended luxury boat (just a step down from the *Emeraude*), the *Jewel of the Bay* runs overnight trips concentrating on eco-tourism that include kayaking, touring, and fine dining. For more information or to book a trip, contact **Buffalo Tours** (© **04/3828-0702**; www.buffalotours.com/jewel). The company runs varying itineraries, including a trip that loops out as far as Cat Ba. Buffalo's boat now has a companion vessel.

Indochina Sails   Run by the people at **Handspan** (© **04/3926-2828**; www. handspan.com), the very popular *Indochina Sails* has a high standard comparable to the *Jewel of the Bay*, and the focus is similarly on hearty eco-tourism and getting away from the crowds.

Attractions

The caves and attractions are listed in the order that you'll reach them on tour from Halong City. All boat trips will point out the prescribed route or provide a map. Most day trips include stops at one or two of the major caves (but not all). Entrance to the caves is usually included in a tour itinerary, but be sure to specify when booking.

Thien Cung Grotto (Heavenly Cave)   A visit to Thien Cung, one of the most popular caves for day trips, starts from the crowded dock area where wooden walkways lead to steep stairs going up to the mouth of the cave—just a short walk. The interior has hokey circus lighting, lots of big rock formations, and the usual interpretive names. This is considered the Cave of the Dragon, where the dragon that created Halong sought refuge, and guides are quick to point out one elaborate stalactite that looks like a dragon (or maybe a hoagie, depending on your interpretation). There's a legend surrounding the cave about a young girl who, in order to end years of oppressive drought, married the presiding dragon in the cave, and their wedding was attended by all in the animal kingdom. It's a "dead cave" in that, unlike many limestone caves, it is no longer dripping water and growing formations of additional deposits or creating new fissures and caves.

4km (2½ miles) directly east off the shore of Halong City. Admission 30,000 VND. Daily 8am–5pm.

Do Go (The Cave of Stakes)   Reputed resting place of the long stakes that Tran Hung Dao used to sink the Chinese fleet that came to attack Halong and Haiphong, Do Go is a massive cave with three chambers, not far from the Thien Cung Grotto (above).

Included with entrance to the Thien Cung Grotto. Daily 8am–5pm.

Surprise Cave ★★ Discovered in 1901, this very large grotto was used by Viet Cong as a hide-out during the war with the United States. A short, steep climb up paved steps leads you to three chambers, the last being the largest. In 1999, the Chinese cooperated to install lights and a safe pathway through the cave. A tour of the cave usually involves a guide leading you on an interpretive stalagmite hunt. Guides like to point out a large phallic formation glowing under a bright red spotlight. Also look for tiger, dragon, and penguin formations, as well as unique "melon ball" stalactites. Toward the top of the cave are viewing platforms overlooking the sprawling bay, with its myriad junks far below.

Admission 30,000 VND. Daily 8am-5pm.

Drum and Virgin Cave Adjoining the most popular place for overnights in Halong Bay, this stunning and quiet nook in the bay is a place where you might be able to interact with some local fisherman, if you can get out on the water in a kayak. The caves are on opposite sides of the calm bay, and each is but a shallow area. Some tours even set up fully catered meals with banquet tables in the caves.

Free admission. Daily dawn-dusk.

Ba Hung Informally called the Indochine Cave (ever since the film starring Catherine Deneuve was shot here), this short grotto leads to a hollowed island lagoon with steep walls of jungle surrounding shallow salty waters. On budget trips to Cat Ba Island, boats stop at the entrance and small shuttle boats will take you to the cave through low openings. The proceeds from admission sales allegedly go to help the small floating school in the nearby floating village (you pass the school on the way).

Free admission. Boat ride is 20,000 VND. Daily dawn-dusk.

CAT BA ISLAND

I first came to Cat Ba in 1998 on an overnight tour by boat from Halong City. At the time, the little bay of Cat Ba was choked with beat-up old fishing junks, and the quiet little oceanside strip had but a few budget hotels. A sturdy Russian Minsk motorbike was the main mode of transport. Oh, how times have changed.

The population of Cat Ba Island is now more than 30,000, the bay has been cleared of junks (all fishing vessels must park a few hundred meters offshore), and the main seaside avenue has been widened. There are a number of midrange high-rise hotels, and even a luxury resort on the Cat Co III beach just north of town. Direct high-speed boat service runs from Hanoi via Haiphong, or, even better, try the direct bus that goes from the town center, rides on a ferry, and delivers you to the center of Haiphong or on to Hanoi. The town is very busy with Hanoi weekenders, especially in the summer, and thus best avoided then (the hotel prices are often nearly double on summer weekends). Most travelers zip through on 1-night package tours, but it's best to arrange your own transport to this area. Tours to Cat Ba limit you to dinner with the group and a strict schedule. I recommend booking a tour with a group for *transport only,* or making Cat Ba your last stop on a budget tour of Halong Bay and then arranging your own hotel and schedule for your time in Cat Ba. This could include any combination of **trekking, mountain biking, sailing,** and **rock climbing** arranged by local tour groups (see "Activities," below). The Cat Ba National Park has some good trails to explore, and the interior of the island and the rocky eastern coast are great places to get off the map (contact any hotel tour desk for an all-day tour of the island). You might want to check out the April 1 festival that commemorates Ho Chi Minh's visit to the island: It's quite a grand fete, with dragon-boat races and a big fashion show.

Getting There & Getting Around

BY BOAT/BUS Most visitors get to Cat Ba on tours through Hanoi's budget cafes, though it's just as easy to go it alone. The typical boat journey on a tour includes an exploration of Halong Bay and an overnight on the island, but more and more folks are now booking their boat journey through Halong with a tour company, then ending the trip in Cat Ba and taking the reins from there. You might even arrange a stop in Haiphong or onward to Ninh Binh.

The best bus-to-boat service from Hanoi to Cat Ba, **Hoang Long Bus Company** (in Hanoi, 28 Tran Nhat Duat, ✆ **04/3928-2828;** in Haiphong, 4 Le Thanh Tong, ✆ **031/355-2866;** on Cat Ba Island, 223 1 April Rd., ✆ **031/268-8008**) runs four times daily from Cat Ba back to the mainland at Haiphong and on to Hanoi. They have air-conditioned buses that pick you up and whisk you to the dock of a high-speed ferry. There are also four buses daily from Hanoi, departing at 5:20, 7:20, 11:20am and 1:20pm. The journey is around 4½ hours, and a one-way ticket will set you back around 200,000 VND.

An alternative is to take a hydrofoil to Haiphong (about 1 hr.), which leaves from the pier at the town center, and then pick up a bus from there. **Transtour** (✆ **031/388-8314**) operates the Mekong Express hydrofoil, which is a swift and comfortable way to go; departure times vary, so call for the latest information. There's a ticket booth at the pier, and the fare is 130,000 VND.

Where to Stay

Room rates fluctuate wildly on Cat Ba, especially during the summer (June–Aug), when the place is overrun with vacationing Vietnamese. At this time hotel owners will bump their rates up as high as they think they can get away with. By contrast, outside this season, they are willing to offer huge discounts to attract guests and give their staff something to do.

Bay View This smart minihotel on the harbor front is run by an English-Vietnamese couple and provides well-maintained rooms with heavy wooded beds at rock-bottom prices. Go for one at the front with the eponymous view; it's as good as any other view in town. There's also a small cafe that turns out great food, so you don't need to go searching at meal times.

Duong 1/4, Cat Ba Town. ✆ **0313/368-8241.** 12 units. $10–$15 double. No credit cards. **Amenities:** Restaurant. *In room:* A/C, TV, fridge, Wi-Fi.

Cat Ba Sunrise Resort ★ This new small resort set a higher bar on little Cat Ba. On a strip of reclaimed land between mountain and beach, the resort is set in a small protected cove called Cat Co III beach. To get to the cove, you have to walk up a flight of steps from the road, then down steps to the narrow beachside strip. Cat Co III Beach connects with the other Cat Co beaches by a high walkway carved into the rocks along the shore. The resort has a midsize central pool overlooking a thin stretch of beach lined with tidy lawn chairs and thatch umbrellas. The space is tight, hemmed in by the dark rocky shore and cliffs that surround the little enclave, but the rooms are of a high standard and the place has enough amenities to cover all the bases. Clean, tiled rooms have beds draped with burgundy covers, matching heavy curtains, and dark-wood built-in cabinets. Suites are large and luxurious, with red-wood trimmings, and the top-floor family suites are great for parents traveling with kids. All units have sea views, and most have balconies. You'll find good dining options in a spacious and lively open-air bar. Beach parties with bonfires are held for special groups.

Cat Co III Beach, Cat Ba Island. www.catbasunriseresort.com. © **031/388-7360.** Fax 031/388-7365. 39 units. $120–$140 double; $220 suite. MC, V. **Amenities:** Restaurant; bar; small health club w/sauna and Jacuzzi; outdoor pool in courtyard; room service. *In room:* A/C, TV, fridge, minibar, Wi-Fi.

Holiday View Hotel ★   Holiday View is the only international-standard hotel on Cat Ba. The 13-story tower, on the north end of the main Cat Ba strip, offers new and neat accommodations, though not particularly luxurious ones. Standard rooms are somewhat compact but offer cool wood floors and tidy coverlets on beds. Everything is clean and not musty. Bathrooms have granite counters but are the guesthouse variety, with shower nozzles that open to the toilet and sink area (kind of a disappointment for this category). Better are the large corner rooms, especially on higher floors with good views of the busy bay out front. Deluxe rooms have bathtubs and a lot more space—they're worth the upgrade. The Holiday View caters mainly to regional businessmen and small conventions, but it's also a good choice for an individual traveler.

Zone 4, Cat Ba Town (north end of the main strip, on the way to the beaches). holidayviewhotel@vnn.vn. © **031/388-7200.** Fax 031/388-7209. 120 units. $65–$75 double; $80–$90 suite. MC, V. **Amenities:** Restaurant; bar. *In room:* A/C, TV, fridge, minibar, Wi-Fi.

Princes Hotel   Just a few feet off the main street, Princes Hotel is an old standby. The staff is friendly as can be, happily accommodating any wish—from hiring guides, to renting motorbikes, to purchasing onward transport—but the place is pretty beat up. Set in a towering courtyard, the rooms have tiled floors and soft lighting. The best are on the top floor with views over surrounding buildings to the bay; otherwise, expect to look at concrete walls.

303 Nui Ngoc Rd., Cat Ba Town (just 20m/66 ft. up a side road off the seaside blvd.). www.catbatravel.com. © **031/388-8899.** Fax 031/388-7666. 80 units. $40–$50 double. MC, V. **Amenities:** 2 restaurants; bar; health club w/Jacuzzi. *In room:* A/C, TV, fridge, minibar, Wi-Fi.

Sunflower One Hotel   A brightly lit lobby of crayon yellow greets you at this hotel, popular among tour groups—if only the staff were so bright and cheery. The clean rooms are comparable to what you'll find at nearby Prince Hotel (see above), but the greeting and service at the Prince is far more kind and genuine. Still, Sunflower One remains the pick for Sinh Café tours, which means folks will keep coming.

Nui Ngoc Rd., Cat Ba Town (just 20m/66 ft. up a side road off the seaside boulevard). www.sunflowerhotels.com.vn. © **031/388-8429.** Fax 031/388-8451. 89 units. $40–$120 double. No credit cards. **Amenities:** Restaurant; bar; room service. *In room:* A/C, TV, fridge, minibar, Wi-Fi.

Where to Eat

Seafood dining on the bay is not what it once was. Gasoline spills abound, and I was paddled out to a seafood joint similar to one I'd visited years ago, and what was brought up from their live well was just a handful of dead shrimp. Cooking conditions are not hygienic, and these folks weigh your catch when wet, then just chop it all up with a cleaver, and cook it. These restaurants are not really atmospheric, and they provide neither good value nor good quality. Stick to dining on the mainland.

The main drag of Cat Ba is chockablock with small storefront eateries. Young hostesses stand out front and try to get your attention, drag you in, and fill you up with seafood by the pound. Prices are reasonable. These places are nothing spectacular but are a good value for local seafood; try **Hoang Y** (see below). Just offshore, **Bien Xanh,** at the north end on the way to the beaches (✆ 031/388-8485; daily 6–11pm), is Cat Ba's only quality floating restaurant. It's connected to shore by a walkway and gangplanks, and inside you'll find a fine-dining area and good fresh fish and seafood much like the town's other oceanside restaurants, but here you're in a quieter and more romantic setting.

Bamboo Café INTERNATIONAL/VIETNAMESE   One of the coziest and most welcoming places along the seafront, this place serves a good range of Vietnamese dishes, such as sweet and sour beef and seafood, as well as some international favorites; portions are generous. The congenial owner Mr. Tuan will help with recommendations if you can't decide what to eat. For seating, choose between the ocean-facing terrace and the snug, bamboo-lined interior.

Duong 1/4 Cat Ba Town. ✆ **031/388-7552.** Main courses 30,000 VND–100,000 VND. No credit cards. Daily 8am–10pm.

Flightless Bird Cafe INTERNATIONAL   Aussie owner Graeme offers a friendly welcome, a pint, or a coffee, and can dispense good information about the area. Flightless Bird is a cozy little streetside cafe and bar in the northern end of the town's main strip. It fills up on weekends with expats and locals.

Zone 4¼ Rd. (ocean side on the northern end of town), Cat Ba Town. ✆ **031/388-8517.** 15,000 VND–40,000 VND. No credit cards. Daily 6:30pm–12:30am.

Green Mango ★ ASIAN/CONTINENTAL   Green Mango is your best bet for a sophisticated meal on the island. Young Chef Hai sidles up to your table and gives you the lowdown on the night's specials in a way that makes you feel like you've just heard about a new club opening. It's a cool, open-air, terra-cotta-tiled, candlelit space on the north end of the main strip, but the hip vibe is sometimes cooled by the presence of local hot shots barking on their cellphones and wandering in and out of a seedy little pool hall next door. The food, from a great tapas menu with lots of daily specials, is presented on cool white plates. I especially like the fresh spring rolls, red snapper spaghetti, and a fresh filet cooked with Thai green curry on a bed of linguine. For dessert, try the delicious crepe with rich pudding. This is a good place to have a good bottle of imported wine and enjoy a leisurely evening in an intimate booth.

Group 19 Zone 4 (ocean side in the south end of town). ✆ **031/388-7151.** Main courses 110,000 VND–240,000 VND. MC, V. Daily 6:30am–late.

Hoang Y SEAFOOD   Of the fairly typical Cat Ba waterfront restaurants, this place is my pick for fresh seafood that's affordable. Go for a steamed fish in any preparation that appeals. They also have a few Western dishes, such as steak and spaghetti, for international tastes. There are several places nearby with similar names, so check that you're at the right address.

197 Duong ¼ (on the seafront at the northern end of town). ✆ **031/388-8199.** 50,000 VND–120,000 VND. No credit cards. Daily 5am–11pm.

Noble House ★ CONTINENTAL   This three-story stylish house is noble indeed. The open-air, first-floor dining is done in a cool mix of rough-hewn timber and stone masonry. The second floor has low tables and floor cushions, and the top is a rockin' bar with a pool table and raised platform seating. Australian owner Peter rules the roost and can share good local information about the town or touring the surrounding area. The food is a savory mix of the familiar. Good "fry-up" breakfasts for the homesick or hung-over (often from a night spent on the same stool) are served all day, and the cheese omelet is done with real cheese. There are also good local stir-fries, lots of grilled or steamed fish dishes, and a popular beefsteak, fries, and salad entree. The steamed crab with ginger is a favorite. You're sure to meet lots of expats and fellow travelers here. (Start with happy hour 6–9pm and go from there.)

Next to the post office on the main oceanside strip. ✆ **031/388-8363.** Main courses 100,000 VND–120,000 VND. No credit cards. Daily 6am–late.

Cat Ba National Park

The Cat Ba National Park, established in 1986, takes up some 50% (15,200 hectares/37,544 acres) of the island's mountain and coastal areas, with vast tracts set aside for "primary care and stringent protection" of endangered species. The park's low peaks—the highest is Cao Vang, at just 322m (1,056 ft.)—are a dynamic, verdant setting. Cat Ba is cool year-round, with an average temperature of 73–74°F (23–24°C). In July, it can get up to 82–83°F (28–29°C), and in January and February, it can go as low as 61–62°F (16–17°C). Rainy season is from April to November. The park is comprised of limestone evergreen forests, upland flooded forests, coastal mangrove forests, inshore coral reefs, and extensive areas of limestone outcroppings laced with caves; all are evergreen tropical monsoon forests.

The park supports a veritable Noah's Ark, with drought-resistant lizards and herbivores, and more than 30 mammals, including langurs, civets, leopards, rhesus macaques, and barking deer. Many species in the park are rare or endangered, especially the **golden-headed langur,** which is unique to this area but has a fragile population of an estimated 70 individuals. Ongoing efforts try to prevent hunting in the park. You might also see pythons, vipers, and water snakes, but your only real chance of catching sight of something special is to take a full-day hike through the park with a guide.

Coastal bird life is astounding, and on any journey along the island's coast, you can see some of Cat Ba's nearly 70 bird species, both tropical monsoon birds and migrants. Water birds, such as the sea eagle, kingfisher, and teal, can be spotted along the island coast. Inland you'll find the likes of the great hornbill, the thrush, and the woodpecker.

This park is geared to domestic tourists, but the scenery is fine and there are a few good hikes. The Educational Center, just on the right after the entry, has one large panel with information (in English) about the park's many rare species, as well as advice about nearby trails. No English speakers are on staff, though, so you're more or less on your own here, which is fine because navigating the park's few trails is a piece of cake, though you can hook up with a tour group in town to explore the place, too.

From the park entrance, walk about 1km (.5 mile) straight back along the wide, clearly marked path, past the rather uninspired zoo with just a few unhappy barking deer in a small field, to the beginning of a good steep grade and signs for the **Kim Giao Forest.** Covering some 20 hectares (49 acres), the forest is home to hardwood prized for furniture making. The trees are not remarkable, however—just squat little things about 5m (16 ft.) high. From here, the path gets treacherous, but just 1.5km

(1 mile) of hiking gets you to the **Kim Giao Peak.** To get to the peak, just pass the turn (on your right) to the Kim Giao Forest and follow the proverbial middle road (the fork to the far left is a steep muddy slope) to the top of the peak. The tiptop requires a good bit of rock scrambling, although there are a few ladders and metal steps set up to make things slightly easier.

Good hikes also go to **Trung Trang Cave** (along the road from Cat Ba Town just before the park entrance), as well as farther into the depth of the park and the Ao-Ech village route to a freshwater reservoir or to the Viet Hai village. Longer routes require a good guide; ask in town about all-day hikes with a boat ride back to Cat Ba Town.

Entrance to the park is just 15,000 VND and 2,000 VND for motorbike parking. Hiring a guide, if you can find somebody, costs about 200,000 VND to go up the peak.

Activities

Cat Ba Island is becoming popular for adventure sports such as **rock climbing, mountain biking, kayaking,** and **trekking.** Most of the **trekking** takes place in the Cat Ba National Park; see above for treks you can do yourself, or join a group at one of the tour operators in town. Two of these operators deserve special mention for their efforts to provide fun activities that don't harm the environment. **BlueSwimmer Adventures** (Ben Beo Pier, Cat Ba Island; © 091/506-3737; www.blueswimmer sailing.com) offers kayaking, sailing, and mountain biking tours including a half-day bike ride ($8), a full-day sailing trip on a catamaran ($50), and a 3-day trip combining all three activities with overnight camping ($140). **Slo Pony Adventures** (Noble House Mezzanine, Duong 1/4 Cat Ba Town; © 091/376-0025; www.slopony.com) specializes in rock climbing, often in combination with kayaking and trips round Halong Bay. Most of their climbing is done in the bay, offering the opportunity to get up close to the sheer limestone cliffs that are a feature of the area. As you can imagine, the number of routes among the thousands of islands is limitless; prices depend on the number in the group, but a full day's instruction ranges between $60 to $100.

Other Attractions

Cat Co Beaches   Cat Co beaches, though just thin strips of hard sand on isolated little bays at the base of the cliffs, aren't a bad place to put your feet up for an afternoon—especially after a long boat trip or before heading back to Hanoi. Cat Co III is home to the Cat Ba Sunrise Resort, making that beach exclusive for anything but walking by and taking a dip. (In other words, you can't use the thatched umbrellas, but nobody owns the water.) Cat Co I and II are open to the public, and you can get there easily by motorbike taxi (about 15,000 VND) or by foot. From the Sunrise Resort on Cat Co III, you can follow the high-cliff walks heading north and enjoy stunning views of the bay on your way to the other beaches.

NORTH-CENTRAL VIETNAM

Most travelers fly over this region between Hue and Hanoi (or take the overnight train), and towns such as Vinh are rarely visited by Westerners (though admirers of Ho Chi Minh go to his birthplace like Elvis fans flock to Graceland). North-Central Vietnam does have some treasures, especially in and around Ninh Binh, a popular place for a day trip or overnight from Hanoi.

NINH BINH

90km (56 miles) S of Hanoi; 110km (68 miles) N of Vinh

The many sights in and around Ninh Binh—just a 30-minute ride south of Hanoi on Highway 1—are often visited as a day trip or with an overnight on a planned tour from Hanoi. Independent travelers arriving in Ninh Binh find themselves in a cluster of shops along busy Highway 1, with little in the way of good food and just one hotel that even passes muster. And, you'll probably end up paying more to do the trip independently. I recommend taking a good, private tour to the area; just choose the sights that most interest you (you can't really do them all in a day) and find a tour operator that makes the trip (see recommended tour operators in the Hanoi chapter, p. 57). The exception to this, and the only place that really merits an overnight—but for nature buffs only—is Cuc Phuong National Park. If you visit Cuc Phuong on a day trip from Hanoi, you arrive at the wrong time of day, when wildlife is hiding, so it's worth an overnight. Otherwise, go with a tour.

Getting There

BY CAR   This is your best bet. Contact Hanoi travel agents to hire your own vehicle with a driver. It's just more than an hour's drive.

BY BUS   There's a regular connection between Hanoi's Giap Bat (Southern Bus Station) and a small station stop just adjacent to the central train station—although some buses will drop you off right on Highway 1. Watch for the hotel of your choosing, best at the Thuy Anh Hotel (see below), and buses will stop for you. You can also connect with Vinh or with Hanoi by minibuses.

BY TRAIN The Reunification Express makes a stop in Ninh Binh, but if you're just making the short trip from Hanoi, it's more of a hassle than going by road.

Visitor Information & Tours

Check with the many tour operators in Hanoi for arranging quality tours of the scenic Ninh Binh area. Go with **Sinh Café** for peanuts, and you'll cover all the bases (for as little as $15 per day); if you book a high-end tour with a company like **Buffalo Tours,** you'll get the best view of local culture and natural sites.

FAST FACTS There's a branch of the **Industrial and Commercial Bank of Vietnam** on Highway 1 at the center of town (Tran Hung Dao; ℂ **030/387-2614**). All hotels provide slow **Internet** connections in lobby terminals, but best is a small Internet nook just across Highway 1 from Thuy Anh Hotel; a small sign leads you down a narrow alley. Cost is just 5,000 VND per hour. The main **post office** is in the south end of town (look for the high radio tower). Open daily 7am to 9pm.

Where to Stay & Dine

In addition to the recommendation below, **Thanh Thuy's Guesthouse & Hotel,** 128 Le Hong Phong St. (ℂ **030/387-1811**), is a bare-bones operation off the main road. Older rooms in the guesthouse start at $6, while smarter rooms in the newer hotel out back go for $15 to $35. They also have a helpful tour desk with reasonable rates. **Queen Hotel,** 21 Hoang Hoa Tham St. (ℂ **030/389-3535;** fax 030/389-3000), outside the train station entrance, is a step up from Thanh Thuy, with doubles from $30 to $45.

Dining in Ninh Binh is only at local storefront restaurants, none more interesting or sanitary than the other. All hotels have decent restaurants, and most people just eat where they're sleeping. Some group tours include meals at **Thuy Anh Hotel**'s (see below) courtyard dining hall or rooftop restaurant (dull, but not bad); and **Queen Hotel** (see above), near the train station, also serves good, affordable one-plate meals. One place worth going out of your way for is the restaurant at the **Xuan Hoa Hotel,** 31D Pho Minh Khai, just off the main highway on the south side of town, where the food gets rave reviews.

Thuy Anh Hotel This place is by far the best in town, and everyone knows it. Thuy Anh is always booked with tour groups, and though the standard is high—for the low price—they don't necessarily court the individual traveler, as tour groups account for most bookings. They do, however, have a helpful front-desk staff and can arrange for motorcycle rentals or a guide for the day. Large rooms are rather plain, with clean white-tile and dark-wood furnishings. Bathrooms are the all-in-one guesthouse variety, but they are clean and have hot water. Dining is a communal affair in the hotel's large courtyard or at the rooftop restaurant.

55A Truong Han Sieu (just a few meters east of Hwy. 1 at the center of Ninh Binh). www.thuyanhhotel.com. ℂ/fax **030/387-1602.** 37 units. $20–$45 double. MC, V. **Amenities:** Restaurant; bar; Internet. *In room:* A/C, TV, fridge, minibar.

Attractions

The sights of Ninh Binh are scattered outside the city, too many to see all in one day. Most travelers visit Ninh Binh on a tour from Hanoi, so it's a good idea to look closely at the sights below before joining a set itinerary. Private tours give you lots of flexibility, and an overnight for some is preferable (especially if you want to visit Cuc Phuong

National Park). A **typical 1-day itinerary** might be either of the following: Tam Coc (the three grottoes), nearby Bich Dong Temple, Hoa Lu (the Old Capital), and Phat Diem Cathedral; or Kenh Ga (Chicken Village), Hoa Lu, and Cuc Phuong. **Note:** Tam Coc and Kenh Ga require boat rides, and visitors usually find one or the other—but not both—to be plenty of floating for 1 day; Tam Coc is more interesting.

TAM COC (THE THREE GROTTOES)

Located near the village of Van Lam, 7km (4¼ miles) southwest of Ninh Binh, the Tam Coc area is a highlight of any visit to Vietnam. Called "The Halong Bay of the Rice Fields" after the UNESCO World Heritage Site north of Hanoi, the stunning limestone karst towers hearken to the famed landscape of the bay, as well as Guilin in southern China—a landscape that has inspired poets for centuries.

The karst towers of Tam Coc are set in wide lowland fields of wet rice. Visitors can take in the stunning scenery on a 1-hour boat ride.

Tam Coc means "Three Grottoes," after the three caves you pass through on the backtracking route. The caves transport you into the misty mountain valley along the meandering stream; there is Hang Ca, Cave One, which is more than 100m (328 ft.)

long; then Hang Hai, Cave Two, at 70m (230 ft.); and last the smaller Hang Ba, Cave Three.

At the large gated entrance, you can buy your ticket (30,000 VND; 60,000 VND for the boat), which entitles you to visit the caves, enjoy a boat ride (you must present your coupon to the rower), and see a few adjoining temple sites. The wooden row-boats leave from a village whose main street is lined with very local linen and embroidery shops—a good selection at very low prices. The rowers are a friendly lot and are happy to chat; some speak English, others smile, and everybody sings as they row, often in unison. Your new friend turns into a salesman by the end of the ride, though. The item up for sale is embroidery, which they'll tell you was executed by the shaking hand of an ailing grandmother—anything to get you to fork over a few dong. If you whip out your wallet, you might as well shout "Free for all! Come and get 'em!"; best to just politely decline and keep your eyes on the passing scenery. In lieu of a purchase, give your rower a small tip at the end.

The time to go to Tam Coc is after 10am (the morning fog obscures the shape of the precipitous peaks). If you arrive too early and the place is still foggy, take a ride out to **Bich Dong Temple,** and then come back for the boat trip. By midday, though, the sun is blistering and the open boats offer no shade. Local hucksters are quick to make the most of your misery and sell (or rent) umbrellas to ward off the sun, but it's best to just bring a good hat and cover up with sunscreen. Along the route you'll see shy kingfishers flitting about, as well as cranes around the paddies and floating weeds. Local fishermen, quite used to the steady stream of tourists, are busy setting nets and paddling about in boats the size of snow saucers. Some fishermen row with their feet, while others use the standing technique of leaning forward and pushing the oars in a heaving forward lunge; the stroke is beautiful to watch, but try doing it and see how difficult it is.

Bich Dong (Jade Grotto) is a stunning cave temple complex at the base of high cliffs about 2km (1¼ miles) past the starting point for boat rides to Tam Coc. A pond is near the entry, and the main temple courtyard gives way to a series of pagodas along the short path up the high rocky hillside: a good vantage point over the surrounding countryside. *Note:* At this sacred place, as at other temple sites, it's best to stay covered up (no shorts).

HOA LU: THE ANCIENT CAPITAL

For a short period at the end of the first millennium (A.D. 968–1009), Hoa Lu was the capital of Vietnam under the Dinh dynasty and the first part of the Le dynasty. The area was chosen because the limestone formations surrounding the site—the same ones that attract tourists by the thousands—were a stalwart natural defense against the Chinese. The temples of Hoa Lu are worth a visit and part of most itineraries out of Ninh Binh. The two temples, both dedicated to respective Le and Dinh kings, are ornate 17th-century re-creations on the site of some ancient ramparts and walls, but what makes the trip interesting is the beautiful scenery of the area, especially along the rural road connecting the site with nearby Tam Coc (see above). The whole valley is hemmed in with high limestone walls of karst, much like the dynamic setting of Tam Coc. One temple honors Dinh Tien Hoang with an imposing statue. The other temple, farther from the road across a large field often used for festivals, is dedicated to Le Dai Hanh, one of Dinh's generals and the first king of the Le dynasty, who grabbed power in A.D. 980 after Dinh was mysteriously assassinated. Hoa Lu can easily be seen on a day trip from Hanoi. The temples are 113km (70 miles) south of Hanoi.

KENH GA: CHICKEN CANAL

Here, tour among floating villages teeming with life, where local oarsmen (and women) row with their feet. Photographers delight. Reach the site by motorbike, either your own rented machine or on the back of a bike with a driver. The village is more than 10km (6¼ miles) west of Highway 1 starting at a juncture 11km (6¾ miles) north of central Ninh Binh. When you arrive, head for the pier where you can hire a boat to take you around the villages for an hour or so for about 50,000 VND.

CUC PHUONG NATIONAL PARK ★★

Ho Chi Minh established Cuc Phuong in 1962 as Vietnam's first national park, and it remains a source of national pride. The park is a lush mountain rainforest with more than 300 bird and 100 mammal species, including tigers, leopards, and the unique red-bellied squirrel. But the park's many visitors—mostly large domestic tour groups, especially on the weekends—might keep you from the kind of wildlife experience you expect in the brush.

   Cuc Phuong National Park (✆ 030/384-8006; www.cucphuongtourism.com) is just 120km (75 miles) south of Hanoi and a 30-minute ride from Ninh Binh. A little town with very basic services (food stall, gasoline stand) is outside the park's first gate. Once in the park, you'll reach the visitor center, where you'll need to pay the 20,000 VND entry fee (children 10,000 VND), as well as an extra 10,000 VND for a (compulsory) guide to lead you around the Primate Resource Center and Turtle Conservation Center. Beyond the visitor center is a small museum.

   A well-paved road runs through the length of the park, and trails and roadside sites are all well marked. Cuc Phuong hosts good hikes, including ones to the park's 1,000-year-old tree, a waterfall, and Con Moong Cave, where prehistoric human remains have been discovered. The park holds 117 species of mammals, 307 types of birds, 110 reptiles and amphibians, 65 species of fish, and 2,000 kinds of insects. The rare Asian black bear and the golden leopard live here.

   The **Endangered Primate Resource Center** ★★★ (✆ 030/384-8002; www. primatecenter.org; daily 9–11am and 1:30–4pm) is the highlight of a visit to the park. Run by an international team of primate experts, mostly from the Frankfurt Zoological Society and supported by zoos worldwide, the project houses some 120 animals in cages, large monkey-houses with swinging bars, and, at the back, a sprawling semiwild jungle enclosure (good for the animals, not great for viewing them). You'll see many species of gibbon, multicolored langurs (including the very rare, protected Catba golden-hair langur and the endangered Delacour's langur), and the cute, bug-eyed slow loris. Animals are lovingly cared for, in the best situation possible, and they put on quite a show—hopping, hollering, and swinging from ropes in large enclosures. **Note:** Though you pass the Primate Center on your way to the main gate, you must still check in at the park's main entrance and backtrack, with a guide, to visit the animals; this policy ensures some measure of control over the number of visitors and their impact on these very intelligent, sensitive creatures.

   The goal of the center is to create stable captive populations of endangered animals and eventually, through socialization and acclimatization in the semiwild habitat, reintroduce animals to the wild. If you visit the park on a day tour from Hanoi, you'll come at the wrong time: midday, when animals are listless and resting from the heat. Folks with an interest in primates will want to spend the night and might even have a chance to meet with staff or researchers who can provide more in-depth information. A small civet-breeding program is next door.

The **1,000-year-old tree** is at the end of a good loop hike that starts at the park's interior visitor center, some 30 minutes' ride past the gate. The path is well marked, mostly paved, and set up with convenient walkways, but the jungle scenery is dense and, if you walk quietly, you might catch a glimpse of some wildlife (especially in the morning or evening).

The **Cave of the Prehistoric Man** is just a roadside attraction, a short hike off the main drag up a hillside with a wide cave. The cave was discovered in 1966, and the remains of an early man, along with his stone tools and relics, are said to date back as far as 12,000 years. The walkway to the site is a good place to sit still and see what kinds of wild things you can spot.

Cuc Phuong is a good day trip from Hanoi, and some tourist cafes offer programs for as little as $35 (depending on the number of people in your group); but a day trip means arriving in the middle of the day, when jungle animals are fast asleep and when the heat and humidity, especially in the hot spring season, can be too much. It's also possible to overnight in the park headquarters or at the visitor information center. They offer basic rooms in a block building at the entrance; doubles go for $10 to $25. One of the most pleasant aspects of visiting Cuc Phuong is the possibility of connecting with visiting naturalists and scientists (when I was there, I met a large contingent from the Philippines), and the overnight accommodations, though rustic, make for a fun evening—especially with a gaggle of scientists in the canteen. There's a lake just inside the park, which is set up like a small summer camp for large groups, usually Vietnamese school kids, and the site echoes with good Vietnamese campfire songs.

Foreigners comprise only a small percentage of the 70,000 people or so who visit the park annually, and the large groups of Vietnamese tourists—and many school groups—are not yet well versed in eco-tourism practices. (I kept coming across a group of more than 50 school kids, all dressed in the same bright yellow T-shirts and wearing oversize straw hats, led by a guide with a bullhorn blaring instructions and information—so much for animal spotting.) Talk to guides about good night-spotting trips and rigorous overnights in the jungle.

PHAT DIEM

Popular in conjunction with a visit to the ancient city of Hoa Lu, a visit to Phat Diem cathedral is an important pilgrimage for the faithful or the architecture buff. Nowhere will you find such a melding of contemporary Christian motifs and Asian-style architecture.

The site is 121km (75 miles) southeast of Hanoi and about 25km (16 miles) south and east of the town of Ninh Binh. The road passes through beautiful areas of lush lowland rice fields and past many lesser cathedrals and Christian burial sites. Note that **Ton Dao Church,** just outside of town, is a particularly imposing edifice with high stone spires, intricate carvings on the lintels and facade, and reliefs of St. Francis ministering to the sick and impoverished. The town of Phat Diem is just a little commercial strip—not much to see, really.

Follow signs to Phat Diem from the main road, down a narrow street that spills onto a broad courtyard at the end of its length. At the center of the courtyard is a pond with an expressive statue of Jesus, and beyond that is your first glimpse of the cathedral.

Enter to the right, but be sure to go back and experience the temple starting at the large Chinese-style gate. The church and grounds uniquely blend East and West. The main cathedral, an imposing wooden structure, has Chinese-influenced parapets, the roofline upturned at the corners, and out front are elaborate lintel bas-reliefs of saints that would elsewhere be Buddhas. All of the structures are decked out in Chinese roofs of terra-cotta tile, and small Chinese pagodas pepper the grounds around the main cathedral. The building stands flanked by a number of small chapels.

The **Cathedral of Saint Joseph**—the first building you reach when making a clockwise circuit around the main temple—was built in 1896 and is made of wood and covered in elaborate engravings and carvings. Behind it is the **Chapel of St. Pierre,** also built in 1896. Usually the interior is closed to the public (most chapels here are), but if you peek along the sides of the altar, which is a 1-ton block of stone, in the back you can see reliefs of the Twelve Apostles and their names in Chinese letters.

Far back on the left is the diminutive **Stone Chapel (Legise de Pierre),** a very refined structure of glossy marble. The chapel is dedicated to the Virgin Mary, and out front is an engraving (in four languages) that reads, IMMACULATE HEART OF MARY PRAY FOR US. Relief works on the cornices of the building depict mythical beasts.

Completing the circuit, and near the entrance of the cathedral grounds, the temple to St. John the Baptist is where locals once came during a cholera epidemic to invoke the help of St. Roch and, when miraculously healed, renamed the building **Roch Chapel.**

The interior of the main chapel is like any Chinese temple, with thick wooden pillars supporting a raised gallery. Red and gold filigree at the altar would be more familiar in a small city temple in Hanoi or Ho Chi Minh City, which makes this cathedral unique. Statues of Mary and Jesus take the place of an expected Buddha, and stained glass depicts both European and Vietnamese martyrs. The main altar was cut from stone block and was consecrated on October 6, 1991, on the 100th anniversary of the temple that was originally built in 1891.

Phat Diem is a working cathedral, and services are ongoing throughout the day.

VINH

300km (186 miles) S of Hanoi; 370km (230 miles) N of Hue

An important bastion of revolutionary thought, the town of Vinh was the scene of a large-scale rebellion led by Le Hong Phong in the 1930s. Bombed beyond recognition during the war with the United States, Vinh was rebuilt with an East German flair, which means that large concrete-block compounds line broad boulevards. Drab and depressing, there isn't much for foreign tourists to see here. What attracts most, and mainly Vietnamese tourists, are the sites dedicated to the city's most famous inhabitant: Ho Chi Minh. Born here in 1890, Ho Chi Minh lived in a small village just 14km (8¾ miles) outside of the city center. A visit to Ho's birthplace, in the adjoining village where his father was a local official, and to the large central square with his statue are the only real sights. Nearby **Cua Lo Beach** is a popular local escape lined with minihotels and beachside coffee shops. Vinh is also a popular way station for those going to or coming from Laos.

FAST FACTS   **Vietcombank** has a branch at 21 Quang Trung St. (© **038/384-2033**) that's open daily from 8am to 5pm (closed for lunch 11:30am–1:30pm). They have an **ATM** and can cash traveler's checks. There is reliable **Internet** service next to the post office. The main post office is at 2 Nguyen Thi Minh Khai St.

Where to Stay & Eat

For **dining** along the Cua Lo strip, the best choice is **Thuy Hang** (© 038/395-1125), at the center of town across the road from the beach. It serves crab, shrimp, squid, and the whole fish as you like. It's the kind of place where you need a bib, but the beauty of it, like most seafood joints in Vietnam, is you can dig in and get your hands dirty, spit shells on the floor, and then wash your hands in the big bucket of water with lemon.

Green Hotel Owned by the conglomerate that owns Maximart, Vietnam's burgeoning version of 7-Eleven, the Green Hotel is a decent choice in the town center, just near the railway station, once you get over the shock of its bright green exterior. Rooms are quite spacious and well equipped with traditional furnishings, a fridge, and satellite TV. The hotel has lots of services, including a small swimming

WHO WAS "uncle ho"?

Ho Chi Minh, Vietnam's greatest revolutionary and patriot, was demonized in the West during the Vietnam War and at the same time canonized as a saint by the Vietnamese, especially after his greatest dream of an independent, united Vietnam was achieved. His martyred image is just as skewed as his vilification in the West.

Ho Chi Minh's life is an allegory of the Marxist struggle in Vietnam, or so young Vietnamese school kids are taught: the ultimate "hero's journey out," where Ho left his homeland, picked up socialist ideals, and returned to raise the flag of revolution. The truth is a bit more complex.

Born **Nguyen Sinh Cung** on May 19, 1890, in the village of Hoang Tru near Vinh, just north of Hue in central Vietnam, Ho spent his young life looking over his father's shoulder as Dad studied to be a mandarin (high government official). While living in Hue, he saw his mother and sister die—experiences that steeled him for a harsh life later. Ho's father was a thinker and had many friends who were active in radical politics, and from an early age Ho was exposed to lots of revolutionary talk. Ho studied only briefly at university before

setting out on his own, walking the length of Vietnam and working as a teacher here and there from 1906 to 1911. He spent time in Nge An, Hue, Quy Nhon, Phan Thiet, and Saigon (all places with "Ho Slept Here" tour spots). Like Che Guevara's motorcycle trip around South America, Ho Chi Minh's formative wanderings in Vietnam were a major part of his identity. He developed his compassion and understanding of the Vietnamese people and also saw up close their struggles under a colonial yoke.

Leaving Saigon in 1911, Ho set sail as a cook on a ship. Reputedly, this was the time when he gained his worldly perspective and began to understand notions of the world as a class struggle, a kind of Darwinian fight that can have only one solution: an ongoing peasant/proletariat revolution. He connected with other free thinkers abroad, working in kitchens in London, and then moved to Paris, where he changed his name to **Nguyen Ai Quoc** ("Nguyen the Patriot"). His ideas began to gain clout among fellow dissidents, and he became involved in underground print journalism while building a Rolodex of fellow revolutionaries.

pool. This is the top choice of the many Vietnamese businesspeople who visit from surrounding provinces.

2 Mai Hac De St., Vinh City, Nghe An Province. ℂ **038/384-4788.** Fax 038/384-8873. 84 units. $32–$45 double. MC, V. **Amenities:** Restaurant; bar; small pool; sauna. *In room:* A/C, satellite TV, fridge, hair dryer, Internet, minibar.

Saigon Kim Lien Hotel Located on busy Quang Trung Street, this government-run, hulking edifice is as good as it gets in Vinh. It was opened in 1990 to commemorate the centenary of Ho Chi Minh's birth, and as such is the town's flagship hotel. The rooms are sparsely furnished (Ho would have approved), but the beds are solid and comfortable. Doubles are not particularly large, so it's worth splashing out on a suite if you want to really relax. There's a good restaurant and a pleasant garden bar, too. Their travel desk can get you a car rental for trips out to Uncle Ho's birthplace or to Cua Lo Beach.

He traveled between Moscow and China, a revolutionary peripatetic, for most of the 1930s, and grew a large following. As a founder of the Indochinese Communist Party (ICP), he was under constant suspicion and surveillance, at one point fleeing to Hong Kong and then on to the south of China, where he formed the League for an Independent Vietnam, whose members, later soldiers, were called the Viet Minh, and then Viet Cong in the war with the United States. Imprisoned by Chiang Kai-shek in 1940, Ho changed his name to **Ho Chi Minh** ("Enlightened One") and returned to Vietnam via surreptitious border crossings and long stays in hide-out caves in the far north (near Cao Bang).

On August 19, 1945, after the surrender of the Japanese in World War II, Ho Chi Minh made his "Declaration of Independence" that borrowed language from U.S. and French documents of freedom. Thus began the armed revolution.

Outwardly an ascetic, Ho was reputedly a ladies' man, and stories of his nighttime dalliances, real or imagined, pepper more recent histories. He is even said to have taken up with a French woman and to have fathered a number of children. Diminutive and delicate, Ho was a leader who lived a spartan existence, upholding the ideals of egalitarian revolution, living in a simple two-room building on the grounds of the former imperial palace (you can see his home near the mausoleum in Hanoi).

Ho Chi Minh died from natural causes in 1969, just 6 years short of seeing his dream of a unified Communist Vietnam. Nearing death, Ho was explicit about his wishes to be cremated, his ashes divided into three separate portions and distributed at sites in the north, center, and south to celebrate the reunification of the country. He asked for no pomp or circumstance, no grand tomb or homage to his remains. The hulking mausoleum, set on the site where he declared independence in 1941, would have him turning in his grave if he weren't, in fact, embalmed and set on a palanquin for general public viewing. A visit to the mausoleum is a quirky highlight of any trip to Hanoi.

Following a long tradition of deifying war heroes, Ho Chi Minh's image is everywhere: on cabs, in shrines, and in long rows of portraits hung in family rooms, sanctified in the family pantheon as one of the great immortals.

25 Quang Trung St., Vinh City, Nghe An Province. ☎ **038/338-3889.** Fax 038/338-8898. 77 units. $40–$55 double; $120 suite. MC, V. **Amenities:** Restaurant; bar; small pool. *In room:* A/C, satellite TV, fridge, hair dryer, Internet, minibar.

Attractions

To truly honor the memory of Ho Chi Minh, visitors to these sights are obliged to buy a bouquet of flowers to lay at three separate places: 1) at the foot of his statue in the central square in the city of Vinh, 2) at his birthplace, and 3) in the nearby village of Kim Lien, where he lived for many years (see listing; below). Going without flowers is, of course, okay, but foreign visitors who follow the tradition get much more respect from the Vietnamese groups. A visit to these sights is a somber one. Docents at each sight speak Vietnamese only, but some will hand you an information card printed in English. *Note:* Especially if you're with Vietnamese friends or tagging along with a group, pretend you're listening; walking away while the docent is speaking is considered rude.

Statue of Ho Chi Minh   In the center of Vinh, the massive square in front of this statue is the city's most popular strolling ground. Western visitors are bombarded by young students eager to practice their English and who want to have their photograph taken with a bona fide Westerner (put on your best grin). The massive statue of Ho at one end of the square is surrounded by a faux mountain range to depict the land of Vietnam, and Ho himself looks downright jaunty, one hand raised as he strides forward, a "revolutionary winning" grin on his bright, silver visage. The steps leading up to the statue are guarded by some surly, jack-booted soldiers who growl at anyone who goes near. The only exception is if you've come with a bouquet for the fallen leader and, leaving your shoes at the bottom of the steps, humbly pad to the foot of the statue and lay your wreath in obeisance (you can stop for a photo on the way down, but don't linger or the lads will bark at you).

At the center of town in Vinh. Free admission. The park and entrance to the statue are open daily dawn–dusk.

Hoang Tru Village   The house where Ho Chi Minh was born belonged to his paternal grandfather and lies in Hoang Tru Village. It's a pilgrimage sight for Vietnamese tourists who come by the busload, especially on weekends and national holidays. Souvenir stalls out front sell busts of Ho, books (some good volumes in English), and bouquets of flowers for placing on the small family altar in Ho's home. The house and furnishings are re-creations, but what strikes any visitor, and is something that Vietnamese almost worship, is the rugged simplicity of these dirt-floored, thatch-wall rooms in which the country's greatest leader sprang from obscurity to spark a revolution. Ho's father was involved in government, and it was in this house, as well as his second home nearby (see below), that Ho first heard the rumblings of discontent from local officials and revolutionary friends of his father. In fact, the likes of Phan Boi Chau, Phan Chu Trinh, and Phan Dinh Phung (names familiar from major city thoroughfares throughout Vietnam) graced the family hearth, and much of Ho's passion for politics came from overhearing these conversations. He was immersed in the cause of peasant revolution. Ho Chi Minh was descended from two generations of teachers, and his studious father endured much to attain the rank of mandarin. Study was therefore a focus for young Ho, too, and his desk and study area are enshrined here, almost like places of worship for Vietnamese, who are so grateful for the high ideals the man held and lived by.

Hoang Tru is 14km (8¾ miles) south of Vinh. Most visitors come by bus or car and then walk to nearby Kim Lien, Ho Chi Minh's second place of residence during his father's shifting career in government.

Free admission. The sights are open daily 8–11am and 1–5pm.

Kim Lien Village   Walking here—it's just 1km (½ mile) from Hoang Tru, along a flat road flanking lush green rice fields—is part of the experience of getting in touch with Ho the man, who, as a young teacher, walked the length of Vietnam going from job to job and searching for a purpose.

The village of Kim Lien features an imposing series of museums and monuments. Display areas with photos of Ho's life and the rise of the revolution grace the walls of two buildings that flank the courtyard entry, and at the back there's a unique building—its interior decorated in red with a great golden bust of Ho Chi Minh—where many lay another bouquet of flowers. It's all strangely like a Buddhist temple, and the vibe is a bit eerie if you're not into worshiping false idols and such (I was with a group of Vietnamese and felt more or less obliged to offer flowers and make an obeisant nod to the bust). Behind this large compound is the house where Ho Chi Minh's father, Nguyen Sinh Sac, lived after his first appointment as a local mandarin. The house (another re-creation) is just as humble as the family's first one, but here you'll see the plaque of the mandarin hanging in Ho's father's office area and a more elaborate family altar. Also on the museum grounds are quiet lotus ponds and a large pavilion with souvenirs (a ceramic Ho Chi Minh bust costs just 20,000 VND) and books, many in English.

Free admission. The sights are open daily 8–11am and 1–5pm.

Cua Lo Beach   The other grand attraction in this region is Cua Lo Beach—wide, wind-swept, and horribly littered—with many services along its length that cater mostly to the Vietnamese holiday crowd (the place is packed on weekends and in the summer). You'll find some great little seafood places on Cua Lo and a few affordable hotels. The beach is just 16km (10 miles) southeast of Vinh, but you shouldn't come here with any illusions, as it's nothing like beaches farther south on the coast.

The last emperor of Vietnam, the "Playboy King" Bao Dai, had a villa here (as he seems to have had in every other town in the country). Now, with lots of little local coffee outlets and romantic picnic areas, the beach is best for strolling (rather than swimming and lying out in the sun). It's a nice escape; don't expect to see other foreign tourists here. Just off the coast, you can see Hon Mat Island in the distance, and tiny Lan Chu Island can be reached on foot at low tide.

Cua Lo Beach is 16km (10 miles) southeast of Vinh.

Phong Nha—Ke Bang National Park   A visit to this national park in Quang Binh Province—which has been designated as a UNESCO World Heritage Site—makes for a good day trip from Vinh. Famous for its massive grottoes, the cave system in this area has still not been fully explored, though several expeditions during the first decade of the 21st century have discovered some truly massive chambers, one of which, the Son Doong chamber, is even bigger than Deer Cave in Sarawak, Malaysia, making it the world's largest cave (the Son Doong discovery was the subject of a story and some stunning photos in the January 2011 issue of *National Geographic* magazine). The main grotto of Phong Nha Cave, and the highlight of a tour here, has 14 "rooms" covering a corridor that is more than 1km long (½ mile) and is illuminated, like the ones in Halong Bay, with multicolored lights that somehow cheapen the cave's grandeur. After clambering up and down several hundred steps to look at the Tien Son Cave (from where there are spectacular views), visitors board boats to travel the length of Phong Nha Cave upstream, then walk back to the cave entrance along a dry route. Note that after heavy rain, boats do not operate, as the water level inside the cave may get too high. Contact tour operators in Hue or Hanoi to visit this stunning natural site. There's no public transportation to the caves.

Nearly 500km (311 miles) south of Hanoi and 55km (34 miles) northeast of Dong Hoi. Admission is 50,000 VND; boat trip is about 200,000 VND. Caves daily 6am–4pm.

CENTRAL VIETNAM

M any of Vietnam's most significant historical sites and some of its best beaches are clustered along its central coast. This is the country's narrowest region; in some places, there's just more than 50km (31 miles) of land between the sea and nearby Laos. Coming from the north, after having passed through (or over) minor cities such as Ninh Binh and Vinh (see chapter 8), the most significant place to visit along the coast is the former Vietnamese capital, **Hue.** With its **Imperial City** and emperors' tombs, the UNESCO World Heritage Site is an important stop for any historical tour of Vietnam.

The next-most important area as you head south is **Hoi An,** another UNESCO World Heritage Site and a historic trading town that had its heyday in the 17th century. Hoi An boasts more than 800 perfectly pre-served classic Chinese and Vietnamese houses and temples laid out in a rabbit warren of streets, preserved as they were hundreds of years ago, thanks to the protection of UNESCO. Formerly the seat of the Cham kingdom from the 2nd through 14th centuries, the central coast also has the greatest concentration of Cham relics and art. Be sure to visit the Cham Museum at **Danang** and the nearby Cham temple site at **My Son.**

Sample the Vietnamese beach scene in its youthful stages at **China Beach** and **Cua Dai,** where luxury resorts are beginning to crowd out fishermen and attract the world's well-heeled. The proximity and conve-nient transportation among the main tour stops in central Vietnam means you'll be able to cover ground efficiently. Danang and Hoi An, for example, are so close (about 30 min. by car) that you can easily stay in one and make day trips to the other.

HUE

Hue (pronounced *Hway*) is culturally and historically significant. It was once Vietnam's Imperial City and later the country's capital under the Nguyen dynasty (1802–1945).

The **Thua Thien–Hue** region was a political football during hundreds of years of early Vietnamese dynastic turf wars with the Cham people in the south and the Chinese in the north. It wasn't until the late 18th cen-tury that the leaders of the **Tay Son rebellion** and Emperor Quang Trung, having routed the Chinese out of the north, established a capital at Hue. Later, the Nguyen dynasty leaders, beginning with powerful Gia

Long, made Hue the capital that served the Vietnamese puppets of the French until the end of World War II. The first citadel and Imperial City was built by Gia Long in 1802 on a former royal site; many of the city walls still stand, battle scarred from fighting with the French as far back as 1873, and later with the Americans during the notorious Battle of Hue in 1968.

Although much of Hue—including most of the walled Citadel and Imperial City—was tragically decimated during wars with the French and the Americans, there's still much to see. And because of the damaged buildings, you'll want to hit the temples with a good English-speaking guide who can bring the place back to life and offer some good background (otherwise, you might see just walls and rubble).

Perhaps most captivating is the daily life on **Perfume River,** with its many dragon boats, houseboats, and long-tail vessels dredging for sand. You can visit many of the attractions, including the tombs of the rather flamboyant and megalomaniacal **Nguyen dynasty emperors,** by boat. The enjoyable town features low-slung, colorful, colonial-style buildings, and strings of lights at outdoor cafes at night draw tourists like moths. Try to sample some of the many local specialties; you'll find fine-dining establishments that specialize in tempering the cuisine to foreign tastes (with varying degrees of success). The **Trang Tien Bridge,** which connects the citadel area with the new town across the Perfume River, is itself a major attraction, a lovers' lane of sorts and a national symbol. You'll see local photographers selling their services in the little riverside park on the new-town side. The bridge is lit up at night with constantly changing bulbs, and lovers stroll the promenade, taking in all of the good Technicolor glistening off the river below. Vendors line the riverside promenade, and it's a good place to buy something sugary.

If you have a special interest in the American War, you may want to plan a full-day excursion to the nearby demilitarized zone (DMZ), the beginning of the Ho Chi Minh Trail, and the underground tunnels at Vinh Moc.

Getting There

BY PLANE   Hue connects to both Hanoi and Saigon with Vietnam Airlines (© **054/382-4709** in Hue). A taxi from the airport costs around 200,000 VND. There's also an airport bus that will drop you off or pick you up at your hotel and covers the half-hour trip to the airport for 45,000 VND. You can buy tickets at a stand in the airport's arrival area, or book through your hotel's front desk or any tour operator.

BY TRAIN   Trains depart daily from both Hanoi and Saigon to the station in Hue (© **054/3822-686**); there are two nightly departures to each place from Hue, at 7 and 11pm to Saigon, and at 3 and 5pm to Hanoi. A trip from Hanoi to Hue takes 14 hours on an express train and costs about $35 in a soft-berth compartment with air-conditioning. From Saigon, in a soft-berth compartment with air-conditioning, it's about $50.

BY CAR   If you're coming from the south, contact any of the tour operators listed below or on p. 178 of this chapter, and they can arrange a car for the 2-hour ride from Danang to Hue for $55 to $65.

BY BUS   Many travelers take a nerve-rattling overnight bus or minivan from Hanoi to Hue. Tickets are $12 for locals and $18 to $22 for tourists through one of Hanoi's tourist cafes (see chapter 5); the trip takes an excruciating 10 hours. Hue is a major

stop on any "open-tour" ticket, and open-tour cafe buses connect with Danang and Hoi An for just 70,000 VND, or Nha Trang for $12.

Getting Around

You can easily get around on foot in the main tourist area along the southern bank of the Perfume River (though the many cyclo and taxi touts would have you think otherwise), but to hit the main sites, you'll need some wheels.

BY TAXI/CAR   Taxis charge 12,000 VND starting out and 14,000 VND for each kilometer after. Flag 'em down or call Mailinh Taxi (© **054/3898-989**). Any hotel front desk can arrange a car and driver for the day, too.

BY CYCLO   Because Hue is relatively small, renting a cyclo by the hour for about 30,000 VND to 40,000 VND works well, but not to the imperial tomb sites outside of town. Red-and-white cyclos stationed outside the Tourist Information Center, 47 Le Loi St., have reasonable fixed rates and planned tour routes.

BY MOTORBIKE/BICYCLE   Even the tiniest hotel provides motorbike rentals at $5 to $7 per day and bicycles for $2 (more for alloy-framed multigear bikes); both are great ways to get out in the countryside and visit the sites. Cycling the Hue riverside areas is particularly memorable. Contact the cheap and friendly Nam Thanh Bike and Bicycle, 48 Le Loi (© **054/3828-951**).

Visitor Information & Tours

You can book boat trips and visits to the DMZ through one of the tour companies in Hue. Every hotel will also be able to assist you, but the tour companies are more affordable, especially for transport. Ask at the Tourist Information Center, for guided private tours. Free maps are also available.

On the budget end, **The Sinh Tourist,** 60 Nguyen Tri Phuong or 12 Hung Vuong St. (© **054/384-5022**; www.thesinhtourist.vn), is open from 6:30am to 10pm. They rent boats for $25 to $35 per day and have very reasonable junkets to the DMZ or around town. A car without guide costs $45 to $50, and a private car to Danang or Hoi An costs $60 to $65. City tours are 200,000 VND.

An Phu Travel, 11 Nguyen Tri Phuong St. or 54 Le Loi St. (© **054/383-3897** or 054/382-0058), arranges reasonable group tours (150,000 VND per person) of the major tombs; tours run daily from 8am to 4:30pm.

[FastFACTS] HUE

Banks & Currency Exchange   Most hotels in Hue change currency. **Vietcombank** is at 78 Hung Vuong St. (© **054/381-1900**), where there's a branch of Western Union as well. VietinBank has an office at 2A Le Quy Don St. (© **054/321-0626**) and ATMs at 12 Hung Vuong St. and on your left as you exit the airport.

Internet   Most hotels and some cafes provide free Wi-Fi, and a few shops on Chu Van An Street provide computers.

Post Office   There's a small post office in front of the Huong Giang hotel. The main post office, 8 Hoang Hoa Tham St., is open from 7am to 9pm.

Telephone   The city code for Hue is 54. You can place international calls at the post office and from most hotels.

Hue

HOTELS ◼
Asia Hotel **17**
The Century Riverside Hotel **9**
Hotel Saigon Morin **8**
Huong Giang Hotel **10**
La Residence Hotel &
    Spa **27**
Orchid Hotel **12**
The Pilgrimage Village **22**
Sports 1 Hotel **13**
Thai Binh Hotel **21**
Thang Long Hotel **21**
Villa Hue **20**

RESTAURANTS ◆
Confetti Restaurant **16**
Hoa Mai Restaurant **10**
Hue Little Italy **18**
La Carambole **15**
Lac Thien **7**
Le Parfum **28**
Mandarin Café **19**
Omar Khayyam **14**

Phuoc Thanh Garden
    Restaurant **15**
Thien Tam Vegetarian
    Restaurant **30**
Tropical Garden **16**
Ushi **14**

ATTRACTIONS ●
Bao Quoc **23**
The Citadel & Imperial City **1**
The Flag Tower **5**
The Forbidden Purple City **2**
Ho Chi Minh Museum **26**
Ho Chi Minh's Home in Hue **11**
Hue Monuments Conservation
    Center **6**
The Imperial Tombs **24**
The Mieu Temple **4**
The Noon Gate (Cua Ngo Mon) **5**
Thai Hoa Palace **3**
Thien Mu Pagoda **29**
Thuan An Beach **11**
Tu Hieu Temple **25**

Local holidays and events abound in Vietnam, but the annual **Hue Festival** is arguably the largest and most colorful. Celebrating ancient Vietnam's richest cultural traditions of dance and theater, the festival has drawn visitors from throughout the country since its inception in 2000. To witness the spectacle, you'll have to book your hotel far in advance—and expect to pay at least double the usual tariff—but you'll enjoy a wild show of floats, dance, and cultural events. **Hue's Imperial Dance** was also named a UNESCO World Heritage vestige of vital "Intangible Culture."

Where to Stay

For the volume of tourists coming through this town, there isn't much of a selection, though things are getting better. Many options are bland, with lots of package tourists arriving to disappointing drab cells ("Honey, it doesn't look like the picture at all!"). Always ask to see your room first. Hotel services in the town's minihotels are limited, but all stops have basic tour services and include breakfast. Prices are flexible, so press for a discount.

EXPENSIVE

The Century Riverside Hotel ★ One of Hue's top choices, this centrally located hotel was recently renovated and is popular with big tour groups. All rooms are clean and fairly comfortable, with new tile and marble bathrooms. Double rooms are rather small, with carved-wood furniture and an impersonal layout that leaves guests feeling rather cold. The river-view rooms are worth the extra money (about $10), and there are great views from upper floors of long-tail boats puttering by or fishermen paddling small dugouts. The pool is in a prime spot by the river, and the Riverside Restaurant offers nice views along with good, familiar fare, if a bit bland.

49 Le Loi St., Hue. www.centuryriversidehue.com. ✆ **054/382-3390** or 054/382-3391. Fax 054/382-3394. 135 units. $155 river-view double; $165 garden-view suite; $250 river-view suite. AE, MC, V. **Amenities:** 5 restaurants; bar; bike/motorbike rental; concierge; gym; outdoor pool overlooking river; room service; 2 tennis courts. *In room:* A/C, TV, fridge, hair dryer, Internet, minibar.

Hotel Saigon Morin ★ The Saigon Morin is a government-run, refurbished colonial block near the main bridge in town. The addition of an executive floor raised their room standard somewhat, but they are no match for nearby La Residence (see below), despite having similar prices. Junior Deluxe rooms have large, stylish bathrooms, which are connected to the bedroom via a fun "peekaboo" shuttered opening. The lower-standard rooms are still the same Chinese business-hotel basic, with old laminated furniture and threadbare carpeting dotted with cigarette burns. The hotel forms a large courtyard around a central garden and pool area with dining. More than 100 years old, the Morin was originally the colonists' address of note, and photos line the halls of this bygone era. The street in front of the Morin was where a young Ho Chi Minh carried his first placard in protest of foreign occupation. The exterior maintains some of that old colonial charm, but common areas are brash and busy, neon-lit, and cluttered with souvenir stalls. Service is a bit hit-or-miss but usually friendly.

30 Le Loi St., Hue. www.morinhotel.com.vn. ✆ **054/382-3526.** Fax 054/382-5155. 184 units. $100 superior; $120 deluxe double; $250–$300 suite. AE, MC, V. **Amenities:** Restaurant; 2 bars/cafe (1 on the

roof w/good views); concierge; gym; Internet; pool; room service; sauna. *In room:* A/C, TV, fridge, hair dryer, Jacuzzi (in executive suites), minibar.

Huong Giang Hotel ★★ This hotel is a veritable Asian wonderland, enamored with carved wood and bamboo furnishings in a faux "Imperial" style. It's tacky, but it's also kind of fun. Standard rooms are clean and comfortable, in basic bamboo, but the bathrooms are a disappointing dormitory style, with plastic shower curtains and no counter space. Try to get a good deal on one of the Royal Suites, with carved-wood walls, grandiose furniture with inlaid mother-of-pearl, and a massive wooden room divider—sort of a minipagoda right in your room. The words *emperor* and *bordello* both leap to mind. The Royal Restaurant, worth a photo for its gaudy gold-and-red-everything design, is for prearranged group dinners, during which the costumed staff serves a fancy, traditional dinner at a hefty price. The River Front Terrace Bar is the best place in Hue to have a drink and watch life on the river, and you can have a fine meal at the Hoa Mai restaurant.

51 Le Loi St., Hue. www.huonggianghotel.com.vn. ℂ **054/3822-122** or 054/3823-958. Fax 054/382-3102. 165 units. $80 garden-view double; $90 river-view double; $180–$200 suite. AE, MC, V. **Amenities:** 4 restaurants; 3 bars; concierge; health club; pool; sauna; spa. *In room:* A/C, cable TV, IDD fridge, hair dryer, Internet, minibar.

La Residence Hotel & Spa ★★ This hotel set the standard for luxury in this ancient city. Set on the banks of the Perfume River, the main building was the former residence of the French government and is the centerpiece of the hotel. In the lobby, you can take in the antique, Art Deco tiles and mounted black-and-white photos depicting colonial life in Indochina in the early 20th century (copies of photos from a museum in France). The rest of the hotel's rooms are found in two separate wings that flank the main building and form an arch around the deep saltwater swimming pool. Most rooms face west and have a small balcony. The unobstructed views of the Perfume River and the outer gate of the Imperial city make for fantastic sunsets. If you can spring for a suite, I recommend the Voyageen Chine; like the other suites, it has a private balcony and large four-poster bed draped in a mosquito net.

5 Le Loi St., Hue. www.la-residence-hue.com. ℂ **054/3837-475.** Fax 054/383-0822. 122 units. $152–$200 double; $219–$344 suite. MC, V. **Amenities:** Restaurant; bar; bikes; concierge; fitness center; outdoor pool; room service; spa w/Jacuzzi, sauna, and massage; tennis court; Wi-Fi. *In room:* A/C, TV, fridge, minibar.

The Pilgrimage Village ★★ If you are looking for a secluded, tropical getaway, this is your best choice in Hue. The resort offers spacious rooms and private villas in a garden setting surrounding a fine-dining pavilion. Some 5km (3 miles) southeast of the town center on the way to the royal tombs and temples, Pilgrimage Village is one of the only independently owned and operated hotels in the area, which explains the laid-back feel and high service standard. Rooms are large with oversize, modern, dark-wood furnishings and exposed brick walls. For a real treat, book one of the three Vietnamese pool houses; huge villas with terra cotta floors and beautiful wood pillars. These houses also come with a small private pool and 2 hours of spa treatments. Pool house rooms have balconies and faux fireplaces, creating a lodgelike ambience. The restaurant, Junrei, is the largest traditional wood house in central Vietnam and serves fine Vietnamese fare. A garden area at the resort's entry is lined with traditional buildings housing craftspeople producing fine embroidery, ceramics, and woodcarving, all for sale. Regular shuttles run to the downtown area, and the very friendly staff can help arrange thoughtful, informative tours to nearby temples and imperial tombs.

130 Minh Mang Rd., Hue. www.pilgrimagevillage.com. © **054/388-5461.** Fax 054/388-7057. 99 units. May–Sept $122–$182 double; $472 pool house; Aug–Apr $129–$202 double; $512 pool house. MC, V. **Amenities:** 2 restaurants; 2 bars; fitness center; large outdoor pool and kiddie pool; room service. *In room:* A/C, TV, fridge, hair dryer, minibar, Wi-Fi.

MODERATE

Asia Hotel ★ Just next to La Carambole Restaurant, this minihotel is popular among regional visitors (mostly Thai). It's near the city center's many shops and restaurants, and just a short walk to the river. Rooms are tidy and clean (though not luxurious), with cheap, fuzzy hotel blankets and drapes. There's a cool top-floor restaurant with great views (this is the tallest building away from the river), and some of the rooms have good river views as well. The pool is like an oversize bathtub in a raised area near the rooftop restaurant, but not a bad place to escape with a book on a hot day.

17 Pham Ngu Lao St., Hue. www.asiahotel.com.vn. © **054/383-0283.** Fax 054/382-8972. 60 units. $50 double; $90–$110 suite. MC, V. **Amenities:** 2 restaurants; bar; babysitting; pool; room service. *In room:* A/C, TV, fridge, hair dryer, Internet, minibar.

Villa Hue ★ This is Hue's best choice in this price range. Villa Hue is run and operated out of the Hue School of Tourism; the rotating management team is made up of teachers, and the hotel staff is comprised of second-year students. The hotel occupies one length of a courtyard, and all rooms face into the central area overlooking the rest of the school. Everyone is friendly, and the teachers/managers are quick to jump in and help when staff stumbles on service (which they do now and again). Deluxe rooms come with cozy beds and overstuffed chairs. Unlike the minihotels in this price category that cram too much into too small a room, everything here is quite spacious; rooms come with comfy, overstuffed furniture, but there's still plenty of wide spaces left to move around. The bathrooms are similarly huge, with slate-colored granite floors, a good-sized tub, and separate shower cubicle in deluxe rooms. Little extras, such as evening chocolates and handmade beaded do-not-disturb signs, make this a charming choice.

4 Tran Quang Khai St., Hue. © **054/383-1628.** Fax 054/383-1627. 12 units. $82 deluxe; $68 superior. Rates include breakfast. AE, DC, MC, V. **Amenities:** Restaurant; room service; Wi-Fi. *In room:* TV, A/C, fridge, minibar.

BUDGET

Apart from the places listed below, the following are worth a look. **Thai Binh Hotel,** 2 Luong The Vinh St. (www.thaibinhhue-hue.com; © **054/382-7561;** 40 units; $20–$35 double), is good in a pinch, with tidy, basic rooms in a quiet location. **Thang Long Hotel,** 18 Hung Vuong St. (© **054/382-6463;** 20 units; $12–$20 double), is a recently renovated budget choice with air-conditioned rooms and a good in-house tour company with a friendly and helpful staff.

Orchid Hotel ★ This popular minihotel is good value for the money. Rooms are comfortable and beds are done up nicely, with charming textiles and accent pillows. There are a few things that veer to the tacky side—faux-wood floors, armchairs made of uncomfortable pleather, and leopard-print silk bathrobes—but on balance, this place is clean and cozy. Family rooms, or triple rooms, are about double the size of standard rooms and come with small balconies; they're an excellent value. Rooms come with free afternoon fruit and cake.

30A Chu Van An St., Hue. www.orchidhotelhue.com.vn. © **054/383-1177.** Fax 054/383-1213. 18 units. $35–$42 double; $57–$60 suite. Rates include breakfast. MC, V. **Amenities:** Restaurant; free airport pickup; room service; Wi-Fi. *In room:* A/C, TV, computer, DVD player, fridge, minibar.

Sports 1 Hotel This place is a good value and one of the town's better budget hotels. The rooms are tidy, beds are decent, and the blond faux-wood interior is pretty inviting. Bathrooms are spotless, which is a major bonus in this price range. The location puts you in the midst of backpackers, which means a good selection of local eateries and popular watering holes. Try to get one of the few rooms that have river views and a decent-size balcony.

15 Pham Ngu Lao St., Hue. www.huesportshotel.com. ☏ 054/382-8096. Fax 054/383-0199. 30 units. $32 double; $39 family room. MC, V. **Amenities:** Restaurant; bar. *In room:* A/C, satellite TV, hair dryer, Wi-Fi.

Where to Eat

Hue cuisine is unique, featuring light ingredients in popular fresh spring rolls. Try *bun bo Hue,* a noodle soup with pork, beef, and shredded green onions; or *banh khoai,* a thin, crispy pancake filled with ground meat and crispy vegetables. Local dishes are best enjoyed streetside, and there are a few good spots with English menus along the river and in the backpacker area, along Hung Vuong.

MODERATE

Confetti Restaurant VIETNAMESE Ever since this place opened in early 2011, it's been a hit, with its classy decor, refined atmosphere, good background music, and attentive staff. Choose from a range of classic Vietnamese dishes such as grilled chicken with lemon grass, or grilled seafood. There's a good list of imported wines. Reservations are advisable.

1 Chu Van An St. **054/382-4148.** confettihue@yahoo.com. Main courses 75,000 VND–185,000 VND. MC, V. Daily 9am-10pm.

Hoa Mai Restaurant ★★ VIETNAMESE Hoa Mai is decked out in kitschy bamboo furnishings in an open area on the top floor of the Huong Giang Hotel. Atmosphere aside, the Vietnamese fare is good, and you'll have great views of the Perfume River. Try *banh rom Hue,* triangular fried rolls stuffed with ground meat, shrimp, and vegetables. Daily set menus are good; mine featured fried cuttlefish with grapefruit, crab soup, and shrimp with fig and rice cake. Be sure to choose a table near the riverside and away from any banquet-size setups that say RESERVED.

51 Le Loi St., 3rd floor, Huong Giang Hotel. ☏ **054/382-2122.** Main courses 45,000 VND–180,000 VND; set menus 200,000 VND–300,000 VND. AE, MC, V. Daily 6am-11pm.

Le Parfum ★ ASIAN FUSION Though the restaurant bills itself as offering Vietnamese cuisine, the menu features a lot of European fare. Pastas are served in appetizer and main sizes. Old standbys such as spaghetti carbonara and even hamburgers and fries are available. The outdoor seating is a quiet setting overlooking the Perfume River and lit by retro gas lamps. It's an excellent place to unwind after a day of temple- and tomb-hopping.

Inside La Residence Hotel & Spa, Hue. ☏ **054/383-7475.** Main courses $6-$28. AE, MC, V. Daily 6am-11pm.

Omar Khayyam ★ INDIAN/VIETNAMESE Hugely popular with tourists and located in the heart of the tourist part of town, this place turns out some great curries as well as the usual extras that go with an Indian meal. It can get crowded some evenings in the high season.

34 Nguyen Tri Phuong. ☏ **054/382-1616.** kafle20082007@yahoo.com. Main courses 90,000 VND–110,000 VND; set menus 110,000 VND-250,000 VND. No credit cards. Daily 10am-11pm.

Phuoc Thanh Garden Restaurant VIETNAMESE/WESTERN   Among lots of budget stops, this large, open-front restaurant borrows its style from the mandarins and temple compounds outside of Hue. It's modern and tidy, and caters mostly to large groups (they ask your nationality when you arrive and deliver your country's flag to your table). It's a good choice for delicious versions of local specialties such as *bun bo Hue* (local noodle soup), *nem ran* (fresh spring rolls), or *banh khoi* (pancakes). A long list of tasty stir-fries, as well as delicious hot pots, rounds out the menu. Set menus include a gourmand's succession of soup, appetizers, and main courses. There's also a small selection of "European dishes" with fish and chips or other familiar eats for the kids.

30 Pham Ngu Lao St. ✆ **054/383-0989.** Main courses 60,000 VND–265,000 VND; set menus 159,000 VND–450,000 VND. No credit cards. Daily 7am–11pm.

Tropical Garden ★★ VIETNAMESE   Though a popular tour-bus stop, Tropical Garden has a laid-back feel. The restaurant, with a sister location called **Club Garden** just down the road (8 Vo Thi Sau St.; ✆ **054/382-6327**), serves fine Vietnamese fare from a good English menu, and there's live music nightly from 7 to 9pm. Even when it's packed, there are enough intimate corners to feel comfortable. The place specializes in "embarrassing entrees," the kind of flaming dishes and multitiered platters that would impress your eccentric uncle. The food is good but a bit overpriced for a la carte items. Set menus are quite reasonable and walk you through some house specialties, such as the banana flower soup and the steamed crab with beer. As an appetizer, don't miss the grilled minced shrimp with sugar cane, wrapped in rice paper and served with peanut sauce. Service is either fawning or forgetful.

27 Chu Van An St. ✆ **054/384-7143.** Fax 054/382-8074. Main courses 50,000 VND–160,000 VND; set menu 240,000 VND–500,000 VND. AE, DC, MC, V. Daily 10am–10pm.

INEXPENSIVE

Hue Little Italy ITALIAN This place, from the same folks behind DMZ Café (see "Cafes, Bars & Nightlife," below), serves pizza and pasta, but it's nothing to write home about. There's a small indoor garden and several private dining areas.

2A Vo Thi Sau St. ✆ **054/382-6928.** www.littleitalyhue.com. Main courses 35,000 VND–150,000 VND. AE, MC, V. Daily 8:30am–11pm.

La Carambole ★★ CONTINENTAL/VIETNAMESE   Good music is the first thing you notice at La Carambole, followed by the cheerful decor: cool lighting, red tablecloths, and playful mobiles hanging from the ceiling. The gregarious French proprietor, Christian, and his wife, Ha, make you feel at home, as does the kind waitstaff. There are good "comfort items" on the menu, such as spaghetti, burgers, pizzas, and various French-style meat-and-potatoes specials. The set menus are a good deal (salad and beefsteak at $6, for example), and portions are ample. There's a game table, and you're sure to meet lots of other travelers.

19 Pham Ngu Lao St. ✆ **054/381-0491.** Fax 054/382-6234. Main courses 70,000 VND–150,000 VND; set menus 120,000 VND–200,000 VND. MC, V. Daily 7am–11pm.

Lac Thien ★ VIETNAMESE   This is one a trio of small restaurants run by extended family members, several of whom are deaf. The neighboring two eateries serve similar fare, but I am partial to Lac Thien for the owner's incredibly friendly personality. The owner also makes simple bottle openers, consisting of a piece of wood and a corkscrew, which are presented to customers as free souvenirs. There's a small mural of photographs on the wall showing customers cracking open beers around the world.

6 Dinh Tien Hoang St. ✆ **054/352-7348.** Main courses 30,000 VND-70,000 VND. No credit cards. Daily 8am-10pm.

Mandarin Café ★ CONTINENTAL/VIETNAMESE   In a busy storefront a short walk from the riverside (near the Saigon Morin), Mandarin is always full of young backpackers for a reason: good, affordable Vietnamese fare, predominantly one-dish items such as fried rice or noodles. Try this place for a casual meal (have a banana pancake) and likely conversation with fellow travelers. The owner, Mr. Cu (pronounced *Coo*), is a practiced photographer and his works—classic images of rural Vietnam—line the walls and are for sale as postcards or prints.

24 Tran Cao Van St. ✆ **054/382-1281.** mandarin@dng.vnn.vn. Main courses 20,000 VND-60,000 VND. AE, DC, MC, V. Daily 6:30am-10:30pm.

Thien Tam Vegetarian Restaurant ★ VIETNAMESE   This is a neat place for a healthy meal on the way to or from the Imperial Tombs. The wide range of dishes are attractively presented and reasonably priced; the hot pots are particularly good, and there are lots of wrap-and-roll dishes, too. Staff is friendly and helpful with kids, and they also offer cooking classes. There's an art gallery attached to the restaurant where you might be tempted to buy an original work.

110A Le Ngo Cat. ✆ **054/3898-220.** Main courses 40,000 VND-110,000 VND. No credit cards. Daily 10am-10pm.

Ushi ★ GERMAN/VIETNAMESE   This restaurant, originally called Hien's Canteen, got its current name after visiting Dutch tourists would tell the owner, Thanh Huong, that she looked like Ushi, a character on a politically provocative Dutch talk show. The menu, however, maintains its German influence, with hearty dishes such as bratwurst, served alongside Vietnamese noodle soup standbys. If you have some time to kill, I highly recommend striking up a conversation with Huong, who will tell you tales of her 6-month motorcycle ride through Europe, or her previous life growing up during Vietnam's closed-economy era.

Across from La Carambole, 42 Pham Ngu Lao St. ✆ **054/382-1143.** ushivietnam@yahoo.com.vn. Main courses 20,000 VND-130,000 VND; set menus 100,000 VND-240,000 VND. MC, V. Daily 7:30am-11pm.

Cafes, Bars & Nightlife

Across from the major riverside hotels is **DMZ Café,** 60 Le Loi St. (✆ **054/382-3414;** www.dmz.com.vn), which stays open late with its beer-swilling frat-party vibe. Along Hung Vuong you'll find a few backpacker bars open 'til midnight, but this is a pretty sleepy town. **Brown Eyes,** 56 Chu Van An (✆ **054/382-7494**), is a late-night bar and cafe that's a short taxi ride from the town center.

Shopping

All along Le Loi Street, you'll find souvenir stalls that vary from cute to the kitschy. You can find good deals on commemorative spoons and velvet Ho Chi Minhs here, but nothing too traditional or authentic. There are, however, a few good silversmiths and some little gems on sale in the glass cases of even the most kitschy tourist boutique.

A few silk shops are worth checking out: **Thuy Silk,** 1A Pham Ngu Lao St. (✆ **054/383-4510**), and **Ken Silk,** 25 Pham Ngu Lao St. (✆ **054/382-5445**), carry the broadest range of products. Riverside Le Loi Street, just across from the Huong Giang and Century Riverside hotels, is also a good place for affordable silk tailors. If you're considering buying a sample of original Vietnamese paintings, drop by **Nhat Quy Art Gallery,** 1A Pham Ngu Lao St. (✆ **054/381-9858**), to see what they have available. **Bambou Company,** 21 Pham Ngu Lao St. (✆ **054/3830-482;** www.bamboucompany.com), next to La Carambole, produces T-shirts of local theme and design in Western sizes. For interesting handmade products, as well as purses, wallets, and *ao dai,* head for **Ella Souvenir Boutique,** 39 Chu Van An (✆ **054/393-9495**).

Attractions

Hue's **Citadel** and **Imperial City** are the main attractions, but a visit here is usually done in conjunction with half-day trips to outlying temples and the many **imperial tombs.** You can bicycle to the Citadel, then along the riverside to **Thien Mu Pagoda,** back to town for lunch, and then out to the tombs (distances are long, but it's a relatively flat ride). You can also hit the sites on a self-guided tour in the comfort of a cyclo. But hiring a guide (see any hotel front desk) is a good idea and offers useful background on the rich history of the town.

The Citadel & Imperial City ★★★ The Citadel is often used as a catchall term for Hue's Imperial City, built by Emperor Gia Long, beginning in 1804, for the exclusive use of the emperor and his household, much like Beijing's Forbidden City. Most of the site is comprised of crumbling stone buildings and walls overtaken by trees and plants. The natural disrepair gives the place an authentic, ancient feeling. Unfortunately, restoration is happening fast, and inner palaces and buildings are being reconstructed and given a fresh coat of paint. The result is rather kitschy, and a theater toward the north end of the city has been set up for scheduled, somewhat cheesy evening dining and entertainment (adults 300,000 VND, children 230,000 VND; ✆ **054/352-9012**). The city actually encompasses three walled enclosures: the Exterior Enclosure, or Citadel; the Yellow Enclosure, or Imperial City, within that; and, in the very center, the Forbidden Purple City, where the emperor actually lived.

The Citadel is protected by a 2km (1¼-mile) wall, 7m (23 ft.) high and 20m (66 ft.) thick, with 10 gates. Although the complex was constructed by a French military architect, it was actually the French who destroyed it many years later. Get a ticket and enter the main entrance through the southwest gate, the Ngo Mon, often called the Noon Gate. And, be sure to get a good English-speaking guide; the site is not spectacular in itself, but the history and traditions are rich, and a good guide can give you a breakdown of what things once looked like and what life was like at the Imperial court. They can also connect you with a dance show of the Imperial Dance Troupe. A short overview is given below.

Admission 55,000 VND. Daily 7am–5pm.

SITES WITHIN THE IMPERIAL CITY

The Flag Tower ★★ The focal point of the Imperial City, a large rampart to the south of the Noon Gate, this tower was built in 1807 during Gia Long's reign. The yellow flag of royalty was the first to fly here and was exchanged and replaced by many others in Vietnam's turbulent history. It's a national symbol.

The Forbidden Purple City ★ Once the actual home of the emperor and his concubines, this second sanctum within the Citadel is a large open area dotted with what's left of the king's court. Almost completely razed in a fire in 1947, a few buildings are left among the rubble. The new **Royal Theater** behind the square, a lookalike of the razed original, is under construction. The partially restored **Thai Binh Reading Pavilion,** to the left of it as you head north, is notable mostly for its beautifully landscaped surroundings, including a small lake with stone sculpture, and the ceramic and glass mosaic detailing on the roof and pillars, favored by flamboyant emperor Khai Dinh.

Catch a performance of the **Royal Traditional Theater** at the Hue Monuments Conservation Center. Eight performances daily, from 9am to 4pm, highlight the ancient art of *nha nhac,* or courtly dance. A VIP ticket (120,000 VND) includes Hue's traditional tea and sweet cakes, while a normal ticket (70,000 VND) includes a bottle of cold water.

Hue Monuments Conservation Center ★ Set in an old picturesque Chinese temple (you're asked to wear shoe covers at the entry in order to preserve the wood), the Hue Monuments Conservation Center is the Imperial Museum of the old capital, displaying all the treasures (or what's left over) from the Nguyen kings. Precious coins, stone carvings, and Ming dynasty pottery from China are just a few of the gifts in this repository of courtly finery presented to Vietnam's 19th-century leaders by visiting dignitaries. The lacquer-framed gong made of stone from China is a special piece. At the back you'll find lacquered palanquins and furnishings for the royal court and procession, and farther back look for the embroidered finery donned by Nguyen kings on parade.

Next door is the **Exhibition of the Resistance Against the American Invader,** which doesn't mince words. The courtyard out front displays some captured war machines. Inside is a rhetorical parade of faded photos and artifacts that tell the story of American aggression from the July 1954 Geneva Agreement to the North Vietnamese Army's jubilant liberation of Saigon, with images of the hard fighting in Hue city in 1968. The exhibition is propagandistic—captions telling of the "lackey" government of "puppet" rulers in the south, and selections of photos depicting Americans as torturers who disemboweled their North Vietnamese prisoners—but that very rhetoric is what's so interesting. History is told by the victors, and the Vietnamese are proud of their victory and of what they had to endure to survive as a sovereign nation. Elsewhere, as with the War Museum in Saigon, which changed its name from "Museum of the American War Crimes," Vietnamese rhetoric about its own recent history is softening, or disappearing altogether.

On the southeast corner of the main citadel entrance. Admission 22,000 VND. Daily 7am–5pm.

The Noon Gate (Cua Ngo Mon) ★★ One of 10 entrances to the city, this southern entrance is the most dynamic. It was the royal entrance, in fact, and was built by Emperor Gia Long in 1823. It was used for important proclamations, such as announcements of the names of successful doctoral candidates (a list still hangs on the wall on the upper floor) and, most memorably, the announcement of the abdication of the last emperor, Bao Dai, on August 13, 1945, to Ho Chi Minh (which took place 12 days later on Aug 25). The structure, like most here, was damaged by war but has been nicely restored, with a classic Chinese roof covering the ritual space, complete with large drums and an altar. Be sure to climb to the top and have a look at the view.

Thai Hoa Palace   Otherwise known as the Palace of Supreme Harmony, this was built in 1833 and is the first structure you'll approach at the entrance. It was used as the throne room, a ceremonial hall where the emperor celebrated festivals and received courtiers; the original throne still stands. The mandarins sat outside. In front are two mythical *ky lin* animals, which walk without their claws ever touching the ground and have piercing eyesight for watching the emperor, tracking all the good and evil he does. Note the statues of the heron and turtle inside the palace's ornate lacquered interior: The heron represents nobility, and the turtle represents the working person. Folklore has it that the two took turns saving each other's lives during a fire, symbolizing that the power of the emperor rests with his people, and vice versa.

The Mieu Temple ★★   Constructed from 1821 to 1822 by Emperor Minh Mang, this temple has funeral altars paying tribute to 10 of the last Nguyen dynasty emperors, omitting two who reigned for only days, with photos of each emperor and his empress(es) and various small offerings and knickknacks. The two empty glass containers to the side of each photo should contain bars of gold, probably an impractical idea today.

Across from The Mieu you'll see **Hien Lam,** or the Glorious Pavilion, to the far right, with the **Nine Dynastic Urns** in front. Cast from 1835 to 1837 by order of Emperor Minh Mang, each urn represents a Nguyen emperor and is richly embellished with all the flora, fauna, and material goods that Vietnam has to offer, mythical or otherwise. It's worth going up close to admire the details, which are impeccably wrought.

IMPERIAL TOMBS

As befits its history as an Imperial City, Hue's environs are studded with tombs of past emperors. Because they're spread out over a distance, the best way to see them is to hire a car for a half-day or take one of the many organized boat tours up the Perfume River. Altogether there were 13 kings of the Nguyen dynasty, although only seven reigned until their deaths. As befits an emperor, each had a tomb of stature, some as large as a small town. Most tomb complexes usually consist of a courtyard, a stele (a large stone tablet with a biography of the emperor), a temple for worship, and a pond. You can visit the tombs on an all-day boat trip, best if arranged with one of the small tour companies (see "Visitor Information & Tours," earlier in this chapter), but also possible with a little haggling at the riverside. Expect to pay as little as $6 for the boat trip, and note that each tomb has a stiff (for Vietnam) entry fee. If going by boat, note that some tombs are far from the riverside and may require a short trip by motorbike, which sometimes doubles the entry fee but saves your muscles for clambering around the sites.

Khai Dinh's Tomb ★★   Completed in 1931, this tomb is one of Hue's wonders. The emperor himself wasn't particularly revered, being overly extravagant and flamboyant (reportedly he wore a belt studded with lights that he flicked on at opportune public moments). His tomb—a gaudy mix of Gothic, baroque, Hindu, and Chinese Qing dynasty architecture at the top of 127 steep steps—is a reflection of the man. Inside, the two main rooms are completely covered with fabulous, intricate glass and ceramic mosaics in designs reminiscent of Tiffany and Art Deco. The workmanship is astounding. The outer room's ceiling was done by a fellow who used both his feet and his hands to paint, in what some say was a sly mark of disrespect for the emperor. In most tombs, the location of the emperor's actual remains is a secret, but Khai Minh boldly placed his under his de facto tomb itself.

Admission 55,000 VND. Summer daily 6:30am–5:30pm; winter daily 7am–5pm.

Tomb of Minh Mang ★   One of the most popular Nguyen emperors—and the father of the last emperor Bao Dai—built a restrained, serene, classical temple, much like Hue's Imperial City, located at the confluence of two Perfume River tributaries. Stone sculptures surround a long walkway, lined with flowers, leading up to the main buildings.

Admission 55,000 VND. Summer daily 6:30am–5:30pm; winter daily 7am–5pm.

Tomb of Tu Duc ★★   With the longest reign of any Nguyen dynasty emperor, from 1847 to 1883, Tu Duc was a philosopher and scholar of history and literature. His reign was unfortunate: His kingdom unsuccessfully struggled against French colonialism, he fought a coup d'état by members of his own family, and although he had 104 wives, he left no heir. The "tomb" was constructed from 1864 to 1867 and also served as recreation grounds for the king, having been completed 16 years before his death. He actually engraved his own stele, which is the largest in Vietnam, at 20 tons. The highlight of the grounds is the lotus-filled lake ringed by frangipani trees, with a large pavilion in the center. The main cluster of buildings includes Hoa Khiem (Harmony Modesty) Pavilion, where the king worked and which still contains items of furniture and ornaments. Minh Khiem Duong, constructed in 1866, is said to be the country's oldest surviving theater. It's great fun to poke around in the wings. There are also pieces of original furniture lying here and there, as well as a cabinet with household objects: the queen's slippers, ornate chests, and bronze and silver books. The raised box on the wall is for the actors who played emperors; the real emperor was at the platform to the left.

Admission 55,000 VND. Summer daily 6:30am–5:30pm; winter daily 7am–5pm.

TEMPLES

The **Thien Mu Pagoda** (see below) is a popular stop on riverboat trips along the Perfume River's north bank and is also easily reached by bicycle or motorbike. The road leading to the imperial tombs south of town affords you a great glimpse of a few working temples—the likes of **Bao Quoc** and **Tu Hieu**—with busy monks, groups of students rushing between classes, and lots of workshops that you can observe.

Bao Quoc   Just past the train station on your way south toward the imperial tombs, little Bao Quoc is a Buddhist temple dating from the 17th century. At the top of the steps leading to the main temple square, you'll see the grand arched entry of a classic Chinese school.

Just south of the train station (away from the river) on Dien Bien Phu St. Daily dawn–dusk.

Thien Mu Pagoda ★★   Often called the symbol of Hue, Thien Mu is one of the oldest and loveliest religious structures in Vietnam. It was constructed beginning in 1601. First called "Linh Mu," the pagoda was then renamed "Thien Mu" by Emperor Tu Duc in 1864. The Phuoc Duyen Tower in front was added in 1844 by Emperor Thieu Tri. Each of its seven tiers is dedicated to either one of the human forms taken by Buddha or the seven steps to enlightenment, depending upon whom you ask. There are also two buildings housing a bell reportedly weighing 2 tons, and a stele inscribed with a biography of Lord Nguyen Hoang, founder of the temple.

Once past the front gate, observe the 12 huge wooden sculptures of fearsome temple "guardians" (note the real facial hair). A complex of monastic buildings lies in the center, offering glimpses of the monks' daily routines: cooking, stacking wood, and whacking weeds. Stroll all the way to the rear of the complex to look at the large graveyard at the base of the Truong Son mountains, and wander through the well-kept garden of pine trees. Try not to go between the hours of 11:30am and 2pm, when the monks are at lunch and the rear half of the complex will be closed.

On the northern bank (same side as the Citadel) of the Perfume River. About 5km (3 miles) southwest of the Citadel entrance. Daily 8am–5pm.

Tu Hieu   At this working Buddhist temple, the many monks and novices clad in brown robes are always busily padding about from class to meditation to worship. Wooden gongs clock the activities of the day. Monks are friendly, and if you time it right (btw. class time or before or after lunch), you are sure to meet up with these cherubic lads, who are all eager to practice their English. I even got some Vietnamese singing lessons. The surrounding ponds and gardens are immaculate, real-deal Zen living. Next door is a nunnery, busier than the monastery and with a small adjoining Bannar house. The approach road to the temple continues on to hilly farmland.

Just past the Nam Giao Esplanade, a large tiered area used by emperors for performances and cere-mony. Stay to the right at the intersection and follow the road about 2 miles to the ornate gated entry to Tu Hieu, a large Buddhist monastery and school. No phone. Free admission. Daily dawn–dusk.

OTHER SITES

Ho Chi Minh Museum   Every city's got one, an homage point for Vietnam's national hero, and this one is actually kind of interesting. In a large rotunda on the road heading from the new town toward the train station, the Ho Chi Minh Museum in Hue is the usual collection of photos and memorabilia telling the story of Ho's early life of poverty in Vinh, here with a stress on the years he spent in Hue during his father's tenure in the university (see Ho Chi Minh's Home in Hue, below). There are images and a reproduction of the boat he sailed on as a galley hand, as well as a picture of Ho working in the kitchen of the Castleton Hotel in London in 1914, when his ideas about Marxism and revolution began to flower. The museum tells the history of Hue, from capital to revolution to the aftermath, in photos. There are also some interesting political cartoons parodying French rule, as well as extensive copies and basic translations of Ho's writings—the likes of the 8 *Requirements of Society,* which Ho presented at the Versailles Conference in Paris in 1919.

On the way to the train station at 7 Le Loi. Free admission. Mon–Sat 7:30–11:30am and 1:30–4:30pm.

Ho Chi Minh's Home in Hue   On the way to Thuan An Beach, a narrow lane leads over a small bridge off of the main road at a curve some 6km (3¾ miles) north of Hue. An immediate right after the bridge brings you along the small river area where Ho bathed during his time here, and just about 100m (328 ft.) farther brings you to the humble home, a reconstruction, and new temple that mark the site where the leader spent formative years during his father's study for examinations to become a mandarin (government official).

6km (3¾ miles) north on Le Loi heading toward Thuan An Beach. Free admission. Daily 8–11am and 1:30–4:30pm.

THUAN AN BEACH

At this local beach site, 12km (7½ miles) north of Hue, the turbulent waves make it less popular for swimming and more popular for hanging in a hammock and taking it all in. To get here, just follow riverside Le Loi Street east and then head north. The place fills up on weekends with young domestic vacationers from the big cities. You pay for parking and seats under an umbrella or a small hut, and are pretty much obliged to buy some snacks or baubles from sellers as you look over a picturesque windswept stretch of coast. You can also sample some fresh seafood.

Unfortunately, these days Thuan An Beach is littered and its thatched-roofed eateries in disrepair. There is an alternative beach: Coming from the direction of Hue city on the main route to Thuan An Beach, there is a new road turning off left, at about the 10km mark, toward Hai Duong village and secluded beaches behind a high sand dune ridge. The picturesque route leads over rice fields, with a total of three bridge crossings over lagoon waters. Circular burial mounds and miniature temple tombs sit amid the rice fields.

THE DEMILITARIZED ZONE

If you're old enough to remember the Vietnam War from television, you'll know **Hue** from the large-scale battles waged here. The 1968 **Battle of Hue,** which heralded the Tet Offensive in the far south, was one of the most gruesome and well-documented battles, and scenes of the fray were depicted in Stanley Kubrick's film *Full Metal Jacket.*

Starting from Hue, a day trip to the nearby DMZ (demilitarized zone) and Vinh Moc Tunnels is a sobering reminder of the tumultuous wartime, and crossing the invisible line of demarcation between north and south is an important part of bringing things full circle for returning veterans and folks who lived through the war years. All of Quang Tri Province is a vestige of the war years really, as this was the site of some of the heaviest shelling and artillery exchanges during the war.

Under the Geneva Accords of 1954, an agreement brought peace to Indochina after its struggle with French colonists. Vietnam was divided into north and south along the **17th Parallel.** What was meant to be a short-term political fix became a battle line known as the **DMZ,** a tangle of barbed wire and land mines bombed and defoliated into a wasteland. The famous American fence, which was called the "million-dollar eye"—a folly of U.S. Defense Secretary Robert McNamara—was an elaborate system of barbed wire laced with electronic sensors that the United States built along the border's length; when sensors in the DMZ were tripped, they triggered American bombers into action. The North Vietnamese regularly foiled U.S. efforts, playing cat-and-mouse with the sensors and sending livestock into no man's land to draw fire. The perimeter was overrun in 1975.

The once-scorched earth of the DMZ is now green with growth and completely unremarkable except for its history. Nearby are strategic sites with names you may recognize: the **Rockpile, Hamburger Hill, Camp Carroll,** and **Khe Sanh,** a former U.S. Marine base that was the site of some of the war's most vicious and deadly fighting. If you take a tour of the area, you'll also visit **Dakrong Bridge,** an official entryway into the Ho Chi Minh Trail region near where the trail begins. The **tunnels of Vinh Moc,** where border troops along with whole families burrowed underground, effectively creating their own underground city, is a testament to the determination and motivation of Viet Cong forces at the north end of the DMZ. A visit here is likely the highlight of any DMZ tour.

Important: If you're interested in tours to the DMZ, your best bet is to pay a little extra and find a knowledgeable guide who can paint a vivid portrait. Except for a few memorial sites and preserved relics, the physical battle scars on the landscape have healed. To make this trip engaging, you'll want to go with someone who knows about the history of the area and can take you to out-of-the-way bunkers and battle sites. Budget tours of the DMZ are often just a full day riding around on a bus, with little time to visit sites and scant information about scheduled stops. "Lots of people fighting here long time ago," your guide might say, pointing to a farmer's field no different than the farmer's field adjoining. It's important to note that the heavy plant growth is only recent, and that this area was the hardest hit of anywhere in Vietnam by the U.S. defoliation campaign Operation Ranch Hand.

The many sites in the DMZ are some 60km (37 miles) north of Hue. Visitors with a serious interest in the history of the area could certainly make it a multiple-day operation; in such instances, but only in such instances, it makes sense to overnight in the town of **Dong Ha,** the jumping-off point to the DMZ and for onward travel to Laos. Most budget tours stop in Dong Ha for lack of options, but this one-stoplight burg is not the kind of place you want to be stranded in for too long. Near Dong Ha, you will cross the Ben Hai River, and most trips stop briefly to take in the old French guard towers and old denuded battlegrounds.

For tours, contact Hue tourist cafes: The best is **Sinh Tourist** on the budget end or **Huong Giang Tourist** for a good private tour. See "Visitor Information & Tours," earlier in this chapter.

Tours leave early in the morning and trace Route 1 north of Hue into Quang Tri Province. The coastal highway passes some lovely stretches of natural inland sand dunes lined with colorful Chinese tombs, some like small temples themselves, before reaching the town of Dong Ha. From here, there are two routes to follow, one up north to the Vinh Moc Tunnels and the other north and then west toward Laos and a number of deserted American bases; most day tours follow both tracks. Some opt to just visit the tunnels of Vinh Moc and a few sites near Dong Ha, making this a half-day tour.

Camp Fuller and the Rockpile These significant mountain outposts were American strongholds throughout the war that came under constant barrage from North Vietnamese regulars. This is the highest ground in the region along a high ridge, so it was valuable turf for artillery units and snipers. The area is now green with foliage (apart from the most heavily bombed mountaintops), but it's a far cry from what was once dense jungle. Operation Ranch Hand, the U.S. defoliation campaign, was relentless in this area.

The Dakrong Bridge and the Ho Chi Minh Trail The current incarnation of the Dakrong Bridge was built in 1975 after reunification. Just west of the main DMZ zone, the bridge was considered the beginning of the Ho Chi Minh Trail network, and during the years of conflict with the United States, this access point was hotly contested. The Dakrong Bridge fell many times, but now it's a grand suspension bridge, a proud thumbed nose as if to say, "You can't knock down my bridge anymore." The road to the bridge leads to the border with Laos, and even the overnight buses that take intrepid travelers over this route will stop for a good look at the bridge, which heads south (buses continue on the main road west to Laos). Across the bridge is a small village that's a popular stop for tour groups, and where most buses turn around and head back to the main highway. The stunning scenery all along Highway 9 is worth the ride.

Note: The **Ho Chi Minh Trail** is a concept, not a road. The trail was a vast network, spread across hundreds of miles of terrain extending far into the interior of Laos, a broad avenue of hundreds of miles of trails that brought supplies to North Vietnamese troops, by hook or by crook, usually on the backs of porters or with giant loads precariously perched on overlaid bicycles. You might call it "the path of least resistance," or the "road less bombed or occupied," really. The trail starts in Quang Tri Province, basically anything from the Dakrong Bridge south, and the Americans were constantly trying to foil the Viet Cong and Gen. Vo Nguyen Giap's relentless end-run around the front line to stage attacks in the south.

Hamburger Hill   Many know the name from the Clint Eastwood film depicting the events of May 10 to May 21, 1969, when U.S. Airborne Troops stood toe-to-toe with heavily dug-in Vietnamese forces in order to stop North Vietnamese movement through the A Shau valley and south. You would only really go to Hamburger Hill if you had some connection with the battle that took place here. The denuded slope is some 100km (62 miles) to the interior from the main DMZ area. To arrange special tours, returning veterans should contact **Huong Giang Tourist Company,** 17 Le Loi St. (© **054/383-2220;** www.huonggiangtourist.com), or DMZ Travel, housed in the DMZ Bar, 60 Le Loi St. (© **054/382-3414;** www.dmz.com.vn).

Khe Sanh ★   If most of the former battle sites in the area require more imagination than many visitors can muster, the base at Khe Sanh is worth the trip for its informative museum and some tangible evidence of American presence and the years of strife in the region. Khe Sanh is where, in January 1968, Viet Cong forces launched a massive attack. It was a diversion to keep U.S. Gen. William Westmoreland comfortable in his illusion that the war was being fought on a single front, and only a few months later the real might of the Tet Offensive landed in the south after skirting the heavily guarded DMZ, but nobody told the two divisions of North Vietnamese troops that it was a diversion. The January 21 attack at Khe Sanh left big numbers of casualties on both sides. The Tet Offensive nearly broke the back of Vietnam's fighting capability (they lost more than 10-to-1 in number of casualties), but it also broke the back of world and U.S. opinion about the conflict, and it was the beginning of the end for support of the war. After the offensive, U.S. forces pulled back to Camp Carol near Dong Ha town.

The large **museum compound** at Khe Sanh is home to a collection of war detritus: an abandoned Huey helicopter, the remains of crashed recon planes, the hulking shell of an M41 tank, a massive CH47 helicopter, and disarmed bombs and shells arranged like a piece of modern art. Inside the museum, a concrete building on stilts, find a good collection of photos and effects that chronicle the events of U.S. buildup, conflict, and withdrawal from this Khe Sanh base. Exhibits have good English descriptions, but captions are as didactic as they are informative. Beneath one photo of wounded U.S. troops struggling for cover, the caption reads, "What was Johnson thinking?" Exhibits make much of the cooperation of local ethnic hilltribe people, a general fabrication, really, as most hilltribe groups supported U.S. efforts to oust ethnic Vietnamese. Ho Chi Minh and later Vietnamese administrators worked hard to bring hilltribe minorities into line, but to this day there is general suspicion in Hanoi about these offshoot groups, many of whom know no borders and move freely from Laos and even as far as Burma or China. An entry ticket is included with most tours, but if not, entrance into the museum costs 30,000 VND.

Vinh Moc Tunnels ★★ The tunnels at Vinh Moc are a testament to human tenacity. Like the tunnels in the south at Cu Chi (see chapter 12), soldiers and civilians went underground, literally, digging more than a mile of tunnels from 1965 to 1966 to support Viet Cong troops and confound U.S. battalions at this strategic position near the line of north-south demarcation. People lived here from 1966 until 1972. An estimated 7 tons of bombs per person living in the Vinh Moc Tunnels were dropped. The initial complex took 18 months to excavate some 6,000 sq. m (64,583 sq. ft.) of red soil that had to be carefully dispersed, usually at night to avoid surveillance, and buried in the nearby sand of the beach. Up to 20m (about 66 ft.) below the surface, multilevel tunnels formed a real community haven, with "living rooms" for families, a conference and performance room, a small cinema, a field hospital, clean facilities, and kitchens complete with elaborate systems to dissipate the smoke of cooking fires. All tunnels also have ingenious exit points inland and along the coast, providing some cross-ventilation. Visitors walk through about 300m (984 ft.) of the tunnels in a main artery that is 1.6m high by 1.2m wide (5⅓ ft. high × 4 ft. wide), going down three stages. Wear your play clothes, because it's dirty, clammy, and a bit claustrophobic. There's a museum at the entrance with survivors' photos and testimonies. The museum houses photos of life among the tunnel families, as well as maps of their labyrinth (including a map that shows where the day's tour will lead) and tools from the excavation of the site. Admission is 30,000 VND, but the price is usually included in DMZ tour prices.

FARTHER AFIELD FROM HUE

Hai Van Pass Towering Hai Van Pass has been an inspiration to Vietnamese artists and poets for centuries. Straddling the highest point on the steep terrain between Danang and Hue, it was a natural defense post during Vietnam's lengthy conflicts, and the large "pill box" fortifications are still in evidence at the peak just above the road. Some tour buses, and even local buses, take a quick pit stop here, and the local vendors descend like their own invading army; but a cloudless day means stunning views north and south. However, there's now a tunnel going beneath the mountain, which saves time and is now used by most traffic passing through. Before arriving at Hai Van from the north, you pass the entrance to Bach Ma National Park and trace the thin strip of land along Lang Co Beach (see listings below) before zigzagging up the slope or through the tunnel.

MACH MA NATIONAL PARK

Bach Ma—with more than 20,000 hectares (49,400 acres) of high mountain trails and sweeping valleys—was once a playground for the French, who built villas on these mountaintops to stay cool when on vacation from Hue. You'll see a number of ruin sites, mostly the remnants of small French resorts and secluded cabins. The park is humid and rainy year-round, but the high elevation (1,712m/5,617 ft. at its peak) makes for cooler temperatures (bring a light windbreaker). The best time to go is in March and April, when the rhododendrons bloom (see "Hiking Trails," below).

Entrance to the park is just 20,000 VND (10,000 VND for children), and fees for hiring a jeep to take you up the road to the park's pinnacle start at 500,000 VND. There's a network of well-marked trails (though nobody has a map), and some cozy lodging at the top. You can hire a guide at the park office for hiking. The park is on the road between Lang Co Beach (at the northern end of the Hai Van Pass) and the town of Hue; at the time of this update, the access road was being upgraded. Many make this a full afternoon before carrying on to Hue, with an overnight in Lang Co (see the next section), or heading over (or under) the hump to Danang or Hoi An. For details, contact (or show up at) the Ecotourism and Environmental Education Center at the base of the hill (the entrance is well marked from Highway 1; ℭ **054/387-1330;** fax 054/387-1329; www.bachma.vnn.vn). The park office is open daily from dawn to dusk.

Where to Stay

There are a number of budget choices in the park, including a small guesthouse at the base. The **National Park Guesthouse** (ℭ **054/387-1330**) or the **Phong Lan Villas** (ℭ **054/387-1801**) can both be found on the road leading to the top but are quite basic. Stick with the Morin, if you can.

Bach Ma Morin Hotel Owned by the same folks behind the grand Saigon Morin in Hue, the Bach Ma Morin might sound luxe, but this mountaintop hotel is a basic collection of simple, fan-cooled rooms in an old, restored, concrete colonial at the park's peak—just adjacent to the fun Summit Trail (see "Hiking Trails," below). Rooms are large and clean, with a guesthouse-style shower and tub. The hotel can muster up some grub in their little canteen and connect you with a guide, but little else. The hotel commonly hosts budget or adventure groups and few individual travelers, but this is your best bet for an overnight in Bach Ma.

At the top of the mountain. ℭ **054/387-1199.** 12 units. $30 double. No credit cards. **Amenities:** Restaurant; bar. *In room:* Fan (high altitude, so A/C not needed), fridge, minibar.

Hiking Trails

Bring lots of water, bug repellent, a swimsuit, a waterproof bag for your camera or other valuables, and another bag for your garbage (always practice ecofriendly tourism). Wandering Bach Ma makes for a good full day or a few hours on your way up the coast.

The trails of Bach Ma are lined with medicinal plants. Ask your guide and look for the Nhe Den (or Curcuma Zedoraria), which is a yellow tuberous root that grows a few feet high and is commonly used to treat cancers of the womb and skin, as well as indigestion. Also keep an eye out for some stunning orchid varieties; growing out of the trunks of trees high up in the spring is the Vani orchid, with lovely fragrant yellow flowers used as an expectorant.

Keep an eye out for Sambar deer tracks; you might even spot the shy animals in the dense wood if you're very quiet. You'll also see the crumbling remains of old colonial villas and homes of Vietnamese who came to work on the area's small farms.

The short **Summit Trail** takes you a few miles past the Bach Ma Morin at the terminus of the park road and brings you to a pavilion with 360-degree views of the surrounding area, usually mist-shrouded and above the clouds. This trail is quite stunning and an easy, paved walk.

Five Lakes Trail starts just along the road from the Bach Ma Morin; the trail is a stunning descent from the road following a small waterfall—the five "lakes" are quaint catch basins along the waterfall's cascade. It's slippery in spots and even technical, with guide wires and ladders as needed. Go with a guide.

The **Rhododendron Trail,** which begins near the National Park Guesthouse, is a great walk. In spring, around March and April when the heat on the coast is at its worst, the rhododendrons bloom, sending explosions of red and clouds of fragrance onto the trails of the park.

Just more than 2km (1¼ miles) of trail hiking brings you to the terminus of the Five Lakes Trail (see above) and to the top of a 300m (984-ft.) waterfall. It's a gradual pitch at the top, and you can test your mettle by looking over the waterfall's edge. Just next to the waterfall is a set of steep stone stairs, and if you've got the chutzpah, the 1-hour hike down (and, more important, back up—it's a dead-end trail) brings you to the bottom. The 689 steps are a killer on the knees: Though there is a good handrail (be careful, because it's slippery), the steps are large, so the descent is bone jarring and each step of the ascent is a haul. But the stunning view from the bottom of the cascade is well worth it.

There are a number of other tracks through the park, and you can hire a local guide at a cost of around $10. Check at the park headquarters.

LANG CO BEACH

A good day stop along Route 1A, between Hue and Danang/Hoi An, Lang Co Beach is a sweeping expanse of sand good for dipping your toes and taking a rest. The absence of group tours and touts is the main draw, and options for overnight stays are growing.

The beach lies at the northern end of Hai Van Pass, and the sands of Lang Co begin just where the mountain switchbacks and the Hai Van Tunnel end. Though the tunnel now connects Danang directly with Hue, it's still worth making the pilgrimage up to Hai Van Pass, especially on a clear day when the views are memorable. Behind the long stretch of beach is a large lagoon, and the lightly populated town area is just a narrow strip of land between sea and lagoon, with most Lang Co villagers in homes along Highway 1. The beach is most popular for fishing and boat repairs, used more as a garbage dump or as a local latrine than for sun-loving tourists, but the southern section of beach near the resorts gets cleaned up on occasion, and this windswept stretch at the base of Hai Van Pass is quite stunning. Starting with the Lang Co Beach Resort, there's a small clutch of cozy budget warrens of bungalows, and more development is slated.

The town has no good dining to speak of, just a few little backpacker places that are popular among passing truck drivers; and where there are passing truck drivers, there are brothels—which seem to be the town's only real industry. The beach is hassle-free; plan to pack your own lunch and drinks, as there are no services on the sands.

Bach Ma National Park (see above) is just a short motorbike taxi ride from Lang Co, and the beach makes a good overnight before a day of hiking and onward travel to Hue. Or, overnight in Lang Co before moving on to Danang and Hoi An.

Where to Stay

Lang Co Beach Resort takes credit cards (and will cash traveler's checks for a hefty percentage), but note that you should come to town prepared to be self-sufficient. There are no services outside of the basic lodgings listed below.

Lang Co Beach Resort ★ This place always seems to be rather empty, so bring a friend. The resort is run by Huong Giang Tourist Company, a large government firm. They do a great job with large package junkets looking to step off the more obvious stops on Vietnam's north-south route. The resort stands over a stunning area of wind-swept beach, and all rooms have large glass sliders that open onto porch areas, some right on the water. Terra cotta-tile floors and dark-wood furnishings are cozy but not particularly luxurious. They have a good restaurant and aim to please.

On the north end of Lang Co Beach, Phu Loc District. www.langcobeachresort.com.vn. 𝒞 **054/387-3555.** 88 units. Oct–Mar $20 double, $45–$65 villa, $110 suite; Apr–Sept $40 double, $100–$120 villa, $200 suite. AE, MC, V. **Amenities:** 2 restaurants; bar; bike rental; outdoor pool; room service; tennis courts. *In room:* A/C, TV, fridge, Internet, minibar.

Thanh Tam Hotel This little seaside stop is constantly growing, with new ameni-ties and bungalows every year, but the place is still pretty rustic. The free-standing bungalows are your best option; the small hotel block at the back isn't really worth it. There's a cozy little grove of seaside pines for lounging, and dining is in a small open-air area. Service is limited, and nobody speaks much English, but you can mime a motorbike-revving wrist twist and get some wheels, and there's a useful list of tour options in English.

Central Lang Co Beach, Phu Loc District. 𝒞 **054/387-4456.** Fax 054/387-3762. 42 units. $28–$60 double. DC, MC, V. **Amenities:** Restaurant. *In room:* A/C, fridge, hair dryer.

DANANG

Danang, the fourth-largest city in Vietnam, is one of the most important seaports in the central region, and the current booming Vietnamese economy has seen an eco-nomic growth (GDP) rate in busy Danang as high as 12.6%. As the most convenient deep-water port in the region, Danang is now greeting more and more international cruise ships, along with a glut of trade vessels.

The city played a prominent historical role in the Vietnam War. It was the landing site for the first U.S. troops officially sent to Vietnam on March 8, 1965. On that day, 3,500 soldiers in beach assault vehicles joined more than 23,000 U.S. advisors who were already in the country.

Danang has nothing in the way of charm, and there aren't any major attractions except for the **Cham Museum,** which has become just a quick stop on the tourist-cafe buses between Hoi An and Hue. But **Furama Resort,** a short ride from the city center, is one of the finest high-end resorts in Indochina, and there are some excel-lent-value hotels in town (some use this as a budget base to explore nearby Hoi An).

China Beach, and also nearby **My Khe Beach,** are worth a stop. This former U.S. recreation base has a light-sand coast with excellent views of the nearby Marble Mountains, and it's beginning to draw more and more international tourists, as well as weekend visits by Danang's growing expat community.

Getting There

BY PLANE You can fly to Danang from both Hanoi and Ho Chi Minh City. The Vietnam Airlines office is at 35 Tran Phu St. (𝒞 **0511/382-1130**). A taxi to or from the airport costs about 60,000 VND.

BY BUS If you're traveling on the "open tour" ticket, Danang is not a specified stop, but the budget tourist cafes can drop you off at the Cham Museum at the southern end of the city. You'll have to call the office in either Hue or Hoi An for pickup when you're ready to leave, or contact **An Phu Travel,** 20 Dong Da St. (in the far north end of town; ☎ **0511/381-8366;** anphu_cndn@yahoo.com), which is the only traveler cafe with an office in town. Catch local buses at the **Interprovince Bus Station,** 33 Nguyen Luong Bang, which is not a bad option for a short hop to Hoi An or Hue (note that these local buses have hourly departures as opposed to traveler-cafe buses, which leave only twice a day). Travelers planning to take the rigorous bus journey onward to **Laos** should contact **An Phu Travel** for buses to **Savannakhet.** Expect to pay about $30 to $35 and expect a long, harrowing journey (honestly, fly if you can).

BY CAR   Danang is about 2 hours by car from Hue, and the route passes Lang Co Beach (good for a stop and a rest) and crosses the very scenic **Hai Van Pass** (p. 194) or goes through the new **Hai Van Tunnel.** You'll pay $65 to take the trip by rented car with driver. From Hoi An, it's about an hour and costs $25. This ride makes a good day trip along with the **Marble Mountains** (p. 202). From either Hoi An or Hue, contact local traveler cafes or travel agents; from Danang, contact An Phu Tourist, or your hotel can make arrangements.

BY TRAIN   All trains stop at the **Danang Railway Station,** 202 Hai Phong St. (☎ **0511/382-1175**).

Getting Around

Danang has the usual contingent of **motorbike taxis** and **cyclos** whose operators are quicker to find you than vice versa. Expect to pay around 40,000 VND for trips in town or 80,000 VND for a ride out to Furama Resort or My Khe Beach. **Taxis** can be called or hailed anywhere, and the initial cost is 12,000 VND, with 14,000 VND for every kilometer after that. Contact **Airport Taxi** (☎ **0511/382-5555**) or **Mai Linh Taxi** (☎ **0511/352-5252**).

Visitor Information & Tours

There are few tour offices in Danang, as most major tour operations are based out of nearby Hoi An or Hue. Any hotel can help with onward travel, either by private car, by minivan, or through budget cafes. Tours can also be booked with any concierge.

An Phu Travel, 20 Dong Da St. (in the far north end of town; ☎ **0511/381-8366;** anphu_cndn@yahoo.com), is the local budget tourist cafe and can arrange any low-budget connections (they also have offices in Hoi An). Their office is in the north end of Danang near the Saigon Tourane Hotel, but they can arrange pickup from your hotel and are generally pretty accommodating.

[FastFACTS] DANANG

Banks & Currency Exchange   Vietcombank is at 12 Phan Chu Trinh, Hai Chau district (☎ 0511/381-7441; www.vietcombank.com.vn).

Hospital   The Family Medical Clinic of Danang offers high-end emergency and general medical services to expatriates and travelers. Their office is at 50–52 Nguyen Van Linh St., Hai Chau District (☎ **0511/358-2699;** danang@vietnammedicalpractice.com).

Post Office   The post office is at 1 Le Duan (☎ **0511/381-7512;** www.danangpt.vnn.vn).

Telephone   The city code for Danang is 0511. You can make international calls from the post office. Danang hosts the usual contingent of budget dial-up Internet shops. Look along Dong Da Street adjacent to the An Phu Travel office, 9 Dong Da St.

Danang

HOTELS ■
Bach Dang Riverside Hotel **4**
Bamboo Green Hotel **9**
Furama Resort Danang **5**
Saigon Tourane Hotel **2**
Tourane Hotel **5**

RESTAURANTS ◆
Apsara **8**
Bread of Life **1**
Kim Do Restaurant **6**

ATTRACTIONS ●
Cao Dai Temple **3**
The Cham Museum **7**

Where to Stay

Look for new hotels from well-known names, as Danang has been attracting some attention lately. Raffles (www.raffles.com) is already working on a new property, but high-end luxury takes time. At press time, their 150-room resort is scheduled to open in 2011, as is a new resort by InterContinental (www.ichotelsgroup.com), their third property in Vietnam (the other two are in Hanoi and Ho Chi Minh). Check the hotel websites for more information.

EXPENSIVE

Furama Resort Danang ★★★   Just a short ride southwest of Danang and elegantly situated near a beautiful sand beach, this popular upscale gem greets you in style with a grand lobby that is more or less the gilded frame to beautiful scenery: sand, sun, and sky. Whether you're a sailor, a beach bum, or a comfort junkie, you'll find what you want here. There are two gorgeous swimming pools: one a multitiered minimalist still life overlooking the open beach, and the other a romantic faux lagoon, complete with small waterfall and bridge. The hotel offers local tours, yoga, tai chi, a spa, and a full salon. Rooms are large and comfortable, with wood floors, Vietnamese-style furniture, and sliding doors to balconies that overlook the ocean or pool. Large

WHO ARE the cham?

There is little recorded history of the Cham. What we do know comes mainly from written Chinese history and from splendid religious artwork the empire created in its prime.

The Cham are of Indonesian descent, and records of their civilization go as far back as the 2nd century A.D. in Tuong Lam, along the central coast of Vietnam, when the Cham fought Chinese incursion. The Cham declared a new land, dubbed the Lin Yi by the Chinese, which extended from Quang Binh to present-day Danang Province. The center of the civilization for most of its existence was in what the Cham called Indrapura, near present-day Danang.

The Cham belong to the Malayo-Polynesian language family, same as Hawaiian islanders and the Maori people near New Zealand and Australia. Traditionally, Cham lived by rice farming; fishing; and trading pepper, cinnamon bark, ivory, and wood with neighboring nations, using Hoi An as a base. Hinduism was their dominant religion, with Buddhist influences and an infusion of Islam starting in the 14th century.

In the middle of the 10th century, internal warfare, as well as battles against both the Khmer to the south and the ethnic Vietnamese, or Dai Viet, to the north, began to erode the Cham kingdom. By the mid–15th century, Cham territories had been almost entirely absorbed into Vietnam. By the early 1800s, there was no longer a separate Cham nation.

Today the Cham are still a distinct ethnic group in Vietnam, and despite years of pressure to assimilate, Cham culture and traditions survive. Cham people have their own language, with a written text derived from Sanskrit, and many of their traditions remain in ancient Hinduism or in Islam, to which many have converted.

marble bathrooms have all the amenities. Small suites are a great option, with large double beds and a sunken sitting area with a large, cushy white couch. Dining choices are great, and their restaurants flank a large, central area with a small reflecting pool in the center. There are shuttles to the city.

68 Ho Xuan Huong St. (ocean side 11km/6¾ miles south and west of Danang). www.furamavietnam. com. ✆ **0511/384-7333.** Fax 0511/384-7666. 198 units. $260–$295 garden-view double; $315–$350 ocean-view double; $420–$720 suite. AE, MC, V. **Amenities:** 3 restaurants; 3 bars; concierge; health club; Internet; 2 pools; room service; spa; 2 tennis courts; watersports equipment/rentals. *In room:* A/C, TV, fridge, hair dryer, minibar.

MODERATE

Bamboo Green Hotel ★★   The best choice in Danang proper, Bamboo Green is also the best of its three properties in town (Bamboo Green II and III are comparable but less luxurious). Rooms are large, and well furnished (except for the hideous polyester bedspreads); request the top floor for a city view. There's a big restaurant with decent Asian/Vietnamese fare and good tour services. The staff is friendly.

177 Tran Phu St., Danang. www.bamboogreenhotel.com. ✆ **0511/382-2722.** 70 units. $45 superior double; $60 deluxe double; $75 suite. AE, MC, V. **Amenities:** 2 restaurants; bar; room service; sauna. *In room:* A/C, TV, fridge, hair dryer, Internet, minibar.

Saigon Tourane Hotel ★   You can expect comfort at a low cost in this nondescript, friendly hotel on the north end of town. Carpeted rooms are clean, and some have good city views from upper floors, but it's certainly not luxurious. The hotel is popular with European tour groups, and the general atmosphere is marked by failing neon signs and worn carpets. Saigontourist owns the hotel and can make any necessary arrangements with little hassle, and the staff couldn't be any kinder. Be sure to ask for a room away—far away—from the karaoke. If you're in a pinch, next door is the **Danang Hotel,** 01–03 Dong Da St. (℃ **0511/382-3258;** fax 0511/382-3431) with budget rooms from $20.

5 Dong Da St., Danang. www.saigontourane.com.vn. ℃ **0511/3821-021.** Fax 0511/3895-285. 82 units. $50–$80 double; $110 suite. MC, V. **Amenities:** 2 restaurants; bar; gym; karaoke; sauna; smoke-free rooms. *In room:* A/C, TV, fridge, hair dryer, Internet, minibar.

INEXPENSIVE

Bach Dang Riverside Hotel   This big riverside hotel has long been a popular expat address. It's pretty beat-up, but rooms are tidy and there are lots of well-maintained amenities. Staff is quite helpful, and you'll find lots of shops and local dining options in the esplanade out front.

50 Bach Dang St., Danang. bdhotel@dng.vnn.vn. ℃ **0511/382-3034.** Fax 0511/382-1659. 99 units. $35–$80 double. MC, V. **Amenities:** Restaurant; bike rental; pool; tennis court. *In room:* A/C, TV, fridge, Internet, minibar.

MY KHE BEACH

Just 3km (1¾ miles) from town across the large lagoon bridge, you'll find a few quiet, little hotels worth the escape on **My Khe Beach.** This stretch of sand is most popular as a local hangout, but it has affordable accommodations.

Tourane Hotel   This hotel has recently undergone extensive renovations. The suites are a good size and very comfortable, with wood floors and high ceilings. The Tourane is a big government hotel, which means it's drab and bare throughout, but it's across the road from the beach and the best choice along this strip.

My Khe, Phuoc My Ward, Danang City. www.touranehotel.com.vn. ℃ **0511/393-2666.** Fax 0511/384-4328. 70 units. $60–$90 double; $100 suite. MC, V. **Amenities:** Restaurant; pool; 2 tennis courts. *In room:* A/C, TV, fridge, Internet, minibar.

Where to Eat

You'll find the best fine dining at Furama (p. 199), but beachside seafood shacks adjacent to the resort also serve good barbecue for a fraction of resort prices. In Danang proper, choices are few—mostly small storefront restaurants. **Apsara,** 222 Tran Phu (℃ **0511/356–1409**), is the fanciest restaurant in the city, serving mostly seafood in smart surroundings, with live traditional music each evening. **Bread of Life,** 4 Dong Da St. (℃ **0511/356-5185;** www.breadoflifedanang.com), is a wonderful cafe/restaurant serving tasty Western fare such as burgers and homemade pies. The owners employ deaf Vietnamese youth, teaching them American Sign Language (quite similar to Vietnamese Sign, both derived from French Sign) and life skills to encourage self-sufficiency. **Kim Do Restaurant,** 180 Tran Phu St. (℃ **0511/382-1846**), is a Chinese restaurant of long standing, with good stir-fries and steamed Cantonese specials.

Attractions

In addition to the listings below, Danang hosts a small enclave of the **Cao Dai sect,** a contemporary Vietnamese denomination incorporating aspects of all religions and science (see the Cao Dai Holy See Temple in chapter 12). Most practitioners of Cao Daism are in the far south, but this Cao Dai temple is one of the largest outside of

Tay Ninh, home of the Cao Dai Holy See. The **Cao Dai Temple** in Danang, 35 Hai Phong St., is open daily dawn to dusk. Someone is usually on-site with a key, but you might have to wake them up to get inside.

The Cham Museum ★★   The Cham Museum was established in 1936 (originally the Ecole Française d'Extrème Orient) to house the relics of the powerful Hindu culture that once ruled vast tracts of central Vietnam. The museum has the largest collection of Cham sculpture in the world, in works ranging from the 4th to 14th centuries, presented in a rough indoor and outdoor setting that suits the evocative, sensual sculptures well. The more than 300 pieces of sandstone artwork and temple decorations were largely influenced by Hinduism and, later, Mahayana Buddhism. Among the cast of characters, you'll see symbols of Uroja, or "goddess mother," usually breasts or nipples; the *linga,* the phallic structure representing the god Shiva; the holy bird Garuda; the dancing girl Kinnari; the snake god Naga; and elephant-headed Ganesha, child of the god Shiva. The sculptures are arranged by period, which, in turn, are named after the geographic regions where the sculptures were found. Note the late-7th-century masterpiece Tra Kieu altar, with carved scenes telling the story of the Hindu epic *Ramayana.* There is a permanent photo exhibition of the many Cham relics *in situ* at various locations throughout Vietnam.

2, 2 Thang 9 St., Hai Chau District, Danang. ⓒ **0511/347-0114.** Fax 0511/357-4801 www.chammuseum. danang.vn. Admission 30,000 VND. Daily 7am–5:30pm. Guided tours daily 8–10am and 2–4:30pm.

The Marble Mountains ✋   The "mountains" are actually a series of five marble and limestone formations, which the locals liken to the shape of a dragon at rest. For the Vietnamese, it is a place of significance, which means you are often climbing with loud tour groups that are trying to elbow past you. The hills are interlaced with caves, some of which are important Buddhist sanctuaries. The caves at the Marble Mountains, like so many in the country, served as sanctuaries for the Viet Cong during the Vietnam War. Each peak is named for an element: Hoa Son, or fire; Mo Son, or wood; Kim Son, or gold; and Tho Son, or earth. The highest mountain, Tho Son, is climbable via a series of metal ladders beginning inside the cave and extending to the surface at the top. Linh Ung Pagoda, a shrine within a cave, is a highlight. The quarries in Non Nuoc village, at the bottom of the mountains, are as interesting as the caves. Fantastic animals and fanciful statues of folk tales and Buddhist figures are carved from the rock. Try to get a good look before you are set upon by flocks of hawkers. What's more, even if you're interested in the items they hawk—incredibly cheap mortar and pestle sets, some very nice chess sets, turtles, and small animals—any amount of marble adds considerable weight to luggage. You can easily see the mountains en route to or from Hoi An; most cafe tour buses stop here.

11km (6¾ miles) south of Danang and 9.5km (6 miles) north of Hoi An along Hwy. 1. All tours stop here. Admission 30,000 VND. Daily 7am–6pm.

HOI AN

Hoi An was designated a UNESCO World Heritage Site in 1999, and a visit to this old-world gem is a sure cultural highlight of any tour in Vietnam. From the 16th to the 18th century, the city was Vietnam's most important port and trading post, particularly of ceramics with nearby China. Today it is a quaint old town of some 844 structures protected as historical landmarks, and the unique influence of Chinese and Japanese traders who passed through (or settled) can still be felt. It's a

Hoi An

HOTELS ■
Betel Garden Homestay **35**
Cua Dai **35**
Golden Sand Resort **35**
Ha An Hotel **21**
Hai Yen (Sea Swallow Hotel) **35**
Hoi An Beach Resort **35**
Hoi An Hotel **20**
Hoi An Riverside Resort **35**
Huy Hoang **24**
Indochine Hotel **35**
Life Resort Hoi An **22**
The Nam Hai **1**
Palm Garden Resort **35**
River Beach Resort **35**
Thanh Binh II Hotel **5**
Victoria Hoi An Resort **35**
Vinh Hung I, II, and III **3, 4, 10**
Vinh Hung Resort **12**

RESTAURANT ◆
Bale Well **19**
Brother's Café **23**
Café des Amis **33**
Cafeteria 22 (Miss Ly's) **28**
Goda **35**
Hoi An Cargo Club & Patisserie **14**
Mango Mango **11**
Mango Rooms **14**
The Mermaid (Nhu Y) Restaurant **25**
Morning Glory **30**
Nam Long **35**
Red Bridge **35**
River Lounge **13**
Sakura **14**
Tam-Tam Café **16**
Van Loc **31**

ATTRACTIONS ●
Cantonese Assembly Hall **9**
Central Market **32**
Fukian Assembly Hall
 (Phuc Kien) **28**
Handicraft Workshop **34**
Hoi An Cathedral **2**
House of Hoi An Traditional
 Handicraft **17**
Japanese Covered Bridge **7**
Museum of History and
 Culture **26**
Museum of Trade Ceramics **29**
The Old House of Phung
 Hung **6**
The Old House of Tan Ky **15**
Quan Cong Temple **27**
Sa Huynh Culture Museum **8**
The Tran Family Home and
 Chapel **18**

OTHER ●
Bank **9**
Post Office **8**
Tourist and Ticket Office **19**

picturesque town, small enough to cover easily on foot, with lots of good nooks and crannies, shops, and gastronomic delights to discover. For many tourists, Hoi An is the highlight of their visit to Vietnam.

Wander among historic homes and temples, perhaps stop to lounge in an open-air cafe, gaze at the oddities and exotic foods in the market, or take a **sampan ride** down the lazy river. In the afternoons when school is out, the streets are thronged with skipping children in spotless white shirts and girls in their *ao dai* uniforms, and you can still see local craftsmen at work in some parts of the city.

During the full moon of every month, local shop owners turn off the electricity and hang lanterns bearing their shops' names. A candlelight procession, complete with a few small floats, makes its way through the Old Town and along the riverfront. It's well worth timing a visit to enjoy the spectacle and the postprocessional festivities. Visit www.hoian-tourism.com to see festival dates.

Getting There

BY PLANE OR TRAIN   Major transport connections go through Danang. From there, you can take a car or a cab to Hoi An for between $18 and $25.

BY BUS   Hoi An is a major stop on all open-tour cafe buses. Connection with Danang is just $3.

Getting Around

Hoi An is so small that you'll memorize the map in an hour or two. Most hotels and guesthouses rent bicycles for 30,000 VND to 40,000 VND a day, a great way to explore the outer regions of the city or head out to Cua Dai Beach. Motorbikes are 120,000 VND to 150,000 VND per day and are not difficult to drive in this tiny city or out busy Cua Dai Road to the beach. However, going by foot or bicycle is the best, quietest option, and increasingly the streets in the heart of the old city are forbidding motorbike traffic (not that anyone follows the rules). **Cyclos** are everywhere; 20,000 VND an hour or so should get you anywhere within the city. Car rental is available anywhere. Try **Hoi An Taxi** (✆ **0511/381-5815**) for a car by the hour or for the day.

Visitor Information & Tours

o **Hoi An Ancient Town,** 1 Nguyen Truong To (✆ **0510/386–1327**), or 12 Phan Chu Trinh St. (✆ **0510/386–2715**), sells the Hoi An World Cultural Heritage tickets. A one-ticket purchase offers limited admission to the town's museums, old houses, and Chinese assembly halls. Ticket booths are at 78 Le Loi, 30 Tran Phu, 12 Phan Chu Trinh, 10 Nguyen Hue, and 5 Hoang Dieu. For more information about the ticket, see "Attractions," on p. 209.

o **Hoi An Tourist,** inside the Hoi An Hotel, 10 Tran Hung Dao St. (✆ **0510/386-1522;** fax 0510/391-1099; www.hoiantourist.com/en), books every type of tour of the city and surrounding areas, including China Beach and the Marble Mountains, and is a reliable operation.

o **The Sinh Tourist,** 587 Hai Ba Trung St. (✆ **0510/386-3948;** www.thesinhtourist. vn), provides bus tours and tickets onward.

o **An Phu Tourist** has an office at 722 Hai Ba Trung St. (✆ **0510/386-2643;** fax 0510/386-4011; www.anphutourist.com), and another in the An Phu Hotel, just out of the town center toward Cua Dai (288 Nguyen Duy Hieu St., away from town toward Cua Dai Beach; ✆ **0510/391-4345;** fax 0510/391-4054).

[FastFACTS] HOI AN

Banks & Currency Exchange The **Vietinbank** branch at 4 Hoang Dieu St. has an ATM, exchanges most major currencies, and does credit card–based cash-withdrawal transactions. Hours are Monday to Saturday 7:30am to 7pm. **Vietcombank** has offices with exchange services at 2 Tran Cao Van St. (✆ 0935/616-129). **Exchange Bureau #1,** across from the Hoi An Hotel at 10 Tran Hung Dao, has exchange services and an ATM. There is also an ATM at the post office (6 Tran Hung Dao St.) You'll find a **Western Union** outlet at Vinh Tours (26 Tran Hung Dao).

Internet Along Le Loi you'll find service at prices of about 5,000 VND to 8,000 VND per hour. **Min's Computer,** 125 Nguyen Duy Hieu, on the northern end of town (✆ 0510/391-4323), is as good as it gets and so popular now that if they are full, just pop into one of the copycat shops that has opened up on the same street (try **123** Internet next door). There's also good Internet service right next to the post office at 4B Tran Hung Dao (✆ 0510/386-1635).

Post Office The post office is at the corner of Tran Hung Dao and Hoang Dieu streets, and is open Monday to Saturday from 6am to 9:30pm.

Telephone The city code for Hoi An is 0510. You can place international phone calls from the post office listed above and from most hotels.

Where to Stay

Hoi An has seen a recent boom in upscale resorts, and there are more on the way along Cua Dai Beach. Large-scale new construction in Hoi An proper is prohibited by UNESCO, but smaller hotels are getting nicer and there are a few new options closer to town. The hotels listed below are broken into four sections: at China Beach, in Hoi An town proper, along Cua Dai Road, and at Cua Dai Beach. With so much competition and so many new resorts going up and posting promotional rates, you can find some great deals for very fine rooms and, with some good bargaining, real steals on a room in the heart of the old city.

AT CHINA BEACH
Very Expensive

The Nam Hai ★★★ This is the best resort in Hoi An, and certainly one of the best luxury destinations in all of Vietnam. Individual villas are discreetly laid out over an immaculately tended 35 hectares (86 acres). The one-bedroom hotel villas are a chic affair of granite stone floors, earthy colors, and dark local wood. The centerpiece is a six-column raised platform topped with lattice woodwork and draped in silk curtains—this is where you'll find the elevated, plush bed facing a huge oceanview window. For in-room entertainment, a flatscreen TV swivels out to face the bed, or there's the iPod loaded with tunes hooked up to a Bose sound system. In-house activities, such as Vietnamese cooking demonstrations or tennis tournaments, are nice when you want to do more than just lounge poolside. Pool villas are styled like traditional Vietnamese courtyard houses. An elevated dining and living room occupies the center of the courtyard and looks out onto the pool and nearby ocean. Multibedroom pool villas are fantastic value if you're a group of four or more, as they come with superluxurious "club benefits" such as return airport limousine transfer, a personal butler, complimentary minibar, and evening cocktails and canapés with free-flowing champagne and wine.

Hamlet 1, Dien Duong village, Dien Ban District, Quang Nam Province. www.thenamhai.com. ☎ **0510/394-0000.** Fax 0510/394-0999. 100 units. $750 1-bedroom villa; $1,360–$3,900 1- to 5-bedroom pool villa. AE, DC, MC, V. **Amenities:** 2 restaurants; bar; badminton court; basketball court; bike rental; health club; library; 3 pools; room service; spa; 4 tennis courts. *In room:* A/C, TV, fridge, hair dryer, iPod/MP3 docking station, minibar, movie library, Wi-Fi.

IN HOI AN TOWN
Expensive

Life Resort Hoi An ★★   This is the only resort within walking distance of Hoi An—a good start. It shut down in 2008 for renovations, and the result is fabulous (enough to be included in *Condé Nast's* 2010 Gold List). The dark-wood furniture and orange and dark champagne accents are a welcome addition to the formerly spartan decorations. Rooms are split-level, with the slightly raised sleeping area done in cool slate tiles. Views of the river are good, and deluxe units have quiet sitting areas out front that are perfect for meditation or a respite from the noonday sun. The dining outlets, housed in a faux-colonial block at riverside, are atmospheric; the quiet, air-conditioned cafe has good coffee and desserts. For location alone, this is a great choice.

1 Pham Hong Thai St. www.life-resorts.com. ☎ **0510/391-4555.** Fax 0510/391-4515. 94 units. $122 double; $158–$286 suite. AE, MC, V. **Amenities:** Restaurant; 2 bars; cafe; outdoor pool; room service; spa. *In room:* A/C, TV, fridge, minibar, Wi-Fi.

Moderate

Hoi An Hotel ★   Still the most convenient in-town address, the Hoi An Hotel was the first high-end hotel in the city, and it works hard to keep its reputation. As a result, it stays busy with lots of tour groups. The friendly staff does a great job and handles large numbers with surprising grace. Don't expect anything fancy, but rooms are unusually large and impeccably clean, with tile floors and comfortable beds—older rooms are just as good for the money. The newest building has upscale rooms with dark-wood floors and a fun, contemporary Chinese theme. The central pool is large, though often overcrowded. Their casual open-air dining facilities are good, and the folks at the tour desk are very helpful. The location is convenient to downtown sites.

10 Tran Hung Dao St. www.hoiantourist.com. ☎ **0510/386-1445.** Fax 0510/386-1636. 160 units. $75–$85 double; $105–$180 suite. AE, MC, V. **Amenities:** Restaurant; bar; babysitting; concierge; Jacuzzi; pool; tennis court. *In room:* A/C, TV, fridge, hair dryer, minibar, Wi-Fi.

Vinh Hung Resort ★   The folks at Vinh Hung have followed a Chinese style of entrepreneurship with the model "Start small; go big." (See also Vinh Hung I, II, and III, below.) Their small, in-town properties have been popular, and they've turned the income from them into this project: a self-contained, midlevel resort on Hoi An Island that is just getting up and running. The area is just a 10- or 15-minute walk from the canal bridge at Hoi An center. Deluxe rooms are the best—large and tidy, with wood floors, Chinese tapestries, and carpeted sitting areas. High-end rooms are enormous, some with Jacuzzis. Rooms encircle a central pool area and, though resort services are limited and everything is a bit compact, this is still an affordable and convenient getaway. Some rooms overlook the wide river; a good choice. They have kayaks for rent, a unique commute (kayaks) to the town center, and cover all basic amenities.

111 Ngo Quyen (An Hoi Islet, across the small bridge connecting to Hoi An near Bach Dang St., and a short ride to the opposite end of the island). www.vinhhungresort.com. ☎ **0510/386-4074.** Fax 0510/386-4094. 82 units. $70–$100 double; $125 suite. AE, MC, V. **Amenities:** Restaurant; bar; babysitting; bike rental; small fitness center; Jacuzzi; pool; room service; sauna; tennis court. *In room:* A/C, TV, fridge, Internet, minibar.

Inexpensive

Betel Garden Homestay ★ Homestays are becoming increasingly popular in Vietnam among visitors tired of impersonal hotels, and Betel Garden certainly offers a more personal and friendly environment than your average high-rise hotel. Located a 10-minute walk from the town center, it features free services including Wi-Fi, bicycles, and laundry. Rooms are well equipped and comfortable, with shady porches surrounded by a leafy garden. Staff is superfriendly and helpful.

161 Tran Nan Tong St. www.betelgardenhomestay.com. ☏ **0510/392-4165.** 7 units. $45–$80 double. MC, V. **Amenities:** Restaurant; pool; room service. *In room:* A/C, cable TV, hair dryer, minibar, Wi-Fi.

Ha An Hotel ★★ This colonial-style place with a courtyard entry is just a short walk from town. Rooms in the faux colonial-style building are compact but tidy and comfortable. The Ha An is basically like minihotels elsewhere, but slightly more spacious and with nice touches such as rattan furniture and wall hangings. There are DVD players and videos available to borrow. The hotel restaurant is cozy, and the staff aims to please. It's a good choice, out of the in-town tourist jumble, and a nice alternative if you can't afford to splash out at neighboring Life Resort.

06–08 Phan Boi Chau St. (just outside the entrance to Life Resort). www.haanhotel.com. ☏ **0510/386-3126.** Fax 0510/391-4280. 24 units. $55–$104. MC, V. **Amenities:** Restaurant; bar; bike rental; Internet; outdoor pool table. *In room:* A/C, TV, DVD, fridge, minibar.

Huy Hoang I ★ The original of this growing local chain is a good bargain option set in a recently refurbished white faux-colonial close to the Central Market. Tidy, basic tile-floor rooms are just $26. There are no phones or other amenities, and only the few $50 rooms are of any substantial size (and also have bathtubs). Breakfast is served in a patio in the back, with views of the river. The staff is exceedingly friendly.

73 Phan Boi Chau St. www.huyhoang1-hotel.com. ☏ **0510/393-6741.** 26 units. $26–$50 double. No credit cards. **Amenities:** Restaurant; bar. *In room:* A/C, TV, no phone.

Thanh Binh II Hotel ★ Thanh Bin II is a better deal than its sister property, **Thanh Binh I** (☏ **0510/391–6364**), which has a good location on Le Loi Street but just basic rooms. Rooms are spacious, but decor is a color-coordinated mishmash. The "suite" is a huge room that sports wood paneling, carved Chinese-style furnishings, a mosquito net over the bed, a nice balcony with beaded curtains, and, in the center of everything, a large wooden Buddha. The staff is really friendly. Another location, **Thanh Binh III,** is at 98 Ba Trieu St. (☏ **0510/391–6777**).

712 Hai Ba Trung St. www.thanhbinhhotel.com.vn. ☏ **0510/391-6364.** 35 units. $15–$25 double. AE, MC, V. **Amenities:** Restaurant; pool. *In room:* A/C, TV, fridge, minibar.

Vinh Hung I, II, and III ★ Vinh Hung I, a downtown property set in an old wooden Chinese house, is a Hoi An institution: Its two signature rooms are almost museum pieces—alone worth a visit—but they're not especially luxurious or comfortable. Standard rooms in both Vinh Hung I and II are large, with wooden appointments and cool retro features such as mosquito nets and Chinese latticework on wood balconies. Vinh Hung II is a tour-group favorite and is often full, but for good reason (the central pool is unique in this price category). However, its popularity means the place is getting a bit rough around the edges. The new Vinh Hung Resort (see above) is an improvement.

Vinh Hung 1: 143 Tran Phu St. www.vinhhungresort.com ☏ **0510/386-1621.** Fax 0510/386-1893. $80–$90 double. Vinh Hung II: Nhi Trung St. ☏ 0510/386-3717. Fax 0510/386-4094. $40–$50. Vinh Hung III: 96 Ba Trieu St. ☏ 0510/391-6577. Fax 0510/391-6359. 119 units. $35–$120 double. AE, MC, V. **Amenities:** Restaurant; pool. *In room:* A/C, TV, fridge, Wi-Fi.

ALONG CUA DAI ROAD

Busy little Cua Dai doesn't offer the most spectacular accommodations, but you can find some small hotels, popular with large groups, along its length (a few even have a pool). Discounts abound, and the prices listed here are just a point of departure for negotiating. If calling for reservations, ask about a "contract rate" or a current discount policy, and begin bargaining for a price for 1 day and ask for less for 2 days or more. The **Hoi An Riverside** is an exception: It's a high-end property.

Expensive

Hoi An Riverside Resort ★★   For upscale, tranquil, and intimate surroundings, you'll find no better than this lush little resort between road and river outside of Hoi An (just 3km/1¾ miles). The place has a cozy feel, as if guest rooms kind of grew around the winding path of the garden and tranquil courtyard pool. Vietnamese- or Japanese-theme rooms have nice wood appointments throughout. The staff is invisible, meaning that this place carries on like an immaculately trimmed golf course that gets a once-over each night. The Song Do restaurant serves fine Vietnamese and Continental fare, and a visit to their Faifo bar hearkens back to another era. The staff is very professional and informative.

175 Cua Dai Rd.. www.hoianriverresort.com. ✆ **0510/386-4800.** Fax 0510/386-4900. 63 units. $99–$159 double. AE, DC, MC, V. **Amenities:** 2 restaurants; 2 bars; babysitting; health club; Internet; pool; room service; snooker/billiards room. *In room:* A/C, TV, fridge, minibar, Wi-Fi.

Moderate

Cua Dai ★★   A good budget gem on the beach road just out of town (like nearby Hai Yen, reviewed below), the Cua Dai is a good marriage of affordability and comfort. It's easy to settle in here, with its open sitting areas and basic but comfy rooms. The kind staff will make you feel right at home. The only drawback is the busy road out front, but all rooms have double glass and are relatively quiet. Rooms in the newer wing in back have fine wooden appointments and creative local decorations; older rooms in the main building are quite large. Cua Dai is a good base for exploring, and a sure bet for meeting some expats and long-stay travelers here on cultural or humanitarian missions.

544 Cua Dai St. ✆ **0510/386-2231** or 0510/386-4604. Fax 0510/386-2232. 24 units. $34–$59 double. MC, V. **Amenities:** 3 restaurants; bike/motorbike rental; pool; room service. *In room:* A/C, TV, fridge, minibar.

Hai Yen (Sea Swallow Hotel) ★   On the edge of the old town (a short walk or ride toward the beach), Hai Yen is a popular choice for big budget-tour groups. Slick diagonal black-and-white (or blue-and-white) tile decorates throughout, and rooms are big but have funky Chinese relief carvings, overly fancy curtains, and shiny polyester spreads. I'd give it an A for effort, but the general effect is kind of unsettling. The small pool is a surprise luxury in this price range. It's all a bit rough around the edges, but the staff is friendly and can help with any detail.

568 Cua Dai St., Hoi An. ✆ **0510/386-2445** or 0510/386-2446. 41 units. $25–$60 double. AE, MC, V. **Amenities:** Restaurant; motorbike rental; pool. *In room:* A/C, TV, fridge, minibar, Wi-Fi.

Indochine Hotel ★   This hotel attracts hordes of French tourists and is always booked. A midrange choice, the faux-colonial is set at a bend in the river about 1km (½ mile) from Cua Dai Beach, set in a U-shaped courtyard. The basic rooms are large and clean, with pricing based on a room's view of the river or garden. There's a fun spirit of camaraderie if you catch the right group, and the rooftop restaurant is a casual evening escape. You'll have to arrange transport anywhere you go, but there's a handy shuttle service.

87 Cua Dai St., Cam Chau Village (about 1km/½ mile back from the beach). www.hoianindochine.com. ℂ **0510/392-3601.** Fax 0510/392-3400. 60 units. $69–$79 double; $99 suite. MC, V. **Amenities:** 2 restaurants; bike rental; Internet (free); room service, free shuttle service. *In room:* A/C, TV, fridge, minibar, Wi-Fi.

AT CUA DAI BEACH

The Cua Dai Beach area is lined with hotels, and surveyors are already lining up for future development. There's some decent swimming and a few very good, affordable accommodations.

Expensive

Golden Sand Resort (Swiss-Belhotel) ★ ☺ This resort is a large open campus on a cleared beach, and all rooms are set in big, square, three-story pavilions. Superior rooms are compact and far from the beach, with limited views (mostly of other superior blocks), but they are done in a clean light-wood interior with lots of good amenities. Deluxe rooms are larger versions of the same, with smart red-wood consoles at the head of each bed and silk-lined lamps. Oceanside suites are absurdly luxurious, with Jacuzzis surrounded by granite tile. The oceanside pool is enormous, 150m (490 ft.) long with funky little bridges spanning narrow channels; there's a good poolside bar and dining. Next to it is a mini water park, with several slides and a big wading area. I prefer Victoria Hoi An (see below), which has similar prices but where you are less likely to share your vacation with a big, noisy tour group.

Thanh Nien Rd., Cua Dai Beach, Hoi An. www.swiss-belhotel.com. ℂ **0510/392-7555.** Fax 0510/392-7560. 212 units. $181 superior double; $231–$251 deluxe double; $482 suite. AE, MC, V. **Amenities:** 2 restaurants; babysitting; bike rental; children's center; health club; Jacuzzi; 2 pools; room service; spa; tennis courts; watersports equipment/rentals. *In room:* A/C, TV, fridge, minibar, Wi-Fi.

Hoi An Beach Resort ★ This government-run resort is across the road from Cua Dai Beach and close to the small restaurant row and popular tourist sunbathing area. Everything from the casual open-air restaurant to the more expensive rooms and suites faces the De Vong River as it approaches the sea, offering a glimpse of everyday riverside life. There's an upscale access point to the beach, where you can sit in private chairs without harassment from beachside sellers. All rooms here are nice, but the villas are certainly worth the extra few bucks: They're quite large, with high ceilings and large private balconies. Villas and suites have vaulted ceilings, and some have separate entrances with a shower area for postbeach cleanup. It's a popular choice for large European tours and can get a bit wild in the busy season. The pools are large, dining is good, and frequent shuttles run to town.

1 Cua Dai Beach. www.hoianbeachresort.com.vn. ℂ **0510/392-7011** or 0510/392-7015. Fax 0510/392-7019. 121 units. $90–$95 double garden deluxe; $110–$115 ocean-view and river-view villas; $165 suite. AE, MC, V. **Amenities:** Restaurant; 2 bars; small health club; Internet; Jacuzzi; 2 outdoor pools; room service; sauna; spa; steam bath. *In room:* A/C, TV, fridge, hair dryer, minibar, Wi-Fi.

Palm Garden Resort ★ This large resort is much like the others (see the reviews for the Victoria, below, or the Golden Sand Resort/Swiss-Belhotel, above) along this open stretch of beach, but it has a bit more charm and thatch. The resort sits on wide, manicured lawns and has an inviting pool. Bungalows on the beach are the best bet and have cool Zen rock gardens at each entry and some laterite stone detail. Beach bungalows have air-conditioned bedrooms and open-air bathrooms with tubs. All rooms have balconies facing the beach, though in varying degrees of proximity. They offer a host of good services and fine dining, and staff is as friendly as can be.

Lac Long Quan Rd., Cua Dai Beach (just 500m/1,640 ft. north of Cua Dai Beach, reached through a warren of streets). www.palmgardenresort.com.vn. ✆ **0510/392-7927.** Fax 0510/392-7928. 188 units. $126–$136 superior garden/ocean view; $146–$166 deluxe garden/ocean view; $195–$235 bungalow garden/beach front; $155 junior suite; $575 palm garden suite. MC, V. **Amenities:** 3 restaurants; 2 bars; babysitting; bike rental; children's center; health club; Internet; Jacuzzi; pool; room service; spa; 2 tennis courts; watersports equipment/rentals. *In room:* A/C, TV, fridge, minibar, Wi-Fi.

Victoria Hoi An Resort ★★ The Victoria offers peace and palm trees just a short ride (4.8km/3 miles) from ancient Hoi An. Rooms are either beachside bungalows, or set in parallel two-story rows to mimic Hoi An's ancient streets; the latter are not displeasing, but a bit like a theme park. Prices reflect beachside proximity. Design and layout vary widely from room to room; some are decorated in French country style, with canopy beds and wicker furniture, and others are Japanese rooms, with open-timber construction, bamboo floors, and tearooms hidden behind sliding doors. There's a certain flow to the public spaces here—from beach to garden and from rooms to common spaces (including a small billiards room with gaming tables and reading nooks)—that invites guests to wander; it's all connected by stone paths. Frequent shuttles connect you to town, or you can rent a motorcycle with sidecar.

Cua Dai Beach, 5km (3 miles) from Hoi An. www.victoriahotels-asia.com. ✆ **0510/392-7040.** Fax 0510/392-7041. 109 units. $170–$235 superior and deluxe double; $280–$300 suite. MC, V. **Amenities:** Restaurant; 3 bars; babysitting; children's play area; health club; Internet; Jacuzzi; small library; pool; room service; spa; 2 tennis courts. *In room:* A/C, TV/DVD (in suites), fridge, minibar, movie library (in suites), Wi-Fi.

Moderate

River Beach Resort ★ This place attracts large groups at cut-rate prices (hence the surly staff), and if you contact the hotel directly, you might get a good contract rate. Rooms are set in a large U shape around a central courtyard with a small pool, and are just a stone's throw from Cua Dai Beach. This is like a high-end minihotel set in a larger-hotel atmosphere. Plan to use the services—travel agents, car rental, and dining—elsewhere, but this is a fine place to lay your head near the beach.

5 Cua Dai Beach (4km/2½ miles from Hoi An Old Town), Hoi An. www.river-beachresort.com. ✆ **0510/392-7888.** Fax 0510/392-7777. 85 units. $109–$129 double; $159–$199 suite. MC, V. **Amenities:** Restaurant/bar; bike rental; small central pool. *In room:* A/C, TV, fridge, minibar, Wi-Fi.

Where to Eat

Hoi An is a feast for the stomach as well as the eyes. Local specialties include *cao lau* (rice noodles with fresh greens, rice crackers, and croutons), white rose dumplings of shrimp in clear rice dough, and large, savory fried won tons. Good, fresh seafood is available everywhere (don't miss the morning market). There are some new high-end options in town alongside some popular standbys, and each of the resorts has its own fine dining (see above). The riverfront road, Bach Dang, has become the de facto "restaurant row," and listed below are a few good spots, but take a stroll down here any time of day, and you'll be besieged by friendly but persistent touts who'll drag you into their restaurants. All the places along Bach Dang are comparable in price and cuisine (fried rice and noodles), and it's sometimes fun to let the restaurant choose you. ***Note:*** If you do eat on Bach Dang, choose a table a bit off the street and say a consistent and calm no to the young Tiger Balm and chewing-gum salesmen.

EXPENSIVE

Brother's Café ★★ VIETNAMESE   Serving similar fine Vietnamese fare as its sister restaurant in Hanoi (p. 82), this is a great choice for cuisine and atmosphere. A bland facade gives way to a lush garden sanctuary. Indoor seating is upscale Indochina of a bygone era, and the courtyard is dotted with canvas umbrellas to while away a balmy afternoon or enjoy a candlelit evening riverside. The fare is gourmet Vietnamese at its finest, with great specials; be sure to ask for a recommendation. It's a good place to try local items such as the white rose, a light Vietnamese ravioli, or *cao lau* noodles. Set menus are great and change daily. This is a great spot for groups to order family style and sample it all. They also feature a cooking school (just ask the staff). Everything's good, the atmosphere is great, and the staff couldn't be friendlier.

27 Phan Boi Chau St. ☎ **0510/391-4150.** Main courses $8–$25; set menus from $30. AE, MC, V. Daily 10am–11pm.

Nam Long ★ VIETNAMESE   This is the place to come for a secluded, riverside view. A hostess leads you through the front garden, past wild lilies, palm trees, and orchids floating in water vessels. The indoor seating is nicer than at Brother's (above), with dark-wood chairs and subdued lighting. However, it's better to stake out a table on the outdoor patio. The steamed sea bass in lemon sauce is delicious, and the staff are friendly.

103 Cua Dai St. ☎ **0510/392-3723.** Main courses $15–$30; set menus from $26. AE, MC, V. Daily 10am–10pm.

MODERATE

Café des Amis ★★ VIETNAMESE   What's on the menu? Well, there isn't one. Simply choose either a seafood or a vegetarian set menu, and wait to see what happens. The result is always good, one of the best meals in Vietnam; guests sign their endorsements in Mr. Kim's lengthy guest book (you'll be asked to sign, too). I enjoyed a leisurely meal starting with a savory clear soup, fried won tons with shrimp, broiled fish, stuffed calamari, and scallops on the half shell. Mr. Kim is careful to explain the intricacies of each dish and even demonstrates how to eat some of the more unusual entrees. A meal here makes for a memorable evening.

52 Bach Dang. ☎ **0510/386-1616.** Set menu 150,000 VND. No credit cards. Daily 8am–10pm.

Cafeteria 22 (Miss Ly's) ★ VIETNAMESE   The menu here is limited, but that means everything is always available and fresh. This little hole-in-the-wall cafe, in the heart of the old town, is the best place to try the town's famous fried won tons, a rice pastry stuffed with meat, shrimp, and onion and topped with Ly's special sauce, onion, and tomato—messy and delicious. Ly has been at it for more than 10 years and has just the right formula. There's nothing fancy here, and that's the appeal for folks who tire easily of trumped-up atmosphere and overpriced, altered versions of local fare.

22 Nguyen Hue St. ☎ **0510/386-1603.** Main courses 35,000 VND–140,000 VND; set menus 120,000 VND–200,000 VND. No credit cards. Daily 9am–10pm.

Goda ★ VIETNAMESE   This locally owned cafe offers a good host of specials: papaya salad, hot pots, local stews, and stir-fries. The place is a contemporary, chic, two-story cafe with a big winding staircase and good jazz music piped in. Located on Cua Dai Street about halfway between the town and the beach, it's a good stop on the way back from the beach for coffee. Goda is a good laid-back place to meet locals.

308 Cua Dai St., Cam Chau Ward. ✆ **0510/392-3644.** www.godahoian.com. Main courses $3–$15; set menus for 2 people from $16. MC, V. Daily 8am–11pm.

Hoi An Cargo Club and Patisserie ★★ INTERNATIONAL   This stylish storefront serves light meals in a lounge bar on the first floor and contemporary Vietnamese cuisine in a refined restaurant upstairs. There are good seafood dishes such as the crab in five spices or jumbo shrimp with tamarind sauce. Sandwiches, soups, and salads are served with fine fresh bread that's baked on site. Upstairs seating is on a cool balcony overlooking the river or a chic indoor space. Curries and good veggie dishes round out a good, affordable menu. They also have the best pastries in central Vietnam. This is a good place to reconnoiter if traveling in a group or to meet other travelers.

107–109 Nguyen Thai Hoc. ✆ **0510/391-0489.** www.hoianhospitality.com. Main courses 115,000 VND–215,000 VND; set menus 150,000 VND–180,000 VND. MC, V. Daily 8am–11pm.

Mango Mango ★★ 🍴 FUSION/VIETNAMESE   This new restaurant, from lively owner Duc, of Mango Rooms fame (see below), is a gem of an addition to Hoi An's dining scene. It has fantastic views of the Japanese Bridge and the river, but without the persistent hawkers that can disrupt your dining experience along Bach Dang Street. Mango Mango's whitewashed walls and orange trim give the place a cool hacienda vibe. The menu's sandwich options make it a good option for lunch. For larger mains, try the "exotic dance," shrimp wrapped in tender slices of beef and served with a soy-garlic sauce. Come after dark to indulge in cocktails, good music, and the great view.

45 Nguyen Phuc Chu (across the river from the Japanese Bridge). ✆ **0510/391-1863.** Main courses $10–$22; set menus $20–$35. MC, V. Daily 9am–10 pm.

Mango Rooms ★★ FUSION/VIETNAMESE   This is the hippest little restaurant between Ho Chi Minh and Hanoi. Owner and chef Duc spent his formative years in Texas before earning his stripes in hotels and fine-dining establishments. He brings his own blend of cuisines and serves cool combinations of California cuisine, down-home barbecue, and Pacific Rim—all stylishly presented. Duc runs the show from an open central kitchen and greets guests with a flamboyant, "Oh man, we're rockin' tonight!" as he steps out from behind the grill to see if he can help you find a seat. Try the likes of La Tropicana, a chicken breast with lemon grass and garlic; the "Asian Sins" of rice noodles pan-fried with vegetables, garlic, onion, and sweet basil; or seared tuna in rice paper. There are daily fresh-fish specials. The drink list is long and the cocktails divine. Try the delicious sticky rice with mango for dessert.

111 Nguyen Thai Hoc (with an entrance on riverside Bach Dang next to Sakura and just across from Tam-Tam Café). ✆ **0510/391-0839.** www.mangorooms.com. Main courses $11–$20; set menus $25–$38. MC, V. Daily 8am–midnight.

The Mermaid (Nhu Y) Restaurant ★★ VIETNAMESE   This quiet spot in the heart of downtown is an ivy-draped, unassuming storefront that serves some of the best authentic Vietnamese food in town (for next to nothing). If you like what you eat, stick around and take a cooking class in the large adjoining kitchen. The spring rolls are light and fresh, with a whole jumbo shrimp in each, and the white eggplant—eggplant covered in spring onion, garlic, and chili, and then pressed, sliced, and served in a light oil—is something special. Everything is good, and the staff, who also teach the classes, are friendly and helpful.

2 Tran Phu St. ✆ **0510/386-1527.** www.hoianhospitality.com. Main courses 38,000 VND–105,000 VND; set menus from 100,000 VND. No credit cards. Daily 10am–10pm.

Morning Glory ★★ VIETNAMESE   This is the crown jewel of local restaurateur Ms. Vy's empire (owner of the Mermaid, White Lantern, and Hoi An Cargo Club). The two-story restaurant is housed in an old colonial building in the heart of the old district. It features an open kitchen on the ground floor, large dining areas on both floors, and a trio of tables on the balcony upstairs. The menu is a delightful selection of Vietnamese street food; it includes tips and recommendations from Ms. Vy on the health properties of ingredients (for example, for cooling the body in hot weather, try the traditional dessert *Che,* made with soft tofu and ginger syrup). Order the morning glory sautéed with garlic for a healthy boost of leafy greens. For mains, I highly recommend the caramelized fish in a clay pot—the portion is a bit small, so if you don't want to share, order two—and the *banh xeo* (crepe-style pancakes stuffed with shrimp, bean sprouts, and other veggies). This restaurant is an absolute must-visit.

106 Nguyen Thai Hoc St. ✆ **0510/324-1556.** Main courses 45,000 VND–195,000 VND. MC, V. Daily 9am–10pm.

Red Bridge ★★ 🍴 VIETNAMESE   In an idyllic riverside location a couple of kilometers from the town center, this place is definitely worth tracking down both for its tempting menu and the opportunity to join an afternoon cookery class. Call for a pick-up in town and enjoy the 20-minute boat cruise to the restaurant, then settle into one of three open-air pavilions to scan the options, which include *banh xeo* (crispy Hoi An pancakes) or countryside soups for starters, and lemon grass beef or a seafood hot pot for mains. Take your swimming gear, as there's a decent pool for guest use. Note that although the restaurant is open for lunch daily, dinner is by appointment only.

Thon 4, Cam Thanh, Hoi An. ✆ **0510/393-3222.** www.visithoian.com/redbridge. Main courses $5–$10. MC, V. Daily 11:30am–2:30pm.

River Lounge ★ 🍴 FUSION   River Lounge is part of the new crop of hip places cropping up north of the river, and its menu was created by a Michelin-star chef. The interior is minimalist white, with turquoise scrawlings on the walls and overstuffed daybeds and lounge chairs upstairs. For dinner, the three-course set menu featuring Hoi An's lovely seafood is a steal. The menu has a healthy representation of Vietnamese influences, but because the owners are a pair of Austrian brothers, there's also excellent Wiener schnitzel, Linzer cake, Linzer torte, and the best Italian coffee in town.

35 Nguyen Phuc Chu. ✆ **0510/391-1700.** Main courses 75,000 VND–158,000 VND; set menu 120,000 VND. MC, V. Daily 8:30am–midnight.

Sakura ★★ VIETNAMESE   Set in the most picturesque period building in town, on a corner overlooking riverside Bach Dang, this Saigon-managed restaurant is as much about atmosphere as it is about dining. Rivaled only by Brother's (see above), the two open floors here reflect true old Hoi An elegance. The second floor has great views of the river and is dramatic, with a high, exposed-tile ceiling and languid ceiling fans. They serve regional dishes such as Hanoi *cha ca* and *mi quang* wide noodles. Presentation is arguably the classiest in town, with fine china, stemware, and lacquered dishes on linen, and the service is professional, if a bit hovering. A good choice for a romantic evening of fine dining, Hoi An style.

119-121 Nguyen Thai Hoc (riverside). ✆ **0510/391-0369.** Fax 0510/391-0436. Main courses 60,000 VND–400,000 VND; set menus from 150,000 VND. AE, MC, V. Daily 10am–10pm.

Tam-Tam Café ★★ CONTINENTAL/ITALIAN   Tam-Tam is the place to be in Hoi An. The brainchild of three French expats, it is historic and laid-back, serving good, familiar food. The decor is authentic and local, with hanging bamboo lamps, a high wooden ceiling, and fantastic wood figurines. The dinner menu is simple—generous portions of homemade pastas, steaks, and salads—but the food is delicious. The dessert menu includes flambéed crepes, sorbet, and hot chocolate. There are two barrooms downstairs: The bigger one to the left of the entry has a pool table, a book-swap shelf, comfortable lounge chairs, and sofas, and is the place to hang out in Hoi An. The extensive drink menu features all kinds of bang-for-the-buck rum specials, and there's even a small counter on the balcony upstairs where you can sip a cocktail and watch life go by on the street below. Be sure to come here, even if it's just for coffee.

110 Nguyen Thai Hoc St. ✆ **0510/386-2212.** Main courses 40,000 VND–205,000 VND. AE, MC, V. Daily 8am–2am.

9 INEXPENSIVE

Bale Well ★★ VIETNAMESE   Bale Well is the epitome of local dining, but they're quite used to foreign visitors and make you feel right at home. This is your chance to experience squat stools and streetside dining, but with a good standard of cleanliness. The meal is simple: a set menu of *nem nuong,* the kind of spring rolls that you make yourself, rolling chicken, beef, or pork with fresh greens and condiments into sheets of rice paper. You might also want to try the pork satay, savory *banh xeo* (pancakes), or fried spring rolls. The restaurant is in a little alley just off of Tran Hung Dao Street. The sign is more or less hidden.

45-51 Tran Hung Dao St. ✆ **0510/386-4443.** Set menu 80,000 VND. No credit cards. Daily 9:30am–9:30 pm.

Van Loc ★ VIETNAMESE   This is where the locals come for *cao lau,* a thick but tender white noodle in light soy with fresh vegetables, garnish, and croutons. It's an open-air place, and the atmosphere is a little rough, but they serve a nice selection of local favorites, too, all for next to nothing. The portions are big and everything's authentic, right down to the kindness in this little mom-and-pop. There are no touts here—it's the food that brings 'em in.

27 Tran Phu. ✆ **0510/386-1212.** Main courses 30,000 VND–150,000 VND. No credit cards. Daily 7:30am–9pm.

Attractions

The whole town is an attraction, its narrow streets comprised of lovely historic buildings buzzing with open-air crafts shops, woodworkers, and carvers. Tran Phu and Nguyen Thai Hoc streets are crowded with the shops of the original Chinese merchants and clan associations. Most Hoi An buildings have been lovingly restored and transformed into cafes, art galleries, and silk and souvenir shops, while still retaining their historical dignity. If you're an artist, bring your sketch pad and watercolors; photographers, bring an extra memory card.

The **Hoi An World Cultural Heritage Organization** (www.hoianworldheritage. org.vn) has the dilemma of financing the restorations and maintaining the old portions of the town. They sell a 90,000 VND ticket that allows limited admission to the sights within the old town, each of which is listed below. "Limited" means a "one from column A, one from column B" formula. One ticket gets you one of the three museums, one of the three assembly halls, and one of the four old houses; entrance to a handicrafts workshop and traditional music concert (10:15am and 3:15pm, respectively, Tues–Sun); plus a choice of either the Japanese Bridge, the Quan Cong Temple, or the local handicrafts workshop. To see everything, you'll have to purchase three tickets. The three-star choices in each category are your best bet if you don't have time to see it all.

MUSEUMS

Museum of History and Culture ★
This tottering building, erected in 1653, houses works that cross 2,000 years of Hoi An history from Cham relics to ancient ceramics to photos of local architecture. There are English explanations, but they are scanty. One interesting tidbit: The name Hoi An literally means "Water Convergence" and "Peace."

7 Nguyen Hue St. (7 is the official address, but it's actually the building on the south side of 11 Nguyen Hue St.). Daily 8am–5pm.

Museum of Trade Ceramics ★★★
Located in a traditional house, this museum describes the origins of Hoi An as a trade port and displays its most prominent trade item. Objects are from the 8th through 18th centuries and include Chinese, Thai, Indian, and Japanese works. While many of the exhibits are in fragments, the real beauty of the place is that the descriptions are in English, giving you a real sense of the town's origins and history. Furthermore, the architecture and renovations of the old house are thoroughly explained, and you're free to wander through its two floors, courtyard, and anteroom. After all the scattered explanations at the other historic houses, you'll finally get a sense of what Hoi An architecture is all about.

80 Tran Phu St. Daily 8am–5pm.

The Sa Huynh Culture Museum ★
After local farmers around Hoi An dug up some strange-looking pottery, archaeologists identified 53 sites where a pre-Cham people, called the Sa Huynh, buried their dead in ceramic jars. The two-room display here includes some of the burial jars, beaded ornaments, pottery vessels, and iron tools and weapons that have been uncovered. English descriptions are sketchy. Upstairs, the little-visited Museum of the Revolution includes such intriguing items as the umbrella "which Mr. Truong Minh Luong used for acting a fortune-teller to act revolution from 1965 to 1967." Huh? This is for connoisseurs only.

149 Tran Phu St. Daily 8am–6pm.

THE OLD HOUSES

The Old House of Phung Hung ★
This private house, constructed in 1780, is two floors of combined architectural influences. The first floor's central roof is four-sided, showing Japanese influence, and the upstairs balcony has a Chinese rounded "turtle shell" roof with carved beam supports. The house has weathered many floods. In 1964, during a particularly bad bout, its third floor served as a refuge for other town families. The upstairs is outfitted with a trapdoor for moving furniture rapidly to safety. You might be shown around by Ms. Anh, who claims to be an eighth-generation member of the family. Tour guides at every house make such claims; however, as at many of Hoi An's old houses, the family really does seem to live here.

4 Nguyen Thi Minh Khai St. Daily 8am–5pm.

The Old House of Tan Ky ★   There have been either five or seven generations of Tans living here, depending on whom you speak with. Built more than 200 years ago, the four small rooms are crammed with dark-wood antiques. The room closest to the street is for greeting visiting merchants. Farther in is the living room, then the courtyard, and, to the back, the bedroom. The first three are open to the public. A guide will hasten to explain how the house is a perfect melding of three architectural styles: ornate Chinese detailing on some curved roof beams, a Japanese peaked roof, and a simple Vietnamese cross-hatch roof support. The mosaic decorations on the wall and furniture are aged, intricate, and amazing. Take your time looking around.

101 Nguyen Thai Hoc St. Daily 8am–5pm.

The Tran Family Home and Chapel ★★   In 1802, a civil service mandarin named Tran Tu Nhuc built a family home and chapel to worship his ancestors. A favorite of Viet Emperor Gia Long, he was sent to China as an ambassador, and his home reflects his high status. Elegantly designed with original Chinese antiques and royal gifts such as swords, two parts of the home are open to the public: a drawing room and an ancestral chapel. One roof tile has been replaced with transparent glass, allowing a single shaft of light to slice through the chapel and onto the altar in the morning. The house does a splendid job of conveying all that is exotic and interesting about these people and their period. The drawing room has three sections of sliding doors: the left for men, the right for women, and the center, open only at Tet and other festivals, for dead ancestors to return home. The ancestral altar in the inner room has small boxes behind it containing relics and a biography of the deceased; their pictures hang, a little spookily, to the right of the altar. A 250-year-old book with the family history resides on a table to the right of the altar. Beside it is a small bowl, containing yin and yang coins, meant to bring good luck. Give them a toss, and if they land one yin and one yang side up, you are on your way to prosperity. I got it on my first try, but the guide will give you three chances. In back of the house are a row of plants, each buried with the placenta and umbilical cord of a family child, so that the child will never forget its home.

21 Le Loi (on the corner of Le Loi and Phan Chu Trinh sts.). Daily 8am–5pm.

THE ASSEMBLY HALLS

Cantonese Assembly Hall   Built in 1885, this hall is quite ornate and colorful. All of the building materials were completed in China, brought here, and then reassembled. The center garden sports a fountain with a dragon made of chipped pottery. Inside, look for the statues depicting scenes from famous Cantonese operas and, in the rooms to each side, the ancestral tablets of generations past.

176 Tran Phu St. Daily 8am–6pm.

Fukian Assembly Hall (Phuc Kien) ★   This is the grandest of the assembly halls, built in 1697 by Chinese merchants from Fukian Province. It is a showpiece of classical Chinese architecture, at least after you pass the first gate, which was added in 1975. It's loaded with animal themes: The fish in the mosaic fountain symbolizes scholarly achievement, the unicorn flanking the ascending stairs symbolizes wisdom, the dragon symbolizes power, the turtle symbolizes longevity, and the phoenix symbolizes nobility. The main temple is dedicated to Thien Hau, goddess of the sea, on the main altar. To the left of her is Thuan Phong Nhi, a goddess who can hear ships in a range of thousands of miles, and on the right is Thien Ly Nhan, who can see them. Go around the altar for a view of a fantastic detailed miniature boat. There are two altars to the rear of the temple: the one on the left honoring a god of prosperity and the one on the right honoring a goddess of fertility. The goddess of fertility is often visited by local couples hoping for children. She is flanked by 12 fairies or midwives, one responsible for each of a baby's functions: smiling, sleeping, eating, and so forth.

46 Tran Phu St. Daily 7am–6pm.

OTHER SITES

Japanese Covered Bridge ★★★ No one is exactly sure who first built this bridge in the early 1600s (it has since been renovated several times), but it is usually attributed to Hoi An's Japanese community. The dog flanking one end and the monkey at the other are considered to be sacred animals to the ancient Japanese, and my guide claimed the reasoning is that most Japanese emperors were born in the year of either the monkey or the dog. The small temple inside is dedicated to Bac De Tran Vu, god of the north, beloved (or cursed) by sailors because he controls the weather.

At the west end of Tran Phu St.

Quan Cong Temple ★ This temple was built in 1653 to honor a famous Chinese dynasty general. Highlights inside are two gargantuan 3m-high (9¾-ft.) wood statues flanking the main altar, one of Quan Cong's protector and one of his adopted son. They are fearsome and impressive. Reportedly the temple was a stop for merchants who came in from the nearby river to pay their respects and pray for the general's attributes of loyalty, bravery, and virtue.

24 Tran Phu St. (on the corner of Nguyen Hue). Daily 8am–5pm.

Handicrafts Workshop ★ Included in the Hoi An Old Town ticket price is a visit to this workshop, where locals are busy making silk lanterns and embroidering panels to show visitors the traditional process of such crafts. It's located in a 200-year-old Chinese trading house, and there are daily performances featuring traditional musicians and dancers at 10:15am and 3:15pm.

9 Nguyen Thai Hoc. ✆ **0510/391-0216.** Daily 7am–6pm.

ATTRACTIONS NOT ON THE WORLD CULTURAL HERITAGE TICKET

Central Market ★★ If you see one Vietnamese market, make it this one. There are endless stalls of exotic foodstuffs and services, and a special shed for silk tailoring at the east end (these tailors charge much less than the ones along Le Loi). Check out the ladies selling spices—curries, chili powders, cinnamon, peppercorns, and especially saffron—at prices that are a steal in the West. But don't buy from the first woman you see; the stuff gets cheaper and cheaper the deeper you go into the market. Walk out to the docks to see activity there (best early in the morning), but be careful of fish flying through the air, and stand back from the furious bargaining (best before 7am).

At Nguyen Hue and Tran Phu sts. along the Thu Bon River on the southeast side of the city.

Hoi An Cathedral The only spectacular thing about this Catholic cathedral is its resilience. Originally built in 1903, the structure was rebuilt in 1964 with the influx of greater numbers of Catholics seeking refuge from persecution in the North. There's a small orphanage out back, and this stalwart working cathedral ministers to more than an estimated 1,000 patricians in the area. Sunday Mass—delivered in Vietnamese—is a well-attended affair. If you go, have a look at the cool contemporary stained glass depicting the early French missionaries alighting in Hoi An.

House of Hoi An Traditional Handicraft ★★   This is basically a silk shop with an interesting gimmick: On the first floor you can see both a 17th-century silk loom and a working, machine-powered cotton one. On the second, you can see where silk comes from: There are trays of silkworms feeding, then a rack of worms incubating, and then a tub of hot water where the pupae's downy covering is rinsed off and then pulled, strand by strand, onto a large skein. They have the best selection of silks, both fine and raw, which come in many colors and weights that are good for clothing and home interiors.

41 Le Loi St. Daily 8am–5pm.

HITTING THE BEACH

Cua Dai Beach ★★ is a 25-minute bicycle ride from Hoi An on a busy road with vistas of lagoons, rice paddies, and stilt houses. Simply follow Tran Hung Dao Street to Cua Dai Street to the east of town and keep going for 3km (1¾ miles). The beach is thin and crowded with hawkers, but there are cozy deck chairs (for a small fee), and the sand, surf, and setting, with views of the nearby Cham Island, are worth the trip. Tour companies tout boat excursions in season (Mar–Sept) to Cham Island, part of a group of seven islands about 13km (8 miles) east of Hoi An; prices vary, but expect to pay about 350,000 VND per person on a group tour. Contact the traveler cafes in town. There are also boat trips on the Thu Bon River from town; just walk along central Bach Dang near the river, and the boatmen will find you.

CHAM ISLAND TOUR

Just 5km (3 miles) off the shore of Cua Dai Beach (see above), Cham Island is a quiet little fishing island populated by ethnic Cham people, an Austro-Asiatic group that fought the north Vietnamese for this territory for centuries (see box on p. 200). A tour to Cham Island is all about diving, as there are some great dive sites just off the island; diving season around here runs from March to September. Contact **Rainbow Divers,** 41 Nguyen Phuc Cu (© **091/422-4102;** www.divevietnam.com), or the **Cham Island Diving Center,** 88 Nguyen Thai Hoc (© **0510/391-0782;** www.chamislanddiving.com), which both charge around $70 to join a dive, or $30 to $40 to snorkel.

You can also make arrangements with sign-waving touts on Cua Dai Beach who will putt-putt you out to the island on tour boats. Some travelers start their trip on the river right in the center of Hoi An and travel by boat to the sea before transferring out into the bay. Contact any hotel front desk or talk with the boatmen themselves along Bach Dang in Hoi An town. Expect to pay about $20 for one person from town to the Cham Islands.

AN EXCURSION TO MY SON

My Son, some 40km (25 miles) from Hoi An (and 71km/44 miles from Danang), is the most important historical vestige of the Cham people, a once powerful Hindu empire. The temples were constructed as a religious center from the 7th through 12th centuries during the height of Cham supremacy. My Son (pronounced *Mee sun*) might have also been used as a burial site for Cham kings after cremation. Originally there were more than 70 towers and monuments at the site, but bombing during the war with America (the Viet Cong used My Son as a base) sadly reduced most buildings to rubble. Additionally, many of the smaller structures and most decorative carvings have been removed to the Cham Museum in Danang. Though comparisons with Angkor Wat are rather fanciful, as so little remains, the complex is a very serene and spiritual setting, and what does remain is powerful and evocative. It's not hard to imagine what a wonder My Son must once have been. The site is deep in the Truong Son Cordillera, and the main temples overlook the 350m (1,148-ft.) Mount Chua, "Mountain of the Gods." My Son is a designated UNESCO World Heritage Site.

The earliest temple constructions are from the 4th century A.D., but much of what remains today are structures built or renovated during the 10th century A.D., when the cult of Shiva, founder and protector of the kingdom, was predominant in the Cham court. Each group had at least the following structures: a **kalan,** or main tower; a gate tower in front of that, with two entrances; a **mandapa,** or meditation hall; and a repository building for offerings. Some have towers sheltering stele with kingly epitaphs. A brick wall encircles the compound.

Architecturally, the temple complex shows Indian influences. Each temple grouping is a microcosm of the world. The foundations are Earth, the square bases are the temple itself, and the pointed roofs symbolize the heavens. The entrance to the main tower faces east, and surrounding smaller towers represent each continent. A trench, representing the oceans, surrounds each group. Vietnamese architecture is represented in decorative patterns and boat-shape roofs. The temple compound is divided into a number of "Groups" built by successive Cham kings and designated by French archaeologist Henri Parmentier with letters of the alphabet. Group A is the most dynamic.

Group A originally had 13 towers. A-1, the main tower, was a 21m-tall (69-ft.) masterpiece before it was destroyed in 1969. Group B bears the marks of Indian and Indonesian influences. Note that B-6 holds a water repository for statue-washing ceremonies. Its roof is carved with an image of the god Vishnu sitting beneath a 13-headed snake god, or **naga.** Group C generally followed an earlier architectural style called Hoa Lai, which predominated from the 8th century to the beginning of the 9th. Groups G and H were the last to be built, at around the end of the 13th century.

Arrange a half-day trip to My Son with any tourist agent in Hoi An (p. 204). Entrance to the site is 60,000 VND, and a private half-day tour with a guide is $36 for a car and $45 for a van. The half-day seat-in-coach tour by Sinh Café costs $6 per person and is nothing more than a ride there, without any explanations. Less frequent tours also depart from Danang (70km/43 miles from the site).

Shopping

Southeast Asia is packed with would-be Buddhists, travelers on a spiritual mission, espousing lives of detachment from material desires. These folks usually walk away with just the "one suit, two shirts, trousers, and a tie" package when they leave Hoi An. Shopaholics wander the streets in a daze, unsure what to buy next.

Hoi An is a silk mecca. The quality and selection are the best in the country, and you'll have more peace and quiet here during a fitting than in Hanoi. **Silk suits** are made to order within 24 hours for about $40 to $45; **cashmere wool** is $50 to $100. There are countless shops, and the tailoring is all about the same quality. A good way to choose a shop is by what you see out front—if you see a style you like, it'll help with ordering. Make sure you take the time to specify your style, down to the stitch (it can come back looking pretty cheap without specifics). Try any of the shops along Le Loi; to recommend one in particular would be like recommending one snowflake over another. The tailoring is very fast but not always great, so it's a good idea to arrange two or three fittings. Be choosy about your cloth, or go to the market and buy it yourself (**Hoi An Cloth Market** is at 01 Tran Phu St.), and haggle. It's not a bad idea to bring an actual suit or piece of clothing for which you'd like a copy made. Get measurements from friends and relatives for good gifts.

There are also skilled cobblers who make custom shoes at affordable rates. Find them near the market on Tran Phu Street.

Tran Phu Street is lined with **art galleries** and good **pottery** and **woodcarving** vendors. Along the river, lots of places sell blue-and-white **ceramics.** However cumbersome your finds are, such as those lovely **Chinese lanterns,** shopkeepers are masters at packing for travel, and will do so before you've even agreed on a price or decided to buy. One place worth checking out is **Reaching Out,** 103 Nguyen Thai Hoc St. (✆ 0510/386–2460; www.reachingout.com), a fair-trade gift shop that employs disabled artisans.

Hand-painted **Chinese scrolls** make a great souvenir, and down the street from the Hung Long Art Gallery (see below), Mr. Ly Si Binh (21 Nguyen Thai Hoc St.; ✆ 0510/391-0721) can script anything from *peace* or *determination* to your best buddy's name in Chinese (if it's wrong, he won't know the difference anyway).

Note: Unless otherwise noted, most stores listed below are open from 8am to late evening (around 9pm), but hours can and do vary.

Adong Silk   This is one of the best of the town's many tailor shops. The tailors here are highly skilled and produce excellent work. 40 Le Loi St. ✆ **0510/386-3170.** www.adong silk.com.

Bambou Company   Bambou produces T-shirts with Vietnamese themes and designs, all in real cotton with big Western sizes available. They also have cool Asian-inspired clothes, such as string-button Chinese shirts, fishermen's pants, and loose shirts. There are two outlets in Hoi An at 90 and 123 Nguyen Thai Hoc St.

Hung Long Art Gallery   This popular gallery features fine lacquer works by artist Nguyen Trung Viet. These stylized images, mostly of young women, are quite appealing. Prices are affordable, and they can ship anywhere on the globe. 105 Nguyen Thai Hoc St. ✆ **0510/386-1924.**

Yaly Couture   If you're confused by the glut of small tailor storefronts and wonder about the quality of the work, Yaly Couture is your answer. Yes, the prices are higher, but quality comes with more of a guarantee and the same efficient service (12-hr. turnaround for a new suit). Their main shop is on Nguyen Duy Hieu Street, but you can pick up their ready-to-wear items in the small showrooms in the town center. 47 Nguyen Thai Hoc: ✆ **0510/391-0474.** www.yalycouture.com. 47 Tran Phu: ✆ **0510/386-1119.** 358 Nguyen Duy Hieu: **0510/391-4995.**

Hoi An After Dark

For the most part, Hoi An is a town that sleeps early, but you can find a few good nightspots. **Tam-Tam Café** (p. 214) has long been a popular spot for travelers, expats, and locals. **Hai Scout Café,** 98 Nguyen Thai Hoc St. (✆ **0510/386-3210**), is a popular late-night hangout for travelers, offering standard bar drinks as well as cappuccino and espresso and some great baked treats. **Treat's Café,** 158 Tran Phu St. (✆ **0510/386-1125**), is usually hopping; it even has a pool table and a guillotine (for show, of course). The owners of Treat's also run **Same Same Not Different Bar,** 93 Tran Hung Dao (✆ **0510/386-2278**). The **Yellow Star Café,** 73 Nguyen

Thai Hoc St. (© 0510/391-0430), serves drinks, yummy Western food, and desserts such as lemon tart, while the next-door **ChamPa,** 75 Nguyen Thai Hoc St. (© 0510/386-2974), has a cozy atmosphere, good wine, and a pool table. **Lounge Bar,** 102 Nguyen Thai Hoc St. (© 0510/391-0480), is a chic, laid-back stop, while nearby **Mango Rooms,** 111 Nguyen Thai Hoc St. (© 0510/391-0839), is similarly hip and mellow.

THE CENTRAL HIGHLANDS

The mountainous Central Highlands are a few hundred very hilly miles inland from Nha Trang, a bumpy ride north from Ho Chi Minh City, or over the paved and very scenic Ho Chi Minh Trail south from Hoi An. The area saw its share of fighting during the war; names such as the **La Drang Valley, Pleiku,** and **Kontum** will ring a bell with veterans or those who watched Walter Cronkite every night. But the scorched earth has now turned green again, and the region prospers as one of the most productive agricultural areas for produce and one of the most prosperous for coffee growing.

10

Called **Tay Nguyen** in Vietnamese, the Central Highlands of five provinces—Kontum, Gia Lai, Dak Lak, Dak Nong, and Lam Dong—stretch along the high ridge of the **Trong Son Mountain Range** of the **Annamese Cordillera,** which serves as a natural border between Vietnam and Laos and Cambodia. With the increase in altitude, the temperature is cool (64°F–77°F/18°C–25°C).

The most accessible city is **Dalat,** a former French colonial outpost nestled among the hills; it retains a serene, formal air of another time, though with some eccentric modern twists. The cooler weather in Dalat is a welcome respite from Vietnam's year-round coastal heat, and the town is full of fun, with hokey local tourist sights, most geared to young Vietnamese honeymooners. Dalat also seems to attract (or create) eccentric local residents, and many Vietnamese artists call this "Petite Paris" their home.

Dalat is also a good jumping-off point for the less-visited towns of the highlands, areas that are still sensitive due to unrest among the local ethnic minority groups, and are sometimes off limits to foreigners. The roads of this rugged region bring you into Vietnam's green and picturesque coffee-growing hills, among diverse hilltribe cultures, and along portions of the old Ho Chi Minh Trail that skirt the border between Laos and Cambodia and were pivotal to Viet Cong supplies and mobility over the decade-long war.

Outside of Dalat, tourist services are limited, and towns such as **Buon Ma Thuot, Pleiku,** and **Kontum** support only bare-bones hotels and dining choices. Riding local buses is just short of masochism; it's best to arrange your own transport or go by tour. Many options, including the fun Easy Riders motorbike trips, start from Dalat, and various options depart from Ho Chi Minh City and Nha Trang.

Central Highlands

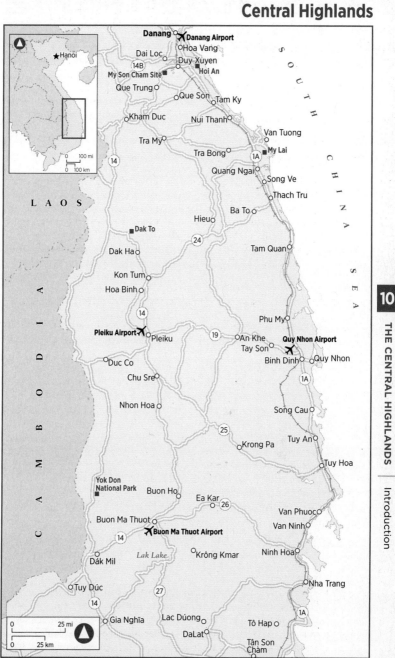

CENTRAL HIGHLAND ETHNIC MINORITY hilltribes

The French called them Montagnards, or "people of the mountains," and these groups have long suffered under more powerful central governments. Hilltribe people paid dues to early Vietnamese kings and later achieved some autonomy under the French, who converted many of them to Catholicism and then conscripted them into labor on roads and bridges in the region. Alliances with American or North Vietnamese forces were just another form of conscription. Even today, disputes with the government over land rights send many fleeing across the border into Cambodia and Laos, and foreign visitors are not permitted into border areas, particularly in Gia Lai Province, without a guide.

The Northern Highland groups (see chapter 6) are known for their more colorful traditional dress, while Central Highland hilltribe people, particularly the men in their Western attire, are often indistinguishable from lowland Vietnamese. But having endured so much for some measure of autonomy, these feisty highlanders still cling to tradition.

The ethnic minorities of the Central Highlands—the M'nong, the Ede, the Jarai and the Bannar, among others—have as much in common as they do differences from one another. Most villages are of thatched single-family houses arranged around a central communal **longhouse** (called a *nha rang* in Vietnamese) raised on stilts at the center of town, where all ceremony and governance take place. Each group has a particular style of *nha rang,* the most dynamic being the Bannar style of a peak of thatch over three stories high, but each kind of *nha rang* is an important symbol of community-respective groups and the center of worship and colorful ceremony. Many hilltribe groups celebrate harvest time or auspicious occasions with the ritual slaughtering of a buffalo, a frenetic event soaked in local whiskey and accompanied by wild dance. Music is important to each group, and each has strong traditions (for example, the Jarai, who woo their brides by serenading, and the M'nong, famed for their drumming).

Many hilltribe groups are matrilineal, where names and even fortunes are passed from mother to child over generations, and almost all practice some kind of animist religion, in which gods are the hills themselves or the natural forces that made them. Funeral ceremonies vary, but all of the Central Highland groups practice elaborate graveside rights, where bodies are interred in elaborate spirit houses decorated with ceremonial carvings and paintings, and later feted and celebrated to the funeral pyre or grave. Musical traditions among hilltribes are elaborate, with gongs, drums, and bamboo flute music playing integral parts of any ceremony.

Catholic missionaries had varied success converting these remote, autonomous groups to Christianity, and the legacy of their efforts still stands in the many churches, orphanages, and missions throughout the region (check out the Catholic seminary in Kontum). E De and Bannar people are among the most commonly converted. Minority groups in the region retain their ethnic traditions and some territorial autonomy, though investments from the Hanoi government have focused more on "enforced primitivism" programs and segregated villages (many open for tour-group visits). There are many opportunities to visit with these minority groups, which are detailed below.

Important: Be very careful when photographing ethnic minorities. Few in the region are used to tourists, and there are many taboos about photography and collecting images of people. Always ask and respect an answer of "no." Often patient persistence pays off—stay and talk to people and explain where you're from and what you're doing. I've often been asked to take a photo by someone after I was initially denied the shot.

Jarai   With an estimated population more than 300,000, the Jarai are the largest group in the highlands. Villages are situated around a central longhouse where village elders hold court over local policy. Jarai people are animistic, with powerful gods of the wind, water, and mountains. Complex Jarai funeral practices start with interring a body in a small spirit house surrounded by a person's effects and ritual statues, followed by cremation. Jarai society follows a matrilineal succession, meaning that family names are passed on from mother to child, and there's a kind of egalitarianism to cooperative villages of hunter-gatherers, river fishermen (villages are usually near water), and subsistence farmers. Jarai people are rumored to have migrated from the central coast long before the "Chinese millennium" some 2,000 years ago, and settled near Pleiku and Kontum, where most Jarai people are found today. Jarai musical talents are renowned (see a whole set of Jarai drums and gongs in the small Hilltribe Museum in Buon Ma Thuot).

E De   The second-largest group in the highlands, the E De have a society quite similar to the Jarai (see above), which centers on a village longhouse on stilts, with one window per family and a large section set aside for communal work and governance. E De are matrilineal and follow rich animistic traditions like the Jarai. Find E De villages on the outskirts of Buon Ma Thuot, mostly in

situations of "enforced primitivism" under the watchful eye of the party.

Bahnar   With a population of almost 200,000, the Bahnar group is about the same size as the E De, but they tend to live farther north, around Pleiku and particularly Kontum. The most striking feature of Bahnar culture is the towering communal house they build in the center of each village, which can reach up to 20m (65 ft.) high.

Sedang   Sedang are notorious warriors. Once known to practice human sacrifice, the Sedang were heavily conscripted as fighters by all sides: France, the U.S., and North Vietnam. Sedang people follow a model of pure egalitarianism in village governance and duties. Find Sedang settlements in and around Kontum, and as far as the Quy Nhon coastal area.

M'nong   You will likely meet M'nong people, the elephant hunters and wranglers of the region, at Lak Lake when you get ferried out across the water by elephant. M'nong are matrilineal and known for their fine small-crafts production and distinct percussion music. The M'nong practice elaborate funeral rituals, placing a coffin in a funeral house decorated with wood statues before burial.

Bru & Ta Oi   Two related groups living in the northern end of the highlands, the Bru and Ta Oi originally inhabited lands near the 17th Parallel, which meant that villages were swallowed in the destruction, and those that didn't flee farther south or to Laos (mostly Bru) were caught up as conscripts of the North Vietnamese (mostly Ta Oi) and played an important role in keeping the Ho Chi Minh supply line moving. Find Bru peoples in and around Khe Sanh.

DALAT

Known as "Le Petit Paris" by the early builders and residents of this hillside resort town, Dalat is still a luxury retreat for city dwellers and tourists tired from trudging along sultry coastal Vietnam. In Dalat, you can play golf on one of the finest courses in Indochina, visit beautiful temples, and enjoy the town's honeymoon atmosphere with delightfully hokey tourist sights.

At 1,500m (4,920 ft.), Dalat is mercifully cool year-round—there's no need for air-conditioning. The town is a blend of pastoral hillside Vietnam and European alpine resort. Alexander Yersin, the Swiss physician and bacteriologist who first traipsed through this pass in 1897, suggested establishing the town as a hill station for recuperating French commanders weary of the Vietnamese tropics. In and around town are still scattered the relics of colonial mansions, some beautifully restored and others gradually crumbling, as well as some serene pagodas in a lovely natural setting; you've escaped from big-city Vietnam for real. A few ethnic minorities, including the Lat and the Koho, live in and around the picturesque hills surrounding Dalat, and you can visit a number of rural villages on local tours.

Dalat is a top resort destination for Vietnamese couples getting married or honeymooning. If the lunar astrological signs are particularly good, it's not unusual to see 10 or so wedding parties in a single day. Many of the local scenic spots, such as the Valley of Love and Lake of Sighs, pander to the giddy couples. The waterfalls are swarming with vendors, men costumed as bears, and "cowboys" complete with sad-looking horses and fake pistols. A carnival air prevails. It's a "so bad that it's good" kind of kitsch that is definitely worth the trip. Emperor Bao Dai, the last in Vietnam, had three large homes here, one of which is now the Dalat Palace Hotel; the other two can be visited on tours.

Getting There

BY PLANE   There are direct flights to Dalat from Ho Chi Minh City (50 min.), Hanoi (1 hr. 20 min.) and Danang (50 min.). In Dalat, call Vietnam Airlines (© **063/383-3499**) to confirm your ticket or with any flight inquiries. Air Mekong (© **063/365-2838**) also operates flights here. Dalat's **Lien Khuong Airport** is 30km (19 miles) south of town. A taxi from the airport to the city is around $14 and takes 30 to 45 minutes, while the Vietnam Airlines shuttle bus costs around $2.

BY BUS   Dalat is the first stop on the **"Open Tour" tickets** from Ho Chi Minh City's budget-traveler cafes. Buses from the south first stop at Phan Rang, an old Cham temple site, where the road turns inland for the hills of Dalat. The ride to Dalat from the coast is winding and spectacular, at one point following hairpin turns underneath a large hydroelectric project. From Nha Trang (to the east) or Ho Chi Minh City (to the south), it's a 7-hour trip and costs $5 to $6 at any tourist cafe. You can make arrangements at your hotel or with one of the tour providers listed below in the "Visitor Information & Tours" section.

Local buses connect Dalat with Nha Trang and Ho Chi Minh City, as well as Buon Ma Thuot, the next town north of Dalat along the highlands ridge—a grueling all-day ride. Buses leave from the Express Bus Station southwest of the city center (get there by motorbike taxi for about 20,000 VND); be prepared to haggle for your ticket.

BY CAR/MOTORBIKE   Take the new highway through the mountains via hired transport in a minivan or car. The trip is just 3½ hours. Also popular are the motorbike trips with Dalat's "Easy Riders" (see box, below). Check the listings below or in

Dalat

Post office
Steps

HOTELS ■
Ana Mandara Villas Dalat **3**
Chau-Au Europa Hotel **11**
Dalat Hotel du Parc **22**
Dalat Palace **21**
Dreams Hotel **1**
Empress Hotel **13**
Golf III Hotel **12**
Hotel Dai Loi (Fortune Hotel) **14**
Ngoc Lan Hotel **6**
Saigon Dalat Hotel **23**
Trung Cang Hotel **16**

RESTAURANTS ◆
ART Café **2**
Café de la Poste **21**
Da Quy **5**
Le Rabelais **21**
Long Hoa **4**
Lyla Hotel Restaurant de Famile **10**
Ngoc Hai Restaurant **8**
Tau Cao **9**
Thuy Ta **18**
V Cafe **15**

ATTRACTIONS ●
Bao Dai's Palace **24**
Dalat Market (Cho Dalat) **7**
Dalat Railway Station
  (Cremaillere Railway) **19**
The French Quarter **20**
Hang Nga's Crazy House **25**
Lake of Sighs (Ho Than To) **19**
Lam Ty Ni Pagoda: Home of Thay
  Vien Thuc **26**
Lang Con Ga (Chicken Village) **20**
Linh Phuoc Pagoda **20**
Prenn Falls **20**
Thien Vuong Pagoda **20**
Truc Lam Zen (Bamboo Forest)
  Monastery **20**
Valley of Love **17**

10

THE CENTRAL HIGHLANDS | **Dalat**

227

Get Your Motor Running!

Do you wish you were "Born to Be Wild," as the song goes, but fear that so far your life has been "Born to Be Responsible"? No experience on motorcycles, but want to make the leap out on the open road and get some proverbial "bugs in your teeth"? Well, here's your chance to have a taste of the open road with none of the road rash or traffic hassles that riding a motorbike yourself brings. Hire the services of an **Easy Rider,** Dalat's now-famous motorbike taxi drivers who haul all over tarnation on a motley mix of motorcycles. You can find the Easy Riders at the **Peace (Hoa Binh) Café,** 64 Truong Cong Dinh St. (② **063/382-2787;** http://dalat-easyrider.com), in the backpacker district. Easy Riders can take you on anything from day trips around Dalat for $15, to longer trips around the region for about $60 to $75 per day, all-inclusive, riding the whole ridge of the highlands up through Buon Ma Thuot, Pleiku, and Kontum, and on to Hoi An over the newly paved Ho Chi Minh Trail, or even farther up or down the coast. *Warning:* Beware of imitations.

Saigon and Nha Trang (a few agents from Nha Trang specialize in tours of the highlands) for more options.

Getting Around

There are no cyclos in Dalat (the streets are too steep), but walking is very pleasant in the cool air. You can catch most of the city sights, such as the market and the lake, **on foot.** For sights outside of town, it's best to rent a motorbike or join a tour.

BY TAXI For taxis in town, try **Dalat Taxi** (② **063/355-6655**) or **Mai Linh Taxi** (② **063/352-1111**).

BY CAR You can **rent a car** with a driver for about $50 to $60 per day with most tour companies. Contact any hotel front desk or the folks at **Dalat Travel Service,** 34 Hoa Binh Square (② **063/351-0993**), just south of the market area in the very center of town.

BY MOTORCYCLE Dalat is a good place to **rent your own motorbike.** The cheapest options are with the streetside places on Nguyen Thi Minh Khai Street, between the market and the lake, for about $5 per day ($6 from hotels and cafes). Be sure to check the brakes and that the horn is working, because you should beep-beep all the way, especially when passing or on curves. The hillside, winding roads will have you feeling like a Hell's Angel if you can forget that you're riding the motorcycle equivalent of a hair dryer. This is a good, adventurous way to get to all the sights outside the city, but you may find it hard to get "into" places such as the Chicken Village or to the closed door of The Lam Ty Ni Pagoda—some attractions are best visited on tours.

Another option is to get a **motorbike with a driver** for the day (about $1–$2 per hour, or fix a rate for the day and the destinations), or hook up with Dalat's famous **Easy Riders** (above).

Visitor Information & Tours

Because many sights are outside city limits, one good option is to take a **half- or full-day tour** organized through your hotel or one of the tour operators below. Some places, such as homes in the weaving villages or at the The Lam Ty Ni Pagoda, require some kind of introduction, so going with a guide or following a tour is smart.

○ **Dalattourist,** 01 Nguyen Thi Minh Khai St. (© **063/382-2520;** fax 063/383-4144; www.dalattourist.com.vn), is located in the center of Dalat with a small kiosk south of the main market. They book classic tours to anywhere in the region and offer good day trips and affordable car rentals. They'll also book you tours with other companies if they don't have the services or prices that fit your needs. In fact, they have a booklet filled with pamphlets and fliers from local budget operators, making this a reliable one-stop shop for a traveler on any budget.

○ **Phat Tire Ventures,** 109 Nguyen Van Troi St. (© **063/382-9422;** fax 063/382-0331; www.phattireventures.com), offers an eco-tourist option. Contact Brian (a U.S. expat), who can arrange anything from day treks to jungle expeditions, plus mountain biking (they have a stable of top-quality bikes and hold daily clinics), rock climbing, rappelling, or canyoning. Daily rates for activities are priced between $20 to $70 and include lunch, transport, and a knowledgeable guide. Safety and environmental stewardship are their trademarks.

BUDGET TOURS

○ **Groovy Gecko Tours,** 65 Truong Cong Dinh (© **063/383-6521;** www.groovygeckotours.net), is a groovy, albeit unoriginal, outfitter providing basic eco-tours in the area.

○ **The Sinh Tourist,** 4A Bui Thi Xuan St. (© **063/382-2663;** www.thesinhtourist.com), has an information and tour office adjacent to Trung Cang, its budget hotel (p. 232). The standard services include arrangements for the open tour and some budget countryside and city tours.

○ **TM Brothers,** 58 Truong Cong Dinh St. (© **063/382-8383**), books standard budget tours from its office on "cafe street" (overlooking the market). They'll pick you up at your hotel and are very professional, especially for their prices.

[FastFACTS] DALAT

Banks & Currency Exchange   **Vietcombank** is at 6 Nguyen Thi Minh Khai St. (© **063/351-0586;** daily 7:30–11am and 1:30–4:30pm). You can exchange traveler's checks here, and you'll also find an ATM that accepts most cards. There's also an ATM at the top of the hill near the central market stalls (just up the street from the Lyla Hotel and Restaurant) and in many other locations around town.

Internet   Reliable Internet connections are provided free in most hotels. If you're stuck, try **Viet Hung Café,** 7 Nguyen Chi Thanh, where Internet use is free with the purchase of coffee or tea.

Post Office   The main office is located at 14 Tran Phu St., across from the Novotel, and it's open Monday to Saturday from 7:30am to 5:30pm.

Telephone   The area code for Dalat is **063**.

Where to Stay

With its long history as a popular resort area for foreigners and Vietnamese alike, Dalat offers some choice lodgings. You'll find plenty of good minihotels, many geared toward Vietnamese weekenders escaping the summer heat in the big cities, and all quite easy on the budget. You'll also find some indulgent colonial villas that pamper guests in every way, such as the Ana Mandara Villas, though naturally these are not so cheap. **Note:** No hotel in Dalat has air-conditioning, but with the year-round temperate weather, none is needed.

VERY EXPENSIVE

Ana Mandara Villas Dalat ★★★   At the risk of sounding trite, this place is magical. The restored colonial villas sit snug on a hillside of towering pines, and the views are spectacular during the day, with the sun shining on the nearby Langbian Mountains and illuminating the town below. Villas are two or three stories high, and each has a common dining area, living room, and kitchen. Families should head straight to Villa 15, which has an attic and lodge tucked under a slanted ceiling—a perfect play area for kids. Floors and furniture are a rustic, dark-brown wood, and everything else is creamy white. There are working stone fireplaces in most bedrooms and living rooms. A retro Art Deco heater whirs away in the corners. Loafers are on hand for roaming around the room, and fleece bathrobes are a bundle of warmth after a hot bath. All the different elements come together for a rustic, cozy ambience that leaves you feeling warm and fuzzy.

Le Lai St., Ward 5, Dalat. www.anamandara-resort.com. ✆ **063/355-5888.** Fax 063/355-5666. 65 units. $159–$759 villa. AE, DC, MC, V. **Amenities:** Restaurant; cafe; bar; concierge; vintage car rentals; heated outdoor pool; room service; spa. *In room:* TV, heating, fridge, hair dryer, minibar, Wi-Fi.

Dalat Palace ★★★   Built in 1922 as the address of choice for French colonists on vacation, and once the home of Emperor Bao Dai, this elegant beauty, with its understated old-world opulence, is one of the finest five-star choices in all of Indochina. From the huge fireplace and mosaic floor in the lobby to the hanging tapestries, oil reproductions of classic European art, and thick swag curtains, it's a French country château with a Southeast Asian colonial flair. The large rooms, with glossy original wood floors and period furnishings, are finished with fine fabrics and throw rugs. The bathrooms feature hand-painted tiles and large claw-foot bathtubs with antique-style fixtures. Genuine antique French clocks and working reproduction telephones complete the picture, yet nothing feels overdone. All deluxe rooms and suites have a foyer and a fireplace. Lake-view rooms open to a huge veranda with deck chairs. The high, high ceilings and huge corridors with hanging lamps contribute to the palatial feeling. Service is superb. All in all, this is an exquisite place that should not be missed. Their in-house dining is unrivaled (see "Where to Eat," below).

12 Tran Phu St., Dalat. www.dalatpalace.vn. ✆ **063/382-5444.** Fax 063/382-5666. 47 units. $172–$202 double; $319–$410 suite. AE, DC, MC, V. **Amenities:** 2 restaurants; 2 bars; children's playroom and outdoor playground; concierge; golf course; horseback riding; motorbike rental; heated pool; room service; spa; tennis. *In room:* TV, fridge, hair dryer, minibar, Wi-Fi.

EXPENSIVE

Golf III Hotel   The Golf is a three-star chain hotel and a good choice in downtown Dalat (Golf I and II are low-end versions). Large rooms are upholstered in purple with gaudy carved-wood details. Some rooms are a bit frayed around the edges. It's worth springing for a deluxe room, a Vietnamese honeymooner favorite, with parquet floors rather than carpet and larger bathrooms with big sunken tubs. The constant stream of Vietnamese wedding parties in and out lends a welcome festive air to the place, and this hotel is at its best when trying to be a little more than it is; blooming bonsais, overstuffed chairs, and a glitzy sheen over the lobby area stand testament. Golf III is right in the center of the busy market area, but set back far enough from the road that rooms are relatively quiet. Amenities are basic and include a rooftop steam, sauna, and massage area (a little seedy), and a lobby restaurant, which serves a fine breakfast.

4 Nguyen Thi Minh Khai St. (near the market), Dalat. www.vinagolf.vn. © **063/382-6042**. Fax 063/383-0396. 78 units. $80-$90 double; $100-$180 suite. AE, MC, V. **Amenities:** Restaurant; bar; gym; room service; sauna; steam room. *In room:* TV, fridge, minibar, Wi-Fi.

Ngoc Lan Hotel ★   Enjoying superb views over the lake, this once-crumbling property has been cleverly restored to four-star status and is now one of the top spots to stay in town. It's just a few steps from the central market and well-positioned for an exploration of Dalat's winding streets. The bright and breezy rooms have wood floors, shuttered windows, flatscreen TVs, Wi-Fi, and well-chosen artwork on the walls; some also have balconies. Facilities such as the fitness center are equipped with the latest gear, making them a pleasure to use. The smart restaurant prepares tasty Vietnamese and international cuisine, and staff are eager to help you plan your stay.

42 Nguyen Chi Thanh St., Dalat. www.ngoclanhotel.vn. © **063/383-8838.** Fax 063/382-4032. 91 units. $65-$95 double; $125-$385 suite. AE, MC, V. **Amenities:** Restaurant; bar; concierge; conference rooms; fitness center; room service. *In room:* Satellite TV, minibar, Wi-Fi.

Saigon Dalat Hotel ★   This grand edifice is one of Dalat's newest offerings; it is built in a colonial style and features a massive lobby with gleaming marble floors. Rooms are a decent size and well equipped with a blend of traditional furnishings and modern facilities such as flatscreen TVs. This government-run hotel appeals to business people as much as tourists, and thus the staff is very efficient and capable. The only downside is that it's a bit of a trek to the town center.

2 Hoang Van Thu St., Dalat. www.saigondalathotel.com. © **063/355-6789.** Fax 063/355-1155. 160 units. $75-$80 double; $100-$230 suite. AE, MC, V. **Amenities:** 4 restaurants; 3 bars; concierge; fitness center; pool; tennis court. *In room:* TV, fridge, hair dryer, minibar, Wi-Fi.

MODERATE

Dalat Hotel Du Parc ★★   Formerly operated by Accor as a Novotel and then as a Mercure hotel, this smart place is located just across the road from the Dalat Palace, and shares its facilities. Lovely renovations converted the 1932 building, and it has now reverted to its original name, Hotel du Parc. The small rooms have attractive historical touches: glossy wood floors, tastefully understated wood furniture, and high molded ceilings. A superior room (the lowest standard) is a bit cramped and not the greatest value, but deluxe rooms are clean, classy, and worth the upgrade. The bathrooms are efficient and spotless, with sleek granite and dark-wood trim. Everything is tidy and convenient, with local artwork throughout and a warm, homey atmosphere. The staff is businesslike and friendly.

7 Tran Phu St., Dalat. www.hotelduparc.com. © **063/382-5777.** Fax 063/382-5888. 140 units. $45-$56 double; $95 suite. AE, MC, V. **Amenities:** 2 restaurants; 2 bars; concierge; golf arrangements; heated pool; room service; sauna; smoke-free rooms; tennis. *In room:* Satellite TV, fridge, hair dryer, minibar, Wi-Fi.

Empress Hotel ★   This Hong Kong/Vietnamese joint venture is a good, upscale, and affordable oasis close to the lake and all the action, and a good alternative to the Ana Mandara or the Dalat Palace. Tucked into the side of a hill, the hotel has rooms that form a courtyard, with the steep gable of a European lodge-style reception and restaurant on one side and two floors of rooms all facing the courtyard on the other. Comfortable rooms have dark-wood walls, terra-cotta tile floors, rattan furniture, good indirect lighting, nice local artwork, and elegant cotton and silk bedspreads.

Bathrooms are large, with granite counters and nice fixtures, some with bathtubs and others with an open arrangement with a combined shower/toilet. The suites are large and luxe, with a sunken tub and large sitting area, but I'd still choose a deluxe room, which is a larger version of a standard and has views of the stone courtyard and lake below. There's a nice restaurant serving good local and Continental fare; if the staff is slightly cool, it's almost refreshingly real of them.

5 Nguyen Thai Hoc St., Dalat. www.empresshotelvn.com. ✆ **063/383-3888.** Fax 063/382-9399. 20 units. $45–$55 double (superior/deluxe); $61–$112 suite. AE, MC, V. **Amenities:** Restaurant. *In room:* TV w/in-house movies, fridge, hair dryer, minibar, Wi-Fi.

INEXPENSIVE

Chau-Au Europa ★　This cozy little hideaway is just around the corner from the imposing Ngoc Lan Hotel (see above), and many rooms enjoy the same views over the lake, though furnishings are not comparable. The real pull here, however, is the friendly family who work tirelessly to ensure guests' comfort. There's a range of rooms here, from windowless closets to spacious, breezy units with good views. Facilities are limited, but all the basics, such as hot-water showers and free Wi-Fi in the rooms, are here.

76 Nguyen Chi Thanh St., Dalat. ✆ **063/382-2870.** 16 units. $10–$25 double. No credit cards. *In room:* Satellite TV, Wi-Fi.

Dreams Hotel ★★　Budget tourists rave about this one, and it's been so successful that there's now a second branch along the road. Dreams Hotel offers large, clean rooms with cable TV and hot water. The owner, Ms. Dung, and her son are very helpful, and this is a good budget base and a place to connect with other travelers. Just at the bottom of the hill from a street with many budget options, this hotel is also close to local tour providers such as Phat Tire (p. 229), as well as the friendly Easy Riders (p. 228), who can take you on fun motorbike trips. Be sure to book ahead, best by e-mail, as Dreams is always fully booked.

151 and 164B Phan Dinh Phung St., Dalat. www.dreamshoteldalat.com. ✆ **063/383-3748.** Fax 063/383-7108. 20 units. $20–$25 double. Rates include breakfast. MC, V. **Amenities:** Restaurant (breakfast only); free Internet. *In room:* TV, fridge, Wi-Fi.

Hotel Dai Loi (Fortune Hotel) ★　If you want value for your money, look no further: this hotel is affordable, comfortable, and still looks fresh. Most other places in this category have musty smells and dingy decor, but this place is spotless. More expensive rooms have two double beds and nice, large bathtubs, and most have balconies. The second-floor restaurant is open and inviting, and the small lobby bar could be airlifted to a museum as a "minimalist installation." The staff members speak little English but are nonetheless quite helpful. The hotel is located far enough from the center of town to be quiet, yet close enough to be accessible.

3A Bui Thi Xuan, Dalat. www.dailoihotel.com. ✆ **063/383-7333.** Fax 063/383-7474. 39 units. $40–$45 double; $50–$55 suite. AE, MC, V. **Amenities:** Restaurant; bar; motorbike rental. *In room:* TV, fridge, minibar, Wi-Fi.

Trung Cang Hotel ★　The Sinh Tourist expands its monopoly on budget-traveler amenities here with this centrally located little gem. Rooms have clean tile floors and basic amenities. Any lack of design (hello, pink ceramic bathrooms) is compensated by clean, airy rooms for next to nothing, though some have nice filigreed ceilings and cool, subdued lighting. The hotel does get its share of groups, and things can get pretty noisy. This is a good budget option, and the folks at The Sinh Tourist are always accommodating when arranging tours or getting you around town. Service is friendly but not always effective.

4A Bui Thi Xuan St., Dalat. ✆ **063/382-2663.** Fax 063/383-6701. 30 units. 250,000 VND–450,000 VND double. Rates include breakfast. MC, V. **Amenities:** Restaurant; Wi-Fi. *In room:* TV, fridge, minibar.

Where to Eat

Dining is one of the great pleasures of a visit to Dalat, due to the huge variety of local produce, particularly fruits and vegetables, which makes for a bewildering range of ingredients. Many small restaurants are located along Truong Cong Dinh and Phan Dinh Phung streets, but some of the best dining is at the many stalls in the central market. Try the artichoke tea and strawberry jam, two local specialties (and good souvenirs to take home from the market). In the evenings, look for the small stalls selling delicious, flavored soy drinks on the main road near the central market.

EXPENSIVE

Le Rabelais ★★ FRENCH   Eating here is an experience in genuine fine dining, French colonial style. Prices are high for this region, but so is the standard of preparation and service. The staff work closely with local organic farms, and all dishes are prepared with the finest fresh produce. Le Rabelais serves from a limited menu, which ensures that everything is done just right. Dinner is a slow progression of delicious courses. The wine list is long, and the staff knows the right suggestions for any given meal—in fact, the staff here is uniquely efficient and professional, attentive without being either fawning or hovering. Certain things do get missed, but overall it's a great place to take that special someone.

12 Tran Phu St. (adjoining the lobby of the Dalat Palace Hotel). ✆ **063/382-5444.** Main courses $25–$52; set menus $65–$85 dinner, $25 lunch. MC, V. Daily 6am–10pm.

MODERATE/INEXPENSIVE

ART Cafe ★ VIETNAMESE   In the heart of the backpacker area along Truong Cong Dinh, ART Cafe serves local cuisine at prices just a tick above the local standard, but in an intimate, semiformal dining room with white linen tablecloths and rattan tables and chairs. The owner (the artist himself) is very friendly and a good source of local information, and the place is packed with young travelers nightly. They serve great stir-fries and have excellent vegetarian options, including delicious spring rolls and savory tofu cooked in lemon grass with a side of steamed vegetables. Portions are large and ingredients are fresh.

70 Truong Cong Dinh St. (near the Peace Café at the bottom of the hill of "Backpacker St."). ✆ **063/351-0089.** Main courses 45,000 VND–75,000 VND. No credit cards. Daily 10am–11pm.

Café de la Poste ★★ CONTINENTAL   This cozy, colonial gem, part of the Dalat Palace Hotel, is located in an open, airy corner building across from the post office (go figure). It's more a restaurant than cafe, really, and has a great selection of light choices, sandwiches, and desserts, in addition to hearty entrees such as spareribs, T-bone steak, and fresh pasta. The salads are big and fresh, and they have a great French onion soup. Don't miss the cheesecake for dessert. Rather stick with Vietnamese? Head upstairs to the elegant **Y Nho Y,** where several gourmet options await. It's pricey for Dalat, but worth it.

12 Tran Phu St. ✆ **063/382-5444.** Main courses $10–$36. MC, V. Daily 6am–10pm.

Da Quy ★★ ASIAN/WESTERN   Just a few steps down Truong Cong Dinh Street from the market brings you to this little gem of a place, where the food and service are top-notch but the check is embarrassingly low. The decor is low-key elegant, with crisp tablecloths topped with glowing candles, and the service is refreshingly unpushy. Try the venison with lemon grass, one of the baked clay-pot dishes, or one of the many Western dishes, and save room for one of their tasty desserts. Add a warming bottle of local wine, and you've got the recipe for a cheap and cheerful evening.

49 Truong Cong Dinh St. ℰ **063/351-0883.** Main courses $3-$12. No credit cards. Daily 7am-10pm.

Long Hoa ★★ CONTINENTAL/VIETNAMESE On a busy street just opposite the hilltop cinema, this small bistro is a Dalat institution. The Long Hoa is bright and tidy but sacrifices none of the old charm. The cozy dining room has checkered tablecloths and an atmosphere that attracts passersby. The owner, a vivacious, self-taught speaker of many languages, is very welcoming and will walk you through menu choices, travel recommendations, or local lore. You'll feel like a regular or will become one even if you are in Dalat for only a few days. The menu is categorized by ingredient (chicken, beef, fish, and so on), and they have various sautéed or steamed dishes, as well as a variety of hot pots and soups that are great on cold Dalat nights. Don't miss the homemade yogurt, a real treat. It's inexpensive, excellent local fare with a French flair.

6 Duong 3 Thang 2 (Duy Tan). ℰ **063/382-2934.** Main courses 45,000 VND-110,000 VND. No credit cards. Daily 11:30am-2:30pm and 5:30-9:30pm.

Lyla Hotel and Restaurant de Famille ★ ☺ CONTINENTAL/VIETNAMESE This longtime expat favorite is real family dining, set in a closed, quiet dining room along Dalat's busy cafe street. The menu is heavy on good French fare—try a "real" Continental meal of French onion soup (absolutely delicious), fries with mayonnaise, and a Niçoise salad—but also has great steaks, pasta, and seafood.

18A Nguyen Chi Thanh. ℰ **063/383-4540.** Main courses 55,000 VND-115,000 VND. MC, V. Daily 7am-10pm.

Ngoc Hai Restaurant ★ CHINESE/VIETNAMESE Just down the street from the market, this local spot is two floors of bright, clean, indoor/outdoor dining. It's nothing spectacular, but the staff is friendly and the menu is ambitious; ask for anything, and you'll hear hearty replies of, "Have. Have." Selections from the Western end of the spectrum include roasted chicken with potatoes and a mock-up of British fish and chips, but go for the Chinese-influenced Vietnamese stir-fries, one-dish meals, and soups. Reasonable set menus vary daily and are a good bet. There are good vegetarian selections, too.

6 Nguyen Thi Minh Khai St. ℰ **063/382-5252.** Main courses 75,000 VND-170,000 VND; set menus 140,000 VND-220,000 VND. V. Daily 6am-10pm.

Tau Cao ★ CHINESE/VIETNAMESE This is a friendly hole-in-the-wall restaurant serving one great dish: noodle soup. Thin yellow noodles are topped with a couple of won tons, minced pork, barbecue pork, and spring onions, all in a tasty broth.

217 Phan Dinh Phung St. (next to Dreams Hotel). ℰ **063/382-0104.** Bowl of soup 40,000 VND. No credit cards. Daily 6am-8pm.

Thuy Ta ★ VIETNAMESE This restaurant, sponsored by Dalat Tourist, stands on a little island over central Xuan Huong Lake, an excellent spot to enjoy a slow breakfast or sundowner. The smartly dressed staff is alert and attentive, and the menu covers a good range of Vietnamese standards and Western favorites. There are often musicians serenading customers in the evening.

01 Yersin St. and 02–04 Tran Quoc Toan St. ℂ **063/382-2288.** Main courses 85,000 VND–130,000 VND. No credit cards. Daily 6:30am–10pm.

V Cafe ★ VIETNAMESE/WESTERN This place, run by V and her American husband, Michael Sterling, is cozy and affordable. The chairs are mismatched and the decor is eclectic. Photography adorns the walls, along with plenty of paper lanterns. Lights with conical hat lampshades are suspended over each table. The food is good and filling; try their barbecue pork Banh Uot Dalat, a dish of barbecue pork over a bed of mushroom-stuffed wide rice noodles, but save some room for one of their yummy homemade cakes. Service is very friendly. If you're an early bird, they've got some comfort breakfast options such as "French Toast—Oh La La."

1/1 Bui Thi Xuan (across the street from Trung Cang Hotel). ℂ **063/352-0215.** Main courses 70,000 VND–120,000 VND. AE, MC, V. Daily 11am–10pm.

CAFES

Nguyen Chi Thanh Street is lined with cafes, one indistinguishable from another in many ways. Each building hangs over the main market street, and all serve ice cream, tea, and beer to cuddling couples and backpackers. Try **Artista Cafe,** 9 Nguyen Chi Thanh St. (ℂ **063/382-1749**), for good ice cream, classic rock, and friendly folks. Next door is **Viet Hung Cafe,** which pretty much has the same menu, but offers free Internet access to patrons as well. For something a bit different, head for **Café Tung,** 6 Hoa Binh Square, right by the market, where the leather chairs and French tunes on the sound system will make you feel you've stepped through a time warp into the 1950s.

Peace Café, 64 Truong Cong Dinh St. (ℂ **063/382-2787**), is the heart of backpacker Dalat—an institution, really. Surrounded by the town's most popular budget guesthouses and minihotels, Peace Café is the place to meet Dalat's **Easy Riders** for tours of the countryside and beyond (p. 228).

For a peek into the local **art scene,** see if you can find Mr. **MPK** (you have to ask him what it means). He makes his home at the back of a little guesthouse overlooking a beautiful valley (Khach San Van Khanh; 11/8 Khoi Nghia Bac Son, up in the hills off Tran Hung Dao St.). MPK is an inspired photographer, best when he's up close to his subject. He shoots with an old rusty camera and turns the lens backward, shooting through a rough-hewn tube to get incredible macro close-ups. Have a coffee, peruse his photos, and buy something (if he's selling).

Attractions

Much of what there is to see in Dalat is natural: Lakes, waterfalls, and dams dominate the tourist trail. Things are spread over quite some distance, so consider booking a tour or renting a car and driver or motorbike.

If touring on your own, try to avoid visiting pagodas between 11:30am and 2pm, when nuns and monks are having their lunch. You might disturb them and also miss a valuable opportunity for a chat. It's also appropriate to leave a few thousand dong in the donation box near the altar.

Typical 1-day itineraries to sights outside the city include a visit to one of the falls, such as Prenn Falls just south of Dalat, followed by a stop at Truc Lam Monastery, the Lat (Chicken) Village, and the Valley of Love. Sights in town include Xuan Huong Lake, a visit with the Crazy Monk, then on to the Crazy House, and ending with a stop at Bao Dai's summer palace or the old train station. Most out-of-town tours make stops at small silk-weaving villages where you can watch the whole process from worm to wear, as well as incense-making workshops, vegetable-growing terraces, and coffee plantations.

Bao Dai's Palace ★ Completed in 1938, this Art Deco villa provided Bao Dai, Vietnam's last emperor, with a place of rest and respite with his family. It features portholes in the walls and a tall pole on the roof that looks like a mast, giving the structure the appearance of a ship. It's the town's most popular stop for domestic tourists, and on a busy weekend in high season, you might get a rush by imagining you're there to liberate the place and are part of the looting masses—that's not hard to imagine, with the crowds ignoring any velvet ropes and posing for pictures on the aging velvet furniture. You'll be asked to go in stockinged feet or wear loose shoe covers, which makes it fun for sliding around the home's 26 rooms, including Bao Dai's office and the bedrooms of the royal family, seemingly frozen in time with period furnishings. You can still see the grease stains on Bao Dai's hammock pillow and the ancient steam bath in which he soaked. The explanations are in English, and most concern Bao Dai's family. There is pathos in reading them and piecing together the mundane fate of the former royals: This prince has a "technical" job, while that one is a manager for an insurance company. Be prepared for an onslaught of souvenir vendors as you leave. There are three other Bao Dai palaces in town, the Dalat Palace Hotel among them, but this is the most popular.

South of Xuan Huong Lake, up the hill behind Hang Nga's Crazy House. Admission 10,000 VND. Daily 7–11am and 1:30–4pm.

Dalat Market (Cho Dalat) ★★★ Huge, crowded, and stuffed with produce of all varieties, this is the top stroll-through destination in Dalat. Here's where you can see—and sample—local specialties. Dalat, in general, is low on the hassling tourist touts that plague the big towns and tourist sights in Vietnam, and entreaties from the merchants are friendly; you can walk around without too much hassle here because the locals are doing all the shopping. The top floor of the market houses a high-end embroidery studio, and shops catering to tourists are on the rise, but mostly what's for sale are good local wines, preserves, and produce. Just outside the market, a number of vendors sell anything from sweetened soy milk to affordable dinners. The place is busy night and day, mostly with domestic tourists wandering the town. A fun vibe pervades it.

Central Dalat.

Dalat Railway Station (Cremaillaire Railway) Built in 1943, the Dalat station offers an atmospheric slice of Dalat's colonial history. You can see an authentic old wood-burning steamer train on the tracks to the rear, and stroll around inside looking at the iron-grilled ticket windows, which are now empty. Although the steamer train no longer makes tourist runs, a newer Japanese train makes a trip just 17km (11 miles) to Trai Mat and the Linh Phuoc Pagoda (see below). The return trip costs around $5 (five daily departures at 7:45, 9:50, and 11:55am, and 2 and 4:05pm).

Near Xuan Huong Lake, off Nguyen Trai St. Daily 8am–5pm.

The French Quarter ★★ The whole town has the look and feel of a French replica, but on the ridge-running road, Tran Hung Dao, don't miss the derelict shells of the many French colonial summer homes once populated and popular; it's where the connected and successful came to escape the Saigon heat in summer. A few of them have been lovingly restored, while others are gradually being reclaimed by nature (an eerie reminder of the recent colonial past). The road itself, one you'll take to many of the sights outside of town, offers panoramic views.

Best visited by motorbike or in a car with driver. Follow Tran Hung Dao Rd. a few miles southeast from town. Some of the houses are on private roads at the end of promontories.

Hang Nga's Crazy House ★★ This Gaudí–meets–Sesame Street theme park is not to be missed. It's a wild mass of wood and wire fashioned into the shape of a giant treehouse and smoothed over in concrete. It sounds simple, but there's a vision to this chaos; just ask the eccentric owner/proprietor and chief architect, Ms. Dang Viet Nga. Daughter of aristocracy, Ms. Nga is well heeled after early schooling in China and has a degree in architecture from the university in Moscow. In Dalat, she was inspired to construct a building with hardly a straight line in sight—it's all curved corners and walls. On a visit here, you'll follow a helpful guide and are sure to have fun clambering around the concrete ladders, tunnels, hollowed-out nooks, and "theme" rooms of this huge fantasy tree trunk. It's an actual guesthouse, too, but it offers more theme than comfort; it's better to visit than to stay. There's a small family shrine in a large common area at the back.

3 Huynh Thuc Khang St. ✆ **063/382-2070.** Admission 30,000 VND. Daily 7am–6pm.

Lake of Sighs (Ho Than Tho) ★ This lake has such romantic connotations for the Vietnamese that you would think it was created by a fairy godmother rather than French dam work. Legend has it that a 15-year-old girl named Thuy drowned herself after her boyfriend of the same age, Tam, fell in love with someone else. Her gravestone still exists on the side of the lake, marked with incense and flowers left by other similarly heartbroken souls, even though the name on the headstone reads "Thao," not "Thuy." The place is crammed with honeymooners in paddle- and motorboats.

Northeast of town, along Ho Xuan Huong Rd. Admission 10,000 VND. Daily 7am–5pm.

Lam Ty Ni Pagoda: Home of Thay Vien Thuc A visit with the "The Crazy Monk" is a highlight for some and just plain creepy for others. The temple itself is nothing special, though the garden in the back is nice; the attraction here is Mr. Thuc's large studio. Thuc, a Vietnamese Zen practitioner, seems to be painting, drawing, and scribbling his way to nirvana. Though locals say he's not a real monk, just a painter and salesman, it's an interesting visit. Thuc has a message of "peace and connectedness" characteristic of the Zen sect, and he conveys that message in Vietnamese, Chinese, French, English, Japanese, German, and Swedish as he continually cranks out poems with small stylized drawings when you talk with him. Your part in the plan is that, for a small donation, he'll scribble an original before your eyes and pose for a photo. You're free to ask him questions, browse his stacks of finished works in the studio, and sign the guest book.

2 Thien My. ✆ **063/382-1775.** Free admission, but most feel obliged (or compelled) to buy 1 of his paintings.

Lang Con Ga (Chicken Village) A village of the Koho minority people, "Chicken" Village is usually part of the all-day tours in the hills around Dalat. Why chicken? Well, there is an enormous cement statue of a chicken at the entry to town—the bird has to do with a village legend (ask your guide—I've heard about four different versions of the story). The Koho people are used to the many visitors who come here every day; you can watch them at work on their unusual "wraparound" looms and buy some colorful pieces of local fabric. Trinket sellers are not pushy, and you are free to walk about this rustic little town at your own pace.

About 16km (10 miles) south of Dalat.

Linh Phuoc Pagoda ★   This pagoda makes an interesting stop at the end of the short train ride from Dalat to Trai Mat, and is another example of one of Vietnam's fantasyland glass-and-ceramic mosaic structures. Refurbished in 1996, this modern temple features a huge golden Buddha in the main hall, and three floors of walls and ceilings painted with fanciful murals. Go to the top floor for the eye-boggling Bodhisattva room and views of the surrounding countryside. In the garden to the right, there's a 3m-high (10-ft.) dragon, made entirely of beer bottles, climbing in and out of a small lake. You'll find cool nooks and crannies to explore. It's all very photogenic.

At the end of Trai Mat St. (30 min. by train). Daily 8am–5pm.

Prenn Falls ★   The falls are actually quite impressive, especially after a good rain. You can ride a rattletrap cable car over them if you're brave, or follow a stone path behind the falling water (prepare to get your feet wet). The true Prenn experience is all about staged photos for Vietnamese tourists: couples preening, boys looking macho, and girls looking wan and forlorn. Professional photographers run the show and pose their willing actors on a small wooden bridge; on the back of a costumed horse, an elephant, or a camel; or perched in one of the cool treehouses (be careful of the loose rungs when climbing up). Come here to have a laugh and observe until you find out that, as a foreign tourist, it's you that's the big attraction; in that case, say *"Xin chao"* (pronounced *sin chow*) or return a few "hellos" and go from there (you'll be getting your photo snapped, for sure). You might walk away with some new chums, not to mention some souvenirs (plastic samurai sword, anyone?). Other falls in the area include the **Datanla Falls,** just 2km (1¼ miles) nearer town, **Gougah Falls,** some 40km (25 miles) south of Dalat, and **Pongour Falls,** 55km (34 miles) south.

At the foot of Prenn Mountain pass, 10km (6¼ miles) south of Dalat. Admission 15,000 VND. Daily 7am–5pm.

Thien Vuong Pagoda ★   Otherwise known as the "Chinese Pagoda," built as it was by the local Chinese population, this structure (ca. 1958) is unremarkable except for its serene setting among the hills of Dalat and the very friendly nuns who inhabit it. It does have three awe-inspiring sandalwood Buddhist statues that have been dated to the 16th century; each one is 4m (13 ft.) high and weighs 1½ tons. Left to right, they are Dai The Chi Bo Tat, god of power; Amithaba or Sakyamuni, Buddha; and Am Bo Tat, god of mercy.

3km (1¾ miles) southeast of town at the end of Khe Sanh St. Daily 9am–5pm.

Truc Lam (Bamboo Forest) Zen Monastery ★★   What's refreshing is that you can walk around Truc Lam with no harassment, unlike many other temples and most pagodas in Vietnam. This is a working temple, and though it's packed with tourists at certain times of the day, you'll be wandering amid meditation halls and classrooms that are utilitarian, not museum pieces. You'll get to see monks at work and have an informative glimpse into the daily rhythms of temple life. The complex was completed in 1994 with the aim of giving new life to the Truc Lam Yen Tu Zen sect, a uniquely Vietnamese form of Zen founded during the Tran dynasty (1225–1400). Adherents practice self-reliance and realization through meditation. The shrine, the main building, is notable for its simple structure and peaceful air, and there is a large relief sculpture of Boddhidarma, Zen's wild-eyed Indian heir, at the rear of the main temple. The scenery around the monastery, with views of the nearby manmade lake, Tuyen Lam Lake, and surrounding mountains, is breathtaking. Truc Lam can be reached by a scenic **cable-car ride** from the top of Robin Hill overlooking Dalat; the 12-minute glide down over the pine forest is a great experience, too, and costs 75,000 VND for the round trip.

Near Tuyen Lam Lake, 6km (3¾ miles) from Dalat. A popular spot on any countryside tour. Daily 7am–5pm.

Valley of Love ★★ The Valley is scenic headquarters in Dalat and a popular stopover for honeymooners. It's a good place to find some really bizarre kitsch, the kind whose precedent can only be roadside America; here, I mean guys in bear suits and huge-headed cowboys with guns that spout "bang" flags. There are a few nice walking paths among the rolling hills and quaint little lakes, and everyone enjoys the antics of Vietnamese honeymooners zipping around on motorboats and posing for pictures with guys in fuzzy jumpsuits. Don't miss it.

Phu Dong Thien Vuong St., about 3.2km (2 miles) north of town center. Admission 10,000 VND. Daily 6am–5pm.

Xuan Huong Lake ★★ Dalat's centerpiece, Xuan Huong, was created from a dam project that was finished in 1923, demolished by a storm in 1932, and reconstructed and rebuilt (with heavier stone) in 1935. It was drained and refilled in 2010. You can rent swan-shape paddle boats, or ride around the perimeter in a pony and trap (high season only). This is Dalat's prime strolling territory (you walk here from the nearby market), and you're sure to see newlyweds, some wearing full wedding regalia, posing for pictures or staring longingly into one another's eyes. It's about 7km (4 miles) around the perimeter, a nice walk in the early evening, passing the Dalat Golf Course and Flower Gardens along the way. Closer to town are some local cafes over the water where you can stop for a *Cafe Sua* (a robust coffee made of locally grown beans and ultrasweet condensed milk).

Central Dalat.

BUON MA THUOT

350km (217 miles) N of Ho Chi Minh City; 200km (124 miles) N of Dalat; 200km (124 miles) S of Pleiku; 180km (112 miles) W of Nha Trang

There isn't much to this little provincial capital unless you're a coffee lover, in which case a visit here is something of a pilgrimage, as this is the heartland of Vietnam's huge coffee industry. Otherwise, it's just a maze of busy streets surrounding the center Thang Loi (Victory) Monument, with its high arch and a statue of the first tank to enter the town during liberation in 1975. Services in Buon Ma Thuot are basic, and the few hotels that exist cater mostly to local coffee growers' expat managers and folks visiting the highlands on agricultural aid projects. The sleepy town has a few beat up old museums hardly worth seeing, but Buon Ma Thuot is a good base for day trips out into the broad-reaching hill areas. Rolling hills covered with the ordered striations of row upon row of coffee plants bring you to far-flung ethnic minority villages of the E De and the M'nong people. You can organize all kinds of trekking and tours in town that include canoeing, hiking, and elephant riding, as well as some great options for overnights and homestays in rural villages, or visit **Yok Don National**

Park just north of town. You can also visit a working coffee plantation. In town, expect little more than local souvenir shopping, mostly for good, fresh coffee and jars of locally brewed whiskey in fired pots of the M'nong people.

Note: This part of the highlands was more or less "off the map" for tourism until recent years, not for want of sights or natural beauty, but because of poor relations between the Vietnamese government and the local ethnic minority groups. The local cadres are really pretty relentless, and independent travel in the region is still not permitted. I met a young traveler putt-putting alone around the region on a rented motorbike out of Ho Chi Minh City; for his troubles, he was made persona non grata in the provinces of Gia Lai and Dak Lak, and the poor guy had to endure lengthy interviews with an irate party cadre before being sent packing. Be sure to arrange a guide to accompany you on any out-of-town exploration.

Getting There

BY PLANE There are direct connections between Buon Ma Thuot and Ho Chi Minh City, and Buon Ma Thuot and Danang. The airport in Buon Ma Thuot is 10km (6¼ miles) from the town center. The office of **Vietnam Airlines** is at 19 Ama Trang Long St. (© **0500/395-4442**). Flight schedules vary, and you should book your flights to and from here in advance (possible from any Vietnam Airlines office countrywide).

BY CAR/MOTORBIKE Probably the best way to arrange transport to Buon Ma Thuot is to hire a car and driver, preferably one who speaks English. The town is a popular stop for the many adventurous travelers who saddle up on a motorbike with one of the highland area's Easy Riders (p. 228). It's not a good idea to ride a motorbike unaccompanied around this region (see note above).

BY BUS Local buses to or from Nha Trang cost around 100,000 VND for the 5-hour ride. Most buses to Nha Trang, Dalat, Pleiku, and Kontum leave in the early morning. The public bus station in Buon Ma Thuot is on Nguyen Tat Than Street (an artery that originates at the large tank and traffic circle at the city center), about 4km (2½ miles) from the town center. Between the station and hotels in town, expect to pay about 30,000 VND for a motorbike taxi.

Getting Around

BY CAR Contact **Damsan Tourist** (© **0500/385-2246**) or **Daklak Tourist** (© **0500/385-2108**) for rentals with drivers. Expect to pay about $60 per day. (See their listings on p. 240.) Also ask at any hotel front desk about rentals or shared vehicles for day trips.

BY MOTORBIKE Choose a bike with English-speaking driver; you'll pay between $15 and $20, depending on where you're going. To Yok Don National Park, for example, you'll pay about $15 for the 1-day round-trip. For Lak Lake, some 55km (34 miles) south, expect to pay $20, and for a trip to Dray Sap Waterfall, pay around $15. For a reliable and helpful driver, contact **Mr. Tam Nguyen** (© **0932/474-242**).

Visitor Information & Tours

The local government agency, **Daklak Tourist**, 53 Ly Thuong Kiet St. (© **0500/385-2246**; fax 0500/384-2115; www.daklaktourist.com.vn), has an office just north of the Thang Loi (Victory) Hotel near the central monument. The company's helpful staff can arrange good trips to just about anywhere in the province, with services comparable to those of Damsan, below. A car with driver is about $60 a day, depending on where you go, and this office is a convenient place to pick up information. They sell a useful local map for 15,000 VND, and are open daily from 7:30 to 11am and 1:30 to 5pm.

Damsan Tours, 212–214 Nguyen Cong Tru St. (✆ **0500/385-0123;** www.damsanhotel.cm.vn), based at the Damsan Hotel, is a very helpful outfit and a good place to pick up information (or a map for 15,000 VND) before hiring a motorbike guide yourself. Their prices match those of Daklak Tourist (see above). It's open daily from 7 to 11am and 2 to 5pm.

FAST FACTS **Vietcombank** has a branch at 6 Tran Hung Dao (✆ **0500/385-7899**), and you'll find a 24-hour ATM at **Vietcombank ATM,** located just west of the Victory Monument in front of the Thang Loi (Victory) Hotel. The **Agribank,** 37 Phan Boi Chau (✆ **0500/385-3930**), can cash traveler's checks, as can most hotel front desks.

Where to Stay

Damsan Hotel ★   The Damsan is about 1km (½ mile) east of the town center and overlooks a quiet valley with coffee bushes across the hill out back. The location might sound like a drawback, but the hotel's very helpful in-house tour company and good dining make this place quite self-contained. Just arrive, and you can plan all of your travels from here. The hotel is comparable to the White Horse but is more convenient. Ask for a room on a higher floor with views of the coffee plantation and pool. They've recently replaced the tennis courts and even upgraded suites and deluxe rooms—it's worth paying the extra $5 for a bigger, newer room. The pool has also been cleaned out (goodbye, algae) and is a nice place to relax in the afternoon. Arrange any kind of trek here, perhaps a long day trip by bus or motorbike that includes canoeing or elephant rides, or spend a night in a hilltribe village.

212–214 Nguyen Cong Tru St. www.damsanhotel.com.vn. ✆ **0500/385-1234.** Fax 0500/385-2309. 68 units. $35–$55 double; $65 suite. AE, MC, V. **Amenities:** Restaurant; bar; Internet; pool; tennis court. *In room:* A/C, TV, fridge, minibar.

White Horse Hotel (Bach Ma) ★   Central and popular, the Bach Ma is a clean place with friendly (though erratic) front-desk service and good support for trips to the countryside or businesses in the area (many of the expat coffee buyers stay here for want of anything better). Nothing about the place is luxurious, but double rooms are huge, with two large double beds dominating a plain, white-tile room. VIP rooms are not worth the extra money; they may come with a computer and a shower curtain, but the carpets are stained and the sitting room is dominated by cheap leather couches.

7-13 Nguyen Duc Canh St. www.bachmahotel.com. ✆ **0500/381-5656.** Fax 0500/381-5588. 70 units. $30–$40 double; $50 VIP double. AE, MC, V. **Amenities:** Restaurant; bar; sauna; steam room. *In room:* A/C, TV, fridge, minibar, Wi-Fi.

Where to Eat

Quan Ngon ★ VIETNAMESE   A big, bright, flashy joint at night, this is the place locals drive by and say, "Expensive," before taking you to their favorite spot around the corner (at half the price). But by Western standards, Quan Ngon is cheap and serves some exotic fare, such as porcupine and pigeon, as well as the usual stir-fries, rice and noodle dishes, hot pots, and seafood brought in regularly from the coast and kept in tanks (I'd stick to land animals, though). The open-air, tin-roofed eatery is always packed for lunch and dinner. The restaurant is about a 5-minute walk east of the central square. The small attached coffee-and-liquor shop sells local wines with strange creatures floating in them, as well as a funky collection of herbs and traditional medicines.

72-74 Ba Trieu. ✆ **0500/385-1909.** Main courses 70,000 VND–250,000 VND. No credit cards. Daily 10am–10pm.

Thanh Van's Nem Nuong (Spring Rolls) ★★ VIETNAMESE   A meal at this shop house is as cheap as it comes—and it's a tasty meal among locals. Here's the drill: Sit down and say "one," or just hold up a finger, and your table will be covered with dishes such as grilled pork and thin pork rind, white rice noodles, pickles, lettuce, a few sauces, and a plate of rice paper. You build the spring rolls yourself, and if you've never done it before, someone will come over to help you. There are lots of variations (learn techniques from adjacent tables), and the only way to do it wrong is to miss your mouth.

20 Ly Thuong Kiet, just west of the Victory Monument. ✆ **0500/385-9561** or 0914/093-990. Spring roll set for 1 25,000 VND. No credit cards. Daily 8am–10pm.

Attractions
MUSEUMS

Ako Dhong Village ★   Situated in the northern outskirts of town, this tidy village of E De longhouses offers a great opportunity to wander around a minority village, though it's so organized that it has the feel of a suburban community. The squat, tiled houses on short stilts are solidly made, and if you hear the clack of a loom at work in one of them, take a peek, and you'll probably be invited in and perhaps be offered the chance to buy a shoulder bag or other sample of the intricate work. There's often the tantalizing aroma of freshly roasted coffee in the air, and the beans spread out to dry, along with the distinctive architecture of the houses, is very photogenic.

At the end of Tran Nhat Duat St., off Phan Chu Trinh St., about 2km (1 mile) north of town.

The Ethnographic Museum   The museum—in a crumbling old colonial-style building adjoining a park and surrounded by huge trees—is hardly organized, but it showcases a good collection of the effects of local hilltribe peoples: the E De, M'nong, Ra-glai, Jarai, Bahnar, and Cham. You'll find an interesting array of traditional dress for each group and displays of everyday items such as the large M'nong whiskey jars, rattan backpacks, wooden mortar and pestles for grinding grain, elaborate musical instruments, and lots of farming and weaving implements. There's a small model of a Rong House and a few interesting examples of the unique pillars used to mark graves, as well as various items of ritual statuary. One room features a hauda (a large, multiperson elephant saddle), elephant riding gear, vicious-looking instruments for taming elephants, and photos of local elephant culture. Sadly, there are few English explanations, but much is self-explanatory. This is the most interesting of the town's three museums.

182 Nguyen Du St. ✆ **0500/385-0426.** Admission 10,000 VND. Daily 7:30–11:30am and 2–5pm.

Revolutionary Museum   Principally for war buffs and history freaks, this faded collection of photos is only worth a visit if you need yet another chance to see the Vietnamese side of the story, though you'll often find it closed during supposed opening hours. Inside are reproductions of classic images from the war, such as the "Girl in the Picture" or "Crossing the River," as well as more obscure shots of early U.S. advisors in the region and ethnic minority actions during the war years. The Hanoi government is still waging a hard-fought—and failing—PR campaign to win hearts and minds of the ethnic minorities in the region, and images in this museum are heavy on "local heroes," or the hilltribe folks who supported the North during the revolution. The whole sequence of the revolution is told in the museum's three rooms, and though there are few English signs, the clockwise progression through the museum is a predictable story and, as always, ends with faded glossies of the happy, fully functioning factories and farms of the present day.

01 Le Duan St. ✆ **0500/385-0426.** Admission 10,000 VND. Daily 7:30-11:30am and 2-5pm.

SIGHTS OUTSIDE OF TOWN

Originating in the high peaks deep inside the highlands' long ridge, the **Serepok River** falls from up high, gouging dynamic ravines in layers of sediment and bedrock to form stunning falls before emptying into the wide, lazy Lak Lake to the far south. Several of Buon Ma Thuot's sights are along the river's length. The best way to see them is to hire a motorbike and driver (from any hotel front desk) or arrange a tour with the town's two tour agencies (see "Visitor Information & Tours," above).

E De Village   Just 15km (9¼ miles) south of town, this tiny parcel is an ethnic enclave set up by the Vietnamese government, something like their own "Strategic Hamlet Program," to deal with the perceived threat of splinter factions among ethnic minorities. It's best to go with a guide, or you may get a cool reception. The first house you come to in the village is the town's English-speaking family, and you'll certainly want to see if anyone's home. One of the younger kids gave me a quick tour of the village, explaining how extended families live in segregated longhouses on stilts and that you can tell how many nuclear families are in one household by the number of windows. Folks are friendly, if shy, and it's okay to take pictures if you ask first. It feels like the village is set up for tourism, and it is (older women march out a few weavings they have on sale), but not too many tourists make it out this way, and the village is quite a welcoming place.

Dray Sap and Gia Long Waterfalls   These two stunning waterfalls (during the rainy season at least) are some 30km (19 miles) south of Buon Ma Thuot. Down opposite forks of the same entrance road (admission10,000 VND), they're a good day trip from Buon Ma Thuot. *Note:* Lak Lake and the falls, though both to the south, are separate day trips; it's too much driving for 1 day.

First, **Dray Sap Falls** has a shaded kiosk area at the entry, a good place to buy a cool beverage after the long, dusty ride. Two paths connect to the falls from the kiosk, the lower road tracing the water's edge up to the falls and the upper path of uneven cobble leading to the top of the falls. Take the low road and go across the small suspension bridge, then follow a narrow path that leads to a great view of **Dray Nur Falls,** which is not as wide as Dray Sap but still very impressive (note that during the late rainy season this path becomes flooded and thus impassable). Back at Dray Sap Falls, you can take a dip at the base of this stunning high waterfall, created by a massive granite shelf, if the current is not too strong. There are some good shaded areas thanks to massive, overhanging banyans and willows. The view from the top of the falls is great, and the rocky path is a fun climb that connects with the cobbled trail leading high above the bank to the kiosk. Nearby **Gia Long Waterfall** (admission 10,000 VND) is just a few clicks down a well-maintained service road, and this waterfall is even more dynamic, not so much for the falling water—which is just a trickle in the dry season—but for its steep rock formations. The whole area around the Gia Long Waterfall is eminently climbable.

Yok Don National Park   North of Buon Ma Thuot, this park is a great place to travel among small communities of ethnic minorities, including skilled M'nong elephant mahouts. It's also one of the only places in Vietnam to get an elephant ride in a natural environment. In this park—Vietnam's largest at more than 100,000 hectares (247,000 acres)—you'll find more than 60 species of mammals, including deer, monkeys, and even wild elephants, as well as a number of rare and endangered animals. You can take an elephant ride with a M'nong mahout, swim in the Serepok River, or take a good day hike to **Ban Don,** a small village set up for tourists (though it's so commercial, you might just want to high-tail it out of there). Yok Don is not only the largest park in Vietnam, but the most temperate, with average temperatures in the mid-70s (mid-20s Celsius) and lots of rainfall. The park is 40km (25 miles) north of Buon Ma Thuot, and a trip here—whether a day trip or an overnight—is best arranged through one of Buon Ma Thuot's travel agents, Damsan or Daklak Tourist (p. 240). Overnight tours stay either in the very drab concrete-block guesthouse near the park entry or in Ban Don village at a longhouse set up for foreign visitors. An overnight gives you a chance to spot animals in the early morning, but most folks do this as a day trip (start early for a chance to see wildlife).

Lak Lake   The bumpy, 1½-hour ride south of Buon Ma Thuot to Lak Lake is a worthwhile day trip and a good access point to visit hilltribe villages. There are many groups of M'nong people, small splinter groups with disparate languages even, represented in the enclaves surrounding the lake. You enter the Lak Lake area via the **Jun Village** and can go by boat or elephant back across the shallow waters to the adjacent **M'Lieng Village.** More adventurous tours take you by boat and then on foot farther back into the bush. When you visit the villages, note the large mounds outside of any enclave: When M'nong die, they put all effects and the body in a raised grave for 1 year, and then cremate it.

If you're visiting the lake on your own, whether by hired motorbike or car, you'll park in busy little Jun Village, worth a stroll to see what rural life along the lake is like, and then explore further by boat. For a 1-hour boat ride on Lak Lake and across to the M'Lieng village, expect to pay about $10 for an hour; you can do the same trip by elephant for $30 (these figures are just points of departure for a bit of bargaining). These trips are included if you book a tour, but you can also arrange them at the water's edge with a bit of casual coffee drinking and shooting the breeze. Look for Mr. Duc, who speaks all of three English words ("You go boat"), at the first little coffee shop near the TOURIST INFORMATION sign. He's a real hoot, and his wife, Mai, cooks the best eats in town. Reach him by phone at ✆ **0500/358-6280** or 0905/371-633, and use a translator (or say, "I go boat").

Note: On a hilltop above the Jun Village area of Lak Lake is yet another former home of Bao Dai, now renovated as a small hotel. **Bao Dai Villa** (✆ **0500/358/6184**), operated by Daklak Tourist, is surrounded by pine and frangipani trees, through which you can peek at great views, and there's a fun "lodge" feel to the place, with old wood floors throughout. Large units are clean, if a bit sparse, but are more stylish than anything near the lake. You can sleep in Emperor Bao Dai's actual former room, with great views of the north end of the lake. The six units range from $30 to $50. Because you're really out in the sticks, this is more or less just a rural slumber party, but the place has a decent restaurant, and the mostly French-speaking staff is kind and accommodating. Be sure to contact Daklak Tourist (p. 240) beforehand, because the place gets booked with big French tour groups. Another good option is the recently restored **Lak Resort,** Lien Son Townlet, southeast bank of Lak Lake (𝄞 **0500/358-6184**), also run by Daklak Tourist. They have small 1950s-style bungalows at the edge of the lake. They're spacious and clean, and a good bargain at $30; serious budget travelers can stay in a longhouse for $8. They also have a small pool.

Shopping

Coffee is the name of the shopping game in Buon Ma Thuot, and just about everyone sells **Trung Nguyen,** the Vietnamese Coca-Cola of coffee (you can buy it or drink it in coffee shops just about anywhere). Trung Nguyen's headquarters are in Buon Ma Thuot (268 Nguyen Tat Thanh St.; 𝄞 **0500/386-5116;** www.trungnguyen.com.vn), and this company sponsors just about every other storefront. You'll find vendors along the streets surrounding the market or the central Victory Monument. Also look for smaller outlets with lesser-known brands such as **Nam Nguyen,** a local producer based at 30 Tran Quang Khai St., near the White Horse Hotel (𝄞 **0500/395-3170**).

All of Buon Ma Thuot's souvenir shops are geared toward Vietnamese domestic weekenders from the larger cities. Large **M'nong-style jugs of whiskey,** a smaller replica of the hilltribe's whiskey containers, are for sale along with the long straws that you use to drink it. The cool ceramic jugs are a nuisance to carry home on the bus/car/plane, but they're not a bad gift if you plan to visit Vietnamese friends.

PLEIKU & KONTUM

Kontum is 50km (31 miles) N of Pleiku; 245km (152 miles) N of Buon Ma Thuot; 198km (123 miles) W of Quy Nhon

The town of Pleiku, capital of Gia Lai Province, is easily recognizable to those who lived through the Vietnam War era. The American Seventh Cavalry, an air brigade and the unit featured in the film *Apocalypse Now,* touched down south of Pleiku near famed Camp X-Ray in the Ia Drang Valley on November 14, 1965. It was the start of open combat between American and North Vietnamese regulars after full American deployment at Danang. The bloody, 3-day battle left hundreds of Americans and thousands of Vietnamese dead, causing the U.S. to claim a tentative victory. It's not a famous battle of scale, but of legend, because it was where warriors on both sides really cut their teeth and sized each other up for what would be 8 more years of war. The clash was also important because it made the war look "winnable" to Americans. The area is hallowed ground to the veterans of both sides who fought here, and hosts many returnees.

These days the authorities in Gia Lai Province insist that tourists get a permit to travel around the province (from Gia Lai Tourist; 215 Hung Vuong, Pleiku; 𝄞 **059/387-4571**), so most visitors give Pleiku a pass and move on to the quieter town of Kontum, where the authorities are much more lax concerning visitors' movements. Kontum played its own important part in the Vietnam War and has a number of interesting sights outside of the city.

Kontum, and the hills surrounding the provincial city (actually more like a small town), were home to some of the heaviest fighting at the war's end in 1972, and again after the "Vietnamization" of fighting, when the last holdout units of South Vietnamese soldiers were pummeled into submission along rocky ridges north of town. A motorbike or car ride north of Kontum brings you to the likes of **Charlie Hill** and **Rocket Ridge,** now denuded peaks near the town of Dak To, and a short ride north up the now-paved Ho Chi Minh Trail takes you among some great mountain scenery. Good tours can be arranged out of Kontum to a variety of ethnic minority villages. The town itself has a distinctive character, with its churches and *nha rong,* towering communal houses of the Bahnar people. It also has a pleasant, recently constructed promenade beside the **Dakbla River.**

Kontum is the last jumping-off point before many travelers hop on the newly built Ho Chi Minh Highway; despite its name, this is not where the Ho Chi Minh Trail once ran. The road, also known as Highway 14, connects Kontum with Danang and Hoi An farther north along the coast. The route is popular for travelers riding along with Easy Riders on motorbike tours out of Dalat (p. 228). Another popular route is Highway 24, which leads down to Quang Ngai on the coast to the northeast of Kontum.

The area around Kontum is home to a number of ethnic minorities: Large populations of Bahnar people (famed for their high-peaked roof houses) live near the city center, and there are Sedang and Bo villages here, too. Accommodations and dining options are spartan, but the interesting sights are worth the journey.

Getting There

Kontum is 50km (31 miles) north of Pleiku and 245km (152 miles) from Buon Ma Thuot. Coastal Quy Nhon can be reached by road, via Pleiku (about 5 hr.), and the new Ho Chi Minh Trail, Highway 14, connects with Danang, far to the north and down along the coast—a 12-hour ride (most Easy Rider tours overnight along the way). All of these routes can be done by local bus—a very uncomfortable, slow option. Going by **private car, motorbike,** or **preplanned tour** are your best options (see "Visitor Information & Tours," in the Dalat section, earlier in this chapter).

Getting Around

This is popular turf for the Easy Riders from Dalat (p. 228), and in fact, you'll be grateful if you have a guide here: Most of what you'll want to see in the countryside, whether coffee plantations or rural homes and workplaces, requires some kind of introduction or an ability with the Vietnamese language. You're sure to meet a few cycling tours in these parts, and if you've got the legs for the hills or can afford a support van, cycling these roads is memorable. You can rent rickety city bikes in Kontum and hit the few sights around town, or even go out to the Konkotu Village some 5km (3 miles) out of town, but otherwise you'll need some good, reliable wheels. Motorbikes can be rented at about $7 per day from the hotels listed below, and all hotels can arrange tours to outlying areas, as can the folks at **Kontum Tourist** (below).

Visitor Information & Tours

Find the **Kontum Tourist** office on the bottom floor of the Dakbla Hotel, 02 Phan Dinh Phung (© **060/386-3333;** www.kontumtourist.com). It's open daily from 7 to 11am and 2 to 5pm. They don't speak much English, but they do have good maps and menus of tours. Transport is a bit pricey: expect to pay around $20 per day for a motorbike driver/guide, or from $60 for a car. If you haven't come with a hired vehicle, these folks are the best bet, but if you're traveling on the cheap, get your own wheels elsewhere (try the folks at Family Hotel, below).

FAST FACTS The **BIDV** bank, 1 Tran Phu St., near Kontum town center (© **060/386-2339**), has an ATM, can exchange dollars, and gives cash advances. In Pleiku, try the **Vietcombank,** 50 Phan Boi Chau St. (© **059/382-8595**), or the **Vietinbank,** 1 Tran Hung Dao St. (© **059/387-1045**), both of which have ATM machines.

Where to Stay

Should you decide to overnight in Pleiku, look for the **Pleiku Hotel,** 124 Le Loi St. (© **059/382-7778**), with basic rooms starting at $25, though they're a bit run-down. Smarter, nicer digs (from $50) and friendly staff can be found at the newish **Hoang Anh Gia Lai (HAGL) Hotel,** 1 Phu Dong Sq. (© **059/351-8459**).

Dakbla Hotel   Named for the neighboring river but oriented to a busy intersection, the Dakbla was once all there was in town and packed in miserable group tours for years. Recently, it's had stiff competition from new places such as the Indochine and Huu Nghi hotels, but it has responded with a long overdue renovation, and now offers clean rooms with all the basic facilities. Probably the best feature of the hotel, though, is the Dakbla Tourist office on the first floor, which can arrange good visits to ethnic minority villages and to sights around Kontum.

02 Phan Dinh Phung St. (riverside). © **060/386-3333.** Fax 060/386-3336. 20 units. From $35 double. MC, V. **Amenities:** Restaurant; bar. *In room:* A/C, TV, fridge, minibar.

Family Hotel   The Family Hotel is your standard budget choice, offering spartan but clean rooms. The folks here, as the name suggests, are friendly and inviting, and can help out with any eventuality in your stay in Kontum, including bicycle and motorbike rentals. Husband-and-wife team Phong and Minh and their kids always wear smiles. The same gang of rugged travelers you meet here will all be hanging out at the Dakbla Restaurant (below) later, and you're sure to make friends. There's now a second hotel location a few doors along the street that has a few bungalows in an attractive back garden.

55 and 61 Tran Hung Dao St. © **060/386-5748.** 28 units. $15–$25 double. No credit cards. **Amenities:** Restaurant (breakfast only); bike/motorbike rental. *In room:* A/C, TV, fridge, minibar, Wi-Fi.

Where to Eat

Other than Dakbla (below), the little storefront places geared to backpackers in Kontum (there are a few near the Family Hotel) aren't worth it, and you're better off at a local *pho* (noodle soup) stand. One nondescript place that is worth looking out for is **Hiep Thanh,** along from the Dakbla Restaurant, on the opposite side of the street at 129 Nguyen Hue; they serve great stir-fries and soups, and the owners are happy for you to point out what you'd like in the kitchen.

Dakbla Restaurant ★ VIETNAMESE/WESTERN   The friendly English-speaking staff greets you heartily, and the place serves good, affordable, one-plate meals, including Vietnamese stir-fries and rice dishes. They offer a few Western specials, such as good sandwiches and fry-up breakfasts. A stop at Dakbla's is also your best bet for hooking up with other travelers in the area and splitting the cost of day tours or an onward connection by hired car. The atmosphere is laid-back, and the restaurant is a good place to kick back in the midday heat and take up a game of backgammon or chess. They sell all kinds of local hilltribe wear and paraphernalia, all of which decorates the walls. They also rent bikes.

168 Nguyen Hue St., Kontum. ℂ **060/386-2584.** Main courses 35,000 VND–90,000 VND. No credit cards. Daily 8am–9pm.

Eva Coffee ★★ ▮ COFFEE SHOP/VIETNAMESE   Mr. An and his wife, Cam, and their three kids bring a bit of the art world to Kontum. This quiet coffee shop on the far edge of town (on the way to or from the Bahnar Rong House to the east) is overflowing with Mr. An's shrapnel sculpture and pieces made of war fallout, as well as his rough-hewn and weathered wood carvings of contorted human faces, a medium inspired by the hilltribe custom of making funerary statues over a grave and leaving the wooden pieces to decay. An grew up in Kontum and later wrote a thesis about hilltribe gardens, his inspiration for designing this hideaway. Grab a cool drink, put your feet up, and prepare for a long talk with the man himself. You'll find a simple menu of snacks and one-plate meals, such as fried noodles, along with a roster of good coffees, teas, and desserts.

01 Phan Chu Trinh St. (on the eastern end of town near the Kontum Village and Bannar Rong House). ℂ **060/386-2944.** evacoffee2002@yahoo.com. Most items less than $1. No credit cards. Daily 6am–11pm.

Attractions in Town

Catholic Seminary and Ethnic Hilltribe Museum

This massive wooden structure of timber and frame was left by aggressive French missionaries who, from a humble skeleton crew in 1848, grew steadily in numbers as they sought to bring the seemingly heathen hilltribe folks into the fold. This seminary was built in 1935 and was at its heyday under **Martial Jasmin,** the first Catholic bishop of the area until 1940. The French were forced to skedaddle as fighting flared up from the 1950s, and activities at the seminary died down. But from the time of reunification in 1975, a Vietnamese bishop was installed at the head, and the seminary now ministers to the needs, both humanitarian and spiritual, of great numbers of hilltribe villagers, all of whom wait in long queues outside the many offices and the clinic here.

The **Ethnic Hilltribe Museum** tells as much about the story of the monastery as it does about hilltribe culture, listing the lineage of bishops with photos of the seminary's many projects over the years—for improved irrigation, agriculture, health, and education. The museum springs from the more modern, post–Vatican II notion of spreading the faith without completely squelching rich local traditions. For instance, some practices, such as the making of large wooden representations of human figures to don graves (the statues decay over time into the most stunning expressionistic pieces), were accepted as part of local Christian practices. You need to visit the museum with a docent, a kind and informative tour guide.

Along Tran Hung Dao heading east of town. Check in at the main desk to contact a docent. Donations accepted. Mon–Sat 8–11am and 2–4pm.

Kontum Konang and Kontum Kopong

These two Bahnar villages are located on the eastern fringe of Kontum and make an interesting walk to explore a typical minority village. Kontum Konang is at the eastern end of Nguyen Hue, the road by the river, while Kontum Kopong is just north of Tran Hung Dao Street as it leaves town to the east. In either village you might see locals weaving baskets from bamboo strips, but to see a good example of a towering *nha rong* (communal house), head for Kontum Kopong.

Old Wooden Church and Orphanage   Built in 1932 on the site of an earlier, more humble structure, Kontum's main church is still a busy place, and on Sunday ministers to a large population of the converted, mostly ethnic hilltribe villagers from the surrounding hills. Check out the intricately carved mantles over the main entrances and the cool, contemporary stained glass featuring modern saints—the likes of French missionaries wearing cravats. The **orphanage** at the back of the main church building is a wild, cacophonous experience. Prepare yourself. A short walk down the steps, and you're attacked by groups of youngsters eager and well accustomed to talking and goofing with foreign visitors (also keen for the sweets and gifts that many visitors bring with them). These children, most orphaned by disease, are cared for by nuns, and visitors are welcome to volunteer their services. In fact, I met a small contingent of Americans doing relief work at the school.

Nguyen Hue, along the river at the town center. Free admission. Daily dawn–dusk.

Outside of Kontum
AN ALL-DAY RIDE NORTH OF KONTUM
Rent a motorbike or join a tour for this all-day ride around the picturesque hills north of Kontum. Many follow this route with an Easy Rider motorbike guide and carry on to Danang or Hoi An.

From Kontum, head north on Phan Dinh Phung past the bus station on the outskirts of town. Concrete storefronts give way to curving roads along mountain tracks and into the hilly expanse that once was the stamping ground of legions of jolly green American giants and sandal-clad Vietnamese forces, a major battleground during the war. Sights up this way include **Dak To,** some 50km (31 miles) north. Centered on a model *nha rong,* a Bahnar communal house, the town of Dak To is quite well developed. Follow signs from here to nearby **Charlie Hill,** the famous battleground where so many gave their lives, though there's nothing to see today.

Continue north on the **Ho Chi Minh Highway** through this area. In 2004, Highway 14, also known as the Ho Chi Minh Highway, was officially opened, giving the country an alternative route from north to south for the first time. Now linking Hanoi with Ho Chi Minh City, it is a superb piece of engineering and a joy to travel as traffic is still not heavy. The road runs the long ridge of the Central Highlands through Kontum, Pleiku, and Buon Ma Thuot, and the section north of Kontum is particularly lovely, with rolling hills and quiet villages. Past Dak To and Charlie Hill—tour guides usually take you to a select few villages along the way—you'll come to the turn-off for the border with Laos at Bo Y, which opened to international travelers a few years ago. From here you can continue riding through stunning scenery toward the north, backtrack to Kontum, or set out a on a whole new adventure in Laos, though you'll need a prearranged visa.

Konkotu and the Villages East of Kontum   Most ethnic villages in the region are situated beside a river—much like villages in nearby Laos—and Konkotu overlooks a wide bend in the Dakbla (a good place to go dip your toes and meet with people swimming, bathing, and doing laundry). At the village center is the high-peaked Bahnar *nha rong,* the communal house of the village. A number of other Bahnar communities border the road—all easily recognizable by their high-peaked *nha rong.* To get to Konkotu, follow central Tran Hung Dao Street heading east out of Kontum. Stay straight, past one *nha rong* on the right, and cross the bridge over the Dakbla. From there, stay left and follow the curving riverside road a few clicks until you come to a large settlement, where you'll see the high roof on your left. Ask to take a photo. The people of Konkotu are used to foreign visitors, and most are glad to pose for a frame or two, but always be sure to ask. Contact Kontum Tourist (p. 246) to inquire about festivals and tours to more far-reaching Bannar and Sedang villages.

SOUTH-CENTRAL VIETNAM

Such-Central Vietnam is a stunning sweep of coastal beaches—some of Vietnam's most popular places to put your toes in the sand and have a colorful drink with an umbrella in it. The area is flanked on the west by the Trong Son Mountains of the Central Highlands (see chapter 10). Traveling south from Danang and Hoi An, you'll first reach the town of **Quy Nhon,** a deep-water port famed for its fine shipbuilding trade. Just outside of town are a number of cool beach areas. You'll find just one luxury resort—the Life Resort Quy Nhon—and a few fun budget stops in town.

Heading farther south, you'll pass mile after mile of fishing villages and open beach areas before arriving in thriving **Nha Trang.** Once geared only to Vietnamese tourists on summer beach vacation, Nha Trang is now home to some of the finest resorts in all of Vietnam, drawing international tourists with daily connecting flights from Hanoi, Ho Chi Minh, and Danang. With good day-trip options, booze cruises, snorkeling, diving, and sailing, Nha Trang has something for everyone. The town also buzzes late into the night with a fun, friendly bar scene—mostly young backpackers. More far-flung resorts on outlying islands and peninsulas mean more and better options for escaping the busy, central backpacker party area of Nha Trang, too.

Between Nha Trang and Ho Chi Minh City (Saigon) in the far south, you'll pass the small town of **Phan Rang** (or Thap Cham), with its high Cham Towers—really just a crossroads for trips up to Dalat (see chapter 10)—before arriving in **Phan Thiet** and the nearby beaches of **Mui Ne.** Just a 3-hour drive from Ho Chi Minh City, the beaches at Mui Ne have become a popular escape for the city's expats, with a growing set of kite-surfing devotees, as well as golf enthusiasts for Nick Faldo's famed course. From here, easy day trips include giant sand dunes and a remote lake; relax at one of these before hitting Saigon (farther south).

QUY NHON

320km (198 miles) S of Danang; 230km (143 miles) north of Nha Trang

A popular saying goes, "It is not the north, it is not the south; nobody trusts the center." Historically fiercely independent, folks in this part of

Vietnam enjoyed their moment in history when two brothers, most notably **Nguyen Hue,** incited what became the **Tay Son Rebellion** in 1772, an uprising against the Nguyen rulers. The rebels marched to Hanoi and struck a crushing blow to a vastly superior Chinese force at Dong Da, and Nguyen Hue became **Emperor Quang Trung**—only briefly, though. He died, and rule passed to Gia Long, the first king of the last Vietnamese monarchy. Quang Trung's feisty spirit is celebrated during the Tet holiday nationwide—his great victory came during the Lunar New Year—and in Quy Nhon with an annual festival and at the local museum.

The small peninsula city of Quy Nhon is sheltered by outlying islands and a curved spit of land like a "cap," which makes this a very effective deep-water port, the most important in a long stretch between Danang and Nha Trang. As a result of this strategic importance, the town was hotly contested for centuries, first by the Chinese and later by the French and the Americans (some of the largest U.S. troop deployments, including the famed "Air Cav" unit, came ashore here at Quy Nhon in 1968).

Although it's long been, and continues to be, more of a fishing port than a tourist destination, Quy Nhon's long central beach is beginning to attract new developments for tourists.

Getting There

BY PLANE Both **Vietnam Airlines** and **Air Mekong** (✆ **08/3846-3666** in HCMC) fly between Quy Nhon and Ho Chi Minh City daily, and Vietnam Airlines also has daily flights to Hanoi. Contact the airline through your hotel front desk or through their local office (55 Le Hong Phong St.; ✆ **056/382-5313**). Quy Nhon's **Phu Cat Airport** is 35km (22 miles) north of the port area, and Vietnam Airlines runs a shuttle bus from town.

BY BUS **Local buses** will get you anywhere in the region: to the Central Highlands via Kontum (about 6 hr.), to the north via Danang (6 hr.), and to the south via Nha Trang (about 5 hr.). Apart from the overnight buses between Nha Trang and Hoi An that sometimes pick up passengers in Quy Nhon at around 4am, the **"Open Tour" buses do not make regular stops here,** so you'll have to use local buses or hire a car for overland travel. The **bus station** in Quy Nhon is about a kilometer (½ mile) from the beach at the far south end of town (about 20,000 VND by motorbike taxi from most points in the city).

BY TRAIN Local trains as well as the Reunification Express connect Quy Nhon with Nha Trang to the south and Danang to the north. The passenger station is far from the city center, and messing around arranging tickets is time-consuming (and frustrating), but most hotels or **Barbara's Backpackers** (p. 254) can arrange it for you for a small commission.

Getting Around

If you're arriving by plane, contact your resort of choice for a transfer (which is usually included, but specify when booking). **Quy Nhon Taxi** (✆ **056/381-5815**) can get you around the peninsula in style for just 10,000 VND per kilometer. **Motorbike taxi drivers** are less pushy in Quy Nhon; in fact, you'll have to hunt them down a bit, which is refreshing. A ride around town starts from 10,000 VND. There are no set places to **rent a motorbike,** but contact your hotel front desk or stop by **Barbara's Kiwi Connection** (p. 254) to get yourself a set of wheels (expect to pay about 100,000 VND). Barbara's also rents bicycles for $1 a day, as do many of the town's

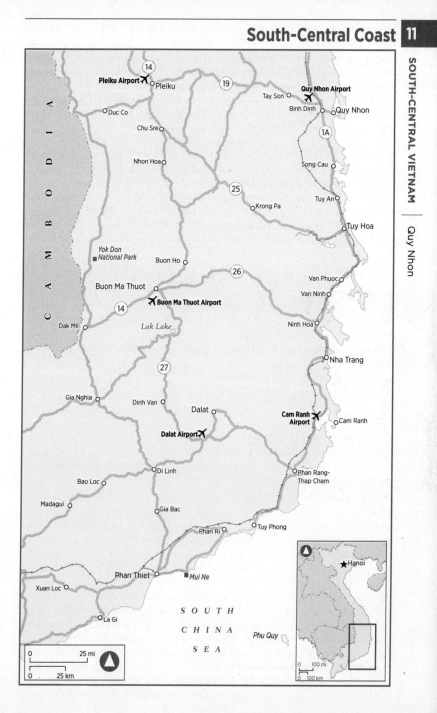

hotels. Biking to the sights in town is doable, but the beaches require a short hill ride, and visiting the Cham towers means navigating city traffic.

ORIENTATION   Quy Nhon is a V-shaped peninsula that, at its narrowest point, is an important deep-water port protected from the stormy seas by outlying islands and a long curve of landmass. Riverside Nguyen Hue Street in the central and northern end of town turns into An Duong as it passes to the south. Quy Nhon is just off the main north-south highway, Route 1, along a spur road, Route 1A. The best beaches in the area are south of Quy Nhon center.

Visitor Information & Tours

Barbara's Kiwi Connection, 19 Xuan Dieu St. (✆ **056/389-2921;** nzbarb@ yahoo.com), is expat- and traveler-information central. Barbara is a very friendly New Zealander who has been in Quy Nhon for many years and helps coordinate the many aid projects coming into the area; she or one of her very helpful staff members can help with any eventuality, arrange tours, find you a motorbike to rent, and give good advice about local happenings (and the food is good, too; see "Where to Eat," below).

[FastFACTS]   QUY NHON

Banks & Currency Exchange   **Vietcombank** has a branch with all services (including ATM) at 152 Le Loi (✆ **056/382-1498**), open Sunday through Friday 8 to 11am and 1:30 to 5pm; Saturday mornings only.

Internet   **Internet access** is provided free in most hotels, or head for the post office (see below).

Post Office   The **Central Post Office (Buu Dien)** is at 197 Phan Boi Chau St. (✆ **056/382-1441;** daily 6:30am–10pm).

Where to Stay

If you're in a pinch, **Saigon Quy Nhon Hotel,** run by Saigontourist, is kind of a mess but offers lots of services. It's located in the middle of town at 24 Nguyen Hue St. (✆ **056/382-9922;** fax 056/382-8128; www.saigonquynhonhotel.com.vn).

EXPENSIVE

Life Wellness Resort Quy Nhon ★★   This resort is a real find, a self-contained hideaway far from the wicked world. Guest rooms are huge, and top-floor rooms have peaked tile roofs. Everyone gets a spacious balcony and unobstructed views of the grand sweep of rocky bay. Most bathrooms have corner shower units that look out over the sea from a floor-to-ceiling plate-glass window (there's a curtain, if you're shy); if you would prefer a tub, request a ground-floor suite. The cool open plan of the rooms is quite cozy, especially when the ocean breezes blow. The resort has a fine spa, with luxurious treatment centers set on a cliff-top area amid lush gardens. The small central pool offers great views of the bay, but I suggest taking up residence on the resort's private beach. Dining at the resort is excellent; try the sea bass seasoned with ginger and lemon grass and steamed in a banana leaf. The resort does have one drawback: its remote location some 16km (10 miles) south of Quy Nhon town. However, there are plenty of in-house activities (free yoga, tai chi, snorkeling trips to a nearby island, and even beginner Vietnamese lessons) to keep you busy in this idyllic resort.

Ghenh Rang, Bai Dai Beach, Quy Nhon City, Binh Dinh Province (16km/10 miles south of town along the coastal road, Rte. 1A). www.life-resorts.com. ✆ **056/384-0132.** Fax 056/384-0138. 63 units. $145–$167 double; $177 suite. MC, V. **Amenities:** Restaurant; bar and lounge; babysitting; free bike; children's center; Jacuzzi; pool; room service; sauna; scuba center; spa w/natural outdoor pool; watersports equipment/rentals. *In room:* A/C, satellite TV, minibar, hair dryer, Internet.

MODERATE/INEXPENSIVE

Hai Au (Seagull Hotel)   This government hotel was one of the first along this stretch. A recent expansion means that rooms are modern and comfortable, if lacking in style. Rooms have plush maroon or orange carpet lines, which, despite the fleur de lis pattern, are distinctly Asian in decor. Double rooms come with small balconies and compact, tidy bathrooms with tubs only, while suites have a separate, spacious shower. Full ocean views are available with most rooms; all have flatscreen TVs.

489 An Duong St. www.seagullhotel.com.vn. © **056/384-6473.** Fax 056/384-6926. 169 units. $45–$70 double; $300–$400 suite. MC, V. **Amenities:** 4 restaurants; bar; room service; sauna; steam room. *In room:* A/C, TV, fridge, minibar, Wi-Fi.

Royal Hotel & Healthcare Resort ★   South of central Quy Nhon, just before climbing the hill out of town, the Royal Hotel is tidy and affordable. It's especially popular with Vietnamese tourists and businesspeople (lots of local conventions). At portside, the resort has a nice sandy beach out front. Wooden boardwalks connect four-unit building blocks, some of which face the sea. Bathrooms are large and have proper tubs and decent amenities. Rooms are the best in town, and sea views of the busy port area are good. They have two pools (the larger pool is quite picturesque and cozy), and unlike other in-town hotels, this resort's beach is kept clean and has shaded lounges. The hotel has three good restaurants: a Western restaurant set in a faux boat at the resort center, a seafood restaurant, and another serving Vietnamese and Chinese cuisine.

01 Han Mac Tu St. (on the farthest end of Quy Nhon's main bay). www.royalquynhon.com. © **056/374-7100.** Fax 056/374-7111. 131 units. $55 garden view; $65 sea view; $120 suite. MC, V. **Amenities:** 3 restaurants; bar; Internet; 2 pools; small spa; 2 outdoor tennis courts. *In room:* A/C, TV, fridge, minibar, Wi-Fi.

Where to Eat

Barbara's Kiwi Connection ★ VIETNAMESE/WESTERN   While many storefront restaurants catering to budget tourists try to do too much, the limited menu here means that they actually *have* everything they list and, more important, do it right. The sandwiches on local baguettes are good; salads are ample, breakfasts are hearty; and you can get good pizza and pasta. Check the blackboard for daily specials. At the very least, pop in for a drink and a chat with Barbara herself or the many young travelers and NGO folks who call the place home (at least for dinner).

19 Xuan Dieu St., Quy Nhon. © **056/389-2921.** Main courses 35,000 VND–100,000 VND. No credit cards. Daily 7am–9pm.

Dong SEAFOOD   Set in a little warren of streets not far from the central market and port area of Quy Nhon, Dong is just one of many little seafood places (also check out **2000,** 3 Tran Doc St. [© **056/381-2787**], just around the corner). The fare is seafood as you like it, and you can order rice and vegetables to go with it. There's an English section toward the back of the menu.

26 Nguyen Lac, Quy Nhon. © **056/382-4877.** Main courses are market price. Expect to pay $5–$7 per plate for small items such as shrimp or squid; $25–$35 per kilo for fish and lobster. No credit cards. Daily 8am–11pm.

Attractions

If you have time for only one attraction here, be sure to check out the huge **boat-building** operation on Phan Chu Trinh Street. Up to 10 large oceangoing boats are in production at any given time, and visitors are free to wander around. The whole place is a great photo opportunity. Craftsmen start with chainsaws and hand planers on rough-hewn planks, light fires to heat and bend the sections that make the curved prows of the boats, and assemble the large frames under a tin-roof warehouse, a track leading from the shop to the sea. You'll see some serious heaving and hauling by gangs of young workers, and can get up close with the more skilled craftsmen or chat with grinning septuagenarians marking planks with neon paint.

Binh Dinh Museum   This small museum has a few good examples of Cham sculpture and pre-Cham Bronze Age pieces. More for school trips than international tourists, but you can expect signs in Vietnamese and English. If you want to continue exploring after this museum, you might check out the **Quang Trung Museum** some 50km-plus (more than 31 miles) west of Quy Nhon—on the site of the original Tay Son Rebellion—but it's mostly for history buffs or as the second leg on a school trip including the Binh Dinh Museum.

Oceanside at 26 Nguyen Hue St. Free admission. Daily 8am–5pm.

Queen's Beach and Quy Hoa Leper Colony   This half-day jaunt starts at **Ghenh Rang Landscape Park** just south of the Royal Hotel & Healthcare Resort (p. 255; take the first left after the resort up the hill). The road from there winds its way high above the coast and affords great views back to the busy port and peninsula of Quy Nhon. Stop for a coffee and chat with locals in one of the little roadside stops along the way.

The road through Ghenh Rang leads over a hump of seaside land directly to the **Queen's Beach** and **Quy Hoa Leper Colony** (2.5km/1½ miles south of the main beach road, either through Ghenh Rang Park or off of Rte. 1A). The beach out front, named for the wife of Bao Dai, the last emperor of Vietnam, is quite inviting, and a good place (albeit no lounge chairs) to put your feet up. It's refreshingly free of touts and sellers, but that also means you have to bring all the stuff—lunch, snacks, an umbrella—yourself. The leper colony is a tidy set of buildings all fenced in, yet surrounded by the homes of former patients who now live quite full lives. The seaside promenade just in front of the leper colony is picturesque; you'll see a small grove of trees and a gallery of busts of famous scientists and great medical innovators from Greece, England, France, and Vietnam (just one woman, a Vietnamese). Look for the bust of Marie De La Passion (1839–1904) near the center of the park; she was a longtime French missionary at the colony. Because of the hard work of colony residents, the whole area is refreshingly free of garbage. You're likely to run into Vietnamese school tours on weekdays, and the *"Hello! Wha choo nay?"* are fast and thick. Say *"Xin chao"* (hello) right back.

Just a few miles up and over the hill on the south end of town (best by rented motorcycle or taxi). Entrance to the park is 5,000 VND plus 2,000 VND with motorbike. Daily 8am–4pm.

Thap Doi Cham Towers   There are many Cham sights outside of the city. In fact, you'll see some of the most dynamic on the ride in from the airport or from the Central Highlands, but Thap Doi is right in town, just off of Tran Hung Dao Street. The two towers are unique in that there are two (Cham towers usually come in groups of odd numbers) and that they're in town (usually on hilltops). The sight is actually less

REVIST THE my lai massacre

March 16, 1968: Chasing an elusive enemy and beleaguered by gruesome casualties from antipersonnel mines and booby traps set by wily North Vietnamese soldiers, the 11th Brigade of Charlie Company, led by Lt. William Calley, marched into the village of **My Lai,** a subdivision of larger **Son My.** Eschewing strict protocol, motivated by hate, and incited by Calley, U.S. troops were given free reign to "search and destroy" in the village as retaliation for the many U.S. casualties. Reports were conflicting, and it was some months after the incident that anything was reported—and even then, only by members of the press—but more than 300 victims (some estimates say more than 500), mostly women and children, died that day in a horrifying massacre. Calley himself supposedly sequestered a group of villagers and executed them in a ditch.

The incident was a sharp thorn in the side of U.S. military policymakers and fuel for fires of dissent and division in the United States. The My Lai Massacre, as it became known, was the beginning of the end of the war at home; the incident incited shouts of "baby killers" from antiwar protesters and brought the brutal reality of the war in Indochina to the attention of the U.S. public. The whole world began to question what many people asked from the start: "Is the U.S. doing more harm than good in Vietnam?" Calley was charged and convicted of murder, but he served only a few years before a successful appeal.

Today a large stone **memorial** and **museum** (daily 8am–5pm; admission 10,000 VND) marks the ground where the atrocities occurred, and a number of small stelae stand in front of specific family homes. The site is 10km (6¼ miles) northeast of **Quang Ngai,** capital of Nghia Binh Province, which is about halfway between Hoi An and Quy Nhon. The small museum consists of grisly photographs that you'll need a strong stomach to look at. Many veterans groups and former war protestors make the pilgrimage here. You can arrange a tour from Hoi An or hire private transport out of Quy Nhon. Most trips visit the sight as a halfway stop between Hoi An and Quy Nhon, or make it a long day trip out of Hoi An (about 4 hr. round-trip). If spending the night in Quang Ngai, try the **Petro-Song Tra Hotel,** 2 Quang Trung St. (✆ **055/382-2665**), or the **Central Hotel,** 784 Quang Trung St. (✆ **055/382-9999**).

spectacular than the walk through this quiet little neighborhood to a sea inlet where you'll find a few local seafood places. The relief work on the tower sculptures is in good shape, particularly the floral lintels, and the little park area around the towers is a pleasant place to rest (but you won't be alone long; folks down this way are friendly).

Just off of Tran Hung Dao on the northwest edge of town. Free admission. Daily 8am–5pm.

NHA TRANG

The capital of Khanh Hoa Province, Nha Trang sees a heavy local and international tourist influx, especially in the summer. The central beachside city area is quite busy and full of cheap guesthouses and small restaurants. The beach and its outlying islands have sprouted some fine new resorts. The surf isn't bad (for frolic, not for surfing) along the vast crescent-shaped beach in Nha Trang's central city, and the bright-blue vista is dotted by more than 20 surrounding islands. There are many good high-end hotels and resorts to choose from, and the high-rises in the town center hearken almost to a large beach town in Florida. Good budget options abound, too. Dining is all about fresh seafood.

Nha Trang is a very popular vacation spot for Vietnamese. In the summer months, the town is chockablock with tourists and young kids out "cruisin' the strip" on the main seaside avenue. The beaches of Nha Trang are a great place to spend 2 or 3 days playing in the surf, snorkeling and diving, or taking a cruise to the nearby islands. And Nha Trang's nightlife is thumping. Centering on the busy backpacker area along Biet Thu Street, the bars hop until late. In fact, the party often starts out on the boats by day and then continues at the bars. Prepare to shake thy booty at the beach.

Culturally, the **Pasteur Institute** offers a glimpse into the life and work of one of Vietnam's most famous expats. Both the **Long Son Pagoda** and the well-preserved **Po Nagar Cham Towers** are interesting sights.

In the winter, the surf can be quite rough, making swimming and watersports less than desirable, and daylong boat trips are less fun. Nha Trang is a good place for **diving** to soft coral sites brimming with reef fish, and a number of very professional dive outfitters can take you there (quite inexpensive by Western standards).

Because Nha Trang expects an increase in regional and international flights, the airport has moved to Cam Ranh Bay, 30 minutes south of town. The logic of the new airport is clear—longer runways for bigger planes—but the old in-town airport is now home to a bevy of military jets, which take off in a deafening roar over the south end of the beach throughout the day. It's kind of cool if you like jets, but not so cool if you like peace and quiet.

Getting There

BY PLANE Nha Trang is 1,350km (839 miles) from Hanoi and 450km (280 miles) from Saigon. Vietnam Airlines makes daily connections with Vietnam's urban centers and nearby Dalat. The **Vietnam Airlines Office** in Nha Trang is at 91 Nguyen Thien Thuat St. (© **058/352-6768**); storefront travel agents can make any reservations for a small fee. The **Cam Ranh Airport** is a 30-minute ride from town along the almost-deserted coastline; the visually exciting trip costs around 320,000 VND for a taxi or 400,000 VND for a minivan/SUV taxi. A shuttle bus runs to the old airport in town for 40,000 VND. The larger resorts offer more affordable group connections or limousine service, and some include free transfers.

BY TRAIN Nha Trang is a stop on the Reunification Express. The ride from Ho Chi Minh City is 7 to 9 hours (445,000 VND on a soft sleeper) and more than 20 hours from Hanoi (1,500,000 VND). Buy your ticket at least 1 day in advance at the Nha Trang train station, 17 Thai Nguyen St. (© **058/382-2113**), or from any travel agent. The overnight connection with Ho Chi Minh City is the most convenient route.

BY CAR If you choose to drive from Hoi An to Nha Trang, it's a 10-hour trip and will cost you about $150.

BY BUS "Open tour" buses connect you with Hoi An (530km/329 miles; 10 hr.; every day at 7am or 7pm) or Ho Chi Minh City (450km/280 miles; 8 hr.; every day at 7:30am and 8pm) for about $8 (less if you book multiple trips with the same company). The overnight schedules to Ho Chi Minh City and Hoi An are long and tiring rides, but a good option if you're short on time and don't want to waste your precious daylight hours looking out the window of a tour coach. Daytime routes connect to both towns as well. Open tour buses also connect with Dalat (214km/133 miles; 6 hr.; daily at 7am) and the beaches at Mui Ne (6 hr.; daily at 7am).

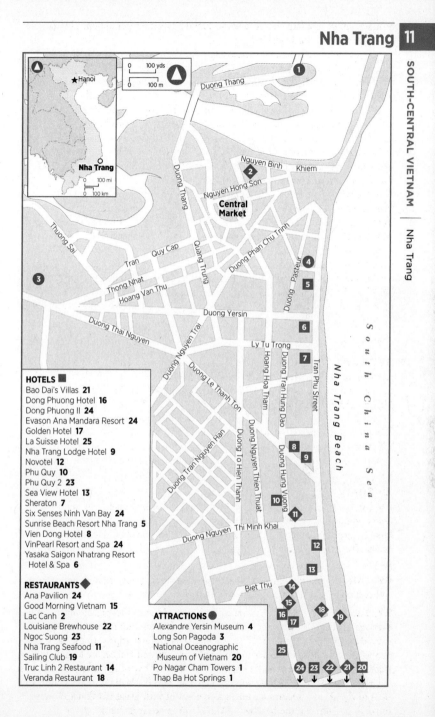

★Hanoi

Nha Trang

0 100 mi
0 100 km

0 100 yds
0 100 m

Duong Thang

Nguyen Binh   Khiem

Nguyen Hong Son

Central Market

Duong Phan Chu Trinh

Thuong Sai

Quy Cap

Tran

Thong Nhat

Hoang Van Thu

Quang Trung

Duong Thang

Pasteur

Duong

Duong Yersin

Duong Thai Nguyen

Ly Tu Trong

Duong Nguyen Trai

Duong Le Thanh Ton

Hoang Hoa Tham

Duong Tran Hung Dao

Tran Phu Street

Duong Thai Nguyen

Duong Tran Nguyen Han

Duong Nguyen Thien Thuat

Duong To Hien Thanh

Duong Hung Vuong

Duong Nguyen Thi Minh Khai

Biet Thu

South China Sea

Nha Trang Beach

HOTELS
Bao Dai's Villas **21**
Dong Phuong Hotel **16**
Dong Phuong II **24**
Evason Ana Mandara Resort **24**
Golden Hotel **17**
La Suisse Hotel **25**
Nha Trang Lodge Hotel **9**
Novotel **12**
Phu Quy **10**
Phu Quy 2 **23**
Sea View Hotel **13**
Sheraton **7**
Six Senses Ninh Van Bay **24**
Sunrise Beach Resort Nha Trang **5**
Vien Dong Hotel **8**
VinPearl Resort and Spa **24**
Yasaka Saigon Nhatrang Resort
  Hotel & Spa **6**

RESTAURANTS
Ana Pavilion **24**
Good Morning Vietnam **15**
Lac Canh **2**
Louisiane Brewhouse **22**
Ngoc Suong **23**
Nha Trang Seafood **11**
Sailing Club **19**
Truc Linh 2 Restaurant **14**
Veranda Restaurant **18**

ATTRACTIONS
Alexandre Yersin Museum **4**
Long Son Pagoda **3**
National Oceanographic
  Museum of Vietnam **20**
Po Nagar Cham Towers **1**
Thap Ba Hot Springs **1**

With droves of tourists wandering about, Nha Trang is notorious for petty crime, particularly the motorbike "snatch and run." Perps cruise the beach and grab bags from the unsuspecting, so be careful on the road, whether walking or in a cyclo. Go by taxi at night. Also, be aware on the beach because, unless you're at a private resort, you'll be hassled by sellers all day; say no, keep an eye on valuables, and leave what you can in a hotel safe.

The **local bus station** is the **Lien Tinh Bus Station,** 23/10 Street, about a 30,000 VND taxi or 20,000 VND motorbike taxi ride from the town center. Buses connect with all points north and south, as well as to towns in the interior Central Highlands (closest is Ban Ma Thuot).

Getting Around

The main street in Nha Trang, **Tran Phu,** runs along a 4km (2½-mile) beach lined with the myriad minihotels and beach attractions that make up the town center. **Biet Thu Street** runs perpendicular to Tran Phu and is where you'll find lots of smaller restaurants and budget tour operators, as well as the city's most affordable accommodations. **Taxis** congregate around the major hotels; most meters start at 15,000 VND for the first 2km (1¼ miles), 10,000 VND for each additional kilometer. **Mai Linh** is a reputable taxi company (✆ **058/381-1811**). Renting a **bike** from your hotel for $1 to $2 a day is a good option, as are cyclos, which you can rent for around $3 per hour from your hotel. A **cyclo** across town will cost about 15,000 VND. In addition, **motorbike taxis** cost around 40,000 VND per hour. All of these prices come with only a bit of friendly bargaining. Note the glut of empty cyclos, and keep walking until you get a reasonable price (and then, if all is okay, give a tip).

Visitor Information & Tours

All hotels in Nha Trang can book city tours, day-boat trips, or onward travel to your next destination. One-day city or countryside tours are worth it, as are the town's popular 1-day boat trips (for more information, see p. 271).

City tours can be booked at any hotel front desk. One-day boat tours can be booked just about anywhere from hotels to Internet shops. The cost is around $8.

For onward tours to the Central Highlands area, trips that connect you from Nha Trang to Ban Me Thuot, and either on to Dalat or north to Kontum, contact the friendly folks at **Highlands Tour,** 54G Nguyen Thien Thuat St. (✆ **058/352-4500;** www.highlandtourstravel.com). Open daily 7am to 9:30pm, these guys help consolidate groups or individuals with similar goals and craft the most economical trip possible (they also offer free Internet in an air-conditioned back room). This tour option is preferable to taking a local bus.

For bus tickets and connections to Dalat, contact any of the following tourist cafe branches. **The Sinh Tourist,** 2A Biet Thu St. (✆ **058/352-2982;** www.thesinhtourist.vn), is the best of the lot, with offices in every town in Vietnam. The in-town competition comes from **TM Brother's Café,** 22B Tran Hung Dao St. (✆ **058/381-4556**).

[FastFACTS] NHA TRANG

Banks & Currency Exchange   **Vietcombank**'s local branch is located at 17 Quang Trung St. (☎ **058/372-2820**). Hours are 7:30 to 11am and 1:30 to 4pm. It offers the usual currency and traveler's check exchange and credit card cash-withdrawal services. Along Biet Thu, some of the tour operators will cash traveler's checks and change money; rates are the same as at the bank (except for a small service fee), and they're open longer hours.

Internet & E-Mail   Most hotels and guesthouses offer free Internet to guests, but if you're stuck, Biet Thu has a few Internet cafes charging 6,000 VND to 8,000 VND per hour.

Post Office & Mail   The main branch is at 4 Le Loi St. (☎ **058/382-3866**). Hours are 6:30am to 10pm Monday to Saturday. DHL express mail services and Internet access are available. There is another branch at 50 Le Thanh Ton.

Telephone   The city code for Nha Trang is **058**.

Where to Stay

There are hundreds of minihotels in Nha Trang; some are a very good value, particularly those around Biet Thu Street, which are geared to Western budget travelers. There's also a small enclave dubbed Hotel Alley, just south of Biet Thu Street (entrance next to 64 Tran Phu) and opposite the beach, where you'll find more than a dozen cheap hotels bunched together. On the luxury end, Ana Mandara and its sister, Evason Hideaway Ana Mandara, stand in a class all their own.

VERY EXPENSIVE

Evason Ana Mandara Resort ★★★   Your luxury stay starts the moment you step off the plane. A Six Senses booth is immediately to your left when you enter the airport. Drop off your tag and staff will retrieve your baggage while you're ushered out of the small, cramped airport and into an air-conditioned van where comfy leather seats, bottled water, and a cool face towel are waiting (you have to book the airport transfer service prior to arrival; it's well worth the $14). The resort itself is on the south end of the beach promenade in Nha Trang. The rooms are beautifully decorated with solid wood furniture. Bathrooms are spacious, and large doors lead to the Jacuzzi bathtub in a private outdoor enclave. If you can, spring for a deluxe beachfront room so that you can almost fall from your balcony onto the sand and surf. It's the little things that make this resort special: native art and handiwork, the bowl with floating flowers in the bathroom, the basin of rainwater on your private veranda for rinsing sandy feet, the burning incense in the open-air lobby. You won't want, or need, to leave this luxury oasis.

Beachside, Tran Phu Blvd. www.sixsenses.com. ☎ **058/352-2222.** Fax 058/352-5828. 74 units. $279–$428 double/villa; $537 suite villa. AE, DC, MC, V. **Amenities:** 2 restaurants; 2 bars; concierge; library; health club; Internet; Jacuzzi; 2 large outdoor pools w/hot tub; room service; smoke-free rooms; spa; tennis court. *In room:* A/C, TV, fridge, hair dryer, Internet, minibar.

Six Senses Ninh Van Bay ★★★   If you aren't someone who's used to a life of luxury, this is the kind of place where, after your butler leaves you alone in your room, you do a little dance of glee. In fact, other hotels in Nha Trang do not hold a candle to this place. The attention to detail here is impeccable. Staff wave you off as the boat pulls away for the 20-minute ride to the resort, and are waiting to greet you when you arrive at Hideaway's jetty. The villas are sanctuaries of cool, off-white stone and blond wood. The main floor has a bathroom the size of a standard living room. Upstairs is the spacious living room, with gorgeous ocean views. Back downstairs is the bedroom, which also faces the ocean; you can take in the view from the window seat big enough for two, the four-poster bed, or the outdoor lounge chairs next to your private infinity pool. Decisions, decisions.

Dining is lovely in a two-story, open-air pavilion at seaside, with great views of the sunset and romantic nooks. On low-tide evenings, diners can enjoy a meal near the surf under the stars. The area is completely secluded, nary a motorbike or car to be found. At night, the skies are so clear it feels like you could reach out and tuck a star into your pocket.

Ninh Van Bay, Ninh Hoa, Khanh Hoa. www.sixsenses.com. 📞 **058/372-8222.** Fax 058/372-8223. 58 units. $688–$1,104 villas; $2,240 presidential villa. AE, MC, V. **Amenities:** 3 restaurants; bar; concierge; dive center; health club; Jacuzzi; library; pool; room service; spa; watersports equipment/rentals (snorkeling, sailboats, water-skiing, and runabouts); 1 villa for those w/limited mobility. *In room:* A/C, TV/DVD, fridge, hair dryer, high-speed Internet, minibar, private pool.

VinPearl Resort and Spa ★ ☺ This enormous new resort on Hon Tre (Bamboo) Island gets an A for effort, starting with the longest sea-crossing cable car in the world (3,320m/10,892 ft.) to get visitors there (you can go by boat if you'd prefer). It's mostly geared toward domestic tourists, and as such, it veers on kitsch. That much is evident as you approach the island and view the word VINPEARL placed in the hills like the famous Hollywood sign; it lights up at night. You'll be away from the main Nha Trang drag, but the hotel is pretty self-contained. Everything on the island, from construction materials to the very water that comes out of the taps, is transported by large tankers—an incredible undertaking. Rooms are large and comfortable, with all the amenities, but plain. The resort is designed in an arc around the vast acreage of the central pool, reputedly the largest in the region at 5,700 sq. m (61,354 sq. ft.), with lots of fun slides, meandering river areas, and bridges, all overlooking a secluded bay. The VinPearl offers lots of activities, group trips, a top-notch watersports facility, a scuba school, and a variety of classes, from yoga to "crazy cricket" (you have to ask what it is)—plenty to keep the kids occupied.

Phu Quy Port, South Cau Da Port, Vinh Nguyen (connect by boat or cable car from the pier on beachside Tran Phu just south of Ana Mandara). http://vinpearlland.com.vn. 📞 **058/359-8188.** Fax 058/359-8147. 485 units. $235–$280 double; from $425 suite. AE, MC, V. **Amenities:** 2 restaurants; 3 bars; babysitting; children's center; concierge; health club; Jacuzzi; pool; room service; tennis courts; watersports equipment/rentals. *In room:* A/C, TV, fridge, hair dryer, minibar, Wi-Fi.

EXPENSIVE

Sheraton ★★ ☺ With a choice location overlooking a gorgeous swath of beach, this new Sheraton has muscled in among other top-end hotels and offers stiff competition with its modern design, comprehensive facilities, and efficient service. Though deluxe rooms are impressive, with eye-pleasing yellow and beige decor and deep mattresses on the bed, it's worth considering an upgrade to a club room or suite, where you'll have superior views, better bathroom amenities, access to the Club Lounge for complimentary breakfast, and free use of the fitness center. Executive suites include a Jacuzzi surrounded by floor-to-ceiling windows with a fabulous view. There's a spectacular rooftop pool and several dining options covering a wide range of cuisines.

26–28 Tran Phu St. www.starwoodhotels.com. © **058/388-0000.** Fax 058/388-2222. 284 units. 3,400,000 VND deluxe; 4,600,000 VND club room; from 5,400,000 VND suite. AE, MC, V. **Amenities:** 3 restaurants; 3 bars; babysitting; children's club; concierge; cooking school; fitness center; 2 pools (1 kids); room service; spa; yoga studio. *In room:* A/C, satellite TV, minibar, Wi-Fi.

Sunrise Beach Resort Nha Trang ★★   The grand edifice of the Sunrise Beach Resort is all polished marble and white columns. The massive hotel is 10 floors of pomp, a bit like an oversize Mafia don's palace, but everything about the place is shiny and new. Large rooms are simple and tastefully decorated in a soothing off-white, all with great views of oceanside Tran Phu Street and the beach. The second-floor circular pool is surrounded by ostentatious columns, but makes for a luxurious getaway. Dining options are many, and the rooftop rotunda houses a classy lounge with views of the big blue beyond.

12–14 Tran Phu St. www.sunrisenhatrang.com.vn. © **058/382-0999.** Fax 058/382-2866. 120 units. $125–$140 double; from $180 suite. AE, MC, V. **Amenities:** 3 restaurants; 2 bars; babysitting; small health club & spa; Internet access; pool; room service. *In room:* A/C, satellite TV, fridge, minibar.

Yasaka Saigon Nhatrang Resort Hotel & Spa ★   On the main strip overlooking Tran Phu and the ocean blue, this Japan/Vietnam joint venture bridges the gap between the ultraluxe resorts and low-end minihotels—a good compromise. Rooms have all the basic amenities and are about as cozy as your favorite highway hotel chain back home. Upper-level units have good views of the sea, some with balconies; the vista from corner suites is quite spectacular and worth the upgrade. The standard superior rooms are comfortable, if bland; the deluxe rooms, on higher floors, are the best bet for atmosphere. Service is friendly, there are lots of good on-site dining options (the Red Onion, on the rooftop, is a local favorite), the pool is small but inviting, and it's just a short hop across busy Tran Phu Street to the beach.

18 Tran Phu St. www.yasanhatrang.com. © **058/382-0090.** Fax 058/382-0000. 201 units. $118–$198 double; from $250 suite. Rates include breakfast. AE, MC, V. **Amenities:** 4 restaurants; bar; nightclub; small health club; Jacuzzi; pool; room service; sauna; tennis court. *In room:* A/C, satellite TV w/in-house movies, fridge, minibar, Wi-Fi.

MODERATE

Bao Dai's Villas ★   Built in 1923 as a seaside resort for then-emperor Bao Dai, the hotel is a cluster of aging colonial-style buildings and a couple of new blocks set high on an oceanside hill south of Nha Trang, so far south that you're in the next town really. There's an interesting Gothic quality to the place, and one could certainly imagine a king wandering the promontory at night, watching the hotel's lighthouse scan the sea and sky, and worrying about the loss of his kingdom, which, in fact, was the case. Unfortunately, service is anything but regal and all facilities are rather run-down. The less expensive rooms are musty monks' cells, but the villa-style rooms have high ceilings and large, shuttered windows overlooking the coast—a better bet. The more top-end rooms vary, but all are palatial in size, even if they're wanting in amenities (the furniture can't keep up with the space). Some of the buildings have creaky old winding wooden staircases and rooftop access.

Cau Da, Vinh Nguyen/Nha Trang. www.vngold.com/nt/baodai. © **058/359-0147** or 359-0148. Fax 058/359-0146. 48 units. $25–$50 standard; $70 superior; $80 suite. MC, V. **Amenities:** 2 restaurants; bike/motorbike rental; Internet; room service. *In room:* A/C, TV, fridge, hair dryer, minibar, Wi-Fi.

Nha Trang Lodge Hotel ★   This lodge calls itself a "business hotel," and indeed it's a well-run and accommodating 12-story high-rise. Average-size rooms are chain-hotel style, with clean carpets, floral bedspreads, and tidy, modern furnishings. If you can, spring for an oceanview room with balcony (on an upper floor away from street noise, if possible). The staff is professional, and this comfortable seaside address covers all the bases with amenities and services. It's a nice, uninspired, affordable place and a bit like the younger, less-accomplished brother of the Yasaka (see above). Don't miss a meal in the popular outdoor seafood barbecue area. It also has one of the most popular discos in town, which can be a blessing or a curse, depending on your perspective.

42 Tran Phu St. www.nhatranglodge.com. ✆ **058/352-1500.** Fax 058/352-1800. 121 units. $75–$95 double; $140 suite. AE, MC, V. **Amenities:** Restaurant; bar; discotheque; small fitness center; pool; room service; sauna. *In room:* A/C, satellite TV, minibar, fridge, Wi-Fi.

Novotel ★ Along with the Sheraton, Novotel is the new kid on the block in Nha Trang. With its clean lines, predictably reliable service, and affordable rates, it provides a solid midrange choice. Like most of the town's top hotels, it enjoys a prominent position on Tran Phu, overlooking the palm-lined beach, and all rooms, brightly lit with modern furnishings, have their own balcony from which to admire the view. It caters both to vacationers and businesspeople, and is equipped with ramps, allowing access for travelers with disabilities.

50 Tran Phu St. www.novotel.com. ✆ **058/625-6900.** Fax 058/625-6901. 154 units. $80–$145 double. AE, MC, V. **Amenities:** Restaurant; 2 bars; fitness center; pool; room service; sauna; spa. *In room:* A/C, satellite TV, minibar, Wi-Fi.

Phu Quy 2 ★ If you'd like to enjoy panoramic views of Nha Trang's beautiful beach without the high price tag, consider this midrange alternative, where most rooms are small but equipped with all the comforts you'd expect of a top-end resort such as bathtubs, solid furnishings, and free Internet. With two other budget properties in town, the Phu Quy team is experienced in providing attentive service, and can help plan your stay to get the most out of the town. There's a tiny rooftop pool, and the best views are from rooms near the top of the 15-story building.

1 Tue Tinh St. www.phuquyhotel.vn. ✆ **058/352-5050.** Fax 058/352-5722. 60 units. $38–$100 double (depending on view and size). MC, V. **Amenities:** Restaurant; bar; pool; room service; smoke-free rooms. *In room:* A/C, satellite TV, hair dryer, Internet (free), minibar.

INEXPENSIVE

Dong Phuong Hotel ★ It's function, not form, in this motel-style block that typifies the budget accommodations in town (this is one of three properties of the same name and standard in Nha Trang). Rooms are bright but spartan, with spotless tile and not much else. Some rooms have a good city view, and if you're lucky, you'll be blessed with a classy nude done in painted tile mosaic in the bathroom (the only decoration I could find throughout). Family rooms are large and a good value, and the penthouse adjoins a huge rooftop area with 365-degree views of town. It's your standard minihotel service, though: just rooms.

103 Nguyen Thien Thuat St. dongphuongnt@dng.vnn.vn. ✆ **058/352-6247.** Fax 058/382-5986. 47 units. $15–$20 double; $30–$40 deluxe (family). MC, V. **Amenities:** Restaurant; pool. *In room:* A/C, TV, fridge, hair dryer, Wi-Fi.

Dong Phuong II This companion to the popular Dong Phuong in the town center (see above) is typical of the many affordable minihotels along this busy section of Tran Phu, south of the town center. The hotel is a real workhorse, with many budget groups calling this home. Rooms are simple affairs; the best are out front with balconies and views of the ocean, although many of these are pretty noisy because they're near the street. Don't expect style or special services here, but it is convenient, affordable, and away from the busy backpacker party scene along Biet Thu.

96A4 Tran Phu St. (on the south end of the Nha Trang strip across from Ana Mandara). dongphuong2@ dng.vnn.vn. ✆ **058/381-4580.** Fax 058/382-5986. 140 units. 300,000 VND–1,200,000 VND double. MC, V. **Amenities:** Restaurant; motorbikes. *In room:* A/C, TV, fridge, minibar, Wi-Fi.

Golden Hotel   It's little more than a surly welcome and room, but with no other expectations than these, you can't go wrong. Private spaces in this oversize minihotel, in fact, are quite nice, done with dark-wood trim, crown molding, and filigree, and more cozy than basic minihotels in the area. Amenities are bare-bones: just good tour services and a lobby safety box.

1K–2K Hung Vuong. ✆ **058/352-4496.** Fax 058/352-4498. 31 units. $20–$60 double. MC, V. **Amenities:** Internet. *In room:* A/C, TV, fridge.

La Suisse Hotel ★   This is one of the friendliest minihotels in town. Tucked down a quiet(ish) lane just south of the backpacker area, bright and colorful La Suisse Hotel offers new, clean, and cozy rooms with air-conditioning and TVs. Decor includes snazzy checked bedspreads and large headboards. There's nothing Swiss about the place except a hokey painting in the lobby of mountain-climbing, horn-blowing Swiss in lederhosen. Upper-floor suites have large curved balconies, and one has a raised wooden platform with a funky shag rug. Staff is extremely friendly and helpful, with genuine sentiment despite an inability to communicate. They can book tours, too.

34 Tran Quang Khai St. (just south of the central backpacker area). www.lasuissehotel.com. ✆ **058/352-4353.** Fax 058/352-4564. 76 units. $15–$30 double; $45 suite. MC, V. **Amenities:** Internet. *In room:* A/C, TV, fridge, minibar, Wi-Fi.

Phu Quy ★   The Phu Quy is one of the longest-standing minihotels in Nha Trang, offering no-frills rooms, helpful staff, and a neat, rooftop chill-out area. The beds are comfortable, but there are no views; still, go for one of the top floors to escape street noise, even though that means climbing lots of stairs. This place has no amenities whatsoever, but breakfasts are good and cheap, and, of course, the hotel will book tickets. This is backpacker central and an anthill of activity, and that, along with the price, makes it worth a stay. The large, shaded rooftop area has hammocks and lawn chairs, and is a good place to relax (they'll deliver food to you there, too). It's family run, and owner Mr. Quy is as nice as they come.

54 Hung Vuong St. phuquyhotel@dng.vnn.vn. ✆ **058/352-1609.** Fax 058/381-2954. 45 units. $8–$16 double with fan; $12–$25 double with A/C. MC, V. **Amenities:** Restaurant/bar. *In room:* A/C (in some), fan (in some), TV (in some), no phone (in some), Wi-Fi.

Sea View Hotel ✦   This is a very good and clean oversize minihotel with an elevator. The Sea View is right in the heart of the busy backpacker area, but you'll have to be on higher floors to garner any actual sea view. Rooms are large, simple, and tidy, with tile floors and balconies (in some). Amenities are few, but the hotel is convenient to the busy downtown and the very helpful staff can arrange anything from rentals to transfers. Being in the heart of backpacker land means hearing rowdy revelers take to the streets when the bars shut down; to avoid this, ask for a room in the back.

4B Biet Thu St. seaviewhotel@dng.vnn.vn. ✆ **058/352-4333.** Fax 058/352-4335. 59 units. $15–$25 double. MC, V. **Amenities:** Pool. *In room:* A/C, TV, fridge, Wi-Fi.

Vien Dong Hotel ★ ✦   A large, government tour-agency hotel, the Vien Dong has just undergone a major renovation and now ranks as one of the best value places in town. It's often busy with tour groups, but it's a relatively comfortable three-star at budget prices. The large pools (one for kids) are a highlight. Small rooms have carpet, simple wood furnishings, and sturdy foam mattresses. There's an inviting outdoor restaurant featuring nightly music and a cultural dance show. You're sure to meet other travelers here, and the general atmosphere is friendly. It's just one row back from the beach. The staff, though taxed by the many large groups coming and going, is kind and helpful.

1 Tran Hung Dao St. www.nhatrangtourist.com.vn. © **058/352-3606.** Fax 058/352-3608. 120 units. $30–$40 double; $70 suite. AE, MC, V. **Amenities:** 2 restaurants; bar; 2 pools (1 kids); room service; tennis courts. *In room:* A/C, TV, fridge, hair dryer, minibar, Wi-Fi.

Where to Eat

EXPENSIVE

Ana Pavilion ★★★ ASIAN/CONTINENTAL   Without question the finest dining on this beautiful stretch of coast, the Ana Pavilion is the jewel in the crown of the Ana Mandara Resort and serves exquisite food in elegant natural surroundings. Whether you're on the oceanfront veranda, under a canvas umbrella in the courtyard, or eating by candlelight over the open ocean on the seaside jetty, the location alone is breathtaking. The food is creatively prepared and beautifully presented, and portions are healthy. Chef Jeevan Thomas serves from an ever-evolving roster of local and seasonal specials ranging from imported Aussie steaks to banana flower salads. Bread is baked on-site. Don't miss the seafood hot pot served in a large, coal-fired crock and brimming with the catch of the day delicately stewed with vegetables. There's an excellent daily lunch buffet, and evening set menus are a great value. This is the best choice for romantic ambience and fine dining.

Tran Phu Blvd. © **058/352-2222.** Main courses 300,000 VND–580,000 VND; chef's signature menu 950,000 VND. AE, MC, V. Daily 6am–11pm.

MODERATE

Good Morning Vietnam ★ ITALIAN   This Vietnamese chain might seem out of place (and kind of redundant, with six locations in tour centers nationwide), but with an Italian manager ensuring good quality, this outlet, the first of the chain, serves familiar Italian fare. It's a nice break after many meals of noodle soup and local beer. Affordable by any standard, everything is cooked fresh and ingredients are of the highest quality. All pastas are homemade. Try the gnocchi dumplings with pesto or Gorgonzola, or the ravioli filled with braised meat. The *fritto misto* of deep-fried squid, shrimp, and sea bass served on the pasta of your choice is a house specialty. The place is not luxurious—just another storefront in and among the town's most popular bars—but Good Morning Vietnam has a nice "grotto" feel and is a cozy respite from the noonday heat. The first-floor lounge with low tables and cushions is a good spot to watch travelers on Biet Thu as the evening's nightlife lights up.

19B Biet Thu St., © **058/352-2071.** www.goodmorningviet.com. Main courses 100,000 VND–190,000 VND. No credit cards. Daily 10am–11pm.

Louisiane Brewhouse ★   This beachfront place is an excellent spot to laze away a sunny afternoon sampling the many goodies on offer, including Vietnamese fare, Japanese sushi, and Western dishes such as pizza, filling sandwiches, and yummy cakes. As the "brewhouse" tag suggests, locally brewed beers are available, and there's also a swimming pool and pool table for guests' use. If you hang around till evening, you'll likely catch a live band drawing in the after-dark partygoers.

29 Tran Phu. © **058/352-1948.** www.louisianebrewhouse.com.vn. Main courses 80,000 VND–240,000 VND. MC, V. Daily 7am–1am.

Ngoc Suong ★★ SEAFOOD Nha Trang has dozens of good seafood restaurants, but this one leads the pack. Whether in the very pleasant thatched outdoor pavilion or the vaguely nautical, softly lit interior, it's "seafood as you like it" served by a helpful, friendly staff. Whole fish and crustaceans can be chosen from a large tank; the day's catch, including shrimp and crab, is ordered by the pound and grilled, fried, or boiled with basic spices such as tamarind or pepper and lemon. The oysters, if they have them, are small but succulent. The name of the restaurant refers to a delicate marinated whitefish salad, one of the specialties and a great appetizer. This is a popular local and expat favorite.

96A Tran Phu (south of the town center at beach side). ⓒ **058/352-5677.** Main courses 80,000 VND–450,000 VND. AE, MC, V. Daily 10am–10pm.

Nha Trang Seafood ★★ SEAFOOD/VIETNAMESE Popular with Japanese groups (or local fat cats out to impress their mistresses), Nha Trang Seafood serves fresh and delicious seafood as you like it: grilled, steamed, or fried. Viet-style preparation is sweet, sour, and/or spicy; grilled items are good, and the shrimp in coconut, clay-pot dishes, and hot pots are affordable and delicious. The atmosphere is simple, best by candlelight on the second floor when the place is crowded. The staff is fun-loving and friendly.

46 Nguyen Thi Minh Khai St. ⓒ **058/382-2664.** www.nhatrangseafood.com.vn. Main courses 40,000 VND–220,00 VND; set menus 90,000 VND–500,000 VND. MC, V. Daily 8:30am–10pm.

Sailing Club ★★ INDIAN/INTERNATIONAL/ITALIAN Sailing Club is a great base for days at the beach. You can rent a chair, order lunch and snacks, and have drinks delivered all day. The prices are a little higher than if you were to rent a chair elsewhere and buy from locals, but the service is good and you can be sure of quality. You have three separate menus from which to choose, along with three seating areas: to your right is Casa Italia, left is Taj Mahal, and Sandal Restaurant is in the back toward the beach; head to Sandal if you want a mix of everything. The place turns into a bar in the late evening, and just as the Sailing Club has been exempted from local building codes, they're also one of the only bars able to stay open until the wee hours. The place has seen constant upgrades over the years and is a very stylish seaside pavilion of thatched-roof indoor seating, low beachside outdoor seating, and a private thatch lounge area on the beach.

72–74 Tran Phu St. ⓒ **058/352-4628.** www.sailingclubvietnam.com. Main courses 100,000 VND–300,000 VND. AE, MC, V. Daily 7am–11pm; bar noon–3am.

INEXPENSIVE

Lac Canh ★★ CHINESE/VIETNAMESE Two words: grilled shrimp. The Chinese-influenced Vietnamese cuisine here is all about its ingredients, so go for the basics. Try the fresh seafood in a light marinade that you cook yourself on a rustic, cast-iron brazier grill. The place is packed with locals and tourists. Try to sit outdoors, because the atmosphere inside is smoky. They don't speak English as well as staff at Truc Linh 2 (see below), but the food is better—and cheaper. This is definitely the local "greasy spoon," and it makes for a fun evening.

44 Nguyen Binh Khiem St. ⓒ **058/382-1391.** Main courses 24,000 VND–140,000 VND. No credit cards. Daily 9:30am–10pm.

Truc Linh 2 Restaurant ★ VIETNAMESE An eclectic menu here runs the gamut from the backpacker standbys of fried rice and noodles to sirloin steak and T-bone. There's a seafood smorgasbord out front from which you can choose your own jumbo shrimp, crab, squid, or fresh fish of the day and then have it weighed and cooked to your taste. They've got fondue and clay-pot specials, barbecued beef on clay tile, and rice-paper spring rolls with shrimp that are delicious. Truc Linh has become one of the hottest spots in Nha Trang, and even folks from the big resorts make it here for at least one meal. Cover the table in seafood to share. Smartly dressed waiters do the "Hurry, hurry, step right up" act out front, but they're hawking good, fresh seafood at budget prices, so let yourself get dragged in. Don't confuse this place with little Truc Linh 1, also on Biet Thu, closer to the beach, which serves simple Viet and Western cuisine (not a bad spot for an afternoon snack or coffee, though).

18A Biet Thu St. ℂ **058/352-1089.** Main courses 70,000 VND–190,000 VND. No credit cards. Daily 7am–10pm.

Veranda Restaurant SEAFOOD/VIETNAMESE   A great location and beautifully presented seafood dishes at rock-bottom prices. The specialty is a seafood hot pot, but they also have items such as spaghetti Bolognese. Try the set menu for $6—you can't go wrong. The decor is cozy contemporary, and it makes a nice respite from the hustle and bustle of the main street.

66 Tran Phu St. ℂ **058/352-7492.** Main courses $1.50–$6.50. No credit cards. Daily 9:30am–10pm.

Cafes

Rainbow Bar ★★   A cool, dimly lit bar and cafe area just off of Biet Thu, the Rainbow Bar is a good place to plan your dive trip over a pint with the professionals, or just enjoy some good basic pub grub, pasta, pizza, and steaks for cheap. Wash it down with imported ales and wine.

90A Hung Vuong St. ℂ **058/352-4351.** www.divevietnam.com. Main courses 90,000 VND–220,000 VND. No credit cards. Daily 7am–10pm.

Romy's Ice Cream and Coffee Bar ★   Look no further if you're an ice cream buff. German owner Fridtjof Rommeley is a trained cook and chef who left the kitchen for the ice cream freezer 2 decades ago. He has run an ice creamery for 16 years in his hometown and now brings his much-needed expertise to Nha Trang. Almost everything, including the waffle cones and garnishes, is homemade, with ingredients imported from Italy. The "Special Dalat" is their bestseller, a huge affair of mostly local fruits and ice cream topped with a healthy dollop of whipped cream. The ice cream was the creamiest I've ever had in Vietnam.

1C Biet Thu St. ℂ **058/352-7677.** Ice cream 30,000 VND–100,000 VND. No credit cards. Daily 10am till last customer.

Attractions

One-day city tours visit Long Son Pagoda, Bao Dai's Villa, the Oceanographic Institute, and the Po Nagar Cham Towers. Country tours take you to Ba Ho Waterfall and secluded Doc Let Beach far to the north, or to Monkey Island. If you get a group together yourself, you can arrange custom trips for very little with any tourist cafe. *Important note:* No matter what anyone tells you, Monkey Island is not worth the trip, especially if you like animals and don't like wasting your time (you can just buy a "monkeys on bikes" postcard and be done with it).

Alexandre Yersin Museum ★★   Here you can get an inkling of the work of one of the few foreigners revered in Vietnam. Swiss doctor Alexandre Yersin was responsible for the founding of Dalat; he also isolated an important plague-causing bacterium and researched agricultural methods and meteorological forecasting, all to the great benefit of the Vietnamese. Yersin arrived in Nha Trang in 1891 and dedicated the better part of his life to scientific discovery from his busy laboratory here until his passing in 1943. He founded the Pasteur Institute in 1895. On display are his desk, overflowing library, and scientific instruments.

In the Pasteur Institute, 10 Tran Phu St. ☏ **058/382-2355.** Admission 26,000 VND. Mon–Fri 8–11am and 2–4:30pm; Sat 8–11am.

Long Son Pagoda ★   The main attraction at this pagoda (ca. 1930s) is the huge white Buddha on the hillside behind the main compound; the 24m-high (79-ft.) statue is an important symbol of Nha Trang. Around the base of the Buddha are portraits of monks who immolated themselves to protest against the corrupt Diem regime; each monk's portrait, carved in relief on a side of the statue, is framed in flames. After climbing the numerous flights of stairs, you'll also be rewarded with a bird's-eye view of Nha Trang.

Thai Nguyen St. Free admission. Daily 8am–5pm.

National Oceanographic Museum of Vietnam ★   The Oceanographic Center, south of Nha Trang, is a fun visit for kids and popular with large groups of domestic tourists. The place is a bit run-down, with outdoor aquarium areas that could use a good scrub and a coat of paint. Despite some rather lackluster presentation—the shark tank, for example, is a big cement pond that you look over from above or from a side window—there is an exacting collection of the kinds of fish you would find in the sea near Nha Trang, and all are labeled in English. The best are the smaller aquariums in the back. Find reef sharks, turtles, living coral, anemones, puffers, lionfish, clownfish, sea horses, and a whole array of colorful reef species, some quite rare. The big turtles out back live in pretty cramped quarters, as do the crocs, but the kids delight at being close-up to these big boys. The aquarium is a fun visit, as the Vietnamese tour groups don't see too many Westerners in their day-to-day lives, and you're as much on display as the fish. The museum area holds more than 60,000 specimens collected over its long history, some full skeletons and others preserved in formaldehyde solution. The institute sponsors ongoing research and community projects, including monitoring aquatic life, developing captive breeding programs, and encouraging preservation and regeneration of local coral reefs.

01 Cau Da St. (at the southern base of the small hilltop on which Bao Dai's Villa sits). ☏ **058/359-0037.** Admission 15,000 VND. Daily 6am–6pm.

Po Nagar Cham Towers ★   Starting in the 8th century, the Cham people, an early Hindu empire in central Vietnam (see box in chapter 9), built the Po Nagar Cham temple complex to honor Yang Ino Po Ngar, mother of the kingdom. Set on the site of an earlier wooden temple burned by the Japanese in A.D. 774, there were originally 10 structures here, of which just three remain. The main tower, or Po Nagar Kalan, is one of the tallest Cham structures anywhere, and its square tower and three-story cone roof are exemplary of Cham style. The towers of Po Nagar have retained structural integrity, giving you a good idea of how it might have looked in all its glory. Two pillars of carved epitaphs of Cham kings are in the vestibule, and two original carved doors are in the sanctuary. The statue inside is of the goddess Bharagati, aka Po Nagar, on her lotus throne. It was carved in A.D. 1050. The Po Nagar temples are still used by local Buddhists who have adopted the site as their own, and the altars and smoking incense add to the intrigue of the architecture. Detracting from the whole experience are kitsch stands and lots of hawkers. To get here, cross the expansive bridge to the north of town spanning the mouth of the Cai River as it flows to the sea. There's a small fish market along the river (take a left to the riverside as you approach the temples), which is a great place to visit in the early morning, when boats are just bringing in their catch. The wide river, with its many bright blue and red fishing boats, is a picture.

2km (1¼ miles) out of the city center at 2 Thang 4, at the end of Xom Bong Bridge. Admission 10,000 VND. Daily 7:30am–5pm.

Thap Ba Hot Springs   Just north of the Po Nagar Cham Towers, a small side road leads a couple of kilometers to this area of hot springs that have been organized into a variety of healthy experiences. The place is hugely popular among Vietnamese and Japanese visitors. If you've never had a mud bath, this is your chance to roll around in a tub of the stuff for 30 minutes, which staff claim will do wonders for your skin due to the minerals contained in the messy ooze. After letting the stuff dry, wash it off with a powerful shower, then head for the mineral water pool or stand under a mineral waterfall. The key mineral here is sodium silicate chloride, which is supposed to ease rheumatism, arthritis, and stress. Prices depend on the treatment chosen (usually $5–$15).

25 Ngoc Son St. (call for hotel pickup). ✆ **058/383-4939.** Daily 7am–8pm.

The Beach

What brings everyone to Nha Trang is the big pond out front, better known as the Pacific Ocean. The waves are more or less a tumbling beachfront break on the best of days, and sea winds can whip up a real chop in the November-to-February monsoon season, but otherwise the beach is a great place for a dip or for lounging in the sun and forgetting it all. Beachside facilities abound, as the long 6km (3¾-mile) park area gets more and more developed with concrete paths and gardens. Nha Trang is a good place to grab a pay-by-the-day beach chair—usually something like 30,000 VND or a promise to buy lunch from smaller vendors. Also, the few large beachside places rent out chairs. Best is the **Nha Trang Sailing Club,** 72–74 Tran Phu St. (✆ **058/352-4628**), where you can order a delicious lunch or have drinks delivered all day. Just a hitch farther south is **La Louisiane,** Tran Phu (✆ **058/381-2948**), which has a tidy little central pool and cafe area, rents shaded lounges for the day, and can arrange any kind of trip. The options below are good for getting out, stretching your legs, and earning some beach time, but don't feel bad about falling into a good novel and relaxing in Nha Trang—that's what it's all about in this sprawling ocean city.

DIVING & SNORKELING

Diving is big in Nha Trang. The best season for weather and visibility is from March to September. There are a number of professional operations, mostly staffed by expat divers and all certified with PADI. Whether you're a beginner or an expert, make your choice based on safety more than anything.

Because of years of large-scale dynamite fishing and bottom dragging, most of the best coral sites are long gone. Most dive trips head straight for **Islands of the Hon Mun Marine Park.** In fact, all of the dive companies surround just a few tiny islands, and it can get quite crowded (a drawback). Underwater life is a colorful mix of hard and soft coral and lots of aquatic life and Technicolor reef fish (for a close-up glimpse of Nha Trang's colorful undersea life without all the bulky gear and expense, head to the National Oceanographic Museum of Vietnam, p. 269). Angelfish, clownfish, puffers, and all kinds of shellfish are in abundance. For less crowded dive sites, contact Jeremy Stein's Rainbow Divers (see below) about their trips to Whale Island (see "Outside Nha Trang," below).

Expect to pay about $50 for a trial dive and from $200 for a multiple-day openwater course. All operators listed below are open from 8am to 8pm.

Jeremy Stein's Rainbow Divers The folks at Rainbow were the first in the area, and in the years since have taken advertising to the level of pollution in Nha Trang, with seemingly every storefront claiming a connection. But whatever your belief is in truth in advertising (or quantity of advertising), these guys are the best in town and you can book just about anywhere. Rainbow also has dive centers throughout Vietnam on nearby Whale Island, on Phu Quoc Island (south of the Mekong Delta), and on Con Dao Island (east of Saigon).

✆ 090/878-1756. www.divevietnam.com. Rainbow Bar: 90A Hung Vuong St. ✆ 058/352-4351.

Sailing Club Divers The Sailing Club has now branched out into diving as well and operates a small outfit from its famous restaurant location on the beach. They offer daily diving and snorkeling trips as well as PADI courses.

72-74 Tran Phu St. ✆ 058/352-4628. www.sailingclubdivers.com.

1-DAY BOAT CRUISES

One-day **boat cruises** to some of Nha Trang's 20 surrounding islands are very popular. For years, Nha Trang was famed for rowdy trips that were more like daytime raves. **Mama Hahn,** 23C Biet Thu (✆ 058/352/2844), one of the boat operators, was once famous for saying, "Smoke and drink! Don't be lazy!" but now the trips have toned down significantly. It's best to fix up through your hotel; you will want to ask for details and maybe leave the kids at home or opt for a private trip without all the "floating bars" and free mulberry wine. The going rate is $8 per day, including a 9am hotel pickup and afternoon drop-off.

Expect a mellow day (depending on the weather) of motoring through some lovely bays. First, you'll hit **Mun Island,** where you're guaranteed some snorkeling, and then **Mot Island,** where you can enjoy a big feast for lunch and a floating bar (this is where the headache juice—some bad grape wine—comes into the picture). Beer and drinks are available all day. The next is **Tam Island,** where you can visit tiny Tam Resort and enjoy some free time for swimming and sunbathing, followed by a visit to **Mieu Island,** where you can visit an aquarium surrounded by cement lobsters and sharks. Though the day out is cheap, you have to fork out for any of the extra activities, including snorkeling (40,000 VND), sitting on a beach at Hon Tam (10,000 VND), and the aquarium (25,000 VND).

OTHER WATER ACTIVITIES

For **sailing,** contact the **Nha Trang Sailing Club** (✆ 058/352-4628), **La Louisiane** (Tran Phu, south of Sailing Club; ✆ 058/352-1948), or the **Ana Mandara** (✆ 058/352-2222). Go for a Hobie Cat if it's available (about $35 per hour), and hire a captain if you're inexperienced. The strong ocean breezes and choppy waters make for a memorable sail. **Runabouts** and **jet skis** are also available at the same locations. **Parasailing** happens just south of La Louisiane.

Shopping

Jean Lou Coiffure De Paris, a French hairstylist and designer, has a little storefront at 13 Biet Thu (✆ **058/352-4159**) and not only does hair and nails, but also serves drinks and does laundry, too. It's open daily from 8am to midnight.

Groove Shack, 89A Nguyen Thien Thuat St. (✆ **058/352-4738**), provides good pirated CDs and media loaded onto your iPod or personal computer. Ethical or legal? No. Convenient? Yes. And you can fill up on good new tunes (or DVDs) for kicking back at the beach. They also sell T-shirts and beach clothes. Open daily from 8am to 10pm.

Bambou, 15 Biet Thu (✆ **058/352-3616;** daily 8am–9:30pm), is a popular T-shirt shop in the heart of the backpacker area of Biet Thu.

In the heart of the busy traveler street in Nha Trang, you can't miss bright **Tashunco,** 17A Biet Thu (✆ **058/352-3035;** daily 7am–10pm), a little grocer that carries familiar Western goods, ranging from Diet Coke to good cheese.

Nha Trang After Dark

Nha Trang has a few lively beachfront bars where tourists congregate to swap stories, and it gets pretty raucous sometimes, especially when boatloads of booze-cruising day-trippers bring the party to the mainland. Bars and restaurants in the city center, and particularly along Biet Thu, are forbidden from staying open much past midnight (though a few do), but beachside Nha Trang Sailing Club and nearby Why Not Bar (see below) pick up the slack.

Crazy Kim Bar   In the heart of the backpacker area, Crazy Kim is the meeting point for the young and wild. Their motto is "Be hot. Be cool. Be crazy. Just be." There are many personified versions of that motto walking around this place. It's especially popular with the diving crowd and the few expats in town. Open until 1am. 19 Biet Thu St. ✆ **058/352-3072.**

Guava   Just next door to popular Crazy Kim (see above), Guava is a similar young scene. They often have good live music acts. Open until 1am. 17 Biet Thu. No phone.

Nha Trang Sailing Club   The Sailing Club, along with Louisiane Brewhouse, are the only bar/restaurants on the beach (all others are across the main road), and this one is extremely popular. They have open-air bamboo huts by the beach, and a large central pavilion with a pool table and dance floor. Open till late. 72-74 Tran Phu St., across from the Hai Yen Hotel. ✆ **058/352-4628.**

Red Apple Club   One of the most popular bars in the budget district, this place often gets packed with revelers looking for short shots or long beers. Open late. 54 Nguyen Thien Thuat St. ✆ **058/352-5599.**

Why Not Bar   A large brick pavilion, this place stays open late thanks to reputed "special" local connections. Live bands and dancing. Open till late. 24 Tran Quang Khai St., just south of the Biet Thu area. ✆ **058/352-2652.**

Side Trips & Overnights from Nha Trang

Cam Ranh Bay ★   Come here now before it gets too touristy, which is sooner than you think. Cam Ranh Bay is adjacent to the airport, so you can't miss this stunning sweep of sand if you're on your way to or from a flight. The high, winding road offers stunning views, and I'm not the first to think so; developers are lining up to have at it with pick and shovel. There's nothing to the beach but sand and a few local hammock-swinging joints. Cam Ranh can be reached by car for about 320,000 VND each way (same as the airport), or by motorbike taxi for about 100,000 VND round-trip.

30km (19 miles) south of Nha Trang.

Doc Let Beach ★★   This beach, with its powder-soft, dazzling white sands, is one of Vietnam's best-kept secrets. It's mostly geared toward domestic tourists—chairs and tables line the surf instead of beach loungers, but that is changing fast and this place is worth considering if you really want to get away from it all. As resorts are so isolated, most places offer a room rate that includes all meals. One cheap and welcoming spot is **Paradise Resort** (✆ **058/367-0480**), with a range of rooms from $20 to $60. Just along the beach, the **Ki-em Art House Resort** (✆ **058/367-0952**; www.ki-em.com) is an esoteric recluse with tastefully decorated rooms that are ideal for artists and start at $160. Probably the most practical base for most folks is the **White Sand Resort** (✆ **058/367-0670**; www.whitesandresort.com.vn), where the well-spaced and comfortably equipped villas provide a great base for a relaxing break. Rates start at around $110. If you plan to stay at one of these places, contact them for advice on transport, otherwise you can get there easily on a rented motorbike (80,000 VND–100,000 VND) or about 500,000 VND one-way if you hire a car.

50km (31 miles) north of Nha Trang.

OUTSIDE NHA TRANG
Jungle Beach

Budget tourists rave about **Jungle Beach.** Run by a Canadian expat, the place is ecofriendly, basic beachside living. Jungle Beach—a quiet, rustic **homestay**—is located 60km (37 miles) north of Nha Trang by road. There are three rooms in a longhouse and 10 basic cabanas made of bamboo catay and thatch (lots of guests even sleep out in the garden looking up at the open sky [under a mosquito net, of course]). This is for folks who like living close to the land and is a low-luxe alternative to the more comfortable Whale Island (see below). Rooms have shared bathrooms. Food, included in the affordable rate, is home-cooked and all you can eat (though not drink; you have to pay for your own booze). They offer trekking trips right from the cabana site, or you can just hang out in a hammock or on the beach. Rooms, including meals, are around 350,000 VND per day/night. Contact them (www.junglebeach vietnam.com; ✆ **058/362-2384**, or 091/342-9144 cellphone) to make a reservation, and they can help you get to the beach. On your own, expect to pay about 500,000 VND by car from Nha Trang (100,000 VND by motorbike). You can also ask tourist or local buses from Hoi An or Nha Trang to drop you off at Doc Let, and from there get a ride with a motorbike taxi driver for around 50,000 VND.

Whale Island

If you ever wanted to be a castaway on a little coconut island, here's your chance. Thanks to great roads, **Whale Island ★★** is just a few hours' drive north from Nha Trang and a 10-minute boat ride offshore. Set in the crook of a long peninsula, not far from the easternmost point in Vietnam, Whale Island is surrounded by tranquil waters year-round, and but for a few small fishing villages, you have the place to yourself. The island has just one all-inclusive resort (www.iledelabaleine.com; ✆/fax

058/384-0501; rate $43–$63 double; meals $25 per person), the brainchild of a longtime French expat and his Vietnamese wife who've been attracting their own small contingent of mostly expat clientele for several years now. Here you can get away from it all, frolic on the beach, or explore the underwater life with the island's exclusive operator, Rainbow Divers. You can also go on hikes around the island, and there are sailboats and canoes for rent.

Word has it that Whale Island was the auspicious site where scuba co-inventor and famous aquanaut Jacques Cousteau, while on assignment as part of a scientific mapping expedition, witnessed pearl divers staying underwater for what seemed an eternity and saw that they were using tubes from the surface. This experience inspired him to create, along with a team of scientists and engineers, the self-contained underwater breathing apparatus system that we rely on now.

Leaving Nha Trang early in the morning on one of the resort's shuttles (included in the package), the road north takes you through some scenic areas, along low-lying rice lands spotted with Chinese tombs and white egrets flying overhead. Near the coast you'll pass by miles and miles of fish farms and rows of rickety stilt houses lining salt flats. As the road approaches the end of the peninsula adjacent to Whale Island, you pass along a spit of high windswept dunes and a high beach buffeted by massive crashing waves.

The short ferry ride to the resort is covered in a zippy oversize runabout (the same boat they use for diving), and there's a speedboat on hand for emergencies. The resort area is just a thin strip of bungalows along a narrow beach. Rooms are simple and rustic with no air-conditioning, but there's 24-hour power for fans and good mosquito nets for nighttime. Bathrooms are small but clean. All rooms have balconies and little garden areas out front. A stay at Whale Island is about getting out into nature, and the rustic accommodations are part of that.

Dining is in a cozy open area overlooking the tranquil bay. In the midst of a small community here, you're sure to meet your neighbors, and guests normally share meals, all from a set menu of delicious local fare—heavy on the good fish dishes. Drinks at the bar afterward or an all-night billiard match in the enclosed library area can cement those friendships for a lifetime.

Diving is shallow coral diving, and visibility is not spectacular but comparable to areas off of Nha Trang. The area has been ravaged by dynamite fishermen, but isolated dive sites, most near Hon Tai (Ear Island), mean you won't be crowded by big groups, and there are good chances of seeing big fish, sting rays, and even whale sharks in the right season. Dive season is from January to October.

There are some great little trails all over the island that lead to secluded beaches, all well marked with signs and paint splotches on the exposed rock areas.

The transfer to the island costs $40, which is taken off your rack rate if you arrive with your own wheels. In addition to the numbers listed above, you may contact the main office on the mainland (2 Me Le Linh St.; © **058/351-3871;** fax 058/351-3873). The resort takes MasterCard and Visa.

PHAN THIET TOWN & MUI NE BEACH ★

Mui Ne is one of the best laid-back getaways in Vietnam. The nearby town of Phan Thiet is a bustling little fishing port—quite picturesque and good for a day's visit—but you'll want to get out to the long, sprawling, sandy stretch of beach at Mui Ne. This is a popular weekend getaway from nearby Saigon, and development in recent years has been rapid. You'll find some very nice upscale resorts and boutique bungalow properties.

Nick Faldo's golf course at the Novotel in Phan Thiet is a big draw, and the consistent winds of Mui Ne Bay bring wind- and kite-surfers from all over the world. Farther east and north along the coast, there are vast sand dunes, like a beachside Sahara, and inland there's the famous and strangely verdant Silver Lake amid the towering, shifting sands—a good day trip. These spots, as well as other small fishing villages, make for great day trips. There are also some local Cham ruins, and the town of Phan Thiet, famous for a brand of fish sauce (*nuoc mam*) made here, is worth exploring (especially the market). Mui Ne is a good getaway from Saigon or to take a break as you make your way down the coast.

Getting There

BY BUS OR CAR   Phan Thiet is just 3 to 5 hours from Saigon (depending on traffic). The tourist cafe buses connect here from Nha Trang and Dalat, as well as Saigon, and **The Sinh Tourist** covers all the bases from their **Mui Ne Resort,** 144 Nguyen Dinh Chieu St., Ham Tien (② **062/384-7542;** www.thesinhtourist.vn). You can also ask at any hotel front desk for car rentals or return bus tickets. A private car can be hired for around $80 to $100 each way. **Vietnam Vespa Adventures,** 169A De Tham St., District 1, Ho Chi Minh City (② **090/240-3055;** www.vietnam vespaadventures.com), is an excellent company running multiday tours to Mui Ne from Ho Chi Minh City. Book with them to roll into town in style on lovingly restored vintage Vespa scooters.

Getting Around

BY TAXI/MOTORCYCLE TAXI   There are two reliable companies. The nation-wide **Mai Linh** taxi company (② **062/389-8989**) has new cars and minivans with meters that start at 12,000 VND for the first 2km (1¼ miles). **Duy Sang Taxi** (② **062/383-3833**) has slightly older four-door sedans, and the meter starts at 10,000 VND. There are also plenty of drivers on motorbikes ready to shuttle you to your destination. Expect to pay 20,000 VND to 40,000 VND for a ride of 2km to 3km (1¼–1¾ miles).

[FastFACTS] PHAN THIET & MUI NE

Banks & Currency Exchange   **Vietcombank** has a branch with all services (including ATM) at 87 Duong 19/4, Phan Thiet (② **062/373-9064;** open daily 8–11am and 1:30–5pm, Sat morning only). In Mui Ne, there are several **ATMs** along the beach strip.

Internet   Most resorts and hotels offer Internet services free to their guests, but if you're stuck, head for Coco Café, 121 Nguyen Dinh Chieu, where rates are 8,000 VND per hour.

Post Office   The **Government Post Office** is on Nguyen That Thanh Street in Phan Thiet (daily 6:30am–10pm). In Mui Ne, there's a post office branch at the **Swiss Village,** 44 Nguyen Dinh Chieu St. (② **062/384-7480;** daily 7:30am–8pm).

Where to Stay

In addition to the recommendations in the section below, the **Novotel** offers the only international standard in the town of Phan Thiet, but most people are heading to the main beaches farther along. Along the beach at Mui Ne, about 9km (5½ miles) to the east, you'll find a growing clutch of luxury resorts that cover all the bases. Many folks plan to stay only a short time but end up in a hammock for a few extra days.

If you plan to kite- or windsurf, consider checking in at **Full Moon Beach,** 84 Nguyen Dinh Chieu, Ham Tien, Phan Thiet (✆ **062/384-7008;** fax 062/384-7160; www.windsurf-vietnam.com), which has the best instructors and equipment in the attached **Jibes Beach Club.** Individually decorated rooms here range from $60 to $90.

Luxurious options just keep opening; at the time of this update, **Anantara** was about to open a five-star property here. Check their website (www.anantara.com) for details.

Note: Most addresses are listed by their distance from Phan Thiet. You'll find **Internet service** at most resorts, though sometimes at inflated prices.

VERY EXPENSIVE

Princess D'Annam ★★★ This new resort, located on an isolated stretch of coast about 20km (13 miles) south of Phan Thiet, is a sight to behold, and I highly recommend ending your Vietnam vacation here. Standard suites are spacious, with raised wraparound wooden foundations for the king-size bed and daybed. The bathroom is equally large, with separate rain showers and a deep tub shaped like an inverted trapezoid. Everything is white or cream, with silk textiles in shades of gold and pale blue. Sepia photographs of Vietnam life adorn the walls. Villas are connected via a narrow stone path, surrounded by a lush tropical garden that is home to a rainbow of butterflies. The stand-alone two-story villas house a couple rooms, are luxurious, and come with an open minibar. There's a spectacular spa right on the beach, and pleasing views of a 19th-century lighthouse on an offshore island.

Hon Lan, Tan Thanh Commune, Ham Thuan Nam District. www.princessannam.com. ✆ **062/368-2222.** Fax 062/368-2333. 57 units. $465 suite; $675–$1,370 villa. AE, MC, V. **Amenities:** Restaurant; 2 bars; babysitting; children's playroom; concierge; health club; 3 pools; 2 tennis courts. In room: A/C, TV, fridge, hair dryer, minibar, Wi-Fi.

EXPENSIVE

Blue Ocean Resort ★★ This is one of the best resorts in Mui Ne. The entire place was given a much-needed makeover in 2008 and is now managed by Life Resorts with an incredibly friendly staff. Skip the standard rooms, if you can, as they are quite small (you have to negotiate your way around the bed) and have tiny bathrooms. Superior rooms have a spacious open layout with large bathrooms. Bungalows are your best bet; they come with his-and-hers sinks and a private outdoor area big enough for the stone tub and rain shower. All units come with private balconies and a pair of daybeds. The entire resort is channeling a breezy Mediterranean decor, with whitewashed buildings livened up with bright orange cushions on the daybeds and colorful accent pillows.

54 Nguyen Dinh Chieu, 200 Ham Tien. www.blueoceanresort.com. ✆ **062/384-7322.** Fax 062/384-7351. 84 units. $121–$144 double; $166–$234 bungalow; $314–$365 family bungalow. AE, MC, V. **Amenities:** Restaurant; bar; babysitting; pool; room service; spa. In room: A/C, TV, fridge, minibar, Wi-Fi.

Coco Beach Resort ★   Coco Beach doesn't look like much from the road—just an ugly pink wall to keep out the noise—but it's a real seaside garden oasis. They were the first to build along the strip at Mui Ne. Rooms are wooden bungalows on stilts, each with a comfy balcony area with a couch and table. It's a nice standard, intimate and tidy, and the real wood and thatch gives it an authentic 1970s rustic atmosphere. Spacious bungalows—the best are the oceanside villas—have high vaulted ceilings, dark beams, exposed thatch roofs, bamboo lanterns, mosquito nets, and subdued, indirect lighting. Service is attentive and genuine, the best along the main strip of Mui Ne. Coco Beach has two restaurants that are the best in town: Paradise Beach Club, the resort's laid-back oceanside seafood venue, and the more upscale Champa (p. 279). There's also a great open-air massage facility.

58 Nguyen Dinh Chieu. www.cocobeach.net. ✆ 062/384-7111. Fax 062/384-7115. 34 units. $110–$135 bungalow; $220–$270 2-room villa. MC, V. **Amenities:** 2 restaurants; bar; Jacuzzi; motorboat and sailboat rental; pool; room service. *In room:* A/C, fridge, minibar, Wi-Fi.

Novotel Coralia Ocean Dunes Phan Thiet ★ ☺   Sandwiched between Nick Faldo's golf course and an open lawn and sandy beach, the Novotel is a popular choice for golfers and Saigon expats on vacation. Rooms are decorated with nondescript carpets and floral prints. There are a few nicks and cracks in the furniture, showing the resort's age. The original hotel is an old Soviet-era resort, and concrete-block rooms are limited by their original build—small and not particularly luxe, but comfy. The two villas on the western part of the resort are a better choice. Where the hotel has a cold, generic Holiday Inn feeling, the villas are warm and charming. Villa rooms have wood floors, and all the furniture is dark wood with bamboo accents. Bathrooms have partially outdoor showers with rock and stone floors. Each villa has a shared common room with a lounge area and bar. The resort is 9km (5½ miles) from the popular beaches of Mui Ne. The beach is narrow and rocky, but the pool area and surrounding yard is expansive and great for kids (there's even a small jungle gym). The hotel has lots of activities and children's programs, and rents jet skis and sailboats.

1 Ton Duc Than St. www.accorhotels.com. ✆ 062/382-2393. Fax 062/382-5682. 123 units. $100–$125 golf/sea villa; $300 villa suite. AE, MC, V. **Amenities:** Restaurant; 2 bars; babysitting; children's playground; concierge; golf; health club; Internet; 2 pools; smoke-free rooms; 2 tennis courts; watersports equipment/rentals. *In room:* A/C, TV, fridge, hair dryer, minibar, Wi-Fi.

Victoria Phan Thiet Resort ★★   The Victoria has a unique layout, with pebble stone catwalks lined with sweet-smelling orchids and tropical flowers connecting the main buildings. The atmosphere is comfortable, laid-back, and private. The pool areas are great places to while away the day, and they have a good massage facility in a seaside grove. Guest rooms are large, private bungalows, some with two tiers and all done in terra cotta, bamboo catay, red earth brick, and dark wood; it's refined comfort with nice touches such as stylish indirect lighting, large ceiling fans, and local artwork. Family bungalows have multiple sleeping areas and a pullout couch. Bathrooms have partially outdoor rain showers with rock and stone floors. The beach is rocky, but the resort overlooks its own quiet cove and there are beachside thatch awnings. Service is good, and the resort has all the amenities of a much larger property, only here it's intimate and friendly. Come for the weekend, and you'll stay for the week.

Km 9, Phu Hai. www.victoriahotels-asia.com. ✆ 062/381-3000. Fax 062/381-3007. 59 units. $190–$240 bungalow; $500 villa. AE, MC, V. **Amenities:** 2 restaurants; bar; children's play area; exercise room; Internet; motorbike rental; 2 pools; tennis court. *In room:* A/C, TV, fridge, minibar, Wi-Fi.

MODERATE

Mia Resort ★★   Formerly the Sailing Club Resort, this seaside spot is owned by the same Aussie folks who run the popular Sailing Club in Nha Trang. Accommodations range from air-conditioned units in an attractive thatched house to top-notch seaside bungalows. Ask to see your room before checking in, as some are a bit musty. All units have terra-cotta tile with bamboo matting, cloth hangings, and bamboo floor lamps. There is an American Southwest feel in the artful beveled edges of the plaster walls and in the similarly rounded built-in nightstands. Large bathrooms are nicely appointed in tile and stripped-wood trim; they're separated from the bedroom by hanging cloths. The high-end bungalows are the best choice and worth the upgrade. The pool is small but set in a picturesque courtyard adjoining the open-air colonial-style restaurant. This is a popular stop for wind- and kite-surfers; both rentals and lessons are available.

24 Nguyen Dinh Chieu St. www.miamuine.com. ℂ **062/384-7440.** Fax 062/384-7441. 29 units. $85 double; $120–$170 bungalow, depending on view. AE, MC, V. **Amenities:** Restaurant; bar; babysitting; Internet access; pool; pool room; room service; spa; watersports equipment/rentals available; Wi-Fi. *In room:* A/C, satellite TV, minibar.

Terracotta ★ ☺   This resort has a fun, childlike look and feel to it, down to its block-lettering logo and a bright yellow-and-blond-wood reception area. Fittingly, it's a perfect place to bring kids. Large, unfinished terra-cotta jugs and vases are everywhere, molded with daisies or flowers and the resort's logo. The garden lawns are decorated with tiny pottery statues of little people in pondering poses. A seesaw made from a varnished log resides on a patch of grass. There's also an activity center set up where you can paint and bake your own ceramic mug and saucer. Rooms have blonde-wood furnishings and small bathrooms. Those in the hotel section are too close to the main road, and you can easily hear the honking and revving of passing cars and motorbikes. For a quieter stay, spring for the bungalow closer to the beach; rooms are spacious and have gray-stone tile floors and a small roof ledge displaying terra-cotta vases.

28 Nguyen Dinh Chieu, Ham Tien. www.terracottaresort.com. ℂ **062/384-7610.** Fax 062/384-7611. 59 units. $95–$130 double; $152–$171 bungalow; $240–$270 suite. AE, MC, V. **Amenities:** Restaurant; 2 bars; gym; Jacuzzi; pool; room service; sauna. *In room:* A/C, TV, fridge, minibar, Wi-Fi.

INEXPENSIVE

Budget accommodations are not as easy to find here as in Nha Trang. Since the mid-1990s, when development in Mui Ne began, the emphasis has been on mid-range or high-end resorts. However, there are a few places offering basic facilities, such as the **Thai Hoa,** 56 Huynh Thuc Khang St. (www.thaihoaresort.com; ℂ **062/384-7320**), with simple but clean rooms starting at $32 a night.

The **Sinh Tourist,** ever expanding their monopoly on the budget tourist market in Vietnam, operates the **Mui Ne Resort,** 144 Nguyen Dinh Chieu St., Ham Tien (www.thesinhtourist.vn; ℂ **062/384-7542**), a 48-room budget hotel on the farthest end of Mui Ne. If you come by one of their buses, they'll strand you there as long as they can in the hopes that you'll stay. Rooms start at $30 and aren't a bad bet. There's a pool and all the basics. A festive atmosphere pervades, with lots of young partiers.

Where to Eat

In addition to the reviewed Paradise Beach Club below, you may wish to try the **Sandals Restaurant** at the Mia Resort, 24 Nguyen Dinh Chieu St., Han Tien Ward

(© 062/384-7440), which serves a blend of Mediterranean and Pacific Rim cuisine at poolside overlooking the ocean. Farther east, **Full Moon Beach,** 84 Nguyen Dinh Chieu, Ham Tien (© **062/384-7008**), is a good stop for coffee or breakfast on your way to Silver Lake or the big dunes north of town.

Thatched-roof eateries line the main beachside road in Mui Ne. **Luna d'Autuno,** Km 12, 51A Nguyen Dinh Chieu, Ham Tien (© **062/384-7591**), a popular Saigon pizzeria, has a cool restaurant serving excellent Italian food and offering an extensive wine list under a high thatched roof. A couple doors down is **Gecko Mui Ne** (© **062/374-1033**), serving French food and some familiar Western dishes. There's also a **Good Morning Vietnam Restaurant,** Km 11.8, Ham Tien (© **062/384-7585**), a countrywide pizza and pasta franchise that serves good, affordable, familiar meals and will even pick you up at your resort.

The **Hot Rock,** 77A Nguyen Dinh Chieu, across from Bien Xanh Resort (© **062/384-7608**), is a casual watering hole with good, basic Western fare. **Jibe's Beach Bar,** 90 Nguyen Dinh Chieu (© **062/384-7405**), is a lively place with a terrace overlooking the ocean. It's a favorite late-night hangout.

Paradise Beach Club ★ SEAFOOD   Set in a soothing seaside pavilion at the popular Coco Beach Resort (p. 277), the Paradise Beach Club is the place for fine fresh seafood and barbecue. Choose from a raw bar, and have your meal cooked to order. For dessert, they make the most unique sundaes I've ever seen. The resort's more upscale restaurant, **Champa,** is also a great choice, but for dinner only.

At the Coco Beach Resort, 58 Nguyen Dinh Chieu, Ham Tien. © **062/384-7111.** Main courses $2–$18. MC, V. Daily 7am–10pm.

Rung (Forest) ★ ☺   This is one of Mui Ne's most atmospheric restaurants, with a jungle feel begging for kids to explore. Minority crafts are on display among the vines and creepers, and the menu is no less exotic. Of course there's the obligatory seafood section, but there's also the chance to taste unusual dishes such as crocodile, snake, and turtle. If you're having trouble deciding, opt for a combination platter such as a farmer's meal or pottery master's meal (both 130,000 VND). Unique to this restaurant is Vietnamese water music, an ingenious system of levers, pulleys, and bamboo pipes that creates a pleasant background melody. They also often stage performances of traditional music.

67 Nguyen Dinh Chieu St. © **062/384-7589.** www.forestrestaurant.com. Main dishes 60,000 VND–160,000 VND. MC, V. Daily 10am–3pm and 6–11pm.

Attractions

Some 20km (12 miles) northeast of town are **Cape Mui Ne's ★★** sprawling sand dunes, and a trip out this way brings you through lots of quaint seaside villages that are well worth a wander. Coming from Mui Ne Beach, you'll first reach a small fishing town and can explore its fine rural market—great in the early morning. Heading inland away from the beach, you'll first come to the towering **Red Dunes ★★.** A walk to the top offers great views of the town and surrounding countryside, and you're sure to be followed by a gaggle of friendly kids trying to sell you on the idea of renting one of their plastic sleds for the ride down the steep dune slopes. It's kind of fun; pay anywhere between 10,000 VND and 20,000 VND for a few runs. From the Red Dunes, if you have time, the **Silver Lake ★★** is reached after a long, bumpy ride, but the views of the coast are dynamic and this verdant lake among the large, parched silver dune makes the trip worth it. It's a long day, though. Ask at any hotel or resort for tours. Expect to pay $10 per person for two or more to go to the tip of the cape and the Red Dunes, and more to go inland.

At the highest point on the road between Phan Thiet Town and Mui Ne Beach, you won't miss the **Po Shanu Cham Towers,** three impressive spires of crumbling brick. The towers date from the end of the 13th century and are worth a stop if you weren't able to catch any of the Cham sites near Hoi An and Danang. Any taxi will be happy to make a brief stop on the way. The most impressive Cham tower in the country is at **Po Klong Garai,** about halfway between Nha Trang and Mui Ne near Phan Rang, and all hotels and resorts can arrange tours.

Outdoor Activities

The wind conditions in Mui Ne are steady and strong in the dry season (Oct–May), and the beach is becoming a real kite- and windsurfing mecca (it has over-12-knot winds for two-thirds of the year). **Jibe's,** 90 Nguyen Dinh Chieu, Ham Tien, Mui Ne (© 062/384-7405; www.windsurf-vietnam.com), a popular rental shop, windsurfer club, and bar, is a good place rent a board and a great opportunity for first-time kite surfers. A day with an IKO-certified instructor starts at just $85; the focus is on safety, of course, and the savings are significant (similar lessons elsewhere cost a mint).

Sailors will want to contact the folks at the **Mia Resort** (formerly the Mui Ne Sailing Club) 24 Nguyen Dinh Chieu St., Han Tien Ward (© 062/384-7440), or at any hotel or resort about renting Hobie Cat and Laser sailboats, Windsurfers, jet skis, or runabouts.

The outstanding Nick Faldo–designed **Ocean Dunes Golf Course,** 1 Ton Duc Thang St. (© 062/382-3366), is a big draw for both domestic and international players.

HO CHI MINH CITY (SAIGON)

S till known as Saigon to its inhabitants, Ho Chi Minh City is no longer threatened by invading forces, though its main attractions are inevitably related to its war-torn past. These include the War Remnants Museum and the **Reunification Palace,** where the fight to reunify the country was finally won. Besides sightseeing, there's a lot to do in this fast-paced city, from shopping for crafts and textiles to tasting some of the country's finest cuisine.

Things to do   The **War Remnants Museum** remembers the country's past conflicts with displays of weapons and photos that are poignant if grim. Many enjoy a visit to the atmospheric **Jade Emperor Pagoda,** with its incense and intricately carved figures, though **Quan Am** and **Thien Hau Temples** in Cholon are equally eye-catching. If you dare, get around by cyclo, a uniquely Vietnamese form of transport.

Shopping   Racks of rainbow-colored silks fill stalls at the **Ben Thanh Market,** the city's biggest market, along with bamboo coasters, souvenir t-shirts, conical hats, and hordes of visitors. Secure your wallet and browse, then make your way along less-crowded **Le Loi Street,** which sells many of the same goods. For hipper shopping, the boutiques of **Dong Khoi Street** sell trendy clothing, original art, and jewelry.

Restaurants & Dining   Good food in Ho Chi Minh City does not have to cost a lot; you can feast on rice and vegetable dishes, noodle bowls, and *che,* a local dessert, at open-air restaurants surrounding **Ben Tanh Market** for next to nothing. For an authentic Vietnamese dinner, head to **Quan An Ngon Restaurant,** where various cooking stations prepare dishes from around the country.

Nightlife & Entertainment   There's no shortage of stylish spots to hang out after dark, including the iconic **Saigon Saigon** rooftop bar at the Caravelle Hotel. Plenty of places feature live music, such as **Seventeen Saloon** and **La Habana.** Over in the budget district, **Go2 Bar** attracts everyone from backpackers to business travelers because it serves alcohol 24 hours a day.

ORIENTATION
Getting There & Away

BY PLANE   Most regional airlines connect with Ho Chi Minh City, including Malaysian Airlines, Thai Airways, Bangkok Airways, Singapore

A veteran's TRIP BACK

Our flight from Honolulu to Vietnam in July 2002 was an hour late. After take-off, I smiled to myself because it took 30 years to return to my adopted second home—late indeed. From May 1967 until March 1972, I was flying into Vietnam or Thailand on support missions, or serving one of three combat tours in Vietnam, Laos, or Thailand. The culture, the food, the language, and the people became part of my heart and soul. Vietnam got a bad rap, in my opinion, in the American psyche from the dark messages of *Apocalypse Now* and *Deer Hunter*. My experiences were quite different; I remembered a beautiful country and great loving people.

On the long flight, I read a book my sister had given me titled *Soul Retrieval,* by Sandra Ingerman. From it, I realized the source of my longing. Part of me was still there, and I felt incomplete. The mission we were sent to complete had no ending—no welcome home. The war had been waged in my head day after day ever since I left.

When I landed at Tan Son Nhat Airport (the name was never changed!) in Saigon, the years were bridged in minutes. All of our old aircraft revetments and bunkers were still there, and the landmarks had not changed. My heart

was pounding with excitement. Ahhh, the hot, humid air hit my face as soon as the door opened, a familiar aroma filled my nostrils, and the high-pitched voices of intense Vietnamese conversation told me I was home. Why had I waited so long? What was I afraid of? The first stop was passport control, facing uniforms of my former enemy, red star and all. What if they kept an "Enemies List"? They could whisk me off and nobody would ever know. The man processing my visa did not react to my Vietnamese greeting, and he seemed to take a long time. I later realized there was simply a lot of information to enter into his computer. My bags were waiting in the baggage claim, Customs waved me through, and 15 minutes after we landed, I was inside the country, free to find my way. There was a crowd of Vietnamese waiting for arriving passengers. As I wheeled my cart down the gauntlet of people, I stopped and raised my arms Rocky style and shouted "Vietnam, Vietnam!" Six young men saw me and thought it was the funniest thing they had ever seen and mimicked me. We exchanged smiles and hearty laughs.

The logistics of getting downtown were painless. There was a choice of a van for $10 or a metered taxi for about

Airlines, Lao Aviation, Garuda Indonesia, Philippine Airlines, United, and Cathay Pacific (from Hong Kong). Vietnam Airlines usually has the best fare, thanks to government controls. If you're flying to Vietnam directly from North America, check with United flights or with Cathay Pacific for good fares and itineraries. Domestically, Saigon is linked by Vietnam Airlines with most major cities in the country.

At the airport in Saigon, you can change foreign currency for VND, but taxi drivers to town don't mind payment in U.S. dollars. Arranging a hotel limousine to greet you will certainly make life a bit easier, but taxis are aplenty outside the arrivals hall. You can also book a taxi at the airport taxi booth just beyond the baggage claim area; the trip to town is around 180,000 VND for a regular taxi or 200,000 VND for an SUV/van taxi. You can contact the **airport lost and found** at © **08/3844-6665,** ext. 7461.

In town, the **Vietnam Airlines office** is on the 16th floor of Sun Wah Tower, 115 Nguyen Hue, District 1 (© **08/3824-4482**), or call its reservations office, which is at 49 Truong Son St., Tan Binh District (© **08/3832-0320**). Just about everyone in

$5. Armed with Vietnamese dong, I chose the taxi and was soon at the Palace Hotel. All of the major accommodations are in the District 1 area. I found a minihotel much more suited to my taste—cozy, friendly, and away from the hustle and bustle, plus one-third of the cost. I hired a van to drive me to the places where I had flown and lived. I went to Long Xuyen, in the Mekong Delta, where I had spent a year. In a stroke of luck, as I was showing 30-year-old photos of my former residence, "Marie House," to people in the old neighborhood, one 70-year-old man exclaimed, "That was my mother-in-law's house until 1975! It's right over here." The front yard where we parked our jeeps was now a pharmacy and our beloved house was a government insurance building. It broke my heart. It wasn't my house anymore, it wasn't anybody's house, but I would never have found it without the gracious help of this gray-haired gentleman half my height. He ran into his nearby house to put on long pants for the photo I took of the two of us, and he hugged me like a son.

After my nostalgic trip through the delta, I went to Dalat, in the hill country. It took about 5 enjoyable hours on the road. A lake in the center of town was the crown jewel of a beautiful Shangri-La. I made friends with the family that owned my favorite Internet cafe. They brought me as the guest of honor to their house for lunch. It was a great time, with lots of laughs, 10 scrumptious dishes, and family love from all 22 family members. Suddenly it hit me: The war is over, and I'm no longer the enemy. We're fellow earth travelers with a common bond.

It was a spiritual journey for me, and much healing took place. My tours in Southeast Asia were the centerpiece of my 28-year career in the United States Air Force, and now Asia has again become part of my life. I have been back four more times to Vietnam, four times to Laos, and 10 to Thailand, which I use as my home base. I'm a different person for having made the trip. It allowed me to recapture my soul and end my war.

—by Mike Cavanaugh

The author of this story retired from the U.S. Air Force as a full colonel and has resided in Honolulu for more than 20 years. He now splits his time among Hawaii, Thailand, Laos, and Vietnam. Mike also served as the air attaché to Afghanistan from 1978 to 1979. He holds the Silver Star and 50 other combat decorations. Half of his 4,000 flying hours were in combat.

town, from the many traveler cafes to hotel front-desk staff or concierge, can book your onward domestic flights on Vietnam Airlines.

To get to town from the **Tan Son Nhat** airport, taxis wait in front of the arrivals area. If you didn't book a taxi at the taxi booth (see above), stick with established companies (see "Scam Alert," below). The ride to most locations in District 1 should cost about 150,000 VND. A fixed price may be negotiated, but going by the fare meter may avoid arguments on added charges at the end of the ride. To get to the airport from town, contact any hotel front desk and agree on a fixed price or use of the meter. Departure taxes are included in the price of air tickets. Below is the contact information for major airlines in Ho Chi Minh City: **Air France,** 130 Dong Khoi, District 1 (© 08/3829-0981); **Asiana Airlines,** 39 Le Duan, District 1 (© 08/3822-2622); **Austrian Airlines,** 11 Dong Khoi, District 1 (© 08/3829-5832); **British Airways,** 170–172 Nam Ky Khoi Nghia, District 1 (© 08/3930-2933); **Cathay Pacific Airways,** 5/F 72 Nguyen Thi Minh Khai, District 3

> ## ⚠ Scam Alert
>
> If you go with a taxi driver, even a metered one, from the airport in Saigon, watch out for the hotel bait-and-switch scam. Drivers get commissions for leading tourists to one hotel or another, and they commonly insist that the hotel you're going to is full, has closed, or has some other problem. The driver will pull a dour face and even sound pretty convincing as he tries to take you to his friend's hotel. Sit tight until you're at your intended destination. It might help for you to have the address clearly written to show the driver. *Important:* Go with established companies when going by metered taxi (choose white Vinasun Taxi, red and white Saigon Tourist Taxi, or white and green Mai Linh Taxi), as many small operators have rigged meters.

(✆ 08/3822-3203); **China Airlines,** 37 Ton Duc Thang, District 1 (✆ 08/3911-1591); **China Southern Airlines,** 21–23 Nguyen Thi Minh Khai, District 1 (✆ 08/3823-5588); **Eva Air,** 2A–4A Ton Duc Thang, District 1 (✆ 08/3822-4488); **KLM Royal Dutch Airlines,** 130 Dong Khoi St., District 1 (✆ 08/3823-1990); **Korean Airlines,** 34 Le Duan, District 1 (✆ 08/3824-2878); **Lufthansa,** 14/F 19–25 Nguyen Hue, District 1 (✆ 08/3829-8529); **Malaysia Airlines,** 37 Ton Duc Thang, District 1 (✆ 08/3829-2529); **Qantas,** 5/F Saigon Centre Building, 65 Le Loi St., District 1 (✆ 08/3823-8844); **Singapore Airlines,** Saigon Tower Building, 29 Le Duan, District 1 (✆ 08/3823-1588); **Thai Airways,** 29 Le Duan, District 1 (✆ 08/3829-2810); **United Airlines,** 7/F 115 Nguyen Hue, District 1 (✆ 08/3823-4755); and **Vietnam Airlines,** 115 Nguyen Hue, District 1 (✆ 08/3824-4482).

BY BUS/MINIVAN   Saigon is the hub of transport in the south, and all bus lines pass through here. Saigon is the terminus of the "Open Tour" ticket for budget bus tours, and Saigon's many **traveler cafes** that line the streets of the Pham Ngu Lao budget travel area are your best bet for cheap and convenient onward travel by road, whether by air-conditioned bus or minivan. See the tour information below for listings.

Tourist buses also connect Saigon by road via the Moc Bai **border crossing** with nearby **Cambodia.** The all-day ride to Phnom Penh leaves daily in either a minibus or a large air-conditioned coach from the De Tham–area tourist cafes (see "Visitor Information & Tours," below). From Cambodia to Saigon, contact the likes of Capitol Tours (www.capitoltourscambodia.com) in Phnom Penh (or any other budget tour office).

Local buses, as anywhere in Vietnam, are a bit harrowing, but Saigon's bus stations are quite well organized and offer myriad routes out from this central hub. See chapter 15 for more information about local buses. Also be sure to leave from the correct bus station (there are three) for your destination.

Mien Dong Bus Station (292 Dinh Bo Linh Rd., Binh Thanh District; www.vexe24h.com) has services to the north of Vietnam, including to the Central Highlands and Phan Thiet. **Mien Tay Bus Station** (395 Kinh Duong Vuong Rd., Binh Tan District; ✆ **08/3877-6594**) serves the Mekong Delta to the south. **Cholon Bus Station** (86 Trang Tu Rd., District 5) connects with nearby towns in the Mekong Delta, as well as west toward Cambodia and the town of Tay Ninh.

BY CAR   The most comfortable and convenient way of getting around is to hire a car and driver. Contact any hotel front desk for arrangements. Many of Saigon's hotels are run by the massive government-run Saigontourist, and they offer lots of affordable in-town and regional tour options by private car (see their listing in "Visitor Information & Tours," below).

BY TRAIN Saigon is the southern terminus of the Reunification Express, Vietnam's north-south rail connection. **Ga Saigon,** or the Saigon station, is in District 3 at 1 Nguyen Thong St. Bookings can be made at the convenient **Saigon Railway Tourist Service Co.,** in the backpacker area at 275C Pham Ngu Lao St. (© 08/3836-7640). The office is open from 8am to 6pm, and they're a pretty surly bunch, but you should find English-speakers in the group. Most popular from Saigon is Nha Trang (about 6½ hr.; 464,000 VND), Danang (15½ hr.; 978,000 VND), Hue (18 hr.; 1,057,000 VND), or all the way to Hanoi (30 hr.; 1,578,000 VND). Prices above are for the fastest trains and comfortable, air-conditioned sleeper berths; budget options are the hard-berth sleepers with six to a car or the masochistic hard seat. Vietnamese trains are quite efficient and a good way to meet locals.

BY BOAT Check out the diverse options between **Chau Doc** in the Mekong Delta and **Phnom Penh.** One option is the weeklong cruise between Saigon (transfer to embark at My Tho) and Siem Reap aboard one of the luxury, shallow-draft **Pandaw Cruise Boats** (www.pandaw.com). Twin shared rooms on the vessel start at $2,258.

Getting Around

BY TAXI Taxis are clustered around the bigger hotels and restaurants. They cost about 12,000 VND at flag fall and 8,000 VND or so for every kilometer thereafter. Call **Mai Linh Taxi** (© 08/3838-3838), **Vina Taxi** (© 08/3815-5145), or **Vinasun** (© 08/3827-2727). Stick with the larger companies listed here, as others (many with copycat names) are famous for doctoring the meter.

BY CAR You can simplify your sightseeing efforts if you hire a car and driver for the day. Contact Ann Tours, Saigontourist, or any hotel concierge. Expect to pay about $95 for a day's rental with driver.

BY MOTORCYCLE TAXI If you can't beat 'em, join 'em. Saigon's crazy motorbike traffic is maddening in a car, which feels something like an elephant in a forest of buzzing mosquitoes, so a motorbike is a great way to weave through the chaos—a short distance is 10,000 VND for the savvy haggler (usually closer to 15,000 VND), while hourly booking can be in the ballpark of $2 to $3 per hour. A bit hair-raising sometimes, but it is a good way to get around. Make sure you wear a helmet (all motorbike taxi riders carry a spare), which is required by law, and a face mask is a good idea, too. Keep your knees in, and keep your bag tucked in front of you, not hanging off your shoulder where it can easily be snatched. You'll come back with some good stories for friends back home.

BY CYCLO Cyclos are available for an hourly rental of about 50,000 VND, but there are some things to consider; some areas are out of bounds to cyclos, there may be language problems, and riding in a slow, open conveyance amid thousands of motorbikes and cars may not be pleasant. A short jaunt around the Dong Khoi area or for hops between some of the city sights is memorable, but all-day cyclo tours are not recommended.

BY BICYCLE & MOTORBIKE Saigon traffic is chaotic, with the right of way generally by assertion, cutting across your path and from any direction, even head-on against traffic or beating lights, so you need to be brave to join the throng. Most hotel front desks can arrange rental at an inflated fee, or try the many little storefronts on Pham Ngu Lao near the intersection with De Tham. A day's bike rental starts at $1 and motorbikes from $6. Wear a helmet and drive slowly, taking your cue from the herd.

SAIGON'S DISTRICTS

Metropolitan Ho Chi Minh City is divided into 24 administrative districts, numbered 1 through 12 and another dozen named, including Tan Binh, Bin Thanh, Phu Nhuan, Thu Duc, Go Vap, Binh Tan, and Tan Phu. Be sure to know the name or number of the district you need when looking for an address, and try to group your travels accordingly (you don't want to try to crisscross too many districts in 1 day). Most of the hotels, bars, shops, and restaurants are in **District 1,** parts of which are easily covered on foot—though you'll want to hop a motorbike taxi or cab to cross the length of a district. District 1 is home to the central **Ben Thanh Market** and includes the city's most busy commercial area, **Dong Khoi,** as well as the **backpacker district** of **Pham Ngu Lao.** District 1 is flanked to the east and south by the Saigon River, which is where Dong Khoi Street terminates and marks the boundary of the most developed part of the city. Saigon's sightseeing attractions are spread among districts 1, 3, and 5 (Cholon). **District 3** is just north and west of the central Dong Khoi area and is home to many foreign business offices and embassies. **District 5** is a fair ride west of the town center and supports the city's large ethnic Chinese population, a number of older temples, and a market area.

Visitor Information & Tours

Every major tourist agency has its headquarters or a branch in Saigon. Some arrange cheap tours for all comers while others specialize in custom itineraries for private groups or individuals countrywide, such as Ann Tours, Exotissimo, Grandeur Journeys, and Sinh Balo. Be wary of small agents who front a desk or counter to sell tours for a cut. They merely pass you on to the operator and will refuse any responsibility if anything goes wrong.

- **Ann Tours,** 58 Ton That Tung St., District 1 (© **08/3925-3636;** fax 08/3832-3866; www.anntours.com), has a great reputation that's well deserved. Ann's specializes in custom tours for individuals or small groups. They can be relatively expensive, but that's in comparison to the seat-in-coach cattle-drive tours. These guys will help you do virtually anything you want to in Vietnam. Ask for director Tony Nong.

- **Exotissimo,** 80–82 Phan Xich Long St., Phu Nhuan District (© **08/3995-9898;** fax 08/3995-9184/5; www.exotissimo.com), can arrange just about any tour in Vietnam and neighboring countries. They are a very professional outfit, and their guides are knowledgeable and speak excellent English. Like Ann Tours, they are on the pricey side, but I highly recommend Exotissimo for their attentive and thorough tours.

- **Grandeur Journeys,** 225 Hai Ba Trung St., District 3 (© **08/3820-0257;** www.grandeurjourneys.com), specializes in tailored, private tours throughout Vietnam, Cambodia, Laos, and Myanmar. They offer good value for the money, and their guides pay attention to detail. If you are looking for special interest options, such as wildlife, photography, or adventure tours, ask for Sarah Nguyen or John Wong.

- **Saigontourist,** 45 Le Thanh Ton St., District 1 (© **08/3827-9279;** fax 08/3822-4987; www.etravelvietnam.com), is a large government-run group, but it'll get you where you want to go and is a far better choice than the budget cafes (see below). Full-day city tours cost from $44, while a seat in a coach to Cu Chi (half-day) is $25.

- **SinhBalo Adventure Tours:** "Sinh balo" means "Sinh the Backpacker," so-called after the company founder and budget-tour pioneer Le Van Sinh, who also gave his name to the very popular (and much copied) cafe tour company for budget tourists (see "Budget Tourist Cafes," below). In 1995, Sinh started this more high-end tour company and has attracted quite a large following. Sinh Balo runs great cycling and motorbiking tours as well as a host of eco-tour itineraries. Their offices are at 283/20 Pham Ngu Lao, District 1 (℃ **08/3837-6766;** fax 08/3836-7682; http://sinhbalo.com).

- **Vietnam Vespa Adventure,** 169A De Tham St., District 1, inside Café Zoom (℃ **09/0240-3055;** www.vietnamvespaadventures.com), runs 4- to 7-day trips to Mui Ne or Nha Trang aboard beautifully restored vintage Vespas. The easy-to-handle scooters, spectacular views, and owner Steven and manager Patrick come together to create an unforgettable experience. They also do 1-day city tours of Ho Chi Minh City.

BUDGET TOURIST CAFES

Saigon's budget tourist cafes, with their many options for affordable seat-in-coach tours in the south and "open tour" bus tickets that run you along the length of Vietnam, are many and all quite similar in the Pham Ngu Lao backpacker area. Sometimes you book with one and go with another tour company. In spite of the slogan "Same, same but different," similar prices and services are the rule. Sinh Tourist (below) is the popular choice, but there are others that offer much the same, including **TNK,** 216 De Tham St. (℃ **08/3920-4766;** www.tnktravelvietnam.com).

Sinh Tourist, 246–248 De Tham, District 1 (℃ **08/3838-9597;** www.thesinhtourist.vn), with an office at 24–26 Pho Duc Chinh St. (℃ **08/3822-2892**), is a good choice for inexpensive trips and tours. On paper, the tours seem exactly the same as others offered at private tour agents. They have computerized air booking and are quite efficient, if usually overrun with the heavy volume of Western tourists.

[FastFACTS] HO CHI MINH CITY

Banks & Currency Exchange As elsewhere in Vietnam, you can change money in banks and hotels. Money changers with shopfront counters in District 1 usually offer better rates. The exchange rate in Saigon is better than in many smaller cities.

Major banks in Saigon include **ANZ Bank,** 2 Ngo Duc Ke St., District 1 (℃ **08/3829-9319**); **Citibank,** 115 Nguyen Hue St. (℃ **08/3824-2118**); **HSBC,** 235 Dong Khoi St., District 1 (℃ **08/3829-2288**); and **Vietcombank,** 29 Ben Chuong Duong, District 1 (℃ **08/3829-7245**). All offer international ATM services.

A good money changer is at 203 De Tham St. (℃ **08/3837-9891**).

Western Union has a number of locations throughout the city. Their main office is at 11/F Saigon Center, 65 Le Loi St., District 1 (℃ **08/3821-0388**).

Dentists International SOS (see "Hospitals & International Clinics," below) has a dental clinic. Try **Westcoast International Dental Clinic,** 27 Nguyen Trung Truc St., District 1 (℃ **08/3825-7999;** www.westcoastinternational.com).

Doctors See "Hospitals & International Clinics," below.

Drugstores Vietnamese drugstores are on every street corner, and they're more or less the "prescribe it yourself" kind, whether you need antibiotics or stomach medicines.

Embassies & Consulates For embassies, see "Fast Facts: Hanoi," in chapter 5. Ho Chi Minh's consulates are all in District 1, as follows: **United States,** 4 Le Duan St. (𝄞 08/3822-9433); **Canada,** 235 Dong Khoi St. (𝄞 08/3827-9899); **Australia,** 5B Ton Duc Thang St. (𝄞 08/3521-8100); **New Zealand,** 8/F 235 Dong Khoi St. (𝄞 08/3822-6907); and **United Kingdom,** 25 Le Duan St. (𝄞 08/3825-1380).

Emergencies For **police,** dial 𝄞 **113;** for **fire,** dial 𝄞 **114;** and for an **ambulance,** dial 𝄞 **115.** Have a translator on hand, if necessary; operators don't speak English, and for any major situation you will want to contact your country's embassy or consulate. For **medical emergencies,** contact one of the clinics listed under "Hospitals & International Clinics," below. For **international calls,** dial the prefix (𝄞 **00**) followed by the country code and phone number.

Hospitals & International Clinics Saigon's large expatriate community gets sick, and when they do, they need doctoring, which means good emergency clinics are available.

Any of the clinics listed below act as a general triage for emergencies and can help coordinate evacuation. They're staffed with both foreign and Vietnamese specialists.

International SOS is at 65 Nguyen Du St., District 1. Open 24 hours all week (𝄞 **08/3823-6520**); emergencies 𝄞 **08/3829-8520.**

The **Family Medical Practice** is at the Diamond Plaza, 34 Le Duan, District 1 (𝄞 **08/3822-7848** or 09/1323-4911).

The **International Medical Center** (1 Han Thuyen, District 1; 𝄞 **08/3827-2367,** or 08/3827-2366 after office hours) offers services similar to what you'll find at International SOS.

Internet Almost every hotel provides Internet services in Saigon, usually for free though, strangely, top-end hotels often charge around $15 a day for the privilege. If you have a laptop, many cafes in the city provide free wireless services to go with your coffee. In the backpacker area, try Highlands Coffee at the T-junction of Pham Ngu Lao and De Tham or Sozo Café at 176 Bui Vien St. If not, Internet cafes in the area charge around 6,000 VND per hour.

Maps The **Tourist Information Center,** 92–96 Nguyen Hue St., District 1 (𝄞 **08/3825-0615;** fax 08/3825-1358), has free detailed city maps.

Post Office The main post office is at 2 Cong Xa Paris, District 1

(𝄞 **08/3827-1149**), across from Notre Dame cathedral. It's open daily from 7:30am to 8pm. Postal service is also available in most hotels and at various locations throughout the city.

Safety The biggest threat to your safety in Saigon is likely to be the traffic. With rarely a break in its flow, when you cross the road, step out at a slow, predictable pace with your eyes to the oncoming traffic and lifting your hand up high helps. The onus is on the motorized hordes to weave around you, so don't panic or stop suddenly.

Pickpocketing is a big problem in Saigon, especially motorbike drive-bys, with someone grabbing or slashing the shoulder strap and driving off. Keep your bag and camera close and away from traffic. Hang on to your wallet, and don't wear flashy jewelry. Be especially wary in crowded places. Women should avoid wandering around alone in the evenings past 11pm. Contact your consulate or your hotel if you have a serious problem. If you insist on going to the local police, bring a translator. But know that the Saigon police tend to throw up their hands at "minor" infractions such as purse snatching or thievery.

Telephone The city code for Saigon is 8. When dialing within Vietnam, the city code should be preceded by the 0 as indicated in the numbers listed in this guide; note that the 0 should be omitted when dialing from overseas.

Toilets There are hardly any public toilets except at bus stations or shopping

malls. Seek out hotels, restaurants, department stores, or public buildings.

WHERE TO STAY

Saigon presents the best variety of hotels in Vietnam, from deluxe business and family hotels to spotless minihotels and cozy guesthouses down busy back alleys. Most hotels are clustered around Nguyen Hue Street and Dong Khoi in District 1, as are the city's best restaurants, shops, and bars.

If you're traveling on a tight budget, head for the Pham Ngu Lao area, the center of which is the intersection of Pham Ngu Lao and De Tham streets, a backpacker haven loaded with guesthouses and minihotels down little rabbit-warren alleys. Here, a fan-cooled room with a cold-water shower goes for as little as $7 per night, or an air-conditioned room with hot water for around $15. Most of these places are basic (and a bit noisy from street traffic), but tidy, well run, and friendly. The area is convenient to the city's many budget travel services and has lots of bars, restaurants with Western or Vietnamese food, and cafes.

Remember that prices listed are rack rates but may rise during holidays, and some hotels base their rates on occupancy. Group bookings, long stays, and promotions in the off season (Mar–Sept) may be a bargain. If you intend to pay in VND, ask for equivalent if quoted in U.S. dollars and check the VAT.

VERY EXPENSIVE

Caravelle Hotel ★★★   Built by the French in 1956 overlooking the Place Garnier, now Lam Son Square, the Caravelle was a wartime hangout for journalists. A joke goes that a bomb targeted at correspondents in 1964 wasn't dropped close enough to the bar. When Saigon fell, a NVA tank aimed at the facade but didn't fire. Renamed the Doc Lap (Independence) Hotel, it lapsed into obscurity before it was revived, and is now an extremely well-appointed and efficient place.

Rooms in the new wing are large and plush with great views higher up. The free Wi-Fi is a great deal, because you have to pay in many other five-star hotels. Its classic character lives on in the old-wing rooftop Saigon Saigon bar, with shuttered windows, checkered floors, and an open terrace for a grand view of the city by sunset. If you let your imagination go, you might just see Graham Greene sidling up to the bar.

19 Lam Son Sq., District 1. www.caravellehotel.com. ✆ **08/3823-4999.** Fax 08/3824-3999. 335 units. $280–$330 deluxe double; $380–$400 signature doubles (with separate check-in and private lounge). DC, MC, V. **Amenities:** 2 restaurants; 3 bars; gaming club; gym; 24-hr. health club; pool; sauna; spa; rooms for those w/limited mobility. *In room:* A/C, satellite TV, fax, fridge, hair dryer, minibar, Wi-Fi.

Grand Hotel ★★   This 1930s colonial, owned by Saigontourist and undergoing a massive expansion at the time of this update (watch out for construction noise!) evokes the era of *Indochine française* with some choice features, such as the lovingly restored iron elevator and colonial decor in the rooms of the original wing. Deluxe rooms in the old building exude a serene, comfortable charm with classic high ceilings, rich wood floors, and marble bathrooms. Amenities are plentiful, with Wi-Fi and 24-hour room service. The central courtyard pool with a bar, overlooked from the balustrade walkway, is a peaceful oasis right in the thick of downtown Saigon. Whether the hotel can retain its refined aura when it adds more than 200 rooms in 2012, however, remains to be seen.

Ho Chi Minh City (Saigon)

HOTELS ■

A & Em V **22**
Asian Ruby **20**
Beautiful Saigon 2 **56**
Bong Sen Hotel **61**
Bong Sen Hotel Annex **62**
Caravelle Hotel **37**
Catina Saigon Hotel **39**
Duxton Hotel Saigon **45**
Empress Hotel **1**
Grand Hotel **59**
Hotel Continental **27**
Hotel Equatorial **3**
Hotel Majestic **44**
Huong Sen Hotel **59**
Indochine **32**
Kim Do Royal City Hotel **39**
Legend Hotel Saigon **29**
Liberty 3 **53**
Liberty 4 **55**
Madam Cuc **57**
May Hotel **20**
Medal Hotel Chuong
  Hoang Yen **24**
Movenpick Hotel Saigon **4**
New World Hotel Saigon **52**
Norfolk Hotel **33**
Orient Hotel **53**
Palace Hotel **42**
Park Hyatt Saigon **28**
Renaissance Riverside
  Hotel Saigon **43**
Rex Hotel **35**
Riverside Hotel **43**
Sheraton Saigon **37**
Sofitel Plaza Saigon **11**
Spring Hotel (Mua Xuan) **19**
Tan Hai Long Hotel & Spa **51**
Windsor Plaza Hotel **3**

RESTAURANTS ◆

Allez Boo **54**
Augustin **36**
Blue Ginger **49**
Camargue **58**
Lemongrass **36**
L'Olivier **11**
Mandarin **21**
Ngoc Suong **2**
Ocean Palace **8**
Opera **29**
Orientica **3**
Pomodoro **38**
Quan An Ngon Restaurant **18**

The Refinery **23**
Sandals **38**
Skewers **60**
Square One **29**
Sushi Bar **15**
Tandoor **23**
Temple Club **48**
Vietnam House **39**
Warda **41**
Wrap and Roll **31**
Xu **38**
ZanZBar **40**

ATTRACTIONS ●

Ben Thanh Market **50**
Bitexco Financial Tower **46**
Botanical Gardens and Zoo **10**
City Hall and Nguyen
  Hue Plaza **26**
General Post Office
  (Buu Dien) **14**
Giac Lam Pagoda **3**
Golden Dragon Water
  Puppet Show **16**
History Museum **9**
The Hoa Binh Noodle Shop **5**
Ho Chi Minh City Museum **25**
Ho Chi Minh Museum **47**
Jade Emperor Pagoda **6**
Notre Dame Cathedral **13**
Reunification Palace **17**
Saigon Opera House (Ho Chi
  Minh Municipal Theater) **30**
Vinh Nghiem Pagoda **5**
War Remnants Museum **12**

8 Dong Khoi St., District 1. www.grandhotel.vn. ☎ **08/3823-0163.** Fax 08/3827-3047. 233 units. $209–$239 double; $259–$419 suite. AE, MC, V. **Amenities:** 2 restaurants; poolside bar; small health club; Jacuzzi; outdoor pool; room service; steam room. *In room:* A/C, satellite TV, fridge, minibar, Wi-Fi.

Hotel Majestic ★   This 1925 landmark on the picturesque, riverside corner of Dong Khoi Street (formerly Catinat) retains its picture-postcard colonial charm with its colonnaded lobby, arched stained-glass windows, chandeliers, and Roman statues. Rooms are classy and comfortable with high ceilings, retro fixtures, tubs in the large bathrooms, and Jacuzzis in the suites. The small central courtyard pool is ringed by French doors and balcony walkways; the best choices are the rooms facing this quiet spot. Suites are larger versions of the deluxe rooms, while standards are small and basic. The staff is the friendliest I've ever met at a Saigontourist-owned hotel. Don't miss the great views from the rooftop Sky-Bar, a good spot to have a chat, and popular for weddings and parties.

1 Dong Khoi St., District 1. www.majesticsaigon.com.vn. ☎ **08/3829-5517.** Fax 08/3822-9744. 175 units. $198 double; $268 suite. AE, DC, MC, V. **Amenities:** 3 restaurants; 2 bars; babysitting; fitness center; small courtyard pool; sauna. *In room:* A/C, satellite TV, minibar, Wi-Fi.

Legend Hotel Saigon ★   This sprawling 17-floor Japanese joint venture along the Saigon River is one step down from the town's best. Rooms are spacious and comfortable with a neat, modern look and cool pastel colors. Bathrooms are stylish, with black granite counters and black-wood trim. Views of the city and river are "legend," especially from higher floors—far enough from the downtown clutter to offer clear views, but close enough for convenient access to the many shops and restaurants on Dong Khoi. The overall scale is large, from a double-height colonnaded lobby, all glass and marble with faux-stained-glass ceiling and large, bronze prancing horses, to the sunken dining area and nice circular pool out back. Everything is clean and neat at this fine downtown standard.

2A–4A Ton Duc Thang St., District 1. www.legendsaigon.com. ☎ **08/3823-3333.** Fax 08/3823-2333. 283 units. $185–$235 double; $425 suite. AE, MC, V. **Amenities:** 3 restaurants; 1 bistro/bar; gym; health club; Jacuzzi; midsize outdoor pool; room service. *In room:* A/C, satellite TV, fridge, hair dryer, minibar, Wi-Fi.

Mövenpick Saigon Hotel ★   Swiss hotelier Mövenpick took over management in 2010 and renovated this former CIA and U.S. Army quarters with an eclectic design with dash of the Orient. Rooms are more spacious the higher up the hierarchy, from Deluxe to Grand Executive Suite, but a flatscreen TV, minibar, safe, and Wi-Fi are standard throughout. The whole affair is rounded out with glass-paneled bathrooms, magnifying mirrors and showers that rain down from ceiling outlets. The drawback is that it is far from the center; 10 minutes from the airport and 15 minutes from downtown. That's okay if you don't want to stay in a tourist area, want somewhere near the airport for an early flight, or enjoy Swiss finesse in cuisine and service.

253 Nguyen Van Troi St., Phu Nhuan (District 3). www.moevenpick-hotels.com. ☎ **08/3844-9222.** Fax 08/3844-9198. 278 units. $200 double; $280–$430 suite. Rates include breakfast. AE, DC, MC, V. **Amenities:** 3 restaurants; 2 bars; babysitting; health club; Jacuzzi; outdoor patio pool; room service; spa. *In room:* A/C, LCD TV, fridge, hair dryer, minibar, Wi-Fi.

New World Hotel Saigon ★★   President Clinton called this first-rate hotel home during his brief stay in Saigon, and British footballer David Beckham also stayed in this huge downtown hotel, a short walk from Ben Thanh Market. The impeccable, plush rooms are done in a soothing array of neutrals, and the bathrooms are a sharp contrast in black-and-gray marble. One-bedroom suites come at a great discount and, with all the extra space and good views, are worth the upgrade. The four executive floors, with an executive lounge, have an impressive list of benefits. If convenience is your game, it's well worth the bump up from a standard double. The staff snaps to it, and service is super efficient. The lounge features live music seasonally and the Dynasty Chinese restaurant's dim sum and roasted duck are about the best I have tasted in Saigon.

76 Le Lai St., District 1. www.saigon.newworldhotels.com. © 08/3822-8888. Fax 08/3823-0710. 533 units. $160–$250 double; $290–$1,600 suite. AE, DC, MC, V. **Amenities:** 2 restaurants; bar; babysitting; concierge; executive/clubrooms; health club; outdoor pool; room service; sauna; smoke-free rooms; spa; tennis court. *In room:* A/C, satellite TV, fridge, Internet, minibar.

Park Hyatt Saigon ★★ From the graceful *ao dai* of reception staff to the toiletries in the bathroom, the Park Hyatt is sleek and sophisticated. Its modernity is set off with touches of Vietnamese and colonial elements; original paintings in the lobby and hallways, and black-and-white photographs of old Saigon in the bedrooms. The rooms come with two-poster beds (mattresses are luxuriously thick), inlaid rugs over the wooden floor, large windows with folding shutters, and ceiling fans. Executive suites include living and dining rooms and kitchenette with a full dining set. The lounge is especially atmospheric with leather armchairs and sofas, the light filtering through wood-framed, vented panels up to ceiling height, a fabulous place to relax with a drink after a hectic day in Saigon.

2 Lam Son Square, District 1. www.saigon.park.hyatt.com. © 08/3824-1234. Fax 08/3823-7569. 244 units. $290–$450 double; $620–$750 suite. AE, MC, V. **Amenities:** 2 restaurants; bar; concierge; health club; Jacuzzi; outdoor pool; room service; spa. *In room:* A/C, satellite TV, fridge, minibar, Wi-Fi.

Renaissance Riverside Hotel Saigon ★ Managed by Marriott, the Renaissance Riverside has great views of the Saigon River from most rooms and the rooftop pool. The lobby's small domed ceiling and spiral stairway is reminiscent of colonial times. Rooms are cream with pastel hued carpeting. Broad glass panels offer unhindered views and give the rooms a light, spacious feel. Beds are comfortable with fluffy pillows, thick mattresses, and cotton sheets. If you are afraid of heights, note that an indoor vaulted atrium runs from the fifth floor to the skylight, and if you're staying on the higher floors, you may have a slight feeling of vertigo.

8-15 Ton Duc Thang St., District 1. www.renaissancehotels.com/sgnbr. © 08/3822-0033. Fax 08/3823-5666. 336 units. $120–$225 double; $375 suite. AE, MC, V. **Amenities:** 2 restaurants; 2 lounges; gym; 7 meeting rooms; rooftop pool; smoke-free floor; spa. *In room:* A/C, satellite TV, fridge, Internet, minibar.

Sheraton Saigon ★★ An excellent hotel in the downtown center with everything on a grand scale. Rooms are stylishly cozy with a late-'70s feel. From the moment your car pulls up front, you'll be given the quality treatment. Executive perks include a separate check-in area, lounge, and meticulous business services. Level 23 (p. 322)—a double-height rotunda space that hosts live bands—is a popular nightspot.

88 Dong Khoi St., District 1. www.sheraton.com/saigon. © 08/3827-2828. Fax 08/3827-2929. 470 units. $200–$400 double; from $500 suite. AE, MC, V. **Amenities:** 3 restaurants; 3 bars; 2 lounges babysitting; concierge; health club; Jacuzzi; outdoor pool; room service; sauna; spa; tennis court. *In room:* A/C, satellite TV, fridge, hair dryer, Internet, minibar.

Sofitel Saigon Plaza ★★ The Sofitel Saigon is the epitome of modern luxury, convenience, and comfort in the heart of the downtown business center. You won't lack any amenities, and the staff is attentive and professional. Rooms are refined, unpretentiously furnished, and bright with harmonized colors and views toward the Saigon River or city. A popular choice for the international business travelers and long-stay executives who enjoy the perks: private lounge, daily buffet, business services, and free in-room Wi-Fi. The hotel is in a relatively quiet spot and only a short walk to historical landmarks such as Saigon's Notre Dame cathedral, the colonial post office, and the Reunification Palace.

17 Le Duan Blvd., District 1. www.sofitel.com. © **08/3824-1555.** Fax 08/3824-1666. 286 units. $210 double; $340 suite. AE, MC, V. **Amenities:** 2 restaurants; 2 bars; babysitting; concierge; health club; rooftop pool; room service; smoke-free floors; spa. *In room:* A/C, satellite TV, fridge, minibar, Wi-Fi.

EXPENSIVE

Catina Saigon Hotel ★ With a prime location along Saigon's main street (Dong Khoi), the Catina must be causing a few worries among the long-established government hotels that make little effort to move with the times. Branding itself as a boutique hotel, the Catina offers bright, carpeted rooms with all the facilities you'd expect of a high-class business hotel, though rates are generally a bit cheaper than the nearby competition. Superior and deluxe rooms are not large but are well equipped with work desks, coffeemakers, and satellite TV. Suites are a bit bigger, and while not huge, have a private balcony. Computers are available for guest use. When it's time to unwind, dk's Wine Bar & Restaurant provides a great spot to relax, while Johnny's Wine Stop is another alternative in the hotel lobby.

109 Dong Khoi, District 1. www.hotelcatina.com.vn. © **08/3829-6296.** Fax 08/3829-6291. 43 units. $112–$147 double; $168–$196 suite. AE, MC, V. **Amenities:** Restaurant; 2 bars; concierge; room service. *In room:* A/C, satellite TV, minibar, Wi-Fi.

Duxton Hotel Saigon ★ Formerly the Prince, before becoming part of the popular Australian chain, the Duxton Saigon is efficient, affordable, and stylish. Beige rooms are a good size, tasteful, and comfortable with marble bathrooms in black-and-white. The lobby, entered by swooping stairs from a circular drive and, inside, circled by a mezzanine, is classy. It's a good downtown meeting point, popular with business travelers, especially those on an extended stay, who come here for all the comforts of home. The staff is efficient and personable. The spa offers body and foot massages, pedicures, and manicures. Cool off after the gym at the small outdoor swimming pool.

63 Nguyen Hue Blvd., District 1. www.duxtonhotels.com. © **08/3822-2999.** Fax 08/3824-1888. 198 units. $110–$150 double; $170–$200 suite. AE, DC, MC, V. **Amenities:** Restaurant; bar; concierge; gym; outdoor pool; room service; sauna; smoke-free rooms; spa; steam room. *In room:* A/C, satellite TV, fridge, minibar.

Hotel Continental ★ This preeminent historic hotel built in 1880 was featured in the movie *The Quiet American* based on Graham Green's book. The author lived in room no. 214 for 2 years during the 1950s. At the La Fayette Restaurant (not quite French cuisine) overlooking the Opera House, I wondered about the intrigues of the colonial elites when the hotel was run by Corsican mobster Mathier Francini from 1930 till the Vietnam War ended. The Dong Khoi address was once Rue Catinat with the Notre Dame Cathedral and post office nearby. Unfortunately, the spacious, comfortable rooms, with beveled furniture, curved headboards, carpeted or wood floors, and tall windows, fail to evoke the era. The hotel staff is friendly but a tad dazed and confused by all the comings and goings. If you are a history buff with imagination, and can forgive the lack of ceiling fans and management foibles of this state-owned property, this is one place to relive old Saigon.

132-134 Dong Khoi St., District 1. www.continentalsaigon.com © **08/3829-9201.** Fax 08/3829-0936. 86 units. $120–$180 double; $250 suite. AE, MC, V. **Amenities:** 2 restaurants; bar; babysitting; small fitness center; room service. *In room:* A/C, satellite TV, minibar, Wi-Fi.

Hotel Equatorial   This large edifice in the far reaches of District 5 has long been a popular regional and international convention venue, with good amenities and service. Nothing about it can be described as luxurious or opulent—more like tidy, utilitarian, and cozy. Rooms are clean cut but dull, which may suit the businessperson who wants no distractions. Upgrade to the Equator Club floor for added perks. There are smoke-free rooms on a few designated floors. Bathrooms are green granite and marble tile with plain tub/showers. The pool bar is a good spot to unwind, and there's the Orientica restaurant and bar for seafood. The hotel is about a 10-minute drive to the Dong Khoi area.

242 Tran Binh Trong St., District 5. www.equatorial.com/hcm. © **08/3839-7777.** Fax 08/3839-0011. 333 units. $150 double; $320 suite. MC, V. **Amenities:** 2 restaurants; 2 bars; airport transfer; concierge; health club; Jacuzzi; outdoor pool w/swim-up bar; room service; smoke-free floors; spa. *In room:* A/C, satellite TV, hair dryer, limited Wi-Fi.

Kim Do Royal City Hotel   This is one of those big, government-run places that has little in the way of character, though it does have a great downtown location. The spacious, cool lobby creates a sophisticated air that isn't maintained in the rest of the property, from the tiny pool and cramped fitness center to the fake wood floors and cheap furnishings in the rooms. Suites are much nicer than the deluxe rooms—big, bright and well equipped—and there are often big discounts for advance online bookings, particularly in the low season.

133 Nguyen Hue Blvd., District 1. www.kimdohotel.com. © **08/3822-5914.** Fax 08/3822-5913. 136 units. $105–$145 double; $195–$215 suite. AE, DC, MC, V. **Amenities:** Restaurant; bar; concierge; Internet; tiny pool; room service; smoke-free floor; steam room. *In room:* A/C, TV, fridge, hair dryer, Internet, minibar, Wi-Fi.

Norfolk Hotel ★★   This snappy little business hotel has one of the highest occupancy rates in town, and for good reason: It's convenient and covers all the bases, though rates are a bit steep. Rooms are large and bright, furnished in slightly mismatched chain-hotel style, but everything is like new. Carpets are still nice and plush, and the beds are soft and deluxe. The marble-finished bathrooms are small, but space has been maximized with sliding doors. Deluxe rooms have a tiny hallway entrance with a small countertop to put keys and wallets—an excellent touch that makes the room feel a bit like home. Guests can also use a swimming pool at a nearby apartment block. Staff is efficient and helpful. The restaurant is bright and upscale, featuring an extensive breakfast buffet (included in the rate), as well as monthly themes and special menus. It's perfect for the business traveler or tourist seeking amenities such as a good business center, health club, sauna, room service, and travel desk to cater to any need.

117 Le Thanh Ton St., District 1. www.norfolkgroup.com. © **08/3829-5368.** Fax 08/3829-3415. 104 units. $120–$135 double; $200–$280 suite. Rates include breakfast buffet. AE, MC, V. **Amenities:** Restaurant; bar/club; concierge; small health club; room service; sauna; smoke-free rooms; steam room. *In room:* A/C, satellite TV, fridge, Internet, minibar.

Rex Hotel ★★   The Rex has an unorthodox history: It used to be a French garage, was expanded by the Vietnamese, and then was used by the United States Information Agency (and some say the CIA) from 1962 to 1970. The hotel was transformed and opened in 1990 as a kitschy, atmospheric place, but a major expansion in 2008–10 pulled it into the 21st century. There's now a new wing with modern rooms that are nicely appointed and mimic the classic decor and furnishings of the old wing, but are not quite on par with the chic and comfortable rooms available at the Park

Hyatt or Caravelle nearby. Rooms in the old wing are large and clean, with fluffy carpets, and have endearing Vietnamese details everywhere—from the bamboo and rattan furniture to the duvet throws with lotus embroidery. The hotel also has two swimming pools on the sixth floor. It's in a great downtown location, across from a square that has a lively carnival atmosphere at night. It is also known for its rooftop bar, with its panoramic Saigon view.

141 Nguyen Hue Blvd., District 1. www.rexhotelvietnam.com. ✆ **08/3829-2185** or 08/3829-3115. Fax 08/3829-6536. 284 units. $130–$145 double old wing; $170 double new wing; $170–$320 suite old wing; $240–$600 suite new wing. AE, MC, V. **Amenities:** 2 restaurants; 2 bars; babysitting; health club; Internet; Jacuzzi; outdoor pool; room service; sauna; smoke-free rooms; tennis. *In room:* A/C, satellite TV, Wi-Fi.

Windsor Plaza Hotel ★   The massive Windsor Plaza is a good distance from the heart of the city, but it's smack in the center of Greater Ho Chi Minh City (District 5)—the developers reckon that, over time, the city center will come to them. This behemoth rises 25 stories from the base of an enormous, low-end shopping compound and contains extensive food and beverage outlets, a two-story nightclub, a casino, karaoke lounges, and a massage facility fit for hundreds. The modern pleasure palace and shrine to excess is a bit much, really.

But for the hotel's current focus—regional businesspeople and investors from neighboring countries—the Windsor offers a comfortable and affordable standard. Standard rooms are done in plain tile with carpet and have dull built-in cabinets and oversize lacquer painting on the walls, while suites are spacious with comfy sofas.

18 An Duong Vuong St., District 5. www.windsorplazahotel.com. ✆ **08/3833-6688.** Fax 08/3833-6688. 405 units. $120 double; $190–$520 suite. MC, V. **Amenities:** 3 restaurants; babysitting; health club; Internet; Jacuzzi; small rooftop pool; room service; sauna; smoke-free rooms. *In room:* A/C, satellite TV, fridge, hair dryer, Internet, minibar.

MODERATE

Asian Ruby ★   One of several new chains offering well-equipped rooms with a touch of luxury at midrange prices, Asian Ruby is proving very popular for its efficient service and attractive design. Dark wood furnishings, colorful artwork on the walls, thick mattresses, LCD TVs, and Wi-Fi come standard. Superior rooms are a bit cramped, so if you plan on staying more than a night or two, it's worth upgrading to deluxe for the extra space. The location is ideal—just north of the downtown shopping district—and there are two other branches at 28 Truong Dinh and 100 Le Lai, both near Ben Thanh market.

26 Thi Sach St., District 1. www.asianrubyhotel.com. ✆ **08/3827-2839.** Fax 08/3827-2836. 80 units. $70–$110 double; $120 suite. MC, V. **Amenities:** Restaurant; bar; fitness center; spa. *In room:* A/C, satellite TV, minibar, Wi-Fi.

Bong Sen Hotel   The Bong Sen (also see the budget Bong Sen Hotel Annex, below) is a bland but affordable and convenient downtown operation. It's right in the heart of the city among the likes of the Sheraton and the Caravelle. The place is always busy, though, so be sure to try to book in advance. Rooms are large and plain, though some are quite dingy, and they have standard amenities; everything is clean and functional. The bathrooms are quite cramped, and sinks and tubs are an unappealing baby blue. If you want deluxe, book the executive Bong Sen Suite, which has a spacious bathroom and a gigantic balcony overlooking Dong Khoi Street. They have two good streetside dining venues; check out the Mangosteen.

117-123 Dong Khoi St., District 1. www.hotelbongsen.com. ✆ **08/3829-1516.** Fax 08/3824-6894. 127 units. $85–$115 double; $120–$180 suite. MC, V. **Amenities:** 3 restaurants; bar; gym; small health club. *In room:* A/C, satellite TV, fridge, minibar, Wi-Fi.

Huong Sen Hotel   Another of the many government-owned places whose service is marked only by varying levels of indifference, but worth a look for its price and downtown location. The decor is a downer, but this hotel is a popular choice for big tour groups, and great group rates (and Internet prices) are available. Rooms are big with simple, colorfully painted wood furniture and floral drapes and headboards. Nice touches include molded ceilings and marble-topped counters in the spotless bathrooms. Some rooms have balconies, and beds are ultracomfortable. The hotel is comparable to any other in this category, but quite bland.

66–70 Dong Khoi St., District 1. www.huongsenhotel.com.vn. © **08/3829-9400.** Fax 08/3829-0916. 76 units. $99–$149 double. Rates include breakfast. AE, DC, MC, V. **Amenities:** Restaurant; bar; fitness center; Internet; Jacuzzi; rooftop pool; room service; sauna. *In room:* A/C, TV, fridge, minibar.

May Hotel ★   This newish hotel seems to have got things right from the start, and is often fully booked, so it pays to reserve in advance. Rooms have pleasant, light-wood furniture and spacious bathrooms. The deluxe rooms come with a small balcony, and there's a large, covered pool on the 14th floor. Staff is super-friendly and efficient, so with its excellent downtown location, the May is a nice place to stay if you want something a bit more upmarket than Spring Hotel, just around the corner.

28–30 Thi Sach St. www.mayhotel.com.vn. © **08/3823-4501.** Fax 08/3823-4502. 117 units. $80–$100 double; $120 suite. Rates include breakfast. AE, MC, V. **Amenities:** Restaurant/bar; pool; room service; Wi-Fi. *In room:* A/C, satellite TV, fridge, Internet, minibar.

Palace Hotel ★   This downtown tower has been around for a while; in fact, it was popular with U.S. soldiers on R&R during the war years, so it has some history. It recently underwent a thorough makeover and is one of the better mid-range options. The modern Art Deco decor and new windows let in plenty of light. Carpets are done in pinstripes of red, brown, and orange, with solid-colored cushions and footstools for contrast. The walls have a fresh coat of cream-colored paint, the furniture is dark wood, beds are covered with cozy white cotton duvets, and the bathrooms are sparkling and new.

56–66 Nguyen Hue Blvd., District 1. www.palacesaigon.com. © **08/3824-4231.** Fax 08/3824-4229. 144 units. $100–$125 double; $145 suite. AE, MC, V. **Amenities:** 2 restaurants; 2 bars; rooftop pool; room service; sauna; spa. *In room:* A/C, TV, fridge, minibar, Wi-Fi.

Que Huong—Liberty 3   As the name suggests, this hotel is part of the little Liberty chain. Liberty 3 is right in the heart of the Pham Ngu Lao backpacker area and arguably the best choice down that way. Unlike most backpacker hotels, the lobby has air-conditioning, which is a welcome relief after a sweaty day of touring the city. Rooms have all the amenities of a proper hotel but are priced just above the average minihotel. You'll find unfortunate thin office carpets and bland decor throughout, but everything is clean. Standard rooms are a bit too small; a superior is your best bet. Be sure to request a window and ask to see your room before you check in, as some are better than others.

187 Pham Ngu Lao, District 1. www.libertyhotels.com.vn. © **08/3836-9522.** Fax 08/3836-4557. 61 units. $110–$190 double. AE, MC, V. **Amenities:** Restaurant. *In room:* A/C, satellite TV, fridge, hair dryer, minibar, Wi-Fi.

Que Huong—Liberty 4 ★   The very tidy, large rooms here are nicely furnished. Service is very efficient, and you'll find lots of in-house services. The hotel is just a skip away from De Tham Street, the busy backpacker area, and rooms out front can be a bit noisy, so ask for one out back. There is a cozy bar, karaoke lounge, and massage area, as befits any Asian business hotel worth its salt, and the rooftop restaurant is intimate and relaxing, a good spot to enjoy the free buffet breakfast, with great views of the city. Standard rooms are nothing special—airless and unpleasant, really—but most superior and deluxe rooms (deluxe have just a bit more space) face the cityscape and are tidy and airy. Be sure to ask to see your room before checking in; they do vary.

265 Pham Ngu Lao St., District 1. www.libertyhotels.com.vn. ✆ **08/3836-4556.** Fax 08/3836-5435. 71 units. $70 double; $110–$150 suite. MC, V. **Amenities:** Restaurant; bar; gym; spa. *In room:* A/C, satellite TV, fridge, minibar, Wi-Fi.

Riverside Hotel   Wedged into an old colonial storefront area between the hulking Renaissance Riverside and the wedding-cake Majestic, the Riverside is a reasonable midrange option in a prime downtown location. The public spaces are pretty banged and battered (worn carpets all around, a dark and not very welcoming lobby), but private spaces are expansive for the price, and everything is clean. It's an old building, and some rooms conform to the angled footprint in unique ways. Bathrooms are huge, plain affairs with small tub/showers, a simple sink, and no counter space—but, again, tidy, if simple. Deluxe rooms are worth the upgrade; they're much larger and have newer carpet and better amenities. Rates include a buffet breakfast and a free massage ticket.

18–20 Ton Duc Thang St., District 1. www.vietnamtourism.com/riverside. ✆ **08/3822-4038.** Fax 08/3825-1417. 73 units. $70–$100 double; $140–$170 suite. AE, MC, V. **Amenities:** 2 restaurants. *In room:* A/C, satellite TV, fridge, hair dryer, minibar, Wi-Fi.

Tan Hai Long Hotel & Spa   With four locations around central Saigon, this award-winning chain is making waves with its top-end facilities and services and competitive rates. This is the most convenient location, just a few steps away from Ben Thanh market and within easy walking distance of both Dong Khoi shops and the budget district. However, it can get a bit noisy out front, so try to secure a room at the back if possible. Superior rooms are tiny (just 22 sq. m/237 sq. ft.), but beds are comfy and such details as flatscreen TVs make them feel snug rather than cramped. It's not quite up to the three stars it claims, but with promotional rates less than half of the rack rates, this place represents excellent value. Check out their latest offers online.

14–16 Le Loi, District 1. http://tanhailonghotel.com.vn. ✆ **08/3827-2738.** Fax 08/3825-6012. 106 units. $65–$70 double; $95–$120 suite. MC, V. **Amenities:** Restaurant; bar; airport transfer; fitness center; spa. *In room:* A/C, satellite TV, minibar, hair dryer, Wi-Fi.

INEXPENSIVE

A & Em V   This is one of several places run by A & Em, a local Vietnamese chain that's something like a Vietnamese version of a Best Western—but with even better prices. The rooms aren't particularly stylish, but the floral patterns and frosted glass in the bathrooms are nice touches. Beds are comfortable, with decent mattresses and cozy sheets. Public spaces have that overly bright, fluorescent lighting popular in Asian hotels and restaurants, but at least it reveals spick-and-span environs. Bathrooms are a good size and come with deep tubs, a true luxury in this price range.

60 Le Thanh Ton St., District 1. www.a-emhotels.com. ✆ **08/3825-8529.** Fax 08/3825-8534. 31 units. $40–$70 double; $72–$90 suite. Rates include breakfast. AE, MC, V. **Amenities:** Restaurant. *In room:* A/C, TV, fridge, minibar, Wi-Fi.

Beautiful Saigon 2 ★   Given the smartly dressed staff, modern furnishings, and well-equipped rooms, you'd expect rates here to be much higher than they are. This newish chain has two locations in the heart of the budget district (Beautiful Saigon 1 is at 62 Bui Vien), though this one is tucked in an alley so is a bit quieter. It also has an excellent restaurant, while the first location serves only breakfast; otherwise rooms in both properties are the same. The hotels aren't huge, but the space is used well and everything works, right down to the in-room computers. Rates include a decent breakfast, and staff is very eager to please.

40/19 Bui Vien St., District 1. www.beautifulsaigon2hotel.com. © **08/3920-8929.** Fax 08/3920-4981. 8 units (22 more at number 1). $30–$60 double. MC, V. **Amenities:** Restaurant. *In room:* A/C, satellite TV, computers (in most rooms), minibar, Wi-Fi.

Bong Sen Hotel Annex ★ This small annex to the large Saigontourist-owned Bong Sen provides many of the same amenities at a lower price. The lobby is bright and welcoming, which is a treat for a minihotel. Rooms are basic but tidy, with light-wood furniture, thin carpet, and blue-tile bathrooms. Everything is kind of on the small side, though, and the economy rooms have only one small window, next to a small balcony. Suites have king-size beds and a separate living room decorated like a college dorm room, but if you're a group on a budget, you can easily fit two extra twin beds next to the couches. Make sure you're getting the Annex and not the main Bong Sen, which isn't much of a value. Service is indifferent, but this is a fine place to lay your head for cheap.

61-63 Hai Ba Trung St., District 1. www.bongsenhotel2.com. © **08/3823-5818.** Fax 08/3823-5816. 57 units. $50–$60 double; $90 suite. Rates include breakfast. AE, MC, V. **Amenities:** Restaurant. *In room:* A/C, satellite TV, fridge, hair dryer, minibar, Wi-Fi.

Empress Hotel ★ This popular colonial-style minihotel is run by the same folks as the Empress Hotel in Dalat City. Rooms have charming sliding windows with wooden slats and bamboo blinds. Rooms are small and cozy. The staff is quite friendly, and the entire hotel is neat and clean. The drawback is the location; they are a bit too far west to be in the center of Saigon's action.

136 Bui Thi Xuan St., District 1. www.empresshotelvn.com. © **08/3832-2888.** Fax 08/3832-8215. 40 units. $33–$45 double; $50–$63 suite. MC, V. **Amenities:** Restaurant; gym; smoke-free floor. *In room:* A/C, satellite TV, fridge, hair dryer, minibar, Wi-Fi.

Indochine Location, location, location. Indochine is across the street from Xu, one of the hippest bars in town, and a couple hundred meters from the top hotels, so it's in the thick of all the downtown action. It's about a tenth the cost of a room at the Park Hyatt, but you get what you pay for. The lobby is a dim, unwelcoming cave. The elevator says it can hold eight people, but I would never ride in it with more than two guests (including me). Some of the rooms have a pervasive cigarette smell, and bathrooms are on the small side. But everything is neat and tidy, and you get cozy duvets rather than the flimsy bedspreads offered at other budget hotels.

40-42 Hai Ba Trung St., District 1. www.indochinehotel.com. © **08/3822-0082.** Fax 08/3822-0083. 33 units. $30–$52 double. Rates include breakfast. MC, V. **Amenities:** Restaurant. *In room:* A/C, satellite TV, fridge, Internet, minibar.

Madam Cuc ★★ 👜 Madam Cuc has a simple policy that works so well that her rooms are almost always full: treat all guests like family, remember their names, help out with transport arrangements, and provide a nourishing, free breakfast (as well as a basic lunch and dinner if you happen to be around) and Internet use. This personal treatment brings a steady stream of repeat customers, and there are now four branches of Madam Cuc's within a short walk of each other in the budget district. Rooms are basic but well maintained, with air-conditioning, satellite TV, and hot-water showers. Reserve through their website to avoid disappointment, and ask for a room out back to escape from the constantly honking car horns on the street.

127 Cong Quynh, District 1, Ho Chi Minh City (main branch). www.madamcuchotels.com. ✆ **08/3836–8761**. Fax 083836–0658. 90 units. $25–$30 double. Rates include breakfast. No credit cards. **Amenities:** Free Internet use. *In room:* A/C, satellite TV, minibar.

Medal Hotel—Chuong Hoang Yen   Medal is another low-end business hotel with clean, basic rooms and limited services. You're just north of Dong Khoi and right in the heart of a good expat dining and nightlife area, which makes this a convenient choice. Just a place to rest your head, though; there's nothing fancy about it.

8A/6D2 Thai Van Lung St., District 1. www.medalhotel.com. ✆ **08/3823-8764**. Fax 08/3823-8761. 54 units. $45–$80 double. Rates include breakfast. MC, V. **Amenities:** Restaurant (breakfast only). *In room:* A/C, satellite TV, fridge, minibar, Wi-Fi.

Orient Hotel   A popular minihotel right in the heart of Pham Ngu Lao, the Orient is a little more grand than the local competition. Large and always busy with budget groups, the hotel has a friendly staff and rooms with basic amenities such as air-conditioning and cable TV; it is otherwise not outstanding—just tidy, with chintzy furnishings and loud checkered bedspreads. The Orient is a good choice if you're between trips to the Mekong Delta and onward travel to the north, as you can make your travel plans easily through the tour operators just outside on De Tham. Go for one of the good-size double or triple rooms facing the front, some with large octagonal windows or balconies facing the busy street below and the city skyline beyond. There are no amenities to speak of, but the neighborhood itself is your best budget resource.

274–276 De Tham St., Pham Ngu Lao Ward, District 1. www.orienthotel.vn. ✆ **08/3920-3993**. Fax 08/3836-9886. 60 units. $17–$40 double. Rates include breakfast. MC, V. **Amenities:** Restaurant. *In room:* A/C, satellite TV, fridge, minibar.

Spring Hotel (Mua Xuan) ★★   If you don't want to spend five-star prices but want to be downtown, look no farther than the Spring, with nicer rooms than many hotels twice its price. Accommodations here are neat and clean, with comfy double and super-king-size beds and nice, solid dark-wood or light rattan furniture. The floral motif isn't bad, and the carpeted floors are impeccably clean. Go as high up as you can to escape street noise, which is the hotel's one failing (though the elevator's kind of slow, too). In-room Wi-Fi is super fast. Lowest-priced "economy" rooms have no windows. Suites are large, with couches in large, separate sitting rooms. The Spring has an unsettling Greco-Roman motif, with statues and filigreed molding, but the rooms are a bit more toned down, utilitarian, and pleasant. The staff couldn't be nicer or more helpful.

44–46 Le Thanh Ton St., District 1. www.springhotelvietnam.com. ✆ **08/3829-7362**. Fax 08/3822-1383. 45 units. $45–$63 double; $77 suite. Rates include breakfast. MC, V. **Amenities:** Restaurant/bar; room service. *In room:* A/C, satellite TV, fridge, minibar, Wi-Fi.

WHERE TO EAT

Saigon offers the widest array of restaurants in Vietnam, and virtually every world cuisine is represented. The area around Dong Khoi is home to many fine-dining choices; ask locals where to eat, though, and they'll point you to the outdoor stalls in places such as the open market area that opens in the evening just adjacent to Ben Thanh Market, or to a small neighborhood storefront. Saigon's famous street stalls serve up local specials such as *mien ga* (vermicelli, chicken, and mushrooms in a delicate soup), *lau hai san* (a tangy seafood soup with mustard greens), and, of course, *pho* (Vietnam's staple noodle soup, popular everywhere). See "Quest for the Perfect Noodle," p. 307, for a few good places to slurp Saigon's delectable noodle dish.

EXPENSIVE

Camargue ★ CONTINENTAL/FRENCH   Camargue is two floors of enchanting renovated colonial. Choose from softly lit interior or spacious outdoor terrace seating surrounded by palm fronds. The menu changes regularly. A sampling from my visit included warm goat-cheese salad, roast pork rondalet, and venison. Camargue also seems to have given tourists the nod by adding ubiquitous, lower-priced pasta dishes. The food, alas, isn't as perfect as the surroundings, and the service is substandard, but it's a quaint, laid-back spot downtown. The first-floor bar, **Vasco's,** is very popular and open late on Friday. Call ahead before you go, as rumor has it that the restaurant's lease is up and they will be forced to move soon.

191 Hai Ba Trung St., District 3. ☎ **08/3824-3148.** Reservations recommended on weekend nights. Main courses 270,000 VND–540,000 VND. AE, DC, MC, V. Daily 6am–10:30pm.

L'Olivier ★★ FRENCH   This hotel restaurant serves incredible delicious French food in a charming atmosphere that feels as bright and cozy as a French countryside home. The food is innovative, with such highlights as perfectly done pan-fried sea scallops balanced over slices of turnip and a touch of mango chutney. For dessert, treat yourself to the chocolate volcano cake, which is injected with a shot of pistachio. This is a fine place to have a leisurely evening repast.

17 Le Duan Blvd., District 1. ☎ **08/3824-1555,** ext. 7731. Reservations recommended. Main courses 140,000 VND–295,000 VND. AE, MC, V. Daily 11:30am–2pm and 6:30–10:30pm.

Mandarin ★ CHINESE/VIETNAMESE   On a quiet side street between busy Le Than Thon and the river, cross the threshold at Mandarin and you enter a quaint, elegant oasis that will have you forgetting the seething city outside. Decor is an upscale Chinese motif with timber beams, fine Chinese screen paintings, and artwork on two open-plan floors. It's plush but not stuffy, and you'll feel comfortable in casual clothes or a suit. The staff is professional and attentive but doesn't hover, and is helpful with suggestions and explanations. Ask about daily specials and set menus. I had an excellent spicy sautéed beef served in bamboo with rice. For a memorable meal, don't miss the famed duck done in a sweet "Mandarin style." The steamed lobster in garlic is as good as it sounds, and their seafood steamboat for four is a real coup. The restaurant features a live classical trio (call ahead for schedule).

11A Ngo Van Nam, District 1. ☎ **08/3822-9783.** Fax 08/3825-6185. Reservations recommended. Main courses $10–$60; set menu from $35 per person (minimum 2). AE, MC, V. Daily 5:30–10pm.

Opera ★ ITALIAN   Excellent, fresh Italian food in a bright, contemporary setting. There's an open kitchen so you can watch them toss fresh fettuccini or linguine with mouthwatering homemade sauces. Staff is attentive and friendly. An addictive loaf of warm ciabatta bread is served with an eggplant and olive oil dip while you wait for your main dish.

1/F Park Hyatt Hotel. ☎ **08/3520-2357.** Reservations recommended. Main courses 210,000 VND–900,000 VND. AE, MC, V. Daily 6am–1am.

Orientica ★★ SEAFOOD/VIETNAMESE   The first thing that strikes you about this restaurant, located on the second floor of the Equatorial Hotel, is the vibrant decor of red, silver, and black, portraying the restaurant's theme of "fire, water and ice." The specialty is seafood, and guests choose their meal either from a bed of ice or directly from a water tank. They can then watch the chefs prepare their food at the city's only teppanyaki "fire bar." Since opening in 2007, the restaurant has been showered with awards, including Best Culinary Establishment of the Year 2009 at the

Vietnam Culinary Challenge. It's a bit of a ride from the city center, but it's a rewarding journey.

Equatorial Hotel, 242 Tran Binh Trong St., District 5, Ho Chi Minh City. (C) **08/3839-7777.** Main courses $18-$42. AE, DC, MC, V. Daily 11:30am-2:30pm and 6:30-10:30pm.

Pomodoro ★ ITALIAN   Good large salads and tasty personal pizzas are popular at Pomodoro, a cozy little dining room with tile floors and brick walls in an arch that gives the place an Italian grotto feel. But the restaurant's actually quite light and airy, and the staff is friendly. Antipastos of bruschetta or prosciutto and melon are great, and if you bring your appetite, you can follow them up with a *primi piatti* of pasta and a rich *secondi piatti* of fish, meat, or poultry. Ingredients are generally fresh, but I ordered a pesto dish and it was delivered in all of 30 seconds; ask to have any pasta cooked to order. The wine menu is deep, with some fine Italian reds. The place is always full.

79 Hai Ba Trung St., District 1. (C) **08/3823-8998.** Reservations recommended. Main courses 200,000 VND-500,000 VND. MC, V. Daily 10am-10pm.

Skewers ★ MEDITERRANEAN   The best food at this chic bistro does, in fact, come on skewers; barbecue entrees, particularly the lamb kabobs, are delicious. Also try the moussaka, baked fish and seafood, grilled Moroccan sea bass, good pastas, or barbecued entrees including vodka-flamed beef or ribs dipped in honey. All the flame-bursting barbecuing is done in an open-air kitchen at the front of the restaurant, which is fun to watch. The salads are large and delicious, and they serve great light meals and appetizers, with great dips such as hummus and baba ghanouj. And to top it all off, they've got the best cigars and whiskey in town. The atmosphere is candlelit and cozy, a great spot for a romantic evening.

9A Thai Van Lung St., District 1. (C) **08/3822-4798.** www.skewers-restaurant.com. Main courses $5-$20. MC, V. Mon-Fri 11:30am-2pm and 6-11pm; Sat-Sun 6-11pm.

Square One ★★ VIETNAMESE/WESTERN   You don't come to Square One to eat; you come to spend an evening paying homage to good food. Dining here is like having a front-row ticket to a fancy cooking show. The menu is divided between traditional Vietnamese starters and Western dishes. The spring rolls—pork, bean sprouts, and mint wrapped in fresh rice paper, and then wrapped in a cabbage leaf and tied together with a strip of pandanus leaf—are light, crunchy, and incredibly fresh. Vietnamese dishes are meant to be shared, so expect large portions for main courses. Early evening lounge music segues into a funkier upbeat tempo after 9pm. Get a table facing one of the five open kitchens—it's better than people-watching.

3/F Park Hyatt Hotel. (C) **08/3520-2359.** Reservations recommended. Main courses $10-$35. AE, MC, V. Daily noon-3pm and 6-11pm.

Sushi Bar ★★ JAPANESE   The food speaks for itself (in Japanese, no less) at this friendly corner sushi bar, which now has four other branches around the city. At the end of Le Thanh Ton, known to some as "Little Tokyo," this is one of many Japanese eateries popping up and is popular among longtime residents. It's a typical busy, big-city sushi bar, complete with a wise-cracking sushi master from Japan. Upstairs there are tatami rooms, and the place always seems full, which is a good sign. Everything's fresh, the lunch specials are a good bargain, and the sushi and sashimi are worth the price.

2 Le Thanh Ton, District 1. (C) **08/3823-8042.** Main courses 28,000 VND-750,000 VND. MC, V. Daily 10am-11pm. Delivery until 10pm.

MODERATE

Augustin ★ FRENCH   On the quaint "restaurant row" Nguyen Thiep (just off Dong Khoi), this bright, lively little place is a favorite with French expats and tourists. The food is simple yet innovative French fare, including beef *pot-au-feu* and sea bass tartare with olives. Try the seafood stew, lightly seasoned with saffron and packed with fish, clams, and shrimp. The seating is quite cozy, especially because the restaurant is always full, and the Vietnamese waitstaff is exceptionally friendly, speaking both French and English. The menu is bilingual, too. A large French wine list and classic dessert menu finish off a delightful meal.

10 Nguyen Thiep. ℂ **08/3829-2941.** Main courses 110,000 VND–220,000 VND. No credit cards. Daily 11:30am–2pm and 6–11pm.

Blue Ginger VIETNAMESE   Also called the Saigon Times Club, this Vietnamese bistro is an atmospheric choice with fine local specialties; as a result, it's a tour-group favorite, but that doesn't spoil the atmosphere. It features a nightly performance of folk music, and the dulcet tones mingle nicely with clinking glasses and the low hum of conversation in the candlelit dining room; it makes for a nice, casual evening. The specialty here is a large seafood steamboat, a veritable cornucopia of seafood done like Japanese *nabe* in a large pot in front of you (for two or more). I had the caramelized pork served in a clay pot, and it was excellent. Desserts include ice cream, crème caramel, and fried bananas.

37 Nam Ky Khoi Nghia, District 1. ℂ **08/3829-8676.** Main courses 94,000 VND–200,000 VND. MC, V. Daily 6:30am–10:30am; 11am–2pm and 5–10pm.

Lemongrass VIETNAMESE   The atmosphere is candlelit and intimate, with cane furniture and tile floors, and its three floors of subdued dining are a still a nice place to duck out of the midday sun. Set lunches are an affordable and light option ($12–$15). The long menu emphasizes seafood and seasonal specials. Particularly outstanding are the deep-fried prawn in coconut batter and the crab sautéed in salt and pepper sauce. The portions are very big, Asian family style, so go with a group if at all possible, and sample as many delicacies as possible.

4 Nguyen Thiep St., District 1. ℂ **08/3823-2036.** Main courses 89,000 VND–600,000 VND. AE, MC, V. Daily 11am–10:30pm.

Ngoc Suong ★ SEAFOOD/VIETNAMESE   This chain of seafood restaurants has become so popular that they are beginning to pop up all over the country. Of the several locations in Ho Chi Minh City, this is the most atmospheric, set in a stylish colonial mansion to the west of downtown and north of the budget district. Try the delectable soft-shelled crab or the clams cooked in white wine.

106 Suong Nguyet Anh St., District 1. ℂ **08/3925-6939.** Main courses $4–$25. AE, MC, V. Daily 10am–10pm.

Ocean Palace ★ CHINESE/VIETNAMESE   Set in a former car showroom with high ceilings, tall windows, and elegant drapes, this newish dining venue features an appealing range of options on its menu, from delicious dim sum at around $2 a serving to crispy roast pork or duck served with a special sauce. The smartly dressed staff is extremely attentive, and the place has quickly become a favorite for business lunches. For sightseers, it fits in well with a visit to the Botanic Gardens or the History Museum, which is directly opposite.

2 Le Duan St., District 1. ℂ **08/3911-8822.** Main courses $5–$10. AE, MC, V. Daily 10am–10pm.

The Refinery ★ FRENCH   This French bistro is built in the former headquarters of the leading opium refinery (hence the name) of old Indochine. They've got a great selection of light and filling food that's made just right. I had the eggplant with tomato-mint sauce, goat cheese, and brown and wild rice—a perfect blend of healthy starches and cheesy indulgence. Being a bistro, they're always ready to serve a coq au vin at the drop of a hat. The understated decor makes for casual, intimate dining. Floors are retro red, white, and black tiles, and seating is that of a Paris bistro—low wooden tables and round chairs. The outdoor terrace is shrouded in plants and a mélange of leather chairs and small tables—you'll forget that you're actually sitting in a *hem* (a small street or alley).

74/7C Hai Ba Trung St. (walk through the traditional yellow gate—it's on your left after about 100m/328 ft.), District 1. ✆ **08/3823-0509.** Main courses 60,000 VND–350,000 VND. MC, V. Daily 11am–11pm.

Sandals ★ MEDITERRANEAN   This restaurant is owned by the same folks who run Sailing Club in Nha Trang (p. 267) and Mui Ne (p. 280), so it should come as no surprise that the food has a beachside comfort quality to it. Sandwiches are hearty and the salads filling—for a salad that packs a carbs punch, try the Lamb Kofta & Harissa (195,000 VND), a mix of Vietnamese salad and greens tossed with grilled lamb and Harissa sauce served over butter roti.

93 Hai Ba Trung St. ✆ **08/3827-5198.** Main courses 145,000 VND–590,000 VND. AE, MC, V. Daily 8am–midnight.

Tandoor ★ 🍴 INDIAN   Bringing north Indian and tandoori cuisine is at its best at this convenient spot just north of the Dong Khoi area. At lunchtime, it's packed with local office workers, a seal of approval in any city. Start with an appetizer of pakora, savory fritters, or samosas. As the name suggests, cuisine at Tandoor centers on the traditional clay oven fired at high heat with charcoal, which is great for grilling meat and browning good Indian breads. The restaurant is best known for their good mutton, chicken, or fish kabobs. They serve all kinds of biryani, unique Kashmiri specials, a host of good curries—great creamy *korma* and spicy *vindaloo*—and *saag* dishes of spinach done with mutton, chicken, fish, or seafood. They have good side salads and yogurt dishes to cool the palate; follow it up with a sweet lassi yogurt drink. They offer set lunches (Mon–Fri) for Saigon's busy business crowd and offer free home (or hotel) delivery.

74/6 Hai Ba Trung St., District 1. ✆ **08/3930-4839.** Main courses $5–$10; set lunch $7–$8. MC, V. Daily 11am–2:30pm and 5–10:30pm.

Temple Club ★★ VIETNAMESE   For atmosphere alone, the Temple Club is a must-see. As the name suggests, this is an old Chinese temple (ca. 1900), with original wood and masonry. The decor is upscale and the food is great, but prices have been creeping up lately. The ceiling is high, and the walls are exposed brick. The floor is terra cotta draped in antique throw rugs, and there are some great Buddhist tapestries and statuary about. There's a classic old wooden bar and a formal but comfortable dining room, as well as a lounge area in the back for coffee and dessert. The cuisine is standard Vietnamese from all parts of the country. This place does a good Hanoi-style *cha ca* (fried monkfish), and the grilled fish *Long Va* style (grilled fish on a bed of spring onions and dill covered in crisp garlic and peanuts) is an excellent choice. For dessert, the homemade Hue cake, a steamed cake made of ground green beans served with a pandan and coconut sauce, is done just right. The coffee is the real thing; they even have cappuccino. This is one of the most atmospheric and romantic spots in town.

29–31 Ton That Thiep St., District 1. ✆ **08/3829-9244.** Main courses 140,000 VND–380,000 VND. MC, V. Daily 11:30am–midnight.

Vietnam House ★ VIETNAMESE   Set in a lovely colonial building with shuttered windows, Vietnam House provides two floors of tables for diners, with traditional musicians playing upstairs and a pianist downstairs from around 7 to 9pm each evening. It's an excellent choice if you happen to be new to Vietnamese food, and the set menus (around $15) provide a good introduction with samples of several typical dishes.

93–95 Dong Khoi, District 1. ✆ **08/3829-1623.** Main courses $4–$12. AE, MC, V. Daily 10am–11pm.

Warda ★ LEBANESE   You walk into this place and get a tiny urge to break into a belly dance. The walls are painted in horizontal stripes (yellow downstairs, blue upstairs); beaded turquoise curtains mark the entrance to a semicircular cave of mirrors (the bathrooms, naturally), and there is an outdoor terrace protected by a patterned awning that looks like something out of Arabian Nights. It's great decor, and the food is excellent to boot. The fish and pear tajine—a braised sea bass marinated in olive oil, parsley, and chili, with thin pear slices—is divine. The fish falls apart at the mere touch of your fork. Drinks have a hint of Arabic style, such as bitter saffron or rose martinis. If you've got a sweet tooth, you'll love the crispy phyllo pastry filled with almond paste for dessert, and for those watching the waistline, an order of apple-flavored tobacco served in a shisha pipe should round out your evening quite nicely.

71/7 Mac Thi Buoi St., District 1.✆ **08/3823-3822.** Main courses $7.50–$14. MC, V. Daily 8am–midnight.

Xu ★★ VIETNAMESE   Co-owner Bien Nguyen left school at 15 to work in the food and beverage industry. An old French couple took him under their wing and taught him, as he puts it, "the A to Z of F and B." Saigon is grateful to that couple and to Bien, who has created one of the finest restaurants the city has on offer. The food is innovative and yet retains the traditional taste and feel of Vietnamese eats. I highly recommend the Sea Bass Taste, a sampler plate that comes with perfect, small portions of grilled sea bass over mashed potatoes, a crispy Vietnamese pancake with fresh veggies, and a sea bass rice flour roll, or *banh cuon.* The decor is modern, with retro wooden chairs fixed with deep purple velvet cushions. The lounge (p. 323) is a great place for pre- and after-dinner drinks.

71–75 Hai Ba Trung, District 1. ✆ **08/3824-8468.** Main courses 190,000 VND–350,000 VND. AE, MC, V. Daily 11:30am–2pm and 6pm–midnight.

ZanZBar ★ INTERNATIONAL   This restaurant has a loyal following among Saigon's expat crowd, and for good reason. I dug in to a generous blackened prawn appetizer, served with an avocado half stuffed with cubed tomatoes and black olives. It was delectable and almost big enough to be a main course. The eatery is small and cozy, but doesn't feel crowded. There's usually a pleasant buzz of activity and energy running well into the evening.

41 Dong Du St., District 1. ✆ **08/3822-7375.** Main courses $9.10–$25. AE, MC, V. Daily 7am–1am.

INEXPENSIVE

Allez Boo ★ VIETNAMESE/WESTERN   This little corner eatery is in the very heart of the Pham Ngu Lao backpacker area. Allez Boo serves affordable one-plate meals, such as pork-steak and mashed potatoes, and a good selection of Vietnamese and faux-Western in an open-air corner bar. Come for dinner and stay for drinks or a game of pool in this busy but cozy spot, all done up in a beachside bamboo-and-thatch theme. The food is good and it's always hoppin' till late. You're sure to meet some fellow travelers. It's pickpocket central, though, so keep an eyes open at the window tables.

195 Pham Ngu Lao. © **08/6291-5424.** Main courses $3-$8. MC, V. Daily 24 hr.

Quan An Ngon Restaurant ★★★ VIETNAMESE *Ngon* means "delicious," and for authentic Vietnamese, this restaurant lives up to its name and gets my vote for the best in Vietnam. Ngon has become a real Ho Chi Minh institution and is always packed with locals and tourists alike; demand is so great that they recently added a couple more floors. The atmosphere is chaotic: a cacophony of laughing, chattering guests, shouting waiters, and clanging pots and pans. The main building is surrounded by cooking stations, each serving a regional specialty. Go with a Vietnamese friend, if you can, but if you're alone, just point. Everything is good. They have Hue-style *bun bo* (beef and noodle soup), a catalog of *pho* (noodle soup), and all kinds of seafood. Meals here are best as leisurely, many-course affairs, but go just for a snack if you're visiting the Reunification Palace or any sights downtown. Don't miss it.

138 Nam Ky Khoi Nghia, District 1. © **08/3827-9666.** Main courses 38,000 VND-200,000 VND. AE, MC, V. Daily 6:30am-11pm.

Wrap and Roll VIETNAMESE This restaurant did for the fresh Vietnamese spring roll what Pho 24 did for beef noodle soup. It's a chain that serves DIY spring rolls in a clean and friendly place. Signature dishes come with your choice of meat or seafood (I had grilled beef wrapped in grape leaves and highly recommend it), along with a big plate of assorted shrubbery such as basil, mint, and lettuce, and a small pile of vermicelli noodles. Roll it all up in rice paper and dip it into the bowl of fish sauce, and it's a perfect sampling of a Vietnamese classic.

62 Hai Ba Trung St., District 1. © **08/3822-2166.** Main courses 38,000 VND-88,000 VND. MC, V. Daily 7:30am-10:30pm.

SNACKS & CAFES

Evening dining in the open areas around the **Ben Thanh Market** is the best opportunity to try real local dishes (from around 6–10 or 11pm daily). These restaurants are quite clean, and most have plastic chairs around large tables for those who don't jibe with squatting low at streetside. Try *pho* (**Pho 2000** restaurant is just adjacent) or *banh khot* (Vietnamese pancakes).

Also note the many riverboat restaurants at the terminus of Dong Khoi Street, near the river ferries and high-speed boats to Vung Tau. **Ben Nghe** (at quay-side Ben Bach Dang; © **08/3823-1475**) is typical of the Christmas-light-draped live stage (or loud karaoke) riverside barges with long tables shared by big groups. The seafood and big fry-ups make for a fun night.

Bach Dang 🛗 A Saigon institution, Bach Dang is three floors of fun. It's always crowded and the best place in town for good ice cream and to meet local people (including beggars if you sit streetside).

26-28 Le Loi St., District 1. © **08/3829-2707.** Daily 9am-midnight.

Café Central Café Central is a great little international deli. Stop in for breakfast or a sandwich any time. If you come at night, you'll be rubbing elbows with the many locals who like to spend their evenings here, watching the world go by.

In the Sun Wah Tower, 115 Nguyen Hue, District 1. © **08/3821-9303.** Daily 7am-midnight.

Cafe 333 Known as Cafe "Ba-Ba-Ba" to locals, this small but smart eatery on busy De Tham, the heart of the backpacker neighborhood, is a good place to put your feet

QUEST FOR THE PERFECT noodle

Pho, or Vietnamese noodle soup, has become a popular dish in the West, but it's a national obsession in Vietnam, eaten any time of day. The simplicity of this dish is the attraction: beef stock with rice noodles garnished as you like, with meat and herbs, all ingredients left to speak for themselves. You can eat *pho* on any street corner and in any market, but here are a few especially good places in Saigon with a high standard of cleanliness:

Pho 2000 Set on Tran Hung Dao just cater-cornered to the Ben Thanh Market, Pho 2000 is a Saigon institution and a beehive of activity day or night. Former U.S. President Bill Clinton even made a visit here, and if Bubba liked it, it must be good.

Pho 24 The most popular outlet of this growing Vietnam chain (they have numerous shops in Saigon and Hanoi) is on Nguyen Thiep Street, a little restaurant row off of busy Dong Khoi. They serve a busy crowd all day in a cool, clean storefront. Also look for Pho 24's other shops in town: Diamond Plaza, at 67 Hai Ba Trung, and at 89 Mac Thi Buoi St., among others.

Pho Hung At 241 Nguyen Trai, a short walk west of the budget district, this place packs them in 21 hours a day (closing just from 3am–6am to catch their breath) with big bowls of delicious, steaming beef or chicken noodle soup with a broth worth savoring.

Pho Quynh With a prominent corner location at 323 Pham Ngu Lau, this is where you can come for the national dish 24 hours a day, and the loyal following makes sure the staff don't get much time to rest.

up and watch the parade of travelers. You'll have to fight off the young gum, lighter, book, and trinket salesmen with a stick, but it's a good place to take it all in and enjoy an affordable breakfast or snack before boarding a budget tour bus.

201 De Tham St. ✆ **08/2221-2746.** Daily 6:30am–midnight.

Café Zoom If you're into people-watching, then here's a spot that can't be beat, with a view of the madness that is the junction of De Tham and Tran Hung Dao streets, just south of the budget district. There's a good range of drinks here, friendly staff, and you can check out what's on offer at Vespa Adventure Tours, who operate out of here.

169A De Tham St., District 1. ✆ **09/0240-3055.** Daily 7am–2am.

Highland Coffee This is the best location of the popular Vietnamese chain (more or less like the Starbucks of Vietnam), with open-air seating in a cool pavilion just behind the historic central Ho Chi Minh City Opera House. There's another branch on the corner of Pham Ngu Lau and De Tham if you want a cool place to wait for an open tour bus.

7 Cong Truong, on Lam Son Sq. just behind the Opera House. ✆ **08/3822-5017.** 193 Pham Ngu Lao ✆ 08/3838-9523. Daily 6:30am–midnight.

La Fenêtre Soleil Though forced to move recently, La Fenetre has managed to replicate the quirky atmosphere of the original, with mismatched sofas, antique chairs, and unfinished wooden tables. They serve two-course set lunches for around $7, and the menu includes all kinds of coffees, cakes, crepes, and cocktails, not to mention the widest choice in town of flavored tobacco for shisha pipes.

2nd floor, 44 Ly Tu Trong (at the corner with Pasteur), District 1. ℂ **08/3824-5994.** Daily 10am–midnight.

Mojo ★   This funky little place belongs to the Sheraton, but it doesn't have the feel of a hotel cafe. It's got simple, Scandinavian-style furniture, and there are loungelike sofas in the back to get cozy with your dining companions. It's a great place to do some people-watching. Hearty sandwiches are served with the crusts cut off.

88 Dong Khoi St., District 1. ℂ **08/3827-2828.** AE, MC, V. Mon–Fri 7am–11pm; Sat–Sun until midnight.

Paris Deli 🎁   Here's an ideal spot for a break while shopping on Dong Khoi, and it will leave enough money in your pocket to continue shopping after. Whether you want a refreshing juice, a strong coffee, a custom-made baguette, or a tasty set lunch for $5, this place can provide it. Place your order, and then head upstairs to the cozy lounge/dining area and settle in for a well-earned break.

35 Dong Khoi St., District 1. ℂ **08/3827-7931.** Daily 7am–10:30pm.

Sozo ★   This shop services excellent coffee and cookies, and all profits are used for staff training, development, and education. It was established in 2005 to help underprivileged Vietnamese families and their kids break the cycle of debt, be trained for employment, and have the opportunity for a new start in life. The upstairs lounge is particularly cozy; a good place for a quiet chat or to collect your thoughts.

176 Bui Vien St., District 1. ℂ **08/6271-9176** or 09/5870-6580. www.sozocentre.com. Daily 6:30am–10:30pm.

EXPLORING HO CHI MINH CITY

The museums and attractions of Ho Chi Minh City are mostly in the downtown areas of Districts 1 and 3. And although the museums are interesting, the multifaceted character of the bustling city itself is the major attraction here.

Typical 1-Day Itinerary

Start the day with the city's top attraction, the **Reunification Palace,** where the jig was up for the Saigon government in April 1975, and then head toward the **War Remnants Museum,** which tells the tale of Vietnam at war with the French and Americans. This museum exhibits some horrific images and ghastly paraphernalia of war, so if you're sensitive, skip this and walk through Reunification Park to the towering **Notre Dame Cathedral** and Saigon's historic **post office.** From there, take a casual saunter down **Dong Khoi,** keeping your eyes open for prominent landmarks such as the **Continental Hotel** and the **Municipal Theater.** The street is lined with fine-looking, refurbished colonial hotels and restaurants, as well as eye-catching window displays that might get you started on a shopping spree.

After a leisurely lunch at **Vietnam House** in the heart of Dong Khoi, take a cab to the **Jade Emperor Pagoda,** a large Chinese compound in the northeast of the city, where you can take some colorful pictures of locals offering incense at the altar. From here, walk or take a cab a couple of blocks south to the **History Museum,** housed in a building that blends Western and Eastern architectural styles. You could spend the rest of the afternoon exploring the 15 galleries here, but I'd recommend just picking the few that interest you most and leaving time for a stroll around the **Botanical Gardens and zoo** before heading back to base.

This still leaves several museums, the pagodas of Cholon, and such markets as Binh Thanh to explore, though the city center is compact enough that it's easy to devise your own itinerary. More than 2 full days in Saigon certainly calls for a day trip out to the **Cao Dai Temple** and/or the **Cu Chi Tunnels.**

Attractions in District 1

Ben Thanh Market ★   The clock tower over the main entrance to what was formerly known as Les Halles Centrale is one of the main symbols of Saigon, and the market might as well be, too. Opened first in 1914, it's crowded, a boon for pickpockets with its narrow, one-way aisles, and loaded with people clamoring to sell you cheap goods (T-shirts, aluminum wares, silk, bamboo, and lacquer) and postcards. Unfortunately, all the fun has gone out of shopping at Ben Thanh, as FIXED PRICE signs appeared over every stall, and there's no longer that good-natured bargaining that can lead to a sale. There are so many people calling out to you that you'll feel like the belle of the ball or a wallet with legs. Out front, near the main entrance, find lots of knockoff brand-name clothes, and farther in are a number of small souvenir stands. Toward the back are a few small cafes serving local cuisine or coffee and *che,* a popular Vietnamese dessert. The wet market at the far back, with its selection of meat, fish, produce, and flowers, is interesting and hassle-free; no one will foist a fish on you. The market has become gradually more geared to tourists over the years, which is a shame because the added hygiene and lack of bargaining comes at the cost of the market's old charm and raw authenticity. In open-air stalls surrounding the market are some nice little eateries that open just as the market itself starts closing down, and this is, in fact, one of the best places to try authentic local cuisine. The adventurous can sample good local specialties including rice dishes, noodle soup, *bun* dishes of vermicelli noodles, or ice cream and dessert for next to nothing.

Note: If you start from Ben Thanh Market and take a walk up Le Loi Street (the main east-west avenue) toward central Dong Khoi, you'll stroll past loads of tourist shops with souvenirs, street booksellers with photocopy knockoffs, watch-repair shops, camera stores, and T-shirt shops. It's as good as—maybe even better than—the sprawling market for souvenirs.

At the intersection of Le Loi, Ham Nghi, Tran Hung Dao, and Le Thanh Ton sts., District 1.

Bitexco Financial Tower   It's perhaps a comment on our shifting priorities that the monuments of yesteryear were associated with religion or the arts (such as the Notre Dame Cathedral and Municipal Theater), while those of the 21st century are built in praise of commerce. This 68-story tower, completed in 2010 and rising 262m (860 ft.) above Saigon's streets, is certain to become one of the city's most recognizable icons, with its slender, tapered shape and distinctive helipad protruding from the 50th floor. Visitors will be most interested in the **Saigon Skydeck** on the 49th floor, where they can take in a 360°-view. It's evident from the number of entire blocks recently razed that Saigon's skyline will have many more changes in the near future.

Ngo Duc Khe, District 1. Saigon skydeck: admission 200,000 VND adults, 130,000 VND children. Sun–Thurs 9:30am–9:30pm; Fri–Sat until 10pm (last tickets 45 min. before closing).

Botanical Gardens and Zoo   Directly opposite the end of Le Duan Street and right next to the History Museum, the Botanical Gardens are one of the city's rare green spaces, providing much needed space for city dwellers to escape the constant blare of car horns. It was established in 1864 by two Frenchmen, but after the American War, the gardens were abandoned for several years. Now they are looking attractive again and make a welcome contrast to the hectic pace of life in District 1. There's a zoo here, too, featuring elephants, camels, and crocodiles, which is a great distraction for kids. **Warning:** Unfortunately you need to be on your guard against bag snatchers and tricksters, who will try to befriend you and offer to guide you around.

Nguyen Dinh Khiem St. Admission 8,000 VND. Daily 7am–7pm.

City Hall and Nguyen Hue Plaza   Saigon's former city hall (now belonging to the People's Committee) was originally a French hotel constructed between 1902 and 1908, a fantastic ornate example of refined colonial architecture. It's not open to the public, but it makes a classic backdrop for photos taken around the Nguyen Hue Plaza, where a statue of Ho Chi Minh with a young girl is another focal point for lenses. Flanking the plaza is the huge Rex Hotel, itself an important vestige of the American years when it housed the CIA headquarters.

Facing Nguyen Hue Blvd.

General Post Office (Buu Dien) ★   In this grand old colonial building, you can check out the huge maps of Vietnam on either side of the main entrance and the huge portrait of Uncle Ho in the rear. The specialty-stamps counter has some great collector sets for sale. It's directly opposite the Notre Dame Cathedral, so you can tick off two places with one visit.

2 Coq Xu Paris, District 1. Daily 7:30am–8pm.

Golden Dragon Water Puppet Show   The art of water puppetry, a uniquely Vietnamese form of theater, was founded in the north, but you can catch a show here or at Ho Chi Minh City's History Museum. It's 50 minutes of slapstick fun, featuring sketches about rearing ducks and catching foxes, unicorns playing with a ball, and a fairy dance. The show is accompanied by traditional music, and kids (and most adults) love it. The early evening show times make it a fun predinner activity.

55B Nguyen Thi Minh Khai, District 1 (on the northern border of Tao Dan Park). ✆ **08/3930-2196.** www.goldendragonwaterpuppet.com. Admission 120,000 VND. Shows daily 5 and 6pm.

The Ho Chi Minh Fine Arts Museum   If you're truly keen on learning about "the scene" in Ho Chi Minh, this is the place to start. Three floors house an evolving modern collection, featuring new and established Vietnamese artists' works in sculpture, oil, and lacquer, as well as a nice collection of ancient Buddhist artwork and some Cham statuary. The museum offers a good glimpse into the local scene. From there, have a look at Lac Hong Art Gallery, located on the ground floor of the museum (✆ **08/3821-3771**), which features the works of many famous Vietnamese artists. Open Tuesday to Sunday 9am to 5pm.

97A Pho Duc Chinh St., District 1. ✆ **08/3829-4441.** Admission 10,000 VND.

Ho Chi Minh City Museum ★   Formerly the Revolutionary Museum, this central behemoth was originally built in 1890 by the French as a commercial museum, and has also been a Governor's Palace and a committee building. The exhibits cover a broad range, from archaeology and ethnic survey to early photos of the city and documents from its founding in the 1600s. The second floor is heavy on Vietnam's ongoing revolution, with displays of weaponry and memorabilia from the period of struggle against imperialism and many flags, placards, and dispatches from the rise of Communism, beginning with the August Revolution of 1945 all the way to the fall of Saigon. The bias is heavy, of course, and it's an important rendering of Vietnam's protracted struggle and ideologies, but it's interesting to note how the displays, not unlike socialist ideals, are a bit frayed around the edges in a land that is going pell-mell toward a market economy. The grounds are picturesque and attract newlyweds posing for photos on the front steps, and there's an interesting collection of captured U.S. fighter planes, tanks, and artillery in the main courtyard. Underneath the building is a series of tunnels (closed to the public) leading to the Reunification Palace, once used by former President Ngo Dinh Diem as a hideout before his execution in 1962.

65 Ly Tu Trong St. ✆ **08/3829-9741.** Admission 15,000 VND. Daily 8am–5pm.

Ho Chi Minh Museum   This large museum commemorates the greatest national hero that Vietnam has ever had. It's housed in the "Dragon House *(Nha Long)* Wharf," a 19th-century building with a European design and Chinese-style roof from which it takes its name. The location is auspicious because this is where the young Ho Chi Minh (then Nguyen Tat Thanh) left to sail for Europe. The museum tells the rags-to-equality story of a self-made revolutionary, but mostly in Vietnamese. The relics of Ho's life are many, and much can be gleaned from photos and what English descriptions you can find. Unfortunately, the presentation is rather unimaginative and cannot compare with its namesake in Hanoi. The museum is south of the city center, just across a small canal off the Saigon River in District 4.

1 Nguyen Tat Thanh Rd., District 4. No phone. Admission 15,000 VND. Tues–Sat 8–11:30am and 2–5:30pm; Sun 8am–8pm.

Jade Emperor Pagoda ★★   One of the most interesting pagodas in Vietnam, the Jade Emperor is filled with smoky incense and fantastic carved figurines. It was built by the Cantonese community around the turn of the 20th century and is still buzzing with worshipers, many lounging in the front gardens. Take a moment to look at the elaborate statuary on the pagoda's roof. The dominant figure in the main hall is the Jade Emperor himself; referred to as the "god of the heavens," the emperor decides who will enter and who will be refused. He looks an awful lot like Confucius, only meaner. In an anteroom to the left, you'll find Kim Hua, a goddess of fertility, and the King of Hell in another corner, who undoubtedly gets those the Jade Emperor rejects.

73 Mai Thi Luu St., District 1. ✆ **08/3820-3102.** Daily 8am–5pm.

Notre Dame Cathedral ★   The neo-Romanesque cathedral was constructed between 1877 and 1880 using bricks from Marseilles and stained-glass windows from Chartres. The Romanesque towers of nearly 60m (197 ft.) loom over a large white statue of the Virgin Mary and the nearby Saigon Post Office. It's an interesting comment on the changing face of this city that these towers, once the tallest points in the city, are now dwarfed by surrounding skyscrapers. The cathedral would pretty much be at home in any European country. The tiles are a cubic pattern done in black, white, and gray. They have a slightly disconcerting 3-D effect, but they are no match for the statue of Mary framed in neon blue lights in the first archway on your left. The atmosphere is fairly serene, and there's something calming about taking a rest on the wooden pews.

Near the intersection of Dong Khoi and Nguyen Du sts., District 1.

Reunification Palace ★   Designed as the home of former President Ngo Dinh Diem, the U.S.-backed leader of Vietnam until his assassination in 1962, this building is most notable for its symbolic role in the fall of Saigon in April 1975, when its gates were breached by North Vietnamese tanks and the victor's flag hung on the balcony; the very tanks that crashed through the gates are enshrined in the entryway, and photos and accounts of their drivers are on display. Built on the site of the French governor general's home, called the Norodom Palace, the current modern building, designed when *modern* meant "sterile," was completed in 1966—it looks something like an old elementary school to my eye now, but modern-design fans love it. Like the Bao Dai Palace in Dalat, the Reunification Palace is a series of rather empty rooms that are nevertheless interesting because they specialize in period kitsch and haven't been gussied up too much. All visitors are required to join a guided tour of the private quarters, dining rooms, entertainment lounges, and the president's office that feel like everybody just up and left one day (they did)—a tour is almost eerie, really. Most interesting is the war command room in the basement, with its huge maps and old communications equipment, as well as the basement labyrinth; it feels as if you've walked onto a movie set. Before starting the tour, visitors are shown a brief movie giving background about the American War, which plays in French, English, Japanese, and Chinese in separate screening rooms.

135 Nam Ky Khoi Nghia St., District1. Admission 30,000 VND. Daily 7:30–11am and 1–4pm.

Saigon Opera House (Ho Chi Minh Municipal Theater)   This magnificent building was built at the turn of the 20th century as a classical opera house to entertain French colonists. The building was renovated in the 1940s, only to be badly damaged by bombers in 1944. A shelter for refugees after the Geneva Accord split the country at the 17th Parallel in 1954, the building would briefly house the parliament before falling under first private and, ultimately, state hands (after reunification) as an opera house and theater. There have been extensive renovations in recent years. The three-story interior houses some 1,800 seats. Today the Municipal Theater does very little in terms of performances, but it is a stalwart atmospheric holdout amid the rising steel-and-glass downtown.

At the intersection of Le Loi and Dong Khoi sts.

Vietnam History Museum ★★   Housed in a rambling concrete pagodalike structure, the museum presents a clear picture of Vietnamese history, with a focus on the south. There's an excellent selection of Cham sculpture and the best collection of ancient ceramics in Vietnam, although some of the artifacts are being held together by tape. Weaponry from the 14th century onward is on display; one yard is nothing but cannons. Room 4 (left of the main entrance) has a fascinating, slightly creepy display of an embalmed body in remarkable shape that dates from 1869. One wing is dedicated to ethnic minorities of the south, including photographs, costumes, and household implements. Nguyen dynasty (1700–1945) clothing and housewares are also on display. There are archaeological artifacts from prehistoric Saigon. Its 19th- and early-20th-century histories are shown using photos and, curiously, a female corpse unearthed as construction teams broke ground for a recent housing project. There are even some general background explanations in English, something missing from most Vietnamese museums.

A small three-row theater inside the museum shows regular water puppet performances. It's an intimate venue, and the performance is more clever and witty than the for-the-tourists water puppet show in Hanoi. Tickets are just 40,000 VND, and performances are held every hour between 9 and 11am and 2 and 4pm Tuesday through Sunday.

Also adjacent to the History Museum is the **Ho Chi Minh City Campaign Museum,** the first address on Le Duan Street, just across from the entrance to the botanical garden and zoo. In the large courtyard outside the museum, you'll find another collection of war detritus similar to what you'll see at the War Remnants Museum and the Ho Chi Minh City Museum, but here you can see the crumpled remains of an American reconnaissance plane shot down, as well as more utilitarian vehicles, troop carriers, and the construction equipment from the U.S. defoliation campaign. The museum has little in the way of English explanations—it's more or less a place for Vietnamese school field trips (there's a long block of classrooms attached)—but Vietnam War enthusiasts can find some weaponry and tools not displayed in other museums in town.

2 Nguyen Binh Kiem. 𝄢 **08/3829-8146.** Water Puppet Theater 𝄢 08/3823-4582. Admission 15,000 VND. Tues–Sun 8–11:30am and 1:30–5pm.

Attractions in District 3

The Hoa Binh Noodle Shop ★   The name means "Peace Noodles," and this little shop is no different from the many others in town, except for a small red plaque above the entrance and a flag of the Communist regime. The plaque, written in Vietnamese, marks this discreet little storefront's important place in history. Its upstairs floors were the staging ground of the Tet Offensive of 1968, a surprise attack on U.S. forces region-wide during a cease-fire that, with thousands of losses, was tantamount to the Viet Cong throwing themselves on their collective sword. However, with the incursions reaching as far as the U.S. Embassy in Saigon, as well as at points throughout the city, this was a turning point in the conflict; it changed popular opinion in the United States and among troops stationed in Vietnam, creating a major diversion from later intensified fighting on northern fronts. Former shop owner Ngo Toai was the Madame Lefarge of the offensive, serving noodles by day and hosting high-level Viet Cong planners by night. The raid blew his cover, and Mr. Toai spent the rest of the war in jail, only to return to his shop in 1975 and pick up the ladle right where he left it, never once betraying the revolutionary zeal that made him a place in history. These days, his children serve up noodles following their father's recipe, and if you show interest, they will produce a dog-eared scrapbook showing articles written about the shop, photos of their father with the many tourists who visit, and a few war photos, too. The noodles are not bad, but not worth the journey alone. This place can be visited in conjunction with Vinh Nghiem Pagoda (see below).

7 Ly Chinh Thang St., District 3. 𝄢 **08/3848-2775.** Daily 7am–11pm.

Vinh Nghiem Pagoda   Located to the north of town on the road to the airport, this pagoda is distinct because of its constant activities at the attached school, as well as for the daily workings of the many monks and nuns housed here. I visited when the place was preparing for a funeral, and it was like the set of a Hollywood movie, complete with egoistic flower coordinators and a bevy of fawning assistants. Housed under large, sloping, Chinese-style roofs, with upturned cornices, the temple has two floors, with a grand sanctuary on the second floor (often closed to visitors) and a more utilitarian hall on the ground floor, as well as large block of classrooms and housing for monks and nuns, some of whom may come out and greet you in the hopes of practicing their English. There's also a seven-story pagoda rising to 40m (130 ft.) above the compound.

Near Vinh Nghiem in District 3, you'll also find the brash pink facade of the wedding cake that is **Tan Dinh Cathedral,** a busy working Catholic church with daily services that stand out like a sore thumb (or a pink elephant) in the busy Saigon streetscape of the Tan Dinh area. The nearby **Tan Dinh Market** is notable for the absence of foreign visitors and the pushy hard sell going on in the popular Ben Thanh Market; Tan Dinh is a good glimpse at the workings of an average city market, with cloth sellers at the front, dry-goods vendors in the center, and meats, vegetables, and fish sold in the back.

339 Nam Ki Khoi Nghia St., District 3. ℂ **08/3848-3153.** Free admission. Daily 7am–6pm; full-moon days until 10pm.

War Remnants Museum ★★ The War Remnants Museum is a comprehensive collection of the machinery, weapons, photos, and documentation of Vietnam's wars with the both the French and the Americans (though the emphasis is heavily on the latter). The museum was once called the American War Crimes Museum, which should give you an idea of whose side of the story is being told here. Short of being outright recrimination, this museum is a call for peace and a hope that history is not repeated. The exhibit begins to the right of the entrance with a room listing war facts: troop numbers, bomb tonnage, statistics on international involvement in the conflict, and numbers of casualties on both sides. Next is a room dedicated to the journalists who were lost during the war. The exhibits are constantly evolving, and the museum is currently expanding and modernizing, improving its presentation and explanations throughout. One room is devoted to biological warfare, another to weaponry, and another to worldwide demonstrations for peace. The explanations, which include English translations, are very thorough. There is a large collection of bombs, planes, tanks, and war machinery in the main courtyard. Kids will love it, but you might want to think twice before taking them inside to see things such as wall-size photos of the My Lai massacre and the bottled deformed fetus supposedly damaged by Agent Orange. There's also a model of the French colonial prisons, called the Tiger Cages, on the grounds.

28 Vo Van Tan St., District 3. ℂ **08/3930-6325.** Admission 15,000 VND. Daily 7:30am–noon and 1:30–5pm (last admission 4:30pm).

Attractions in District 5

Cholon ★★ Cholon is the predominately Chinese district of Saigon and probably the largest Chinatown in the world. It's a sizable district bordered by Hung Vuong to the north, Nguyen Van Cu to the east, the Ben Nghe Chanel to the south, and Nguyen Thi Nho to the west. The Chinese began to settle the area in the early 1900s and never quite assimilated into the rest of Saigon, which caused a bit of resentment among the greater Vietnamese community. You'll sense the different environment immediately, and not only because of the Chinese-language signs. Cholon is where you might have found dark, exotic opium dens and brothels in the French colonial time, the same opium dens and brothels that greeted American troops. Story has it that a huge number of U.S. troops went AWOL in Cholon during the war—when the fall of Saigon was imminent, U.S. expeditionary forces advertised a period of amnesty for U.S. citizens on the run in the district—only one dazed and confused soldier came stumbling out.

A bustling commercial center, Cholon is a fascinating maze of temples, restaurants, jade ornaments, and herbal medicine shops. You can lose yourself walking the narrow streets, but it makes sense to take a cyclo by the hour to see the sights. Many of the city tours (see "Visitor Information & Tours," earlier in this chapter) start at Giac Lam Pagoda and make a few stops in the district, including the large market.

If you're on your own, start with a motorbike or taxi ride to the **Binh Tay Market ★★**, on Thap Muoi Street, which is even more crowded than Ben Thanh and has many of the same goods, but with a Chinese flavor. There's much more produce, along with medicines, spices, and cooking utensils, and you'll find plenty of hapless ducks and chickens tied in heaps. From Binh Tay, head up to Nguyen Trai, the district's main artery, to see some of the major temples on or around it. Be sure to see Quan Am, on Lao Tu Street off Luong Nhu Hoc, for its ornate exterior. Back on Nguyen Trai,

Thien Hau pagoda is dedicated to the goddess of the sea and was popular with seafarers giving thanks for their safe trip from China to Vietnam. Finally, as you follow Nguyen Trai Street past Ly Thuong Kiet, you'll see the Cholon Mosque, the one indication of Cholon's small Muslim community. Other sights in Cholon include the following:

Chua Quan Am (12 Lao Tu St.) is a classic Chinese temple with the scent of incense and the soothing sounds of music wafting in the air—but crackling speakers at high decibels mean different things to different people. Nearly 20 resident monks and an abbot are on hand and welcome visitors. In fact, they'll even take the time to show you around and allow you to take photos for a small donation in the alms box at the altar. Buy one of the oversize incense sticks—the size of a large flashlight—and make a wish for your journey (in Vietnam or in life). The temple is heavily gilded in snazzy gold and red paint, and don't miss the cool mechanized rotating offering stands. This is a "working temple," and that means the place is busy day and night with visiting supplicants. Just outside the entrance, don't miss the busy cabinetmakers at work in a large streetside collective.

Cha Tam is Cholon's small Catholic church, with high vaulted ceilings and surrounded by the Stations of the Cross. A statue of Mary stands in a small grotto out front amid offerings, placards, and prayer entreaties at her feet. This little cathedral is a cool place to take a break and visit an imposing white statue of Jesus or a standing statue of St. Francis of Assisi. Don't miss the large relief of the Last Supper.

Thien Hau—The Lady Temple was originally built by a Cantonese congregation in the early 19th century. The temple pays homage to a special psychic lady, Thien Hau, born A.D. 940, who was said to be able to predict the weather and protect sailors. The classic Chinese temple has a wooden entry, the roof of which is lined with tiny figurines. Small central ponds are flanked by heavy, bright red pillars and all around are elaborate carvings of gods and monsters. The place is busy all day and echoes with sounds from the adjacent schoolhouse. The huge coils of incense hanging over the central courtyard space make for great photos.

Giac Lam Pagoda ★   Giac Lam Pagoda, originally built in 1744 and remodeled in the early 1900s, is the oldest pagoda in Saigon. The front garden features the ornate tombs of venerated monks, as well as a rare bodhi tree. Next to the tree is a regular feature of Mahayana Buddhist temples, a huge statue of Avalokitesvara, a bodhisattva seated on a lotus blossom, a symbol of purity. There's also a seven-tiered pagoda dedicated to Avalokitesvara that you can climb for distant views across the crowded city. In the temple, there are just two simples rules: no hats and no smoking (though most do); wearing shoes is permitted. Inside the temple is a spooky funerary chamber, with photos of monks past, and a central chamber chock-full of statues. Notice the aged, dark, carved wood of the double-height hall. Walls are lined with funerary portraits, from large red-and-yellow plaques to small wallet-size photos, and there is some very elaborate statuary about and an altar with gilded figures. There are three altars at the back: The central is Ho Chi Minh, who is flanked by photos of the recently deceased. The monks are busy but quite friendly (when they're not chatting on their cellphones). For a small fee, monks don yellow prayer robes over their daily temple attire and perform beautiful chanting services, accompanied by bells, for visiting supplicants. One well-known monk ministers to the sick and suffering (and tells fortunes) in a side room. Don't miss the large outbuilding just to the right of the entrance—inside are aisles of shelves with colorful urns of ashes, Chinese pots with red lights, candles, and offerings.

118 Lac Long Quan St., Tan Binh District. Daily 5am–noon and 2–9pm.

Day Trips from Ho Chi Minh

Can Gio Island   The Can Gio beach, just west of the Vung Tau Peninsula, is not spectacular, nor set up for fun and frolic, but it's a place where Vietnamese families come to picnic—and that's the main allure. The journey is really what it's about. Rent a motorbike ($6–$10 a day from any of the shops along Pham Ngu Lao in Saigon's backpacker district) and head south (it's about 1½ hr. away), going through the Nha Be area, a wide, wet plain, followed by a ferry crossing. The island's mangrove forest area and beach (low mudflats and hard sandy shores) are good for a long walk and to escape Saigon's pollution and honking traffic. You can get a bite at one of the local seafood shacks. Note that taking a vacation alongside locals might mean being invited to a good barbecue and cup after cup of rice whiskey; be careful if you've driven yourself here.

Cao Dai Holy See Temple ★★   The Cao Dai religion, less than 100 years old, is a broad, inclusive faith that sprang from Buddhist origins to embrace Jesus, Muhammad, and other nontraditional saints such as Louis Pasteur, Martin Luther King, and Victor Hugo. About two million Vietnamese people (mostly in the south) practice Cao Daism, but you'll see temples far and wide, recognizable by the "all-seeing eye," which looks like the eye on the U.S. dollar. The temple at Tay Ninh (often included with trips to the Cu Chi Tunnels) is the spiritual center and the country's largest. Visitors are welcome at any of the four daily ceremonies, but should wear trousers below the knee, remove their shoes, and act politely, quietly observing the ceremony from the balcony area (great for pictures). The temple interior is colorful, with bright murals and carved pillars. Cao Dai supplicants wear either white suits or colorful robes, each color denoting what root of Cao Daism they practice (Buddhist, Muslim, Christian, or Taoist).

On the way from Saigon to the temple, you'll pass through the town of **Trang Bang,** site of the famous photo of 9-year-old Kim Phuc, who was burned by napalm and whose story is told in the popular book *The Girl in the Photo.* The road also passes **Nui Ba Den,** the Black Virgin Mountain, which is just 11km (6¾ miles) northeast of Tay Ninh (100km/62 miles from Saigon). The story goes that a young girl was forced to marry a wealthy Mandarin, but rather than do so, fell to her death from the peak. The mountain is dotted with small temples. Most tours just drive by, as your guide recounts a bit of the history. Ba Den also marks the end of the Ho Chi Minh Trial, as the supply line descended from the north to reinforce the North Vietnamese guerrillas, including the people of Cu Chi (see below). Despite relentless fighting throughout the war, U.S. forces were never able to clear the North Vietnamese from the area.

Cu Chi Tunnels ★★   The Cu Chi Tunnels are definitely worth the day (or half-day) trip out of Saigon. Vietnamese are proud of their resolve in their prolonged history of struggle against invading armies, and the story of the people of Cu Chi is indicative of that spirit. Just 65km (40 miles) northwest of Saigon, the Cu Chi area lies at the end of the Ho Chi Minh Trail and was the base from which Ho Chi Minh guerillas used to attack Saigon. As a result, the whole area became a "free-fire zone" and was carpet-bombed in one of many American "scorched-earth" policies. But the residents of Cu Chi took their war underground, literally, developing a network of tunnels that covered a staggering 250km (155 miles) at its height, and included meeting rooms, kitchens, and triage areas—an effective network for waging guerrilla warfare on nearby U.S. troops. The U.S. Army's 25th Infantry Division was just next door, and there are detailed maps denoting land that was either U.S. held, Vietminh held, or in dispute.

Visitors first watch a war-era propaganda film that's so over the top it's fun. The sight supports a small museum of photos and artifacts, as well as an extensive outdoor exhibit of guerrilla snares and reconstructions of the original tunnels and bunkers (widened to accommodate Western frames). Wear your "play clothes" if you choose to crawl through the tunnels; the experience is dirty and claustrophobic. There is also a shooting range where, for around $1 per bullet, you can try your hand at firing anything from a shotgun to an AK-47. Souvenir hawkers abound. A half-day trip can be arranged with any tour company in Saigon, or a full day trip including a visit to the Cao Dai Temple (above).

65km (40 miles) northwest of Saigon. ✆ **08/3794-8842.** Admission 80,000 VND. Daily 7am–5pm.

Golf

There are two excellent 18-hole golf courses at the **Vietnam Golf and Country Club.** Fees are $108 during the week for nonmembers (though there are cheaper rates: $50–$65 on Mon and Wed) and $142 on Saturday and Sunday. The clubhouse is at Long Thanh My Ward, District 9 (✆ **08/6280-0124;** fax 08/6280-0127; www.vietnamgolfcc.com).

Along with its two internationally accredited 18-hole courses, the Vietnam Golf and Country Club offers extensive pro services, a driving range, locker facilities, a pro shop, a swimming pool, and tennis courts. The first course was built in 1994, and the second (1997) was designed by Lee Trevino. Just 20km (12 miles) from Saigon, the club is open to nonmembers. Reservations are required.

Spa & Massage

Most of the major hotels listed have extensive spa and massage facilities, and Saigon now plays host to lots of little storefront spas. Busy Dong Khoi Street is lined with affordable foot-massage shops and manicurists; young ladies in traditional *ao dai* dress stand out front and pass out flyers. Back-alley places in the same area might offer more services than you want, but the foot-massage spots are okay and a bargain. Prices start from $10 for a bone-crunching massage. **L'Apothiquaire** (100 Mac Thi Buoi St.; ✆ **08/3822-2158;** www.lapothiquaire.com) offers a long roster of affordable pampering, from facials and scrubs to massage and manicures. Open daily 9am to 9pm. Call for an appointment.

Anam QT Spa (26–28 Dong Du St., District 1, near Dong Khoi; ✆ **08/3825-1250**) is sponsored by Clinique and does it all—you can get facials, manicures, waxing, body treatments, and massages ($35 for a 1-hr. oil massage). Open daily 10am to 10:30pm.

Jasmine (45 Ton That Thiep, District 1; ✆ **08/3827-2737**) is a highly rated day spa offering a wide range of treatments with prices ranging from $10 to $95. Open daily 9am to 8pm.

SHOPPING

Saigon has a good selection of silk, fashion, lacquer, embroidery, and housewares. Prices are higher than elsewhere, but the selection is more sophisticated, and Saigon's cosmopolitan atmosphere makes it somewhat easier to shop, meaning that shop owners, especially in more upscale boutiques, aren't immediately pushing you to buy. Stores are open 7 days a week from 8am until about 7pm. Credit cards are widely accepted (often with a charge of 3%–5%), except at local markets and streetside places.

Dong Khoi is Saigon's premier shopping street. Formerly Rue Catinat, it was a veritable Rue de la Paix in colonial times. The best blocks are the last two heading toward the river, but the whole area is loaded with shopping opportunities. With the glut of Japanese tourists, there are lots of Japanese Zakka shops with cute, though overpriced, jewelry, accessories, and shoes. You'll also find little watch shops, repair shops, and old camera vendors (the street adjacent to Dong Khoi, Nguyen Hue, is lined with camera shops). Good silk tailors abound. Below is just a short selection of the many choices. Explore.

Shopping A to Z

ART GALLERIES

In addition to the galleries reviewed below, a few other popular galleries in town include the **Apricot Gallery,** 50–52 Mac Thi Buoi St., District 1 (© **08/3822-7962**), and **Particular Art Gallery,** 3/F 123 Le Loi St., District 1 (© **08/3821-8330**). If these galleries pique your curiosity about contemporary Vietnamese art, pick up a copy of *The Word:HCMC* or *Asialife,* two local happenings guides, for further listings and special shows.

There are galleries selling reproductions of well-known paintings throughout the city, many clustered around Dong Khoi and near all the major hotels. Here you can get some great deals (reproduction being a big industry in town), and those with deep pockets will find easy introductions to the artists or their representatives themselves. For a price, you can also turn any photo into an enormous oil painting.

Lotus Gallery Stop by this large gallery space and view superb examples of impressionist art as well as work by traditional and contemporary Vietnamese artists, well organized into different sections. There's a lot more upstairs, too. Open daily 8am to 8pm. 67 Pasteur St. © **08/3829-2695.** www.lotusgallery.com.

BOOKSTORES

The city's best-stocked foreign-language bookstore, **Fahasa,** has two convenient locations (40 Nguyen Hue and 60 Le Loi). It carries some coffee-table books on Vietnam, a limited selection of classics in English and French (mostly geared to Vietnamese readers), as well as some foreign-language newspapers, good regional maps, and locally published volumes for foreign students of Vietnamese. Daily 8am to 10pm.

Better if you're just looking for a good read are the many small bookshops on De Tham Street and the nearby alleys in the backpacker area of town. Here you'll find hole-in-the-wall shops carrying photocopied titles and used books. Some of these places do swaps, but you're certain to come away frustrated. Just come ready to spend a few bucks instead of trading that old novel.

Elsewhere in the city—pretty much anywhere tourists herd and congregate, really—you are sure to run into wandering booksellers with a meter-high stack perched on their hip, offering the same collection of books about Vietnam, from guidebooks to popular nonfiction about the Vietnam War years, as well as the current popular novels and backpacking classics, all photocopied (so well that you might take them for originals) at one of Vietnam's many reproduction factories and quite cheap (usually $2–$5).

CAMERA SHOPS

Good camera stores, the likes of **Thien Ngan** (46 Nguyen Hue St.; © **08/3822-0327;** daily 8am–10pm; MasterCard and Visa accepted), line busy Nguyen Hue Street (just parallel to Dong Khoi) and can print and burn to DVD as well as fix or replace most amateur equipment. You'll also find lots of good deals on used 35mm equipment—but be warned that much of it has been reconditioned and comes with no guarantee.

CLOTHING & ACCESSORIES

Gaya ★★ This store carries a beautiful selection of clothing, home decor, and furniture from one local Vietnamese and four expat designers. Everything is of serious quality. The linens are from Catherine Denoual (see below), so expect a beautiful collection. Clothing is by Cambodian-born, France-raised Romyda Keth. The beautiful dresses are often multicolored and touched with embroidery or a bit of sparkle. It can look like too much on the hanger, but more often than not looks smart and sophisticated once you put it on. The quality of material and cuts are amazing, and the staff has an excellent eye for fit. Open daily 10am to 8pm. 1 Nguyen Van Trang St., District 1 (at the corner of Le Lai St.). ℰ **08/3925-1495.**

Ipa Nima The place to get funky, original handbags decked out in tassels, patterns, and busy prints. Their Saigon stores are not as large and expansive as their flagship in Hanoi (p. 107), but there is still a great selection on offer. Open daily 9am to 9pm. 71 Pasteur St.: ℰ **08/3824-2701.** 77-79 Dong Khoi St; District 1. ℰ 08/3822-3277.

La Bella Come here for a fine collection of silk, jersey, and cotton separates and dresses, as well as silk sleep and loungewear. Some designs are simple (long, Roman-style jersey dresses) and others are eccentric (silk wraparound halters and sequined skirts). Open daily 9am to 9pm. 85-87 Pasteur St. ℰ **08/3823-0172.**

Mai's ★ This store has original, contemporary clothes that look like a cross between high-street Vietnamese fashion and Roberto Cavalli. The fabrics and cuts are of excellent quality, with prices to match. Open daily 9:30am to 9:30pm. 132-134 Dong Khoi St. ℰ **08/3827-2733.**

DAILY GOODS

Annam A fine selection of imported goods, with Italian and French wines, as well as European chocolates and other comfort foods. Open Monday to Saturday from 8am to 9pm, and Sunday from 9am to 8pm. 16-18 Hai Ba Trung, District 1. ℰ **08/3822-9332.**

Bacchus Corner Expat communities bring their luxury tastes with them, and this stylish storefront carries hundreds of fine vintages for the discerning, including an amazing selection of imported wines. Open Monday to Saturday 9am to 9pm; Sunday 11am to 7pm. 158D Pasteur St., District 1. ℰ **08/3829-3306.** www.bacchuscorner.com.

Veggy's This cool little grocery caters to the most finicky expat from any country. Find fresh daikon along with expensive, imported condiments and staples from Japan; fresh cheeses, yogurt, and wine for Westerners; and good fresh vegetables and special cuts of meat brought in fresh—not frozen—from Australia and New Zealand. It's all in a big walk-in freezer that clients are welcome to peruse. Open daily 8am to 8pm. 29A Le Thanh Ton St., District 1. ℰ **08/3823-8526.**

DEPARTMENT STORES & OUTLETS

There are a number of newer department stores and budget outlets for fashion and footwear. Try the following:

Diamond Department Store More or less a museum to Western luxury for most cash-strapped Vietnamese, the hulking Diamond is a good place to pick up any essential from home you might have forgotten. The top floor of Diamond has a large entertainment area with video games, a bowling alley, and a movie theater that often runs popular Western features (though only sometimes in English with subtitles, so be sure to check ahead). This is a good place to bring the kids for a dose of quarter-plunking, mind-numbing entertainment when tired of touring the busy city. Major credit cards are accepted. Open daily 9:30am to 10 pm. In the Diamond Plaza just north of Notre Dame Cathedral, at 34 Le Duan St. ⓒ 08/3822-5500.

Saigon Square 👜 Go to either of Saigon Square's locations for cheap local and Chinese-imported copies of designer sportswear, anything from the latest temples for your toes to winter coats. The quality is, well, fake, but the price is right and the stuff is good and rugged. It's not a bad place to stock up on travel items or on things you'll need heading home in wintertime. The complexes also house all manner of small budget fashion boutiques, jewelry sellers, and accessories vendors (a good place to pick up copies of the latest Prada or Burberry bag). Open daily 9am to 9pm. 78-89 Nam Ky Khoi Nghia St., District 1 (Saigon Square 1) or 7-9 Ton Duc Thang St., District 1 (Saigon Square 2).

HANDICRAFTS, GIFTS & SOUVENIRS

Note: Unless otherwise stated, most stores listed below open daily at 9am and close around 9pm, but regular hours aren't always (or often) followed. Be prepared for somewhat random opening and closing times, based on the whims of storekeepers.

Alphana Jewelry Gold, silver, and precious stones for all budgets. Accepts MasterCard and Visa. Open daily 8am to 8pm. 159 Dong Khoi St., District 1. ⓒ 08/3829-7398.

Catherine Denoual–Maison ★ This store has exclusive linen and silk cotton blends in elegant neutral tones of white and cream. Bedding, cushions, and runners are designed with tasteful embroidery, and everything has a luxuriously high thread count. Open daily 9am to 9pm. 15C2 Thi Sach St., District 1, opposite the May Hotel. ⓒ 08/3823-9394.

Dong Duong (Comtoir De L'Indochine) Soapstone carvings and fine statuary. Open daily 9am to 7:30pm. 45 Dong Khoi St., District 1. ⓒ 08/3827-3748.

Mai O Mai Tiny shop just off Dong Khoi selling a wide range of handmade accessories and handicrafts, especially necklaces and earrings, as well as some striking bags. Open daily 8am to 10pm. 67 Mac Thi Buoi St. ⓒ 08/3829-4007.

MC Decoration Unique, tasteful, hand-embroidered pillows, table linens, and hand-woven fabrics, as well as fine furnishings, can be found at this stylish outlet. 92C5 Le Thanh Ton, across from the Norfolk Hotel. ⓒ 08/3822-6003.

Nga The lacquer furniture on display here is certainly colorful and eye-catching, and you might just find something that will fit in well back home. Open daily 8am to 10pm. 41 Mac Thi Buoi St., District 1. ⓒ 08/3823-8356.

Red Door Deco Large, contemporary copies of classic Asian-theme furnishings, colonial and Chinese motifs, as well as fine modern pieces. Open daily 8:30am to 8:30pm. 31A Le Thanh Ton, District 1. ⓒ 08/3825-8672.

Saigon Crafts Lacquer crafts and gifts. Accepts MasterCard and Visa. Open daily 8:30am to 9:30pm. 74 Dong Khoi St., District 1. ⓒ 08/3829-5758. www.saigoncrafts.com.

Sapa Crafts and fashions from Northern Vietnam, particularly embroidery of the Flower Hmong that sells like hot cakes. There are several outlets, of which the one on De Tham is probably most convenient. Open daily 8am to 9pm. 209 De Tham ⓒ 08/3836-5163.

Tombo The best of Ho Chi Minh City's many Japanese Zakka shops. What is a Zakka shop? More or less a collection of lady's accouterments, from shoes and wraps to earrings and fine jewelry, the kind of stuff Dad brings home to Mom after a long business trip. This is one of Ho Chi Minh City's most popular—with everything short of Hello Kitty in the mix. Accepts MasterCard and Visa. Open daily 8:30am to 9pm. 145 Dong Khoi St., District 1. ✆ **08/3827-5973.**

SILK

Kenly Silk A brand-name supplier with some of the best ready-to-wear silk garments in the town. Open daily 9am to 8pm. 132 Le Thanh Ton St. ✆ **08/3829-3847.** www.kenlysilk.com.

Khai Silk With outlets throughout the country, Khai Silk is one of the best places for ready-made and tailored silk in Vietnam. The signature store is right downtown, but they have shops throughout the city in some of the finer hotels. Good business sense says, "If something works, then copy it," so there are lots of Khai Silk lookalikes, but Khai is the best. Open daily 9am to 10pm. Smaller shops are at 38 Dong Khoi St., the Legend Hotel, the New World Hotel, and the Sheraton Saigon Hotel and Tower. 107 Dong Khoi St. ✆ **08/3829-1146.** www.khaisilkcorp.com.

SAIGON AFTER DARK

When Vietnam entered the world scene in the mid-1990s, Ho Chi Minh City quickly became one of the hippest party towns in the East. The mood has sobered somewhat, but it's still fun, especially around the Pham Ngu Lao area, where some bars stay open 24 hours. Everything is clustered in District 1; ask expats in places such as **Saigon Saigon** or **Level 23** about underground club happenings, or check out listings in *The Word:HCMC* or *Asialife* magazines. All bars open in the evening and usually keep running until the last customer. As for cultural events, Saigon is sadly devoid of anything really terrific, except for a few dinner and dance shows.

For a nonbar experience, **Bonsai Cruise** (3/F, 101 Nguyen Van Thu St., District 1; ✆ **08/3910-5095;** www.bonsaicruise.com.vn) operates dinner cruises on the Saigon River for $35 per person. Boats depart from a pier just south of the Renaissance Riverside hotel.

Bars & Clubs

The Pham Ngu Lao area stays up late, and there are a number of good watering holes that cater to young travelers. On De Tham Street, about 100m (328 ft.) off Pham Ngu Lao, you'll find a host of little cafes, restaurants, and bars. For a club or chilled lounge vibe, stick to the streets around the Opera House. Also see the box "Saigon Nights: *Bia Hoi* on the Sidewalk Stools," below.

Allez Boo With a prime location at the corner of Pham Ngu Lao and De Tham, this is a classic travelers' bar, serving all kinds of food and a wide range of drinks, with a background soundtrack of current popular hits. It's a great spot to run into people you've met before on your travels, as well as strike up new relationships. Open daily 24 hours. 195 Pham Ngu Lao St., District 1. ✆ **08/6291-5424.**

Amber Room ★ This funky lounge is the new "it" place of Saigon. It's got a slick New York–bar feel to it, with dark wood, overstuffed sofas, and fine cocktails. By day, the music and atmosphere is relaxed and loungelike. The tunes are funkier come night-fall, but the mellow vibe remains. 59 Dong Du St., opposite the Sheraton. ✆ **08/6291-3686.**

Crazy Buffalo In classic copycat style, this place stands opposite to and mirrors the format of super-successful Go₂ Bar (see below), but hasn't yet started drawing the same crowds; perhaps they need some more insistent barkers. There's a happy hour each night from 9 to 11:30pm and shisha pipes. 212 De Tham St., District 1. No phone.

Go₂ Bar ★ This four-story bar, under the same management as Allez Boo, is in the backpacker district, but you'll find everyone from backpackers to businessmen in this place, one of Saigon's top night spots. It has a well-regimented staff of barkers patrolling in front who succeed in packing the place night after night, and it never closes. The terrace spills onto the street, and the party regularly rocks on until dawn. 187 De Tham St., District 1. ✆ **08/3836-9575.**

La Habana Havana meets Saigon in this cozy Mediterranean-style bar, with a nod to Germany in the form of imported beers and food. There's always something going on here, whether it's salsa classes or a live band. Order a mojito and a cigar, close your eyes, and imagine you're in the Caribbean. Open daily 8am to late. 6 Cao Ba Quat St., District 1. ✆ **08/3829-5180.**

Latin Cafe Hope you weren't expecting Latin dancing here. This place is a sports bar through and through, with big TVs on hand to show the latest football matches and other international sporting events. 17 Dong Du St. ✆ **08/3827-9339.**

Level 23 Level 23 is a rotunda with two-story-high ceilings overlooking town. It hosts an all-out disco scene on the weekends and features good live bands. The bar is pretty dead on weeknights, so opt instead for the outdoor patio, a great place to have a chat over late-night drinks. 88 Dong Khoi St. (23rd floor of the Sheraton Hotel). ✆ **08/3827-2828.**

O'Briens If it's good drinking and darts or pool you want, you've come to the right place. This brick-walled Irish pub always packs 'em in, and if you don't know anybody when you walk in, you're sure to know somebody by the time you walk out. Also serves some great pizza. 74A Hai Ba Trung. ✆ **08/3829-3198.**

163 Cyclo Bar Just down the street from Allez Boo (see above) is this busy bar. It rocks from 4pm until late (4 or 5am). The scene is a little seedy sometimes; hang on to your valuables (or leave them in a hotel safe). 163 Pham Ngu Lao St. ✆ **08/3920-1567.**

Pacharan ★ This is a happening place in a perfect location beside the Caravelle and across the street from Park Hyatt. A flatscreen TV is tuned into sports on the first floor, live bands are often playing on the second floor, and the outdoor terrace is on the top floor. A great place to grab a beer, some Spanish wine, or (my personal favorite) a pitcher of sangria. The Spanish tapas here make for good nibbles, but check your bill before leaving, lest you be paying for baskets of bread and aioli dipping sauce that—though tasty—you didn't even order. 97 Hai Ba Trung, District 1. ✆ **08/3825-6024.**

Saigon Saigon On the top floor of the old wing of the Caravelle Hotel, this very popular spot features live music (usually a Filipino cover band) and a terrific view from the balcony seating area. This is undoubtedly the most classic of Saigon experiences (journalists hung out here during the Vietnam War), with great views through heavy wooden shades and under slow-turning ceiling fans of Lam Son Square and the Opera House. Open daily 11am to late. 19 Lam Son. ✆ **08/3823-4999.**

Sax 'n Art This narrow bar is a must for all jazz fans, as there's a very competent live band from 9pm each night, sometimes with talented vocalists, too. As well as mainstream classics, you're likely to hear some bluesy numbers and others influenced by sounds from the Central Highlands. The only problems are the pricey drinks (more than 100,000 VND for a small beer) and a cover charge (65,000 VND) that is slipped in with the check. Open daily 6pm to midnight. 28 Le Loi St., District 1. ✆ **08/3822-8472.**

Seventeen Saloon Yee-hah! Dig out your cowboy outfit and get into the mood at this huge Wild West bar, where three Filipino bands alternate sets and belt out rock classics from the likes of Bon Jovi and U2. Located just east of the budget district, it's very popular among Vietnamese and occasional groups of backpackers. Open daily 7pm to 1am. 103A Pham Ngu Lao St., District 1. ✆ **08/3914-0007.**

Sheridan's Something like O'Briens, above, Sheridan's is a good, friendly, local watering hole—Irish style. There are live bands most nights. Open daily 8am to midnight. 17/13 Le Thanh Ton St. ✆ **08/3823-0793.**

Vasco's Bar This chic, open-air bar twinkles with Christmas lights and the town's elite. It's especially popular with the French crowd. Friday nights really hop. Open daily 4pm to midnight (later on Fri nights). 74/7D Hai Ba Trung, District 1. ✆ **08/3824-2888.**

Xu ★ This is a groovy place with big comfy couches and urban lounge tunes playing in the background. It's not so loud that you have to yell, and not so slow that you fall asleep. The cocktails are excellent—the coconut martini is near-addictive. This is the perfect evening lounge spot in the hotel district. Open daily 11am to midnight. 71-73 Hai Ba Trung St., District 1. ✆ **08/3824-8468.**

Yoko ★ If you start feeling that all nightlife in Saigon is just a poor imitation of bars and clubs back home, check out this cool music venue named after John Lennon's wife in the backstreets of District 3. The huge, low-ceilinged room has a wonderful intimacy and vibrancy to it most nights from around 9pm, as local musicians inject the audience with their enthusiasm. Each night there's a theme such as blues/rock, country pop, or soft jazz. Staff is friendly and drinks are a reasonable. Open daily 8am to late. 22A Nguyen Thi Dieu St., District 3. ✆ **08/3933-0577.**

Music & Theater

A few hotels stage traditional music and dance shows at dinner theaters. The **Rex Hotel** (141 Nguyen Hue Blvd.; ✆ **08/3829-2185**) has regular performances as well. Call ahead of time to check the performance schedule.

SIDE TRIPS FROM HO CHI MINH CITY

Vung Tau

130km (81 miles) SE of Ho Chi Minh City

Just a boat ride from Ho Chi Minh City, Vung Tau is a popular playground for Saigon's expat community, a low-luxe version of the usual beach resort, popular mostly for its convenience to the city. You wouldn't fly around the world to get here, but if you have an extra day in Ho Chi Minh and want some beach time, Vung Tau is a good choice (more picturesque beaches around Mui Ne and Nha Trang require an overnight stay).

Originally called Cape Saint Jacques by French colonists who once vacationed and sailed out of here, the small peninsula and town area today is just a port, but more and more vacation villas are popping up on the surrounding beachside hills. The

🎁 Saigon Nights: *Bia Hoi* on the Sidewalk Stools

The best local nightlife is out on the street at the city's many *bia hoi* stands. In these places, which generally start serving from around 4pm, customers usually squat on a tiny stool and quaff glass after glass of this refreshing brew (fortunately the alcohol content is low so you can manage a few) at around 5,000 VND a pop. Many of these places also serve Vietnamese-style tapas (savory snacks that keep the beer flowing).

In the Dong Khoi area, look for the **Dai Ly Bia Hoi,** 4 Thi Sach, a big fluorescent-lit hall that's usually full of local imbibers at sundown. In the budget district, head for **Bia Hoi 102,** 102 Bui Vien, which is nothing more than a tiny shopfront with stools packing the sidewalk in front; your fellow drinkers here are likely to be other travelers staying in the area, so dust off your travel tales and prepare to pick up some useful tips for your remaining itinerary.

better hotels in Vung Tau City proper are geared to serving European and regional petrochemical workers—offshore oil and gas deposits are mined, shipped to offshore refineries, and then reimported for domestic use. The town also has a thriving hostess-bar scene catering to the same set. There are a few fine beach developments just a short ride from the city, and you'll find good, fresh seafood here.

For some reason, the town has inspired builders of oversize sculpture. On the small mountain to the south of town, look for the giant statue of Jesus, a smaller version of the statue in Rio De Janeiro, and to the north of town, a grand Madonna and Child, plus a big Buddha on a lotus leaf. A sizable Christian population accounts for the Christian statuary, as well as the town's large central cathedral.

ESSENTIALS

GETTING THERE & AWAY   A boat connection is your best option. The 1½-hour trip costs just $10 ($5 for kids), payable in U.S. dollars or Vietnamese dong (200,000 VND/100,000 VND). With two companies sending out boats, there are hourly departures to or from Vung Tau. Boats are rarely full, but departures can be crowded on weekends, so buy a ticket in advance if leaving Saigon on Friday evening or returning from Vung Tau on Sunday; otherwise, you can just show up and see which company has the next departure. Contact **Vina Express** at their riverside ticketing booth, either at the dock area or at their main office at 91 Le Quoc Hung, District 4 (*©* **08/3825-3333**). They have departures starting in the morning at 6am (then at 8:30am, 9:30am, 10:30pm, 12:30pm, 2:30pm, and 4:30pm). Competitor **Petro Express,** 20 Truong Cong Dinh St., in Vung Tau (*©* **064/353-0775**) sells tickets at dockside. The high-speed, Soviet-built boats hydroplane across the surface. Tracing the Saigon River, you get a good look at the boom in import/export traffic from the country's largest port area. The ride is smooth until the mouth of the river, where the boat crosses a short stretch of open sea and bounces around a bit. There's a bathroom on board, and attendants provide complimentary water. Connecting by road from Ho Chi Minh is also a quick and easy trip, just 1½ hours by rented car or minivan. Local buses leave Ho Chi Minh's **Mien Dong Station** in District 3 and take about 2 hours to reach Vung Tau.

ORIENTATION   The city of Vung Tau is spread out over the wide peninsular area, ending to the south with hills and the town's large statue of Jesus. The town center is easy to cover on foot, but the beaches are a bit spread out, so it's a good idea to rent some wheels: bicycle, motorbike, or car with driver. The beaches on the west side of the peninsula are called **Front Beach** and **Mulberry Beach;** the better one on the east is **Back Beach.** Hotels line the busy western port area. The large statue of Tran Hung Dao, at the terminus of the road by the same name, is a good orientation point—many restaurants and services surround this central square, and the road that originates here extends north through town. Tran Phu Street runs along the west side of the peninsula and leads to the town's good seafood restaurants and a few sights.

GETTING AROUND   You'll be swamped by taxi drivers when you pull in at the port; just pick someone. Metered taxis—the best is **Mai Linh taxi** (© **064/356-5656**)—are available all over town. Motorbikes are for rent right at the pier for 120,000 VND, and motorbike taxi drivers and cyclos are available at negotiable rates (about $2 per day or 10,000 VND–15,000 VND for short trips in town).

FAST FACTS   **Vietcombank** has a branch at 27 Tran Hung Dao St. (© **064/385-2309**) with ATM service and can exchange currency or traveler's checks (daily 8am–4pm, with a break for lunch). Internet connections are available in a few storefronts along central Tran Hung Dao Street, with charges around 6,000 VND per hour.

WHERE TO STAY

A few budget choices are along Hoang Hoa Tham Street, leading west from the town center. **Thuy Tien** is just across from Mulberry Beach and adjacent to the large Madonna (84 Tran Phu St.; © **064/3835-220**); they have clean, very spartan rooms in a three-story hotel block for 350,000 VND per night.

Binh An Village 🎁 ★★   By far Vung Tau's nicest place to stay, this secret garden with just four rooms and five suites is a really magical place. From the moment you step through the massive wooden gate in the high wall, you feel you have entered a different world. Inspired by traditional Vietnamese architecture, with solid wood pillars and roofs made of terra cotta tiles, the rooms are all individually decorated in a tasteful blend of period and modern furnishings. Most rooms have an outdoor living room with views across the endless ocean, and there are also libraries of movies and music to choose from. Some suites also have private gardens and pool.

1 Tran Phu St., Vung Tau City. www.binhanvillage.com. © **064/335-1553.** Fax 08/3810264. 9 units. $100–$130 double; $170–$280 suite. MC, V. **Amenities:** Restaurant; 2 bars; saltwater and freshwater pools; room service. In room: A/C, satellite TV, DVD player and movie library, fridge, Wi-Fi.

Palace Hotel   The most popular and busiest of the affordable central lodgings for the town's petrochemical workers (you might feel out of place without a helmet and oily jumpsuit), the Palace has a good array of services and makes for a quick and convenient overnight in Vung Tau (quite close to the ferry pier and the town's expat area). It's nothing special, with large, basic, tidy rooms, but there are lots of good in-house services, including a large, open pool area, a good restaurant overlooking a funky little fountain, a big bar, and massage services. The staff is used to international clients, and service is quite efficient for the price. The **Grand Hotel** (2 Nguyen Du St., Vung Tau; © **064/385-6888;** fax 064/385-6088; www.grandhotel.com.vn), just next door, is slightly more polished, with rooms at the same price, and the two hotels are in negotiation to combine as one.

01 Nguyen Trai St., Vung Tau City. www.palacehotel.com.vn. © **064/385-6411.** Fax 064/385-6878. 94 units. $90–$110 double; $120 suite. MC, V. **Amenities:** Restaurant; bar; small fitness center; Internet; outdoor pool; tennis court. In room: A/C, satellite TV, fridge, Internet, minibar.

Paradise Resort ★   The name is pushing it, but for work-weary residents of Saigon, or tourists looking for a quick escape from steamy city touring, Paradise is something special. The resort is a collection of free-standing beachside bungalows surrounding a small, central pool. Half of the units are older with rough-hewn balconies and exteriors of bamboo and wood sheathing; newer units have a stucco exterior. Both are air-conditioned and tidy, if lacking in style; shiny bedspreads and tacky drapes are kind of a shame, as is the fact that they're a bit dark. But everything is clean, there's a good restaurant, and the resort is adjacent to the town's popular golf course (under the same ownership). The central area has fun, white-plaster Greek statues of scantily clad goddesses and a large lion presiding over the whole scene. You'll need to bring your own wheels or call cabs, but it's only 4km (2½ miles) back to Vung Tau, and you won't likely need to get there much.

On the far north end of Back Beach (in-town sales office: 01 Thuy Van, Vung Tau City). ☏ **064/381-1559.** Fax 064/358-5894. 98 units. $50–$70 double. No credit cards. **Amenities:** Restaurant; bar; golf course; pool. *In room:* A/C, satellite TV, fridge, minibar.

Petro House ★   A grand circular drive and a boutique, colonial lobby greet you at busy Petro House, a popular choice of European expat workers, many on long stay with the petrochemical companies that operate in Vung Tau. Rooms are large and very clean, if sparsely decorated and not quite on par with the hotel's stylish public spaces, but the mattresses are comfy, and the larger suites are great. Hotel staff does all they can to support their guests, even dig up information and contact support for projects. A "can-do" attitude prevails. Their Monte Carlo restaurant serves good Continental cuisine. The bar is always busy and is a good place to grab a game of pool and get the lowdown on the local scene. The Petro House also has fine serviced apartments.

63 Tran Hung Dao St., Vung Tau. www.petrohouse-vungtau.com. ☏ **064/385-2014.** Fax 064/385-2015. 71 units. $55–$65 double; $72 suite. MC, V. **Amenities:** 2 restaurants; bar; fitness center. *In room:* A/C, satellite TV, fridge, minibar, Wi-Fi.

WHERE TO EAT

In addition to the two recommended venues below, consider **Monte Carlo,** at the Petro House Hotel (63 Tran Hung Dao St., Vung Tau; ☏ **064/385-2014**), which serves fine French food; or, at 15 Nguyen Trai, **Whispers,** which is a popular expat haunt that serves up traditional roast dinners and other Western fare.

Nightlife in little Vung Tau is pretty seedy. The places with English signs surrounding the central Tran Phu Square are hostess bars that do a brisk business with Vung Tau's many sailors in port. One spot where you can just enjoy a chat and background music is **Blue Note** on the corner of Tran Hung Dao and Truong Cong Dinh.

Binh An Village INTERNATIONAL/VIETNAMESE   As often happens, the best place to sleep is also the best place to eat. The ambience at this lovely seafront restaurant is as intimate as you could want. Chunky, traditional chairs and tables, as well as relaxing sofas are discreetly spaced, and *objets d'art* are scattered everywhere. Preparation and presentation is immaculate, and everything tastes great. If you've got an appetite, go for an imported steak, or if you're not famished, select some grilled seafood. If you happen to be here on a Saturday evening or Sunday lunchtime, you might be serenaded by a jazz trio.

1 Tran Phu St., Vung Tau City. ☏ **064/335-1553.** Main courses $16–$30. MC, V. Daily 6:30am–10pm.

Ganh Hao SEAFOOD/VIETNAMESE   Serving delicious, fresh seafood from a cool ocean-side promontory, Ganh Hao is the second best place to dine in Vung Tau (next-door Binh An is tops, but this is the locals' pick for seafood). Choices here include lobster with butter or tamarind, fried soft-shell crabs, crabs steamed with beer, jumbo shrimp dishes, oyster, and squid, as well as great whole-fish dishes such as goby, snake-head fish, sea bass, or red tilapia. The Ganh Hao Fish Salad of white-fish lightly sautéed in butter with onions and peanuts, wrapped in a rice paper roll with coriander, basil leaves, and lettuce, and dipped in sweet sauce or fish sauce is absolutely delicious. The view of the ocean from the terrace makes for a pleasant afternoon or evening. If it's too windy, try the large, two-story restaurant section. Take a taxi here; it's about 4km (2½ miles) up Tran Phu Street along Front Beach.

03 Tran Phu St., Vung Tau. © **064/355-0909.** Main courses 55,000 VND–115,000 VND; luxe seafood can run up to 500,000 VND. No credit cards. Daily 9am–10pm.

Good Morning Vietnam ITALIAN   This unoriginal chain of eateries can be found in almost all of the tourist spots in Vietnam, but each one's individually owned and managed. This is a good one, with an effusive Italian owner who hosts lots of international business clients looking for a taste of the familiar. Portions are large, ingredients are fresh, and the pizza is tops.

6 Hoang Hoa Tham St., Vung Tau. © **064/385-6959.** Main courses 75,000 VND–210,000 VND. No credit cards. Daily 9am–10pm.

ATTRACTIONS & ACTIVITIES

Thic Ca Phat Dai is the name of the temple and large Buddha statue that stands high above the seaside about 5km (3 miles) north along Tran Phu Street at Front Beach. Climb the hill, first to the small temple, and then on up the steps to the large open area with the big Buddha overlooking the port below, as well as other statuary and little pavilions. One gazebo has inscriptions from the Buddhist precepts about the delights of passionless meditation, cultivating good in oneself, the impermanence of the body, and the belief that viewing the world as a fragile bubble, a mirage, fends off fear of death. Heady stuff. Just before reaching the big Buddha, meet the giant Madonna standing over another stretch of beach. Both sights are free, but with plenty of suggested donation boxes, and are open from dawn to dusk.

The **Giant Jesus statue** on the small mountain to the south of town can be reached by climbing a path up from the coast, and you can even clamber up inside for a heavenly view from the statue's shoulder. It's open from 7:30 to 11:30am and 1:30 to 5pm; admission is free. Also on the small mountain, just north of the giant Jesus statue, is a century-old **lighthouse** that can be accessed by a winding road leading up from near the hydrofoil jetty. Once again, there are great views out to sea and along Back Beach.

One of Vung Tau's newest attractions is a cable car leading to Cloud Lake Cultural and Ecotourism Park at the top of the big mountain (240m/787 ft.) to the north of town; tickets cost 100,000 VND. The cable car station is just north of Front Beach.

If you're interested in golf, check out the **Paradise Resort** (on the far north end of Back Beach; see "Where to Stay," above), which hosts the popular beachside **Paradise Ocean Noon Golf Club,** a recently renovated course of 27 holes with a small dining area, club rentals, and a pro shop. Contact the clubhouse directly at © **062/382-3366.**

A Side Trip to Long Hai

120km (75 miles) SE of Ho Chi Minh City; 40km (25 miles) NE of Vung Tau

Just a short trip north along the coast from Vung Tau—or a direct drive from Saigon—Long Hai is a secluded getaway along an attractive piece of coastline. It can be blissfully peaceful on weekdays, but like everywhere within driving distance of Ho Chi Minh City, it's packed with day trippers at the weekend. The town itself is a Fellini-esque place, but the many kids flying massive kites of sharks and dragons make it a sight (and *really* Fellini-esque), while the resorts are a few kilometers away.

GETTING THERE

From Vung Tau, it's a short 20km (13-mile) ride west to Long Hai along a newish coast road that runs almost as far as Phan Thiet and has made many stretches of beach accessible that were previously impossible to get to. From Saigon, it's 120km (75 miles; follow signs from the turnoff in Ba Ria).

WHERE TO STAY

Anoasis Resort ★★ This aptly named resort has long been a favorite of Saigon's expats. In an area where the last emperor, Bao Dai, once came to play, Anoasis Resort is run by a French expat and his wife, a helicopter pilot of local fame. It can get pretty busy on the weekends (when rates are about 10% higher) with folks fleeing the city heat. Whether in their large pavilion rooms or a smaller bungalow, the accommodations are neat, characterized by double-height thatch roofs, oversize bamboo furnishings, and lots of comfortable areas to sit back and put your feet up (bathrooms are a bit small, though). The service is impeccable. The place is arranged along a hillside overlooking a picturesque bay where the wind howls and the surf rolls in, mesmerizing in the cool of a hammock at seaside. The central pool is large and has great shaded lounges and places for the kids to frolic—even basketball hoops. The hilltop restaurant is stunning, with French and familiar Western gourmet cuisine.

Road 44, Long Hai, Ba Ria, Vung Tau. www.anoasisresort.com.vn. ✆ **064/386-8227.** Fax 064/386-8229. 46 units. $110–$179 bungalow; $280–$800 villa. MC, V. **Amenities:** Restaurant; bar; small fitness pavilion; outdoor pool; tennis courts. *In room:* A/C, satellite TV, fridge, minibar, Wi-Fi.

Long Hai Beach Resort Sprawling Long Hai Beach Resort is more of a classic resort than the idiosyncratic Anoasis, with a large, ostentatious lobby and wide walkway leading down to oceanside colonnades and a picturesque pool perched over the rocky beach. Public spaces are stylish, but rooms are tacky in terra-cotta tile and faux-Chinese furnishings. The large thatched-roof restaurant is quite stunning, though, and views of the pool and shore are great. It's geared mostly to tour groups and business conventions, but can be a relaxing place if no groups are in residence. Rates go up around 10% at weekends.

Next to Anoasis Resort along Road 44, Long Hai, Long Dien District, Ba Ria, Vung Tau. www.longhaibeachresort.com. ✆ **064/366-1355.** Fax 064/366-1356. 110 units. 3,500,000 VND deluxe double; 4,500,000 VND bungalow; 5,900,000 VND suite villa. MC, V. **Amenities:** 2 restaurants; bar; bikes; children's center and playground; small fitness center; Jacuzzi; outdoor pool at beachside; room service; spa. *In room:* A/C, satellite TV, fridge, minibar, Wi-Fi.

Thuy Duong This isolated, low-luxe resort complex is located on a nice stretch of beach shaded by casuarina trees. Popular with vacationing Vietnamese, it's got a kitschy beachside vibe (lots of little cottages, playgrounds, and busy coffee shops overlooking the sea). Rooms in the hotel block are clean and nondescript but comfortable; go for the superior rooms, which are larger and have decent furnishings, offer windows with views, and are less prone to must. The pool is a postage stamp. The hotel is in Phuoc Hai, a few miles north of the two fine resorts at Lang Hai; it is, however, pretty self-contained, with a host of activities, including boat and jet-ski rentals, a large nightclub with karaoke, and a massage parlor. Especially popular with Vietnamese tourists.

Phuoc Hai Village, Long Dat Do District, Vung Tau Province. www.thuyduongresort.com.vn. ✆ **064/388-6215.** Fax 064/388-6180. 113 units. $50–$185 double. No credit cards. **Amenities:** 2 restaurants; bar/nightclub; small outdoor pool; tennis; watersports equipment/rentals. *In room:* A/C, satellite TV, fridge, minibar, Wi-Fi.

ATTRACTIONS

The beach is the real attraction here, and you'll likely spend all of your time at your resort; there are, however, a few fun day trips, either from here or Ho Chi Minh City. The beach at **Ho Coc,** some 30km (19 miles) farther along the coast, is the best you'll find on a day trip from Ho Chi Minh City, and there are a few resorts there, too, including the massive **Furama Resort** (www.furamahococ.com), scheduled to open in 2012 with more than 500 rooms. The **Binh Chau Hot Springs** (www.saigonbinhchauecoresort.com; ✆ **064/387-1131;** admission 20,000 VND), some 15km (9 miles) farther on from Ho Coc, offers visitors the chance to plunge in hot mud or soak in a steaming bath of soothing mineral water at the "Dreamy Spring Pool," and boil an egg for a snack over the scalding water of a geothermal opening. Near the Thuy Duong Resort in Phuoc Hai, you might also consider a visit to the **Minh Dam Caves,** a former Communist bolt-hole located near the top of a hill, from where there are great views of the coast and rice paddies.

A Side Trip to Con Dao Archipelago: Con Son Island

180km (97 nautical miles) SE of Vung Tau

There's an old saying on Con Son: On days when the water surrounding this remote island's rocky cliffs is windless and still, locals say that, with the shimmering reflection in the deep blue-green water, it's as if the "birds swim in the sea and the fish fly in the clouds."

Con Son, the main island of 14 in the Con Dao Archipelago, possesses a kind of solitary beauty that inspires poetry, but the island also evokes the haunting memory of the thousands who suffered and died in the notorious prisons that date from the French colonial era to the end of the American War. Many Vietnamese, war veterans, and former prisoners travel to the island to pay homage to the fallen at temple shrines and tombs, many of which are unmarked at the Hang Duong memorial cemetery.

The island was known by its Malay name, Poulo Condore, during the era of European maritime exploration and the scramble for wealth and power in the East. The British East India Company laid claim to the island in 1702, but their stay was short-lived. In 1787, the island was ceded to the French by Nguyen Anh (who later became Emperor Gia Long) in return for military support for his efforts to consolidate the throne. Ironically, the French later came to dominate all of Vietnam, and, in 1861, Con Son became a prison island for political prisoners. Perhaps the most tragically poignant story of Con Son's prisoners is that of Vo Thi Sau, executed by the French at 19 years of age for lobbing a grenade at French soldiers when she was only 14. These days there is something of a cult surrounding her, and her grave is one of the most visited of the many in the Hang Duong Cemetery. The battle of Dien Bien Phu ended French power in 1954 and Vietnam was divided at the 17th Parallel, after which prisons in the south were controlled by the South Vietnamese and their new American allies. It became notorious for its "tiger cages" when photos by Tom Harkin (now Iowa's U.S. senator) were published by *Life Magazine* in July 1970. Freedom finally came at the end of the war in 1975.

The archipelago is one of the last frontiers for conservation in Vietnam, and although much of its land and coastal waters are national park zones, the state of its natural environment remains in delicate balance. The unique diversity of the archipelago's topography and microclimate host a menagerie of terrestrial, aquatic, and avian species, some of which are endemic. Among its unique natural features are the dune marshes, unfortunately dissected by a grid of roads for a housing development that never materialized. Migratory herons and egrets in breeding plumage can be seen at Quang Trung Lake in March and April, and the brown noddy and brown booby nest at Trung Islet north of Con Son. In the forest the endemic black giant squirrel and macaques are common sightings.

The unpopulated outer islands are a boon to **sea turtles** that nest on deserted beaches, such as Cat Lon beach on Bay Canh Island, and 300 annual nestings have been recorded in past years. **Dugongs** feed in the seagrass meadows of shallow bays but are now increasingly rare. The World Wildlife Foundation and other international NGOs have supported conservation efforts, and the island's National Park office maintains a museum and hands out information and visitor permits to protected areas where park rangers are stationed.

Just getting here by plane is an adventure: Looking out of the ports of the turbo-prop planes, you see the murky estuaries of the delta spilling into swirls of blue sea as the plane is buffeted about in the strong seasonal winds of the South China Sea. The winding ride into town hugs the cliff face with the surf pounding below, and as you swoop down to the island's little runway, you see the rugged island peaks and outline of reefs and land emerge.

The town fronting Con Son Bay doesn't have the usual bars or glitzy trappings found in most Vietnamese beach resort towns. Instead, the colonial buildings, streets lined with huge trees, and fishing boats bobbing at anchor in the small port lend a nostalgic, peaceful atmosphere to this oceanic outpost. Secluded beaches are without the usual thatched cone shelters, sun loungers, or itinerant vendors and masseurs. Cool sea winds make the island rather temperate year-round, but wind conditions and poor visibility make **diving** a tacky proposition between November and January. **Cycling** along the narrow track bordering the reed- and water lily–filled Quang Trung Lake to the huge expense of sand dunes is a great outing. The dunes forested with acacia trees are often used by the army garrison as a training ground and shooting range, complete with bunkers, foxholes, and mock tanks, so take care when in this area.

GETTING THERE

Con Dao is 45 minutes by air from Ho Chi Minh City with daily morning and after-noon flights, though these are occasionally delayed or canceled due to inclement weather. **Vasco Airlines** (Vietnam Air Service Co.), a division of Vietnam Airlines, operates twin-engine turboprop planes from **Ho Chi Minh City**'s Ton Sa Nhat Airport (one-way flights cost from 1,000,000 VND). Be sure to make prior arrangements for transport from the airport to your hotel. If you arrive without arrangements, there may be coaches from resorts you can hop on to get into town. There are no regular taxis, and motorbike taxis are uncommon.

Buy tickets through any Ho Chi Minh travel agent, or drop by any of the Vietnam Airlines ticketing offices, listed on their website (www.vietnamairlines.com).

Locals often take the ships plying between Con Dao and Vung Tau (outlying port) leaving at 5pm, but I don't recommend this. The cheap overnight sea crossing takes 12 hours with bunk beds provided, but departures are irregular and tickets snapped up quickly.

ORIENTATION

The airport on the northern part of Con Son Island is a 20-minute ride to town, winding along the steep cliffs overlooking the sea, past the new Six Senses Resort at Dac Doc beach, and leveling out as you pass Lo Voi Cape. The small town in the middle of the island on the eastern coast fronts Con Son Bay. The main road continues south out of town, hugging the hilly scenic coastline, ending at Ben Dam Port on the south western tip. There is no road on the western side of the island with rugged mountains sloping to the sea.

FAST FACTS   The Vietinbank on Le Duan Street in Con Son Town provides basic banking services and an ATM. The better hotels accept credit cards, but bring enough local currency just in case. Most resorts, some minihotels, and a few cafes have Wi-Fi. The **post office** is at 48 Nguyen Hue, next to the radio tower.

WHERE TO STAY & DINE

With the exception of the Six Senses Resort, all **accommodations** on the island are quite affordable, though advance booking is advisable in high season (Dec–Jan) as there are a limited number of rooms available.

The best **dining** options are in the better hotels, and while the food is often fine, service leaves something to be desired in most places. The **Con Dao Sea Travel Resort,** 6 Nguyen Duc Thuan St., has a good seafood restaurant, while the **Saigon Con Dao Resort** (see below) is a reliable standby with both Vietnamese and international dishes. For a real splurge, book a table at the Six Senses Resort's restaurant, **By the Beach,** where the menu consists mostly of Asian fusion dishes. If you want to dine as the locals do, there are stalls near the small central market selling noodles, baguette sandwiches, grilled skewered meats, and soya curd. Take your phrase book along or just point out what you want.

Resort A   This converted French administration building retains its colonial look with terra cotta roofing, timber rafters, and colonnaded verandas. Some villas date from 1936, but new blocks, poorly modeled after the real thing, lack ambience. The rooms are modestly furnished and rather plain but fairly comfortable. It's a good option for small groups or families who want a place all to themselves since some "villas" are in small separate compounds. The sea is just across the road from the embankment wall that skirts the town's waterfront at Con Son Bay. Rates are reasonable for the historical ambience and convenience of its central location.

8 Ton Duc Thang St. © **064/383-0666.** Fax 064/383-0111. 52 units. $40 double; $182 suite (with private pool). **Amenities:** Restaurant. *In room:* A/C, TV, minibar.

Saigon Con Dao Resort ★   Once housed in converted prison administration buildings of the 1930s, this resort has now moved down the road to smart new digs that are managed by government-run Saigontourist. It can be a little noisy when filled with locals or government officials, but there are plenty of facilities such as a swimming pool and tennis court. Rooms are smart, if rather plain, with all the basics you'd expect.

18-24 Ton Duc Thang St. www.saigoncondao.com. © **064/3830-336.** Fax 064/3830-567. 115 units. $65–$85 double; $110–$150 suite. Rates include breakfast. MC, V. **Amenities:** Restaurant; motorbike/car rental; pool; sauna; tennis court. *In room:* A/C, TV, minibar.

Six Senses Con Dao ★★★   This super stylish resort opened in December 2010, instantly placing Con Dao on the international luxury resort map. Nestled cozily on a private beach at Dat Doc Bay and backed by a forested ridge, it is a world unto itself. The individually furnished villas with wood paneled interiors have huge soft beds draped with opaque mosquito nets, looking like something out of the Arabian Nights. This princely vantage point looks over the private pool, as well as the beach, sea, and sky. The complex blends into the natural landscape with a re-created "fishing village" on an elevated timber walkway with a deli, restaurant, media library, and artisan houses. As usual at Six Senses resorts, each villa has a private butler, and leisure activities include water sports, boat trips, and cooking classes.

Dat Doc Beach. www.sixsenses.com. © **064/383-1222.** Fax 064/383-1456. 50 units. From $600–$900 pool villa; $1,760–$2,205 2-4 bed villa. **Amenities:** Restaurant; bar; media library; beachside pool; sauna; spa; watersports equipment/rentals. *In room:* A/C, TV, minibar, fridge, hair dryer, Wi-Fi.

ATTRACTIONS

Lady Phi Yen Temple   This small temple was built in homage to Lady Phi Yen, wife of the Nguyen Dynasty Emperor Gia Long. Just south of town, the temple is a 1958 remake of the late-19th-century original (destroyed by the French). The story goes that Phi Yen accompanied her husband in exile after defeat at the hands of the Tay Son. Under threat and desperately seeking French support to retain his throne, the Emperor made many concessions including ceding Con Dao to the French. It was to herald the beginning of Vietnam's colonization by the French. His wife expressed doubt, advocated peace, and was suspected by Gia Long of treason. After he left the island—fleeing the Tay Son—Lady Phi Yen was thrown into an isolated cell and left to die, but she survived with the help of mythical creatures (a monkey and tiger), only to commit suicide later. The temple honors her tragic tale, her fortitude, and her love of peace.

On the southern end of the town just off the main road. Arrange for a guide at your hotel. Dawn–dusk. Free admission.

HISTORICAL VESTIGES

The main attractions of Con Dao make a stark contrast; the rugged beauty of the landscape and the sad vestiges of its inhumane past. For Vietnamese visitors, a trip to Con Dao is tantamount to a pilgrimage to pay respect to those who gave their lives in the struggle for independence, and while it's worth visiting the museum, prison buildings, and the cemetery, these aspects of the island can be depressing. Fortunately, taking time to explore the island and its surrounding waters is the perfect antidote to the island's painful history. The below can all be seen with one ticket (35,000 VND, purchased at the Con Dao Museum), and are by appointment only. Contact the museum or your hotel front desk to arrange a visit.

Con Dao Museum   Located in the center of town by the waterfront, adjacent to the long jetty where prisoners were disembarked onto the island, the Con Dao Museum was once the home of island governors—French, South Vietnamese, and American. The building was converted to a museum after the island was liberated by the Viet Cong in 1975, and is now a good place to begin an exploration of the island's brutal history.

The exhibits include photos of emaciated prisoners shackled together, artwork of their desperate conditions, and the very rifle butts and clubs that were used for beatings. The last room in a clockwise loop through the building chronicles the liberation of Con Dao, the reconciliatory return of many prisoners, and a rather faded collection of German and Russian state gifts to the people of Vietnam. Several members of the current Hanoi administration did tenure in the horrific prison chambers, and the museum displays their pictures with an account of their experience. There are good

English-language descriptions of the island's history, lists of official French and U.S. policies toward prisoners, and information about the many uprisings and armed resistance by prisoners.

Ton Duc Thang St. Admission is free. Mon–Sat 7:30–11:30am and 1:30–5pm

Phu Hai Prison   Built in 1862, this is the oldest of the island prisons. Originally Bagne 1 (Prison 1) under the French, it was later called Camp II by the South Vietnamese and then renamed Phu Hai. Low guard towers loom over the open courtyard, and thick, high walls are topped with shards of glass. At the center of the broad space is a small Christian chapel built in 1963, a bit of irony considering the atrocities committed here. Comprising the bounds of the courtyard are the sloping terra-cotta-tiled roofs and shaded cellblock walkways. Where in other colonial strongholds of Vietnam the faded yellow plaster, heavy timbers, and umber tile work of colonial architecture looks quaint and inviting, here it takes on a rather sinister aspect.

The first cell on the left, no. 9, is set up to re-create prison conditions in their heyday, when more than 5,000 men were held here, with 80 to 100 shackled together in large common cells. Concrete mannequins, disturbingly lifelike, are rendered in all manner of contorted positions, just as the inmates were. Docents light a handful of joss sticks, and visitors are invited to make an offering at a small Buddhist altar.

Closest to the Con Dao Museum. Contact the museum directly or arrange at one of the better hotels or resorts.

Phu Son Prison   Just adjacent to Trai Phu Hai, this prison is about the same: a large courtyard surrounded by large common rooms of high yellowed walls. The prison's claim to notoriety is its most heroic revolutionary prisoners—the likes of Le Hong Phuong, and later Le Duan, who succeeded Ho Chi Minh as the president of Vietnam at the end of the war. Plaques listing the names of famous internees are next to each door. At Trai Phu Son, your guide may take you into a small isolation cell and close the door, shutting out all light, leaving just the smell of dank cement in disorientating darkness to give you an idea of what solitary confinement was like.

At the town center, just adjacent to Trai Phu Hai. Contact the museum directly or arrange at one of the better hotels or resorts.

The Tiger Cages and Hang Duong Cemetery   The tiger cages were built by the French and later used by the southern regime allied to America. Here, from 1940 to 1955 under French authority and again during the Vietnam War, prisoners were kept in walled pits with bars overhead from which their jailors could look down. Prisoners were often tormented with buckets of limewash poured down on their suppurating wounds. Most tours of Con Dao's historical vestiges end at the Hang Duong Cemetery, where there are nearly 2,000 prisoners' graves, mostly unmarked. Your guide will no doubt point out the grave of Vo Thi Sau, shot by a firing squad when she was just 19; combs and mirrors are made as offerings for the girl who loved to comb her hair.

To arrange a private tour with an English-speaking guide, contact the museum directly or arrange at one of the better hotels or resorts.

OUTDOOR ACTIVITIES
Diving
Rainbow Divers, based at the Six Senses Con Dao, is a franchise of the popular PADI certified dive operator in Nha Trang. The expat dive masters and instructors are friendly and competent at arranging day or night dives and snorkeling trips. They also

instruct Open Water Courses or "try dives" for beginners off the beach or in the pool, and activities on the outer islands. The best time to go is between May and July; low season is from January to March.

Con Dao has the most diverse range of dive sites in Vietnam, and several species listed as common sightings include frogfish, paperfish, devil scorpionfish, nudibranches, and giant moray eels. Every diver hopes to see the elusive manta rays and reef sharks known to be in these waters, or the turtles that come to nest at Bay Canh Island, but it is the macro life that has distinguished Vietnam's waters. Sightings of the **dugong,** a large sea mammal that feeds on seagrass, have been documented in Con Dao but are rarely seen. There's also a wreck.

Prices for snorkeling or just tagging along on a boat trip start at $50; diving off the beach $100; two daytime dives $200; and a night dive $145. Dig deeper into your pockets for an Open Water Course ($510).

Six Senses Resort, Dat Doc Beach, Con Dao. *C* **09/0557-7671.** www.divevietnam.com.

Trekking

Trekking in protected forest areas requires a permit. Your guide can make arrangements, or you can visit the **Con Dao National Park Office,** 29 Vo Thi Sau St. (*C* **064/363-0443;** www.condaopark.com.vn), a few miles from the town, adjacent to Quang Trung Lake. The office is open from 8 to 11:30am and 1 to 5pm.

A small museum at the office features natural history exhibits including a preserved dugong carcass and informative materials and photographs.

The popular So Ray forest trail is well marked and takes you up and down to emerge at Ong Dung beach, where rangers are stationed. Chattering birds flit through the canopy, and giant black squirrels forage among the fruiting trees.

A longer trek explores the knoll and remote beaches near the airport, best attempted with a guide from the park. Other trips include day boat trips to outlying islands, particularly to **Bay Canh Island,** where you can trek to the old French lighthouse. The sand dunes north of Quang Trung Lake are another option where no permit or guide is necessary.

A Side Trip to Cat Tien National Park (Vuon Quoc Gia Cat Tien)

145km (90 miles) N of Ho Chi Minh City; 195km (121 miles) S of Dalat

Covering a massive area of more than 70,000 hectares (173,000 acres) shared by three provinces—Lam Dong, Binh Phuoc, and Dong Nai—the Cat Tien National Park was first established in 1978 and enlarged (nearly doubled) in 1992. It's one of the top bird- and game-spotting preserves in the region, important not only as one of the last standing evergreen and semievergreen old-growth forests in the south of Vietnam, but as a habitat for some of the region's most endangered species, particularly the Javanese rhinoceros. Once ranging widely throughout Southeast Asia, the rhinos were thought completely extinct until a few were spotted in 1999 by tripwire cameras in the park. The sad fact is that these are the last few of a nearly extinct breed, but part of the park's mission is to create the right conditions of wide grasslands and damp, swampy wallows so that the rhinos will see resurgence in numbers. Other rare animals—tigers, sun bears, and Asian wild dogs—are known to range freely, and the park has been quite successful in growing a population of the threatened Siamese crocodile. You're unlikely to see anything too rare, but even the shortest walk in the dense forest or along the park access road means sightings of squirrels, monkeys, and small game such as civets and miniature forest deer.

Con Dao by the Bells

For Vietnamese, a visit to Con Dao is something akin to standing in front of the Liberty Bell in Philadelphia or the Magna Carta in the British Library. As such, old Communist cadre decorum is the rule, and like back in the day when the state ruled every move for citizens, there is a system of bells and announcements telling you what to do. Starting at 5am, you'll hear wake-up music and announcements. At 5:30am, music and instructions follow for exercise time. The lunch bell sounds at 11am, and 1pm is the end-of-lunch (or wake-up-from-siesta) bell. The bell at 5pm signals an end to the workday, and at 6pm you'll hear the news.

But the park's birds bring most visitors here. You could meet anyone from eccentric amateur birders to professors of **ornithology.** The park's canteen, in fact, looks something like a panel in one of Gary Larson's *Far Side* cartoons, with peculiar scientists comparing eyeglass prescriptions and zoom lenses, and swapping their experiences in spying all that is ruby-crested, struts, and shows plumage. The park publishes a comprehensive guide listing the many rare species here. I had the good fortune to see a massive yellow hornbill, as well as various large egrets, heron, and rare water fowl.

The park is sponsored by the folks at the World Wildlife Foundation and, under their tutelage, Vietnamese rangers have reduced the number of people living in the park to a few thousand (subsistence farmers are given good incentives to move, and support thereafter), and steps are being taken to eliminate dangerous detritus, the kind that is not just an eyesore, but can harm animals, such as fishing nets and rope traps. The park supports more than 100 varieties of mammals, 350 species of bird, more than 100 types of fish, 79 reptile species, 41 amphibians, 457 butterflies, and thousands of insects. The tally of protected animals is as follows: 18 mammals (including the endangered Indo rhino), 20 birds, 12 reptiles, 1 amphibian, and an orange-necked partridge—which is endangered—in the proverbial pear tree. The nice part is, unlike other parks in Vietnam, the animal population density is high and you're sure to spot some critters. You're also sure to see some massive, ancient ficus trees on many of the park's hiking trails. The grasslands and wetlands that give life to the park's animals and plants drain into the **Dong Nai River,** which runs near the park entry.

The park area was also home to ancient Oc Eo settlements from Vietnam's early history, and you can find some information about them, and the ancient Phu Nam dynasty, at the visitor center.

The best news is that Cat Tien National Park is very organized. At information counter you can organize tours, borrow bicycles, rent jeeps, and hire guides at very reasonable rates (**night viewing** by jeep is 200,000 VND per person, with descending rates per person for larger groups).

Be sure to visit **Bai Sau,** otherwise known as **Crocodile Lake,** largest of the park's wetland areas and the best opportunity for seeing larger game. (I saw a small herd of Sambar deer, civets, and, yes, crocodile eyes glowing on the lake at night.) The lake is 10km (6¼ miles) from the park office, and the lakeside ranger station is a stunning 5km (3-mile) forest walk. You must hire a guide for the trip. You can overnight at the lake for the best chance to see wildlife at night, but the experience is very basic; imagine an aging Boy Scouts' camp minus any frills.

For further information, contact the park office at Tan Phu District, Dong Nai Province (© **061/366-9228;** fax 061/366-9159; www.namcattien.org).

GETTING THERE

Hiring a car for the one-way trip from either Dalat or Ho Chi Minh is the best option. Expect to pay around $100 to get you to the park gate, but it'll save you some hassle. Alternatively, sign up for a small group tour of the park with a reliable Ho Chi Minh City tour operator such as Sinhbalo Adventure Tours.

The park is located 24km (15 miles) north of Hwy. 20 between Dalat and Ho Chi Minh (the turnoff to the park is 125km/78 miles from Saigon and 175km/109 miles from Dalat). You can arrange a ride to kilometer 125 from Ho Chi Minh or Dalat, but you'll have to watch for the turnoff and remind the driver before you get there. Budget tourist cafe buses also follow these routes daily and are good about dropping you off in the right spot.

The motorbike taxi drivers at the turnoff are some of the hungriest bunch of crocodiles I've ever met, and the sad news is that once you hop off the bus, they have you over a barrel. The bargaining starts at 400,000 VND, but if you're patient and persistent, you should get it for a quarter of that. Park entrance is 50,000 VND. Walk 100m (328 ft.) down the road to the free ferry, and then to the park information and check-in center, where the very helpful folks will help you sort things out.

WHERE TO STAY & DINE

The best and priciest accommodation option is **Forest Floor Lodge** (www.vietnam foresthotel.com; © **061/366-9890**), located on the fringe of the national park, where you can choose between deluxe tents or wooden Vietnamese houses, with rates from $135 to $155. Rooms and bungalows operated by the park are basic but clean, with much cheaper rates ($20–$30). The entrance area to the park is a cozy little campus, and there is a fun fraternal vibe among the many visitors here, most of whom are avid birders and eager to connect with fellow members of that rare species. Dining at the canteen is reasonable and quite good; they also have a selection of local wines that really gets the conversation flowing. Expect to meet people here and be able to arrange shared tours to the woods together.

One other option is to spend the night out at Bai Sau, Crocodile Lake. Accommodations here are spartan, but they do have running water and toilet facilities. Rooms have no fan and just a hanging mosquito net, but the less-than-basic, rustic comforts ensure a good chance to spot rare animals at lakeside in the early morning or at night.

THE MEKONG DELTA

The Mekong Delta is one of Vietnam's most interesting and scenic regions. An organized tour, even the most low-budget version, offers action-packed days with bus and boat trips to small crafts villages, mangrove swamps, island orchards, and spectacular **floating markets.**

The Delta is a web of Mekong River waterways covering an area of about 60,000km (37,200 miles) across 13 provinces. The region is one of the most densely populated in Vietnam with around 20 million souls, most engaged in farming and fishing. The Mekong Delta accounts for more than 50% of all rice and produce in the country, exporting between 4 and 5 million tons of rice per year, earning it the title of the country's "rice basket." The land is tessellated with bright green rice paddies, fruit orchards, sugar-cane fields, and vegetable gardens, and its waters stay busy with boats and fish farms. Rice production and harvest still involves water buffaloes instead of tractors, as well as backbreaking hand planting of rice shoots, weeding, and harvesting.

Impoverished under socialist agricultural programs, the region benefited greatly from the 1980s Doi Moi reforms, and rice paddies that once yielded just one crop now produce three crops per year, an important part of Vietnamese economic self-sufficiency.

The Delta was a hotbed for Viet Cong guerrillas during the war with the U.S., and some tours will take you to the vestiges of old Viet Cong hide-outs, complete with ambush holes and a ride among the mangrove swamps where stealth forces disappeared after raids in Saigon.

A 1-day trip isn't quite enough to fully delve into the Delta, so plan on an overnight—best in the Delta's urban centers of Can Tho or Chau Doc near Cambodia (try to stay at the Victoria in either location). For more specific advice on tour options, see p. 338.

VISITOR INFORMATION

To cope with necessary logistics in the Mekong Delta, use a tour agent, who can offer everything from day trips to long adventure tours and longer homestays. Cycling the Delta has become popular, and many of the operators (I recommend Sinhbalo and Ann Tours) are now offering cycling tours that take you along the dusty paths that line the area's canals and link rice paddies between small towns. Again, even on a bike, go with a tour operator to avoid the crowded roads in the region and get to the back of beyond. Many tours conclude in Chau Doc, and lots of travelers make their way to Phnom Penh from there, while others prefer to wind up their Delta adventure with some toes-in-the-sand time on Phu Quoc Island. Tour operators are flexible and can accommodate any special plans.

Tour Operators

My pick for classic tours to the Mekong Delta is **Sinhbalo Adventure Travel,** 283/20 Pham Ngu Lau St., District 1 (© **08/3837-6766;** fax 08/3836-7682; www. sinhbalo.com or www.cyclingvietnam.net). Their custom tour takes you off the beaten path (from $35 a day with a group) to homestays and offers plenty of chances to bike along country lanes and kayak along narrow canals. Another reliable operator is **Exotissimo,** 80–82 Phan Xich Long St., Phu Nuan District (© **08/3995-9898;** fax 08/3995-9184; www.exotissimo.com). Their prices are steeper than other tour operators, but their guides are very knowledgeable and their level of professionalism is unrivaled. They arrange private, customized tours, which means you travel away from groups and on your own time schedule.

Ann Tours, in Ho Chi Minh City at 58 Ton That Tung St., District 1 (© **08/3925-3636;** fax 08/3832-3866; www.anntours.com), is a long-running and efficient operator that specializes in customized tours for individuals, couples, or small groups. They can help you develop an itinerary and then quote a price for transport, guide, and accommodation.

Victoria Hotels, main office in Ho Chi Minh City, second floor, 101 Tran Hung Dao St., District 1; www.victoriahotels-asia.com; © **08/3837-3031;** fax 08/3836-4108), runs the two finest hotels in the region (in Chau Doc and Can Tho). If you book through the hotel directly, consider taking advantage of their excellent tour services—all with private driver, guide, transfers, and good local tours using one—or both—hotels as a base. They have luxury day-cruisers in Can Tho and offer a standard course of floating market tours from both Can Tho and Chau Doc. Also check out their high-speed connection—on board a zippy runabout—between Chau Doc and Phnom Penh, Cambodia.

You'll also find many **eco-tour options** in the Delta, with trips that combine cultural touring and cycling trips (the area is mercifully flat). Contact **Innoviet Tours,** 158 Bui Vien, District 1 (© **08/6291-5407;** www.innoviet.com), which runs 2- and 5-day cycling tours for small groups (max. 8 people), with lots of time in the saddle. On the budget end, **Delta Adventure Tours,** 267 De Tham, District 1 (© **08/3920-2112;** www.deltaadventuretours.com), runs lots of routes and houses you in their floating hotel at Chau Doc.

The **tourist cafes** all run standard, affordable tours. Contact **The Sinh Tourist,** 246–248 De Tham St., District 1 (© **08/3836-9420;** www.sinhcafevn.com), or **TNK,** 216 De Tham St. (© **08/3920-4766;** www.tnktravelvietnam.com), in the Pham Ngu Lao area of Ho Chi Minh City. All of the budget cafe tour companies offer 2- and 3-day tours starting at around $20 per day (with optional connection to Cambodia), and for that low price, expect little in the way of good tour leading and explanation. Accommodations on these trips are very basic, and one gets the sense of being on a cattle drive (as cattle, not cowboys), and though they do hit all of the relevant sights, I highly recommend going with a more upmarket tour (see Sinhbalo or Ann Tours, above) to see the Delta in style and with informed guides and helpful tour leaders.

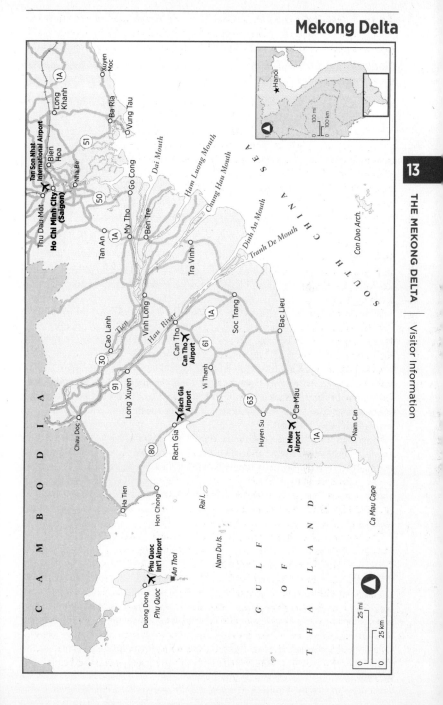

Typical Itineraries

The trips below are the most common itineraries on bus tours. Custom itineraries offer myriad deviations from these now well-tracked paths, including options for **homestays** with rural families, as well as more off-the-map destinations such as **Ben Tre** and parts of **Vinh Long Province.** Generally, the more you pay—such as with **Sinhbalo** or **Ann Tours**—the better the trip.

Many travelers make their Mekong Delta trip a one-way adventure, going **on to Cambodia** overland from the town of **Chau Doc.** For information about this and tours that will take you directly to Cambodia's capital, Phnom Penh, check with Saigon's many **tourist cafes** (see "Visitor Information & Tours," in chapter 12).

Tours can also be extended to include some beach time at **Phu Quoc Island,** which lies just off the coast of the Delta to the west, near Chau Doc. Your options are to overland (by car or local bus—ouch) from Chau Doc to the coastal town of **Ha Tien** or **Rach Gia** and then go by boat, or take a short flight from **Can Tho** or **Rach Gia.** There are also several daily flights between Phu Quoc and Saigon.

2-DAY TOUR   Start in the early morning from Saigon, with a visit to the **Cai Be Floating Market** near My Tho, and then various handicrafts sights. The trip is done by boat, with stops at island orchards and rural villages—including a walk over a shaky "Monkey Bridge" across a canal—and the first day ends in the city of **Can Tho,** where you'll spend the night.

On the second day, take a 3-hour boat trip with plenty of stops and photo ops at places such as a rice vermicelli factory, a raw-rice processing plant, and rural orchards. You'll also stop at the large **Cai Rang Floating Market** before returning to Saigon in the evening (around 7pm). These 2-day itineraries are jam-packed, and you're always on the go by bus, boat, and foot.

3-DAY TOUR   A 3-day tour expands on the 2-day itinerary to include far-flung **Chau Doc,** set on the Bassac River (the lower arm of the Mekong). Lots of travelers call this their last port of call in Vietnam and carry on into Cambodia by boat from here.

Day 1 follows the itinerary of the 2-day tour above, but the morning of **Day 2** takes you to floating houses and ethnic Cham villages near Chau Doc. You'll then travel up **Sam Mountain,** a knob of a pilgrimage peak that gives you a great vantage over the wide, flat Delta, and return to **Can Tho** for an overnight.

The morning of **Day 3** takes you to the **Cai Rang Floating Market** near Can Tho (a bonus is that you'll be there early in the middle of the action), with stops at more local cottage-industry workshops before making your way back to Saigon in the evening.

MY THO

70km (43 miles) SW of Ho Chi Minh City; 104km (65 miles) N of Can Tho; 179km (111 miles) N of Chau Doc

As the closest Mekong Delta town to Ho Chi Minh City, My Tho—capital of Tien Giang Province—is the most common jumping-off point for short day trips around the Mekong Delta. The city is just a small riverside grid along the Mekong. Most boat trips from My Tho include a visit to **Thoi Son (Unicorn) Island,** the nearest to the mainland, with its sprawling fruit orchards, as well as **Tan Long (Dragon) Island,** which is thick with banana and coconut plantations. Another popular destination for day tours is to **Cai Be Floating Market,** a short way west of My Tho, where a boat

Space isn't wasted in the densely populated Mekong Delta—any empty plot is used for farming, mostly of lowland "wet rice," which is grown in flooded paddies separated by dikes. Technology, from industrial pumps to spring-loaded hand scoops, is used to irrigate the fields. First, seeds are planted in flooded paddies and then replanted to avoid rot. Everything is done by hand, and even harrowing and plowing is still done by a buffalo. The Communist model of cooperation, particularly by way of sharing water resources, has served the Vietnamese well, and since the inception of the Doi Moi economic reforms, which made Mekong growers personally accountable for their output (in other words, it hit them in the pocketbook), the country has made great leaps in catching up with nearby rice-growing giants Thailand, Japan, and the western United States. Now, due to high productivity and improved technology, the only concerns are keeping salinity levels down and avoiding contamination from fertilization. Rice exports from Vietnam reached around 6 million metric tons in 2010; shipments to the Philippines alone totaled a million tons.

trip around the market is combined with visits to local workshops producing rice paper and candy. You could conceivably visit My Tho on your own by arranging transport from Ho Chi Minh City, and from My Tho organize a boat tour through local **Tien Giang Tourist,** 6, 30 April St. (✆ **073/387-3184;** www.tiengiangtourist. com). My Tho also makes a good base for an exploration of **Ben Tre** to the south, accessed by a massive bridge that was completed in 2009.

CAN THO

175km (109 miles) SW of Ho Chi Minh City; 104km (65 miles) SW of My Tho; 75km (47 miles) NW of Chau Doc

With a population of more than a million, Can Tho is the largest city on the Mekong Delta and the fourth-largest city in Vietnam, just behind Haiphong. Set at a confluence of two branches of the Mekong (the Hao Giang and the Can Tho rivers), it makes a great base for canal tours to the surrounding countryside. Can Tho's quaint riverside location has given rise to several semiluxe hotels, and as such it has the Delta's best accommodation options. A visit to the floating markets, the city's massive central market, or outlying riverside towns is memorable. Travel in and around Can Tho is best arranged with a tour group or good private guide who can take you to all the right places: the impressive floating market, rice-paper-making and weaving villages, small factories, and picturesque rural canals.

A fine park on the riverside promenade, a pleasant place for an evening stroll, showcases a large, shiny statue of Ho Chi Minh overlooking the busy water's edge and large neon advertisements for local beer—would he approve? Check out the small Chinese Temple across from Ho Chi Minh's statue, a good example of the places of worship for Can Tho's large Chinese community, who faced heavy recrimination in the late 1970s when China and Vietnam butted heads over Vietnamese involvement in Cambodia. Also at riverside, just in front of the city's fresh market, is a large covered market selling souvenirs.

Getting There

All of the tour agents (see "Visitor Information," above) provide extensive services to Can Tho. A new airport opened here in 2011 (on the site of the former U.S. air base), with flights connecting the city with Hanoi, Ho Chi Minh City, Phu Quoc, and the Con Dao Islands. A new highway and bridge (the longest cable-stayed bridge in Southeast Asia) have cut down journey time from Ho Chi Minh City to less than 4 hours. Local buses—should you be so brave and patient—arrive and depart from Can Tho's bus station about 1km (half a mile) south of the town center (take a motorcycle taxi to or from the riverside for 20,000 VND). Can Tho is about 3 hours to/from Chau Doc, in the other direction. Express minibuses to Ho Chi Minh City cost around 80,000 VND and to Chau Doc around 60,000 VND. Your hotel can arrange transport to the bus station.

Getting Around

The busiest part of sprawling Can Tho is along the riverside area, all of which, including taking in the town's museums and shopping, can be done on foot. You can also hop on motorbike taxis.

Visitor Information & Tours

Most travelers come to Can Tho on group or private tours out of Saigon. If you've got plenty of time and need a break from the 3½- to 4-hour ride to Can Tho, I recommend stopping at Vinh Long for a **bike ride** through the orchards and gardens on Anh Bin Island. Most outfitters can arrange for bike rentals and lunch along the way.

If you're on your own and hoping to set up trips to Can Tho's nearby floating markets and mangrove swamps, contact **Can Tho Tourist Company,** 50 Hai Ba Trung, along the riverside at the center of town; ℭ 0710/382-1852; www.canthotourist. com.vn), who can help you arrange boat trips to the markets and homestays. Prices are a bit higher than the tourist cafes, but the service is better, and if you need help with your onward travel, these folks can help with that, too. All tours take you to **Cai Rang** floating market, the nearest market to town, or to **Phong Dien,** a little farther away.

Private boat operators gather at the riverside and approach you like they're trying to sell you something illegal—and they are. The government, in cooperation with Can Tho Tourist (above), has put the kibosh on local independent tour operators, claiming that they were getting bad reports from tourists. Private boat hire starts at around $15 for half-day trips, and these guys are eager for work and very accommodating. If you have your own group, this is a good choice. Don't listen to anyone telling you that you'll be arrested—it's the boat driver who'll have trouble with police, not you. It's best to take a look at the boat first, though, as many have no shelter from the sun or rain.

[FastFACTS] CAN THO

Banks & Currency Exchange   Look for the **Vietcombank** branch, where you'll find international **ATM service,** at 7 Hoa Binh (ℭ **0710/382-0445;** daily 8–11am and 1:30–4pm).

Internet Service   Try the post office (see below), as independent shops are now hard to find (they're all closing since Wi-Fi has become universal).

Post Office The large central post office is near the bank and museum area, just a few hundred meters from riverside, at 2 Hoa Binh St.

Where to Stay

Golf Hotel Can Tho The star of the Golf chain (there are three hotels in Dalat; see p. 230), this hotel along the river is popular with newlyweds; coincidentally, it looks a bit like a wedding cake. Rooms try to be fancy, with high ceilings, built-in cabinetry, and heavy filigree, but the thin office carpet is a letdown. Large deluxe rooms are done in the same decor, but with lots more space. The best rooms have balconies with great views of the riverside and harbor—worth the upgrade. There's a quiet pool area, extensive massage facilities, a basement club, and a very kind and helpful front-desk staff.

02 Hai Ba Trung St., Ninh Kieu District. www.vinagolf.vn. © **0710/381-2210.** 107 units. $147–$180 double; $338–$417 suite. MC, V. **Amenities:** 3 restaurants; 2 bars; pool; room service. *In room:* A/C, TV, fridge, hair dryer, minibar, Wi-Fi.

Saigon Can Tho Saigon Can Tho is best for a quick overnight in a pinch, as it's close to everywhere in the center. Deluxe rooms are huge—like the Golf Hotel—at a fraction of the price, though furnishings are a bit bland. Rooms with balconies are great but come with lots of street noise. The place is affordable, and Saigontourist runs a helpful tour desk in the lobby.

55 Phan Dinh Phung St., Ninh Kieu District. www.saigoncantho.com.vn. © **0710/382-5831.** Fax 0710/382-3288. 46 units. $42–$73 double. MC, V. **Amenities:** 2 restaurants; sauna; steam room. *In room:* A/C, TV, fridge, minibar, Wi-Fi.

Victoria Can Tho ★★ After more than a decade of operations, the Victoria Can Tho still offers the best digs in this bustling Mekong city. Like all Victoria properties, rooms here are large, upscale, and charming, with natural woods, elegant silk hangings, and a puffy comforter on a big, sumptuous bed. River-view rooms are the best choice and have balconies overlooking busy river traffic. The hotel is just a short trip from the city by bicycle or taxi, but better to arrive in style aboard the hotel's wooden sampan boat, a free shuttle service, which drops you off at the Can Tho Market.

Cai Khe Ward, Can Tho City. www.victoriahotels-asia.com. © **0710/381-0111.** Fax 0710/382-9259. 92 units. $185–$195 double; $265 suite. AE, MC, V. **Amenities:** Restaurant; bar; bike rental; concierge; fitness center; Internet; pool; room service; spa. *In room:* A/C, TV, fridge, minibar, Wi-Fi.

Where to Eat

Dining at the Victoria Hotel's **Spices Restaurant** comes at a price, but everything is good. In town, restaurants are along the riverside; most are just open-air storefronts serving good local cuisine and seafood.

Note: For good snacks to take on day trips, look for the **Coop Mart,** 1 Hoa Binh Blvd., near the Can Tho Museum (© **0710/376-3586**), an extensive supermarket, open daily 8am to 10pm.

Mekong Restaurant 🍴 VIETNAMESE The food here—at this quiet little storefront with an air-conditioned room out back—is hearty and healthy. It's a real no-frills spot, but the staff is very attentive and the kitchen turns out some great dishes (check out the chateaubriand steak). You'll find good vegetarian options and a laid-back "diner" feel.

38 Hai Ba Trung, at riverside right next to Nam Bo. © **0710/382-1646.** Main courses 55,000 VND–140,000 VND. No credit cards. Daily 8am–2pm and 4–10pm.

Sleeping on the Mekong

Frenchman Benoit Perdu pioneered luxury cruises on the Mekong River with the *Bassac I* ★, a rice barge with a solid teak hull crafted into an elegant two-deck ship. The fleet now includes the *Bassac II* and larger *Bassac III,* plus several Mystic Sampans for day cruises. I took the hallmark overnight cruise from Cai Be to Can Tho, which includes fine dining and shuttles in a small boat up narrow canals to rustic farms. On the spacious deck, we watched languid scenes of river life till sunset and a starry night with glasses of wine. The air-conditioned cabins have hot showers and thick bedding. The boat was quietly anchored for the night, and I slept soundly. Sunrise found us amid a small flotilla of retail vendors, and the upper deck was a great vantage point for pictures. Cruising on to the largest wholesale floating market at Cai Rang, we arrived early to embark on a Mystic Sampan and get up close into the thick of the waterborne bustle. Overnight cruises cost, on average, $232 from the Delta towns.

Contact **Transmekong**, 97/10 Ngo Quyen (✆ 071/382-9540; www.transmekong.com), or depart from Saigon with Grandeur Journeys (✆ 08/3820-0257; www.grandeurjourneys.com).

Nam Bo ★ INTERNATIONAL/VIETNAMESE   Set in a riverside corner colonial just across from its previous location, this is the coolest perch in town. The dining area has smartly laid tables over two floors, and the menu features pizzas, steaks, and several appealing Vietnamese fusion dishes such as prawns with mango sauce. On the rooftop there's a boat-shaped bar and wine cellar, with a few tables for diners as well. The rest of the property is taken up by Nam Bo's latest venture—a boutique hotel (nearing completion at the time of this update) with just a handful of compact rooms at around $150 a night.

1 Ngo Quyen. ✆ **0710/381-9138.** Main courses 65,000 VND–150,000 VND. MC, V. Daily 9am–10:30pm.

Sao Hom ★ VIETNAMESE/WESTERN   Run by Benoit Perdu, the owner of Nam Bo and *Le Bassac* boats, this restaurant has an idyllic riverside location. It's located inside the old Can Tho Market Hall and occupies prime real estate next to the pier where his luxury boat docks (see the box on p. 344). It's an open restaurant with cheerful yellow paint and outdoor seating. This is a good place to come when you're looking for some Western comfort food or a safe experience with Vietnamese dishes.

Old Can Tho Market Hall, Ninh Keu Pier. ✆ **0710/381-5616.** Main courses 90,000 VND–180,000 VND. MC, V. Daily 6am–11pm.

Attractions

The real attractions in Can Tho are the floating markets and riverside life. Most days in this part of the Delta begin early, around 6am. You'll go by boat on a circuitous route to a number of rural sights, including the large **Cai Rang Floating Market,** where you're not sure who's watching whom as your tiny long-tail boat makes its way among busy sellers in packed sampan-style boats—great photo opportunities and best early in the morning. A number of handicrafts villages are in the area, and boat trips make stops at some rather canned tour attractions, the likes of a weaving village, rice-paper factory, vermicelli-production plant, rice mill, and "monkey bridge" made of vines, as well as a large island orchard. The riverside scenery is beautiful and the sights, though touristy, are quite interesting. The other, less-frequented floating market is at **Phong Dien,** which is often paired with a cruise along narrow canals to sample local fruits in orchards. If you arrive in the city in the midafternoon and have some free time on tour or while in transit back to Saigon, check out the few sights below.

Army Museum   The Army Museum is an interesting visit and just across Hoa Binh Street (away from the river) from the Can Tho Museum (see below). An interesting display of weaponry, maps, photos, stained glass, and memorabilia from Vietnam's long struggles are on display. At the center is a small "hooch," or thatched building, housing a mannequin meeting of high-level Viet Cong guerrillas on the Delta. Note that the upper floors are closed and locked. Wonder what goes on up there?

On Hoa Binh just across from the City Museum. Free admission. Daily 7:30–11am and 1:30–5pm.

Can Tho City Museum ★   A comprehensive and colorful museum of local history, industry, custom, Chinese population, and the region's role during colonial repression, as well as during the war years with the United States. Maps are detailed but indecipherable. You won't find any signs in English, but that doesn't matter, as most exhibits, like the scenes and images of the Delta's history, are interesting and self-explanatory. Go with a guide if you want to get background information. The second floor is a patriotic display of war remnants. There's also a model Chinese apothecary and temple in homage to the region's large Chinese population, local musical instruments, and a large diorama of a wedding procession. You'll see a bust of Ho Chi Minh and other Vietnamese patriots in the lobby. A visit here combined with a tour of the Army Museum (see above) is a good little city walk.

06 Phan Dinh Phung St. Free admission. Daily 7:30–11am and 1:30–5pm.

Riverside Market and Can Tho Market Hall   Riverside market is a typical, local wet market located near the center of town. Come here to wander through the stalls with the locals and see the varied aquatic life (turtles, fish, snakes) and veggies on offer in the Mekong Delta. It's located near the river, but unfortunately everything is indoors, so there's not much of a view and pretty much no ventilation. If you're squeamish about dirty feet, wear closed-toe shoes when you visit. In front of the market is the old Can Tho Market Hall, which dates back to 1913. It's now a tourist market selling mostly clothes and trinkets, housed in a bright, cheery yellow building that's very neat and tidy. The Sao Hom restaurant (see above) at the back of the market is my top choice for a coffee break.

71 Ha Ba Trung St. Free admission. Daily 7am–midafternoon.

CHAU DOC

285km (177 miles) SW of Saigon; 75km (47 miles) SW of Can Tho; 180km (112 miles) SW of My Tho

This little riverside border town—worth a visit in and of itself—is the main stopover for travelers going to and from Cambodia (see "Getting There," below). Chau Doc is a bustling center of trade and river transport, yet also a lazy, riverside burg and a throwback to another time. You'll still see old-style Ho Chi Minh surreys, called *xe loi,* a two-wheel cart on the back of a regular bicycle, instead of the standard cyclo. And though most boats have long-tail motors, many fishermen and small-time traders still row their own boats in the standing, forward-pushing style. A large floating market and nearby ethnic Cham villages are popular for early morning tours (usually part of a larger Mekong Delta package), as well as the small pilgrimage peak called **Sam**

Mountain just outside of town. There are a few good hotel options (best is the Victoria), and dining is at alfresco eateries near the market, as you take in the busy comings and goings.

Getting There

Contact a tour agent in Ho Chi Minh City (see "Tour Operators," p. 338). Chau Doc is 285km (177 miles) southwest of Saigon, and the all-day bus ride combines visits to other hamlets in the Delta, boat trips, and lunch stops—it's a fun, full day.

Local **buses** leave and arrive from the bus station a few miles east of town on the way to Long Xuyen (connect by motorbike taxi for about 20,000 VND). There are regular connections on reliable shuttle buses to Ho Chi Minh City (200,000 VND) and Can Tho (120,000 VND).

Boats from Chau Doc to Phnom Penh (and vice versa; $10–$26, plus $26 for a Cambodian visa) leave at 7, 8, and 8:30am, and 1:30pm, arriving 4 to 5 hours later. Contact any local tour operator in Saigon, or make arrangements with tour operators in Chau Doc (see below) or, coming from Cambodia, with Capitol Tours in Phnom Penh.

Visitor Information & Tours

If you're crossing over from Cambodia and looking for onward connection by cafe bus, tiny **Mekong Tours,** 14 Nguyen Huu Canh (✆ **076/386-8222;** www.mekongvietnam.com), offers good tours and bus connections to other parts of the Delta or with Saigon.

[FastFACTS] CHAU DOC

Banks & Currency Exchange There are a few small banks in little Chau Doc, including **Sacombank,** 88 Doc Phu Thu (✆ **076/626-0262**), where you can exchange dollars or withdraw from the ATM. It's best to bring enough money for on-tour incidentals (usually few) and carry a few U.S. dollars if you're coming from Cambodia.

Internet There's a small Internet counter with rather slow service for 8,000 VND per hour on the post office grounds (see below),

Post Office The main branch is at 2 Le Loi St. (✆ **076/386-9200**), just adjacent to the large riverside park. The main office is open from 6am to 10pm.

Where to Stay

There are a few minihotels around town. If you come on a budget tour, you'll be put up at one of several simple but clean places near the town center.

Song Sao Hotel This is a basic minihotel overlooking the town's main square. Some rooms are pretty stinky with disinfectant and others are a bit beat up, so ask to see the room first.

12-13 Nguyen Huu Canh St., on the main square in town. ✆ **076/356-1776.** Fax 076/386-8820. 24 units. $12–$15 double. No credit cards. *In room:* A/C, TV, Wi-Fi.

Trung Nguyen Hotel This minihotel gets kudos for its clean, basic rooms stacked high above the marketplace. They have no services to speak of, but the staff is friendly as all get-out, and basic rooms—at the same price as some of the grittier choices in this category—have cable TV, working air-conditioning, and no bad odors (yet).

86 Bach Dang St., near the market. www.trungnguyenhotel.com.vn. (C) **076/386-1561.** Fax 076/386-8674. 15 units. $15–$19 double. No credit cards. **Amenities:** Bike rental; Internet. *In room:* A/C, TV, fridge.

Victoria Chau Doc ★   The riverside Victoria Chau Doc stands proud on the banks of the Bassac, a busy but captivating stretch of the Mekong. The resort is beginning to look worn around the edges, but it's still your best option in Chau Doc, and the staff remains friendly and eager to please. Rooms are a good size, with wood floors and fine detail throughout—a tidy, comfortable colonial copy. Prices are based on the view (an extra $15 for a view of the river). The beds are grand in size, with thick, comfy mattresses. Halls are done in a comfortable antique tile, and the general atmosphere of this old riverside dandy is quite pleasant. There's a small pool and decks with great views. They have a private boat for tours or connections to Cambodia, and the helpful front-desk staff can arrange any local tours.

32 Le Loi St. www.victoriahotels-asia.com. (C) **076/386-5010.** Fax 076/386-5020. 92 units. $185–$210 double; $275 suite. MC, V. **Amenities:** Restaurant; bar; free bikes; concierge; fitness center; Internet; pool; room service; spa. *In room:* A/C, TV, minibar, fridge, Wi-Fi.

Where to Eat

The fine **Bassac Restaurant** at the Victoria Chau Doc (above) serves fine Vietnamese and Western cuisine in an air-conditioned dining room or on a picturesque terrace. Behind the basic **Thuan Loi Hotel,** 18 Tran Hung Dao St. ((C) **076/386-6134**), lies a charming floating restaurant serving basic Vietnamese fare. The restaurant is made up of a trio of thatched huts balanced on sticks over the river. Be sure to book ahead, as even a small tour group can take over the entire place; have your hotel concierge reserve the corner table in the main hut for unobstructed views of the river.

Chau Doc's other local dining options are in and around the market, particularly at the end near the city center and busy square, or in one of the town center's basic storefront eateries that serve good local fish, among other Vietnamese specialties. Try **Hong Phat,** 77 Chi Lang St. ((C) **076/386-6950**), for Chinese and European facsimiles (daily 9am–9pm).

Attractions

The sprawling riverside market at the town center, a crossroads for goods to and from nearby Cambodia, is the real attraction. A stroll in the central market on any given morning is a feast for the eyes (and the nose), and there are some small temples to visit in the small downtown area. Even the most budget tour will take you to the **floating villages ★★** in wooden sampans rowed in the Vietnamese-style "forward stroke" (give it a try). You'll get to see a unique way of life and visit one of the many catfish farms that collectively are taking the world market by storm.

About 7km (4¼ miles) out of town to the west, and not a bad day trip by bicycle, is the **Sam Mountain ★**, a popular local pilgrimage peak. There's a colorful temple at the base of the mountain, and the path up is dotted with smaller spots for worship and shade-giving awnings where you can buy a Coke, stretch out in a hammock, and enjoy the view. It's a tough hike, but this is the only high spot—some 230m (755 ft.)—for miles, and the view is like looking at a map of the Mekong's overflowing tributaries.

Easily arranged at any hotel or tour desk in Chau Doc, a visit to **Tuc Dup Hill** is a revisiting of some of the Delta's worst history. Here, U.S. forces tried—but failed—to put a stop to small-time insurgencies and logistical support from Cambodia. Called the "Two Million Dollar Hill" for the kind of resources the U.S. poured into taking the hill, Tuc Dup was successfully defended by the Viet Cong throughout a 4-month U.S. assault. Near Tuc Dup at **Ba Chuc,** you'll see a grisly memorial of stacked skulls and graphic images recording a massacre of more than 3,000 villagers by the Khmer Rouge in April 1978.

Chau Doc After Dark

Just west of the market, the town's central square lights up like a wonderland at night. Trees are strung with lights, faux electric fireworks spark atop poles surrounding a central temple area, and there's a lit-up Buddha of Compassion. The square is a good place to strike up friendly conversation with locals. Grab a lawn chair at one of the many coffee bars serving the sweet local gelatin called *che,* and say *"Chao chi/em/anh"* to the person sitting nearest you (see chapter 16 to find out which is best for whom).

PHU QUOC ISLAND

120km (75 miles) W (over sea) from Rach Gia (Rach Gia is 250km/155 miles S of Saigon by road)

The same size as Singapore, the island of Phu Quoc lies off the west coast of Vietnam's Mekong Delta. Also claimed by Cambodia, which calls it Koh Tral, the island is now like an armed fortress of the Vietnamese navy, and 70% of the island is protected as the Phu Quoc National Forest. Exploring the dirt-track byways of the forested isle, among picturesque pepper plantations and long stretches of deserted beach, is a hoot. A visit to Phu Quoc is a good, affordable opportunity to relax, spend time on the beach, and snorkel or scuba-dive.

Phu Quoc is most famous for its production of *nuoc mam,* the noxious fish sauce that is part of any meal in Vietnam. U.S. pilots flying over the island during the Vietnam War joked that the fumes from *nuoc mam* factories of Phu Quoc were enough to blow out the torch on a jet engine. Find a guide on the island, and you'll be able to get up-close and personal with the aromatic production of Vietnam's most versatile condiment.

Phu Quoc was an off-the-map tourist destination for many years, but the developers, led by Saigontourist's large Saigon Phu Quoc Resort and followed by international chains, such as Accor, are coming in droves. Services remain limited, though things are constantly improving, such as more dining choices, a sealed road linking resorts, and the imminent opening of a new international airport. For now, however, the quiet, undeveloped quality of this beach escape—just a short, easy hop from Saigon—is the real attraction.

Weather on the island, thanks to cool ocean breezes, is always temperate and thus a great escape from sultry Saigon. The coolest time to go to Phu Quoc is from December to February. **Note:** The island is quite rainy and exposed to monsoon storms from May to November.

Getting There

Vietnam Airlines offers daily flights from Ho Chi Minh City, Can Tho, and Rach Gia, a small coastal town adjacent to Phu Quoc on the Mekong Delta mainland. Some flights actually hop from Ho Chi Minh to Rach Gia and then on to Phu Quoc. From Ho Chi Minh, the flight is about 45 minutes on a midsize turboprop plane. The cost is 1,200,000 VND for the one-way trip. Flights leave Saigon's **Tan Son Nhat** domestic terminal several times daily (depending on season). Contact Vietnam Airlines in Ho Chi Minh directly at their office at 200 Nguyen Son St., Long Bien

A UNIQUE BREED: THE PHU QUOC ridgeback

Found only on the island of Phu Quoc, the medium-size Phu Quoc Ridgeback is a bit taller and sturdier than the average curly tailed street mutts you find elsewhere in Vietnam. Tenacious hunters, intelligent, and loyal, Ridgebacks are credited with nearly completely ridding the island of all things that crawl, walk, or creep. Locals still employ the dogs to hunt small game. Usually black, with a distinctive line of hair growing upward along the spine, Ridgebacks are not under any specific control or pedigree breeding, so they come in all shapes and sizes.

As elsewhere in Vietnam, dogs roam free and travel in packs, which means you should be mindful if out on the beach or rural roads late at night; I saw one of the worst dogfights I've ever seen in my life on this island. The dogs are said to breed only on the island, and controlled breeding on the mainland has been unsuccessful.

District (© **08/3832-0320**). *Note:* Try to book at least a week in advance; residents of Phu Quoc often travel to Ho Chi Minh City for daily shopping trips and errands, so these flights fill up fast. Any travel agent can make arrangements for a small fee. A metered taxi from the airport to Long Beach is around 60,000 VND to 120,000 VND, depending how far along the beach your resort is. An international airport is just about complete and is slated to open sometime in 2012, though it's already been delayed several times, so don't hold your breath.

There are regular hydrofoils that connect Phu Quoc with Rach Gia and Ha Tien on the mainland. The 2½-hour, 140km (87-mile) trip to Rach Gia is relatively smooth (in the low season) and costs just 240,000 VND, while the shorter (1½-hr.) trip to Ha Tien costs 210,000 VND. This route is very popular since the international border opened at Xa Xia (near Ha Tien), allowing beach bums to move easily between Phu Quoc and Sihanoukville in Cambodia. Boats connect with Phu Quoc by the east coast ports of Ham Ninh and Vong Beach; it's a 40,000 VND motorbike taxi or 60,000 VND minibus ride between the ports and the Long Beach area; expect to pay 250,000 VND to 300,000 VND for a taxi to Long Beach or more to Ong Lang. **Superdong,** 14 Tu Do St. (© **077/387-7742,** and 10, 30 April St., © **077/398-0111** on Phu Quoc), and **Vinashin Rose,** 21 Nguyen Troi (© **077/260-0155** on Phu Quoc), are the two main companies; both have early-morning and early-afternoon departures. Be sure to buy boat tickets at least 1 day in advance; just about every resort can help with bookings.

Note: The boat can get overcrowded and may have the unfortunate lingering odor of previous passengers' weak stomachs. The journey is pleasant and smooth during the low season but is often beset by jarring waves during the high season; hotel staff can advise you of ocean conditions. Taxis and motorbikes in Rach Gia can shuttle you to the bus terminal (some 6km/3¾ miles out of town). From there, public buses can take you onward to Ho Chi Minh City, Can Tho, or Chau Doc. I recommend flying directly from Ho Chi Minh City to Phu Quoc, but another good option is a multiday trip on the Mekong Delta ending in Can Tho, from where you can hop on a short flight to Phu Quoc before returning by flight to Ho Chi Minh.

The **local bus station in Rach Gia** is at 260A Nguyen Binh Khiem St. Buses connect regularly with Chau Doc, Can Tho, and on to Ho Chi Minh's Mien Tay Bus Station.

Orientation

The island is more than 50km (31 miles) in length and just 20km (12 miles) at its widest. The Phu Quoc Airport is currently near **Duong Dong,** the island's largest town, a fishing port on the western shore, though it will shortly be moving south to the center of the island. From Duong Dong, Tran Hung Dao Street runs south behind **Long Beach,** which stretches around 20km (12 miles) to the island's southern tip. Most of the island's resorts are located along the northern 6km (3¾ mile) stretch of Long Beach, south of which the beach is deserted. Ong Lang Beach is about 6km (3¾ miles) north of Duong Dong. At the northernmost point of the island, you're just 15km (9⅓ miles) from Cambodian waters.

Getting Around

Taxis wait just outside the **Phu Quoc Airport** (✆ 077/384-6742) arrival terminal. Starting rates are 12,000 VND for the first 0.7km (½ mile) and 2,000 VND per 200m (656 ft.) thereafter. **Mai Linh Taxi** (✆ 077/397-9797) is a reliable company. Phu Quoc is also a great place to putter around on a motorbike—the dirt roads are mostly smooth, and there is hardly any traffic. An all-day motorbike rental will set you back around 120,000 VND to 180,000 VND.

[FastFACTS] PHU QUOC

Bank & Currency Exchange The **Vietcombank** branch on 20, 30 April St. (✆ **077/398-1036;** Mon–Sat 7–11am and 1–4pm; www.vietcombank.com.vn) has comprehensive services, including cashing traveler's checks, currency exchange, and an **ATM.** There's a branch of **Western Union** at the post office.

Internet There's decent **Internet** service next to the post office.

Post Office The **post office** is in the town center, just down 30 April St. from the Vietcombank (✆ **077/384-6177**). It's open from 7am to 8pm (closed Sun).

Where to Stay & Eat

Because most visitors go to Phu Quoc to relax on the beach, choosing a resort is the most important decision you'll make. Most people opt to stay on **Long Beach,** by far the busiest beach on the island, as it means you have several alternatives for dining nearby. If you really want to get away from it all, head for **Ong Lang Beach** or **Cua Can Beach,** both farther north along the west coast, or **Sao Beach,** on the southeast coast. But, be prepared to dine at your resort, as they are all rather cut off from each other.

Just between the town of Duong Dong and Long Beach, on **Vo Thi Sau Street,** you'll find lots of cheap food stalls each evening at the **night market.** Along the northern stretch of **Tran Hung Dao,** which runs behind the resorts on **Long Beach,** are several restaurants offering Italian, Spanish, and German cuisine as well as Vietnamese. Among these is **Chez Carole,** 88 Tran Hung Dao (✆ 077/384-8884), which serves excellent seafood specialties and familiar Western fare such as wood-oven pizzas. **Chez Carole** also runs a small but exclusive resort on the remote beach at Cua Can (✆ 077/370-3793), where the cute villas go for around $150 a night.

For something special, head for **Pepper Tree** at La Veranda Resort (see below), where the colonial ambience and attentive service imbues all diners with a sense of importance. Rainbow Divers' **Rainbow Bar** (✆ 0913/400-964) is a little beachside place serving good burgers and familiar Western fare.

Note: Room rates are given for high season; in low season and when booking online, expect considerable discounts. Most places offer free pickup from the airport.

LONG BEACH

Long Beach is where you'll find the island's best choice of accommodations. The beach is getting busier with touts and sellers, but a friendly, laid-back atmosphere prevails.

Beach Club ★ Located toward the southern end of the string of resorts on Long Beach, budget Beach Club is a great choice for a few days of quiet and fun in the sun. British owner Mike and his Vietnamese wife, Thien, are the most gracious and helpful hosts. Accommodations are basic—large, tidy rooms in a small block set back from the beach, and a similar standard in free-standing beachside bungalows—but the friendly staff and laid-back feel of this hideaway draws you in. There are hammocks in every spot of shade, and the hotel's dogs, fine specimens of the Phu Quoc Ridgeback (see box on p. 349) are friendly and playful. The food here is tops, and this is a good place to meet other travelers. Mike is a wealth of information on the area; he can happily provide maps and arrange any rentals or tours.

On the south end of Long Beach. www.beachclubvietnam.com. ✆ **077/398-0998.** 10 units. $30 for hotel block room; $40 for bungalow. No credit cards. **Amenities:** Restaurant; bar; motorbike rental. *In room:* Fan (w/mosquito netting), no phone.

Eden Resort ★ One of the newest resorts on the island, Eden seems to have got everything right, from the beautifully landscaped gardens to the well-appointed rooms. Staff is superefficient and capable, and the resort offers everything you need—a huge swimming pool, inviting restaurant, and fitness center. Rooms are tastefully furnished throughout, but for a bit of privacy, go for one of the bungalows rather than rooms in the main building. Rooms are priced according to view, and many have balconies with sea views. Rates include an excellent buffet breakfast. A second phase is being built, so construction noise could be a problem until it's complete.

Cua Lap Hamlet, Long Beach, Phu Quoc (about 7km/4 miles south of Duong Dong town). www.eden resort.com.vn. ✆ **077/398-5598.** 64 units. $139 double; $169–$199 suite; $229 bungalow. AE, MC, V, DC. **Amenities:** Restaurant; bar; pool; watersports equipment/rentals. *In room:* A/C, satellite TV, DVD player (in suites), minibar, Wi-Fi.

La Veranda ★★★ Now a M Gallery property (part of the Accor chain), La Veranda is easily the best resort on the island in every respect, from the well-equipped rooms and top-notch facilities to the capable staff. Resort bungalows are laid out around a small natural garden or ocean side; I highly recommend springing for the latter. All bungalows come with private balconies and cozy beds; beachside bungalows have bigger bathrooms. Art Deco is the theme throughout, though with a twist of modernity, such as glassed-in louvered windows. The main house is a classic colonial mansion with a restaurant on the second floor (Pepper Tree) serving a fine selection of French fare (main courses $20–$30) and sumptuous Vietnamese food ($8–$15). Dining at the resort is an excellent choice not only for the food, but for the view and the relaxing ambience created by the sound of live jazz piano from the downstairs bar.

Tran Hung Dao St., Duong Dong Beach. www.mgallery.com. © **077/398-2988.** Fax 077/398-2998. 43 units. $328–$434 room/villa; $646 La Veranda suite. AE, MC, V. **Amenities:** 2 restaurants; bar; Jacuzzi; pool; room service; spa. *In room:* A/C, satellite TV/DVD, hair dryer, minibar, movie library, Wi-Fi.

Saigon Phu Quoc Resort ★   Occupying a prime slice of beach frontage, Saigon Phu Quoc is a sprawling campus on a slight rise overlooking the sea. Lounging in the hotel's large central pool and bar area, and lying under one of their large, beachside thatched awnings, is a great way to spend the day. They have extensive services, including a spa area, small gym, tennis courts, and golf driving net and putting green. Rooms aren't anything special—just large, bland, clean spaces. Free-standing Star Cruise bungalows at seaside are worth the upgrade. I'd opt for one of the nearby budget stops (the others listed here), as you can use Saigon Phu Quoc's services as an outside guest for a small negotiable fee.

1 Tran Hung Dao, Long Beach, Phu Quoc (just a few miles south of Duong Dong Town). www.sgphu quocresort.com.vn. © **077/384-6999.** Fax 077/384-7163. 90 units. $149–$189 double; 259–$319 family room and suite; $389 beachfront villa. MC, V. **Amenities:** 3 restaurants; 2 bars; babysitting; bike rental; children's center and small playground; health club; Internet; putting green; room service; tennis court; watersports equipment/rentals (kayaks). *In room:* A/C, TV, fridge, hair dryer, minibar, Wi-Fi.

Sao Bien—Sea Star Resort ★   Sea Star is one of those little workhorse resorts that has come to its own by not trying to be too much. Rooms are basic, two-unit, free-standing concrete bungalows with tile floors, hard but cozy beds, air-condition-ing, and TV—all clean and without much style, but who needs style when your pri-vate balcony leads to a sandy beach, as many of the rooms do? Large rattan rockers are great for putting your feet up. Wi-Fi may not reach all rooms.

Ba Keo—Khu Pho 7—Duong Dong, Phu Quoc (about 3km/1¾ miles south of Duong Dong Town). © **077/398-2161.** 43 units. $40–$75 double. No credit cards. **Amenities:** Restaurant; bar; bike/motor-bike rental. *In room:* A/C, TV, fridge, minibar, Wi-Fi.

ONG LANG BEACH

Just 6km (3¾ miles) north of Duong Dong town, a left turn leads to this beach, which is broken up into several separate bays by rocky headlands, offering a degree of pri-vacy to each resort here.

Chen Sea Resort & Spa ★★   This fancy resort, formerly called Chen La, has now been taken over by the Centara Group and offers four-star luxury on the quiet, southernmost stretch of Ong La Beach. There's a diving and water sports center, an infinity pool, solarium deck, fitness center, and spa with a comprehensive range of treatments. The spacious villas are a minimum of 78-sq. m (840 sq. ft.), and some have private pool and Jacuzzi. Furnishings are a mix of rustic and modern, and the full-length windows allow superb views of the beach.

Bai Xep, Ong Lang Beach, Phu Quoc. www.centarahotelsresorts.com. © **077/399 5895.** $290–$350 villa; $585 pool villa. MC, V. **Amenities:** Restaurant; bar; bike rental; fitness center; library; spa; tennis court; watersports equipment/rentals. *In room:* A/C, satellite TV; DVD player; minibar; Wi-Fi.

Mango Bay Resort ★   Billed as a "low-density resort" with an eye to the environ-ment and in harmony with the surroundings, Mango Bay is an excellent off-the-track collection of cozy bungalows along a picturesque, rocky bay. Sandy paths connect simple, spacious, free-standing units, each separated from the next by a good distance, which affords you privacy. It's boutique rustic, with finely molded pale-yellow concrete set against dark wood and high thatch ceilings. Bathrooms are enormous outdoor areas with a low bamboo fence for privacy. Room details are stylish; older wooden units are more atmospheric. There are also budget hotel-block rooms. All rooms have big balcony areas.

Ong Lang Beach, Phu Quoc Island. www.mangobayphuquoc.com. ☎ **090/338 2207.** 31 units. $90 hotel block double; $125 plantation or family bungalow. MC, V. **Amenities:** Restaurant; bar. *In room:* Fan, no phone.

Exploring the Island

Phu Quoc's quiet dirt roads are a great place to get your motor running. Motorbike rental costs around $6 to $10 a day, depending on the type of bike, and can be arranged at any hotel front desk.

Before heading out to the island's far-flung corners, you can get a good introduction to Phu Quoc culture at the **Coi Nguon Museum,** 149 Tran Hung Dao (☎ **077/398 0206;** www.coinguonmuseum.com), a private museum that displays a fantastic array of shells, fossils, endemic plants, sea-life skeletons, and information on the island's history. It's on the east side of Tran Hung Dao Street about 5km (3 miles) south of Duong Dong Town, and is open daily from 7am to 5pm daily (admission 20,000 VND).

Heading north from Duong Dong town along the west coast of the island, you'll come first to the beach area of **Ong Lang,** which hosts a small clutch of resorts and services along a quiet stretch of sand; a small turnoff from the main road takes you there. Continuing north, follow long stretches of open beach, lined with fish and squid out to dry on large bamboo mats. There are lots of opportunities along the way for complete seclusion. The coastal road reaches **Ganh Dau,** a small town of busy *nuoc mam* (fish sauce) factories. *Note:* Don't buy bottles of *nuoc mam* as souvenirs; the pungent sauce is banned from Vietnam Airlines and virtually all flights out of the country. Farther out on the peninsula, you'll find a few local hangout spots with hammocks under shade trees by the beach.

From Ganh Dau, you can turn inland and make a long clockwise loop. It's 13km (8 miles) along jungle road to the town of Rach Vieu, and another 6km (3¾ miles) east brings you to the **Suai Cai Crossroad.** From there you can go 13km (8 miles) to the beaches of Bai Thom (a military base on the far north end of the island), or even get motocross for the long trip down the treacherous trails on the island's east side; most take the short loop inland some 16km (10 miles) heading back to Duong Dong town.

Going south from central Duong Dong town, toward the An Thoi Port area on the far southern tip of the island, are a few attractions. The west coast road south of the resorts is unpaved and bumpy, but for long stretches provides postcard views of unspoiled palm-fringed beaches.

Along the coast, **Phu Quoc Pearl Farm** (Duong To Village, 10km/6¼ miles south on the western coastal road, Tran Hung Dao; ☎ **091/399-3202;** www.treasuresof thedeep.com) is a relaxed roadside stop overlooking a long stretch of open beach along the dusty coastal road, with good explanations about the complex process of pearl farming and a very high-end boutique with some very unique colored and clear pearls in fine gold and silver settings. Stop here if you're heading to Sao Beach (Bai Sao) in the far south.

Nha Tu Phu Quoc is the old jail where the French housed Vietnamese dissidents. The sight is just an enclosed field with old fallen-down sheet metal Quonset huts, but there is an adjoining museum with some photos and information (daily 7–11:30am and 1:30–4pm).

The town of **An Thoi** in the far south is little more than a turnaround point, but the busy port is worth a wander.

One-day **boat trips** from Phu Quoc to the **An Thoi Archipelago** off the southern tip of the island are fun. Local tour operators run regular trips to this chain of 15 small islands and islets surrounded by deep blue waters; the all-day tour costs $15 to $20, which includes a lunch and snorkeling gear rental.

Tour operators also run evening **squid fishing trips.** You're sure to see the lights of squid fishermen far out on the horizon each evening; it looks like a small city out there at certain times of year. The tour leaves at 4:30pm, and you motor out to join the large fleet. Fishermen catch squid by attracting them with a light and hooking them near the surface, a fun and playful jigging technique. Kids love it. Book through your hotel.

On the southeast coast, just north of the prison, a bumpy track leads east from the main road down to **Sao Beach,** a stretch of brilliant-white, powder-soft sand lined with palms and azure waters. On clear days, it's great for snorkeling, and in the monsoon season it's much calmer than Long Beach, where the angry sea often gets too dangerous for swimming. Sao Beach is still thankfully free of the developers' shovels, though there are a couple of low-key resorts offering rooms, the better of which is the **Lang Toi** (✆ 077/397-2123), with just a few fan-cooled rooms at $45 a night. There are a few lazy beachside shacks with low tables under umbrellas and lots of hammocks in the shade where you can sip a cool drink, order lunch, and watch the day go by. It's a popular beach for domestic tourists, though, so it gets pretty crowded on the weekends.

Scuba & Snorkeling

As in their other locations in Vietnam (Nha Trang, Whale Island, and Can Dao Island), **Rainbow Divers** (✆ 0913/400-964; www.divevietnam.com) runs a very professional outfit here on Phu Quoc. Check out their small office near the boat-booking offices at 11 Tran Hung Dao, just south of Duong Dong town, or at their beachside **Rainbow Restaurant** and at most hotel front desks (as in Nha Trang, the Rainbow Divers folks are already going a little overboard with exposure). There are other small dive companies on Phu Quoc, but Rainbow is the most professional and has access to all of Phu Quoc's coral dive sites in the north, as well as in the south at the An Thoi Islands. The diving season is from October to May, depending on currents.

CAMBODIA

Cambodia is unpredictable—very unpredictable—but that's the allure for many travelers who come here. Traffic is chaos, corruption is law, poverty is endemic. Less than half of Cambodians have access to clean water and sanitation facilities. Children suffer from malnutrition and inadequate immunizations against polio, measles, and diphtheria. The political situation is uncertain. And although the good news is that years of rampant violence and anarchy are over and a stable coalition government is now in power, strong destabilizing elements remain, and a powerful criminal underworld still exists—which means that things are never as they seem.

14

The sign on the ride from the airport reads: ABUSE A CHILD IN THIS COUNTRY, GO TO JAIL IN YOURS, and speaks of multilateral participation with foreign governments to crack down on child abusers, but foreign "sexpats" and fugitives from the law still find Cambodia a nice, cozy place to crawl under the rug. Ownership is tenuous, at best, and many foreign investors watch their investments simply evaporate. Illegal logging of old-growth teak is still common practice, despite the best efforts of regional and international bodies.

In Cambodia, you can pay to fire heavy weaponry left over from violence of the Kmer Rouge era. It's a place where sometimes you have to just keep dialing in the hopes of getting a phone connection that works—and where everything is going to happen in "just 15 minutes," which inevitably stretch into hours. What brings so many here is their desire to help; humanitarian-aid workers are the majority in places such as Phnom Penh, but tourists also flock here for the incredible temples of Angkor Wat and rural journeys that were too dangerous until only recently.

The situation is grim in this small agrarian kingdom, but things are improving. Following years of war, the chaos and genocide of Pol Pot's Khmer Rouge, and a long period of civil and political instability, Cambodia was for years an armed camp, closed to foreign visitors (except maybe travelers of the danger-seeking variety). The first wave of intervention troops from the United Nations did as much to bolster vice in the country as they did to establish order; armed anarchy and banditry ruled until very recent years.

Fortunately, Cambodia is now beginning to heal, and though this process will take years, the country is enjoying a period of relative stability. Strict gun laws and more tenacious policing of offenders mean that the disarming of Cambodia has sped up. Cambodia offers travelers a host of experiences, from the legacy of ancient architecture to a growing urban capital and beautiful countryside. Even the shortest visit is a window into a vibrant ancient culture and a chance to meet with very kind and resilient people.

What brings so many to this Buddhist land of smiles is **Angkor Wat,** the ancient capital and one of the man-made wonders of the world. The temple complex at Angkor is stunning, a monumental Hindu/Buddhist temple compound of behemoth block temples, towering spires, giant carved faces, and ornate bas-reliefs. It's a pilgrimage point for temple aficionados and a place of spiritual significance to many—seeing Angkor is a once-in-a-lifetime experience. Most travelers limit their visit to a few days at the temples and major sites in the growing capital, **Phnom Penh,** which is tatty shabby but charming, with crumbling French colonial architecture and a splendid palace.

Getting off the track in Cambodia is a glimpse of a beguiling, unpredictable land. Travel in rural Cambodia, once unheard of, is improving, but you still need some tolerance for bumpy roads and rustic accommodations. Cambodia is resplendent with natural gifts such as the **Mekong River**—the country's lifeline that connects with **Tonle Sap (Great Lake),** Southeast Asia's largest lake, surrounded by fertile lowlands.

Bouncing around the hinterlands of Cambodia still begs caution, though, and travelers should be aware of the massive amount of UXO (unexploded ordnance, or land mines) and the absence of proper medical services. Any of the larger tour operators are a good bet for arranging trips to the likes of mountainous **Rattanakiri** in the northeast, the Thai border area, or rural riverside towns along the Mekong. The country's only port, **Sihanoukville,** is a popular beach destination. Intrepid travelers commonly rent motorcycles or brave rattletrap buses.

Known for warm, beguiling smiles that have weathered great hardship, Khmer people are very friendly, approachable, and helpful; but be warned that the hard sell is on in Cambodia, and you're sure to be harried, especially by the persistent young sellers at Angkor Wat. Nevertheless, travelers here are sure to meet with great kindness.

Tourism is growing in leaps and bounds. Many **nongovernmental organizations (NGOs)** here have done their part to rebuild and support the growing nation. Their activities, centered in offices in Phnom Penh, are what keep social services and the infrastructure at subsistence levels. If you're interested, volunteer opportunities abound, and you can effect great change as a volunteer or through donations. The number of foreign aid workers means increased quality of services; hotels and restaurants in Siem Reap and Phnom Penh are on par with any in the region, although outside of these two centers, they are sparse.

The trip to Cambodia is worth it, even if it's just to see the Angkor temples. This beguiling land that's shaking off the shackles of a devastating recent history is an exciting, emerging tourist destination.

GETTING TO KNOW CAMBODIA
The Lay of the Land

Cambodia, comprising some 181,035 sq. km (69,898 sq. miles), has 23 provinces, bordered by Laos in the north, Vietnam in the east, Thailand to the west, and the Gulf of Thailand to the south. The marine port in Cambodia, Sihanoukville, is connected to the capital and largest city, Phnom Penh, via a major U.S.-built highway.

The mighty Mekong enters from Laos to the north and nearly bisects the country. The river divides into two main tributaries at Phnom Penh before it traces a route to the delta in Vietnam, and most areas of population density lie along the river valleys

Cambodia

and fertile plains of this great river and its tributaries. Near Siem Reap, the Tonle Sap (Great Lake) is the largest lake in Southeast Asia. In the monsoon summer months, when the Mekong is swollen from the snows of Tibet, the river becomes choked with silt and backs up on the Mekong Delta. The result is an anomaly: The Tonle Sap River relieves the pressure by changing the direction of its flow and draining the Mekong Delta hundreds of miles in the opposite direction and into the Tonle Sap Lake.

The northeast of the country, Rattanakiri Province, and areas bordering Vietnam are quite mountainous and rugged, as are the Thai border areas defined by the Dangrek Mountains in the northwest and the Cardamom Mountains in the southwest. These jungle forest regions are a rich source for timber in the region, and steps toward preservation come slow.

A Look at the Past

Some 2 millennia ago, a powerful people known as the Khmer ruled over much of present-day Southeast Asia, including parts of what are now eastern Thailand, southern Vietnam, and Laos. Theirs was a kingdom that seems to have been created in a dream: wondrous temples, magnificent cities rising from steamy jungles, and glorious gods.

357

The story of Khmer civilization is one of a slow decline from the zenith of the powerful Angkor Civilization of the 11th century. War and years of alternating occupation by neighboring Thailand to the west and Vietnam to the east, later by the French and Japanese, had Cambodia bouncing like a strategic Ping-Pong ball, and the Khmer kingdom's size was chiseled away considerably. Remaining is what we know today as Cambodia, a tiny land half the size of Germany.

The name Cambodia is an Anglicized version of the French *Cambodge,* derived from the tribe of northern India from which the Khmer are said to descend. Citizens are alternately referred to as Khmer or Cambodian; the language is Khmer. Whatever the origins, the name Cambodia hardly evokes thoughts of ancient glory: especially in the West, Cambodia suggests instead a history of oppression, civil war, genocide, drug running, and coup d'état. Constant political turbulence, armed citizenry, bandits, and war fallout, such as unexploded mines and bombs, have given the country a reputation as one of the world's most dangerous places to travel rather than a repository of manmade and natural wonders. It's important to have perspective on the country's troubled history in order to understand the present. Only then can we appreciate the present civil order and the fact that citizens have been or are being disarmed, and that Cambodia is making the slow push into this new century.

A Turbulent Political Past

Cambodia is populated by people of the **Mon-Khmer** ethnic group, who probably migrated from the north as far back as 1000 B.C. It was part of the kingdom of Funan, a Southeast Asian empire that also extended into Laos and Vietnam, to the 6th century, when it was briefly absorbed into a rebel nation called Chenla. It then evolved into its glorious Angkor period in the 8th century, from which sprung many of Cambodia's treasures, most notably the lost city of Angkor.

By the late 12th century, however, the Angkor kingdom began a decline, marked by internal rebellions. Angkor was lost to the Kingdom of Siam in 1431, and Vietnam jousted with Siam and also had a hand in controlling the kingdom, to some degree, beginning in the early 17th century. The French took over completely in 1863, followed by the Japanese and then the French again. Cambodia finally regained independence in 1953 under the leadership of **Prince Norodom Sihanouk.**

Vietnamese Communist outposts in the country, however, drew Cambodia into the Vietnam War. It was heavily bombed by U.S. forces in the late 1960s. A U.S.-backed military coup followed in 1970, but in 1975 the infamous **Khmer Rouge,** led by the tyrannical **Pol Pot,** took over Cambodia, renamed it Democratic Kampuchea, and established a totalitarian regime in the name of communism. Opposition—even imaginary opposition—was brutally crushed, resulting in the death of more than two million Cambodians. The civil and Vietnam wars decimated Cambodian infrastructure. It became, and still is, one of the world's poorest nations, with a mainly agrarian economy and a literacy rate of about 35%.

In response to Khmer Rouge infractions in its country, Vietnam invaded Cambodia in 1978 and occupied it until 1989, installing a puppet regime led by Hun Sen as prime minister. When Vietnam departed, the United Nations stepped in and engineered a fragile coalition government between the Sihanouk and Hun Sen factions. There was never full agreement, however, and Hun Sen took over in a violent 1997 coup. The Khmer Rouge subsequently waned in power, and Pol Pot died in 1998.

Saloth Sar, aka Pol Pot

Saloth Sar is known by many names—Pouk, Hay, Pol, "87," Grand-Uncle, Elder Brother, First Brother, and later as "99" and Phem—but there's one name that might be most fitting: monster. A man who rose from relative obscurity to the highest post in Cambodia, riding on the rungs of a growing socialist movement that, somewhere along the line and mostly due to his leadership, became genocide, Saloth Sar is responsible for the deaths of untold numbers—estimates range from one to two million.

Born (1925) in Kompong Thom, south of Cambodia, Pol Pot's path to power was tangential. He attended some of Cambodia's finest schools and studied abroad in France, where he came in contact with Marxism and socialist ideals that he later bent to create his chaotic kingdom. He worked as a teacher briefly and then took up the mantle of revolutionary, working first alongside and then separately from the Vietnamese Communists. Pol Pot lived on the jungle fringes between Cambodia and Thailand, carrying on his violent ideological revolution until his death in 1998.

In November 1998, a new coalition government was formed between the two leading parties, leading to relative political peace. The war-crimes tribunal for four Khmer Rouge perpetrators drags on, while the rest of the country wants to leave behind its vicious and bloody past and move forward.

The Present

July 2003 elections went off without incident, but it took nearly a year for negotiation of a government coalition. Hun Sen still reigns as prime minister. In the fall of 2004, King Norodom Sihanouk, Cambodia's longtime standard-bearer through the many violent regime changes and trying times, abdicated, selecting his son Norodom Sihamoni, a retired ballet dancer, to take up the symbolic post of king.

Cambodia's economy is experiencing an annual growth rate of around 5%, mostly due to tourism, garment exports, and construction, but the scene in rural Cambodia is bleak. Basic medical services are nonexistent; education and job training are out of reach for rural peasants; and international monitors and aid organizations look to this young population (some 60% under the age of 20), the survivors and the next generation after genocide, to foster peace and productivity. The forecast is not good. The proliferation of new AIDS cases in Cambodia, and the inability to treat patients, is a major concern. Rural travel entails following safety precautions to the letter (see "Safety," below) and staying abreast of the political situation—instability being the hallmark. Know that the Cambodia of today, however, is a much safer and saner land than only a few years ago, and tourist dollars are a big help.

The Khmer People

Ninety percent of Cambodia's 15 million people are ethnic Khmer, the remainder a mix of ethnic Vietnamese, Chinese, hilltribes, and a small pocket of Cham Muslims. Cambodia's history is a road map of incursions and invasion. Cambodia is a geographic and cultural crossroads of the two powers, India and China, that shaped Southeast Asia and, more than any country in the region, reflects the French term *Indochine*. Khmer culture, like nearby Laos, is defined by Theravada Buddhism.

Etiquette

Traditions and practices in Cambodia, as in neighboring Thailand and Laos, are closely tied with Theravada Buddhism. Modest dress is expected of all visitors, and bare midriffs or short shorts are an offense to many and will cause a stir. Men and women should go easy on public displays of affection. As in all Buddhist countries, it is important to respect the space around a Buddhist monk; women especially should avoid touching and even speaking to the men in orange robes outside the temple.

In personal interaction, keep it light and friendly, especially when bargaining or handling any business affairs. If Khmer people are confused, misunderstand, or disagree, they do what many Westerners find inconceivable: smile, nod, and agree while whole in the knowledge that they will do something different. This is difficult to understand, but try to remember that if you're angry and lots of people around you are smiling, you're unlikely to have achieved your desired aim (in short, you're doomed). Direct discourse is certainly not standard procedure here, and many Western visitors can feel cheated by that misunderstanding. Be clear in what you expect from someone—whether a guide, a motorbike driver, or a business associate—and get firm affirmation of that fact. Listen closely to what comes after the *but* in "Yes, but . . ."

On the line of cultural "no-nos," remember that the feet are considered dirty and that the head is sacred and pure. This means that even pointing the feet in the direction of another or stepping over someone, thus exposing the soles of the feet, is impolite. Touching someone's head, even tussling a child's hair, should be avoided.

Hospitality has its own elaborate rules, and, like in any culture, it is important to accept when possible, or comfortable, and say thank you, *"Awk koun."*

Cuisine

A crossroads of culture, Cambodia is also a crossroads of cuisine, with a mixture of Thai, Laotian, and Vietnamese, as well as newcomers Chinese and French. Just as for its neighbors, rice is the staple of the Khmer diet, but not even the devastating cultural purge of Pol Pot, in which all foreign food and customs were banned, could remove the French-infused tradition of eating baguettes and specialty breads with good milk coffee at outdoor cafes (you'll even see folks playing boules, aka petanque, in provincial towns). Don't pass up a snack at one of the many glass-sided bread carts that roam city streets, particularly in Phnom Penh; sweet breads and good baguettes bought at these mobile stalls are good to have on all-day bus rides and long day trips. You can find lots of stands selling Vietnamese baguettes stuffed with pâté as well.

Dining Khmer style is a long, jocular affair, with cover-the-table spreads of various dishes shared by many over long hours of drinking and chat. Fish is the most prized entree, and Khmer *amok,* a dish of fish steamed in bamboo leaf with coconut milk and curry, is not to be missed. Fried veg and meat dishes abound, some with fiery spices and chili, similar to Thai fare.

Dessert is sweet cakes and breads, or treats made of glutinous rice, or sticky rice, in coconut milk. The list of good local fruit is long, topped by mangos (when in season), papaya, mangosteens *(mankut),* durian, rambutan, jackfruit, citrus treats, and all kinds of spiky, horned things you're sure to see at the market. Just ask how much and ask the vendor to cut it open for you.

Language

The language of Cambodia is called *Khmer,* a term that refers to the ethnic majority of the country but is used to describe all things Cambodian: Khmer people (the

Khmer), Khmer food, culture, and so on. Unlike in neighboring Thailand and Laos, the Khmer language is not tonal and is thus more merciful to the casual learner. Basic pronunciation is still frustrating and difficult, though. Khmer script is based on a south Indian model and is quite complex.

Khmer has borrowed many words from French, Chinese, and now English, especially technical terms. Older Khmers still speak French, and young people are keen to learn and practice English. In the major tour centers, speaking slowly and clearly in basic English will do the trick, but a few choice phrases in Khmer will get you far.

USEFUL KHMER PHRASES

English	Khmer	Pronunciation
Hello	**Soa s'day**	Sew sadday
Goodbye	**Lia haoy**	Lee howie
Thank you	**Awk koun**	Awk coon
Thank you very much	**Awk koun chelan**	Awk coon chalan
How are you?	**Sohk sabai?**	Sook sabai?
I am fine.	**Sohk sabai.**	Sook sabai.
Yes (man)	**Baat**	Baht
Yes (woman)	**Jaa**	Jya
No	**Te**	Tay
I'm sorry	**Sohm To**	Sum too
Do you have . . . ?	**Men awt men . . . ?** (literally, do you have or don't you?)	Men ought men . . . ?
Water?	**Tuhk?**	Took?
Toilet?	**Bawngku uhn?**	Bangku oon?
How much?	**Th'lai pohnmaan?**	Tlai bawn mahn?
Can you make it cheaper?	**Som joh th'lai?**	Sum joe tlai?

PLANNING YOUR TRIP TO CAMBODIA

Visitor Information

You'll find a wealth of information at www.gocambodia.com, or click on "Cambodia" at www.visit-mekong.com. The Cambodian Embassy to the United States sponsors www.embassyofcambodia.org.

- **In the U.S.:** 4530 16th St. NW, Washington, DC 20011 (© **202/726-7742;** fax 202/726-8381; www.embassyofcambodia.org). **In New York:** 866 U.N. Plaza, Ste. 420, New York, NY 10017 (© **212/223-0676;** fax 212/223-0425).
- **In Australia/New Zealand:** No. 5 Canterbury Crescent, Deakin, ACT 2600, Canberra (© **02/6273-1259;** fax 02/6273-1053; www.embassyofcambodia.org.nz).
- **In Thailand:** No. 185 Rajdammri Rd., Lumpini Patumwan, Bangkok 10330, Thailand (© **02/254-6630;** fax 02/253-9859).

Working with a Tour Operator

Many visitors choose to see Cambodia with the convenience of a guided tour, which is a good idea: It's not only safer and easier, but it also means that you won't miss the finer details of what you're seeing and can visit rural Cambodia in as much comfort as possible. Being part of a larger group tour is a good, affordable option. Even if you travel independently, you might want to sign up with a local tour operator (like Diethelm or Exotissimo, below) once you're there.

RECOMMENDED TOUR OPERATORS

International

- **Abercrombie & Kent.** 1411 Opus Place Executive Towers West II, Ste. 300, Downers Grove, IL 60515 (✆ **800/554-7016;** www.aandktours.com).

- **Asia Transpacific Journeys.** 2995 Center Green Court, Boulder, CO 80301 (✆ **800/642-2742** or 303/443-6789; fax 303/443-7078; www.asiatranspacific.com).

Regional

These regional agents are reputable operators with foreign management and a high level of service—whether transport and rooms or all-inclusive tour itineraries. All three act as on-the-ground operators for international travel agents.

- **Diethelm Travel.** No. 65 Street 240, P.O. Box 99, Phnom Penh, Cambodia (✆ **023/219-151;** fax 023/219-150; www.diethelmtravel.com). **In Siem Reap:** House No. 470, Krous Village, Svay Dongkum Commune, Siem Reap, Cambodia (✆ **063/963-524;** fax 063/963-694).

- **Exotissimo.** 6th Floor, SSN Center, 66 Norodom Blvd., Phnom Penh (✆ **023/218-948;** fax 023/426-585; www.exotissimo.com). **In Siem Reap:** New Building B, 20–21 Street 60MK, Siem Reap (✆ **063/964-323;** fax 063/963-621).

Also, just as Vietnam has its budget "traveler cafes," Cambodia hosts a roster of good budget tour options. The folks at **Capitol Tour,** No. 14AEO, Street 182, Phnom Penh (✆ **023/217-627;** www.capitolkh.com), offer affordable, no-frills tour and transport options. Also try **Mekong Express** for reliable ground transport.

Entry Requirements

All visitors must carry a passport and visa. Applying online (www.mfaic.gov.kh/e-visa/vindex.aspx) for a 1-month e-visa costs $25. The procedure is simple, straightforward, and will save you time and energy at the airport/border crossing. Visas can also be issued on arrival at the Phnom Penh or Siem Reap airports for $20, as well as at almost all border crossings. For example, an overland visa-upon-arrival is available from both Thailand (overland from Poipet) and Vietnam (by boat from Chau Doc or by bus through Moc Bai) for $23. Bring one 4×6-inch passport photo for your application.

Tourist visas can be extended three times for a total of 3 months. Any travel agent can perform the service for a small fee. Business visas, for just $25 upon entry, can be extended indefinitely.

Customs Regulations

For visitors 18 years and older, allowable amounts of goods when entering are as follows: 200 cigarettes or the equivalent quantity of tobacco, one bottle of liquor, and a reasonable amount of perfume for personal use. Currency in possession must be declared on arrival. Cambodian Customs on the whole is not stringent. With a long, sad history of theft from the Angkor temples, it is forbidden to carry antiques or Buddhist reliquary out of the country, but Buddhist statues and trinkets bought from souvenir stalls are fine.

Money

Cambodia's official currency is the riel, but the Cambodian economy is tied to the fate of its de facto currency, the U.S. dollar. Greenbacks can be used anywhere. The exchange rate at the time of publication was **4,000 riel = $1.** It's important to have riel for smaller purchases, but there's no point in exchanging large amounts of foreign currency. Prices for all but the smallest purchases are in U.S. dollars and are thus listed in this chapter. The **Thai bhat** is widely accepted in the western region of the country. You'll commonly receive small change in riel. The riel comes in denominations of 100, 200, 500, 1,000, 2,000, 5,000, 10,000, 50,000, and 100,000. You cannot change Cambodia's riel outside the country, so anything you carry home is a souvenir.

ATMS **ANZ Bank** and **Canadia Bank** have ATMs throughout Cambodia with reliable international service.

CURRENCY EXCHANGE You can change traveler's checks in banks in all major towns. Because the U.S. dollar is the de facto currency, it's not a bad idea to change traveler's checks to dollars for a 1% or 2% fee and make all purchases in U.S. cash.

TRAVELER'S CHECKS Traveler's checks are accepted in most major banks for exchange, but not commonly at individual vendors. American Express is a good bet and is represented by **Diethelm** (p. 362).

CREDIT CARDS Cambodia is a cash economy, but credit cards are becoming more widely accepted. Most large hotels and high-end restaurants accept the majors, but you'll want to carry cash for most transactions, and certainly in the countryside.

When to Go

CLIMATE Cambodia's climate falls into the pattern of the southern monsoons that also hit neighboring Thailand and Vietnam from May to November. The seasonal temperature varies little, meaning that it's always hot (a yearly mean of about 82°F/28°C), and the best time to go is in the dry season from December to April. Wear light, loose clothing, preferably cotton, and bring a hat.

PUBLIC HOLIDAYS & EVENTS **Independence Day** is November 9 (1953) and is celebrated throughout the country like the American Fourth of July. October 31 is **King Sihanouk's Birthday,** and **Khmer New Year** is in the middle of April, celebrated with water splashing. The **Bon Om Touk** festival features boat races on the Tonle Sap in October or November, though unfortunately a stampede at this event in 2010 led to the deaths of 375 people. The **Angkor Festival** is also held in November.

Safety

Check with your home country's overseas travel bureau or with the **United States Department of State** (click "Travel Warnings" at www.state.gov) to keep abreast of travel advisories and current affairs that could affect your trip.

The days of the Khmer Rouge taking backpackers hostage are long gone, and the general lawlessness and banditry that marked Cambodia as inaccessible and dangerous only a short time ago has abated. Gun-toting thugs, once a common sight in any town, have been disarmed, but old habits die hard and, in general, travelers should take caution. Poverty in rural areas breeds desperation and a volatile climate. Below are some good guidelines.

SOME IMPORTANT safety TIPS

○ Remember that the police and military of Cambodia are not there to protect and serve. Any interaction with the constabulary usually results in frustration and/or you coming away short a few dollars. Contact your embassy for major problems, and call for police assistance only in cases of theft or extreme danger. Demand a ticket if threatened with a fine of any sort, although often, especially for small traffic infractions, it's best to just cough up a buck or two.

○ Rural travel is opening up, and you'll find a hearty welcome in even the most remote hamlet, but travelers may find some roads a bit rough. Know, too, that you're really on your own out in the sticks, with no hospitals and limited support

services. Banditry has lessened, but still be sure to travel by day (also because of road conditions).

○ As in most big cities, travelers should stay aware, especially at night; purse snatching is not uncommon in Phnom Penh, and pickpockets are as proficient here as anywhere in the region.

○ Land mines and unexploded ordnance (UXOs) still lie buried in rural areas in Cambodia, especially in Battambang, Banteay Meanchey, Pursat, Siem Reap, and Kampong Thom provinces. Don't walk in heavily forested spots or in dry rice paddies without a local guide. Areas around small bridges on secondary roads are particularly dangerous.

DRUGS

Cambodia is one of the world's biggest producers of cannabis—not to mention heroin, amphetamines, and other substances—and peddlers abound. You might be tempted to buy or sample substances offered, but if caught, you could face a lengthy jail sentence, which is guaranteed to be uncomfortable. Enough said.

HEALTH CONCERNS & VACCINATIONS

In chapter 15, I outline the health essentials for Vietnam, which are quite similar to Cambodia. Health considerations should comprise a good part of your trip planning for Cambodia, even if you're going for only a few weeks. You'll need to cover all the bases to protect yourself from tropical weather and illnesses, and you will need to get special vaccinations if rural areas are on your itinerary. You should begin your vaccinations as necessary (ask your doctor how many weeks before your trip you need to allow to give them time to take effect). If you follow the guidelines here and those of your doctor, however, there's no reason you can't have a safe and healthy trip.

Malaria is not a concern in Phnom Penh or any of the larger towns, but upcountry and even in and around Siem Reap and Angkor Wat it's quite common. Many travelers take preventative medication. Check with the Centers for Disease Control and Prevention (CDC) at www.cdc.gov for current information. An **antimalarial prophylaxis** is recommended everywhere but in Phnom Penh. Take atovaquone proguanil (brand name Malarone) or doxycycline. If you plan to travel extensively in the rural areas on the western border with Thailand, primaquine is the only effective preventative.

Other mosquito-borne ailments, such as **Japanese encephalitis** and **dengue fever,** are also prevalent. Your best protection is to wear light, loose-fitting clothes from wrist to neck and ankles, use a bug repellent with DEET, and be particularly careful at sunset or when out and about early in the morning.

Hepatitis is a concern as in anywhere else (see chapter 15), and reliable statistics on **AIDS** are not out, but with rampant prostitution and drug abuse, Cambodia is certainly fertile ground for the disease. Recent efforts to educate needle users about the dangers of the substance and the importance of clean needles, as well as increased condom use, are positive signs, but recent statistics show that the tide of new AIDS cases is rising.

FOREIGN EMBASSIES IN CAMBODIA

If you encounter problems during your visit, go to your embassy. Addresses for embassies in Phnom Penh are as follows:

- **U.S.:** 1 Street 96, at the corner of Street 95 and Street 51 (✆ **023/728-000;** http://cambodia.usembassy.gov).
- **Australia** (also serves New Zealanders): Villa No. 11 Senei Vinnavut Oum (Street 254; ✆ **023/213-470;** www.cambodia.embassy.gov.au).
- **U.K.:** No. 27–29 Street 75 (✆ **023/427-124;** http://ukincambodia.fco.gov.uk).

Getting There

BY AIR International flights to Cambodia from neighboring countries are numerous and affordable. Cambodia's two main hubs, **Siem Reap Airport** and **Phnom Penh International Airport,** are served by the following: Bangkok Airways and Air Asia from Thailand; Malaysia Airlines from Kuala Lumpur; Lao Airways from Vientiane; Vietnam Airways from Ho Chi Minh City and Hanoi; and Silk Air from Singapore and Shanghai Air, EVA, President, and China Southern connections between Phnom Penh and points in China.

Note: There's a hefty **$25 international departure tax** ($13 for children 12 and under) when you leave that is *not* included in ticket fees.

BY BOAT Daily boat connections run between Chau Doc in Vietnam and the town of Neak Loeung, some 2 hours south of Phnom Penh in Cambodia. You can arrange the trip through any budget travel agent in Vietnam, and many include the onward boat connection to Phnom Penh as part of a multiday Mekong Delta trip. *Note:* Budget tour operators **Sinh Café** (✆ **08/3838-9593** in Ho Chi Minh City) and **Capitol Tour,** No. 14AEO Road 182, Phnom Penh (✆ **023/217-627**), are now working together, so when you cross borders, the other company adopts you. It's an all-day journey in a diesel-belching tour boat, but views of life on the wide, lazy Mekong are worth it. *Also note:* A visa is available upon arrival when entering Cambodia, but you have to have a prearranged visa for entry to Vietnam.

⚠ **Medical Safety & Evacuation Insurance**

The Cambodian medical system is rudimentary at best and nonexistent at worst. Make sure that you have medical coverage for overseas travel and that it includes emergency evacuation. For details on insurance, see chapter 15. There are a few clinics in Phnom Penh and Siem Reap, but for anything major, evacuation to Bangkok is the best option.

I don't recommend going by prearranged tours on Thailand's Khao San Road or Sukhumvit Road with dodgy tour agents. Scams abound: overcharging, price fixing at remote border points with extortive fees, and arriving late in Siem Reap in the hopes that you'll stay at the company guesthouse. If you're game for the overland route from the Thai capital, take a local bus from Bangkok's Mo Chit (Northern) Bus Station to Aranyaprathet, follow the border procedures (do not enlist the help of anyone who will charge you later); then, once across the border, go by a Toyota Camry taxi for 1,000 Thai baht ($33) to Siem Reap. It's best to fly, though.

For good, constantly updated information about crossing the Thai border, check the useful website **www.talesof asia.com**.

For a luxury option, the **Victoria Chau Doc Hotel** (✆ 076/386-5010) offers an expensive private transfer from Chau Doc to Phnom Penh on a speedy runabout boat.

BY BUS Buses connect with neighboring **Vietnam** at the Moc Bai border area—at the town of Svay Rieng on the Cambodian side. From Saigon in Vietnam, contact **Saigontourist** (✆ 08/3824-4554) or **Sinh Café** (✆ 08/3838-9593) for direct connection to Cambodia—Sinh Café and Capitol Tour (also called Capitol Guesthouse) are in cahoots, and one carrier takes up your transport at the border. Going in either direction (to or from Cambodia), you'll cross the border around noontime and the bus drops you at your destination sometime after 3pm. The overland border procedure is quick and easy going into Cambodia. You just have to fill out some forms and pay the 2,000 VND tax (payable in any currency). The Capitol/Sinh office is just across the border and has nice "chill-out chairs" (low lawn chairs) where you can get a coffee and wait for the buses to fill. Sinh buses are clean and have air-conditioning, and some even make a quick stop at Psah Goki, a sprawling marketplace on the road between the one-time enemy countries. Going from Cambodia to Vietnam, ask at any travel agent or hotel, or the Capitol Guesthouse (discussed later), and be sure that you have a prearranged visa for Vietnam. A visa is available upon arrival at any land crossing in Cambodia. It's a manageable route but draining, and I highly recommend **going by air** in or out of Phnom Penh or Siem Reap from Vietnam or Thailand.

Getting Around

BY AIR Connection between Phnom Penh and Siem Reap is frequent and regular on Cambodian Angkor Airways. *Note:* There's an $18 domestic departure tax in both Phnom Penh and Siem Reap.

BY BUS Most travelers find local buses rough but a great way to connect with local people. Most routes depart from Phnom Penh.

Mekong Express, 87 Sisowath Quay, Phnom Penh (✆ 023/427-518) connects Phnom Penh and Siem Reap with daily luxury buses for just $12 and runs various routes (also boats) throughout Cambodia. Bus rides come with a snack, and there's a bathroom onboard. They make good time: 5½ hours with one 15-minute break. *Tip:* Earplugs are your friend on this bus ride (and any bus ride, really), which plays Khmer karaoke songs and various Asian pop music videos.

Capitol Tour, No. 14AEo Road 182, Phnom Penh (© 023/217-627), is a long-popular choice for inexpensive seat-in-coach connections and tours throughout the country. Buses leave early from Siem Reap and Phnom Penh. At their office in the capital, they serve good cheap breakfasts, are open 6am to 9pm, and a loudspeaker lets you know when the bus is leaving with something like, "For the traveler who him going to Siem Reap, please get on the bus now!"

BY CAR/MOTORBIKE   Hiring a car with a driver, driving yourself, or going by rented motorbike is a great way to see Cambodia's rural highways and byways. Rough country roads mean that you'll need to rent the most durable of vehicles, with good suspension. Hiring a driver is recommended; traffic is unpredictable. Contact hotels and travel agents. In Phnom Penh, **Lucky! Lucky!,** 413 Monivong Blvd. (© 023/212-788), is the best place to rent quality motorbikes ($7–$8 a day) and other vehicles. You'll have to leave your passport, but these folks are reliable and trustworthy. Next door is **New! New!,** a friendly competitor copycat.

BY BOAT   Speedboats make the 5-hour trip between Phnom Penh and Siem Reap. The cost is $35, and any hotel can arrange a ticket. Boats leave from the pier near 106 Street in the north end of town or connect with Siem Reap's Tonle Sap docks by taxi.

Tips on Accommodations

Be warned that accommodations often fill up in the winter high season, especially the finer hotels nearest Angkor Wat. *Note:* There's a 10% VAT charge at most major hotels. Expect discounts in the low season. Phnom Penh and Siem Reap both have the highest concentrations of comfortable accommodations at international standards, but there are developments in small towns as well. Sihanoukville, Cambodia's little seaside resort south of the capital, boasts a fine high-end resort, the Sokha Beach, but in rural stops such as Battambang, you'll find only budget rooms. Some of the most convenient choices are the smaller, foreign-owned guesthouses where you're likely to meet up with other travelers and can get the inside scoop on what's going on in the area.

Tips on Dining

In this old French colony, the cuisine is heavily French, all affordable, and often quite good. You'll also find tasty Thai, and tourist centers are chockablock with storefronts that serve reasonable facsimiles of Western favorites.

Tips on Shopping

You'll find antiques stores and boutiques in the major centers, but shopping for trinkets and memorabilia is best at the big markets: the Russian Market and Central Market in Phnom Penh, and the Old Market in Siem Reap. The temple town of Siem Reap is fashioning itself as a chic international destination, and along with the many luxurious hotels and fine dining comes good boutique shopping and galleries. In Siem Reap, you'll find fine art photography by noted expatriate artists and some good original artwork and pleasing reproductions from the temples, a far cry from refrigerator magnets and collector spoons (but you can find those along the road to the temples).

Important note: The treasures and carvings of Angkor and Cambodia have been looted for centuries, and those treasures are still being sold. **Do not buy any antique stone carving or temple reliefs in Cambodia.** Some reputable galleries are willing to arrange backroom deals for authentic Khmer antiquities, and even make it look legitimate. For more information, go to www.heritagewatchinternational.org.

Krama Chameleon

The *Krama* is all things to all people: it's a scarf, a towel, a curtain, a headband, a headdress, a baby sling, a belt, a sash, a mask to cover the nose and mouth on dusty roads, an over-the-shoulder satchel, a carrier for a fighting rooster, a cushion for carrying water jars on the head, a bandage, a hankie, and a shawl. The woven cotton scarf, usually of a two-tone checked pattern but in many variations, is essential for rural travel. They're convenient and make great gifts. If you don't have a *Krama,* the young sellers at the temple sites in Angkor or on the streets of Phnom Penh are sure to remind you that you need one (or another one).

[FastFACTS] CAMBODIA

Business Hours Vendors and restaurants tend to open at about 8am and close at 9 or 10pm. Government offices, banks, travel agencies, and museums are usually open from 8am to 4 or 5pm, with an hour break for lunch.

Crime Where violence and banditry was once an everyday occurrence, Cambodia has become much safer. The civilian population is more or less disarmed and civil authorities have firm control, but stay on your toes. Try not to be on the roads late at night, and be careful to lock your valuables in hotel safes. In the event of trouble—as in a holdup—comply and report it to local officials.

Drug Laws Availability might look like permission, but that's not the case. It's a time-tested rule that you can bribe your way out of (or into) anything in corrupt Cambodia, but it's best not to test it. Police are crooked and may be the ones selling the drugs (out of uniform) in order to collect the bribe. Dabbling in this arena makes you friends in all the wrong places, and Cambodia is not a good place to have the wrong friends.

Electricity Cambodia uses 220-volt European standard electricity, with rounded, two-prong plugs requiring an adaptor. Bring a surge protector for delicate instruments.

Emergencies In Phnom Penh, dial ✆ **117** for police, or ✆ **119** for an ambulance.

Hospitals You'll want to take care of any medical or dental issues before arriving in Cambodia. The **SOS Clinic** in Phnom Penh, No. 161 Street 51 (✆ **023/216-911**), is your best bet in a pinch.

Internet Reliable service can be found in the major centers; prepaid wireless connections have recently become available. Prices for connections range from 50¢ per hour at budget Internet cafes to $3 per hour for wireless DSL connections. Note that local Internet cafes can be a bit frustrating; without the proper protective software, bothersome pop-ups and very slow connections are common. Pay more and get more is the rule.

Language The Cambodian language is Khmer. English, French, and Mandarin are also widely spoken.

Police Khmer police exist to harass and collect, not to protect and serve. Contact them only in the event of a major emergency, at ✆ **117,** or the tourist police at ✆ **097/778-0002.**

Post Office Hotels usually sell stamps and send postcards. See "Fast Facts" for Phnom Penh and Siam Reap for locations in these cities.

Publications The *Cambodia Daily* and the twice-monthly *Phnom Penh Post* are good local rags with nitty-gritty news from Cambodia, as well as stories from international wire services. You can also find

Thailand's *Bangkok Post* and the *Nation*, as well as the *International Herald Tribune* and the standard array of international news mags (*Time, Newsweek,* and the *Economist*). Free local magazines are chock-full of good insights. Look for the useful **Asia Life Phnom Penh** (or visit www. asialifeguide.com), a free listings-and-entertainment monthly geared to English-speaking expats, and free listings guides published by **Cambodia Pocket Guides,** which are updated regularly.

Telephone & Fax   Phones in the major centers are reliable, and international direct-dial is common. See "Telephone Dialing Information at a Glance," below.

Time Zone   Cambodia is 7 hours ahead of Greenwich Mean Time, in the same zone as Bangkok. It's 12 hours ahead of New York City and 3 hours behind Sydney.

Tipping   Tipping is not obligatory but appreciated. A blanket 10% to 20% is exorbitant. Best to just round up any check or leave a buck or two.

Toilets   Public toilets are a little rough—mostly of the Asian "squatty-potty" variety—and rather grungy, with an attendant at the door charging a small fee for entrance and a few squares of gritty paper. Not a bad idea to bring your own roll and some hand sanitizer. Facilities in Western accommodations are more familiar.

Water   No tap water is potable. Buy bottled water, available everywhere.

PHNOM PENH

Founded in the mid–14th century as a monastery by the Khmers, Phnom Penh replaced Angkor Thom, a city at the Angkor temples, as the country's capital a century later. The city has long been a vital trading hub at the confluence of three rivers: the Mekong, Tonle Sap, and Bassac. Perhaps the city's most auspicious period was actually when it lay vacant; following an eviction order from Pol Pot, the city was deserted in a period of hours, and almost all of Phnom Penh's residents moved to the countryside in 1975, not to return until 1979 under the authority of Vietnamese troops.

It has been a long road to the peaceful and growing Phnom Penh of today. There were many years of frontier-style anarchy after the city was repopulated in 1979. Drugs and prostitution remain a big downtown commodity, but it's unlikely that you'll be caught in the crossfire, which you couldn't say a decade ago. Today Phnom Penh enjoys its own kind of harmony of opposites and offers visitors peaceful moments of a sunset at riverside, as well as its dusty, motorbike-choked labyrinthine alleys and busy markets. The city is an incongruous cluster of crumbling French colonials, and the central riverside area is great for wandering, especially in the evening when half the city's inhabitants turn out for a bit of exercise and a chat. Things are changing fast however. One indication of this is that Boeng Kak Lake at the north end of the city was being drained at the time of this update to provide space for condominiums and a shopping center. The east bank of the Tonle Sap River is also now the site of intensive construction, including new riverside hotels.

Despite this frenzied development, there's still much of historical interest in Phnom Penh. Its **Royal Palace** is a stone showpiece of classical Khmer architecture, and the **Silver Pagoda,** on the palace grounds, is a jewel-encrusted wonder. Throughout the city, you'll see the faded glory of aged **French colonial architecture.** There are also many notable *wats,* Buddhist temples with resident monks. Of more grisly interest is the **Tuol Sleng,** or Museum of Genocide, a schoolhouse-turned-prison where up to 20,000 victims of Pol Pot's excesses were tortured before

telephone DIALING INFORMATION
AT A GLANCE

○ **To place a call from your home country to Cambodia:** Dial the international code (011 in the U.S., 0011 in Australia, 0170 in New Zealand, or 00 in the U.K.), plus the country code **855,** the city code (**23** for Phnom Penh, **63** for Siem Reap), and the phone number (for example, 011+855+23/000-000). *Important note:* Omit the initial 0 in all Cambodian phone numbers when calling from abroad.

○ **To place a call within Cambodia:** Dial 0 before the city code (as numbers are listed in this book). All phone numbers are 6 digits after the city code.

○ **To place a direct international call from Cambodia:** Most hotels offer international direct-dialing, but with exorbitant surcharges of 10% to 25%. Faxes often have high minimum charges. To place a call, dial the international access code **(001)** plus the country code, the area or city code, and the number (for example, to call the U.S., you'd dial 001+1+000/000-0000).

○ **Here are international country codes:** Australia 61, Myanmar 95, Canada 1, Hong Kong 852, Indonesia 62, Laos 856, Malaysia 60, New Zealand 64, the Philippines 63, Singapore 65, Thailand 66, U.K. 44, U.S. 1, Vietnam 84.

○ Post offices and Internet cafes all rent time on direct lines. If you can manage the static and the delays, affordable Internet phone service is available at Internet cafes. Also keep your eyes open for the many streetside stalls with cellphones on loan, a good choice for regional calls.

being led to the **Choeung Ek,** otherwise known as "The Killing Fields," about 16km (10 miles) from Phnom Penh.

It's a town certainly worth exploring for a few days. Phnom Penh has a pace all its own, and you'll find a lot to catch your eye, whether it is the glut of luxury vehicles, anything from big sport-utility vehicles to European sports cars all rolling around with tinted windows and no license plates, or sprawling local markets.

Visitor Information & Tours
DELUXE

○ **Diethelm Travel,** No. 65 Street 240, P.O. Box 99, Phnom Penh, Cambodia (✆ **023/219-151;** fax 023/219-150; www.diethelmtravel.com). In Siem Reap: House No. 470, Krous Village, Svay Dangkum Commune, Siem Reap, Cambodia (✆ **063/963-524;** fax 063/963-694).

○ **Exotissimo,** 46 Norodom Blvd., Phnom Penh (✆ **023/218-948;** fax 023/426-586; www.exotissimo.com). **In Siem Reap:** New Building B, 2021 Street 60MK, Siem Reap (✆ **063/964-323;** fax 063/963-621).

BUDGET

○ **Capitol Guesthouse Tours,** No. 14AEo Street 182, Sangkat Beng Prolitt (✆ **023/217-627**). This is the town's budget travel cafe and a good place to

CAMBODIA

Phnom Penh ★

CHRUOY CHANGVAR

HOTELS ■
Amanjaya Pancam Hotel **8**
The Billabong **30**
Blue Lime **10**
Boddhi Tree Aram **33**
California 2 **4**
Golden Gate Hotel **22**
Goldiana **24**
Hotel Cambodiana **19**
Hotel InterContinental
  Phom Penh **29**
The Pavilion **20**
The Quay **7**
Raffles Hotel Le Royal **1**

RESTAURANTS ◆
Boddhi Tree Umma **27**
Café Metro **9**
Comme à la Maison **23**
Foreign Correspondents
  Club (FCC) **13**
Friends (Mith Samlanh)
  Restaurant **11**
K West **8**
La Résidence **32**
Le Wok **12**
112 Restaurant **2**
Origami **18**
Pacharan **16**

Riverhouse Asia Bistro **6**
Romdeng **31**
Titanic **5**
Topaz **25**

ATTRACTIONS ●
Independence Monument **21**
The Killing Fields & Choeung
  Ek Memorial **26**
National Museum **14**
Royal Palace **15**
Silver Pagoda **17**
Tuol Sleng Museum of
  Genocide **28**
Wat Phnom **3**

arrange inexpensive rural and local tours and onward connections by bus and boat. Remember that you get what you pay for, but the services are convenient.

- Small tour operators and ticket shops abound along Sisowath. For flights and other services, try **K.U. Travel and Tours,** at No. 77 on Street 240, in the cafe and gallery area (© **023/723-456;** www.kucambodia.com).

- For buses and onward land and water connections, contact your hotel front desk, which in turn will likely contact one of the following consolidators: **Mekong Express,** 87Eo Sisowath Quay (© **023/427-518**), which offers the most deluxe services at slightly higher rates, with clean and very efficient air-conditioned buses; **Neak Krorhrom Travel and Tours,** No. 4 Street 108, on the Wat Phnom end of Sisowath Quay (© **023/219-497**); **PTM Travel and Tours,** 200 Eo Monivong (© **023/986-363**); or **World Express Travel and Tours,** No. 148 Eo Street 169 (© **023/884-574**). These are just a few of the many. *Note:* Avoid booking full-package-tour connections to Bangkok.

Getting There

BY AIR   All major airlines in the region connect here. **Phnom Penh International Airport** is just a 15-minute drive from the city center; a cab costs $9, a tuk-tuk $7, or a ride on the back of a motorbike just $3. Buy tickets from the taxi stand outside the departure terminal under the archway to your left.

BY BOAT   Speedboats connect Phnom Penh with Siem Reap and leave every morning from the main dock on the north end of town. Tickets are available just about anywhere in town. The price is $35 from most hotels or the Capitol Guesthouse (see above). See the "Getting There" section at the beginning of this chapter for information about boat connections from Vietnam.

BY BUS   Phnom Penh is a hub for buses throughout the country—best are the many budget tourist companies offering affordable daily connections to anywhere from the far south to Siem Reap. A tourist bus to Siem Reap takes 6 hours and costs from $5. **Sorya Transport** (© **023/210-859**), with an office just west of the central market, sells tickets to all the major stops and minor hamlets in the country. **Mekong Express** has daily connections to Siem Reap on an air-conditioned bus for $11. Their buses make the trip in about 5½ hours.

Getting Around

Phnom Penh's downtown is accessible on foot, and it's reasonably easy to find your way because the streets are arranged in a numbered grid. However, not all streets are numbered at each corner, and numbers along a street often follow an illogical progression, making it difficult to find some places. For sites farther afield, such as the Killing Fields or any temples, you'll need wheels. Metered taxis are around, and any hotel can arrange daily car rental (with driver).

   Motorcycle taxis, called *motodups,* can be hired anywhere and cost about $1 for short trips in town. Bargain hard. These guys are everywhere, especially on the riverside, and the competition is in your favor. Then again, what the heck is $1? Tip, and you'll have a friend for life.

   Tuk-tuks are the best choice and available anywhere. The name is taken from the Thais, but these tuk-tuks have nothing to do with the noisy Bangkok three-wheeler. Cambodia's tuk-tuks are a two-wheeled surrey pulled by a standard motorbike. They are shaded, and the padded seat is great for two. There's a smaller seat at the front of the cart in which, at a pinch, you can seat two more, but it's not very comfy. Pay between $1 and $3 for trips around town; a ride farther out, say, to the Killing Fields, will set you back around $15.

Lucky! Lucky!, 413 Monivong Blvd. (© **023/212-788**), rents high-quality motorbikes for rural touring (available for long-term rental), as well as jeeps and even luxury cars. Next door is **New! New!**, a friendly competitor. Rates are $5 to $9 per day.

[FastFACTS] PHNOM PENH

American Express For basic American Express services, contact **Cambodia Asia Bank,** No. 246Eo Monivong Blvd. (© **023/224-280**).

Banks & Currency Exchange **ANZ Bank** has many reliable international ATMs in town, the most convenient being at their riverside branch, 265 Sisowath Quay (© **023/726-900**). **Canadia Bank,** No. 265–269 Street 114 (© **023/215-285**), and **Mekong Bank,** 1 Street 114 (© **023/217-112**), are also in the downtown area and can cash traveler's checks and give cash advances. A **Western Union** office is at 349Eo Sisowath Quay (© **023/220-381**).

Clinics The **International SOS Medical and Dental Clinic,** No. 161 Street 51 (© **023/216-911**), is the best place to handle minor emergencies. **Naga Clinic,** No. 11 Street 254 (© **023/211-300**), is

another. For any major emergency or injury, however, you'll want to arrange medical evacuation.

Emergency For police, dial © **117;** for fire, dial © **118;** and for the expat hot line, dial © **023/724-793.**

Internet Internet outlets line riverside Sisowath Street. Hourly access starts at 50¢. **Friendly Web,** near Capitol Guesthouse, has good access from its office at No. 199Eo Street 107 (at the corner of Rd. 182; © **012/843-246**). **Sunny Internet Cafe** has several flatscreen computers serving up fast ADSL connections in a bright location at 351 Sisowath Quay (© **023-986-629**). **KIDS** is an NGO where American owner Bill Herod brings Internet technology to Khmer students. They have good, inexpensive access in their offices at No. 17A Street 178 (© **023/218-452;** kids@camnet.com.kh).

Post Office The post office is in the north end of town on Street 13, east of Wat Phnom. It's open daily from 6:30am to 5pm and has standard delivery service and an international phone. **DHL** has an office on No. 353 Street 110 (© **023/427-726**), and **FedEx** is at No. 71 Street 242 (© **023/216-708**). There's also a post office at the airport in the outdoor archway between arrivals and departures (across from the Dairy Queen).

Telephone The local code for Phnom Penh is **23.** International direct-dialing is available in most hotels and at the post office. Storefront Internet cafes along Sisowath do inexpensive Internet calls or direct-dialing. Cellphones are very popular, and you'll find streetside stalls on wheels where you can make local and international calls for next to nothing, with a good cellular connection.

Where to Stay

There are some choice hotels in town, from old, upscale gems to budget minihotels, and even a few small boutique properties. I recommend spending a little more for bargain luxury because the midrange properties of Phnom Penh are run-down, at best. Always ask about seasonal rates.

VERY EXPENSIVE

Hotel InterContinental Phnom Penh ★ This luxury behemoth has every amenity and in-room convenience. The downside is the location; the self-contained hotel is pretty far from the city's action. Rooms are done in tidy carpet, dark-wood furnishings, patterned couches, and striped raw-silk curtains that match the spreads on the king-size beds. Everything is large and luxe, and beds are fluffy and comfortable. Well-appointed bathrooms have separate showers and tubs with Art Deco faucets. Oak desks and huge windows give guests that "power broker" feel (even if you're just a small fish). The large outdoor pool on the third floor has an Angkor Wat theme, with stone carving decorations, a centerpiece fountain with three elephant heads, and an elegant water-level bar.

296 Blvd. Mao Tse Toung. www.intercontinental.com. *☏* **023/424-888.** Fax 023/424-886. 345 units. $177 double; $457 executive suite; $3,000 Royal suite. AE, MC, V. **Amenities:** 2 restaurants; bar; snack bar; concierge; fitness center; pool; room service; sauna; spa; Wi-Fi. *In room:* A/C, TV, fridge, high-speed Internet ($15 per day), minibar.

Raffles Hotel Le Royal ★★★ This is my favorite high-end hotel in Phnom Penh. Built in 1929, this is the city's most atmospheric hotel, an authentic Art Deco and colonial classic. Everything from the vaulted ceilings in the lobby to the classic original central stairs breathes history and charm. Walking down the arched hallways, with sunlight bouncing off the black-and-white floor tiles and streaming in through stone columns, is like walking smack into the extravagance of Indochina. Rooms are done with fine tiled entries, high ceilings, indirect lighting, a sitting area, and ornate touches such as cabinets with antiques and fine drapery. Landmark rooms, just one step above the standard, are a good choice in the old wing and are larger, with claw-foot tubs and Art Deco faucets. The central pool area is a tranquil oasis divided by a pavilion, and the amenities throughout, such as the fine spa facility, are luxe. The staff is attentive and very professional.

92 Rukhak Vithei Daun Penh (off Monivong Blvd.), Sangkat Wat Phnom. www.raffles.com. *☏* **023/981-888.** Fax 023/981-168. 170 units. $220–$330 double; $350–$2,100 suite. AE, MC, V. **Amenities:** 2 restaurants; 2 bars; babysitting; children's club; concierge; health club; Internet; Jacuzzi; 2 pools; room service; sauna. *In room:* A/C, TV, fridge, hair dryer, minibar, Wi-Fi.

EXPENSIVE

Amanjaya Pancam Hotel ★★ Riverside at Sisowath Quay, this three-story corner building is a true house of style. The porous laterite walls of the lobby—the same stone used in Angkor—and Buddhist statues throughout contribute to a cool boutique vibe. Though sparse in services and amenities, rooms are spacious, done in rich red-silk hangings and bedspreads, in bold contrast with dark-wood trim and floors. All rooms have king-size beds. For the same price as the standard suites at the Quay nearby (see below), Amanjaya's deluxe suites are far more spacious and come with a small balcony. Rooms vary in size and shape; best are the corner suites with panoramic views of the river and busy street below. There's also a new rooftop bar with fine views over the river. Noisy traffic is the only drawback.

No. 1 Street 154, Sisowath Quay. www.amanjaya-pancam-hotel.com. *☏* **023/219-579.** Fax 023/219-545. 21 units. Apr–Sept $120–$220 suite; Oct–Mar $155–$250 suite. MC, V. **Amenities:** Restaurant; bar; room service. *In room:* A/C, TV, fridge, minibar, Wi-Fi.

Hotel Cambodiana ★★ With a convenient location, atmosphere, and all the amenities, this is a good jumping-off point for the sites downtown. The building looks like a giant gilded wedding cake, and its vaulted Khmer-style roofs dominate the sky in the southern end of downtown. The lobby is abuzz with activity, whether it's visiting dignitaries or disembarking tour buses, but the helpful staff handles it all with grace. The large riverside pool is great, and there are some fine choices in international dining. Everything is tidy, but decoration is a chain-hotel style in plain wood and office carpet; it's a bit dull, and some floors reek of pungent deodorizers. The high-end suites are richly decorated and unique, and executive privileges on the top floors are luxe. They have wireless Internet (with prepaid cards) available in all public spaces. All rooms have picture windows and good views of town or the river.

313 Sisowath Quay. www.hotelcambodiana.com.kh. © **023/218-189.** Fax 023/217-059. 238 units. $180–$225 double; $400–$500 suite. AE, MC, V. **Amenities:** 2 restaurants; bar; concierge; executive-level rooms; small health club; Jacuzzi; pool; room service; sauna; tennis court; Wi-Fi. *In room:* A/C, TV, fridge, minibar.

The Quay ★★   This chic new riverside hotel is giving nearby Amanjaya a run for its money. I advise skipping the small, windowless (though, admittedly, still very stylish) standard rooms and booking yourself into a panorama suite. For the extra $50, you get a room twice the size, with large balconies with unobstructed views of the river and a cozy sitting area with Arne Jacobsen swan chairs. The decor of light wood, champagne-color textiles, and cream walls and furniture creates a truly soothing escape from the chaos of Phnom Penh. The rooftop Jacuzzi is luxurious, if a bit uncomfortable, as there is also a popular rooftop bar, so you may have to shimmy your way past patrons for a soak.

277 Sisowath Quay. www.thequayhotel.com. © **023/992-284.** Fax 023/224-893. 16 units. From $105 standard suite; from $160 panoramic suite. AE, MC, V. **Amenities:** Restaurant; Jacuzzi; room service. *In room:* A/C, TV, fridge, minibar, Wi-Fi.

MODERATE

Blue Lime ★★   Blue Lime is the latest oasis from the group that brought the Pavilion (see below) to Phnom Penh. Rooms are spacious, especially if you bump up to the superiors; the extra $5 gets you a nice private balcony. The pool is surrounded by four-poster daybeds and tall, leafy tropical trees. Staff here is friendly and extremely efficient and thoughtful. A room on the top floor offers lovely views of the curved rooftop of the National Museum in the distance. Rooms are, on balance, spotless, but there was an ant problem in mine, so be sure to throw food and sweets in the fridge. Blue Lime is already popular with travelers in the know, so book far in advance.

No. 42 Street 19Z (in the alley off Street 19; btw. 181Eo and 179B Street 19). www.bluelime.asia. © **023/222-260.** 23 units. $40–$60 double; $75 pool room (Dec 15–Jan 15 add $10). MC, V. **Amenities:** Restaurant; bar; saltwater pool. *In room:* A/C, TV, DVD player, fridge, hair dryer, minibar, Wi-Fi.

Boddhi Tree Aram ★   This cute boutique hotel, which occupies two roomy houses on a quiet street just a short walk from the Royal Palace and National Museum, is a good place to escape the clamor of Phnom Penh. Rooms are decorated in a soothing off-white with modern furnishings, potted plants, tasteful artwork, and indirect lighting. It's got all the comforts you'd expect from a place in this price range, including tea- and coffeemaking facilities, but there's no minibar or fridge, which can be a drawback on a hot day. There's no swimming pool either, though guests can use the pool at the nearby Himawari Hotel. Balconies around the buildings are ideal for catching the breeze and are decked with bright flowers. Staff is superattentive, and the small restaurant serves tasty Khmer and Western dishes.

No. 70E Street 244 (just south of the Royal Palace). www.boddhitree.com. ✆ **023/211-376.** 12 units. $76–$82 double. MC, V. **Amenities:** Restaurant; room service. *In room:* A/C, TV, Wi-Fi, no phone.

The Pavilion ★★   Hidden behind big, heavy wooden doors and long white walls, The Pavilion is an absolute oasis in this city of honking, jostling tuk-tuks and motorcycles. Stepping into the central courtyard garden is incredibly calming. Daybeds with overstuffed pillows, friendly staff, and a compact pool offer much needed comfort after touring the city. Double rooms are basic, with firm beds and a few silk decorations. For a splurge, book one of the pool rooms, which come with nice private toe dippers. This is a very popular boutique hotel, so make sure to book ahead and get confirmation in writing or by e-mail. All guests must be 16 or older to ensure tranquility. *Note:* The Pavilion's sister hotel, **Kabiki,** 22 Street 264 (✆ **023/222-290**), was built specifically for families. It has a very similar ambience and level of service.

No. 227 Street 19. www.thepavilion.asia. ✆ **023/222-280.** 20 units. $40–$80 double; $90 suite or pool rooms (Dec 15–Jan 15 add $15). MC, V. **Amenities:** Restaurant. *In room:* A/C, TV, DVD player, fridge, minibar, Wi-Fi.

INEXPENSIVE

The Billabong ★   This hotel attracts a laid-back group of travelers who want something a little more luxe than the basic $15 backpacker deal. Everything is done in navy blue and white and feels a bit like an old-fashioned cabana or low-key country club. Rooms are basic, with navy sheets and red silk bed throws. Staff is ultrafriendly, and the pool is an excellent oasis after a day of touring the city. Spring for a room with a poolside view; it's worth the extra $3.

No. 5 Street 158. www.thebillabonghotel.com. ✆ **023/223-703.** Fax 023/998-472. 20 units. $36–$39 double; $58 superior; $62 deluxe. MC, V. **Amenities:** Restaurant; Internet. *In room:* A/C, TV, fridge, minibar.

California 2   This reliable riverfront guesthouse has recently moved to the northern end of Sisowath Quay, and its handful of rooms have all you might need (air-conditioning, cable TV, and hot-water showers). Most lack windows, but if you're out sightseeing all day, as most visitors are, this is no problem. The owner, Jim, is an American biker with a wealth of local info, and the bar/grill (p. 384) is a cool, fun place to hang out.

79 Sisowath Quay (just west of Wat Phnom). www.cafecaliforniaphnompenh.com. ✆ **077/503-144.** 10 units. $27 standard double; $35 deluxe double. No credit cards. **Amenities:** Restaurant, bar (24-hr.). *In room:* A/C, TV, minibar, Wi-Fi.

Golden Gate Hotel   This is a popular spot for long-staying expat business visitors and NGO folks. Standard rooms are basic but clean; deluxe rooms are larger but just as plain; and the suites, with kitchenette and small living room, are like one-room apartments. Rooms are done in either tile or office carpet, and have mismatched but tidy cloth and rattan furniture. The best choice is a deluxe room on a higher floor (with view). Be sure to ask to see the room first, as they really vary.

No. 9 Street 278, Sangkat (just south of the Independence Monument). www.goldengatehotels.com. ✆/fax **023/427-618.** 105 units. $28 double; $35 deluxe double; $45 suite (monthly rates available). MC, V. **Amenities:** Restaurant; room service; Wi-Fi. *In room:* A/C, TV, fridge, Internet (in deluxe and suite only), minibar.

Goldiana ★   A labyrinthine complex, the result of many construction phases, the Goldiana is one of the best budget choices in the Cambodian capital. It's also another top choice for NGO workers and those working in diplomatic circles. The hotel is just south of the Victory Monument and a short ride from the main sites. It's low-luxe but squeaky clean. Rooms are large and have either carpet or wood flooring. The hotel's maintenance standard, unlike similar hotels in town, is meticulous. The third-floor pool is a real bonus in this category. The staff is kind, helpful, and used to the questions and concerns of long-staying patrons, tourists, and business clients.

No. 10–12 Street 282, Sangkat Boeng Keng Kang 1. www.goldiana.com. ✆/fax **023/219-558.** 147 units. From $38 double; $68-$98 suite. MC, V. **Amenities:** Restaurant; gym; Internet; pool; room service. *In room:* A/C, TV, fridge, hair dryer, Internet, minibar.

Where to Eat

Between remnants of French colonialism and the recent influx of humanitarian-aid workers, international cuisine abounds in the Cambodian capital. Some restaurants themselves are actually NGO projects designed to raise money for local causes or provide training. Ask Khmer folks where to eat, and you'll certainly be pointed to any of the streetside stalls or storefront Chinese noodle shops south of the Central Market, but good eats can be had from one of many options along riverside Sisowath or in and among the lazy alleys of the town center.

For an interesting evening of local fun and frolic, cross the Cambodian–Japanese Friendship Bridge on the Tonle Sap River in the north end of town, and follow the main road a few short miles to the town of **Prek Leap,** a grouping of large riverside eateries always crowded with locals on the weekend. Some of these places put on popular variety shows: It's the universal language of slapstick in play here and a good chance to eat, talk, and laugh with locals. All the restaurants serve similar, good Khmer and Chinese fare. Go by taxi and pick the most crowded place; the more, the merrier.

EXPENSIVE

Foreign Correspondents Club (FCC) ★ CONTINENTAL   With a long history as Phnom Penh's place to see and be seen, the FCC is as much a tour stop as a restaurant. Once the gathering place of the dust-caked, camera-toting, intrepid breed who came to chronicle the country's troubled times, the FCC is now a multifloor affair of hotel, restaurant, bar, and shops done in dark wood and terra cotta. There are low reclining chairs in the cafe area, a fine dining room, and a dark bar as the stalwart centerpiece. The whole third floor is oriented to the fine views of the river and busy Sisowath below. The food is uninspired Western, but you come here more for the atmosphere than a fine meal. The pizza is rather bland, but try the nachos and enchiladas. The fourth-floor bar is popular at weekends and often has cover bands playing live music.

No. 363 Sisowath Quay. ✆ **023/724-014.** Main courses $7-$14. MC, V. Daily 6am-midnight.

La Résidence ★★ FRENCH   If you splurge on only one meal in Phnom Penh, do it here. Housed in a former imperial mansion, this is fine dining at its best. Waitstaff are discreet and attentive, the setting is romantic without being stuffy, and the food is fantastic. Book ahead to get a table by the garden window. The chef previously worked in Michelin two- and three-star restaurants. The menu consists of classic and modern French food. Anything from the foie gras list is rich and decadent, but I suggest the stuffed ravioli with duck liver in Parmesan cream sauce, a dish worthy of the zillion-calorie intake. A three-course dinner will likely set you back at least $50; if money is tight, opt for a more frugal three-course set lunch menu.

No. 22-24 Street 214. ☏ **023/224-582.** www.la-residence-restaurant.com. Reservations recommended. Main courses $10-$80 (average is about $25); set lunch menu $15-$28. AE, MC, V. Mon–Fri 11:30am–2pm and 6:15–10pm; Sat–Sun 6:15–10pm.

112 Restaurant ★ FRENCH   You found it—the new French restaurant highly favored by the expats in this area of town. The decor is a bit busy, with brown and white embroidered table settings and chairs, wrought-iron lamps and light covers everywhere, and tall potted trees curving around the arched ceilings. Music is hit and miss—one moment it's Ella Fitzgerald and "My Funny Valentine," the next moment it's the Carpenters' "Yesterday Once More"—but the food is excellent. They have signature French dishes, such as steak tartare, and an impressive salad menu. The green salad with goat cheese on toast and walnuts is crisp and tangy, and a meal unto itself.

No. 1A Street 102 (Colonial Mansions). ☏ **023/990-880.** Reservations recommended. Main courses $15-$40. AE, MC, V. Daily 11am–2pm and 6–10pm.

Origami ★★ JAPANESE   Sushi in Cambodia? Go figure. There are a number of Japanese restaurants in town, in fact, but Origami serves fine sushi and all manner of good, authentic Japanese. From *tonkatsu* (deep-fried pork over rice) to real Japanese ramen (noodle soup), Ms. Kimura, the genial proprietor, covers all the bases. Essential ingredients are imported from Japan, and everything is well priced. The sushi is the real deal; the presentation and decor of this little park-side gem could have been lifted straight out of Tokyo. Popular with Japanese expats on humanitarian assignment, the restaurant is an NGO offering Khmer kids training in Japanese language and culture.

84 Sothearos St. (near the main downtown sites). ☏ **012/968-095.** Main courses $3-$20; set menu $10-$40. V, MC. Mon–Sat 11:30am–2pm and 5:30–9:30pm.

Riverhouse Asia Bistro ★★ ASIAN/FRENCH   One of many along the riverside, this bar and restaurant stands out by virtue of size and style. A classic corner colonial, its downstairs is an open-air bar area with quaint cushioned chairs under canvas umbrellas, while inside there's an elegant air-conditioned dining room. Red velvet chairs, two stately bars in wood and glass, and the fine linen and silver presentation are luxe far beyond the price tag. The food is excellent, characterized by fine French specials such as duck, salmon tournedos, and imported steaks. Upstairs is the Riverhouse Lounge; come for a romantic dinner and stay for dancing.

157 Sisowath Quay. ☏ **023/212-302.** Reservations recommended. Main courses $7-$22. AE, MC, V. Daily 10am–2am.

Topaz ★★ CONTINENTAL/FRENCH   Good familiar food and atmosphere that's sophisticated but not stuffy are the hallmarks of Topaz, a stylish French bistro. In air-conditioned comfort, diners sit at elegant tables with fine linen, silver, and real stemware in a formal dining room unrivaled in town. The menu features great steaks, pasta, and salad. The Caesar salad is noteworthy. Daily specials are contingent on the day's imports of fish or fine steaks. Wine racks line the room beside the entrance, with some great choices. Everything's good.

182Eo Norodom Blvd.☏ **023/221-622.** Reservations recommended. Main courses $8-$90. MC, V. Daily 11am–2pm and 6–11pm.

MODERATE

Café Metro ★ ASIAN/INTERNATIONAL   This stylish, contemporary restaurant serves excellent food in a cornerside location overlooking the river. The food is top notch, mostly seafood and Australian beef. They've got a nice selection of "small plates" for those who want lighter portions. On the large-plate menu, the grilled tenderloin served with a side of fries will knock out any hunger pangs. There's free Wi-Fi access and an extensive martini menu, too.

271 Street 148 (on the corner with Sisowath Quay). ☏ **023/222-275.** Main courses $8–$20. MC, V. Daily 9.30am–1am.

Comme à la Maison ★ CONTINENTAL   Expats love this place—it's quiet. They have great bread; in fact, on a weekend morning there's a steady stream of deliveries leaving their bakery. Light fare tops the bill: good soups and salads sopped up with something freshly baked. Comme à la Maison also features heartier French entrees, meats, and cheese platters, as well as good pizzas, pastas, and daily specials. Follow up with fresh yogurt, fruit, and good desserts. The quiet courtyard area is at the top of the list for escaping the chaos of busy Phnom Penh.

No. 13 Street 57 (around the corner from the Goldiana, southwest of the town center). ☏ **023/360-801.** www.commealamaison-delicatessen.com. Main courses $6–$13. No credit cards. Daily 6am–10:30pm.

K West ★★ KHMER/WESTERN   In the lobby of the Amanjaya Hotel, one of Phnom Penh's coolest boutique properties, this chic little international bar and bistro is French owned and managed. The menu features an array of savory salads. Fine pastas are made fresh and cooked to order, and you'll find good meat and poultry entrees, seafood specials, and a host of good Khmer dishes. Dessert is a cornucopia of cakes and pies, ice cream, and "The Colonel," lemon sherbet and vodka. The air-conditioned interior has cozy wooden booths for privacy and is flanked by a long wooden bar area, popular among expats. The place is a busy catwalk in the evening.

No. 1 Street 154, Sisowath Quay, Phnom Penh. ☏ **023/214-747.** Main courses $6–$20. MC, V. Daily 6:30am–midnight.

Le Wok ★ INTERNATIONAL/KHMER   Conveniently located across from the National Museum, Le Wok is worth checking out for its adventurous menu, which gives a twist to many traditional dishes. I tried the Parma ham risotto with mushroom sauce, which proved to be a delightful blend of tastes and textures, though there are plenty of other intriguing items to choose from. The decor is relaxing, and cool jazz in the background makes guests want to linger after eating.

No. 33Eo Street 178. ☏ **092/821-857.** Main courses $6–$12. MC, V. Daily 8am–11pm.

Pacharan ★ SPANISH   This hip place serves reliable tapas. They've got all the favorites: patatas bravas, cured meats, Spanish tortillas. Portions are small, and you're meant to order plates to share among friends. The calamari is excellent, but skip the lackluster chicken croquettes. They also have a fine selection of Spanish wines.

389 Sisowath Quay. ☏ **023/224-394.** Tapas $2–$10. MC, V. Daily 11am–11pm.

Titanic ★ INTERNATIONAL/KHMER   Firmly attached to the riverbank, this is the only restaurant along Sisowath Quay with a true riverfront location (the view from all others looks out across a noisy and busy road). The Titanic features a great combination of delicious dishes and cozy atmosphere. There's a lengthy, breezy terrace overlooking the water and comfy armchair seating, and an extensive menu of local and international cuisine, all at reasonable prices. I went for the set menu of spicy beef salad, amok fish (a mild curry served in a coconut shell), and crispy pineapple rolls, all for $12, and was delighted with the choice. They also serve burgers, steaks, pizzas, and a wide range of drinks. Staff is superfriendly and helpful, making this an ideal spot for a long, lazy lunch or a romantic dinner.

North end of Sisowath Quay (next to the ferry pier). ℂ **023/427-209.** Main courses $6–$15. MC, V. Daily 6am–10pm.

INEXPENSIVE

Boddhi Tree Umma ★ ASIAN/KHMER   The Boddhi Tree is a good spot to collect your thoughts after visiting vestiges of Cambodia's late troubles at nearby Tuol Sleng (p. 382). Named for the tree under which the Buddha "saw the light," this verdant garden courtyard and rough-hewn guesthouse has comfy balcony and courtyard seating and serves as much calm as coffee, tea, and light fare. All the curries are good, the baguette sandwiches have generous fillings, and there are weekly specials. Established in 1997 as a way to drum up funds and support for Khmer kids and families in challenging circumstances, the folks here welcome your suggestions and invite visitors to get involved in their important work.

No. 50 Street 113, Beong Keng Kong (across from Tuol Sleng museum). ℂ **023/211-397.** www. boddhitree.com. Main courses $3–$6. V. Daily 6:30am–10pm.

Friends (Mith Samlanh) Restaurant ★★ INTERNATIONAL/KHMER   This friendly gem, an NGO project where Khmer street kids are given shelter and taught useful skills for their reintegration into society, is not to be missed. The food, an ever-changing tapas menu of local and international favorites and a host of desserts, is great. I had delicious sweet sticky rice with a nice mix of local fruit. This is a great spot to cool off and have a light bite while touring the city center (right across from the "must-see" National Museum). The space is an open-air colonial in a courtyard of primary-color murals of the kids' drawings. The name of the restaurant means "Friends," and you might meet some here as you find yourself giving English lessons, laughing, and smiling with these young survivors.

No. 215 Street 13 (across from the entrance to the National Museum). ℂ **012/802-072.** www.mith samlanh.org. Main courses $2.50–$4.75. V. Daily 11am–9pm.

Romdeng ★★ KHMER   Romdeng serves tasty Khmer food in an original, atmospheric French colonial house. Run by the same NGO as Friends Restaurant (see above), the menu is similar, but the decor is a bit cozier, with small, separate dining areas and alfresco seating set around a small outdoor pool and garden. Try the fish and pumpkin curry in coconut sauce, a delicious savory dish that packs just the right amount of spice and is big enough for two.

No. 74 Street 174. ℂ **092/219-565.** www.mithsamlanh.org. Main courses $4.50–$6.25. V. Daily 11am–10pm.

SNACKS & CAFES

Java Café and Gallery, No. 56 Sihanouk Blvd. (ℂ **023/987-420**), is a good spot in town to relax and escape the midday heat. Just south of the main sights (near the Independence Monument), this popular spot has casual seating on a large balcony and an open gallery interior. They serve coffee, cappuccino, and good cakes and other baked goods; they sometimes feature live music in the evening. It's open 7am to 10pm.

The **Deli,** No. 13 Street 178 (ℂ **012/851-234**), is a favorite among expats for a good sandwich and excellent pastries.

The **Shop** is a stylish cafe on popular Street 240 (ℂ **023/986-964**), with a newer, equally comfortable location on the north end of Sisowath Quay. Come here for baked goods (try the raspberry chocolate tart), filling paninis and toasted sandwiches, tea, and coffee. There are neat details such as butcher-block tables and fresh flowers, and they can arrange picnic lunches for day trips from Phnom Penh.

Chocoholics *must* visit **Chocolate by The Shop** ★, 35 Street 240 (© **023/998-638**), next door, which serves fantastic Belgian truffles, chocolates, and frozen bonbons all for reasonable prices.

Sugar Palm, No. 19 Street 240 (© **023/220-956**), is a gallery featuring local crafts and also serves good Khmer dishes at streetside or from their upstairs balcony.

Pizza can be found at any number of storefronts on the crowded riverside; **Herb's Happy Pizza,** No. 345 Sisowath Quay (© **012/921-915**), is among them. Beginning with the name, there are cute little codes in play here, so to cut through it all, say "Please don't put marijuana on my pizza," unless you want it. Same drill at **Ecstatic Pizza,** 132F Norodom Blvd. (© **023/365-089**); both are good and will deliver, pot or not.

Attractions

All sights in the city center can be reached on foot, but you'll want to hire a car with a driver or, for the brave, a motorbike taxi to reach sights outside the city center. **Tuol Sleng** and the **Killing Fields** can be visited together, and arrangements can be made at any hotel.

Central Market   This Art Deco behemoth, built in 1937 but recently renovated, is a city landmark and, on any given day, a veritable anthill of activity. The building, perhaps of more interest for its architecture than its market stalls, is a towering rotunda with busy wings extending in four directions. On the periphery you'll find T-shirts, hats, and all manner of trinkets and souvenirs, as well as photocopied bootlegs of popular novels and books on Cambodia. Goldsmiths and watch-repair and -sales counters predominate in the main rotunda, and you can find some good deals. Spend some time wandering the nooks and crannies, though, and you might come across something that strikes your fancy, whether that's a chaotic hardware shop, a cobbler hard at work with an awl, or just the cacophony and carnival-barker shouts of salesmen and haggling shoppers. Be sure to bargain for any purchase. The **Russian Market** in the south end of town is comparable and equally worth a visit (it's a good stop on the return trip from the Killing Fields).

Btw. streets 126 and 136 in the town center. Daily 5am–5pm.

Independence Monument   Built in the late 1950s to commemorate Cambodia's independence from the French on November 9, 1953, this towering obelisk is crowned with Khmer Nagas and is reminiscent of Angkor architecture and Hindu influence. The area is at its most majestic when all lit up at night (or from afar while squinting).

South of the town center at the intersection of Norodom and Sihanouk.

The Killing Fields & Choeung Ek Memorial ★★   Originally a Chinese cemetery before becoming the execution grounds for the Khmer Rouge during their maniacal reign under Pol Pot from 1975 to 1979, the site is a collection of mounds, mass graves, and a towering monument of cataloged human skulls. The monument is 17 stories high, reminding visitors of April 17, 1975, the day the Khmer Rouge took over Cambodia. As a sign of respect, take your shoes off before mounting the steps to view the monument up close. Human skulls, arranged by age and gender, are arranged at eye level, while other bones are placed on higher levels. The Killing Fields are often visited in conjunction with a tour of Tuol Sleng (see below).

15km (9¼ miles) south of Phnom Penh. Arrange a private car or motorbike. Admission $3. Daily 8am–5:30pm.

National Museum ★★★   This museum, opened in 1920 by King Sisowath, is an important storehouse holding artifacts and statuary from all regions of Cambodia. (many pieces, unfortunately, were plundered and smuggled out of the country before they could get here). Nevertheless, this grand red sandstone edifice has a beautiful and informative collection of Khmer pieces. From the entrance, begin on your left with a room of small prehistoric artifacts. A clockwise loop around the central courtyard walks you through time, from static, stylized pieces of stiff-legged, standing Buddhas to contra-posed and contorted forms in supplication. There are good accompanying descriptions in English, but this is not a bad place to have a knowledgeable guide (ask in the lobby). The central courtyard features a shiva lingum and large temple fragments. At the more significant works—the statue of Jayavarman VII, for example—elderly women, looking like museum docents, hand out incense and flowers and instruct visitors to place them on makeshift altars. Don't feel obliged, but feel free to do so and just drop a few riel or even $1.

Just north of the Royal Palace at Street 178, a short walk from the river. Admission $3. Daily 8am–5pm.

Royal Palace and Silver Pagoda ★★★   Don't miss this glittery downtown campus, the ostentatious jewel in the crown of Cambodia's monarchy. Built in the late 1860s under the reign of Norodom, the sight is comprised of many elaborate gilded halls, all with steep tile roofs, stupa-shape cupolas, and golden temple nagas denoting prosperity. The grand **Throne Hall** at the center is the coronation site for Khmer kings and the largest gilded cathedral in the country. Don't miss the many royal busts and the gilded umbrella used to shade the king when in procession. The French built a small exhibition hall on the temple grounds, a building that now houses the many gifts given to the monarchy, among them cross-stitch portraits of the royal family and all manner of bric-a-brac. Just inside the door, don't miss an original by Cézanne, which sadly suffered terrible water damage and hangs in a ratty frame. The balcony of the exhibition hall is the best bird's-eye view of the gilded temples. The facade of the neighboring **Royal Residence** is just as resplendent and is still the home of the now-abdicated King Sihanouk and his son and successor.

The **Silver Pagoda** is just south of the palace, and entrance is included with the same ticket. The floors of this grand temple are covered with 5,000 blocks of silver weighing more than 6 tons. The temple houses a 17th-century Buddha made of Baccarat crystal, and another made almost entirely of gold and decorated with almost 10,000 diamonds. That's not exactly what the Buddha had in mind, perhaps, but it's quite beautiful. The temple courtyard is encircled by a covered walkway with a contiguous mural of Cambodia's history and mythology. On the southern end of the complex is a small hill covered in vegetation and said to model the sacred Mount Meru; there's a large Buddha footprint and a small temple that provokes devout practice in Khmer visitors.

Btw. streets 240 and 184 on Sothearos. The entrance is on the east side facing the river. Admission $6.25. Daily 7:30–11am and 2–5pm.

Tuol Sleng, Museum of Genocide ★★   The grounds of this former high school are just as they were in 1979 at the end of Cambodia's bloody genocide. During the recent violent history in Cambodia, the two-story compound became one of the most notorious concentration camps, essentially a torture chamber before people were slaughtered in the Killing Fields. From 1975 until 1979, an estimated 17,000 political prisoners, most just ordinary citizens, were tortured at Tuol Sleng and died, or were executed in the nearby Killing Fields. A visit here is a visceral revisit of some horrible events, too much for some visitors. Be prepared to be greeted by some ghoulish characters showing off their deformities and holding out a cap for any donation you can spare.

If you don't come with a guide, it's a good idea to hire one at the entrance, although you're free to roam the grounds on your own. Local guides often have personal experience with the prison and are vital sources of oral history. They are open to questions, but go easy on any debate. Recrimination against the arbiters of these horrific events is an important issue here; just as Cambodians hope to move on into the future, they fear revisiting the past in the current international tribunals. The prison population of Tuol Sleng, also known as S-21, was carefully cataloged; in fact, the metal neck brace employed for holding subjects' heads in place for the admitting photograph is on display. There are some written accounts in English, paintings done by a survivor, and gory photos of the common torture practices in the prison, but perhaps what is most haunting is the fear in the eyes of the newly arrived; one wing of the buildings is dedicated to these very arrival photos. This sight is a bit overwhelming, so give it a miss if you're a sensitive type.

South of town at the corner of streets 350 and 113. ℂ **023/216-045.** Admission $2; guide $6. Daily 7:30am–5:30pm.

Wat Phnom ★★ This is Cambodia's "Temple on the Hill." Legend has it that sometime in the 14th century, a woman named Penh found sacred Buddhist objects in a tree that was dragged out of the nearby river and placed them here on the small hill that later became a temple. *Phnom,* in fact, means "hill," so the name of the city translates to "Penh's Hill."

The temple itself is a standard Southeast Asian *wat,* with Naga snakes on the cornered peaks of the roof and didactic murals of the Buddha's life done in Day-Glo allegories along interior walls. At the time of this update, however, it was closed for re-roofing and extensive renovations. There is a two-story **museum** on the northeast slope of the hill (admission $2; 8am–6pm), where the exhibits consist largely of dioramas depicting Penh's story and other significant events in the city's history. Interestingly, those relating to the Khmer Rouge era, on the second floor, are shown in two-dimensional cutouts, as if the memory is still too painful to portray with three-dimensional models.

The hillside park around the temple was once a no-go zone peopled by armed dealers and pimps, and in the evening you should still be careful, but now it's a laid-back park. You're sure to meet with some crafty young salesmen who'll offer you the chance to show your Buddhist compassion by buying a caged bird for a dollar and letting it go; if you stick around long enough, you'll see the bird return to the cage.

Intersection of Street 96 and Norodom Blvd.

Shopping & Galleries

The best shopping in town, for everything from souvenirs and trinkets, is at any of the large local markets. The **Central Market** (see "Attractions," above) shouldn't be missed, but the **Russian Market,** between streets 440 and 450 in the far south of town, is where the real deal on souvenirs can be had (go by cab). It takes hard haggling to get the good deals on items such as opium paraphernalia, carvings, and ceramics. It's all authentic-looking, even if made in China.

Shops and galleries are growing in number in the developing capital. All along Street 178, interesting outlets are springing up and include a few affordable silk dealers such as **Sayon Silkworks,** just west of the National Museum at No. 40 Street 178 (www.sayonsilkworks.com). **Asasax Art Gallery,** No. 192 Street 178 (✆ **012/217-795;** www.asasaxart.com.kh), features local works. **Silk & Pepper,** 33 Eo Street 178 (✆ **023/222-692;** www.silkandpepper.com), has some great silk accessories and kimonos. Take a stroll along Street 240, which is home to a fantastic cafe culture and a few antiques shops and boutiques such as **Bliss,** No. 29 Street 240 (✆ **023/215-754**), which sells beaded and embroidered cushions and quilts, or **Le Lezard Bleu,** No. 61 Street 240 (✆ **023/986-978**), which features traditional and contemporary artworks and top-notch framing.

Bazar, 28 Sihanouk Blvd., near the Independence Monument (✆ **012/776-492**), has a small but refined collection of Asian antiques and furniture.

For upscale, original clothing, **Ambre** ★, No. 37 Street 178 (✆ **023/217-935;** closed Sun), is a two-story store that carries the whimsical, beautifully cut designs of Cambodian-born, France-raised Romyda Keth. Keth has a love affair with jersey and often layers clothing with funky embroidery or gorgeous swaths of organza.

For CDs, DVDs, cool T-shirts, and hip-hop fashions, stop by the **Boom Boom Room,** on Street 93, in the backpacker area near Boeung Kak Lake (✆ **012/709-096**).

For essentials and Western groceries, stop by the **Lucky Market,** No. 160 Sihanouk Blvd. (✆ **023/215-229**), the most popular shopping center for Phnom Penh's many expats. "The Lucky" is just west of the Victory Monument traffic circle. For fresh, organic produce and fine canned goods, **Veggy's,** No. 23 Street 240 (✆ **023/211-534**), carries a similar line of familiar comfort foods from back home, whether home is Arkansas, Tokyo, Paris, or Seoul.

Monument Books, No. 111 Norodom Blvd. (✆ **023/217-617**), has a great selection and is a good spot to find books on the Khmer language and culture. Upstairs you'll find Monument Toys for the kiddies. There are also stores at 53 Street 426 (✆ **023/217-617**) and in the airport at the international departure level. Also check out the **Sorya Shopping Centre** (✆ **023/210-018**), just south of central market, which carries brand-name international goods as well as discount copies.

Phnom Penh After Dark

Phnom Penh is commonly referred to as "party town," as it has lots of bars and nightclubs that stay open through dawn. It's also notorious for some of the seediest nightlife in all of Southeast Asia. There are some good, friendly bars, though many are the "hostess bar" variety.

The downtown area along the riverside is chockablock with small storefront bars shoulder-to-shoulder with fancy, upscale spots. **Green Vespa,** 95 Sisowath Quay (✆ **012/887-228;** www.greenvespa.com), near the north end of the riverside road, is a funky bar decked out in a Vespa theme—dig the cool green Vespa on display over the door. It's popular with expats and open daily from 10am until late. Nearby **California 2,** 79 Sisowath Quay (✆ **077/503-144;** www.cafecaliforniaphnompenh. com), is a 24-hour bar and grill with a pool table that's also popular among local expats. **Chow,** 277 Sisowath Quay (✆ **023/224-894**), the rooftop bar at the Quay hotel, is a personal favorite. Sip a proper cocktail while perched on tall riverside bar stools, or curl up in one of the chic daybeds that line the wall. Drinks are half-price during happy hour (4–8pm).

Just north of the National Museum, streets 178 and 172 are packed with cozy bars and restaurants where you can enjoy a reasonably priced drink and a chat. For a more boisterous night out, head for **Heart of Darkness,** 26 Street 51 (℃ **023/222-415**), where the dance floor heaves on weekends, or **Sharky's,** 126 Street 130 (℃ **012/228-045**), which has several pool tables and frequent live bands.

Spa Services

Amara Spa, on the corner of Sisowath Quay and Street 110 (℃ **023/998-730;** www.amaraspa.hotelcara.com), is along the riverside just opposite the popular River-house Asia Bistro (p. 378). They offer a range of treatments, from a simple foot massage for $12 to signature treatments that combine a body scrub with Swedish massage and deep cleansing for $95.

Comparable, though with a focus on European techniques, is **In Style,** No. 5 Street 51 (℃ **023/214-621**). **Bliss Spa,** 29 Street 240 (℃ **023/215-754**) is popular among expats.

Budget **Island Massage,** 329 Sisowath Quay (℃ **023/991-950**), a small storefront with air-conditioned comfort, offers excellent foot massages, great after a day of touring, as well as a list of basic health and relaxing body massages at low prices. They also have two other locations at Street 94 (℃ **023/992-282**) and 43 Street 86 (℃ **023/991-273**).

Day Trips from Phnom Penh
OUDONG
Following defeat at Angkor by the Thais, the Khmer capital moved to Oudong, and kings ruled from there for more than 100 years until the power center shifted to nearby Phnom Penh in 1866. The area was a monastic center, and the 13th-century temples, like most others, pale in comparison to those of the Angkor complex. Still, the hills of Oudong offer breathtaking views. It's 1 hour west of Phnom Penh and is best reached by rented vehicle.

PHNOM CHISOR & TONLE BATI
If you've been to or are going to Angkor Wat, these temples will pale in comparison, but the ride through the countryside and among rural villages makes for a good day. Tonle Bati (33km/21 miles south of Phnom Penh) is a small collection of Angkor-style temples. Entrance costs $3. Nearby Phnom Chisor is a group of 10th-century ruins atop a picturesque hill. Phnom Penh travel agents can make all the arrangements.

SOUTHERN CAMBODIA

When you think of Cambodia, visions of tranquil beaches probably aren't the first things that come to mind, which is a shame. It isn't much when compared with the quality and quantity of beach living in nearby Thailand, or even along the coast of Vietnam, but the southern coast of Cambodia boasts some fine sandy stretches worthy of putting your feet up for a few days, especially after some heavy-duty temple touring or bouncing around rural roads.

Route 4, which connects Phnom Penh with Cambodia's only port at Kompong Som, or **Sihanoukville,** was built by the United States to facilitate Cambodian trade and the influx of aid starting from the mid-1960s. Just adjacent to the busy Sihanoukville port, you can find some lovely beach areas, most of which are speckled with budget bungalows and groovy bars owned by Western expats, as well as a fine resort called the Sokha Beach Resort (p. 389). The town of **Kampot** is a lazy river town, just a grid of mostly colonial-style houses, but another good place to kick back. You might also visit nearby **Kep,** which was a French colonial vacation spot whose 1950s to '60s-era villas lay in ruin. **Bokor Mountain,** a short ride from Kampot, was the cool mountaintop retreat of the French, but is currently closed for renovations. Connections by bus with Sihanoukville are convenient, and many choose to do this region in a rented vehicle or even by affordable local taxicab. So if you're stuck in Phnom Penh for a few days waiting out a Vietnam visa, hit the beaches. You'll be surprised.

Kampot & Kep

148km (92 miles) S of Phnom Penh; 112km (70 miles) E of Sihanoukville

The French colonists built many luxury vacation homes along the coast here. Development continued in the high plateau of Bokor Mountain with a large hotel, casino, church, and school. The two towns are some 25km (16 miles) apart, and today most choose to stay in Kampot and make a side trip to Kep. Kampot is just a quiet riverside town with views of the mountains and a lazy grid of old colonial houses. There are a few nice hotels and little to do but wander, chat with locals and expats at cafes, and peep the sunset over Bokor. Kep has a large crab market sitting on a busy bay of fishing vessels; hit Kep to check out the classic colonial homes (some day they'll probably all be boutique resorts or private dwellings again). This area is a laid-back stop on your way to Sihanoukville.

ESSENTIALS
Getting There

The road from Phnom Penh is a good, thin ribbon of asphalt. Your best bet is to arrange a taxi from Phnom Penh. There are no tourist bus services directly to Kampot or Kep. Connection with Sihanoukville by taxi costs about $20 for a 3-hour ride.

Getting Around

Kampot is a tiny riverside town easily traversed on foot (if you can pull yourself from the guesthouse hammock). Kep is just 25km (16 miles) east of Kampot, easily reached on rented motorbike, motorbike taxi, or tuk-tuk.

If you're off to Kep beach or the caves near Kampong Trach, take a motorbike with driver for just $4 per day trip, or $2 one-way if you stay in Kep overnight. Renting your own little 100cc Devo machine is just $3; the 250cc Honda Degree bike, which has good suspension and can take the bumpier roads, is $11. Maintenance at the town's two rental agents is limited. The price is quite low, but so is the quality. Contact **Sean Ly,** No. 27 DSoeng Ngoc Rd. (✆ **012/944-687**), just south of the central traffic circle; it's your best bet for picking up a motorbike. Next door, nearer the traffic circle, **Cheang Try** (✆ **012/974-698**) looks less efficient but offers the same bevy of beat-up bikes at the same price. It's $3 for a 100cc putt-putt mobile, and $5 for a 250cc Honda Degree with heavy suspension. The same offices also rent cars or four-wheel-drive vehicles for $20 per day.

For more extensive tour services, **Art Suriya Travel** (✆ **012/501-742**) offers custom tours of the surrounding area or other parts of the region. Costs are higher than the storefront tour offices, but you get the full custom treatment. Contact **Sok**

Lim Tours, in front of Blissful Guesthouse (below; ✆ 012/719-872), for adventure trips and jungle-trekking tours around Bokor.

From **Kep,** check out the $10 day trips out to **Rabbit Island** ★, which has pretty, quiet beaches good for swimming.

WHERE TO STAY
Kampot

Blissful Guesthouse An old colonial villa fashioned with heavy wooden beams, Blissful Guesthouse has hammocks swinging from every veranda and under every tree, a quiet upstairs sitting area, and lots of cozy papasans and couches to curl up with a book and rest. Rooms are guesthouse basic, but everything's clean. Angela, the friendly Danish owner, is a font of local information. The bar hops late, and this is a great place to meet up with other travelers.

Just a short walk east of the river, past the "2000" monument. www.blissfulguesthouse.com. ✆ **092/494-331.** 10 units. $4–$8 double. No credit cards. **Amenities:** Restaurant; bar; motorbikes. *In room:* Fan, no phone.

Bokor Mountain Lodge This old colonial, lined with cool travel photos, has the best location, along the riverside, in town. Rooms are bright, and open colonnaded walkways overlook the busy street below and river beyond. Breakfast is included, and there's a good in-house tour company that can arrange excursions. They've got Wi-Fi access, but it can be finicky.

Riverfront Dr. (riverside at the center of Kampot). www.bokorlodge.com. ✆ **033/932-314.** 6 units. Oct–Apr $35–$45 double, $60 family suite; May–Oct $30–$40 double, $50 family suite. Rates include breakfast. MC, V. **Amenities:** Restaurant; bar. *In room:* A/C, TV, Wi-Fi.

Homestay Cafe The owners of former Little Garden Guesthouse have relocated to a smaller, cozier place conveniently situated near the town center. The two-floor building has just four basic rooms, but all either share or have their own private balcony, and there's a separate lounge with cable TV. The cafe serves tasty breakfasts and familiar Western dishes for lunch and dinner. These folks are involved with the local orphanage and can get you connected to offer some service during your trip.

Just northeast of the bridge. www.homestaycafe.com. ✆ **077/526-443.** 4 units. $5–$15 double; long-term rates available. No credit cards. **Amenities:** Restaurant. *In room:* A/C or fan, Wi-Fi, no phone.

Kep

Knai Bang Chatt ★★ Knai Bang Chatt marks the arrival of luxury in Kep. Rooms at this seaside property are in villas (one new, three renovated), built in the New Modern Khmer style of the 1960s. Rooms are spacious and done in mellow, neutral colors, such as champagne and beige, and mixed with subtle mauves and khaki green. Beds are extremely cozy. Everyone gets a huge private terrace overlooking the garden or the ocean. The outdoor infinity pool faces some stiff competition from the nearby ocean, where you can take a midnight dip among phosphorescent plankton.

Phum Thmey, Sangkat Prey Thom. www.knaibangchatt.com. ✆ **012/349-742.** 11 units. Apr–Sept $160–$225 double; Oct–Mar $165–$325 double. MC, V. **Amenities:** Restaurant; bar; pool; spa. *In room:* A/C, TV, fridge, minibar, Wi-Fi.

Veranda Natural Resort ★ On a hilltop overlooking the town, Veranda is the best budget choice in the area. Rooms have an, attractive, boutique flavor, housed in rustic thatch and wood units on stilts overlooking the sea; they're compact but tidy. Go for an oceanview room with an outdoor daybed, and you've got a little low-luxe private oasis. If you're splurging, check out the Residence House, which has newer, more luxe rooms that come with private balconies. The bar is a popular spot for sunset views over Bokor Mountain in the distance. The restaurant serves good faux-Western and Khmer—a good thing, because you're pretty much stranded up here (expect to pay $5–$10 for main courses).

Far up the hillside overlooking town, opposite ASPECA orphanage. www.veranda-resort.com. ℂ **012/888-619.** 29 units. $38–$75 double; $195 villa. MC, V. **Amenities:** Restaurant; bar; motorbikes. *In room:* A/C (some rooms), TV (some rooms), Wi-Fi, no phone.

WHERE TO EAT

The expat owner of **Homestay Cafe** (p. 387; ℂ **077/526-443;** www.homestaycafe.com) serves good Western cuisine and sponsors programs for a local orphanage. Stop in, and you're likely to meet up with other like-minded travelers.

For good Khmer food, stop by the open-air **Restaurant Phnom Kam Chay Thmey** (ℂ **012/602-505**), an affordable joint right next to the bridge.

After dinner and a brief walk around town, the only thing going on is the bar at Blissful Guesthouse. You could also grab a fruit shake at one of the stalls just west of the central monument area; ask for no sugar unless you like it super sweet.

Bamboo Light Café ★ SRI LANKAN Here you'll find cheap, tiptop eats. Curries are red or yellow, mild or fiery—prepared to your tastes. The mutton dishes are especially good, as are the Sri Lankan Kottu roti dishes (pancakes cut up and mixed with potato and curry). The very clean interior has cool, indirect lighting in bamboo stanchions. Great breakfasts of bacon and eggs, as well as good sandwiches and Western meals, are served all day. With an Internet cafe upstairs, this is a good place to beat the heat.

River Rd. (near the bridge) in central Kampot. ℂ **012/681-530.** bamboo_vana@yahoo.com. Main courses $2.50–$4. No credit cards. Daily 7am–10pm.

Sihanoukville

230km (143 miles) S of Phnom Penh; 112km (70 miles) W of Kep

A popular summertime spot for Khmers, Sihanoukville is really a port town, but the beaches are good, there are some good accommodations choices, and it's very affordable. Trips to outlying islands for scuba diving and snorkeling are attracting more and more Western tourists.

ESSENTIALS
Getting There
BY CAR The U.S.-built Route, 4 between Phnom Penh and Sihanoukville, is a long, straight, smooth ribbon of highway, but it means that people drive like lunatics on this road, and there are many (at times fatal) accidents. Be extremely careful should you choose a self-drive option along this stretch. Renting a private taxi is your best bet, and the 3-hour ride to or from Phnom Penh goes for about $40 per vehicle. The cost can jump up to $60 if you depart Phnom Penh in the late afternoon. A taxi connection with Kampot to the east (see the section above) is $25 for the 3-hour ride. Contact any hotel front desk.

BY BUS Frequent, convenient buses connect Sihanoukville and Phnom Penh. The 3-hour ride costs $5 (including a snack) in an air-conditioned bus with **Mekong Express** (ℂ **023/427-518**), and $3 to $4 with other budget carriers. **Capitol Tours** (ℂ **023/217-627**) and **Sorya Transport** (ℂ **023/210-359**), among others, offer daily connections to and from Phnom Penh, usually leaving in the morning.

ORIENTATION

Sihanoukville is set on a wide peninsular area jutting south and east into the Gulf of Thailand. The peninsula is shielded by islands—Koh Rong, Koh Rong Sam Leuem, Koh T Kiev, and Ko Ses are among the many. Starting on the north end of the peninsula, find the busy port area, just south of which, tracing the coast, you'll find Victory Beach, Independence Beach, Sokha Beach, and Ochheuteal Beach to the far south. Ekareach Street turns inland at the terminus of Route 4, just past the busy port, and cuts a path across the peninsula to the downtown market area before ending at the Golden Lion Monument near Ochheuteal Beach. Signs point the way from Ekareach to the beaches along its length.

GETTING AROUND

Motodups, the ubiquitous motorcycle taxis, are everywhere in Sihanoukville and your best bet for ferrying to and from the beaches. Bicycle and motorbike rentals are also available. Distances and the many hills along Ekareach Street make hopping a moto or renting one worthwhile, but once at the beach, you can easily walk around town.

FAST FACTS Canadia Bank (ⓒ **034/933-490**) and **Mekong Bank** (ⓒ **034/933-867**) both have convenient branches, with cash exchanges, in the downtown area along Ekareach Street. The telephone code for Sihanoukville is **34,** and IDD phone services, as well as cheap Internet phone connection at the Internet cafes, abound. Most hotels and guesthouses offer free Internet service. **Ocean Mart** is a handy supermarket in a convenient location close to the major beaches and next to the main traffic circle (beside Golden Lion Traffic Circle). Emergency services in Sihanoukville are nonexistent, and any major medical issue means evacuation to Phnom Penh or on to Bangkok. The **CT Clinic,** 47 Boray Kamakor (ⓒ **034/934-222**), in the center of town offers basic first aid, and the **Sokha Beach Resort** (ocean side at Sokha Beach; ⓒ **032/935-999**) has a doctor on call at their own private clinic.

WHERE TO STAY
Expensive

The Independence Hotel ★   This restored hotel has an excellent location on a private strip of sand on Independence Beach. The hotel used to be a showpiece of the royal family and once played host to elite dignitaries. Former King Norodom Sihanouk himself was responsible for the interior design of the hotel back in the 1960s. The rooms are large and airy with smart, tiled floors and solid furnishings in a classical style. The corner deluxe suites are particularly roomy, with panoramic ocean views, while other deluxe rooms are situated in more recently constructed buildings and have private balconies. There's a beautiful garden walkway at the base of a rocky outcrop along Independence Beach. Staff is very friendly and very eager to please.

Street 2 Thnou, Sagkat No. 3, Khan Mittapheap. www.independencehotel.net. ⓒ **034/934-300.** Fax 034/933-660. 71 units. $170–$190 double; $300–$750 suite. MC, V. **Amenities:** Restaurant; bar; concierge; Internet; fitness center; pool; room service. *In room:* A/C, TV, fridge, hair dryer, minibar.

Sokha Beach Resort ★ ☺   While the Independence (above) is cool and modern architecture, Sokha Beach Resort is finely executed kitschy Khmer. You can see the traditional, winged, red-tile roofs from a distance, and the public spaces are decorated with carved stone reliefs and Khmer statues. Room decoration is functional, with bamboo rattan chairs and tables and terra cotta floors. Club suites have swanky '70s-style circular beds, and all suites have an ocean view. If you're looking for something special, rent one of their villas; originally military housing units, they maintain their '50s/'60s box-style architecture. Each villa has a small living room and a separate garden space, so you're really set apart from other hotel guests.

Street 2 Thnou, Sangkat 4, Mittapheap District. www.sokhahotels.com. ✆ **034/935-999.** Fax 034/935-888. 391 units. $200–$220 double; $350–$380 villa; from $250 suite. MC, V. **Amenities:** 2 restaurants; 3 bars; babysitting; bike rental; children's play area and activities; health club; room service; spa; tennis courts; watersports equipment/rentals; Wi-Fi. *In room:* A/C, TV, fridge, hair dryer, minibar.

Inexpensive

Malibu Bungalows ★ Owned and operated by Ms. Lina, a Khmer-born U.S. resident and friendly raconteur, Malibu is a cool collection of beach bungalows on a steep hillside overlooking the beach. There's also a small hotel block farther back. The hotel is at the crest of a dynamic promontory, such prime turf that the Khmer government decided they would like to commandeer the land for their own use; Ms. Lina and her connections with Khmer royalty keep the area—there are a few nearby guesthouses—from being gobbled up. There's a cozy sitting area near the entry, and the hotel's restaurant offers great views of Sokha Beach below and the vast sea beyond. The breakfast buffet is delicious, and Ms. Lina can, upon request, arrange for a Khmer-style royal meal. The rooms are simple, free-standing bungalows lining the precipitous steps along a verdant hillside path; at the bottom is a relaxing bar area and small private beach. There are also comfy air-conditioned apartment blocks near the entry at the top of the hill. Rooms are rustic, and electricity can be erratic. Mosquito nets and bamboo furnishings give the place a certain Robinson Crusoe feel.

Group 14, Mondol 4, Sangkat 4, Khan Mittapheap (on a small rise above the Sokha Beach Resort). ✆ **012/733-334** or 011/422-787. 19 units. $40–$60 double. No credit cards. **Amenities:** Restaurant. *In room:* A/C (in rooms only), TV, fridge, minibar, no phone.

Orchidee Guest House This guesthouse is popular with expats and returning guests. Simple rooms have air-conditioning and satellite television. It's affordable, and a fun party vibe pervades. The standard rooms are big, with white tiles, and the best choice (better than the red-carpet rooms). Get a room next to the pool, and you're likely to make lots of friends.

23 Tola St. (1 block back from Ochheuteal Beach). www.orchidee-guesthouse.com. ✆ **034/933-639** or 012/380-300. 69 units. $13–$28 double; $30–$40 family room. No credit cards. **Amenities:** Restaurant; motorbike rental; pool. *In room:* A/C, TV, fridge, minibar.

Reef Resort This small guesthouse is casual and laid-back. Rooms are neat and tidy, and the bamboo furniture, silk lamps and wall hangings, and knit blankets give the place a charming appeal. Most rooms come with a small poolside terrace. The bar has a proper pool table and a large flatscreen TV for movies or sports; it's a great place to while away the evening with a couple beers.

Road from Golden Lion to Serendipity. www.reefresort.com.kh. ✆ **012/315-338.** 11 units. $35–$65 double; $70–$80 family room. MC, V. **Amenities:** Restaurant; bar; pool. *In room:* A/C, TV, DVD (family rooms only) fridge, minibar, Wi-Fi, no phone.

WHERE TO EAT

Dining in Sihanoukville means mostly good, cheap seafood, and there are lots of oceanside stops. Expats are putting up shingles around town advertising tastes of home and cocktails. Sokha Beach Resort (see above) has a fine seafood restaurant.

Chez Claude ★ FRENCH/KHMER It's worth the trip to this hilltop spot above Sokha Beach for the view alone (there's a tiny cable car to take you up), but the food also happens to be some of the best in the country. Seafood is the specialty here, and the clay pot is particularly memorable. There's a decent choice of French wines, and when a fresh breeze is blowing, there's no better place in town. They also have some rustic rooms for rent with the same spectacular view.

2 Thnou Beach Rd. (behind and above the Sokha Beach Resort). © **034/934-100.** www.best cambodia.com. Main courses $4–$15. MC, V. Daily 7am–11pm.

Mick and Craig's ★ WESTERN   These guys are the originals in Sihanoukville, and backpackers and expats alike flock here. Some of the best food in town is served in a casual open-air setup with good tunes, a busy bar, and a billiards area. You can sign up for trips with their in-house eco-tour company, pick up a good read in their book corner, or even stay in their new guesthouse (the whole place has just moved to a new location near Serendipity Beach, just behind the Lion traffic circle). They offer lots of favorites from home: pizza, sandwiches made with bread baked on-site, snacks such as nachos and potato skins, steaks, bangers and mash, grilled fish, and veggie offerings (including a yummy veggie burger), as well as lots of good Khmer dishes. Dessert is apple crumble or ice cream. Extensive breakfasts are the best cure for that Sihanoukville hangover: muesli and fruit or a full-on fry-up.

Just adjacent to the Golden Lion Traffic circle at the head of the road leading to Serendipity Beach. © **034/650-500.** www.mickandcraigs.com. Main courses $5–$9. No credit cards. Daily 7am–11pm.

Snakehouse INTERNATIONAL   This part restaurant, part jungle, on a hill above town, makes for a fun evening. Parrots, snakes, turtles, and crocs are displayed (and well taken care of), but not on the menu. The food, a selection of Russian dishes and standard international fare, ranges from spaghetti to steak.

Soviet St., on the hilltop near Sihanoukville's busy backpacker ghetto. © **012/673-805.** Main courses $4–$9. No credit cards. Daily 8am–11pm.

Starfish Café INTERNATIONAL   Set up as an NGO to train and employ people with physical disabilities, many of whom are victims of antipersonnel mines, the Starfish Café gives hope to a group of people who are systematically shunned by Khmer society, funding local literacy programs and serving as a drop-in point for clients of the Starfish Project. The place offers a time-tested formula of good sandwiches, baked goods, and light local fare. The friendly staff can offer good information about tours and travel. There's an upstairs reading area and a shaded courtyard. They sell popular T-shirts, as well as products from the Snar Dai Project, which sells goods made by mothers of street kids.

Just behind the Samudera Market at the town center. © **012/952-011.** www.starfishcambodia.org. Main courses $3–$4.50. No credit cards. Daily 7am–6pm.

ATTRACTIONS

Apart from sticking your toes in the sand and sipping cocktails, tours to outlying islands are the main attraction in Sihanoukville. The friendly folks at **Eco Sea Dive,** Samudera Market, Town Center (© **012/654-104;** www.ecosea.com), arrange great day tours with stops in remote coves where clients can snorkel or take a scuba course. The diving is mostly shallow and the visibility varies, but Eco Sea Dive is a very professional outfit, and a day on their boat—whether diving, snorkeling, or taking in the scenery over their tasty lunch buffet (or diving off the top deck)—is alone worth the trip down to Snooky (Sihanoukville).

For tours to outlying hills, contact the friendly folks at **Eco-Trek Tours Cambodia,** next to Mick and Craig's, Serendipity Street (© **012/987-7073** or 016/876-200;

ecotrektourscambodia@yahoo.com). For car and taxi service on to any other parts of the area, contact any hotel front desk.

SIEM REAP & ANGKOR WAT

The ruins of the ancient city of **Angkor**, capital of the Khmer kingdom from A.D. 802 until 1295, are one of the world's marvels. The "City of Kings," Angkor boasts some of the largest religious monuments ever constructed; it's a vast and mysterious complex of hulking laterite and sandstone blocks. Unknown to the world until French naturalist Henri Mouhot literally stumbled onto it in 1861, the area of Angkor existed for centuries only as a myth—a wondrous city (or cities, to be exact), its exact location in the Cambodian jungle unknown. After Mahout in 1861, archaeologists flocked here, only to be foiled by years of conflict that left the temples in the hands of the Khmer Rouge. Many temples were damaged and pillaged. Tourists were the subsequent invaders, from the late 1990s. Today the sight is mobbed, but you can still find those quiet moments in communion with this amazing manmade wonder.

The temple complex carries the remains of passageways, moats, temples, and palaces that represent centuries of building in the capital. Days spent scrambling about and exploring the temples are memorable, and this is a great place to bring adventurous kids who like to get their play clothes dirty.

The temples are served by the nearby town of Siem Reap, some 6km (3¾ miles) to the south. Siem Reap means "Victory over the Thais" and refers to the 16th-century victory that solidified the Khmer kingdom—though animosity between the two neighbors remains to this day. All of western Cambodia was once under Thai control, and Khmer people are very proud of their survival in the face of so many invaders, the very reason that an image of Angkor Wat graces the national flag.

Siem Reap, once just a dusty track with a few storefronts, now supports a host of large five-star hotels and resorts, fine-dining options, and the kind of good services, shops, galleries, and spas that make the little city a new oasis of luxury in parched western Cambodia. The town's central market is a great stop for souvenir purchases, and the nearby downtown area is abuzz day and night with quaint bars and party spots.

A 3- or 4-day visit will suffice (though many do it in less time) to come away with a newfound love for ancient cultures, Asian religions, and sunsets. Good options abound for visiting more far-flung temple ruins (in fact, one of the most common complaints is about the large crowds that now visit Cambodia's "Disneyland of Temples"), and trekking or boat trips to remote mangrove swamps and a large bird sanctuary are enough to keep you busy. Bring your sense of adventure, your camera, and a youthful sense of wonder. You won't be disappointed by amazing Angkor.

Getting There

BY PLANE **Cambodian Angkor Air** (© **023/212-564** in Phnom Penh, or 063/969-268 in Siem Reap; www.cambodiaangkorair.com) is currently the only airline running the 1-hour connection to Siem Reap from Phnom Penh. One-way fares are $70.

If you just want to see the great temples at Angkor, the process is simplified with international arrivals: Vietnam Airlines flies directly from Ho Chi Minh City, Bangkok Airways flies directly from Bangkok, and you can check flights by Silk Air and Lao Aviation for other routes.

Siem Reap

HOTELS ■
Allson Angkor Hotel **1**
Amansara Resort **3**
Angkor Palace Resort and Spa **1**
Angkor Village Hotel **24**
Angkor Village Resort **5**
Auberge Mont Royal d'Angkor **32**
Bopha Angkor **18**
City River Hotel **17**
FCC Angkor **13**
Hôtel de la Paix **34**
La Noria **11**
La Résidence d'Angkor **16**
Le Meridien Angkor **5**
Passaggio **25**
Pavillon d'Orient **10**
Pavillon Indochine **3**
Raffles Grand Hotel d'Angkor **7**

Sofitel Royal Angkor **5**
Sokha Angkor **4**
Soria Moria **22**
Two Dragons **15**
Victoria Angkor Hotel **9**
Viroth's Hotel **19**

RESTAURANTS ◆
Abacus **2**
Beaches **21**
Blue Pumpkin **29**
Butterflies Garden Restaurant **23**
Café Indochine **37**
Chivit Thai **14**
Curry Walla **36**
8th Street Brasserie **28**
FCC Angkor (Foreign
  Correspondents Club) **13**

Khmer Kitchen
  Restaurant **29**
Le Bistrot de Siem Reap **8**
Madame Butterfly **2**
Meric **34**
Nest **35**
The Red Piano **27**
The Sugar Palm **33**
Tell Restaurant **31**
Viroth's Restaurant **20**

ATTRACTIONS ●
Angkor National
  Museum **6**
Land Mines Museum **6**
Psar Leu, the New Market **12**
Night Market **30**
Psar Chas, the Old Market **26**

GIVE OF "yourself" IN SIEM REAP

They want your blood in Siem Reap. Many humanitarian-aid agencies use Siem Reap as a base for raising funds and treating rural peoples. The **Kantha Bopha Hospital,** on the main road to the temples, and the **Angkor Hospital for Children** (contact them through www.fwab.org or ☎ **063/963-409**) are always looking for blood donors to help young patients through the most trying periods of acute dysentery and hemorrhagic fever. Patients often make it to these centers from rural parts in dire circumstances and need immediate blood transfusions to make it through their first days. Just show up at either clinic to make a donation of blood, time, and/or money—all of which are desperately needed.

I highly recommend flying into town. The international airport is relatively new and beautifully designed, using traditional Cambodian architecture. *Note:* The international departure tax (from both Phnom Penh and Siem Reap) is $25; the domestic tax is $6.

BY BOAT   A ride on the 5-hour boat connection between Phnom Penh and Siem Reap costs $35, though the service is dwindling as most people opt to go by bus or plane. Contact any hotel or travel agent (they all sell the same tickets at the same price). There are also boats to Battambang. In the rainy season, the ride is 6 to 8 hours, but in the dry season (Feb–May) it can take 8 to 10 hours or more and isn't recommended. The price is $25.

A luxury option is the 8-day cruise between **Angkor Wat** and **Ho Chi Minh City,** passing through **Chau Doc** and **My Tho** in Vietnam's Mekong Delta aboard one of the luxury, shallow-draft **Pandaw Cruise Boats** (www.pandaw.com). Twin rooms on the vessel start at around $1,400.

BY BUS   Your hotel front desk can arrange bus transportation for you at no additional cost. **Mekong Express** (☎ **023/427-518**) connects Phnom Penh and Siem Reap with daily luxury buses ($11 for the 5½-hr. ride). Bus rides come with water and a snack, and there's a bathroom on board. *Tip:* A set of earplugs is your friend on this bus ride (and any bus ride really), as they play Khmer karaoke songs and various Asian pop-music videos. **Capitol Tour,** No. 14 Road 182 (☎ **023/217-627**), also runs daily minivans between Phnom Penh and Siem Reap ($5 for the 5-hr. ride), as well as to destinations farther afield such as Battambang or Poipet at the Thai border. **Neak Krorhorm Travel and Tour** (☎ **023/219-496** in Phnom Penh, or 063/964-924 in Siem Reap, near the Old Market) provides similar services.

Getting Around

You'll need some kind of wheels to make your way around Siem Reap and to and from the temples. Any hotel front desk or travel agent can make arrangements for you.

A rented **car with driver** is about $25 to $50 (depending where you're going). This is your best bet if hitting the temples farther afield, but if just doing the main temple circuits, I recommend one of the open-air options below.

Tuk-tuks are the best choice and available anywhere. The name is taken from the Thais, but these tuk-tuks have nothing to do with the noisy Bangkok three-wheeler. These are a two-wheeled surrey pulled by a standard motorbike. They are shaded, and the large, padded seat is great for two. There's a smaller seat at the front of the cart, and in a pinch you can seat two more, but it's not very comfy. Pay $15 for the whole day, $1 to $2 for short trips in town.

A **motorcycle taxi,** called a *motodup,* is a good, cheap option for $8 to $15 per day. Helmets are generally available, though few wear them (I recommend wearing one). This is a good choice for solo travelers going to the temples without a guide. For sights farther afield, it can be a bit tiring. Riding **your own motorbike** was once the most popular choice, but local officials put a stop to it, citing many road accidents.

The temple roads are flat and well paved, so **bicycles** are a good option. You can rent one for $1 to $2 per day from guesthouses and hotels. Take care in the scorching midday heat, and drink plenty of fluids. On a bike, you can go where you please, as you please. When parking at temples, vendors implore you to park near them and they'll mind your bike. Agree to nothing, but tell them that maybe you'll buy something later; when you do need the inevitable bottle of water, buy from your new friend.

Visitor Information & Tours

Siem Reap is full of helpful traveler services and information. In fact, most hotels and guesthouses can help you arrange all of the essentials. Below are a few service providers I'd recommend, among the many others you'll see in the area.

EXPENSIVE

o **Beyond,** Sivutha Boulevard, 1 block west of the Old Market (© 077/562-565; www.beyonduniqueescapes.com). This downtown tour operator offers day tours of the temples, Tonle Sap, and local villages, with rates ranging from $20 to $35 a day. They also run cooking courses in a rural village out of town for similar day rates.

o **Diethelm,** House No. 470, Krous Village, Svay Dangkum Commune, Siem Reap (© 063/963-524; fax 063/963-694; www.diethelmtravel.com). Providing all local and regional services, Diethelm is a top international tour operator, offering classic tours in Angkor, as well as anywhere in the region.

o **Exotissimo,** No. B20–21 Street 60MK, Siem Reap (© 063/964-323; fax 063/963-621; www.exotissimo.com). Like Diethelm (see above), Exotissimo is a large conglomerate, with offices throughout the region that can arrange any inevitability. Mostly for larger budgets.

o **Osmose** (© 012/832-812; www.osmosetonlesap.net). Offering high-end tours to the far-flung coastal areas of the Tonle Sap Lake, Osmose levies high fees for its popular eco-tours in order to maintain high standards of low environmental impact and to fund its efforts at encouraging sustainable development and preservation in the region.

o **Terre Cambodge,** 668 Hup Guan St. (© 092/476-682; www.terrecambodge. com). Catering to many of the French tourists who flock to Siem Reap and have deeper pockets, Terre Cambodge arranges adventure trips to the farther-flung reaches in the area, ranging from off-the-map destinations along Tonle Sap to little-known jungle temples far from Angkor.

BUDGET

Here are a couple of the more reliable, less expensive companies. Hotel or guest-house front desks, for free or a small fee, can arrange tickets with one of the companies listed below. In fact, popular **Capitol Guesthouse** and more upscale **Mekong Express Tours** don't even have offices in town and must be booked through hotel front desks.

- **Neak Krorhrom Travel and Tours,** just adjacent to the Old Market (east side; ℂ **063/964-924**), is a good one for onward bus connections to rural stops such as Battambang. In fact, book with one of the other operators and you'll likely end up waiting for the bus out in front of these offices.
- **PTM,** right in the heart of the bar street near the Old Market (ℂ **063/964-388;** fax 063/965-486; www.ptm.com.kh), offers basic bus services and can book flights.

[Fast FACTS] SIEM REAP

Banks & Currency Exchange **Canadia Bank,** on the western side of the Old Market (ℂ **063/964-815**), and **ANZ Royal Bank,** 566–570 Tep Vong St. (ℂ **063/969-700**), are the best options for services. **ANZ** has several ATMs around town, including one at the central branch and two 24-hour ATMs in the heart of the Old Market just south of Red Piano Bar. You can change traveler's checks in some hotels and in any bank.

Emergency There's a tourist police station near the entrance to the temples. For local police, dial ℂ **117.** In the event of a medical emergency, contact **International SOS Clinic** in Phnom Penh (ℂ **023/216-911**).

Internet Wi-Fi is offered free in many hotels and guesthouses, as well as many bars and restaurants, so you probably won't need an Internet shop. If you do need one, small storefront offices surround the central market area, and there are several more along Sivutha Boulevard. Almost all Internet shops can burn CDs or DVDs if you need to empty your camera's memory card. Most are open 7am to midnight.

Post Office The post office is on Pokambor Avenue at riverside near the town center (next to the FCC; see "Where to Dine," later in this chapter). It's open daily 7am to 5:30pm and can handle foreign and domestic regular and parcel post.

Telephone The city code for Siem Reap is **63.** Most hotels have international direct-dialing (IDD), but many of the Internet cafes around the Old Market have better rates and offer callback service or Internet phone services.

Where to Stay

Tourist numbers are high, and development is revved up in tiny Siem Reap. Visitors can choose from some of the finest upscale accommodations in the region.

For midrange hotels (below $100), there are a handful of nice boutique choices in town. In the high season, high-end accommodations often fill up, so be sure to book ahead. In low season, be sure to ask for a discount. Most hotels levy a 10% VAT.

VERY EXPENSIVE

Amansara Resort ★★ *Aman* means "peace" in Sanskrit, and the suffix *sara* refers to Khmer Apsara dancers. Set downtown in an old guest villa once owned by King Sihanouk, the suites of the Amansara are done in a cool, contemporary, minimalist design of white stucco and dark timber all surrounded by shade trees. The outside world melts away when you step into this complex. Large bedrooms with adjoining sitting areas lead to a private outdoor courtyard area. Decor is simple; the bedroom wall has a white stone bas-relief of a banyan tree, the courtyard has a lotus pond with goldfish. The services at Amansara are unrivaled: private driver and guide, personalized excursions to the temples and town, high tea with freshly baked cookies and cake, stocked bar, wine and cheese cellar, and the list goes on. The idea is that Amansara is your home, so you can wander into the central house and mix yourself a gin and tonic or grab a cookie whenever you fancy. Unfortunately, the compulsory daily $100 "half-board charge" per person *on top* of the rather steep room fees feels like you're being nickel-and-dimed (or Benjamin Franklin–ed!) here. That said, service is in its own category here and it is a remarkable experience for Siem Reap.

Road to Angkor, Siem Reap. www.amanresorts.com. ⓒ **063/760-333.** Fax 063/760-335. 24 units. $800 suite; $1,000 pool suite. AE, MC, V. **Amenities:** Restaurant; bar; complimentary bikes (with or without guide); library; 2 saltwater pools; room service; luxurious Aman spa. *In room:* A/C, TV, bar, fridge, hair dryer.

Angkor Palace Resort and Spa ★★   The acres and acres of open space afforded by the Angkor Palace Resort's location—far from the action—wins this one kudos. Plus you'll find plenty of elbow room, fine gardens, a large pool, and tennis courts in a town where real estate is at a premium. This high-end resort offers a friendly and casual atmosphere. The pool area is large, open, and inviting, with bridges connecting walkways, and you'll find extensive services, including a fine Italian restaurant, in-house Internet services, and any kind of tour services or vehicle rental you might need. Rooms are enormous and done in dark wood with white silk bedspreads and fine local wall hangings. First-floor rooms have direct access to the pool area. The spa has a host of fine massage and facial treatments, but planning and construction are underway for a much larger project. You'll find a good sauna and steam area, as well as a poolside Jacuzzi.

No. 555 Phum Kruos, Khum Svay Dang Khum, Siem Reap. www.angkorpalaceresort.com. ⓒ **063/760-511.** Fax 063/760-512. 259 units. $160–$180 deluxe; $330–$450 suite; $800–$1,500 villa. AE, MC, V. **Amenities:** Restaurant; concierge; driving range; health club; Internet; pool; room service; smoke-free rooms; free shuttle service into town; spa; tennis courts. *In room:* A/C, TV, fridge, minibar, Wi-Fi.

Hôtel de la Paix ★★★   This chic, modern hotel is a personal favorite in Siem Reap. The original design—a sort of Art Deco meets minimalist meets Khmer decor—is a refreshing change from the colonial-heavy influence of popular hotels like the Raffles or the Victoria (see below). Staff is incredibly friendly and appears invested in providing a wonderful guest experience. Spacious deluxe rooms come with black-and-white color schemes, accent pillows in deep purple, and silver wall hangings and lamps. A white marble bathtub lies a couple of feet away from the foot of the bed. If you decide to splash out on the two-story spa suite, get the corner unit (room no. 346), which comes with a huge balcony equipped with a private stone tub, lounge chairs, a love seat, and a cozy dining table. There's a large, partially outdoor pool with an indoor enclave at one end. If you are around at noon, make sure to glance at the marble Apsara statue in the main lobby—a single ray of light filters through a cleverly placed hole in the ceiling and shines on the statue's head. The moving design is a good indication of the thoughtful touches throughout the hotel that pay tribute to the architecture found at nearby Angkor Wat.

Sivutha Blvd. www.hoteldelapaixangkor.com. ⓒ **063/966-000.** Fax 063/966-001. 107 units. $300 double; $420–$650 suite. AE, MC, V. **Amenities:** Restaurant; lounge; cafe; babysitting; concierge; fitness center; Jacuzzi; pool; sauna; spa. *In room:* A/C, TV, DVD (in suites), fridge, hair dryer, iPod/MP3 docking station, minibar, Wi-Fi.

La Résidence d'Angkor ★★   This stylish, self-contained sanctuary is managed by luxury Orient-Express. Cross a small moat to enter the cool interior of the steeply gabled, dark-wood lobby with its grand Angkor-inspired reliefs. The tranquil central courtyard is lined with palms and dominated by a small but stylish pool fed by a stylized Shiva-lingum. The resort area is small, but everything from the gardens to the room decor is tidy and designed for privacy. Rooms are large, well appointed, open,

14

CAMBODIA   Siem Reap & Angkor Wat

and elegant, with cloth divans, retro fixtures, and nice local touches. Large bathrooms connect with bedrooms by a bamboo sliding door, and another glass slider from the bedroom opens to a small private balcony with cool loungers and views of the courtyard. The lobby restaurant is good fine dining, and there are some great open sitting areas for drinks, as well as a library with books and chess.

River Rd. www.residencedangkor.com. © **063/963-390.** Fax 063/963-391. 62 units. $335–$395 double; $485–$585 suite. AE, MC, V. **Amenities:** 2 restaurants; bar; motorbike rental; saltwater pool; room service. *In room:* A/C, TV, fridge, hair dryer, minibar, Wi-Fi.

Le Meridien Angkor ★★   The massive monolith of the Le Meridien looks something like a spaceship landed on the road running north to the temples. Three stories and square, the building is beveled, with the larger edge at the top, and is surrounded by a moat and large open areas, all stylistic nods to the temple architecture nearby; accents of culture include fine Apsara sculptures in each room and tinted photos of the temples. Done in dark wood, rooms are clean and elegant, with silken bed comforters, cane floor matting, and Khmer-style contemporary divans. Deluxe and superior rooms differ only slightly in size. Dining options range from buffet to a fine Italian restaurant, all set in large glassed-in spaces overlooking a lush central courtyard where a many-headed Ganesha statue holds court. The pool is a unique esplanade of smaller, tiered pools connected with waterfalls and traversed by interlocking raised pathways and Greek-style colonnaded arches.

Vithei Charles de Gaulle, Khum Svay Dang Kum, Siem Reap (on the temple road, just north of town and the Kantha Bopha Hospital). www.lemeridien.com or www.angkor.lemeridien.com. © **063/963-900.** 223 units. $190 superior double; $250 deluxe double; $390–$450 suite. AE, MC, V. **Amenities:** 2 restaurants; bar; concierge; health club; pool; room service; spa. *In room:* A/C, TV, high-speed Internet, minibar.

Raffles Grand Hotel d'Angkor ★★★   Right in the center of town, this is simply the best hotel in Siem Reap; it remains unrivaled for luxury, charm, and service. If arriving by air, hotel staff will pick you up and escort you to a waiting limo. At the hotel, a doorman outfitted in the hat and uniform of the old Royal Guards whisks you into the Conservatory, a bright alcove bar overlooking the expansive outdoor pool. Guest rooms are large, with classic French doors and windows, beautiful black-and-white-tile entries, fine furnishings, and antique standing lamps, and most come with a balcony. Landmark rooms, the next-higher standard, have four-poster beds, wooden floors spread with rugs, and a balcony with rattan furniture. Cabana suites are gems: each has a unique theme, color, and decor, and balconies are large enough to hold a table and chairs for two and a cozy daybed. The courtyard pool (lit by fairy lights and tiny candles in the evening) is large and inviting, and the spa facilities are indulgent.

1 Vithei Charles de Gaulle, Khum Svay Dang Kum, Siem Reap. www.raffles.com. © **063/963-888.** Fax 063/963-168. 119 units. $405–$450 double; $530–$950 suite; $3,000 2-bedroom villa. AE, MC, V. **Amenities:** 4 restaurants; 2 bars; children's club; concierge; health club; Jacuzzi; pool; room service; sauna; spa; 2 tennis courts. *In room:* A/C, TV, fridge, hair dryer, minibar, Wi-Fi.

Sofitel Royal Angkor ★★   Sofitel is famed in the region for bringing life back to classic hotels of old Indochina, but in Siem Reap they started fresh, with a project limited only by the designer's imagination. The lobby is an old-world Indochine replica with antique Khmer pagoda and a menagerie of overstuffed European furniture. Design and decor nicely marry Khmer and French styles, with vaulted Naga roofs high above the sculpted central garden and tranquil pond area. The courtyard pool is large, open, and fun—great for kids, with a short river meander crossed by a small bridge. The spa is tops, and the private massage areas are resplendent, with private bathrooms. Rooms are spacious, with dark-wood floors and rich touches such as designer throw rugs and elegant built-in cabinetry. All bathrooms are large, with tubs and large granite counters. Spring for a superior room with a balcony and view of the central courtyard: It's worth it. Be sure to take a moment, preferably near the magic hour of sunset (but any time will do), and take it all in from the island pagoda in the central pond.

On the way to the temples, just north of the town center. Vithei Charles de Gaulle, Khum Svay Dang Kum, Siem Reap. www.sofitel.com. © **063/964-600.** Fax 063/964-609. 238 units. $220–$290 double; $300–$450 suite. AE, MC, V. **Amenities:** 5 restaurants; 3 bars; bike rental; concierge; 18-hole golf course; health club; Jacuzzi; pool; room service; sauna; smoke-free floor; spa. *In room:* A/C, TV w/in-house movies, fax, fridge, hair dryer, minibar, Wi-Fi.

Sokha Angkor   Maybe this is what Angkor Wat would have looked like if it was a pleasure resort rather than a place of worship. The lobby is gigantic, with big columns framing a bronze-and-sheer-glass chandelier. A blown-up photograph of a Banteay Srei temple is plastered over the elevator doors. In the courtyard, a large stone pediment with a waterfall empties into the pool. Big stone lions at the back and lingas at the front are minifountains, spitting out streams of water that also empty into the pool. Rooms are, thank goodness, more subtle. Blond-wood furniture gives things a light feeling, and a floral spritzer gives everything a springtime-fresh smell.

Rd. No. 6 and Sivutha Blvd. www.sokhahotels.com. © **063/969-999.** Fax 063/969-998. 276 units. $160–$170 double; from $350 suite. AE, MC, V. **Amenities:** 3 restaurants; 2 bars; lounge; concierge; health club; pool; room service; spa. *In room:* A/C, TV, fridge, high-speed Internet, hair dryer, minibar.

Victoria Angkor Hotel ★★   Victoria Angkor is a tasteful replica of a French colonial-era hotel, but with the amenities and functionality of a modern resort. Public spaces are done in earth tones, rattan and wood accents, and Art Deco floor tiles in mustard-yellow tones. The central pool is a private oasis surrounded by a minijungle, with massage salas nestled in the flora. Rooms are large, luxurious, and decorated with retro oil paintings of peaceful jungle scenes and framed photographs of everyday life in Siem Reap. Floors are wood with a border of fine tile that matches luxurious woven bedspreads. All rooms have balconies. Colonial suites have individual themes, and the best ones are the corner suites, with large, covered outdoor balconies. Fine dining at their Le Bistrot (see below) is tops.

Central Park, P.O. Box 93145, Siem Reap. www.victoriahotels-asia.com. © **063/760-428.** Fax 063/760-350. 130 units. $155–$165 double; from $450 suite. AE, MC, V. **Amenities:** 2 restaurants; bar; babysitting; bike rental; children's center; concierge; Jacuzzi; saltwater pool; room service; spa. *In room:* A/C, TV, fridge, hair dryer, minibar, Wi-Fi.

EXPENSIVE

Angkor Village Hotel ★★   In a quiet neighborhood not far from the main market, this peaceful hideaway is a maze of wood bungalows connected by covered boardwalks surrounding a picturesque ivy-draped pond. Rooms are rustic wooden affairs with high bamboo catay ceilings, wood beams, built-in cabinetry, comfortable beds, and decorative touches such as traditional Khmer shadow puppets and statuary. Top units have balconies overlooking the central pond. Bathrooms are all large, with tub/shower combos and sinks set in oversize ceramic cauldrons. The pool is small but picturesque in a verdant courtyard at the rear. The Auberge de Temples Restaurant is on a small island in the central pond and serves fine French and Khmer cuisines. The hotel's **Apsara Theater Restaurant,** just outside the gate, has Khmer-style banquet dining and performances of Khmer Apsara dancing nightly. The whole place is infused with Khmer culture and hospitality, and so popular is the original that they've expanded (see **Angkor Village Resort,** below). Angkor Village is often full, so be sure to book ahead.

Wat Bo Rd. www.angkorvillage.com. ℃ **063/963-361.** Fax 063/963-363. 46 units. $79–$169 double. AE, MC, V. **Amenities:** Restaurant; bar; bike rental; Internet; library; pool; room service. *In room:* A/C, TV, fridge, minibar, Wi-Fi.

Angkor Village Resort ★

This campus of luxury rooms is located a few steps closer to the temples (it all counts when you're racing for the sunrise). The resort offers the same standard of comfort and style as its sister hotel (see above), but with a fun pool as well as large ponds of Japanese koi, fountains, and lush landscaping. The resort does a good job of creating a sanctuary far away from town, but unfortunately the loud music from nearby developments occasionally overpowers the tranquil buzzing of cicadas. Rooms are stylish but lean more to the cozy than to the austere, with firm four-poster beds completing the cozy effect. All rooms have balconies overlooking the pool. Bathrooms are large, with raised shower units open to a tile room with a one-piece wooden counter set with two bright, free-standing porcelain sink bowls; pale-green tile and cool, indirect lighting are quite pleasing. The toilet area is separate. The staff is as friendly as they come. Breakfast of fresh breads and crepes by the pond is a treat.

Phum Traeng (on the north end of town nearer the temples), Siem Reap. www.angkorvillage.com. ℃ **063/963-561.** Fax 063/963-363. 40 units. $189 double. AE, MC, V. **Amenities:** Restaurant; bar; bike rental; Internet; library; pool; room service. *In room:* A/C, minibar, fridge, Wi-Fi.

FCC Angkor ★

This modern hotel is located behind high walls and shaded by towering tropical trees. All the rooms have names (Basil, Lychee, and so on), not numbers, to give things a personal feel. Rooms have low beds on wooden frames and modern amenities such as flatscreen TVs and hip furniture. The decor is similarly minimalist cool, with pale-yellow tile floors paired with fun block-color paintings hanging on the walls. The narrow outdoor pool is great for an afternoon cool-off, though not for laps.

Pokambor Ave. (next to the Royal Residence and just north of the post office). www.fcccambodia.com. ℃ **063/760-280.** Fax 063/760-281. 31 units. May–Sept $135–$150 double, $270 suite; Oct–Apr $170–$190 double, $340 suite. AE, MC, V. **Amenities:** Restaurant; bar; saltwater pool. *In room:* A/C, satellite TV/DVD, fridge, minibar, Wi-Fi.

Pavillon d'Orient ★★

Another Art Deco colonial hotel arrives in Siem Reap, but this one stands out for its boutique charm. Pavillon is a great choice in this price range, as it comes with nice perks such as free tuk-tuk transportation to the temples. Rooms are large, and all have private balconies overlooking the central garden. This buzz-worthy place is often full, so make sure to call ahead; if it's booked, you'll find similar standards of service and friendliness at its sister hotel, Pavillon Indochine (below).

Rd. 60, Siem Reap (on the new road to the temples). www.pavillon-orient-hotel.com. ℃ **098/655-738.** 18 units. $80–$110 double. AE, MC, V. **Amenities:** Restaurant; bar; pool; room service; spa. *In room:* A/C, TV, fridge, minibar.

MODERATE

Allson Angkor Hotel ★   Of the many hotels along the airport road, Route 6, the Allson is the best (and only slightly more expensive than the rest). Popular with group tours, the hotel is large and ostentatious, with high, Khmer-style roofs and large reproductions of temple statuary in the entry. Everything is clean and comfortable, if a bit sterile. Ask for a room in the new building in the back. Guest rooms are bland but large, with crown molding, clean carpet, and good, familiar amenities such as a minibar and safe. The bathrooms are a little small. This is a good, comfortable step down from the glitzier hotels in town, and the best choice if they're full. The lobby is always busy with tour groups, but the staff remains friendly and expedient. The hotel is sufficiently self-contained, with good basic amenities, a outdoor pool in the courtyard, a good restaurant, and all the necessary services. The two caged bears in the hotel's garden are enough to make you cry, though.

Rte. 6, Phum Sala Kanseng. www.angkor-hotel-cambodia.com. © **063/964-301.** Fax 063/964-302. 193 units. May–Sept $70 double, $74 deluxe double, $150 suite; Oct–Apr $75 double, $85 deluxe double, $160 suite. AE, MC, V. **Amenities:** Restaurant; bar; basic gym; Internet; pool. *In room:* A/C, TV, fridge, hair dryer, minibar.

Bopha Angkor   With its gaudy, red-and-gold decor and cheap imitations of Angkor statuary, there's a certain "cultural theme park" vibe to this place, but Bopha Angkor is tidy and affordable and offers a culturally infused visit to Siem Reap. Rooms are arranged in a U-shaped courtyard around a lush central garden. Private spaces are large but not luxe and feature fun local accents such as mosquito nets and souvenir-shop trinkets on the walls. The staff is friendly and the hotel is close to the old market area.

No. 0512 Acharsvar St. (across the canal from the market). www.bopha-angkor.com. © **063/964-928.** Fax 063/964-446. 38 units. $50–$87 double; $120 suite. MC, V. **Amenities:** Restaurant; bar; pool. *In room:* A/C, TV, fridge, minibar, Wi-Fi.

City River Hotel   If the Bopha Angkor sounds a bit over the top, its neighbor is much less pretentious. Though it's popular with tour groups, the tidy City River Hotel handles it all with ease. As the name suggests, you're right on the Siem Reap River, a short walk from the popular Old Market area. Rooms are spartan but clean and quiet. The price is reasonable, though there are few amenities, apart from a small rooftop pool and a massage service.

No. 0511 Achasva St., Wat Bo, Siem Reap. www.cityriverhotel.com. © **063/763-000.** Fax 063/963-963. 60 units. $45–$58 double; $85 suite. AE, MC, V. **Amenities:** Restaurant; room service. *In room:* A/C, TV, fridge, hair dryer, Internet, minibar.

Pavillon Indochine ★   This converted traditional Khmer house and garden is the closest you'll get to the temples and is quite peaceful, even isolated, in a quiet neighborhood. The upscale guesthouse is charming and surprisingly self-contained, with a good restaurant and a friendly, knowledgeable French proprietor whose staff can help arrange any detail in the area. Rooms are large, clean, and airy, in terra-cotta-tile and wood trim, but they're not particularly luxe. The courtyard area is a picturesque garden dotted with quiet sitting areas.

On the back road to the temples, Siem Reap. www.pavillon-indochine.com. © **012/541-003.** 24 units. $50–$55 double; $70–$75 suite (discounts in low season). AE, MC, V. **Amenities:** Restaurant, pool. *In room:* A/C, cellphone available upon request, Wi-Fi.

Soria Moria ★ This is one of the best of a glut of boutique hotels that have opened in recent years, not just for the attractive building and comfortable rooms, but also for the management's caring policy of supporting local charities and for the enthusiastic staff. Facilities are generous considering room rates, and include a spa, a fusion restaurant, rooftop bar and Jacuzzi, plus a boutique shop that sells some stylish textiles. Rooms are spacious and simply decorated, while the bathrooms have tubs and smart fittings. Rates include both breakfast and airport pickup.

Wat Bo Rd. www.soriamoria.com. ℂ **063/964-768.** 38 units. $50–$65 double. MC, V. **Amenities:** Restaurant; bar; Jacuzzi; spa; sundeck. *In room:* A/C, TV, minibar, Wi-Fi.

Viroth's Hotel ★★ ✦ You'd be hard-pressed to find another hotel that is this chic and affordable. The boutique Viroth's provides a private, intimate experience. The rooms are minimalist and modern, with sleek geometric furniture, including cozy lounge beds, and soft touches, such as dark-brown leather desktops and coffee-colored coverlets and accent pillows, keep it warm and inviting. Most rooms have private balconies. The best room is no. 3, on the ground floor; it comes with a large poolside corner terrace. The small pool is surrounded by cream-colored sun beds. Breakfast is served on the rooftop restaurant. It's lit with fairy lights at night and is an excellent place to spend the evening, looking out over the rooftops of Siem Reap.

0658 Wat Bo Village (behind City River Hotel). www.viroth-hotel.com. ℂ **012/778-096.** 7 units. From $90 double. AE, MC, V. **Amenities:** Restaurant; bar; rooftop Jacuzzi; saltwater pool; room service; small spa. *In room:* A/C, TV, Wi-Fi.

INEXPENSIVE

The downtown area of Siem Reap, on either side of the main road, is brimming with budget accommodations.

Auberge Mont Royal d'Angkor ★ ✦ Down a lazy lane just to the west of the town center, Auberge is an excellent choice for budget travelers. Terra cotta tile covers all open areas and rooms, and there are atmospheric touches such as canvas lamps, carved-wood beds, cushions, and traditional hangings, curtains, and bedspreads. The traditional decor is pleasant and inviting. Pool villas are well worth the upgrade. More rooms and a second pool are opening soon.

West of the town center. www.auberge-mont-royal.com. ℂ **063/964-044.** 39 units. $37–$57 double; $66 pool villa. MC, V. **Amenities:** Restaurant; bar; Internet; pool, spa. *In room:* A/C, TV, fridge, minibar.

La Noria ★ La Noria is a mellow group of bungalows connected by a winding garden path. The guesthouse is near the town center, but you wouldn't know it in the hush of this little laid-back spot. Rooms are basic but have nice local touches. Terra-cotta floors, wooden trim, and small balconies are all neat and tidy, and fine hangings and details, such as shadow puppets and authentic Khmer furniture, round out a pleasing traditional decor. The place is light on amenities but has a small pool and makes up for any deficiency with gobs of charm. The open-air restaurant is a highlight, serving good Khmer and French cuisine. The hotel is affiliated with Krousar Thmey, "New Family," a humanitarian group doing good work, and there's a helpful information board about rural travel and humanitarian projects.

Down a small lane off Rte. 6, to the northeast of town. www.lanoriaangkor.com. ℂ **063/964-242.** Fax 063/964-243. 28 units. $39 double. No credit cards. **Amenities:** Restaurant; Internet; pool. *In room:* A/C.

Passaggio ★　This small boutique hotel is convenient to downtown and adjoins its own helpful travel agent, Lolei Travel. Rooms are large and tidy, but not much more; the three floors here are something like a motel in the U.S., complete with tacky art. The family room has a bathtub; all others have stand-up showers in bathrooms that are nondescript in plain tile but are neat and new. The friendly staff can arrange any detail and is eager to please.

Watdamanak Village (across the river to the east of town). www.passaggio-hotel.com. ℭ **063/760-324.** Fax 063/760-163. 17 units. $32–$45 double. AE, MC, V. **Amenities:** Restaurant; free Internet; pool; free airport transfers (one-way). *In room:* A/C, TV, fridge, minibar, Wi-Fi, no phone.

Two Dragons ★　Two Dragons is a good budget spot for picking up reliable information on the temples and onward travel, as well as for meeting up with other travelers. Rooms are spartan but very clean. There's a little patio on the second floor, and free tea and coffee are available 24 hours a day. Good camaraderie pervades this place. The restaurant serves terrific Thai and Khmer cuisine. The staff is as friendly as they come and can help arrange good guides to the temples.

110 Wat Bo Village (on a side street off Wat Bo Rd.). www.twodragons-asia.com. ℭ **063/965-107.** 14 units. $15–$25 double. MC, V. **Amenities:** Restaurant; bar; bike rental. *In room:* A/C, fridge (in some), Wi-Fi, no phone.

Where to Eat

Dining in Siem Reap is not a pricey affair. The major hotels all have fine upscale eateries, and there are also several good free-standing spots. The area around the Old Market is a cluster of storefronts, most of little distinction from one another, but all are affordable and laid-back.

EXPENSIVE

Le Bistrot de Siem Reap ★★　FRENCH　The atmosphere in this restaurant is wonderfully charming, with old French music playing lightly in the background, light gray walls with the ceiling trim and accent walls painted warm maroon, and black lacquer tables with mixed wooden and rattan chairs. The walls are adorned with old posters advertising voyages to the Far East, but the cuisine is a superb culinary trip to France, with dishes such as snails in garlic butter. There's an extensive wine list, and a good selection of Cuban cigars. It's a wonderful, tasty slice of old Indochine.

Central Park, P.O. Box 93145, Siem Reap. ℭ **063/760-428.** Reservations recommended. Main courses $15–$26. AE, MC, V. Daily 6:30am–midnight.

Meric ★★　KHMER　This is a slick, trendy restaurant located in the equally stylish Hôtel de la Paix. I prefer the Western dishes to the Khmer tasting menu, but both are constantly changing, with the latter often offering off-the-beaten-path specials such as mashed snake or frog. The steaks here are the best in town, and service is tops. There is outdoor dining around a stately Boddhi tree in the central courtyard, or indoor tables near the open kitchen.

Sivutha Blvd. ℭ **063/966-000.** Reservations recommended. Main courses $18–$26. AE, MC, V. Daily 6am–10:30pm.

MODERATE

Abacus ★ ASIAN/FRENCH   This restaurant has recently moved to a gorgeous garden setting, where guests can eat either on the leafy terrace or in the elegant, air-conditioned interior with ceiling-to-floor windows. Starched tablecloths and fine silverware adorn the tables. The menu is written on a chalkboard, and you can choose from a good selection of either Asian rice bowls or Western mains such as grilled lamb with rosemary or duck with orange sauce. There's also an extensive selection of wines.

Just north of Rte. 6 on the way to the airport. ℂ **012/644-286.** www.abacuscafe.com. Main courses $8.50–$19. No credit cards. Daily 11am–late.

Cafe Indochine ★★ ASIAN   On the north end of the busy central road that leads to the temples, Cafe Indochine is a cool, Indochina throwback. Set in an old wooden building that's been newly renovated, this little perch is a pleasant place to watch life go by on the busy street out front and unwind from a busy day at the temples. The menu is an eclectic list of Khmer and French dishes. Try a shared set menu for $15 and get a short course in local cuisine such as *chas kruang* beef; fine curries; *amok* fish; a number of whole-fish dishes; and beef, chicken, or vegetable stir-fries. Follow up with good ice cream or coffee.

44 Sivutha Blvd. ℂ **012/804-952.** Main courses $5–$9. AE, MC, V. Daily 10am–3pm and 5–11pm.

FCC Angkor (Foreign Correspondents Club) ★★ INTERNATIONAL   The glowing white, modern cube of the FCC would be at home in a nouveau riche California suburb or a Jacques Tati film, but it is a bit jarring canal side in the center of Siem Reap. The first floor offers some of the finest boutique shopping in the city, and the second floor is an elegant open space with high ceilings. There's a bar, low lounge chairs at the center, and standard dining space on the balcony. The main room is flanked on one end by an open kitchen. The FCC holds numerous functions and hosts live music. The menu is the same as the original FCC in Phnom Penh, with soups, salads, and Western standards such as pasta, steaks, and wood-fired pizzas, as well as Khmer favorites such as amok curry.

Pokambor Ave. (next to the Royal Residence and just north of the post office). ℂ **063/760-283.** Main courses $8–$25. AE, MC, V. Daily 7am–midnight.

Madame Butterfly ★ KHMER/THAI   Serving the finest authentic Khmer- and Thai-influenced cuisine in town, Madame Butterfly is worth a visit for the setting alone. In a converted traditional wooden home, seating is in low rattan chairs, and the decor is characterized by a tasteful collection of Buddhist and Khmer artifacts. Candlelight mingles with mellow indirect lighting, and the whole effect is casual and romantic. There are daily specials, and the menu is heavy on good curries and hot-pot dishes. I had a delicious dish of poached fish in coconut sauce with sticky rice. The Masaman curry is divine, and the *mchou pous,* a chicken-and-shrimp bisque, is rich and tasty.

A short ride west on No. 6, airport rd. ℂ **016/909-607.** Main courses $6–$15. V. Daily 6–11pm.

Nest ★★ INTERNATIONAL/KHMER   Be prepared for some pleasant surprises when you visit Nest. First is the striking design: a futuristic, multilayered tent envelops a wide space that is liberally sprinkled with palms and other tropical plants. On the left are comfy loungers and daybeds where you can enjoy a cocktail and chat, while on the right, the starched tablecloths and smiling staff invite diners. The next surprise are the menus, both the Khmer tasting menu, which offers several local dishes for $20, or the larger menu, which features tempting items such as a yin yang combination (tenderloin steak crab ravioli, pumpkin puree, and tom yam gravy; $22). Preparation and presentation of dishes is excellent.

Sivutha Blvd. (next to Mekong Bang). ✆ **063/966-381.** www.nestangkor.com. Main courses $8-$25. AE, MC, V. Daily 10am-midnight.

The Red Piano ★ INTERNATIONAL Angelina Jolie and cast and crew of the film *Lara Croft: Tomb Raider* made this atmospheric bar their second home while filming at the temples, an act that has guaranteed the success of the place since. Imported steaks, spaghetti, sandwiches, salads, and international specialties such as Indian samosas and chicken *cordon bleu* round out a menu of familiar fare. Everything is good, and this place is always hoppin' late into the night. If it's full downstairs, check out the second floor.

50m (164 ft.) northwest of the Old Market. ✆ **063/964-750.** Main courses $4-$8. No credit cards. Daily 7am-late.

The Sugar Palm ★★ TRADITIONAL KHMER This is where food and beverage managers from nearby five-star hotels come to feast. Co-owner Kethana serves old-fashioned, flavorful, and hearty Khmer food. The restaurant has a warm and inviting ambience with subdued, covered lighting; a wall painted in sunny yellow; and vaulted ceilings. The furniture and bar are done in dark sugar palm wood, and most of the seating is on the wraparound balcony, partially covered from the outside world with roll-down bamboo blinds. On the menu, the pomelo salad is excellent. Fleshy pomelo tendrils are played off the sharp taste of dried shrimp and crunchy chopped peanuts. Strips of spicy red pepper give it an extra kick. For mains, I recommend the chicken stir-fried with ginger. The meat is tender and the sauce is loaded with tender slices of sautéed ginger.

Ta Phul Rd. (400m/1,312 ft. south of the Caltex gas station). ✆ **063/964-838.** Main courses $5-$8. MC, V. Mon-Sat 9:30am-3pm and 5:30-11pm. Bar till late.

Tell Restaurant ★★ GERMAN/INTERNATIONAL Tell Restaurant serves hearty German fare, catering to the many expats and travelers longing for a bit of home (mostly Germany and Scandinavia). Savory entrees, such as Vienna schnitzel, German sausages, stroganoff, and a signature raclette special or enormous cheese fondue ($23; enough for two or more), are quite impressive. You walk away with a bit of a heavy belly into the steamy Khmer evening, but after a day touring the temples (and usually another one planned), a hearty meal might be just the ticket.

No. 374 Sivutha Blvd. (200m/656 ft. north of the Old Market). ✆ **063/963-289.** Main courses $3-$12. V. Daily 10am-11pm.

INEXPENSIVE

8th Street Brasserie INTERNATIONAL/KHMER Competition among restaurants and bars is fierce along Pub Street (aka Bar Street or 8th Street), but this roomy brasserie, located just along from the super-successful Red Piano, stands out with its dark wood floors, large mirrors, and maroon walls. The menu includes several Khmer favorites as well as burgers, pastas, and salads. The extensive drinks list, featuring a variety of cocktails, is another reason to hang your hat here awhile. If the street action seems too noisy, head for the upstairs terrace, where things are a bit calmer.

Pub St. (just north of the Old Market). ℂ **017/692-997.** Main courses $3–$6. No credit cards. Daily 7am–late.

Beaches INTERNATIONAL/KHMER/THAI You probably never expected to sit on a beach in Siem Reap, but here's your chance. This new, Thai-run place, located in the up-and-coming Wat Bo area, has a funky vibe, and "the beach" (actually a sandy garden) is a relaxing setting with big, soft seats that are ideal to enjoy a fresh fruit juice or a cocktail. The restaurant is on the terrace of a wooden, stilted house, where the menu covers a range of local and international dishes from steaks to pizzas, and a pool table tempts diners to linger for a game after their meal.

Wat Bo Road (just west of the temple). ℂ **063/659-4343.** Main courses $3–$6. No credit cards. Daily 8am–11:30pm.

Chivit Thai ★ THAI Here you'll find authentic Thai cuisine in an atmospheric streetside restaurant, though avoid tables by the roadside, which can be noisy. The food is great, the price is low, and there's casual floor seating and a rustic charm to the place, which is quite romantic in candlelight. Name your favorite Thai dish, and they do it here. The tom yum (sour, spicy Thai soup) is excellent, and they have good set menus ($5–$9) comprised of many courses that are much finer than their low price tag. Dishes are sometimes toned down for Western tastes, so if you like your food spicy, just tell them.

130 Wat Bo Rd. (across the river from the FCC, near the intersection of Rte. 6 going out of town). ℂ **012/830-761.** Main courses $3–$8. No credit cards. Daily 7am–10pm.

Curry Walla INDIAN There's nothing fancy about the decor here (it's a simple shopfront place), but the fantastic curries, ranging from an explosive vindaloo to a mild korma, keeps customers coming back. Besides the many chicken, lamb, and beef dishes, there are some great deals in *thalis,* which give you a taste of a few different dishes. If you can't decide what to go for, the owner is usually on hand to make recommendations. There's a second branch in the Night Market.

No. B05 Sivutha Blvd. (just north of the Old Market). ℂ **063/965-451.** Main courses $3–$5.50. No credit cards. Daily 10:30am–11pm.

Khmer Kitchen Restaurant ★ KHMER This busy little storefront hides itself down an alley on the north end of the Old Market, but it draws a nightly crowd for big portions of simple, delicious Khmer fare. In fact, it's so popular that it has taken over neighboring properties, and reservations are advisable. Good curries and stir-fries share menu space with dishes such as baked pumpkin. It's about the food here, not the service, but these folks are friendly enough, considering how busy they usually are.

Down an alley just north of the Old Market. ℂ **063/964-154.** www.khmerkitchens.com. Reservations recommended. Main courses $2–$4. No credit cards. Daily 11am–11pm.

Viroth's Restaurant ★★ KHMER This is a cool spot to enjoy top-class Khmer cuisine without the big price tag. Like its sister hotel two streets down (p. 402), Viroth's Restaurant boasts a sleek and stylish interior. Unlike the hotel, which is still a well-kept secret, the restaurant is popular and loved. The food is traditional Khmer cuisine and is mighty tasty. The amok fish is a perfect blend of coconut milk and lemon grass, and unlike at other restaurants, the fish is completely deboned. The spacious dining area is on a raised wooden platform, and ceiling and floor fans keep a cool breeze going and send ripples through the strips of sheer saffron sheets suspended from the ceiling and hanging between tables.

246 Wat Bo St. (behind La Résidence Hotel). ℂ **063/760-774.** Main courses $4–$8. MC, V. Daily 10:30am–2pm and 5:30–10pm.

SNACKS & CAFES

Blue Pumpkin   This is a stylish cafe on the northeast end of the Old Market. Blue Pumpkin is a longtime local favorite serving great pastries, coffee, and burgers and sandwiches. They'll pack you a lunch for the temples, too.

563 Mondol 1. ℂ **063/963-574.** MC, V. Items $1–$4. Daily 8am–11pm.

Butterflies Garden Restaurant ★   Don't miss this netted enclosure with a butterfly farm and meticulous menagerie of local flora and fauna, including a pond filled with Japanese carp. There are detailed descriptions of all plants and some individual butterflies. They serve Khmer and international cuisine. Vegetarians will also enjoy an extensive selection here.

Across the Siem Reap River north of the Old Market. ℂ **063/761-211.** http://butterfliesofangkor.com. Items $2–$5. No credit cards. Daily 8am–10pm.

Café Central   Here's a neat spot to relax over a coffee and snack while watching tourists drift by in the Old Market. Tables are well spaced, and there's a laid-back vibe. They also serve sandwiches, burgers, pizzas, and ice cream in case you want to settle in for lunch and dinner.

Corner of sts. 9 and 10 in the Old Market. ℂ **017/692-997.** Items $2–$6. No credit cards. Daily 7am–11pm.

DINING AT THE TEMPLES

Across the busy parking lot closest to Angkor Wat, the snazzy **Angkor Café** (ℂ **017/692-370**) serves, for a mint by Khmer standards, good coffee, tea, and sandwiches, all provided by **Blue Pumpkin** (above). It's the best thing going on the Angkor compound, and, apart from the good food, the building is air-conditioned. The attached **Artisans d'Angkor** boutique (p. 419) offers high-end silver and stone reproductions of the temples, as well as silk and other souvenirs. Open daily from 8am to 6pm. No credit cards.

In and among all the major temples, you'll see lots of small **thatch-roofed eateries,** and all will implore you to enter. The competition means that you have more leverage when haggling: "Are you sure this Coke is $2? Someone over there said it was . . ." You get the picture. You'll be swarmed by vendors when you approach these restaurants. Just pick one quickly, and the rest will split. Prices are slightly inflated, but it's a tourist sight and folks need to make a living (and probably have to pay some heavy kickbacks). A few bucks will get you fried rice, noodles, or vegetables. Most of these places have shaded hammock areas out back (mostly for drivers, but a good place to rest) and basic toilets. Carrying your own hand sanitizer is a good idea.

Attractions

Angkor Wat is the Disneyland of Buddhist temples in Asia. The temple complex requires a few busy days to get around the major sights thoroughly. Everyone has a favorite, but I've highlighted a few must-sees below. Plan carefully and catch a sunrise or sunset from one of the more prime spots; it's a photographer's dream. **Note:** The temples are magnificent, and days spent clambering around them are inherently interesting, but be careful not to come away from a visit to ancient Angkor with a memory of an oversize rock collection or jungle gym. There's much to learn about Buddhism, Hinduism, architecture, and Khmer history; it's useful to hire a well-informed guide ($20–$30 a day) or join a tour group. There are also subtleties to temple touring, and a good guide is your best chance to beat the crowd, catch the intricacies, or be in the right place for the magic moments of the day. Contact any hotel front desk or the tour agencies listed earlier (p. 395).

THE TEMPLES

Entrance fees for Angkor Wat are as follows: A 1-day ticket is $20, a 3-day ticket is $40, and a 1-week ticket is $60. The tickets were recently restructured, extending the validity of 3-day passes to 1 week instead of 3 consecutive days. Similarly, 1-week passes are now valid for 1 month. Tickets are good for all sights within the main temple compound, as well as Banteay Srei, to the north, and the outlying temples of the Roluos Group. Other sights, such as Beng Melea or Koh Ker, require an additional fee. The temples open at dawn, and you can buy a ticket as early as 5am to get there for sunrise. At dusk, around 6pm, temple attendants start gently nudging visitors out of the park.

My strongest recommendation is to get a guide, at least for 1 day of temple touring. A guide not only provides the most useful information that will serve as a background for your further exploration, but makes the logistics of that first day much easier. Contact any hotel front desk or tour office, and they can arrange something for you. Guides are certified and come from the same school, so dispense nearly the same information, but, of course, some are better than others. Ask around for recommendations.

Tip: The temple sites listed below are more or less in the usual order you might visit them. A visit to Angkor is now a noisy romp among large Korean, Thai, Chinese, and European groups. An average guide will take you along in the heart of the herd, following the standard temple routine, but a good guide knows how to get you out of the pack. Insist on it.

Important note: The Angkor complex is constantly undergoing restoration, so you may find certain sections hidden behind scaffolding or closed off to visitors.

Angkor Wat ★★★   The symbol of Cambodia, the five spires of the main temple of Angkor are known the world over. In fact, this is the most resplendent of the Angkor sites, one certainly not to miss even in the most perfunctory of tours.

Built under the reign of Suryavarman II in the 12th century, this temple, along with Bayon and Baphuon, is the very pinnacle of Khmer architecture. From base to tip of the highest tower, it's 213m (699 ft.) of awe-inspiring stone in the definitive, elaborate Khmer style. From base to tip of the highest tower, it's 65m (213 ft.) of awe-inspiring stone in the definitive, elaborate Khmer style. The temple moat is 1.5km×1.3km (1 mile×¾ mile) around and 190m (62 ft.) wide, crossed by a causeway with long naga statues on each side as railings from the west; in fact, Angkor is the only temple

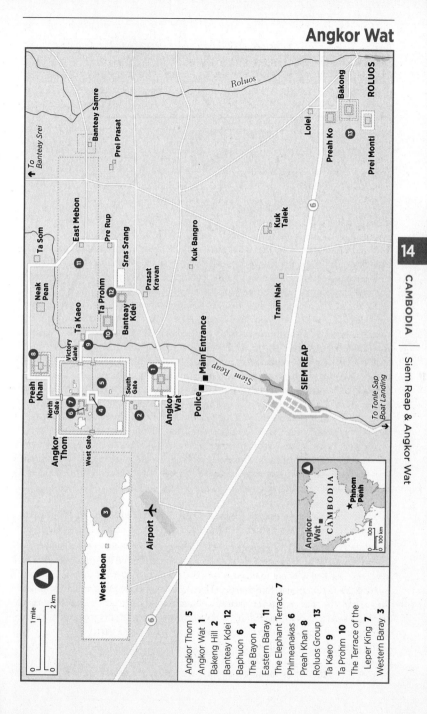

Roluos

To
Banteay Srei

Banteay Samre

Prei Prasat

Lolei

Preah Ko

Bakong

ROLUOS

Prei Monti

East Mebon

Pre Rup

Sras Srang

Kuk Bangro

Kuk
Talek

Ta Som

Neak
Pean

Ta Kaeo

Prasat
Kravan

Banteay
Kdei

Ta Prohm

Tram Nak

Main Entrance

Preah
Khan

Victory
Gate

Angkor
Wat

Police

Siem Reap

SIEM REAP

North Gate

South
Gate

West Gate

To Tonle Sap
Boat Landing

Angkor Thom

West Mebon

Airport

CAMBODIA

Angkor
Wat

Phnom
Penh

CAMBODIA

100 km

Angkor Thom **5**
Angkor Wat **1**
Bakeng Hill **2**
Banteay Kdei **12**
Baphuon **6**
The Bayon **4**
Eastern Baray **11**
The Elephant Terrace **7**
Phimeanakas **6**
Preah Khan **8**
Roluos Group **13**
Ta Kaeo **9**
Ta Prohm **10**
The Terrace of the
Leper King **7**
Western Baray **3**

1 mile

2 km

entered from the west (all others from the east). Angkor Wat is the only Angkor monument that is a mausoleum—all others are temples or monasteries—and its main temple is dedicated to Vishnu.

Approaching the temple, you'll first cross the causeway over the main moat, restored in the 1960s by the French. Enter the compound across the first gallery, the Majestic Gallery, with some carvings and Brahma statuary, and then pass into the large, grassy courtyard housing the main temple. This next causeway is flanked on either side by two small library buildings, as well as two small ponds. (**Hint:** A shot of the temple's silhouette reflected in this pond at dawn is one of the iconic views of Angkor.)

An outdoor staircase sits at the approach to the main temple. From there, you'll enter the richest area of statuary, galleries, and bas-reliefs. The famous bas-reliefs encircling the temple on the first level (south side) depict the mythical "Churning of the Ocean of Milk," a legend in which Hindu deities stir vast oceans in order to extract the elixir of immortality. This churning produced the Apsaras, Hindu celestial dancers, who can be seen on many temples. Other reliefs surrounding the base of the main temple show Khmer wars, and corner towers depict Hindu fables.

The most measured and studied of all the sites, Angkor Wat is the subject of much speculation: It's thought to represent Mount Meru, home of Hindu gods and a land of creation and destruction. Researchers measuring the site in *hat,* ancient Khmer units of measure, deduce that the symmetry of the building corresponds with the timeline of the Hindu ages, as a map or calendar of the universe, if you will. The approach from the main road crosses the baray (reservoir) and is an ascending progression of three levels to the inner sanctum. The T-shirt hawkers are relentless, and the tricky steps and temple height are a challenge to those with vertigo, but the short trip is awe-inspiring and the views from the top are breathtaking. **Note:** There's a guide rope on the southern face (and often a long line up).

It's a fair walk up to the second level, a flat, open space that overlooks the main temple square, the famed Angkor *prangs* or parapets on each corner. From here, it's a steep climb (use the staircase with roped handrail on the south side of the temple) up to the third and final level (at the time of writing, this level was closed to visitors). There are four large courtyards surrounded by galleries, and balcony overlooks from the base of the prangs at each corner. These high perches are great for watching the sunset over Bakeng Hill (though, lately, the guards try to get folks down earlier and earlier).

Angkor Wat is the first temple you pass when entering the complex, but depending on your guide, you might save it for the evening and head directly to nearby Angkor Thom.

Bakeng Hill ★★   Just past Angkor Wat, Bakeng Hill is meant to resemble Mount Meru, the center of the earth in the Hindu cosmology. The hill makes a great spot for sunrise or sunset viewing, with great views down over Angkor Wat itself, and gets crowded like a mosh pit in high season. The hike up is a good way to limber up and break a sweat predawn, but the crumbled steps and slippery mud are a bit much for some. Consider taking the trek in style high upon an elephant's back in a houda. Elephants for hire start at about $20 and wait at the bottom of the hill.

Angkor Thom ★★★   The temple name means "The Great City" in Khmer and is famed for its fantastic 45m (148-ft.) central temple, **Bayon,** and nearby **Baphuon.**

The vast area of Angkor Thom, over a mile on one side, is dotted with many temples and features; don't miss the elaborate reliefs on the Bayon's first-floor gallery or of the **Terrace of the Leper King** and the **Terrace of Elephants.** The **Angkor Thom Gates,** particularly the south gate, are good examples of the angelic carving of the Jayavarman head, a motif you find throughout the temple sites. The bridge spanning the moat before the south entrance is lined with the gods and monsters said to have been in competition to churn the proverbial sea of milk that would cause creation of the world. The line of statues with the gate in the background is a classic Angkor scene.

The Bayon ★★★   The **Bayon** is the very centerpiece of the larger Angkor Thom city and, with its classic carved faces, is one of the best loved of the Angkor temples. Bayon is a Buddhist temple built under the reign of prolific Jayavarman VII (A.D. 1190), but the temple was built atop a previous Hindu site and adheres to Hindu cosmology; with its central tower depicting Meru and its oceanic moat, it can be read as a metaphor for the natural world. The Bayon is famous for its huge stone faces, usually set in groups of four around a central *prang,* or tower, and each face indicating an ordinal direction on the compass. The curious smiling faces are done in deep relief at Bayon—and also in different forms at the entrance gates to Angkor Thom, at Ta Prom, and at Banteay Kdei—and the image is the enigmatic Mona Lisa of Southeast Asia, at once recognizable as an image of compassion and equanimity. The face is also said to depict Jayavarman VII, the temple's very builder and benefactor. You approach the Bayon along a forested area at the city center, cool and misty, where streams of light come through in visible rays and the drone of cicadas is deafening (you might even see some monkeys). Elephant trekkers also line the road to the temple.

The three-level Bayon is nearly square. The first level is surrounded by an intricate **bas-relief gallery** depicting stories of Khmer conquests and battles, as well as daily life and ritual among the early Khmers. A good guide can lead you to the juicy bits of the fun story, and you can spend a good bit of time sorting out the details for yourself, too (kids love it). Look for the unique pairs of Apsara dancers on columns near the gallery (Apsaras usually dance alone). On the South Wall, find three tiers depicting Khmer battles with the Cham from 1177 to 1181, a battle that took place on the waters of the Tonle Sap Lake in boats—look for the grisly images of crocodiles eating the carcasses of the fallen. Also note the Chinese figure with beard, topknot, and lance on a horse. Khmer soldiers ride elephants and have short hair, a spear, and a magic string for invincible fighting; they also carry shields and banners. A good guide can point out details such as a lady crouching and getting burned on a fire, a man handing a turtle to a chef, and a scene of a cockfight and soldiers sacrificing a buffalo to ensure good luck in battle. There's a real sense of humanity to these images.

The second level has some Apsara reliefs and porticos with lingum, but the third level is the most interesting, where you can get up close with the many **Apsara Faces** thought to resemble a serene Jayavarman. Each of the 54 small towers is adorned with a face, or a number of faces, and you can have a ball with your zoom lens. There are a number of porticos with small lingum statues, and elderly matrons sell incense sticks and a chance to make merit by making an offering. The large central tower, or prang, is 25m (82 ft.) in diameter, with 16 small coves for meditation of kings and high priests. In 1933, French archaeologist George Groslier excavated the main prang, only to find a massive statue of Jayavarman hidden underneath. The statue, called **Jaya Bot Mohania,** is a seated Jayavarman with a seven-headed naga snake looming over him; it is now on display at a small temple near the **Victory Gate** (just east of the Bayon).

One of the greatest views of the many faces of the Bayon is from the ground at the northern end of the temples, just before a large snack, refreshment, and shopping area. Stop here on your way to the Baphuon (reviewed below) by foot.

Baphuon   Just north of the Bayon is the stalwart form of the **Baphuon,** a temple mount built in 1066 and an important Khmer capital. Early French archaeologists sought to restore the crumbling mount and began to disassemble the temple block by block, but their efforts were interrupted by war, and it would be some years before archaeologists would return to find a confused jigsaw puzzle of a dismantled temple, and, *mon dieu!,* someone had misplaced the plans. Bilateral efforts are underway to solve the puzzle and put the temple back together, and these ongoing efforts give visitors an idea of what original temple construction might have been like. The Baphuon was the last capital in the Angkor period.

The east gate of the Baphuon is the only remaining part of what was once a large laterite wall. A narrow causeway with moats on either side connects the gate with the main temple. The temple has five levels that are all the same height, which makes the site more like a pyramid and unique among Angkor temples. *Note:* From the Baphuon, you can make a clockwise loop, first to Vimean Akhar, then to the Terrace of the Leper Kings and the Terrace of Elephants (all on foot), before you return to the vendors' area and your awaiting chariot to go on to Preah Khan or via the east gate to Ta Prohm.

Pre Rup ★   With its three central spires, **Pre Rup** looks a bit like a mini Angkor Wat. Pre Rup was built by King Rajeindravarmen II in 961 and was dedicated to Shiva. The best views are from the Hindu temple's south side. It is made of gray sandstone, which is a less durable material than the pink sandstone of Banteay Srei. As such, time and weather have had their way with the temple, and many of the intricate carvings and details have been worn away by rain and erosion, but it's still completely awesome in size and structure. Plants have begun to grow on the central towers, and you can see bright green leaves working their way through the stone. You'll be scrambling over the fallen rock and debris near the bottom of the temple, and you'll still feel like a humble, insignificant mortal. Climb to the top of the temple and look west; on a clear day, you can see Angkor Wat's spires (roughly 12km/7½ miles away) peeking out over the treetops.

Phimeanakas ★   Continuing north of the Baphuon—and still within large Angkor Thom—you reach the "Palace of Air," or **Phimeanakas,** which was a royal palace built by three successive kings (Jayavarman II and V and Suryavarman I) over time from 944 to 1045. This Hindu temple dedicated to Shiva is some 12m (39 ft.) high with three levels; each of the three levels represents one of the kings who helped build it. Each side has steep steps, and the shallow moat is full in rainy season. The top of the temple is a narrow pillared gallery. The steep climb is best attempted to the left (west) when approaching from the Baphuon (there's a handrail). Have a drink or a fresh coconut in a shaded area at the bottom of the other side.

Adjacent to the Baphuon are two large ponds: The biggest is 125m (410 ft.) long and was where the king himself bathed; the smaller ponds were for the king's courtiers.

Note: The eastern entrance of the Phimeanakas has a Sanskrit inscription with a brief history of construction and orientation. Most are in museums, and this is one of just a few that you can still find on the temple site.

THE MAGIC HOURS AT angkor wat

The skies over Angkor always put on a show. With just a bit of prior planning, you can see the dawn or the day's afterglow framed in temple spires, glowing off the main *wat* or reflected in one of the temple reservoirs. Photographers swoon. Here are a few hints for catching the magic hours at the temples.

The sunrise and sunset views from the upper terraces of **Angkor Wat,** the main temple, are some of the best, though it's a tough climb for some. At dusk, temple staffers start clearing the main temple area just as the sun dips. Smile, avoid them, and try to stay for the afterglow.

For the classic photographer's view of Angkor Wat at sunset—with the image reflected in a pool—enter the first wall of the temple compound, walk halfway down the front gangway, and then take a right or left down the set of stairs and out into the field. The view from the water's edge, with warm light bouncing off the temple, is stunning. The pond on the right nearly disappears in dry season but has natural edges, not stone, and makes for a nicer shot. At dawn the same view produces a graphic silhouette of the temple spires, and if you're lucky, with a golden background of the sun rising behind the temple.

It's a bit crowded, but views from **Phnom Bakeng (Bakeng Hill),** a short drive past the entrance to Angkor Wat, are stunning at both sunrise and sunset. It's a good climb up the hill, and those so inclined can go by elephant for about $20.

The open area on the eastern side of **Banteay Kdei** (see Angkor Wat map, above) looks over one of Angkor's many reservoirs, **Sras Srang,** which serves as a great reflective pool for the rising glow at sunrise. See the "'Get High' at Angkor" box, below, for other options.

If money is no object, contact **Helicopters Cambodia Ltd. ★**, 658 Hup Guan St. (✆ 063/963-316). For $200, you can get a 20-minute flight to see the sights from any angle you choose. Be sure to specify your needs and interests, and they can create an itinerary that suits.

More affordable is a ride with **Angkor Balloon.** Just $15 gets you a 10-minute ride up to 180m (500 ft.) above the ground. The balloon basket is large, good for walking around and taking in the view from different sides. The balloon is controlled from the ground by tether, a very sophisticated contraption brought to Cambodia by French developers. It's a bit like an amusement park ride really. The takeoff is 1km (a halfmile) west of the main entrance to the temples (you're sure to see them from afar throughout the day). Flights start at sunrise and end at sunset (depending on the weather; no flights if it's windy or rainy), and the prime times fill up quickly. Call them at ✆ 011/886-789 to book a ride. In the middle of the day, it's first-come, first-served.

The Terrace of the Leper King ★★ Built by Jayavarman, this section is the northern half of a long north-south shelf (the Elephant Terrace, below, is the southern half) of what was supposedly a main viewing stage for the king and his entourage to watch elaborate shows in the open area out front. Approach the terrace from its most northern point. Outside you'll find an image of the guardian of hell, because the area site was a crematorium. The top of the terrace is a statue of the king with leprosy (a copy of the original). The long terrace is made of two walls, and visitors pass through a shaded walkway on the interior. The whole site is lined with rich relief carving and has been lovingly restored and propped up with a new concrete wall that maintains

Like many of the world's great monuments, the temples of Angkor are laid out over massive spaces, with miles of temple wall on the side of each temple, as if a sign to the gods. Visitors approaching temples on foot experience the temple like Khmers of the Angkor period would have, in procession from one side to the other, but we see only one section of the main gate, for example, or experience only the inner sanctum of the temples without being able to see the whole. It is important to remember that the Angkor temples were each self-contained cities or large monasteries, with populations in the hundreds of thousands. Now choked with jungle, these wider areas are best appreciated from above, where the scope of the building at Angkor is best understood. The rule is that there's a 1km (half-mile) "no fly" radius around the temple compound, and the trips above know just where that is and can take you as close as they are allowed.

the integrity of the original. **Note:** There are portable toilets at the far north end of the Terrace of the Leper King.

The Elephant Terrace   This terrace is the south end (near the Bayon) of a long performance terrace of the king, so named because of its elaborate reliefs of elephants, whose trunks make decorative columns. The long concourse (about 350m/1,148 ft.) depicts images of circus acrobats, wrestlers, and elephant hunters in the wild.

Preah Khan   Built by Jayavarman VII in 1191, the name of the temple means "Sacred Sword." It's rumored that this was where Jayavarman called home during the building of the Bayon. You approach the Preah Khan through a walkway lined with low lantern towers (note that the Buddhist reliefs were changed to divine vultures during the iconoclastic period). The compound is surrounded by wall and moat. The moat represents the ocean, the wall is a mountain, and the temple is Mount Meru—the mother mountain of Hindu creation. Four gates face the ordinal directions, and each gate has a god and demon statuelike entry to Angkor Thom, but just a tower, no Apsara face. Stop in at the small visitor center for information about preservation. The temple is a monastery, like Ta Prohm and Banteay Kdei, and is thought to have been built in homage to Jayavarman's father. The site plan is much like Ta Prohm. The temple passage has lots of meandering galleries and side rooms with statues (most broken or missing) and Shiva Lingum. Many Buddha reliefs here have been chiseled off. Interior walls are lined with cross-legged, bearded forest hermits in relief. The central tower is a stupa for ashes of a later king, dating from the 16th century and replacing a large Buddha statue of Jayavarman VII that was found by the French in 1943, and then summarily lost. One side room has a headless Buddha perfect for that canned "Put your head on the seated Buddha" photo. The many empty pedestals and lintels are courtesy of the Khmer Rouge and many tomb raiders.

Enter the temple from the west, and then make the long and winding walk along the central axis, exiting through the east gate where you see a massive Spoong tree (like a Banyan tree). From here, make your way back to the west entrance and your transport.

Ta Prohm ★★★   The jungle foliage still has its hold on this dynamic temple, which was left in a ruinous state when early archaeologists freed the temples from the jungle. Ta Prohm is a favorite for many; in fact, those very ruinous vines appeal to most. As large around as oak trees, the Khmer Spoong tree is something like a banyan tree, and it's often encased in the wandering tendrils of the *charay*, a thick vine. The powerful Spoong and the charay vines cleave massive stones in two or give way and grow over the top of temple ramparts. It's quite dynamic, and there are a few popular photo spots where the collision of temple and vine are most impressive. Sadly, Ta Prohm was looted quite heavily in recent years, and many of its stone reliquaries are lost. The temple was built in 1186 by Jayavarman VII as a monastery dedicated to the king's mother and spiritual teacher. There are 39 towers connected by numerous galleries. The exterior wall of the compound is 1,000m × 700m (3,281 ft. × 2,297 ft.), and entrance gates have the classic Jayavarman face. Most visitors enter from the west gate—some drivers will pick you up on the other side. A line of small open-air eateries, just outside the main entrance to Ta Prohm, is a popular place for a snack or lunch.

Ta Kaeo ★   What's most interesting about Ta Kaeo is that it was never completed. Legend has it that the temple was struck by lightning during its construction, and all work was abandoned at a stage where the main structure was complete, but no adornment had been added; as such, it serves as "Temple Structure 101." Also unique is the fact that Ta Kaeo is made of a rich green sandstone (elsewhere it's a deeper brown or grayish color). Built in the 10th century by Jayavarman V, the temple was dedicated to Shiva. The central prang once housed a lingum, and the three levels are all encircled by sandstone galleries. The climb to the top is very steep, a bit of "four-points" rock climbing, really, but the view is well worth it. Few visitors bother with this temple, so it's a good place to escape the throngs of tourists.

Banteay Kdei   The first temple built by Jayavarman VII in 1181, Banteay Kdei is just opposite the large **Sra Serang Reservoir,** a lovely lily pond that is 300×700m (984×2,296 ft.) and surrounded by sandstone steps of Khmer Vintage; the reservoir is a popular place to watch the sunset gleaming off the water's surface. Sra Serang once housed a small island temple where the king liked to meditate, and now local folks bathe here or steer the water to local rice farms. The four gates of Banteay Kdei have Jayavarman's iconic smiling face, like those at the famed Bayon. The east entrance brings you past an area lined with lions and nagas along an open terrace once used for performances. There's a moat around the second interior gate. The Buddha at the entrance is an original, intact statue, quite unique to the Angkor compound where so many pieces have been stolen or destroyed (beheaded).

Some portions of the main interior temple area are held together with strong rope and cable. Look for a small offering house with columns just inside on the right used to gain merit through gift-giving. Also watch for the refined Apsara carvings on the main temple. Exit via the west gate—look for more Jayavarman heads—and walk the verdant fields around the side of the temple back to the east gate and your wheels, or take a short walk, through a gauntlet of young hawkers, to the Sra Serang Reservoir.

Attractions Farther Afield

Banteay Srei ★★   True temple buffs won't want to miss this distinct complex. Some 32km (20 miles) north of the main temples, the 10th-century buildings of

Banteay Srei are done in a style unique to the high spires of Angkor. The collection of low walls surrounds low-rise peaked structures of deep red sandstone. It is the only building to have been built with pink sandstone, a high-quality mineral that can withstand tougher elements. As such, the carvings and bas-reliefs on this temple are some of the most intricate, best-preserved carvings you'll find in Angkor. Translated as "The Citadel of Women," it has relief carvings on the squat central buildings and intricate tellings of ancient Hindu tales. Walking through the temple, there's a real feeling of "work in progress." Some of the doorways flanking the central pathway were originally framed in wood and have weakened with age. As such, the sandstone pediments that once stood on top crashed to the ground and broke into large pieces. They've since been reassembled and lie at the foot of the doorways like some ancient jigsaw puzzle. After the first gate and walkway, you'll come to a small entranceway that has a square pedestal with a round piece in the middle that used to hold a linga (it was stolen some years ago). Look at the frame of the square. It isn't smooth and straight, as you would expect, but completely warped and oddly worn away. The Khmer Rouge used to sharpen their knives here. The hallmarks of the temple are the three temples. The middle one is dedicated to Shiva and is flanked by temples honoring Vishnu and Brahma. I highly recommend you go with a guide who can explain the finer details of temple inscriptions. Be prepared to join a crush of other visitors, as it's crowded from dawn till dusk, and also steel yourself to pass the gauntlet of pushy vendors who assail you as you are forced to leave through a cluster of souvenir shops.

Beng Melea ★★   Truly the aficionado's temple, Beng Melea is where to go if the Angkor temples seem tame, if you are longing to go "Tomb Raider" and clamber around the crumbling stones of an undiscovered temple that has been claimed back by the jungle. Squint or use your imagination, and you can feel like Indiana Jones. The kids will love it. Beng Melea is 60km (37 miles) east of Siem Reap and often arranged as a day trip after a stop at the Roluos Group. If you go by motorbike—good luck—wear a *Krama* or a good mask, as the route can be dusty. The temple has three gallery walls and a moat entry. No one has ever found the Sanskrit inscription on the temple, but Angkor Wat's builder, Suryavarman, supposedly put it up in the 12th century. The interior temple area is a big, fun pile of rubble, great for trouncing around. The area has just been cleared of mines, and the temple, long a secret enclave for temple buffs, is now attracting more visitors. The east entrance is closed because of the many rocks fallen here, but enter just to the right of this main entrance and follow a wooden walkway that allows access to much of the site. Look out for the relief images of the god of fire over the first door as you approach the gallery, and then an image of a three-headed elephant born of the mythical churning-of-the-ocean-of-milk Hindu creation legend. A small library is inside this first gallery area. The raised walkway takes you around what remains of the site, including the pile of massive stones that was once the central temple. Everywhere, strangling fig trees grasp the remaining walls in a fierce embrace, making for dramatic images, and carvings of upside-down apsaras protrude from the rubble. You are free to clamber around the rest of the site, but do so at your own risk. Be particularly careful after rain, when the rocks can be slippery. Get here as early as you can, and you'll have the place to yourself. The ride is 1 hour by car at a cost of about $50 with a driver, and about 1½ hours by motorbike, about $30 with a driver. North of Beng Melea is **Koh Ker,** another popular off-the-map temple.

Kabal Spean ★★ 🏕　Known as the "River of a Thousand Linga" (a *linga* is a phallic symbol representing the Hindu god Shiva), Kabal Spean lay undiscovered by Westerners until a French researcher stumbled across it recently. Dating from the early 11th century, the relief carvings that line the streambeds are said to purify the water before it fills the reservoirs (called *barays*) of Angkor. It's the journey here that's really interesting—through rural villages north of Banteay Srei—and there's a fun forest hike of 1.5km (1 mile), clambering over tree roots and boulders, to reach the site. There's something spell-binding about these carvings in a natural, rather than temple, context, and guides will point out carvings of crocodiles and frogs that are not immediately obvious. The place is more impressive during the rainy season, when many carvings are submerged but still visible, though it's an amazing spot to visit at any time.

5km (3 miles) north of Banteay Srei. Admission $3.

Land Mines Museum　You won't find signs leading you to this seemingly impromptu museum; Cambodian officials prefer their own rhetoric to that of the owner and curator, Mr. Akira. The museum itself is just a corrugated-roof area stacked high with disarmed ordinance and detailed data about the use, effects, and statistics about UXO (unexploded ordnance) in the country. Most interesting is the small grove out back, an exhibit of how mines are placed in a real jungle setting. The museum is a call to action for demining in the country. Resist any temptation to volunteer (unless properly trained), but you're sure to have a chance to chat with Mr. Akira, peruse his recent book on the subject, and sign a petition (he's hoping to achieve NGO status).

On the main road to the temples, just before the checkpoint and a few clicks east. Go by motorbike or taxi. www.cambodialandminemuseum.org. Admission $1. Daily 7am–5pm.

Roluos Group　About 13km (8 miles) east of the town center, these three are best viewed in context of Angkor architecture's progression, as the forefathers of the more dynamic of Angkor's main temples. A visit to these temples is included in the temple ticket but will cost you a bit extra for transport.

Tonle Sap Lake　Day trips on the Tonle Sap Lake fall into two categories, so be careful what you're signing up for. First, avoid the 1½-hour tours out of the boat ferry jetty, Chon Khneas. These trips sound like fun, and for just $15 per boat or $10 per person, you can go with a driver and guide out onto the Tonle Sap. You do glimpse a bit of river life, the net-twirling fishermen, floating schools donated by Korean NGOs, and the commercial boat traffic on the Tonle Sap's main inlet, but once out on the water of the lake, you get a quick ride among ethnic Vietnamese, Khmer houseboats, and fisherman; then stop at a large tourist-trap barge with crocodile pits, small fish farms, and perhaps an aquarium with some sickly looking turtles, snakes, and fish choking on dirty water. It's all about the $1 Coke or souvenirs you might buy. Not worth the trip, so be sure to avoid rides to just Chong Khneas. The only exception to this is the fine upmarket evening cruises along this same route through the company **Terre Cambodge** (see below). The cost is $20 per person and doesn't include the fine cocktails you might enjoy while watching the sun dip into the cool lake.

　　The best day trips are one of the full-day options that take you to far-flung floating villages such as **Kampong Phluk** in canoes among low mangrove or to a lush bird sanctuary, called **Preak Toal.** Following these routes with the larger tour operators comes with a hefty price tag for Cambodia, from $80 or so per day, but it's worth it.

Contact **Terre Cambodge** (www.terrecambodge.com), **Beyond** (www.beyond uniqueescapes.com), or talk with your hotel's tour desk. All services are consolidated through the same providers, so you get the same trip wherever you buy it. Be sure and specify the exact sights you want to see and any inclusions you'd like, such as lunch. One unique find is the folks at **OSMOSE** (www.osmosetonlesap.org), whose main focus is conservation but who run fine tours as well.

These trips are best in rainy season because the mangrove swamps are dried up at other times. The birds at the bird sanctuary are best viewed from December to April. The Tonle Sap basin is lush and green when the water recedes in the dry season, but the water is so low that getting around on the lake, which drops from 12m (39 ft.) down to 4m (13 ft.) in depth—a third of its rainy season size—is quite difficult.

If you're connecting onward with Siem Reap or Battambang by boat, you'll get a glimpse of life along the aquatic byways of Cambodia. The road heading south to the lake follows the Siem Reap River and gives you a glimpse into communities of precarious stilt houses that look ready to totter any second and farmers herding groups of domesticated ducks along canals. To get to the boat, you follow a long dirt causeway lined with shanty houses and elbow among trucks overloaded with minnows and small fish caught in the lake, squishing and leaking and bouncing precariously. Out on the open water on the speedboat to or from Phnom Penh, it's just hot sun and blue water—not especially picturesque, but fun when the water is high in the rainy season.

In Siem Reap Town

Angkor National Museum   This museum beckons visitors from the main road to the temples. It houses an impressive collection of artifacts from Angkor, many of which are on loan from the National Museum and the Conservation d'Angkor, a treasure trove that was heretofore closed to the public. Highlights include a room displaying 1,000 Buddhas, and an Angkor Wat exhibition with a model of the famed temple. It's a good place to see carvings and statue details up close and with decent explanations on hand; audio guides are available for an extra $3. It's an excellent introduction to a temple visit if you know nothing about Angkor; otherwise, your time and money are better spent at the temples.

968 Vithei Charles de Gaulle, Khrum 6. ✆ **063/966-601.** www.angkornationalmuseum.com. Admission $12. Daily 8:30am–6:30pm.

Shopping

Shopping in the Angkor temple town has boomed, and new boutiques pop up daily. The old standbys, such as the market and smaller boutiques, are also benefiting from increased numbers of tourists and expats.

You can find good **reproductions of temple statuary** anywhere in town, but it's a pretty cumbersome buy unless Siem Reap is your last stop before, say, Bangkok and a flight home. **Rubbings** of temple bas-relief can be found anywhere and are easily transported, best in a light poster tube. Original artwork and photography are available at every turn. Silk hangings and clothing are on sale in many boutiques, but "buyer beware" of price and quality before making a big investment. The vendors below are the best of many, and the Old Market area, where most are concentrated, is within easy walking distance.

Because you are likely to spend most of your days marveling at the temples, the **Night Market,** located just northwest of the Old Market and opening at around 6pm, is an ideal spot to pick up all your souvenirs, with hundreds of stalls that sell an amazing array of items lining a maze of alleyways. Just in case you arrive early, the **Noon Night Market** is situated at the entrance to the Night Market, so you needn't walk away empty-handed. For something a bit classier, don't miss the chic FCC compound and its upmarket shops and galleries.

Large, mall-style souvenir venues line the road just north of town on the way to the temples and are a good stop for the obligatory collector's spoon or plastic replica of the temples, but are mostly set up for bus tours.

You'll find lots of small **convenience stores** in and around town. Star Mart is a familiar convenience store open 24 hours (on the airport road), though just one among many. It's not a bad idea to stock up on a few snacks before a day of temple touring.

Artisans d'Angkor The artisans here are all disadvantaged youth who have been trained in the crafts of stone carving, silk weaving, and lacquerware. The work is of exceptional quality, so it's worth dropping by to pick up a treasured memento of your stay. There are other branches at Angkor Café by the temples (p. 407) and at the airport. American Express, MasterCard, and Visa accepted. Open daily 7:30am to 6:30pm. Stung Thmey St. (west of the Old Market) ⒞ **063/963-330.** www.artisansdangkor.com.

Colors of Cambodia A project set up to fund Cambodian schools, this shop sells framed artwork of young Khmer kids who visit the temples or depict their daily life in Technicolor crayon. Some of the work is quite expressive, and a purchase here certainly goes a long way to helping out. No credit cards are accepted. Open daily from 8am to 7pm. House No. 270, Mudull 1 Village (northwest side of the Old Market). ⒞ **063/965-021.** colorsofcambodia@yahoo.com.

John McDermott Photography Just next door to the FCC, American John McDermott displays his stunning silver gelatin prints, some very classic images of the temple, in a cool, tiled contemporary space. The gallery is inspiring for more amateur photographers shutter-bugging at the temples, and these fine prints make great gifts. Small postcards are available for $2, larger reproductions just $35, and poster-size prints start at $300. Due to popularity, a beautiful two-story second gallery has opened in the heart of the Old Market. The second floor features exhibitions by other artists. MasterCard and Visa are accepted. Another branch is on the Passage, near the Old Market (& 012/274-274; www.mcdermottgallery.com). Both open daily from 10am to 10pm. On the north end of the FCC compound on Pokambor Ave. ⒞ **012/615-695.**

Monument Books An expansion of the popular Phnom Penh outlet, Monument Books carries the best in new volumes about the temples, from coffee-table tomes to guidebooks and histories, as well as international newspapers. Open daily 8am to 8pm. Inside Lucky Mall on Sivutha Blvd.

Psar Leu, the New Market Recently rebuilt, the New Market is distinct from the old in that it caters to local tastes, so it's not the place to hunt for souvenirs, but a great place to witness everyday Cambodian life. This makes it good for a wander and for taking some photos. Open daily from dawn to dusk. On Rte. 6 west of the town center.

Psar Chas, the Old Market The very heart of tourist Siem Reap, this is the best place to find Buddhist trinkets and souvenirs such as T-shirts, as well as good books on the temples. The market is a fun wander, and friendly folks here are used to foreign visitors, so you can easily haggle in English (or by passing a calculator back and forth to display your offer on an item). The many food stalls on the north end of the market are a good way to sample local cuisine for next to nothing. Most businesses in town give their address in relation to the Old Market, so it's a good place to know for orientation purposes. Open daily from dawn to dusk. Riverside in the south end of town.

Rajana Rajana is an NGO-based souvenir and handicraft shop producing fair-trade products using traditional Cambodian skills with contemporary design. Items on sale include silk paintings, silver jewelry, bamboo crafts, as well as local coffees and condiments. American Express, MasterCard, and Visa accepted. Open Monday to Saturday 9am to 9pm. 153 Sivutha Blvd (just north of the Night Market). ☏ **012/481-894.**

Senteurs d'Angkor Carrying good contemporary Khmer arts and crafts, statuary copied from Angkor's greats (a good place to pick up that Jayavarman VII bust), traditional leather shadow puppets, silver jewelry, Khmer silks, *Kramas* (Khmer scarves), traditional local spices (pepper and lemon grass), potpourri, local teas, rice brandy, and fragrant handmade soaps, Senteurs d'Angkor is a good stop to satiate your shopping appetite before a flight back home. Great souvenirs at reasonable prices. Open daily 7am to 9:30pm. No. 275 Psaa Chas, cater-cornered to the northeast end of the busy Old Market. ☏ **063/964-801** or 012/954-815.

Spas & Massage

After a day of scrambling, sweating, and climbing the temples, there's nothing like a bit of pampering to round things out, and with the tidal-wave rise in tourism in Siem Reap, all kinds of services are popping up. On the high end of the scale, contact the **Sofitel Hotel** (on the way to the temples on Vithei Charles de Gaulle; ☏ 063/964-600), the **Raffles Grand Hotel d'Angkor** (at the very town center; ☏ 063/963-888), or the **Angkor Palace** (☏ 063/760-511).

In town, try **Visaya Spa** at the plush FCC complex (Pokambor Ave. just north of the post office; ☏ 063/760-280), which has three stylish treatment rooms and a roster of high-end services, including body scrubs, wraps, facials, aqua therapy, and massages, all at high prices for this part of the world (a 90-min. massage is $65) but worth it. Contact them to make a reservation, or just stop in. Open daily from 10am to 10pm.

Frangipani, 616–617 Hup Guan St. in the area north of the Old Market, offers a fine roster of treatments, from facials and aromatherapy to oil massage and traditional massage. A good little find with a professional staff offering services starting at just $25 per hour for a traditional massage. For booking, call ☏ **012/982-062.**

Bodia Spa, at the eastern end of Bar Street above U-Care pharmacy (entrance is in the adjacent narrow lane; ☏ 063/761-593), is a stylish place offering a range of treatments, such as a 1-hour head and shoulder massage for $24, or an "Apsara Indulgence," which lasts 90 minutes and costs $55.

On the lower end of the scale, where you can expect to pay as little as $6 for an hour massage, try any of the small storefronts on Sivutha Boulevard just north of the Old Market, in the popular tourist area. Around here, and especially in the Night Market, you'll find plenty of places offering the novel attraction known as **fish spa.** This involves dangling your feet in a tank while schools of tiny fish nibble at your feet, cleaning off the dead skin. It's certainly a different experience but can be very ticklish. For good Khmer massage, similar to Thai massage, try **Islands Traditional Khmer**

Massage (north of Psar Chas; © 012/757-120). It's a little more expensive than most other places ($8 per hour), but the service is reliable. The most affordable massage in town, and a great way to support local enterprise, is at one of the many massage schools for the blind. Trained by international volunteers, blind masseuses—who in Khmer society might have little other chance in life than to rattle a cup or string flowers onto leis as temple offerings—are able to make a comfortable living. One convenient and very professional location is **Seeing Hands IV** (© 012/286-316), on central Sivutha near the Tell Restaurant and the Dead Fish Tower bar. Trained by Japanese and endorsed by Aus Aid and the Blind Care Foundation, masseuses are professional, and for only $5, you can't go wrong. Most folks tip heavily here and come away with a unique connection. Call or just stop in.

Siem Reap After Dark

Siem Reap is a town where most visitors are up with the sun and out visiting the temple sites, but there are a few good evening options.

Apsara dance is an ancient art in Cambodia. Dancers in traditional gilded costumes practice their slow art: elegant contortions of a dancer's wrists. Contact the folks at the **Angkor Village Hotel** (© 063/963-561) to make reservations for the nightly show, combined with a fine set Khmer menu in the traditional indoor banquet-house theater. Dinner begins at 8pm, and the show starts at 8:30pm (tickets cost $25).

The **Raffles Grand Hotel d'Angkor** has a similar show, though this one includes dances illustrating other aspects of Khmer culture, staged in a pavilion behind the swimming pool (around $40, including a buffet dinner). Times and performances vary, so be sure to call © 063/963-888 in advance. Most hotels have a performance space, and many small restaurants have shows of varying quality.

Okay, admittedly, this one is pretty kitschy, but the kids might like it: **Cambodia Cultural Center,** far west of Siem Reap on the airport road (Svay Dongkum; © 063/963-836), holds a host of shows and all-day events, including a mock Khmer wedding and Apsara dance. Call for current offerings, as the program varies. If you don't like the performance, you can walk the grounds, set around a large central pond, spend some time in Cambodia's only wax museum, walk among all of Cambodia's sights done in miniature, or visit various exhibits of village life and rural skill. You can even get around in an electric car. This one's most popular with Asian tour groups.

Dr. Beat (Beatocello) Richner plays the works of Bach and some of his own comic pieces between stories and vignettes about his work as director of the **Kantha Bopha Foundation,** a humanitarian hospital just north of the town center. Admission is free, but donations are accepted in support of their valiant efforts to serve a steady stream of destitute patients, mostly children, who suffer from treatable diseases such as tuberculosis. Dr. Richner is as passionate about his music as he is about his cause. You're in for an enjoyable, informative evening. Performances are every Saturday at 7:15pm just north of the town center on the road to the temples.

BARS & CLUBS

There are a few popular bars near the Old Market in Siem Reap. Below are just a few. Most nightlife centers on what has become the de facto "Bar Street" in the center of the Old Market area, where lots of hip little spots hop into the late evening (usually till 2am and sometimes later). It's a great place to swap tales of temple touring and meet up with other travelers.

The **Angkor What?** (Pub St., 1 block west of the Old Market) was the first—and still the most popular—bar here, more or less where it's at in Siem Reap. Sign your name on the wall and say "Hi" to all the folks you met that day at the temples or on highways and byways elsewhere. **Easy Speaking Café and Pub,** next to the busy Angkor What?, handles the spillover, as does **Temple Club,** right opposite.

Laundry (© 016/962-026) is the funky side of Siem Reap. When the temple town gets psychedelic and stays up really late, this is where it happens. On a side street to the north of the Old Market, it's open nightly but usually hosts special events that you'll see promoted all around town.

Linga (North of Old Market; © 012/246-912) is a gay bar that attracts a decent mixed crowd to a corner location overlooking the small side street and the traffic on Mundul 1 Village St. The walls have psychedelic paintings of Buddhist monks.

Molly Malone's, Bar Street, across the street and west of Red Piano Bar (© 063/963-533), is one of the hippest pubs in town, though it also functions as a steakhouse. They've got local expats playing live music some nights, a mix of original songs and covers of crowd-pleasers like old Beatles and Roberta Flack numbers. The bar is fully stocked with a fine selection of Irish whiskey, and they've got a good stock of imported beer.

If you're looking for a stylish spot to chill out, check out the **Art Lounge** at the Hotel de la Paix on Sivutha Boulevard (© 063/966-000), where you'll find huge daybeds for lounging, a good range of cocktails, and probably an art exhibition. Another laid-back place is **Nest** (p. 404), one of Siem Reap's hippest new nightspots, offering gourmet food, wine, and cocktails in a futuristic setting.

BATTAMBANG

180km (112 miles) from Siem Reap; 290km (180 miles) from Phnom Penh; 150km (93 miles) from Poipet

The west of Cambodia is made for the hearty traveler, a place to get off the track if you have the gumption. The far west, areas such as the southwestern Cardamom Mountains and the northern border region with Thailand, are virtually off-limits to all but the most hearty vehicles, but Battambang is quite accessible and boasts a few interesting sights, offering a glimpse into the daily rhythms of rural Cambodia.

Travel west of Siem Reap means bumpy, dusty roads, best in a rented taxi (cheap to share). Where once it was just dusty pickup trucks along a pitted track notorious for banditry, the road east of Siem Reap to Phnom Penh, National Highway 5, is wide and paved, and means just a few hours of air-con cruising before you make the capital.

Poipet, the border town where most overland travelers enter or exit Cambodia with Thailand, is just a collection of dodgy casinos and persistent touts circling like hawks over the cattle-chute of tourists who pass through this bottleneck daily (see the "Border Hassles: Thailand to Cambodia Overland" box at the beginning of this chapter). Avoid Poipet at all costs, or just fly through on your way to or from Cambodia.

From Sisophon, to the west of central Tonle Sap Lake, the road splits; National Highway 6 connects with Siem Reap and National Highway 5 goes south to Battambang, both roads reconnecting a few hundred miles away in Phnom Penh.

After visiting the temples of Angkor, you can connect with Battambang by boat or bus, and from there carry on to Phnom Penh, via Pursat, or directly to the Thai border via Sisophon. It is some beautiful countryside, in places a flat plain dotted with palms and cattle grazing what appears to be sand; in others, especially near Battambang, it is lush and green, a bread basket of Cambodia.

Second only to Phnom Penh in size, little Battambang is third in per-capita income, eclipsed by the rising star of Siem Reap. Over the centuries, the town switched hands between Thailand and Cambodia, and was under Thai control as late as the 1940s. The people of Battambang did resist the initial coup d'état of the Khmer Rouge in the late 1970s but succumbed under heavy fighting, and the area became a Khmer Rouge stronghold.

Battambang sits on the west bank of the Sangker River, which connects with the Tonle Sap; irregular boats carry tourists along this picturesque route (best to avoid in the dry season, though). The city is also the heart of one of the country's most productive farmlands, and the surrounding area is lush with growth. Fields of mango, papaya, jackfruit, and milky fruit, as well as peanuts, corn, and green beans, are well irrigated (note the long green hoses connecting fields), and a tour out into the countryside by car or motorbike is what is really on offer here. Battambang also has a strong colonial history, evident in the town's many French-style villas and storefronts, and there's a certain cozy ease to this riverside burg.

At the traffic circle on the eastern end of the city, find a large statue of Ta Dumbong, the legendary Khmer King who founded order and security in the town and surrounding area with what is the town's namesake, a *Bat Dambang,* or a "Disappearing Stick."

Important warning: Battambang was heavily mined during Cambodia's late troubles, and many of the NGO folks you'll meet out this way are here in support of teams that do the very dangerous jobs of removing land mines from rural areas. As such, do not venture too far afield in the countryside, at least not by yourself, and stick to well-worn paths wherever possible.

Essentials
GETTING THERE
Though government sources are projecting an air connection to Battambang, at press time, flights weren't going there. The nearest air connection is at Siem Reap.

BY BUS   Daily air-conditioned tourist buses connect Battambang with Siem Reap, east to Phnom Penh via Pursat, or west to Poipet and the Thai border area via Sisophon. All buses leave between 6 and 8am. Bus companies are near the Psah Boeung Choeuk on the east end of Battambang, and most buses arrive near there. Contact **Capitol Tour** offices in Phnom Penh (14AE0 Road 182, Sngkat Beng Prolitt; ✆ 023/217-627), or near the Psah Boeung Choeuk in Battambang. **Neak Krorhorm Travel and Tour** (in Phnom Penh, ✆ 023/219-496; in Siem Reap near the Old Market, ✆ 063/964-924; or in Poipet, ✆ 012/970-067; neaktour@yahoo. com) also has regular buses and an office near the market in Battambang (✆ 053/953-838). You can book bus tickets at your hotel's front desk. It's $4 between Siem Reap and Battambang, and $5 between Battambang and Phnom Penh.

BY RENTED TAXI OR MINIVAN   You can commandeer a Toyota Camry or a Japanese or Korean minivan just about anywhere in Cambodia; it's just a question of ponying up a big fee for one-way use. Expect to pay $40 to $50 for a car from Siem Reap to Battambang, for example, but more common routes, from the Thai border to Siem Reap or from Phnom Penh to Kampot or Sihanoukville in the south, come at reasonable rates of about $20 to $25 for a 3- or 4-hour ride. All-day car rentals at Angkor or for day trips from certain areas start at around $30 per day. If you're looking to keep your costs low, you can usually find other travelers looking to share expenses;

just pop in at a cafe or a bar and meet a possible travel companion. Contact your hotel front desk or any tour agent in Siem Reap or Phnom Penh to make arrangements.

BY BOAT   Boat connection between Battambang and Siem Reap makes for a pleasant morning when the water is high but should be avoided in dry season, when the trip must be completed in a bone-shaking pick-up across bumpy fields. Boats are becoming less regular these days as most people make this trip by bus or taxi. Starting at the ferry docking area on the Tonle Sap nearest Siem Reap, boats depart in the early morning, from 7am, and the 6-hour trip (8–9 hr. when navigating narrow canals in the dry season) costs $20 to $25. Book a boat ride through your guesthouse or a tour company such as Capitol Tour or Neak Krorhorm Travel (see above).

ORIENTATION

The town lies on the north side of the Sangker River. A new bridge connects National Rte. 5 with the south bank of the river, and a smaller iron bridge, built by the French, crosses at the center of town. On the south bank, at the intersection of Route 5 and the airport road, you can see a statue of the town's founder holding the stick that is the town namesake. Hotels and services are clustered at the town center. Bus company offices are in the east of town near the Psah Boeung Choeuk. Nearby Psah Nath is another large market good for a wander.

GETTING AROUND

You can walk around the town center, but for sights farther afield, hiring a motorbike taxi driver, or *motodup,* is the easiest and most affordable way; the downside is that, short of the highways, Route 5 from Sisophon and Route 10 going to Pailin, roads are very dusty. If you do take a motorbike, be sure to bring a scarf or a Khmer-style *Krama,* or ask the driver to stop at a streetside stall for a cheap facemask. Find drivers in front of the main hotels; try to find someone who can speak a bit of English, as you'll be together for a long day. Most of the younger drivers are well informed about the area's temples and flora and fauna, and are eager to practice their English. Expect to pay about $12 per day for transport. All-day rentals of a Toyota Camry start at $30. Contact any hotel front desk.

FAST FACTS   The Thai baht is accepted widely, and at a rate better than you'll get in Siem Reap (usually about 30B for $1). ANZ Royal, Canadia Bank, and UCB are located in front of Phsar Nath (the main market), and all have ATMs.

Where to Stay & Eat

Among Battambang's dining options, the popular **White Rose,** House No. 102/8 on Street No. 2 (in the very heart of town, just 1 block from the river; ✆ **012/536-500**), is a worthy find and makes good use of the surrounding countryside's abundant produce. Serving good, authentic Khmer and a laundry list of Chinese-style stir-fries, Thai soups and treats, and some Western cuisine, the White Rose is the most popular choice among humanitarian workers visiting Battambang. Prices are from $2 to $3. On Street No. 3, just a block north of White Rose, **Gecko Café** (✆ **017/712-428;** www.geckocafecambodia.com) serves pizzas, burritos, and a good range of drinks on the balcony of an old colonial house. On the east side of the river, **La Villa** (✆ **053/730-151**) is the upscale choice for Western dining in town, also offering reliable Asian food.

Bambu ★ 👜   This smart new hotel is an oasis of calm on the east side of the river and just a couple of minutes from the town center. The 16 rooms are spread through four traditional-style buildings, and there's a great saltwater swimming pool in the grounds, too. Rooms are well equipped, with flatscreen TVs, DVD layers, Wi-Fi, and iPod docks. There's also a good restaurant and bar here in case you're too lazy to make the short journey into town.

Phum Romchek 5, Sangkat Rattanak, KO St., Battambang. www.bambuhotel.com. ✆ **053/953-900.** 16 units. $80–$95 double; $110 suite. MC, V. **Amenities:** Restaurant; bar; saltwater pool; room service. *In room:* A/C, TV, DVD player, minibar, MP3 docking station, Wi-Fi.

La Villa ★   This is the best option in Battambang, and most people know it, so make sure to book ahead. The charming hotel is set in a 1930s colonial house done in sunny yellow with white shutters over arched windows. Rooms are spacious and come with gorgeous Art Deco tile and four-poster beds. Suites come with balconies or terraces overlooking the river. Tall guests should stay on the first floor, as second-floor rooms come with sloping ceilings that are charming only when you aren't accidentally bashing your head on them. Bathrooms are large and modern; some come with awkward, though sizable, tubs.

N 185 Pom Romchek 5 Kom Rattanak Srok, Battambang. www.lavilla-battambang.net. ✆/fax **053/730-151.** 7 units. $60 double; $85 suite. MC, V. **Amenities:** Restaurant; bar; Internet; pool. *In room:* A/C, TV/DVD, fridge (suites only), hair dryer (suites only), minibar (suites only).

Attractions

A wander among Battambang's classic crumbly colonials, all of which are colored a deep yellowish tan that lights up in the morning and evening, makes for nice city walking. A few Buddhist temples are scattered around town, and south of the city is the large statue of a kneeling **Ta Dambong,** the legendary founder of peace and stability in the region, holding the "Disappearing Stick" from which Battambang gets its name.

The real sights in this area are the rural temples and beautiful countryside. A 1-day trip can get you to all of them, and as much fun are the rural stops in between: a visit to a farmer's field, perhaps, or to roadside juice stands. A trip to Wat Phnom Sampeou and Wat Banang is a good circuit, beginning at Route 10 on the west end of town and then returning along the river. For $5, most motorbike drivers will try to talk you into a trip back on a small metal-and-bamboo, motor-driven platform that sits on top of the train tracks, a common form of transport now that train services have been terminated. A visit to Wat Phnom Ek is an additional trip in the other direction.

Just a short 8km (5-mile) drive from Wat Phnom Sampeou (see below) and included in most day trips out of Battambang, the Angkor-era ruins of **Wat Banang** (admission $2) are nothing in comparison with the stunning temples of Angkor, of course, but for temple buffs or burgeoning archaeologists, Wat Banang's five Angkor-style towers, which predate the penultimate Angkor era, are a unique insight into the development of building styles. Reached by a long, steep staircase of 358 laterite steps, the temples themselves are hewn in rough laterite, with some of the original sandstone facing and Apsara decorations, many with the faces chipped off during one of Angkor's iconoclastic revolutions, still intact. Views from the top are lovely.

Wat Ek Phnom (admission $2), on the north end of town, is another pre-Angkorian ruin. The hilltop temple of Wat Ek Phnom is, like Wat Banang above, in relatively good condition, with some carving intact.

Wat Phnom Sampeou A 2002 reconstruction of a Buddhist temple built in 1964, Wat Phnom Sampeou is a dynamic little hilltop temple, its towers jutting out of the top of a steep hill, one of the only high points in a wide, flat plain. The temple is best known as Battambang's "Killing Fields," like Choeung Ek outside of Phnom Penh, where thousands of concentration-camp victims of the Khmer Rouge were killed. At Sampeou, victims were slaughtered and thrown into deep caves, two of which now house small temples and monuments. A visit here follows a circuit, first to the caves and a small temple that was once the prison building of the concentration camp here, and then to the nearby hilltop temple. The temple itself is not incredibly interesting—just a few spires and some shaded meditation areas and statuary—but the views across the plain are stunning and the monks are quite friendly and talkative. The path then leads back down a steep path to the entrance.

When you arrive at the base, you'll be swarmed by a group of young guides. For just $1, one of the lads can take you the easy way up the hill and point out the poignant sights, saving you some time scouting around on your own. Most speak just a bit of English but are happy to talk with you and can tell you some details about the temple legend, a very confusing and ambling tale meant to be told over hours and hours about a girl named Rumsay Sok, who was courted by the Khmer king and—through a series of magical events and the intervention of chickens, crocodiles, and a storm at sea—used her magical hair to dry up the valley and create the mountains that represent characters in the legend. Your guide can point out the nearby Crocodile Mountain, as well as a small statue of the magic girl. Watch out for the gangs of macaques that roam around the summit, looking to grab any unattended bags in search of food.

16km (10 miles) from Battambang. Admission $2. Guide hire $1. Daily dawn–dusk.

PLANNING YOUR TRIP TO VIETNAM

Obtaining a visa and buying a ticket are all you need to prepare for a safe and exciting trip to Vietnam. But the information below helps you plan your finances, decide whether to go on your own or by tour, and follow some important health considerations. For the lowdown on taking a side trip to Cambodia, see chapter 14.

GETTING THERE

Getting to Vietnam

BY PLANE

The three international airports in Vietnam are **Tan Son Nhat International (SGN)** in Ho Chi Minh City, **Noi Bai International (HAN)** in Hanoi, and **Danang International (DAT)** in Danang (central Vietnam). Vietnam Airlines has hubs in both Tan Son Nhat and Noi Bai. Most carriers connect to Vietnam's three international airports via **Singapore, Bangkok** (Thailand), **Hong Kong, Taipei** (Taiwan), or **Seoul** (South Korea).

To find out which airlines travel to Vietnam, please see "Airline, Hotel & Car Rental Websites," p. 447.

Getting into Town from the Airport

In Hanoi, taxis queue up just outside the arrivals door and will zip you into town for around 300,000 VND. Taxis to and from Danang's airport will cost 60,000 VND. Down south, a ride into Ho Chi Minh City is around 180,000 VND.

BY CAR

The overland route from Phnom Penh to Ho Chi Minh City is safe and quite accessible. You can arrange transfers with any of the Phnom Penh travel agencies, which makes for a relatively fluid connection between the Cambodian capital and Ho Chi Minh City; the best is budget **Capitol Tours,** No. 14 Road 182, Phnom Penh (ⓒ **023/217-627;** www.capitol tourscambodia.com). *Note:* You must have a prearranged Vietnamese visa when entering Vietnam (visa on arrival is available in the other direction, from Vietnam to Cambodia). Buses leave from the Capitol Tours office in the early morning, arriving in Ho Chi Minh in the midafternoon, depending on the efficiency of the connection.

FROM LAOS

I wouldn't recommend this long overnight road trip from Vientiane or Savannakhet. You're dropped off smack in the center of Vietnam, at Dong Ha Province just north of Hue (makes for a more limited itinerary or backtracking). It's better to fly from Vientiane to Hanoi or Ho Chi Minh City on Vietnam Airlines or Laos Aviation. Note that any connections with the city of Luang Prabang must go through the Laos capital, Vientiane.

BY TRAIN

There is a regular connection between Vietnam and China at Dong Dang, north of Lang Son, which eventually leads to Beijing, though it involves changing trains at Dong Dang. The more popular route from Hanoi via Lao Cai to Kunming in Yunnan Province, China, has not operated in recent years. Note that you need prearranged visas for entrance into China and Vietnam, so be sure to plan ahead if traveling in either direction.

BY BOAT

You can cross to Vietnam by boat from a port near the Cambodian capital of Phnom Penh to Chau Doc, a small Vietnamese border town in the Mekong Delta. Contact budget **Capitol Tours** in Cambodia for connections.

A more luxurious option is the weeklong cruise from Angkor Wat all the way to Saigon on one of the luxury, shallow draft **Pandaw Cruise Boats** (www.pandaw.com). Twin cabins on the vessel start at $2,261 for the 1-week duration (discounts for early-bird bookings).

GETTING AROUND

You'll find good local travel agencies in every tourist stop in Vietnam, all ready to book your plane, bus, and boat tickets or to rent cars. Competition among service providers works to your advantage, and you can find affordable deals for getting around with just a bit of shopping.

BY PLANE

It's a good idea to fly the longer hops along Vietnam's length: from Hanoi to Hue, from Danang to Nha Trang, and from Nha Trang to Ho Chi Minh City (or vice versa). Vietnam Airlines runs the most domestic routes in Vietnam, while budget carriers Air Mekong and Jetstar Pacific offer healthy competition on the tourist routes (namely to-and-fros btw. Hanoi, Ho Chi Minh City, Danang, and Nha Trang).

BY CAR

If you've got the budget for it, renting a car and driver (preferably English-speaking) is the best and safest way to see Vietnam. Self-drive is still not an option in Vietnam except those with a driving license from Vietnam and other ASEAN countries (so you might see a few expat residents driving around). It's probably just as well; there are rules on the road, but to the uninitiated, driving is chaotic.

For car-rental options, see "Visitor Information & Tours," in each destination chapter. Most hotels will rent wheels for day trips at inflated rates; budget hotels and guesthouses offer the best rates. Budget travelers often pitch in for a rented car between sites (from Hue to Nha Trang, for example), where going by private car means you can set your own schedule and stop at places such as Bach Ma National Park, Lang Co Beach, and atop Hai Van Pass.

BY TRAIN

The Reunification Express runs the entire length of Vietnam's coast—from Ho Chi Minh to Hanoi, with routes out of Hanoi to the likes of Sapa, Lang Son, and coastal Haiphong. Riding the length of the country takes nearly 40 hours. The most popular hops are from Hanoi up to Sapa, where special luxury trains with dining cars cover the route, or from Hanoi down the coast to the old capital of Hue, and from there to Danang (less popular) or all the way to Nha Trang and Ho Chi Minh. There are a number of classes, from third-class hard seat to air-conditioned cushioned seat to sleeper, but in general the more comfortable seats are affordable. Be warned that you need to book trains a few days in advance, especially for weekend travel. Popular trips to Sapa are best organized through a tour company (for a small fee) from home or well in advance when on the ground in Vietnam. *Warning:* Along some sections of the Saigon-Hanoi route, kids throw stones at the windows (and passengers) for sport. Conductors know these sections and often ask passengers to lower the metal grille as they pass.

BY BUS

Local buses are either a nightmare or a delight, depending on your expectations. If you're prepared to be the main character in a piece of bad, chaotic performance, then your appetite will be pleased; if you want grist for the travel journal, you will find it; if you want to get somewhere efficiently and with all of your sensory nerve endings intact, you will be disappointed.

Local buses depart from stations usually a good distance from the town center (it usually requires a ride on the back of a motorbike taxi to get there), and station touts are all over you, pulling you this way and that (this is the best piece of "bad performance art"). Buses leave only when full—and "full" means that everyone is uncomfortable, two to a seat, produce hanging, bags under your feet, and bird flu be damned, chickens in bags and on people's laps. Just when you think the bus is completely full, when not one more person could possibly squeeze in, the driver pulls to the side of the road and, like a circus clown car, the bus swallows one more body. All buses honk wildly as they navigate the chaotic traffic of Vietnam's bumpy roads, and all transport travels at a lumbering 50kmph (31 mph).

In the bigger cities and on longer routes, you'll find regular schedules and bus stations with ticket booths and marked prices, but when you're out in countryside, you often have to negotiate a price with the driver or bus tout—a frustrating operation when you just want to catch the @#%! bus. It is a real visceral adventure, and going by local bus is the best way to meet Vietnamese people and learn the local language, but it can be too overwhelming for some.

One good alternative is to buy a ticket with assigned seat on the **small air-conditioned minivans** that ply most major routes in Vietnam (the **Mai Linh Express** is a reliable option). Ask at any hotel front desk, and expect to pay (often) double the local bus price (still very affordable) and ride in relative style among locals but without the hassles.

The **"open tour" ticket** is a convenient way to plan your overland travel all the way up or down the coast of Vietnam; it is a one-way, multistop ticket, and you can catch buses from each town going from Hanoi south, all the way to Ho Chi Minh City, or vice versa. It sounds like a great idea, and folks in the sales offices will regale you with tales of ease and comfort as you explore the length of the Vietnam coast, but don't be fooled: These are rock-bottom budget tours, and though the buses are usually in pretty good shape and have air-conditioning, it can be a pretty unpleasant cattle-herding situation among lots of complaining backpackers. Buses stop only at big tourist-shopping complexes, and you get little interaction with locals. That said, these tour buses are good for short hops between cities, but I try to mix it up, catching the train where possible (especially on long hauls from Hanoi to Hue or Danang to Nha Trang), and even getting together with fellow travelers and hiring your own car for a day along the coast (not much more costly). Don't be taken in by the easy "open tour" ticket, as, for just a few bucks extra, you can buy individual journeys from each town as you head south.

TIPS ON ACCOMMODATIONS

Affordable luxury is the name of the game in Vietnam. For what you'd pay to get a cracker-box room in U.S. and European big cities, you get to go in style in Indochina. Pay more than $100, and you stay like royalty. Budget travelers and young backpackers flock to the region, and a big part of the charm is spending $10 to $20 per night. If your trip is short, live it up: Go for a luxury room, or at least a good midrange option; and take advantage of affordable health, beauty, and spa treatments (for a fraction of what you'd pay elsewhere). Midrange boutique hotels and rustic ecofriendly rural resorts are also a new trend as developers discover that "refurbished" is cool and that location—whether overlooking the Mekong or set in a tropical rainforest—is everything.

Many of the major chains are in the region. **Sheraton** and the **Mövenpick** have hotels in Ho Chi Minh City and Hanoi. **Hilton** has properties in Hanoi, and there's a **Park Hyatt** in Ho Chi Minh City. The French hoteliers at **Accor** host a number of **Sofitel** and **M Gallery** hotels in Vietnam. Many of the big-city properties are aimed at the business market, but in Vietnam, the unique, refurbished **Sofitel Metropole** takes the cake. There are also a number of good individual brands in Vietnam: the likes of **Hotel Nikko** in Hanoi, or the **Rex** and the **Caravelle** in Ho Chi Minh City.

Budget accommodations generally mean the ubiquitous **minihotel.** Quality varies, but these small, several-story hotels usually have air-conditioning, hot water, and cable TV starting at around $15. Some minihotels in Hanoi and Ho Chi Minh are going boutique—a good trend. **Hanoi Moment** in Hanoi is a good bet for a boutique hotel in a good location.

Whatever your financial situation, you will be greeted by high standards with good amenities and services at low cost in Vietnam.

A good way to secure an affordable room is booking through an **on-the-ground tour agent in Vietnam.** Check the "Visitor Information & Tours" sections of specific destination chapters in this book. Travel agents do, of course, tack on a fee for their services, but that's on top of a very low contract rate they have negotiated directly with the hotel. Vietnam-based online hotel booking is a singularly dodgy affair, but many report success with small local consolidators, exemplified by the likes of **www.asia-hotels.com** or **www.vietnamhotels.biz**.

Prices in this book have been categorized as Very Expensive (more than $200), Expensive ($100–$200), Moderate ($50–$100), and Inexpensive (less than $50).

HEALTH & SAFETY

Health concerns should comprise an important piece of your preparation for a trip to Vietnam, and staying healthy on the road takes vigilance. Make it a priority. Tropical heat and mosquitoes are the biggest dangers, other than motor vehicle accidents, and travelers should exercise caution over the extreme change in diet and sanitary standards in Vietnam—especially if eating at local joints. But with just a few pretrip precautions and general prudence, you can enjoy a safe and healthy trip. Consult with a health practitioner or someone specializing in travel health before your trip about inoculations. Stay abreast of international monitors, such as the **U.S. Centers for Disease Control and Prevention** (✆ **800/CDC-INFO** [232-6348]; www.cdc.gov) or the **International Association for Medical Assistance to Travelers** (**IAMAT;** ✆ **716/754-4883,** or 416/652-0137 in Canada; www.iamat.org), for tips on travel and health concerns, as well as the most current information on any outbreaks of infectious diseases in the region.

General Availability of Health Care

The only high-quality health care facilities are located in Hanoi and Ho Chi Minh City (Saigon)—for specific listings, see "Hospitals" below and also in chapters 5 and 12. Hanoi and Ho Chi Minh City each have a branch of the International SOS clinic. Hanoi also supports the Hanoi Family Medical Practice, as well as the Hanoi French Hospital. Your options in rural areas are quite limited, and any major medical issue usually means an uncomfortable transfer to one of these centers or an evacuation to Singapore, Bangkok, or Hong Kong.

In rural areas, the local apothecary shop often acts as a catchall triage for what ails you, and over-the-counter medications are available anywhere from small storefront pharmacists who, with little more than a brief chat and description of a problem (with the use of a phrase book or some creative charades), will dole out affordable prescriptions for anything from antibiotics to sleeping pills. However, there are a lot of fake medicines for sale, and storage conditions may be poor. I would recommend calling

SOS, Family Practice, or your home country's embassy for recommendations of reliable pharmacies.

When you're heading for the boonies, I recommend taking a small kit of medicines that includes antidiarrheal medication, rehydration salts for the almost inevitable bout with diarrhea, antibacterial cream and bandages, and a pain reliever such as ibuprofen or acetaminophen.

Common Ailments
TROPICAL ILLNESSES

Most of the real "baddies" in Vietnam and Cambodia are tropical diseases carried by mosquitoes: the likes of **malaria, dengue fever,** and **Japanese encephalitis.** Quite simply, the best way to avoid mosquito-borne diseases is to avoid being bitten. Repellents that contain between 25% and 50% **DEET** are the most effective. The more gentle alternatives, including oil of eucalyptus (see baby-care products in any pharmacy) provide terrific DEET-free mosquito protection but are not as effective. Picaridin also offers DEET-free protection. It's an excellent repellent, but at 7% concentration, it lasts for a shorter period of time; go for a concentration of around 20%. Also be aware that malaria mosquitoes bite most frequently around dawn and dusk, so exercise caution especially at those hours (wearing long sleeves and long trousers and burning mosquito coils is a good idea). Dengue-fever mosquitoes bite during the day. Always sleep under a mosquito net where needed—and if they are needed, they are usually provided—and make sure it has no holes (or at least patch them up with tape). If you are purchasing your own mosquito net, it is most effective if it has been pretreated with permethrin, which is a very safe insecticide.

MALARIA   Some 250 million people are infected with malaria yearly, with nearly one million deaths, particularly in developing countries. The disease has four strains, including deadly cerebral malaria (common in Africa), but all are life threatening. Malaria is caused by a one-cell parasite transmitted by the female Anopheles mosquito. The parasite travels into the liver, lies dormant, and grows; then symptoms occur when the parasite enters the bloodstream. Symptoms include high fever, painful headaches in the front of the head, nausea, vomiting, dizziness, and confusion. If experiencing any degree of these indicators, seek treatment. Keep in mind that malaria symptoms look like a number of diseases (even just a flu).

Malaria is a concern for travelers in Vietnam. But don't stress out over the bogus information you might hear and read—the kind of stuff that would keep you up all night listening for skeeters or vacationing somewhere else. Arm yourself with correct information, and forget the rest.

First, know that visitors to the major cities and standard coastal tour areas in Vietnam have a very low chance of contracting malaria—very low. Travelers venturing off the track and up into the bush in the Central Highlands or the interior in the central, north, or Mekong Delta will want to take a **malaria prophylaxis.** In farther "off-the-track" border regions near Myanmar, Laos, and Cambodia—areas where a resistance to standard medications has developed—travelers should take Doxycycline.

Your best insurance is to take care when sleeping: Ensure that windows are closed (when you have air-conditioning) and that you have a good mosquito net when needed (typically provided). Also, cover up in Vietnam—wear a long-sleeve shirt and trousers in the evening; this not only keeps the mosquitoes at bay, but modest attire is also the social norm in conservative Vietnam. Put bug spray (preferably with DEET) on exposed areas of the skin, and avoid swampy marshes or heavy jungle at dawn and dusk. Take these precautions—as needed—and all will be well.

However, no antimalarial drug is 100% effective. If you develop fever and chills while traveling or after your return home, seek medical care and tell the provider that you have traveled to a malarious area and need to be checked.

DENGUE FEVER   **Dengue fever** is possible to contract just about anywhere in Southeast Asia. Dengue is a viral infection spread by the Aedes-Aegypti mosquito. Symptoms include headache, high fever, and muscle pain. Unlike malaria and Japanese encephalitis, which survive and spread mostly out in rural areas, dengue knows no bounds and urban outbreaks are common. There is no prophylaxis and no treatment— and some cases are fatal—but with dengue, it is just a matter of suffering it out with cold compresses, fever-reducing pain relievers, and lots of hydration. A real drag.

JAPANESE ENCEPHALITIS   **Japanese encephalitis** is viral, transmitted by mosquitoes, and is endemic to the region—especially after rainy season (July–Aug). Symptoms include headache, fever, nausea, upset stomach, and confusion—all quite similar to malaria and dengue fever. When outbreaks occur, or if traveling widely in rural parts, vaccination is recommended, but note that vaccination is not 100% effective.

HEPATITIS

Another common but preventable ailment in Vietnam is **hepatitis A,** which causes inflammation of the liver. Hepatitis A is contracted from contaminated water or food, and the pathogen of hep A is rather stalwart, staying alive in the air and on the skin for some time. The best preventative is to wash your hands thoroughly before eating and stick to bottled water and food cooked to order (not sitting out). Symptoms include fever, general ill health (nausea and vomiting), lack of appetite, and jaundice.

For anyone over 2 years old traveling in Vietnam, I'd recommend a hepatitis A vaccination. The inoculation requires just one shot and a booster after 6 months.

Hepatitis B is contracted through contact with blood of an infected person (needle, sexual contact, splashed blood, or even sharing a toothbrush or razor—insist on a new razor if you get a haircut and shave). Nurses, for example, are commonly immunized in any country, and the three shots (over a 6-month period) are recommended for a longer stay in the region.

RABIES

Rabies is a fatal viral infection carried by animals. The disease is transmitted by a bite or contact with the saliva of an infected animal. Rabies is a concern in rural Vietnam, among populations of dogs, as well as monkeys and bats. If exposed in any way—a puncture wound of any kind from a suspected animal who exhibits strange behaviors such as foaming at the mouth or ataxia—seek treatment immediately and follow a series of vaccinations over a 1-month period—commonly the Verorab brand. Adventure travelers or health workers who will spend lots of time in the countryside and the bush might just want to consider a **pre-exposure vaccination,** which makes post-exposure treatment far more simple, as it decreases the number of shots required as well as prevents the need for rabies immune globulin, which may not be available and

aids IN VIETNAM

Statistics on AIDS in Vietnam are unreliable because of limited testing, but with increased border crossings from China and rampant prostitution—including, sadly, a great deal of child prostitution—the prognosis is not good. Estimates report that there were about 14,000 AIDS-related deaths in 2009 and about 0.3% of the general population in Vietnam is infected with HIV. However, this proportion can be much higher in commercial sex workers (possibly up to 60%–70% in some areas) and intravenous drug users (possibly up to 60%–80% in some areas).

Unprotected sex with an anonymous partner is very risky behavior. Although condoms are widely available in Vietnam, be aware that certain groups still have very high HIV/AIDS infection rates. International monitors with the U.S.

Centers for Disease Control and Prevention and other agencies are working with the Hanoi government on HIV/AIDS prevention, care, and treatment. An increasing campaign is promoting the use of condoms—you'll see lots of signs with cartoon character condoms smiling and waving from the roadside, needle users underneath skull and crossbones, or a happy young couple embracing, a condom in the young man's hand. These measures appear to be having some success, as the number of HIV cases has leveled out in recent years. But generally speaking, Vietnam's remaining fears of outside influence and continued tight control on information—combined with a certain shame over even talking about issues of sex—are ripe ground for the disease to spread. Time will tell.

thus may require a trip elsewhere for care (for example, Bangkok). Another group at high risk is children. They are more likely to touch or play with stray dogs and are less likely to report a bite.

TYPHOID

A bacterial illness that is transmitted through contaminated food, typhoid is life threatening, especially to children and the elderly, but early detection and a course of antibiotics is usually enough to avoid any serious complications. There are a few different vaccinations available in both oral and injectable forms. Though they are only between 55% and 70% effective, the vaccine is recommended for travelers in the region.

TUBERCULOSIS

As in so many developing countries, tuberculosis is quite common, especially in rural Vietnam. Caused by poor hygiene and unventilated overcrowding, TB is a bacterial infection of the lungs that can spread to other parts of the body and, if left untreated, kill. The vaccination requires a TB screening 6 months prior to inoculation.

SEXUALLY TRANSMITTED DISEASES

Anyone contemplating **sexual activity** in Vietnam should be aware that **HIV,** the virus that causes AIDS, is rampant in many Southeast Asian countries, including

Vietnam. Also concerning are other **sexually transmitted diseases (STDs),** such as gonorrhea, syphilis, herpes, and hepatitis B. A latex condom is recommended second to abstinence. For more information on AIDS, see the box below.

OTHER DISEASES

Other diseases common in the region include schistosomiasis and giardia, both of which are parasitic diseases that can be contracted from swimming in or drinking from stagnant or untreated water in lakes or streams. **Cholera** epidemics sometimes occur in remote areas. Keep an eye on the CDC website or other international health monitors to stay informed of any health hot spots.

Dietary Red Flags

Unless you intend to confine your travels to the big cities and dine only at restaurants that serve Western-style food, you'll likely sample some new cuisine. Initially, this could cause an upset stomach or diarrhea, but it usually lasts just a few days as your body adapts to the change in your diet.

Always drink bottled water (never use tap water for drinking). To be safe, you should even brush your teeth with bottled water. The old adage of "Boil it, cook it, peel it, or forget it" is important to remember in Vietnam. Be sure to peel all fruits and vegetables and avoid raw shellfish and seafood. Also beware of ice unless it is made from purified water. Any suspicious water can be purified by boiling for 10 minutes or treating with purifying tablets. If you're a vegetarian, you will find that Vietnam is a great place to travel; vegetarian dishes abound throughout the region (just say *Toi ahn jai,* which means "I eat vegetarian").

In terms of hygiene, restaurants are generally better options than street stalls. But don't forgo good local cuisine just because it's served from a cart or dining is on squat stools at street side—this is where you'll find some of the best food in Vietnam, as well as the highest likelihood of a stomach cootie. It is acceptable—in fact, customary—to wipe down utensils in restaurants, and in some places locals request a glass of hot water for just that purpose. Carrying antiseptic hand-washing liquid is also not a bad idea.

So how can you tell if something will upset your stomach before you eat it? Trust your instincts. Avoid buffet-style places, especially on the street, and be sure that all food is cooked thoroughly and made to order. I've been plenty sick my share of times and have found that each time I get into trouble, I've usually felt a certain sense of dread from the start. If your gut tells you not to eat that gelatinous chicken foot, don't eat it. If your hosts insist but you're still nervous, explain about your "foreign stomach" with a regretful smile and accept a cup of tea instead. Be careful of raw ingredients, common as garnish on Vietnamese dishes. Questions such as, "Are these vegetables washed in clean water?" are inappropriate anywhere. Use your best judgment or simply decline.

Bugs, Bites & Other Wildlife Concerns

All kinds of creepy critters live in a tropical climate. Mosquito nets in rural accommodations are often required and, if so, are always provided by hoteliers. Check your shoes in the morning (or wear sandals) just in case some little scorpion is taking a nap in your Nikes. Keep an eye out for snakes and poisonous spiders when in jungle terrain or when doing any trekking. Having a guide doesn't preclude exercising caution. **Rabies** is a concern in rural areas of Vietnam, and extreme care should be taken when walking rural roads, especially at night, when you might want to carry a walking stick or umbrella as a deterrent to any mangy mutts. Vietnamese street mutts, the ones who escape the stew pot, have all been hit with stones; if you are threatened by a dog, the very act of reaching to the ground for a handful of stones is often enough to send the beast packing. Some travelers, especially those spending a lot of time in the back of beyond, get a **rabies pre-exposure vaccine** (for more information, see the "Common Ailments" section, above). If you are bitten, wash the wound immediately and, even if you suffer just the slightest puncture or scrape, seek medical attention and a series of rabies shots (now quite a simple affair of injections in the arm in a few installments over several weeks). The best advice: Stay away from dogs.

Respiratory Illnesses

SARS hit the region hard in the winter and spring of 2003. Singapore reported some cases and essentially closed to tourism, and though most other countries in the region reported no cases of the disease, places such as Thailand, Vietnam, and Cambodia suffered the fallout of the region-wide scare. At press time, there are no new cases in the region.

Following right on the heels of the SARS crisis, which was devastating to tourism in Vietnam, the **avian influenza,** also called the "bird flu," caused another public-relations nightmare throughout the region. The danger of humans contracting bird flu is still rather low, and limited to people working in poultry slaughterhouses. Millions of chickens suspected of carrying the illness have been culled, and the countries affected have been unusually forthright about reporting new cases and combating outbreak. Human-to-human transmissions—caused by a mutation of the poultry-borne disease—have not been reported. For more information, check the CDC website for the most up-to-date information about the disease. It is important to note that you cannot contract bird flu from consuming cooked chicken.

Air quality is not good in the larger cities such as Ho Chi Minh City, Hanoi, Haiphong, and Danang; with no emissions standards, buses, trucks, and cars belch some toxic stuff. Visitors with respiratory concerns or sensitivity should take caution. **Tuberculosis** is a concern in more remote areas where testing is still uncommon.

Sun/Elements/Extreme Weather Exposure

Sun and heatstroke are a major concern in Vietnam. Locals wear those cool conical hats and long-sleeve shirts and trousers for a reason. Limit your exposure to the sun, especially during the first few days of your trip and, thereafter, from 11am to 2pm. Use a sunscreen with a high protection factor and apply it liberally. Asian people are still big fans of parasols, so don't be shy about using an umbrella to shade yourself (all the Buddhist monks do), but note that it is a decidedly feminine choice of accessory. Remember that children need more protection than adults.

Always be sure to drink plenty of bottled water, which is the best defense against heat exhaustion and the more serious, life-threatening heatstroke. Coffee, tea, soft drinks, and alcoholic beverages should not be substituted for water; they are diuretics that dehydrate the body. In extremely hot and humid weather, try to stay out of the midday heat, and confine most of your daytime traveling to early morning and late afternoon. If you ever feel weak, fatigued, dizzy, or disoriented, get out of the sun immediately and go to a shady, cool place. To prevent sunburn, always wear a hat and apply sunscreen to all exposed areas of skin.

Be aware of major weather patterns; many island destinations are prone to typhoons or severe storms.

What to Do if You Get Sick Away from Home

Reliable emergency service is limited to Hanoi and Ho Chi Minh City (see the "Hospitals" listing, in "Fast Facts: Vietnam," below). Any foreign consulate can provide a list of area doctors who speak English. If you get sick, consider asking your hotel concierge to recommend a local doctor or nearby pharmacist. Some larger hotels and resorts have on-call nurses and doctors available for "room calls." Do not get involved with local hospitals, many of which have an archaic standard of care, unless in the most dire situation or as a base for an evacuation.

For travel abroad, you may have to pay all medical costs upfront and be reimbursed later. Medicare and Medicaid do not provide coverage for medical costs outside the U.S. Before leaving home, find out what medical services your health insurance covers. To protect yourself, consider buying medical travel insurance. (For information on traveler's insurance, trip-cancellation insurance, and medical insurance while traveling, please visit www.frommers.com/planning.)

Very few health insurance plans pay for medical evacuation back to the U.S. (which can cost $10,000 and up). A number of companies offer medical evacuation services anywhere in the world. If you're ever hospitalized more than 150 miles from home, **MedjetAssist** (② **800/527-7478;** www.medjetassistance.com) will pick you up and fly you to the hospital of your choice virtually anywhere in the world in a medically equipped and staffed aircraft 24 hours a day, 7 days a week. Annual memberships are $250 individual, $385 family; you can also purchase short-term memberships.

U.K. nationals will need a **European Health Insurance Card (EHIC)** to receive free or reduced-cost health benefits during a visit to a European Economic Area (EEA) country (European Union countries plus Iceland, Liechtenstein, and Norway) or Switzerland. For advice, ask at your local post office or see www.nhs.uk/nhsengland/Healthcareabroad.

I list **hospitals** and **emergency numbers** in the "Fast Facts: Vietnam" section, below.

If you suffer from a chronic illness, consult your doctor before your departure. Pack **prescription medications** in your carry-on luggage, and carry them in their original containers, with pharmacy labels—otherwise, they won't make it through airport security. Carry the generic name of prescription medicines, in case a local pharmacist is unfamiliar with the brand name.

Safety

An old Asia hand I know says this: "Your best insurance policy for any trip in Vietnam is to stay off motorbikes. Don't ride one yourself. Don't ride on the back. And watch out for them on the streets."

He's right, but the sad fact is that motorbikes and motorbike taxis are the best and most common way to get around most Vietnamese towns. In some cases, a ride on a bike is the only choice for covering short city hops or getting to the bus station, for example. The decision is yours, of course, but be careful: Tuck your knees in, wear a helmet, and ask the driver to slow down (say *dii cham* or give a thumbs-down gesture) if he gets going too fast.

The greatest danger to your safety when traveling Vietnam is in fact road travel: Getting around by car or bus means throwing your lot into a system where might is right, and the fastest vehicles or the ones that look and sound most like the apocalypse have the right of way. Even major highways are narrow and require a bit of "chicken"—or "forced giving way"—when opposing vehicles meet. An estimated 30 people die every day on roads in Ho Chi Minh City alone.

The good news is that anonymous violent crime is almost nonexistent in Vietnam. Petty thievery and pickpocketing is an issue, but you'll have no problems if you practice some vigilance with valuables (keep your passport and cash in a concealed travel wallet or in a hotel safe). Also, try to stick more to the well-traveled roads, especially at night—walking down dark alleys is never safe in any country. In general, foreign visitors have no problems with crime in Vietnam unless they're doing something wrong themselves.

Vietnam is politically very stable, so don't worry about getting caught up in any insurgency, though tensions and mistrust do continue between Vietnam's ethnic hilltribe communities and the central Vietnam administration. Terrorism is nonexistent because the visa restrictions are so tight, and because anyone doing anything funny under the watchful eye of the Party—and that means you—just gets the boot. There have been a number of cases of journalists and members of evangelical religious denominations being detained and having materials confiscated.

Corruption in government on all levels is rife, and, if you find yourself talking with the local constabulary, know that you won't be "protected and served" in Vietnam, but "harassed and collected from." Road violations are usually handled with an expected small bribe at curbside, for example, and you can typically bribe your way out of—or into—any situation. In general, however, local law agents don't want anything to do with foreigners unless there is a clear road to a quick profit. If in doubt in any circumstance, contact your country's embassy or consulate.

Marijuana may appear legal in Vietnam, considering its widespread availability—especially in beach towns such as Nha Trang—but don't be fooled. The same guy who sold it to you collects a few dong for informing a crooked cop, who then collects his dong bounty and a few dollars from you—or, worse, jail time if you can't produce the requisite bribe. Not worth it.

DEALING WITH DISCRIMINATION

Western visitors of all races are treated as a collective oddity in Vietnam; no one gets particular attention, really. In certain rural parts, the arrival of a Westerner draws a crowd. Foreign visitors are greeted everywhere with spastic shouts of "Hello"—often genuine, but for local kids, especially, it's usually something like shouting "punch buggy" when you see a Volkswagen. Say hi back and you've made someone's day, but responding to everyone—especially when it's not too genuine—is a bit much. Vietnamese are motivated by a friendly curiosity with foreigners, and that often translates to pushing boundaries of physical space: tugging at arm hair (not unusual for Vietnamese) or grabbing at your personal items (not to steal, just to see). It's okay to push people away, but know that Vietnamese are motivated by curiosity and operate under different definitions of personal space.

Women alone rarely run into any special problems in Vietnam, but all should take caution when alone at night. If unmarried, or traveling sans spouse, the pity is laid on pretty thick.

Gay travelers should note that there are laws against homosexuality in Vietnam, but the laws are more or less institutionalized prejudice—and the impetus for harassment and police blackmailing scams. Raids on homosexual establishments are not uncommon. Beware of homosexual touts and escorts, many of whom act in cahoots with police on scams. A large gay culture does exist in the big cities, but it's kept well under the table.

[FastFACTS] VIETNAM

Area Codes   The area codes for the provinces of Vietnam are as follows: An Giang 076, Bac Can 0281, Bac Giang 0240, Bac Lieu 0781, Bac Ninh 0241, Ben Tre 075, Binh Dinh 056, Binh Duong 0650, Binh Phuoc 0651, Binh Thuan 062, Ca Mau 0780, Can Tho 0710, Cao Bang 026, Da Nang 0511, Dak Lak 0500, Dong Nai 061, Dong Thap 067, Gia Lai 059, Ha Giang 0219, Ha Nam 0351, Hai Duong 0320, Haiphong 031, Hanoi 04, Ha Tinh 039, Ho Chi Minh City 08, Hung Yen 0321, Hoa Binh 0218, Khanh Hoa 058, Kien Giang 077, Kontum 060, Lai Chau 0231, Lam Dong 063, Lang Son 025, Lao Cai 020, Long An 072, Nam Dinh 0350, Nghe An 038, Ninh Binh 030, Ninh Thuan 068, Phu Tho 0210, Phu Yen 057, Quang Binh 052, Quang Ngai 055, Quang Ninh 033, Quang Tri 053, Soc Trang 079, Son La 022, Tay Ninh 066, Thai Binh 036, Thai Nguyen 0280, Thanh Hoa 037, Thua Thien-Hue 054, Tien Giang 073, Tra Vinh 074, Tuyen Quang 027, Vinh Long 070, Vung Tau 064, Yen Bai 029.

Business Hours   Vendors and restaurants tend to be all-day operations, opening at about 8am and closing at 9 or 10pm. People are up and about very early in the morning in Vietnam—in fact, some towns still follow the old socialist bell system over outdoor speakers that start with waking bells at 5am, exercise regimen at 5:30am, siesta bell at 11am, return-to-work bell at 1pm, finish-work bell at 5pm, and the news piped in at 6pm (this mostly in remote areas). Note that locals eat an early lunch, usually just after 11am, and some restaurants are all but closed at 1pm. Government offices—including banks, travel agencies, and museums—are usually open from 8 to 11:30am and 2 to 4pm. Streets are often very quiet during the siesta hours of the day, when the sun is most merciless. Restaurants usually have last orders at 9:30 or 10pm, and, with the few exceptions of city clubs, bars are rarely open past midnight.

Cellphones The best way to get connected with your own phone in Vietnam is to **buy an affordable GSM phone** and set up a simple prepaid account. Local calls are less than 10¢ per minute, and incoming calls are free.

Most cellphone operators in the West sell "locked" phones that restrict you from using any other removable computer memory phone chip card (called a **SIM card**) other than the ones they supply. Buy an **unlocked phone** that accepts a prepaid SIM card (found at a local retailer for as little as $40) that gives you a new account and phone number and can be exchanged for a new card in your next destination (such as nearby Cambodia or Thailand). Buy new and reconditioned cellphones at local department stores in the major cities or in any of the small storefront vendors popping up everywhere. When signing up for a local calling plan (for as little as $20, including a first batch of anytime minutes), you will get a local phone number and the staff can help you set it up (be sure to ask for help getting the phone set to "English," or *tien Anh,* if searching the LCD monitor yourself). In Vietnam, service providers include **Vinaphone** and **Viettel,** and cards are sold at retailers around the city.

Mobiphone is a similar service and has good service in urban areas, but is not as effective as Vinaphone or Viettel out in the provinces. Retailers for these popular providers are just about anywhere, and at any post office in the country.

Note: **Phone rental** is unavailable in Vietnam; buying a phone and setting up a prepaid account is the way to go.

Customs If you are entering the country as a tourist, you do not need to declare electronic goods and jewelry if these things are for personal use. Declaration forms are only to make sure you're not importing goods without paying a tariff. You must declare cash in excess of $7,000 or the equivalent. You can also import 400 cigarettes, 1.5 liters of alcohol, and perfume for personal use.

It is unlikely that you will be hassled in Vietnam for bringing anything in, but be careful if bringing excessive equipment. Adventurers with bicycles or special kites for kite surfing will have to prove that they will be taking their expensive items home with them and not selling them in Vietnam. Commercial photographers or amateurs who work with professional, high-end equipment should be wary

of bringing the whole studio with them.

For information on what you're allowed to bring home, contact one of the following agencies:

U.S. Citizens: U.S. Customs & Border Protection (CBP), 1300 Pennsylvania Ave., NW, Washington, DC 20229 (© **877/287-8667;** www.cbp.gov).

Canadian Citizens: Canada Border Services Agency (© 800/461-9999 in Canada, or 204/983-3500; www.cbsa-asfc.gc.ca).

U.K. Citizens: HM Customs & Excise at © 0845/010-9000 (from outside the U.K., 020/8929-0152), or consult their website at www.hmrc.gov.uk.

Australian Citizens: Australian Customs Service at © 1300/363-263, or log on to www.customs.gov.au.

New Zealand Citizens: New Zealand Customs, The Customhouse, 17–21 Whitmore St., Box 2218, Wellington (© 04/473-6099 or 0800/428-786; www.customs.govt.nz).

Drinking Laws There are surprisingly no age restrictions limiting when or where you can buy or consume drinks. Laws against drinking and driving are not enforced, so it is not uncommon to find that your motorbike or taxi driver has had a few. Be cautious, especially at night.

Electricity Vietnam's electricity carries 220 volts, so if you're coming from the U.S., bring a converter and adapter for electronics. Plugs have either two round prongs or two flat prongs. If you're toting a laptop, bring a surge protector. Big hotels will have all these implements.

Embassies & Consulates Embassies are located in Hanoi at the following addresses: **Australia,** 8 Dao Tan (ℭ 04/3774-0100); **Canada,** 31 Hung Vuong (ℭ 04/3734-5000); **European Union,** 83B Ly Thuong Kiet (ℭ 04/3941-0099); **New Zealand,** 63 Ly Thai To (ℭ 04/3824-1481); **United Kingdom,** 31 Hai Ba Trung (ℭ 04/3936-0500); **United States,** 170 Ngoc Khanh St. (ℭ 04/3850-5000).

Emergencies Nationwide emergency numbers are as follows: For police, dial ℭ **113;** for fire, dial ℭ **114;** and for ambulance, dial ℭ **115.** Operators speak Vietnamese only.

Holidays Banks, government offices, post offices, and many stores, restaurants, and museums are closed on the following legal national holidays: New Year's Day (Jan 1), Tet holiday (usually a few days in late Jan/early Feb on the Gregorian Calendar—see "Vietnam Calendar of Events," in chapter 2), Gio To Hung Vuong Day (1 day, usually in Apr on the Gregorian Calendar—see "Vietnam Calendar of Events," in chapter 2), April 30 (Saigon Liberation/Reunification Day), and September 2 (National Day).

For more information on holidays, see "Vietnam Calendar of Events," in chapter 2.

Hospitals In Hanoi, the expatriate choice for comprehensive services is the **Hanoi French Hospital,** south of the town center at 1 Phuong Mai (ℭ **04/3577-1100**). For emergencies or minor medical issues in Hanoi, stop in at the **International SOS** medical center at 1 Dang Thai Mai St., just beside West Lake; call the 24-hour service center for emergencies at ℭ **04/3934-0666.** They have both Vietnamese and foreign doctors on call. Also in Hanoi, find the **Hanoi Family Medical Practice** at Van Phuc Diplomatic Compound, 298 Kim Ma (ℭ **04/3843-0748**).

In Ho Chi Minh City, **International SOS** is at 167A Nam Ky Khoi Nghia St., District 3 (ℭ **08/3829-8424,** 24-hr. hot line). The **International Medical Center,** 1 Han Thuyen, District 1 (ℭ **08/3827-2367** for emergencies), offers services similar to what you'll find at International SOS.

Insurance Travel insurance is a very good idea for Vietnam. In the event of, say, a motorbike accident or a stomach ailment, seeking treatment at the international hospitals is very expensive. A consultation with a doctor at International SOS alone will set you back close to $200, let alone medicine and fees for setting broken bones or treating an acute case of diarrhea.

For information on traveler's insurance, trip-cancellation insurance, and medical insurance while traveling, please visit www.frommers.com/planning.

Internet Access Internet cafes are disappearing fast in Vietnam as Wi-Fi and broadband ADSL connections become widespread, and usually free, though you'll still find a few Internet shops (they rarely serve coffee or anything) catering to the few game-playing kids who don't yet have their own computer or iPhone, and charging around 6,000 VND per hour. The Internet is controlled by the government post office in any town, and most post offices have adjoining cybercafes that are a good bet for fast, affordable service. In rural areas, it can get frustrating; the good

When you change money, ask for some small bills, which will come in handy for tipping and public transportation. Consider keeping the change separate from your larger bills so that it's readily accessible and you'll be less of a target for theft. Keep a good supply of $1 bills and/or 20,000 VND bills; these will come in handy when paying for cab and motorcycle rides.

ADSL line that starts at the post office gets split and spliced in its path to rural parts, creating patchy service or, if someone's been digging in the wrong place, unavailable service. The other drawback is that these places are often smoky and packed with screaming kids playing online shoot-'em-up games. Check the listings in individual chapters, or inquire at any hotel front desk to find an Internet cafe.

To find cybercafes in your destination, check **http://cybercaptive.com** and **www.cybercafe.com**.

Most major airports have **Internet kiosks** that provide basic Web access for a per-minute fee that's usually higher than cybercafe prices.

Wi-Fi has taken Vietnam by storm and is now the most common method of getting online in the country, with everywhere from the cheapest hostel to the most expensive resort providing the service either for free or for a fee.

Most business-class hotels in Vietnam offer dataports for laptop modems and increasingly offer high-speed Internet access using an Ethernet network cable or in-room Wi-Fi. You can bring your own cables, but most hotels will gladly loan them. A growing number of hotels in Vietnam offer free in-room Internet service.

Wherever you go, bring a **connection kit** of power and phone adapters, a spare phone cord, and a spare Ethernet network cable (some of the better city hotels can provide what you need). The current in Vietnam is 220V. Most laptops can plug directly into Vietnamese outlets, but bring a three-prong-to-two-prong adapter and a surge protector.

Language Vietnamese is the official language of Vietnam. Older residents speak and understand French, and young folks are busily learning Chinese these days. While English is widely spoken among folks in the service industry in Hanoi and Saigon, it is harder to find in other tourist destinations. Off the beaten track, arm yourself with as many Vietnamese words as you can muster (see chapter 16) and a dictionary.

Legal Aid   The legal aid system in Vietnam is tenuous for its own citizens, let alone international travelers. If you find yourself on the wrong side of the law, contact your embassy or consulate immediately.

Mail   A regular airmail letter will take about 10 days to reach North America, 7 days to reach Europe, and 4 days to reach Australia or New Zealand. Mailing things from Vietnam is expensive. A letter weighing up to 10 grams costs 15,000 VND to North America, 12,000 VND to Europe, and 10,000 VND to Australia/New Zealand; postcards cost between 7,000 VND and 15,000 VND. Express mail services such as FedEx and DHL are easily available and are usually located in or around every city's main post office.

Money & Costs   Frommer's lists exact prices in the local currency wherever possible, though the

WHAT THINGS COST IN VIETNAM

Cup of coffee	15,000 VND–40,000 VND
Taxi from the airport	180,000 VND–300,000 VND
Three-course dinner without alcohol	120,000 VND–300,000 VND
Moderately priced hotel	600,000 VND–1,200,000 VND

Note: Prices vary in smaller towns.

U.S. dollar is used widely in both Vietnam and Cambodia: In fact, the dollar is the de facto currency in Cambodia, and packing some U.S. greenbacks will come in very handy. Rates fluctuate, so before departing, consult a currency exchange website such as **www.oanda.com/currency/converter** to check up-to-the-minute rates.

During your trip, the most useful Vietnam Dong bills will be upwards of 10,000 VND, which is worth about 50¢. There are smaller bills (which are also physically smaller than the more frequently used bills of 10,000 VND and up) of 1,000 VND, 2,000 VND, and 5,000 VND, which are handy when buying snacks from street vendors, or for giving exact change to cab drivers. Every now and again, a bronze 5,000 VND coin might land your way, though you may never see a coin at all. For the most part, bills are distinguishable by color: The 500,000 VND is light blue, 100,000 VND is green, and 20,000

VND is dark blue. Be mindful of the 10,000 VND, 50,000 VND, and 200,000 VND notes—all are done in pinkish-red hues that are quite similar to each other.

ATM service is good in all cities and the machines accept four-digit PINs. However, if heading off into the countryside, take cash. Credit cards are also widely accepted, though many smaller companies, such as tour agencies or boutique hotels, will charge a 2% or 3% commission. All hotels accept U.S. dollars, though often at an unfavorable rate, so you pay for the convenience. Aware of foreigners' difficulties in mentally converting huge sums, most vendors will happily quote prices in U.S. dollars, though again to their advantage. Big-ticket items are best handled with greenbacks instead of large stacks of local currency.

Dealing in U.S. dollars can make things less complicated, but always try to make an approximate conversion so that you know if

you're being charged the correct amount or are given the correct change (usually in Vietnamese currency). With the current exchange rate of around $1=20,000 VND, this is quite easy ($5=100,000 VND, $10=200,000 VND, $50=1,000,000 VND, etc.), but unfortunately exchange rates have been volatile during recent years. In this book, I've listed **hotel, restaurant, and attraction rates** in whatever form the establishments quoted them—in local currencies where those were used, and in U.S. dollars (designated by the dollar sign: $) where those were quoted.

Newspapers & Magazines *Viet Nam News* (http://vietnamnews. vnanet.vn) is the country's English-language daily newspaper. You can find copies at bookstores in the major cities.

Passports See www. frommers.com/planning for information on how to obtain a passport. See "Embassies & Consulates," above, for whom to contact if you lose your passport while traveling in Vietnam. For other information, please contact the following agencies:

For Residents of Australia Contact the **Australian Passport Information Service** at ℂ **131-232,** or visit the government website at www.passports.gov.au.

For Residents of Canada Contact the central Passport Office, Department of Foreign Affairs and International Trade, Gatineau QC K1A 0G3 (ℂ 800/567-6868; www.ppt.gc.ca).

For Residents of Ireland Contact the Passport Office, Setanta Centre, Molesworth Street, Dublin 2 (ℂ 01/671-1633; www.irlgov.ie/iveagh).

For Residents of New Zealand Contact the Passports Office at ℂ 0800/225-050 in New Zealand, or 04/463-9360, or log on to www.passports.govt.nz.

For Residents of the United Kingdom Visit your nearest passport office, major post office, or travel agency, or contact the **United Kingdom Identity and Passport Service** at ℂ **0300/222-0000** or search its website at www.homeoffice.gov.uk.

For Residents of the United States To find your regional passport office, either check the U.S. State Department website or call the **National Passport Information Center** toll-free number (ℂ **877/487-2778**) for automated information.

Police You won't find a helpful cop on every street corner. Count on them only in cases of dire emergency, and learn a few words of Vietnamese to help you along. Moreover, police here can sometimes be part of the problem. Especially in the south, you and your car/motorbike driver might, for instance, be stopped for a minor traffic infraction and "fined." If the amount isn't too large, cooperate. Corruption is the rule, and palm-greasing and graft pose as police process. Be aware.

Smoking "No smoking" areas are rare in Vietnam, and even those that exist are often not well ventilated. Like other countries in the region, Vietnam is a smoker's paradise, and complaining about secondhand smoke is often met with confusion.

Taxes A 20% VAT is charged for hotels and restaurants, but expect variation in how it's followed. Upscale establishments might add the full 20%, and some might even tack on an additional 5% service charge. Others might absorb the tax in their prices, and still others will ignore it entirely. Inquire before booking or eating.

Telephones For domestic calls, visit the post office, where public phone service is offered at affordable rates, or buy a domestic phone card at any post office or phone company branch, usually at a rate of about 1,000 VND per minute. Local calls from hotels come with exorbitant surcharges and are best avoided.

The best way to make international calls from Vietnam is using an international calling card program, the likes of AT&T or MCI. Most hotels offer international direct-dialing, but with exorbitant surcharges of 10% to 25% on already inflated rates. International calls from any post office are more affordable, but without a calling card it is usually more than $1 per minute.

Internet phone service is available at most Internet storefronts. You can buy a card that gives you rates as low as 3,000 VND per minute, but many Internet shops don't allow you to use cards purchased elsewhere and levy a small surcharge on top of the 3,000 VND per minute. Internet phone quality ranges widely, best from the larger cities, and there is always a slight "walkie-talkie" delay, but it is the most affordable way to stay connected.

If you have a GSM cellphone that accepts SIM cards, you can buy an affordable plan at any post office or telecommunications center. The trick here is that receiving calls from anywhere is free of charge, so you can buy someone back home an affordable international phone card and arrange times when they can call you.

To call Vietnam: If you're calling Vietnam from the United States:
1. Dial the international access code: 011.
2. Dial the country code: 84.
3. Important Note: City codes are listed in this book with a 0 in front of them, as is required when dialing domestically. Do not dial the city code's prefix of 0 when dialing from abroad. When dialing a number (as listed in this guide), such as ✆ 04/555-5555, from abroad, you dial as follows: ✆ 011 (for international), + 84 (for Vietnam), + 4 (the city code minus the 0) + 555-5555. Looks like ✆ 011-84-4-555-5555.

To make international calls: To make international calls from Vietnam, first dial 00 and then the country code (U.S. or Canada 1, U.K. 44, Ireland 353, Australia 61, New Zealand 64). Next you dial the area code and number. For example, if you wanted to call the British Embassy in Washington, D.C., you would dial 00-1-202-588-7800.

For directory assistance: Dial ✆ 116 if you're looking for a number inside the country.

For operator assistance: If you need operator assistance in making a call, dial ✆ 110.

Toll-free numbers: Calling a 1-800 number in the States from Vietnam is not toll-free. In fact, it costs the same as an overseas call.

Time Vietnam is 7 hours ahead of Greenwich Mean Time. There's no daylight saving time in Vietnam, meaning that in the summer months, it's 12 hours ahead of the U.S. East Coast, in winter months 11 hours ahead; it's 14 or 15 hours ahead of the U.S. West Coast, and 3 or 4 hours behind Sydney, Australia.

Tipping Tipping is common in Hanoi and in Saigon. In a top-end hotel, feel free to tip bellhops anywhere from 10,000 VND to 20,000 VND. Most upscale restaurants throughout the country now add a service surcharge of 5% to 10%. If they don't, or if the service is good, you might want to leave another 5%. Taxi drivers will be pleased if you round up the bill (again, mainly in the big cities). Use your discretion for tour guides and others who have been particularly helpful. Contrary to rumor, boxes of cigarettes as tips don't go over well. The recipient will say regretfully, "I don't smoke," when what he really means is "Show me the money." Exceptions to this are chauffeurs or minibus drivers.

Toilets You won't find public toilets or "restrooms" on the streets in most cities in Vietnam, but they can be found in hotel lobbies, bars, restaurants, museums, department stores, railway and bus stations, and service stations. Be sure to carry tissues, as many of the restrooms in the railway and bus stations do not have toilet paper. Large hotels and fast-food restaurants are often the best bet for clean facilities. Restaurants and bars in resorts or heavily visited areas may reserve their restrooms for patrons.

Visas Vietnam grants **5-year visa exemptions** to all overseas Vietnamese in more than 90 countries. The exemption applies to individuals who have Vietnamese nationality and foreign nationals of Vietnamese origin. If you are the spouse or child of someone who qualifies, you can have your very own visa-free status, so long as your husband, wife, or parent has obtained the exemption first. Check out http://mienthithucvk.mofa.gov.vn for instructions and regulations. It can be a lengthy process, so apply at your nearest Vietnamese embassy or consulate well ahead of your trip.

Residents of the United States, Canada, Australia, New Zealand, and the United Kingdom need both a passport (valid for at least 6 months) and a **prearranged visa** to enter Vietnam, which can be arranged at your local embassy or online; in the latter case you will get the **visa on arrival.** A tourist visa lasts for 30 days and costs around $65. You'll pay a bit more through an agent but will save yourself some paper shuffling. **_Note:_** If you're planning a side trip to Angkor Wat but your return flight leaves from Vietnam, make sure to get a multiple-entry visa to get back into the country. A multiple-entry 90-day visa costs $110. A visa takes 5 to 7 days to process. Applicants must submit an application, a passport, and two passport photos. U.S. citizens can obtain a visa application from the Vietnam Embassy in Washington, D.C., online at **www.vietnamembassy-usa.org**, or by calling ℂ **202/861-0737.** Mail the completed application with your passport and your passport photos using an express carrier (Federal Express, US Express, or Priority Mail with delivery confirmation) to the embassy (1233 20th St. NW, Ste. 400, Washington, DC 20036), including a self-addressed stamped envelope from an express carrier (with delivery confirmation). Processing time is usually 5 days, but for a small fee, you can expedite it to as few as 2 days, and even less in last-minute circumstances (call to see what you can arrange). The embassy is open Monday to Friday from 9:30am to 12:30pm. The fax number is 202/861-0917.

Australian citizens can obtain up-to-date visa information from the **Vietnam Embassy** at 6 Timbarra Crescent, O'Malley, ACT 2606 (ℂ **02/6286-6059;** www.vietnamembassy.org.au), or at the **Consulate General of Vietnam** at Ste. 205, Level 2, Edgecliff Centre, 203–233 New South Head Road, Edgecliff, Sydney, NSW 2027 (ℂ **02/9327-2539;** www.vietnamconsulate.org.au).

British and **Irish** subjects should contact the **Vietnam Embassy** at 12–14 Victoria Rd., London W8 5RD, U.K. (ℂ **0207/937-1912;** fax 0207/937-6108) or download an application form at **www.vietnamembassy.org.uk**.

Canadian citizens can apply through the **Vietnam Embassy** at 470 Wilbrod St., Ottawa, ON K1N 6M8 (ℂ **613/236-0772;** www.vietnamembassy-canada.ca).

Citizens of **New Zealand** can obtain up-to-date visa information by contacting the **Vietnam Embassy,** Level 21 Grand Plimmer Tower, 2–6 Gilmer Terrace, Wellington 6011 (ℂ **4/473-5912;** www.vietnamembassy-newzealand.org).

Getting the visa online at www.vietnamvisa.com saves a lot of time, and is a speedy and efficient service. You can apply for 1- or 3-month visas, single or multiple entry, and fees are a bit cheaper than through the embassy. Within a day of applying and paying the fee, you will receive confirmation, which you should print out and present with your passport and photos at the **Visa on Arrival** desk at your point of entry in Vietnam. The only downside is that you'll need to queue up to get the passport stamped before you go through immigration when you arrive, though since few people use this service as yet, the process is quite swift.

Because 3-month visas are now available, it is unlikely that you will need an extension, but if you do, this can be arranged by any tour operator; see the Tourist Information section of any chapter for recommendations.

You no longer need to specify an entry point; Vietnam visas are good for any legal port of entry—land, sea, or air—but remember that your visa begins on the date that you specify on your application.

In a bid to boost investment and cooperation, Vietnam has lifted visa requirements for Japanese and Koreans—a good sign that visa restrictions for Western visitors might loosen up even more soon.

Visitor Information

In Hanoi and Ho Chi Minh City, head to the **Tourist Information Center** (7 Dinh Tien Hoang St. in Hanoi, ✆ **04/3926-3366;** or 92–96 Nguyen Hue St., District 1 in Ho Chi Minh City, ✆ **08/3822-6033**) for free detailed tourist maps and general information. In the north, Sapa's new **Tourism Information Center** (✆ **020/387-1975**) is a good resource for local hiking conditions and decent maps. Recent stats and general information on the country and local holidays can be found at the state-run tourism site www.vietnamtourism.com.

Water Water is not potable in Vietnam. Outside of top-end hotels and restaurants, drink only beverages without ice, unless the establishment promises that it manufactures its own ice from clean water. Bottled mineral water, particularly the reputable La Vie and A&B brands, is everywhere. Counterfeits are a problem, so make sure you're buying the real thing, with an unbroken seal. Beware of big typos: "La Vile" water speaks for itself.

AIRLINE, HOTEL & CAR RENTAL WEBSITES

Major Airlines

Air France
www.airfrance.com

Air New Zealand
www.airnewzealand.com

British Airways
www.british-airways.com

China Airlines
www.china-airlines.com

Japan Airlines
www.jal.co.jp

Korean Air
www.koreanair.com

Lufthansa
www.lufthansa.com

Northwest Airlines
www.nwa.com

Qantas Airways
www.qantas.com/au

Philippine Airlines
www.philippineairlines.com

Thai Airways International
www.thaiair.com

United Airlines
www.united.com

Vietnam Airlines
www.vietnamairlines.com

Budget Airlines

Jetstar Pacific (Australia)
www.jetstar.com

Air Mekong
www.airmekong.com.vn

Major Hotel & Motel Chains

Hilton Hotels
www.hilton.com

Hyatt
www.hyatt.com

InterContinental Hotels & Resorts
www.ichotelsgroup.com

Life Resorts
www.life-resorts.com

Mövenpick Hotels
www.moevenpick-hotels.com

Six Senses
www.sixsenses.com

Sofitel Hotels
www.sofitel.com

Sheraton Hotels & Resorts
www.starwoodhotels.com/sheraton

Victoria Hotels & Resorts
www.victoriahotels-asia.com

Car Rental Agencies

Budget
www.budget.com.vn

TNK Travel Vietnam
www.tnktravelvietnam.com

THE VIETNAMESE LANGUAGE

The ancient Vietnamese language, though not complex structurally (subject, object, verb with no plurals), is tonal and therefore difficult for Westerners to master. In its earliest written form, Vietnamese was based on the Chinese pictographic writing, called **Chu Nom,** and you'll see remnants of that tradition on temple walls—in fact, young people still study written Chinese in school. But in the 17th century, a French missionary named **Alexandre de Rhodes** developed **Quoc Ngu,** the Romanized Vietnamese alphabet that's used today. Unlike other languages in the region, many of which use Sanskrit as a base, Vietnamese looks almost readable to a Westerner, and though the easy recognition of Romanized letters makes finding street addresses much easier, the system of diacritical marks is complex and pronunciation is difficult. There are no dialects of Vietnamese, but regional accents are quite distinct, and many words are completely different in the north and south.

To really learn Vietnamese, you'll need to work with a pronunciation coach, and the best part about traveling in Vietnam is the willingness of people to listen, laugh, and correct or model for you as you bludgeon their precious language. Learning just a little goes a long way.

Today most city dwellers seem to speak at least a little English, and the older generation speaks some French. With increased influence from China—the Chinese comprise well over 50% of international visitors in Vietnam—younger people are increasingly studying Mandarin. Students especially will be eager to practice English with you (as well as French or Mandarin). Solo travelers, being less intimidating, are at an advantage; you'll have many opportunities (and invitations) to have a squat on a street corner, drink a *bia hoi* (local draft beer), and practice pronunciation.

Note: For useful **food terms** and names of popular dishes, see p. 18.

Who Do You Think You're Talkin' To?

It's important to know whom you're speaking to, especially in Vietnam, where the pronoun *you* is used widely and denotes the relationship of the two people speaking. If you're just saying "Hello" to someone, you need to say the equivalent of "Hello older man" or "Hello young person." In fact, when peers meet, there's a moment of figuring out who is older/younger—sometimes folks even ask so that they know what to call you. The second-person pronouns are important and easy to learn. Say hello as follows:

○ Use *Chao ong* for a man significantly older, an elder or grandfather.

○ *Chao ba* is polite for a married woman older than you, an auntie or grandma.

○ *Anh* is the word for a young man (only if older than you) or brother; if you're elderly, everyone is *Em* and *Anh* to you.

○ Say *Chao chi* to an older or middle-age woman.

○ Use *Chao co* when referring to an older single woman or teacher.

○ *Chao em* is the proper pronoun for someone younger than you, male or female. *Note:* A man saying this to a woman is considered too informal—as if it were a come-on—so the more neutral *Chi* or *Co* is better. Also note that shouting *"Em"* or *"Em oi!"* is the best way to get a waitress's attention. If the waitress is much older, though, be sure to use *"Ba oi!"* instead.

THE BASICS
Useful Vietnamese Phrases

English	Vietnamese	Pronunciation
Hello	**Xin chào**	Seen chow
How are you?	**Em/Ông/Bà Khỏe không?**	Em/Ong/Ba Kwe kong?
I am very well, thank you.	**Khoẻ, cảm ơn.**	Kwe, kam un.
Good morning	**Chào buổi sáng**	Chow boy sang
Good afternoon	**Chào buổi chiều**	Chow boy chew
Good evening	**Chào buổi tối**	Chow boy toy
Thank you	**Cảm ơn**	Kam un.
You're welcome/Not at all	**Không có chi** (north) **không có gì** (south)	Kawng co chi/kawng co yi
Goodbye	**Tạm biệt**	Tam bee-et
Please	**Làm ơn**	Lahm uhn
Yes	**Vâng**	Vung
No	**Không**	Kawng
Excuse me	**Xin lỗi**	Seen loy
May I take a picture?	**Tôi có thể chụp ảnh?**	Doi kaw tay joop ayn?

Numbers

English	Vietnamese	Pronunciation
0	**Không**	Kawng
1	**Một**	Mawt
2	**Hai**	Hi
3	**Ba**	Bah
4	**Bốn**	Bawn
5	**Năm**	Nam
6	**Sáu**	Sow
7	**Bảy**	Bay-ee
8	**Tám**	Tam
9	**Chín**	Cheen
10	**Mười**	Mooey
11	**Mười một**	Mooey mot
12	**Mười hai**	Mooey hi
20	**Hai mươi**	Hi mooey
21	**Hai mươi một**	Hi mooey mot
30	**Ba mười**	Bah mooey
100	**Một trăm**	Mot jam
243	**Hai trăm bốn mươi ba**	Hi jam bawn mooey bah
1,000	**Một ngàn**	Mot ngun
10,000	**Mười ngàn**	Mooey ngun
100,000	**Một trăm ngàn**	Mot jam ngun
1,000,000	**Một triệu**	Mot true

Note: Numbers 11 to 20 continue with *Möôøi* (10) plus ordinal numbers. In other words, 12 is "ten two" and 19 is "ten nine."

Emergency

English	Vietnamese	Pronunciation
I need a doctor.	**Tôi cần bác sĩ.**	Toy kahn back see.
Hospital	**Bệnh viện**	Ben vee-in
Antibiotic	**Kháng sinh**	Kahng sin

Getting to Know Someone

English	Vietnamese	Pronunciation
What is your name?	**Anh tên là gì ?**	Ayn ten la zee?
Where are you from?	**Anh từ đâu đến?**	Ayn du dow den?
I come from . . .	**Tôi đến từ . . .**	Toy den tu . . .
America.	**Mỹ.**	mee.
Australia.	**Úc.**	ook.
Britain.	**Anh.**	ayn.
New Zealand.	**Tân Tây Lan.**	tan tay lan.
Do you have a boyfriend/ girlfriend?	**Anh/Chò có baïn trai/ gaùi?**	Ayn/chi co ban dray/ban guy?
Are you married?	**Anh có vợ chưa? (to a man)**	Ayn co vuh choo-ah?
	Chị có chồng chưa? (to a woman)	Chi co chong choo-ah?
Where were you born?	**Quê bạn ở đâu?**	Gay ban er dau?
I am studying Vietnamese.	**Tôi học tiếng Việt.**	Toy hoc tieng viet.
I like . . .	**Toâi Thích . . .**	Toy tick . . .
studying Vietnamese.	**học tiếng Việt.**	hoc tieng Viet.
ice cream.	**ăn kem.**	ahn kem.
traveling.	**đi du lịch.**	dee zoo lick.
How long have you been in Vietnam?	**Anh/Chị ở Việt Nam bao lâu rồi?**	Ayn/chi er Vietnam bow low roy?
One week/month/year	**Moät tuaàn/thaùng/năm**	Mot too-ang/tang/nan
What is your job?	**Ông/Bà/Anh/Chị làm nghề gì?**	Lam ngay zee?
I am . . .	**Toâi laø . . .**	Toy la . . .
a writer.	**nhà văn.**	nya van.
an artist.	**họa sĩ.**	ho-a see.
a teacher.	**giáo viên.**	gee-ow vee-en.
in business.	**thương gia.**	too-ong yee-a.
a student.	**sinh viên.**	seen vee-en.
retired.	**về hưu.**	vay hoo.
Good	**Tốt**	Tawt
You are clever!	**Anh thông minh!**	Ayn tong min!
Oh, my gosh!	**Ôi, chúa ơi!**	Oh, zoi oi!
How old are you?	**Ông/Bà/Anh/Chị bao nhiêu tuổi?**	Bow nyew too-ee?
I am 34 years old.	**Tôi ba mươi bốn tuổi.**	Toy ba mooey bawn too-ee.
See you again.	**Hẹn gặp lại.**	Hen gup lie.

Talking About Language

English	Vietnamese	Pronunciation
Do you speak English?	**Biết nói tiếng Anh không?**	Biet noy tieng Ayn kohng?
I speak a little Vietnamese.	**Tôi nói nhỏ người Việt Nam.**	Toy noy nyo nuey Vietnam.
How do you say . . . in Vietnamese?	**Làm thế nào để bạn nói . . . tiếng Việt?**	Lam te nao de ban noi . . . tieng Viet?
I don't understand.	**Toâi khoảng hieẩu.**	Toy kawng hew.
I understand.	**Tôi hiểu.**	Toy hew.
Please speak slowly.	**Xin oâng/baø noùi chaăm laïi.**	Seen owng/ba noy chum lie.
Please repeat that.	**Xin oâng/ba lòng lặp lại.**	Seen owng/ba long lap lie.

GETTING AROUND
Getting There

English	Vietnamese	Pronunciation
Where is . . .	**. . . ở đâu?**	. . . er dow?
the bus station?	**trạm xe buýt?**	cham say bwit?
the train station?	**trạm xe lửa?**	cham say loo-a?
a hotel?	**khách sạn?**	kak san?
a guesthouse?	**nhà khách?**	nya khat?
a restaurant?	**nhà hàng?**	nya hahng?
the toilet?	**nhà vệ sinh?**	nya vay shin?
a hospital?	**bệnh viện?**	ben vien?
my embassy?	**Đại sự quan?**	dai sher kwa?
the road to . . .?	**đường đi . . . ?**	doo-ang dee . . . ?
Where can I buy a map?	**Toâi coù theẩ mua baûn ñoà ôû ñaâu?**	Doi kaw tay mua ban do ou do?
Turn right.	**Rẽ phải.**	Ray fie.
Turn left.	**Reõ traùi.**	Ray chai.
Where are you going?	**Ông/ Bà/Anh/Chị đi đâu?**	Owng/ba/ayn/chi dee doe?
I am going from . . . to . . .	**Tôi đi từ . . . đến . . .**	Doy di two . . . den . . .
I want to go to . . .	**Tôi muốn đi đến.**	Toy Moo-an dee den. . .
When?	**Luùc naøo?**	Look now?
Yesterday	**Hôm qua**	Home gwaa
Today	**Hoâm nay**	Home ngai
Tomorrow	**Mai**	My
What time do we leave?	**Mấy giờ đi?**	May zuh tee?

English	Vietnamese	Pronunciation
What time do we arrive?	**Mấy giờ đến?**	May zuh den?
Is it far?	**Xa kohng?**	Saa kawng?
Very far	**Rất xa**	Rat saa
Fast	**Nhanh**	Nuan
Slow	**Chậm**	Jam

Touring

English	Vietnamese	Pronunciation
I want to see . . .	**Tôi muốn xem . . .**	Doi moo-an same . . .
temple	**đền**	den
pagoda	**chùa**	choo-uh
church	**nhà thờ**	nya thuh
mountain	**núi**	nu-y
cave	**hang**	hang
river	**song**	song
lake	**hồ**	ho
beach	**bãi biển**	bye byen
It is very beautiful!	**Rất đẹp!**	Rat dep!
I'm tired.	**Tôi mệt mỏi.**	Toy met moh.

Transportation

English	Vietnamese	Pronunciation
airport	**sân bay**	shun bai
taxi	**tắc xi**	taxi
I want to rent a car.	**Tôi muốn thuê một chiếc xe hơi.**	Toy moo-un tuay mot chic say hoy.
motorbike	**xe máy**	say my
motorbike taxi	**xe ôm**	say ohm
bicycle	**xe đạp**	say dap
bus	**xe buýt**	say bwit
train	**xe lửa**	say loo-ah
baggage	**hanh ly**	han lee
backpack	**ba lô**	ba lo
pedicab	**xích lô**	sick low

Restaurant & Self-Catering

English	Vietnamese	Pronunciation
Please bring me . . .	**Xin mang cho tôi . . .**	Seen mang cho toi . . .
It is delicious, thank you.	**Raát Ngon, caùm ôn.**	Wreck ngawn, kam un.
bread and butter	**bánh mì và bơ**	bun me vuh bo
egg	**tröùng**	chung
vegetable	**rau**	rau
beef/chicken/fish	**thòt boø/thòt gaø/ caù**	tit baw/tit ga/ka
fried/boiled/grilled	**chiên/ luộc /nướng**	chi-yen/loo-uk/noo-wong
one cup of coffee/tea	**moät taùch caø pheâ/traø**	mot tak kafay/cha
I can't eat spicy food.	**Tôi không thể ăn thực phẩm gia vị.**	Toy khong te ahn took fam ha vi.
Check, please!	**Xin, tính tiền!**	Seen, tin tee-un!

Hotel

English	Vietnamese	Pronunciation
Do you have any available rooms?	**Có còn phòng không?**	Co con fong kawng?
I want a . . . single room.	**Tôi muốn . . . một phòng đơn.**	Doi moo-an . . . mot fong der.
double room	**một phòng đôi**	mot fong doi
I want a room with . . .	**Tôi muốn có một căn phòng với . . .**	Doi moo-an co mot can fong veuy . . .
hot water..	**nước nóng.**	noo-uc nawng.
air-conditioning.	**máy lạnh.**	my la-n.
a bathroom.	**bồn tắm.**	fawng tam.
a phone.	**điện thoại.**	di yen twye.
Can I see the room?	**Coù theå xem phoøng ñôõïc khoâng?**	Kaw tay same fong kawng?
I need a . . . pillow.	**Tôi cần . . . gối.**	Toy can . . . goy.
blanket.	**chăn.**	chan.
towel.	**khăn.**	kan.

Laugh from Your Mistakes

The Vietnamese language, with its six tones, has an enormous capacity for puns, and Vietnamese people get a kick out of foreigners' mistakes. Words that mean "progress with sales," if pronounced incorrectly, come out as "very hungry." Bawdy mistakes by foreigners who think they're ordering pork but are naming a human body part, for example, send Vietnamese people into a tizzy.

Shopping

English	Vietnamese	Pronunciation
Please give me . . .	Cho tôi . . .	Jya toy . . .
Do you have . . .	Coù khoâng . . .	Kaw kawng . . .
mineral water?	nước khoáng?	nook kwang?
iced tea?	trà đá?	chaa da?
a beer?	bia?	bee-ah?
soap?	xà phòng?	sa phong?
How much does it cost?	Bao nhiêu tiền?	Bow nyew tyen?
Expensive! (Too much!)	Maéc quaù! (south)	Mak gwa!
	Ñaét quaù! (north)	Dat gwa!
Cheap!	Reû!	Ray!
Do you have something . . .	Coù . . .	Kaw . . .
better?	tốt hơn?	tawt hawn?
bigger?	lớn hơn?	lawn hawn?
smaller?	nhỏ hơn?	nyaw hawn?

Index

See also Accommodation index, below.

General Index

A

Abercrombie & Kent, 29, 362
Absolute Asia, 29–30
Academic trips, 25–26
Accommodations, 430–431. *See also* Accommodations Index
  Ban Lac and Pom Coong, 131, 134
  best, 5–6
  Buon Ma Thuot, 241
  Cambodia
    Battambang, 425
    Kampot, 387–388
    Phnom Penh, 373–377
    Sihanoukville, 389–390
  Can Tho, 343
  Cao Bang, 144
  Cat Ba, 158–159
  Cat Tien National Park, 336
  Chau Doc, 346–347
  Cho Ra, 143
  Con Son, 331–332
  Dalat, 229–233
  Danang, 199–201
  Dien Bien Phu, 138–139
  Doc Let Beach, 273
  Dong Van, 142
  Haiphong, 148, 150
  Halong City, 152–153
  Hanoi, 65–76
  Ho Chi Minh City, 289–300
  Hue, 180–183
  Lang Co Beach, 196–197
  Lang Son, 145–146
  Long Hai, 328–329
  Mach Ma National Park, 195
  Muong Lay, 140
  Nha Trang, 261–266
  Ninh Binh, 164
  Phan Thiet and Mui Ne, 276–278
  Phu Quoc, 350–354
  Pleiku, 247
  Quang Ngai, 257
  Quy Nhon, 254
  Sapa, 125–127
  Siem Reap, 396–403
  Son La, 135
  Vinh, 170–171
  Vung Tau, 325–326
  websites, 448
Active Travel Vietnam, 50
Active vacations and organized adventure trips, 49–54
A Dong Photo Company (Hanoi), 110
Adong Silk (Hoi An), 220

Adventure and wellness trips, 27–29
AIDS, 434
  Cambodia, 365
Airline websites, 447
Air quality, 436
Air travel, 427, 428
  Buon Ma Thuot, 240
  Cambodia, 365, 366
    Phnom Penh, 372
    Siem Reap, 392
  Can Tho, 342
  Con Son, 330
  Dalat, 226
  Danang, 197
  Dien Bien Phu, 138
  Hanoi, 55–57
  Ho Chi Minh City, 281–284
  Hue, 176
  Nha Trang, 258
  Phu Quoc, 348–349
  Quy Nhon, 252
Ako Dhong Village (Buon Ma Thuot), 242
Alexandre Yersin Museum (Nha Trang), 268–269
Allez Boo (Ho Chi Minh City), 321
Alphana Jewelry (Ho Chi Minh City), 320
Amara Spa (Phnom Penh), 385
Amber Room (Ho Chi Minh City), 321–322
Ambre (Phnom Penh), 384
American Express, Phnom Penh, 373
Ana Mandara (Nha Trang), 271
Anam QT Spa (Ho Chi Minh City), 317
Angkor (Cambodia), 392
Angkor Balloon (Cambodia), 413
Angkor Festival (Cambodia), 363
Angkor Hospital for Children (Siem Reap), 394
Angkor National Museum (Siem Reap), 418
Angkor temple compound, 408–418
Angkor Thom (Cambodia), 410–411
Angkor Thom Gates (Cambodia), 411
Angkor Village Hotel (Siem Reap), 421
Angkor Wat (Cambodia), 356, 392, 408–411, 413
Angkor What? (Siem Reap), 422
Annam (Ho Chi Minh City), 319
Ann Tours, 58, 286, 338
An Phu Tourist, 204
An Phu Travel, 178, 198
An Thoi, 354
An Thoi Archipelago, 354
Antiques, Hanoi, 104–106
A-1 Hill (Dien Bien Phu), 139
Apricot Gallery
  Hanoi, 108
  Ho Chi Minh City, 318

Apsara dance (Cambodia), 421
Apsara Faces (Cambodia), 411–412
Area codes, 439
Army Museum (Can Tho), 345
Army Museum (Hanoi), 96
Art galleries
  Dalat, 235
  Hanoi, 108
  Ho Chi Minh City, 318
  Hue, 186
Artisans d'Angkor (Siem Reap), 419
Art Lounge (Siem Reap), 422
Art Vietnam (Hanoi), 108
Asasax Art Gallery (Phnom Penh), 384
Asia Transpacific Journeys, 26, 29, 30, 362
ATMs and banks. *See* Banks and ATMs
Au Delice (Hanoi), 111
Au Lac, 11
Avian influenza (bird flu), 436

B

Ba Be Lake, 142–143
Ba Be National Park, 141–143
Bacchus Corner (Ho Chi Minh City), 319
Bac Ha Market (near Sapa), 128
Bach Ma National Park, 196
Bach Ma Temple (Hanoi), 86, 88, 94
Ba Chuc, 348
Backroads, 30–31
Ba Dinh District (Hanoi), 60
Bahnar people, 225
Ba Hung (Halong Bay), 157
Bai Chay (Halong City), 152
Bai Sau (Cat Tien National Park), 335
Bai Tu Long Bay, 154–155
Bakeng Hill (Cambodia), 410, 413
Bamboo district (Hanoi), 93
Bambou (Nha Trang), 272
Bambou Company
  Hoi An, 220
  Hue, 186
Ban Don, 244
Ban Gioc Waterfall, 141, 144–145
Banks and ATMs, 443
  Buon Ma Thuot, 241
  Cambodia, Sihanoukville, 389
  Can Tho, 342
  Cao Bang, 144
  Chau Doc, 346
  Con Son, 331
  Dalat, 229
  Danang, 198
  Dien Bien Phu, 138
  Haiphong, 148
  Halong City, 152
  Ho Chi Minh City, 287
  Hoi An, 205
  Hue, 178